COMPUTERS AND INFORMATION PROCESSING

AN INTRODUCTION

COMPUTERS AND INFORMATION PROCESSING

AN INTRODUCTION

WILLIAM L. HARRISON
Oregon State University

WEST PUBLISHING COMPANY
St. Paul New York San Francisco Los Angeles

50 West Kellogg Boulevard
P.O. Box 64526
St. Paul, MN 55164-0526

Printed in the United States of America

Library of Congress Cataloging in Publication Data

Harrison, William L. (William LeRoy), 1937-
Computers and information processing.

Includes bibliographies and index.
1. Electronic data processing. 2. Electronic digital computers. I. Title.
QA76.H294 1985 001.64 84-29152
ISBN 0-314-85245-X

Cover Art: Kevin McMahon
Cover Design: Henry Taly
Composition: Parkwood
Copy Editor: Flora Foss
Artwork: Art Axya

Cartoon Credits

p. 15 Drawing by Jonik; © 1981 The New Yorker Magazine, Inc. **p. 60** Drawing by Robert Weber; © 1969 The New Yorker Magazine, Inc. **p. 86** Drawing by W. Miller; © 1965 The New Yorker Magazine, Inc. **p. 205** Drawing by H. Martin; © 1970 The New Yorker Magazine, Inc. **p. 238** Drawing by Chon Day; © 1971 The New Yorker Magazine, Inc. **p. 276** Reprinted by permission. © Copyright King Features Syndicate. **p. 430** Drawing by Shirvanian; © 1969 The New Yorker Magazine, Inc. **p. 469** Reprinted from INFOSYSTEMS July 1980. Copyright © Hitchcock Publishing Company. **p. 492** Reprinted from INFOSYSTEMS March 1980 Copyright © Hitchcock Publishing Company. **p. 494** Drawing by Lorenz; © The New Yorker Magazine, Inc. **p. 519** Drawing by Stevenson; © 1977 The New Yorker Magazine, Inc.

Intext Photo Credits

Part I: Courtesy of Sperry Univac Corporation. **Chapter 1:** Woodfin Camp & Associates. Photo by Sepp Seitz. **Fig.1.1** Courtesy of Information Systems. **Fig. 1.2** Courtesy of Bethlehem Steel. **Fig. 1.3** Courtesy of General Dynamics. **Fig. 1.4** Ford Motor Company Photo. **Fig. 1.5** Reprinted by permission of International Business Machines Corporation. **Fig. 1.6** Courtesy of NCR Corporation. **Fig. 1.10** Reprinted by permission of International Business Machines Corporation. **Fig. 1.11** Courtesy of Sperry Univac Corporation. **Fig. 1.12** Courtesy of Bell Laboratories. **Fig. 1.13** Courtesy of Fairchild, Inc. **Fig. 1.14** Courtesy of Motorola, Inc. **Fig. 1.15** Courtesy of Apple Computers, Inc. **Chapter 2** Courtesy of Amdahl, Inc. **Fig. 2.2** Reprinted with the permission of International Business Machines Corporation. **Fig. 2.3** Courtesy of Taurus Pictures. **Fig. 2.4** Courtesy of The Historical Pictures Society. **Fig. 2.5** Courtesy of Sperry Corporation. **Fig. 2.6** Courtesy of Iowa State University of Science and Technology. **Fig. 2.7** Courtesy of Sperry Corporation. **Fig. 2.8** Reprinted with the permission of International Business Machines Corporation. **Fig. 2.11** Courtesy of NCR. **Fig. 2.12** (a) and (b) Courtesy of Computervision and (c) Courtesy of Sorcim, Inc. **Fig. 2.13** (a) Courtesy of Aiplicon and (b) Courtesy of Recognition Equipment, Inc. **Fig. 2.14** Courtesy of Sperry Univac Corporation. **Fig. 2.15** Courtesy of Digital Corporation. **Fig. 2.16** Reprinted with the permission of International Business Machines Corporation **Fig. 2.18** Courtesy of the Sperry Univac Corporation. **Fig. 2.19** Courtesy of Motorola. **Chapter 3** Woodfin Camp & Associates. Photo by John Blaustein. **Fig. 3.1** Courtesy of Radio Shack. **3.2** Courtesy of the Institute for Advanced Study. **Fig. 3.3** Reprinted with the permission of International Business Machines Corporation. **Fig. 3.5** Courtesy of Marathon. **Fig. 3.6** Courtesy of Marathon. **Fig. 3.8** Courtesy of Marathon. **Part II** Woodfin Camp & Associates. Photo by Robert McElroy. **Chapter 4** Woodfin Camp & Associates. Photo by John Blaustein. **Fig. 4.1** Courtesy of Quotron, Inc. **Fig. 4.3** Reprinted with the permission of International Business Machines Corporation. **Fig. 4.7** Reprinted with the permission of International Business Machines Corporation. **Fig. 4.8** Courtesy Mannesman Tally. **Fig. 4.9** Courtesy of CPT Corporation. **Fig. 4.10** Courtesy Lear Siegler. **Fig. 4.11** Courtesy of Tektronix, Inc. **Fig. 4.12** (a) Courtesy of Hewlett-Packard and (b) Courtesy of Sorcim. **Fig. 4.13** Courtesy of Control Data Corporation. **Fig. 4.14** Courtesy of Hewlett-Packard. **Fig. 4.15** Courtesy of Teleqenix. **Fig. 4.17** Courtesy of Nicolet-Zeta. **Fig. 4.18** Courtesy of Calcomp Corporation. **Fig. 4.19** Courtesy of Bausch and Lomb. **Fig. 4.20** Courtesy of Infodetics, Inc. **Fig. 4.21** Copyright © 1981 by CW Communications/Inc. Framingham, MA. Reprinted from COMPUTERWORLD. **Fig. 4.25** Courtesy of Dataproducts Corporation. **Fig. 4.26** Courtesy of Qume. **Fig. 4.27** Courtesy of NEC Information Systems, Inc. **Fig. 4.28** Courtesy of Honeywell, Inc. **Fig. 4.32** Courtesy of Hewlett-Packard. **Fig. 4.33** Courtesy of National Semi-Conductor. **Chapter 5** Woodfin Camp & Associates. Photo by David Burnett. **Fig. 5.1** Courtesy of Holiday Inn. **Fig. 5.2** Reprinted with the permission of International Business Machines Corporation. **Fig. 5.5** Courtesy of Hewlett-Packard. **Fig. 5.6** Courtesy of NCR. **Fig 5.7** Courtesy of NCR. **Fig. 5.8** Courtesy of Dataproducts Corporation. **Fig. 5.9** Courtesy of NCR. **Fig. 5.10** Courtesy of Chase Manhattan. **Fig. 5.11** Courtesy of Paradyne. **Fig. 5.12** Copyright © 1983 by C.W. Communications/ Inc. Framingham, MA. Reprinted from COMPUTERWORLD. **Fig. 5.15** Photo courtesy of Jerry Bushey. **Fig. 5.16** Courtesy of Headrix Corporation. **Fig. 5.18** Courtesy of Pacific Gas and Electric. **Fig. 5.19** Courtesy of GTCO Corporation. **Fig. 5.20** Courtesy of Bausch and Lomb. **Fig. 5.21** Courtesy of Mouse Systems Corporation. **Fig. 5.22** Courtesy of Firestone. **Fig. 5.23** Courtesy of the Voice Connection, Inc. **Fig. 5.24** Courtesy of the Coca Cola Company. **Chapter 6** Courtesy of Tandem Corporation. **Fig. 6.1** Courtesy of AT&T. **Fig. 6.2** Courtesy of General Dynamics. **Fig. 6.3** Courtesy of Apple Computers, Inc. **Fig. 6.4** Courtesy of Cray Inc. **Fig. 6.5** Courtesy of Hewlett-Packard. **Fig. 6.11.** Copyright © 1982 Datamation. Reprinted with permission. **Chapter 7** Blackstar. Photo by Dennis Brack. **Fig. 7.4** Courtesy of AT&T. **Fig. 7.6** Courtesy of Conrail. **Fig. 7.7** Courtesy of Adage. **Fig. 7.17** Courtesy of Boise Cascade. **Fig. 7.18** Courtesy of Dysan. **Fig. 7.19** Reprinted with the permision of International Business Machines Corporation. **Fig. 7.24** Courtesy of Control Data Corporation. **Fig. 7.26** Courtesy of Memorex. **Fig. 7.29** Courtesy of Bell Laboratories. **Fig. 7.30** Courtesy of Hitachi Sales Corporation of America. **Chapter 8** Courtesy of Texas Instruments. **Fig.**

Credits are continued following the index.

Contents-In-Brief

Contents

3
Computer Fundamentals—Software 59

PART II
DATA PROCESSING FUNCTIONS 81

4
The Production of Information: Output 83

5
The Entry of Data: Input 125

6
COMPUTATION: Central Processing Units and Operating Systems 165

18
Computers and the Quality of Life: Today and Tomorrow 537

Appendix A
Problem Solving and Programming 569

Appendix B

Appendix C

Color Sections

Preface

This text has been designed to be used as part of a first course in data processing, especially in those disciplines where the emphasis is on the use of computing devices to serve organizational needs.

The course may include hands-on computer work—either the learning of a computer programming language or the utilization of previously written software packages. The treatment of BASIC in the appendix provides an introduction to programming. As more and more students are introduced to programming in high school, junior high or elementary school, instructors may want to add exercises in word processing, spreadsheet analysis, or other areas.

This is a user-oriented text, written for the person who expects to use a computer in order to accomplish some data processing activities in support of his or her role in an organization, whether that organization is a business, a government agency or some other not-for-profit organization.

This text is designed to allow maximum flexibility. In particular, the first eight chapters are divided into three major parts—*Concepts, Tools,* and *Technology.* Instructors can emphasize the particular elements essential to the individual course goals.

Short sections called *Historical Perspectives* within each of the chapters are utilized to present historical material to avoid having a full chapter on the history of computing. This allows the historical material to be used to develop perspective on the part of students so that the presentation of current materials will be better understood and more fully appreciated.

Computing Challenges—short, hypothetical cases—are used to motivate students and to focus their attention on issues relevant to the chapter at hand. Additionally, real cases are included at the end of the chapter for those instructors who utilize case discussions in their classes.

The sections on *Newest Developments* in each chapter represent an attempt to identify developments on the leading edge of the technology of computing.

Several bibliographic references are given at the end of each chapter for those students who seek additional study. Discussion questions and exercises have also been provided.

Not until one writes a textbook does the importance of this next portion of the preface become apparent. It simply is not possible to give adequate credit to those who helped create this text. Initial encouragement comes, of course, from the sales representatives of textbook publishers. Ralph Protsik gave me an early opportunity to write a study guide for another data processing text, an effort which helped me believe I might be able to write a full text. Many editors and reviewers of the early materials had an impact on the direction the manuscript took. Brian Hinshaw was especially helpful.

Many reviewers tried to help me make the book better. I would like to thank them for the suggestions they gave which became part of the book. In particular I am grateful to:

Gertrude W. Abramson
Rockland Community College, New York

C. Nathan Adams
Middle Tennessee State University

Robert Behling
Bryant College, Rhode Island

A. G. Buckman
California State University, Hayward

Jeffrey G. Collins
Santa Monica City College

Allen P. Corbett
University of South Carolina

William R. Cornette
Southwest Missouri State University

Marilyn J. Correa
Polk Community College, Florida

Ronald L. Ernst
Northern Arizona University

Robert S. Fritz
American River College
California State University, Sacramento

Lee L. Gremillion
Boston University

Rodney J. Heisterberg
Austin Community College

Grace Hertlein
California State University, Chico

Ron Jones
University of Missouri, Kansas City

Daniel R. Rota
Robert Morris College, Pennsylvania

Robert A. Schultheis
Southern Illinois University

Gilbert L. Simmons
Univerity of Arkansas

Robert D. Smith
Kent State University, Ohio

J. Wayne Spence
North Texas State University

Steve Teglovic
University of Northern Colorado

Walter J. Wadycki
University of Illinois, Chicago

Charles M. Williams
Georgia State University

My friend, Roger Hirsch helped establish a working relationship with West Publishing, for which I am grateful. Clyde Perlee of West, contributed a lot of his insight and energy to the project and the book benefitted greatly from his contributions. Carole Grumney also helped a great deal as did the many editors, artists, and other professionals of the West Publishing organization.

Many students, friends and family members helped with various activities in support of the text. I would like to thank Beth Neideigh, Molly O'Donnell, Deborah Jacobs, Amy Harrison, JoAnne Roberts, Megan O'Donnell, Jill Robbins, Mark Harrison, Rick Smith and Carolyn Vock. Donna Carsner and Betty Harrison helped with the word processing chores. The manuscript was created through the use of Word Juggler* word processing software on an Apple ///.**

A separate Study Guide is available for students who might want to increase their knowledge through the use of additional study materials provided there. An instructor's manual is also available containing annotated lecture outlines coordinated with a complete set of teaching slides. The instructor's manual also contains an extensive test bank. The test bank is also computerized on WesTest II for mainframes and MicroTest II for microcomputers.

Students, I hope you learn many exciting facts and concepts from reading the book and that your learning process is an enjoyable one. Suggestions for improvements in the text or any of the supplemental materials will always be welcomed.

In my classes at Oregon State University I share many poems with my students. They insist that I include at least one in this book. I have chosen the following poem in the hope that it might have meaning in your life, as it has in mine.

A Peaceful Day

It was a peaceful day,
Just you and me,
No conqueror,
No conqueree.***

William L. Harrison
Corvallis, Oregon
July, 1984

*Word Juggler is the registered trademark of Quark Engineering.
**Apple is the registered trademark of Apple Computer.
***From *Listening to Quiet Voices* by W. L. Harrison and J. L. Shane.

We are moving toward the twenty-first century with the very great goal of building a Computopia on earth, the historical monument of which will be only several chips one inch square in a small box. But that box will store many historical records, including the record of how four billion world citizens overcame the energy crisis and the population explosion; achieved the abolition of nuclear weapons and complete disarmament; conquered illiteracy; and created a rich symbiosis of god and man without the compulsion of power or law, but by the voluntary cooperation of the citizens to put into practice their common global aims.

Yoneji Masuda

Part I

An Overview of Data Processing

PART PREFACE

The quotation from Yoneji Masuda suggests that computers will record how we, as a society, overcame the crises of insufficient supplies of energy, exploding populations, excessive nuclear weaponry, and pervasive illiteracy through the pursuit of common global aims. Computers would undoubtedly be very useful in achieving those worthwhile goals, but where do we start?

The purpose of this preface, and the ones for each part of the text which follow, is to give some direction to the reader's journey. Without it, the journey might be inefficient.

Part I of the text is intended to provide the reader with an overall understanding of the perspective within which this study of data processing will take place. The first chapter discusses organizations, the nature of decision making within organizations, and the role of data processing in support of those decision-making activities. Then, Chapters 2 and 3 present an overview of data processing by examining data processing's fundamental building blocks: hardware and software.

This overview is presented early in the text so that the reader will be able to build an early, but full-view picture of the entire operation. This overview, though quick, is pretty shallow. Depth is built throughout the rest of the text. Additionally, an early overview allows the student to begin using the computer at a point very early in the course.

Active experiences such as hands-on exercises with computers will help the reader learn more about data processing and be happier about the process. Whenever possible, the student should strive to talk with people about their uses of data processing, arrange a visit to a computer center, and try to gain additional hands-on experience with computing equipment. Such experiences will help the preliminary material in this part come alive.

Chapters in Part I are:

- Chapter 1 *Information Processing in Organizations*
- Chapter 2 *Computer Fundamentals—Hardware*
- Chapter 3 *Computer Fundamentals—Software*

1

Information Processing in Organizations

CHAPTER PREVIEW

Computers challenge us as we have never before been challenged. They challenge not only our society, but us as individuals. The challenge is not whether we humans can maintain the upper hand, as we often see it portrayed in the movies or read about it in the popular press. The challenge is: Can we take full advantage of the computer's potential while minimizing its potential for negative impacts? A computer can perform millions upon millions of operations per second, store and provide access to billions and billions of elements of data. But, can we use the computer to make our lives better? Can we use our knowledge of computers to improve our lives? We must learn what we can in order to ensure that the computer's impact is as positive as possible.

In many areas, technology seems to limit the extent to which we can improve the quality of our lives. We continue to seek the technological breakthroughs that could give us an unending energy supply, or an adequate (and adequately distributed) food supply, or peace, or even a more adequate (and less painful) education. That is not to say that, in all cases, technology is the limiting factor. In many cases the technology already exists, but other factors, such as selfish interests, politics, and lack of motivation, keep us from desired goals.

Our use of computers is limited by the level of technology in many cases, by cost considerations in others, and in still other instances by our lack of motivation. With computers, however, a large factor in limiting their use to improve our well-being is our general lack of knowledge about *how to use them most effectively*.

Computers can make great contributions to our lifestyle, relieving us of tedious tasks (accounting), entertaining us (video games), educating us (computer-assisted instruction), and allowing us to work in a lakeshore cabin and communicate with our co-workers via satellite (telecommuting). If only we were smart enough to use them effectively. Consider the following example.

Figure 1–1 Taming a Computer

COMPUTING CHALLENGE: *Foggy Bottom Runners' Club*

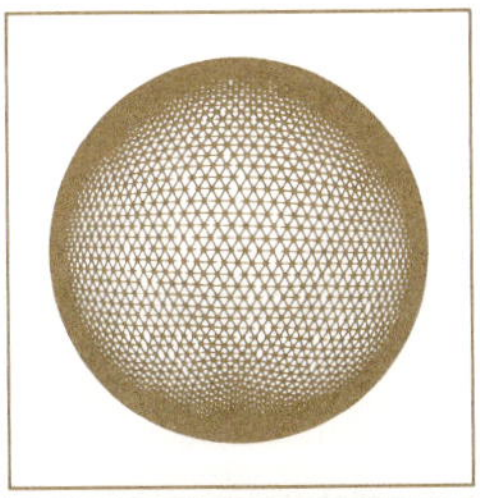

Jamie Schwindel is the president of the Foggy Bottom Runners' Club in Eugene, Oregon. Many joggers, would-be runners, runners, and world class marathoners belong to the club. The club sponsors numerous long distance running events throughout the year. One of the attractive features of being a member of the club is that running statistics on all members are kept and distributed with the monthly newsletter.

Members can record their daily mileage at several stores specializing in running shoes or at other apparel shops in Eugene, at the University track office, or at the YMCA. They can even mail their running log to the club office if that is more convenient. In addition, runners' finishing times and places are recorded for all club-sponsored races. With the monthly newsletter the club sends race results, monthly and daily average distances, and other running statistics. Previously, all of this data had been recorded manually on ledger sheets, and the statistics calculated by club officers using hand-held calculators.

This system worked well when there were only fifty members. In recent years the club has grown; its present membership is 3,150. The officers of the club began investigating the use of a computer to record mileages and calculate statistics. Several clubs in the East were known to use computers to record finishing times and the order of finish for races.

What do we know about computers which might help Jamie and the running club? Do we know anything about computer outputs, inputs, computation, or storage? Do we understand the computer's role in information processing? Although we may not be runners, are we involved in organizations which might be faced with similar problems? And if we were in such an organization would we know enough about computers to be part of a solution to those problems, or would we be so unknowledgeable as to be part of the problem?

The challenge is clear. The solution requires more knowledge of computing. We must read on and begin the task of becoming part of the solution. This chapter represents the first step. After successful completion of this chapter, the reader should be able to:

1. *Describe the role of information in the decision-making activities of managers.*
2. *Differentiate between data and information as each is used in data processing.*
3. *List the four functions which combine to form what we know as data processing.*
4. *Explain some ways in which computers might be used in organizations.*

HISTORICAL PERSPECTIVE

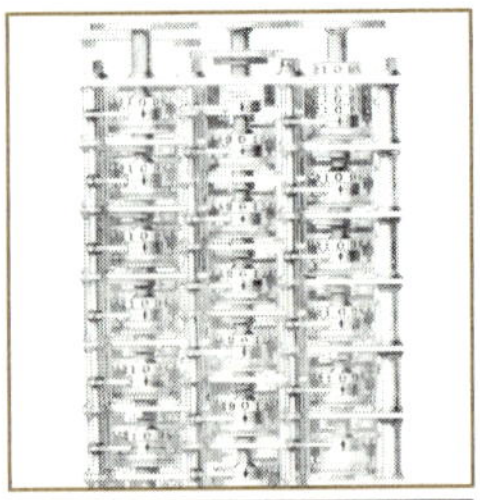

Most of the organizations with which we interact grow larger with the passing of time. It may be that we are moving through a series of increasingly large organizations, as we do when we progress from elementary school to middle school to high school to college; or, it might be that the organizations to which we belong are themselves getting larger—for example, businesses merge, forming larger businesses.

As organizations grow, their record-keeping tasks become larger. Membership lists grow. The list of people or organizations with whom an organization interacts becomes larger and in many cases the number of activities the organization undertakes gets larger. The organization must have more filing cabinets, more typewriters, more clerks, more telephones, more paper, more pencils—all tools for keeping track of activities.

In many cases the increased workload of record-keeping becomes too large for manual systems. One solution, which has found frequent use, is to use a computer to make it easier to handle large quantities of information.

The increased size of organizations is not the only factor leading to an increasingly complex environment within which we all function. We also find that laws become more complex, the products of businesses become more complex, and so on. Many organizations have turned to *computerized data processing systems* to help them keep track of activities in an increasingly complex world, and to help with the increasing load of processing generated by the many transactions completed daily. This growth in the use of computers has contributed greatly to our economy. U.S. companies now sell approximately $100 billion of computer-related goods annually.

Concepts: The Processing of Data into Information

Throughout this text we will be exploring the use of computers to assist the members of organizations in **transaction processing** and **decision-making** activities. Before we can go very far in that direction, it is necessary to make sure we all start from a common point of understanding.

The purpose of this introductory chapter is to enable us to share a few concepts which are basic to decision making and a few which are basic to computerized data processing. Virtually none of this material will be startlingly new to even the novice, but we do it with a *precision* that is important to fully understand the material to be presented later.

Organization

People join together to form organizations in order to attain goals which can be achieved through the combined efforts of the members. Social organizations exist to provide their members with a desired level of social interaction. Churches, synagogues, schools, fraternal organizations, clubs, and societies are formed so that their members may join together in pursuit of organizational goals while, at the same time, satisfying individual needs.

Most organizations require some managerial effort to maintain communication among the members, to identify tasks and sub-tasks, to assign work, to provide tools and services, to plan, to maintain control, and so on. In some organizations the managerial effort is very informal, while in others it has become quite sophisticated. Within a small, informal organization the managerial functions may be performed by a single person, or be quite informally distributed among several members.

As the organization grows, several changes usually occur. Several levels of managerial activity exist in larger organizations, forming, in most cases, a hierarchy or ordering of managers on the basis of their authority. Managers at the upper levels exercise their authority over those at lower levels while lower level managers supervise the work force. These organizations typically become very formal in the manner in which they operate. Rules, guidelines, and standard operating procedures are developed to help define the roles of managers at the various levels.

The lower levels of managerial activity are those most closely connected with the day-to-day operating activities essential to the survival of the organization. Think, for example, about the typical fast-food outlet. Workers are assigned to the various tasks of order-taking, food preparation and clean-up. Assistant managers usually work very closely with the working group to fill in for absent employees, alleviate bottlenecks, and train new people. The manager is usually somewhat removed from the day-to-day activities in order to be able to plan, order supplies, and interview potential employees.

On the other hand, managers at the top of the hierarchy take on the role of long-range planning to set the direction the organization is to take in the future. For example, bank presidents must concern themselves with the long-range goals of the bank in terms of demand deposits, savings deposits, consumer loans, real estate loans, commercial loans, and many other areas. In between the top level of long-range planning and the lower level of operations we find one or more levels of middle managers, who must translate the long-range plans into the controls that are applied to operational levels to make sure the organization does, in fact, move in the desired direction.

Lower levels in the hierarchy need information about day-to-day activities. Middle managers are more interested in trends and summaries, while the information needs of managers at the upper level are sometimes quite difficult to characterize. We will find that computers have been useful in supporting the needs of managers at all levels of the organization.

We should not, of course, fail to recognize that virtually all members of an organization have information needs. Clerks, secretaries, and workers of all types have need for information to support their daily activities. Much of the effort to improve information processing within organizations is directed at improving workers' access to information as well. Computers help supply information to virtually all members of the organization.

We will see, as we progress through the text, just exactly how computers

Figure 1–2 Process Control at Bethlehem Steel Corporation

are used in organizations to help with the processing of information. In the next section we begin to provide some structure to the discussion of computer use.

Uses of Computers

Computers are used in many ways—too numerous to list completely. Schools use them to process students' enrollments and grades; social organizations use them to maintain mailing lists, while government agencies and businesses use them across the full range of their activities.

In chemical processing plants they are used to monitor temperatures, pressures, and flow rates at important locations in the process, and then to send signals to the various regulating devices to control the chemical process itself; hence the name of this use: *process control* (see Figure 1–2). Computers are used in sawmills to calculate optimum cutting patterns, in airplanes to assist the navigator, in industry to control machines (Figure 1–3) and robots (see Figure 1–4), in medical laboratories to perform analyses, in hospitals to aid diagnosticians and surgeons, and so on. This book is *not* about any of those uses, though they are obviously very important.

The *transaction processing* activities of computers will be treated in some detail, but transaction processing probably does not require much of an introduction. Most readers of this book will have already experienced a computerized transaction processing system. Most will have used an automatic teller machine at a bank, a point-of-sale cash register terminal at a supermarket or department store, or a computerized airline reservations system (see Figures 1–5 and 1–6). Not so obvious, perhaps, are the uses of automated systems to clear checks in the banking system, to process credit card purchases, and to provide daily summaries of sales and shipping activities. These activities all represent the use of computers to automate the processing of some of the many transactions created within a modern business. These systems also provide a collection system for the capture

Figure 1–3 Numerically Controlled Machine at Work

Figure 1–4 Robot

Figure 1–5
Automatic Teller Machine

of the data which will be used by managers in their decision-making activities.

This book is also about the use of computers to process data into information so that managers in organizations in our society can perform their managerial tasks with greater efficiency and effectiveness. Many of the organizations in which we are involved are business organizations, and for that reason almost every topic discussed throughout the book is applicable to business organizations. However, we are involved in many other, nonbusiness organizations, such as churches, synagogues, recreational clubs, governmental agencies, and social clubs. We will keep these other organizations in mind throughout the book, for there are many similarities be-

Computers in Action 1

Meeting the Challenge

1

2

3

1. A personal computer proves to be a very handy tool in maintaining records for any kind of organization, from the Foggy Bottom Runners' Club to the Senior Citizens Quilting Circle. **2.** This is one of the most attractive personal computer designs, the Apple IIc from Apple Computer Co. **3.** Another Apple Computer Co. product, the Macintosh, ushered in a new era of personal computer graphics on an easy-to-use machine.

4

5

4. Establishing the starting time for runners in a race is a relatively simple task, even though runners in the back of the pack start at a slight disadvantage. **5.** Recording finishing times for all runners can be a major information processing task, however. Personal computers have been found to be quite useful in recording race results. **6.** This Radio Shack microcomputer, the TRS-80, was one of the first of the popular machines.

6

7

7. This Compaq was one of the most successful of the early portable microcomputers. The Foggy Bottom Runners' Club used a Compaq to record finishing times for their first "computerized" race. **8.** A world-class runner makes use of a Hewlett-Packard portable computer to compute splits for an assault on his personal best time as he rides the train to the site of a marathon. **9.** Here a sponsor of a large marathon uses his GRiD Compass microcomputer to analyze race revenues and expenses.

8

9

10. Foggy Bottom Runners' Club officers hope to use a color plotter to produce maps showing the route, mileage markers, and locations of aid stations for next year's marathon. **11.** Graphics tablets help enter important data during the actual monitoring of the race itself. **12.** Some runners use home computers to analyze their food intake for purposes of relating nutrition to performance.

10

11

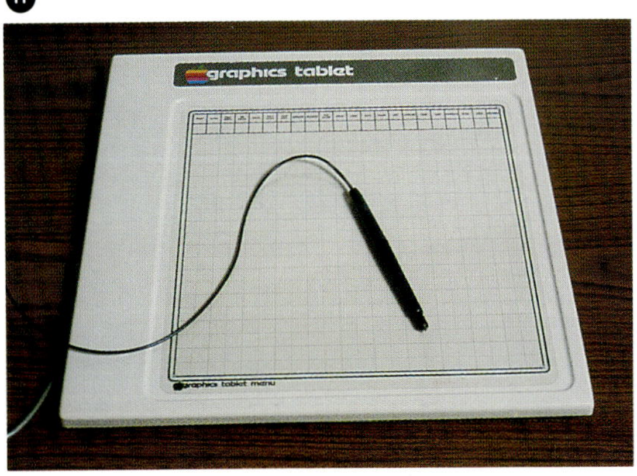

12

Figure 1–6 Point-of-Sale Terminal

tween the decision-making activities of managers in business organizations and those in other organizations.

A word or two about the use of the word **manager** is also in order. Manager is used in its most general sense as a person who makes decisions about the allocation of the organization's resources. I do not refer only to the manager at the top of some segment of the organization chart but to all people who do some managing within the organization. For example, a program chairperson must *manage* the development of a program to attract participants to meetings, and government employees must collect information from the public to guide the *management* of their programs in fisheries, wildlife, forest, range, and park management.

The Role of Information in Decision Making

Each of us could probably make a good attempt at defining data and decision making. Some of the definitions would not be precise enough for the purists; but, in a sense, we all know what decision making is and we all know what data are. (To be grammatically correct we must use a plural verb with data because it is the plural form of the word datum.) *Data* are the raw materials from which information is derived.

Decision making is the act of choosing between two or more possible activities or states. Decision making takes place as doctors decide how to treat symptoms, as social directors decide which programs are most attractive to club members, and as legislators decide how to vote on issues of importance to their constituents. Within businesses, managers must decide upon an allocation of the firm's resources to the tasks at hand.

Definitions of key terms in data processing play an important role in allowing us to communicate efficiently with each other. We must be sure to work new words into our vocabulary correctly. We quite properly describe the data entering the computer system as input, but we stretch the rules when we talk of "inputting" the data. Input and output are nouns, and "inputting" and "outputting" represent improper usage. The use of acronyms, the taking of the first (or first few) letters of several words to form a new word, provides an additional challenge. Most specialized fields use acronyms to make the process of communication between professionals more efficient. Thus we have CORE (Congress On Racial Equality), SAC (Strategic Air Command), COBOL (COmmon Business-Oriented Language), and MADD (Mothers Against Drunk Driving). Many data processing entities are known by their acronyms, and learning about data processing will require you to learn some.

While I do not want to oppose the gradual changing of our language to reflect current usages, I would also not want to see it improperly used. If, on the other hand, we all grow up using *input* and *output* as verbs, the dictionaries will eventually reflect that usage as proper.

I assume, in this text, that a *manager* is a person in an organization who has some responsibility for making decisions which affect the future path of the organization. Some of these decisions are major ones, made by managers at the highest level in the organization. Other decisions turn out to be minor in scope, made by the participants at lower levels. The manager is continually faced with a number of different choices which could be made; we call them **alternative courses of action.** Each course of action, if selected, would interact with the environment within which the organization operates to produce a result, or **outcome.** The manager's problem (depicted in Figure 1–7) is to select the course of action which results in the best outcome given the existing conditions. For example, managers must decide which applicants to hire, which grade of raw materials to use, which design would make the best product, which advertisements to use, and so on.

Determining which outcome is best is often a complex problem in itself. Some outcomes are best in terms of profitability, while others are best because they are most efficient, least disruptive, least costly, most humane, or, simply, easiest. Computers are often very helpful in allowing us to quickly explore many alternatives.

Let us be a little more precise. Let us characterize the "real world" as a collection of **events** which are taking place. Events give off **signals.** In fact, we observe the signals to determine that an event has taken place. Perhaps an example will help. In 1980, events were taking place within a mountain in the Pacific Northwest known as Mt. St. Helens. The observable signals included earthquakes, releases of steam, and releases of ash. People ob-

Figure 1–7 Manager Choosing Between Two Alternative Courses of Action

served these signals, tried to determine the events which had taken place, and tried to decide what the mountain might do in the future.

There are other examples. Lawmakers read their mail and try to decide how voters feel about important issues. Recruiters look at personal data sheets and try to determine whether a candidate would be a suitable employee. Financial analysts look at firms' annual reports and try to decide whether or not an investment is wise. (Figure 1–8 illustrates that events in the real world give off signals and information systems must capture the appropriate signals to generate information.)

People who are faced with decision-making opportunities try to gather information to help them decide which course of action they should take. Through the use of computers, they can analyze many more decision problems more thoroughly and generate better decisions. In the context of Figure 1–7, the manager tries to gather information which will help in the evaluation of the many different paths available to the organization. That evaluation will enable him or her to choose the course of action which leads to the best outcome. Notice that we are, at this point, ignoring a very

Figure 1–8
Information Systems are Designed to Capture Signals

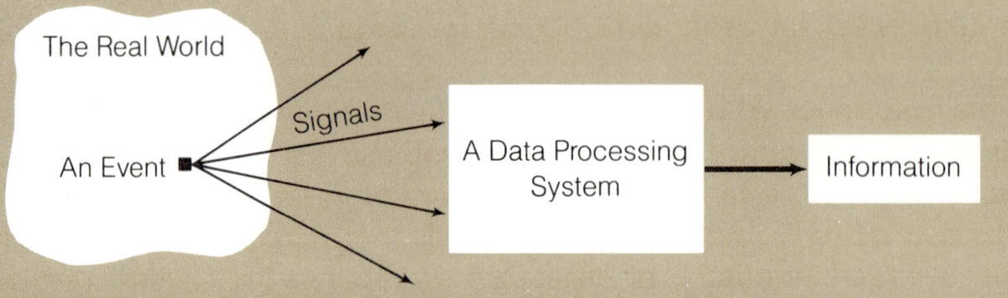

Example:

Event:	• Student adds a class
Signals:	• Student's appearance in classroom • Paperwork submitted to the registrar • Tuition paid to cashier • Homework turned in to instructor • Student buys book(s) for class
Information:	• University enrollment statistics • Student's transcript • Instructor's class list

important part of the manager's problem: what exactly is the meaning of the word *best*? Much study is required to begin to understand the nature of *best* in most decisions.

Challenge Update

Jamie Schwindel should now be able to understand the role of information in decision making.

We will call the signals that indicate an event has taken place **data.** In earlier examples, the lawmaker's mail, the recruiter's personal data sheets, and the analyst's annual reports are data. A manager must make sure that a system is constructed to collect, store, and process the organization's data. Once data have been processed and transformed into a useful form, it is called **information.** Most often, data are processed into information under the assumption that the information will be useful. Information is useful to a manager if it helps in the manager's choice of a course of action. To be precise, information is said to have value if, and only if, it *reduces the uncertainty* in the manager's decision problem. Information which helps a manager evaluate a particular alternative or determine the likelihood of a particular state reduces the uncertainty in the original problem.

Challenge Update

The distinction between data and information should now be clear. For example, individual runners' times in a race are data, but summaries provide information for race management.

A brief review is in order. A manager in a decision situation is faced with several possible alternatives, and the outcome which will result from each alternative, if chosen, is uncertain. A manager tries to build a system to capture, store, and process data (signals) into the information needed by the manager to reduce the uncertainty of the situation.

"Now, *that's* a welcome sight! I was just beginning to miss decision-making."

The Role of Data Processing in Management

Researchers are sometimes very careful about the distinction between data and information. Before any processing takes place they assume we have only *data,* and that *information* arises only from the processing of data. Confusion, however, arises when we consider that the information used by one manager may undergo further processing to become information for another manager. For example, a sales representative collects orders (data) from customers in order to compute product sales (information) and commissions (information) resulting from those sales. The production manager uses summaries of product sales (data) to schedule future production (information). The production schedule (data) is used by upper level managers to analyze productive capacity (information). Thus, the effort to maintain the distinction between data and information becomes difficult *unless the exact context of its use can be specified.* Wherever possible we will try to focus on the usefulness of information in a particular decision-making situation, recognizing that it may have existed in some prior, unprocessed form as data.

Data and information are both resources of an organization. Other scarce resources—in particular, money and people's time—are expended in collecting, storing, and processing data so that costs are involved in the data processing operation. A manager obviously cannot build a data processing system which captures all the data with complete accuracy and processes them correctly to produce a true picture of the real world. Many compromises are required. The manager hopes to maximize the value of information available while minimizing the cost of producing that information.

A favorite classroom trick of some teachers is to write the numeral 13 on the blackboard and ask how many students believe that it is the number thirteen. All but the very suspicious respond that, of course, it is the number thirteen. The teacher then erases the "13" from the blackboard and claims thereby to have destroyed the number thirteen as it clearly no longer exists. Of course, the "13" was only a symbol for the number thirteen, and only the symbol was destroyed.

To be precise about the processing of data, we must recognize that we process **symbols** which have been used to represent the data. The symbols we use are called **characters.** There are three types of characters in most data processing systems:

1. The numeric characters (0, 1, 2, . . ., 9).
2. The alphabetic characters (A, B, C, . . ., Z).
3. The special characters (+, −, /, :, *, etc).

If the symbols used to represent data are only numbers, then the data are called **numeric data.** If the symbols are only letters, the data are **alphabetic data.** If the symbols are a mixture of numbers, letters, and special characters, the data are called **alphanumeric data.** Data processing systems must handle all three types of data, but they typically handle them differently. Most data manipulated by computers falls into the category of either numeric or alphanumeric data. An extensive amount of work is being done in the field of pattern recognition to make computers more capable symbol processors. People, of course, process graphs, pictures, sounds, smells and many other data representations.

Data Processing

Four principal functions are involved in the processing of data into information. They are **output, input, computation,** and **storage,** as shown in Figure 1–9. We will discuss them in the order in which they are considered in the design of a data processing system. In terms of their operational sequence, input of course precedes output. An important principle of system design states that we must first determine what output is desired from the system. The requirements of the output must control the computation, storage, and input requirements. We will treat the topics in the order of their design consideration so as to emphasize the importance of that order.

Challenge Update

Jamie could now consider how the four functions might be represented in a computing system for the runners' club.

The output from a data processing system should be the information needed by managers and other users in support of the organization's transaction-processing and decision-making activities. We determine not only the contents of the output during this first phase, but also the manner in which it will be presented to a manager. A manager must be able to find and understand the output before it can be useful in making decisions.

Once the output is determined, consideration of the remaining three functions can be pursued at the same time. We look at the input, storages

Figure 1–9 The Four Basic Data Processing Functions

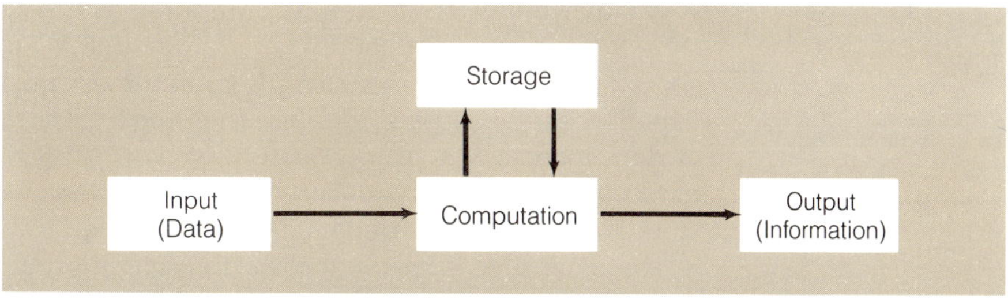

and computation functions simultaneously because they are extensively interrelated. A comparison of the desired output to the available input determines the computations which must be done to transform the incoming data into information. The requirements of the output and input determine, basically, the storage requirements.

We will study how each of the functions of output, input, computation, and storage is accomplished in a computerized data processing system. Consider, for a minute, some of our own roles as human information processors. As students, we want to know first what it is that teachers want us to know (or be able to do) by the end of the term, an *output*. Second, we want to know the reading and homework assignments, the *inputs*. Then we try to figure out how we can compute and store the data and information necessary to produce the desired output.

The Computer's Role

Within this text we will be studying the computer's role in data processing activities in support of managerial decision making and in the processing of transactions. In particular, we will be looking at those features of computers which make them good tools in this service. Other features may account for their role in process control (they never go to sleep) or in machine control (they never get bored).

In the support of decision making, a computer's help may be sought because of the *speed* with which it is able to perform routine tasks. A computer can process a lot of data in a very short time. (Most computer systems can execute millions of instructions per second.)

Another invaluable feature of the computer is its *accuracy*. Although computer errors are the basis for many cartoons and anecdotes, the fact of the matter is, computers are very accurate devices. Most so-called computer errors turn out to be errors caused by humans. A single location where data is stored within a computer can be expected to fail (make an error) on the average of once every 7,500,000 years. Of course, millions of these elements can be incorporated into a machine establishing an environment in which an error might occur once every six weeks. If the computer is performing a million instructions per second, an error rate of once in six weeks is quite small. Even that rate, however, could be significant if allowed to go unchecked. The rate at which computers make errors is, therefore, greatly improved by the use of many error-detecting techniques built into the machines themselves.

Another important feature of computers is the ability of the machine to store large volumes of data in such a way that we can retrieve the data on short notice. In large systems, there is almost no limit to the amount of data that can be stored, although the time it takes to find a particular item of data increases as the collection of data gets larger. Smaller machines have correspondingly smaller storage areas, as a rule. Modern computer storage areas are now quite small as illustrated in Figure 1–10.

The computer is best suited for the role of processing huge amounts of data in a short amount of time, where the processing tasks are routine or repetitive. This latest feature will be more fully understood later, when we have developed an understanding of the nature of programming. Computers are not presently adept at handling nonroutine, unstructured tasks, although research efforts continue to improve their capabilities in these areas.

Figure 1–10
Computer Chip Memory

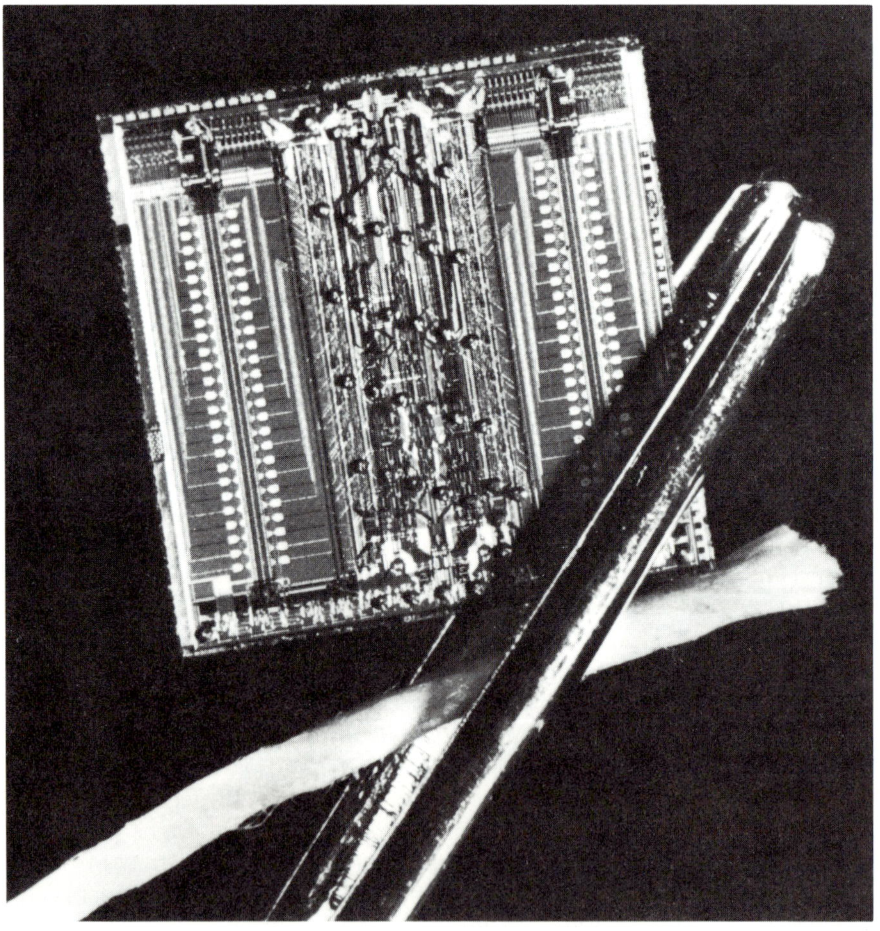

Challenge Update

By now Jamie should begin to understand how computers might be used in organizations of all types.

Tools: The Types of Machines Which Process Data

Classes of Data Processing Tools

The tools through which the computer works to bring about the processing of data are the subject of a large part of the book. Each will receive comprehensive treatment at the appropriate time. In this section of the chapter, we will see how the computer itself is distinguishable from the other data processing tools.

It would be foolish to suggest that all of the world's data processing should, or even could, be done on computerized systems. Many data processing operations are very satisfactorily accomplished by manual means. We have only to visit a few offices to confirm that much of the data processing work being done is still being done through noncomputer means. Short memoranda, telephone messages, entries in the copying machine log, training material compilations, small computations, appointment calendars up-dates, and many other data processing tasks still rely primarily on manual means, even though electronic alternatives might be available.

We can classify the tools which are used in organizational data processing into three classes, as follows:

1. Mechanical
2. Electro-mechanical
3. Electronic

The continuing efforts toward product improvement and the declining costs of electronic devices have led to a gradual movement toward the use of electronic data processors.

In spite of this gradual movement to electronic means, many manual systems, which provide only a small amount of mechanical advantage, are still in evidence. Thus, we still find filing cabinets, 3 × 5 card files, and some files stored in small tubs (called tub files).

Mechanical. What data processing equipment of the mechanical class (machine-like, but not electrically driven) do we find in current use? Manual typewriters are still around, as are some really old mechanical (not electro-mechanical nor electronic) calculators. We still find some accounting machines which use paper with pre-punched holes along the margin to align the rows and columns for manual entries to accounting ledgers. There are even mechanical time clocks still in use. The proprietor of a wonderful Chinese restaurant in Berkeley still uses an abacus to calculate the customer's bill.

Figure 1–11 Vacuum Tubes–the First Electronic Components for Computer Storage

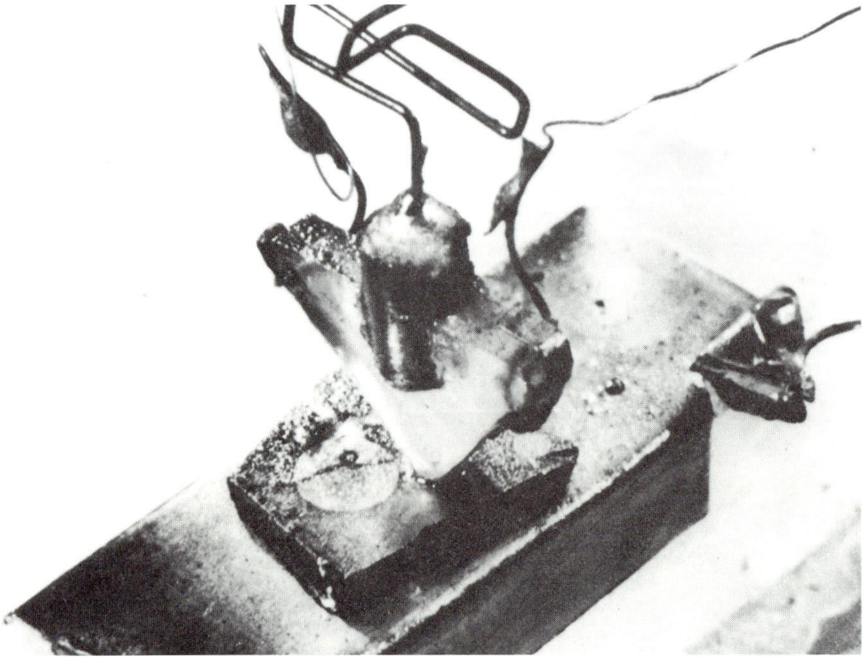

Figure 1–12 An Early Transistor

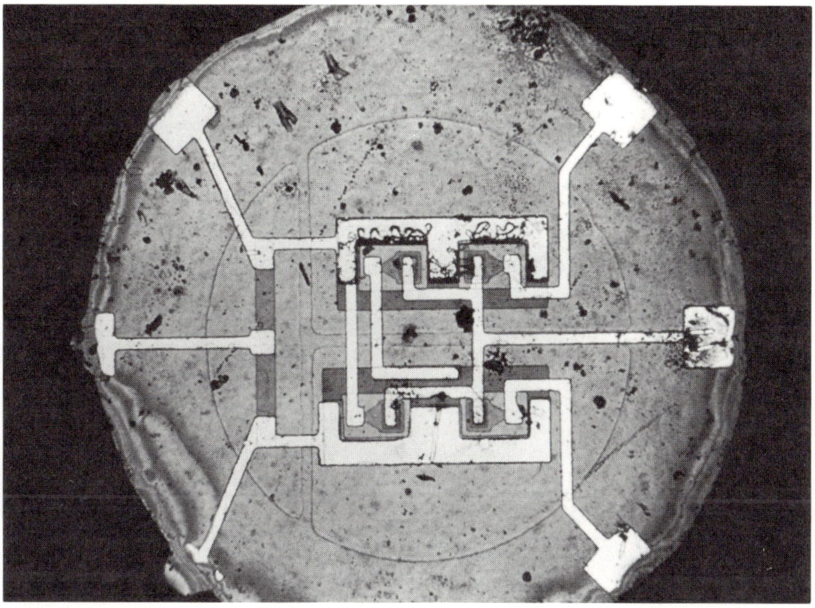

Figure 1–13
Integrated Circuit Module

Electro-Mechanical. In the electro-mechanical class (machine-like, electrically driven) it is easy to find examples. Electric typewriters and cash registers still abound. The telephone system was primarily electro-mechanical but is being converted to electronic. Copy machines are moving from electro-mechanical to electronic operation. Many calculators were originally electro-mechanical.

Electronic. Computers, of course, belong to the electronic class (relying on the physics of electrons), but many of the functions in a complete computer system are still electro-mechanical, as we shall see. The electronic basis of the early computers was the **vacuum tube** (shown in Figure 1–11). The second generation computers were built around semiconductor devices known as **transistors,** giving rise to "solid state" electronics (see Figure 1–12). Numerous transistor circuits were later combined into **integrated circuits,** or **ICs,** which became the basis for the third computer generation (Figure 1–13). The fourth generation machines are based upon an extension of the integration of transistor circuits on a very large scale (see Figure 1–14). Transistor circuits have been combined beyond integrated circuits to **large-scale integration (LSI)** and **very large-scale integration (VLSI).** Perhaps some day we will have very, very large scale integration (VVLSI).

Defining Characteristics of Computers

It is no longer easy to define *computer*. In the "good old days," before digital watches, hand-held calculators, programmable microwave ovens, and the like, it was an easier task. Constructing an adequate definition is somewhat

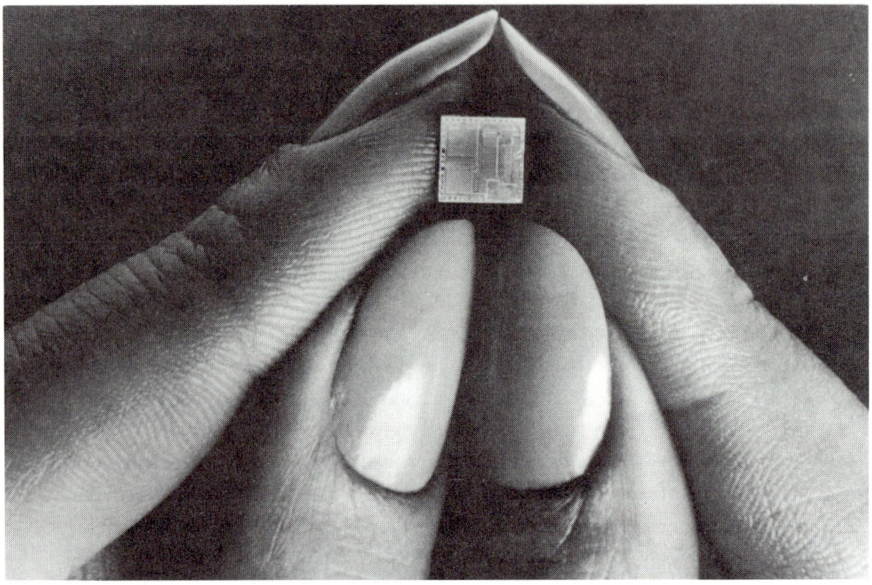

Figure 1–14 Relative Size of a Microchip

Figure 1–15 A Personal Computer

like publishing the rules for correct spelling in the English language. Given a rule, someone can find the exception. Perhaps if we add a little structure to the discussion we can then arrive at a definition which will satisfy, if not please, most people.

At the outset let us exclude from our consideration all the historical antecedents to the modern computer. The abacus is a computing machine, as are the slide rule and various other relics.

The definition we seek must recognize that computers exist in a wide variety of sizes, from large ones (called **mainframes**) to small ones (called **microcomputers**). We will see that the smallest of these, the microcomputers, are bringing drastic changes to our daily lives. We differentiate between the microcomputer and a piece of electronic equipment known as a microprocessor. The **microprocessor** is an electronic device that carries out many of a computer's functions according to electronic logic that is programmed into it at the time of manufacture. That is, its functions are fixed the moment it is manufactured. The microcomputer, on the other hand, is built in such a way that its programming can be varied by the user. Microcomputers used for personal information processing tasks are called **personal computers,** one of which is shown in Figure 1–15.

Digital watches, microwave ovens, hand-held calculators, and other devices operate by the use of limited function microprocessors. Programmable calculators present another problem. If *programmable* means only that a sequence of preprogrammed functions may be used, then the device is not a computer.

What, then, is a computer if it is not a microprocessor nor a programmable calculator? The distinguishing characteristics of a computer are as follows:

1. It must be electronic (as opposed to mechanical or electro-mechanical). That is to say, data are represented electronically and moved or processed through the use of electronic impulses.
2. It must have the capability of storing within it one or more sets of instructions (called programs) as well as some portion of the data for these programs.
3. It must be able to interpret and execute the instructions described in 2 above.
4. Based upon data to which it has access, or the result of arithmetic or logical manipulations, the computer must be able to choose between two or more possible paths through the program.

A device satisfying these four criteria is said to be a computer. For now, these characteristics merely represent a definition. Throughout the book we will be developing an understanding of the computer which will make a definition unnecessary.

Technology: The Digital Nature of Computers

Throughout the text, material presented under the "Technology" heading will help the reader understand the inner workings and hidden features of computer systems, but it is not, for the most part, material which is absolutely essential to making effective use of a computer. The technological details do help us understand why the system performs in a particular way, but they represent a level of detail beyond that required for many users.

Many drivers are quite satisfied to know how to start the car, put it into motion, direct its energy to following a certain route to a desired destination, stop it, and shut it off. Others may want to know the details of the combustion cycle, drive chain, and exhaust system before they feel comfortable using a car. Using a computer is, in that sense, analagous to using a car. Some users want only to know how to use it, while others want to know the finer details of its operation.

In this segment of this chapter, we will discuss just what *digital* means with respect to data processing and, in passing, how digital computers differ from analog computers. It is interesting but not absolutely essential information.

Digital computers are built on a design principle that uses only two discrete states to form patterns to represent data. It is exactly as if we were required to express ourselves using only two symbols, say 0 and 1. If we restricted our vocabulary to yes or no, the two symbols would be adequate: 0 could mean yes and 1 could mean no. Trouble arises if we need to say maybe! Two symbols would no longer be adequate.

In a digital computer we represent each letter, number, and special character by some unique pattern of the two available states. The two states may be ON/OFF, 1/0, magnetization one way (north pole) versus magnetization another (south pole), the opening or closing of an electronic gate, or some other means. The pattern used to represent each character is

Figure 1–16 A Comparison of Analog and Digital Signals

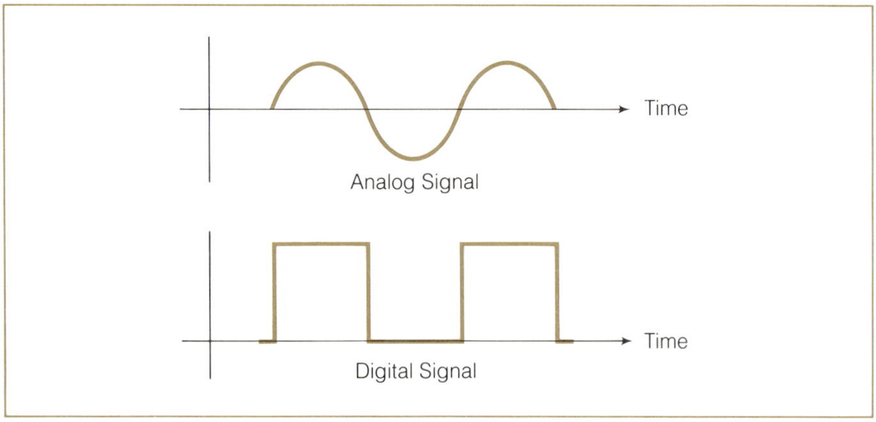

specified by an **encoding scheme,** which defines a different pattern for each character.

In an analog system the representation of data is done differently. Devices in an analog computer use continuous functions to record a full range of values from one extreme to another. A light bulb with the typical ON/OFF switch would be a two-state, digital device. A light bulb with an infinitely variable dimmer switch would be an analog device. An analog wave pattern and a digital wave pattern are represented in Figure 1–16.

Analog computers do exist, but the emphasis in this text will be on digital computers. Virtually all business data processing computers are based upon the digital technology. Many process control computers are analog, however.

Newest Developments

The earliest successes in terms of computer applications were in transaction processing systems. It was relatively easy to use computerized systems to enter orders, record sales, note shipments, and acknowledge receipt. The use of computers has vastly improved the productivity of those people involved in the processing of transactions essential to an organization. Attention was then directed at the use of computers to support managerial tasks. Although many people predicted that computers would eventually displace many managerial workers, that has not yet happened to any great degree. The displacement of managers by computers and the displacement of factory workers by computer-controlled devices (robots) may have a profound impact on employment. This topic is explored in some detail in Chapter 18.

There is hope, however, that we will be able to make progress in the productivity of managerial workers through the intelligent use of computing machines. There are efforts to bring about an automated office, designed to improve clerical and managerial productivities. A lot of work is now being done on decision support systems, designed primarily to improve managerial productivity. These are both relatively new developments with a lot of promise. They also receive a thorough treatment later in the text.

The "Newest Developments" section of each chapter will be used to introduce the reader to the newest concepts, tools, and technologies. Some of these ideas will thrive, others will fade away. Only time will tell which will become important parts of future data processing systems.

COMPUTING CHALLENGE: *A Final Note*

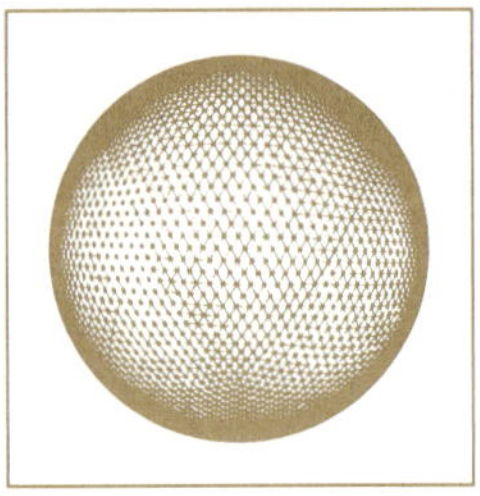

A return to the COMPUTING CHALLENGE will help us gauge our progress in each chapter. We will use these visits to pose interesting questions and, perhaps, provide a few answers.

What can we now say to Jamie Schwindel, the president of the running club? A few questions are provided to help direct our attention. Formulating answers to these questions will not be easy. We must know more.

1. *Of what computer capabilities (speed, accuracy, and large storage capacity) will the club officers be taking advantage in:*
   a. *recording mileages?*
   b. *calculating statistics?*
   c. *recording finish times?*
2. *The club officers know very little about computers. Where might they seek help in this project? Hint: Where would the reader look for help in similar circumstances?*
3. *The club obviously does not own a computer. In what ways might they be able to acquire the needed computing capability? Could they buy one? Rent one? Borrow one?*
4. *How are each of the four functions of data processing reflected in tasks for which the running club would likely use a computer?*

Our study of data processing is under way. Although much lies ahead, some important material is already within our control. Our capabilities will increase with each chapter.

SUMMARY

- Virtually all organizations find it necessary to transform data into information.
- As organizations become larger and the environments within which they operate become more complex, their data processing tasks become more difficult.
- Organizations are faced with processing huge amounts of data to accomplish two major functions: (1) to process the many transactions and (2) to generate information which might be useful in reducing the uncertainties of the environment.
- Computers can be used to reduce the unit costs of processing transactions and in the generation of information.
- The four data processing functions of output, input, computation, and storage are represented in all computing systems.

- Computers are used in process control, machine control, and robotics in addition to their role as support to managers in decision-making activities.
- Computers have impressive capabilities in terms of speed, accuracy, and storage capacity.
- Computers are defined as electronic devices capable of executing stored programs and modifying the path of execution.
- Computers are responsible for a revolution in the way in which organizations are managed.
- Computers have evolved through three generations (vacuum tubes, transistors, and integrated circuits) to a fourth based upon the very large-scale integration of electronic components.
- Digital computers are used by most organizations for information processing while analog computers are used more often for process control.

CASE: Computer Saves Waiting at AVIS

The automobile renting business is a very competitive one. Rental agencies are always trying to improve the level of service they are able to offer their customers. For example, customers dislike having to wait in line to get a rental car or to return one.

AVIS, one of the largest automobile renting companies, uses a specially designed computer system called Wizard II to reduce the time spent by customers waiting at the reservation desk. The system was designed and built for AVIS to meet the special needs of rental agents and customers. Before Wizard was installed, customers spent a considerable amount of time waiting, either to check out or check in a rental car. The new, computerized system has greatly improved service. Check-out time has been reduced by 40 percent and check-in time has improved by 55 percent with Wizard's help.

A small terminal with television display at the agent's fingertips displays all required information and entries made. Data entered can be reviewed and errors can be easily corrected. The new system has reduced the time spent entering rental data, which increases the rental agent's productivity. It also reduces the amount of time that customers must wait for service. In addition, Wizard can quickly produce legible rental contracts and billing forms. On checking out a car, the customer can have a printed contract in only twelve seconds, and on checking in, a bill in twenty seconds.

For credit purchases, the credit cards can be passed through an automatic reading device connected to the system, which instantly checks the validity of the card. Then, with a single command, the appropriate entries are automatically made to stored information to complete the transaction. To further improve the rental process, the customer may obtain a Wizard number which provides for an instant recall of previously-stored information from the system's memory. The stored customer information is all that is needed to fill out the rental contract.

Speed and accuracy are the most important characteristics of the counter transactions for automobile rental agencies. Wizard has helped AVIS accomplish a quick and accurate process. The benefits of Wizard II are twofold. Not only does it make service fast and accurate for its customers, but it improves the productivity of its rental clients by reducing their nonproductive time waiting in line.

"Rental Agents Provide Faster Service with Terminal System," *Infosystems*, November 1981, p. 102.

Questions for the Case

1. What two fundamental events (or transactions) are handled by Wizard?
2. What signals does AVIS probably capture from these events?
3. What information does AVIS probably generate from these signals?
4. What are Wizard's outputs? Inputs?
5. What computations are usually necessary in car rentals?

DISCUSSION QUESTIONS AND EXERCISES

1. Consider a manufacturing company. For what transactions might they be using a computerized system? What transactions might they consider for conversion to computerized processing?
2. Think for a few minutes about a bank. For what transactions might they be using computers? What else might they consider for conversion to computerized processing?
3. Consider a church, synagogue, or other religious or social organization. For what transactions might they be using a computerized system? What transactions might they consider for conversion to computerized processing?
4. Imagine how a wholesale grocery warehouse might operate. What important decisions must managers make? What information would they find useful in making those decisions?
5. In what ways do the capabilities of computers exceed the capabilities of human beings?
6. In what ways do the capabilities of human beings exceed the capabilities of computers?
7. What general characteristics of transaction processing activities make them suitable for conversion to computerized processing?
8. Define a computer.
9. Explain the difference between digital and analog. Are most business computers digital or analog?
10. List the three clearly identifiable generations of computers. On what principle is the fourth generation based?
11. Think about the information processing needs of a student. How might a computer help in the student's information processing tasks?
12. Cite some examples in which the use of computers brings benefits to our society. Describe some negative aspects of these uses.

13. Describe a decision-making situation which might be faced by a bank manager. What information would be helpful in making the decision? What data would be useful in generating the information?
14. Make a sketch to show the various elements (employees, suppliers, and customers) of a fast-food outlet. Indicate on the sketch the most important information flows. What happens as the organization gets larger and the number of employees, customers, and products increases?

ADDITIONAL READINGS

Feigenbaum, Edward A., and Feldman, Julian. *Computers and Thought.* New York: McGraw-Hill, 1963.

Graham, Neill. *The Mind Tool.* St. Paul: West Publishing, 1976.

Harris, Sidney. *What's So Funny about Computers.* Los Altos, CA: William Kaufmann, 1982.

McWilliams, Peter A. *The Personal Computer in Business Book.* Los Angeles: Prelude Press, 1983.

Metropolis, A., et al. *A History of Computing in the Tenth Century.* New York: Academic Press, 1980.

Pattis, Richard E. *Karel the Robot: A Gentle Introduction to the Art of Programming.* New York: John Wiley & Sons, 1981.

Van Tassell, Dennie L. *The Complete Computer,* 2d ed. Palo Alto, CA: Science Research Associates, 1982.

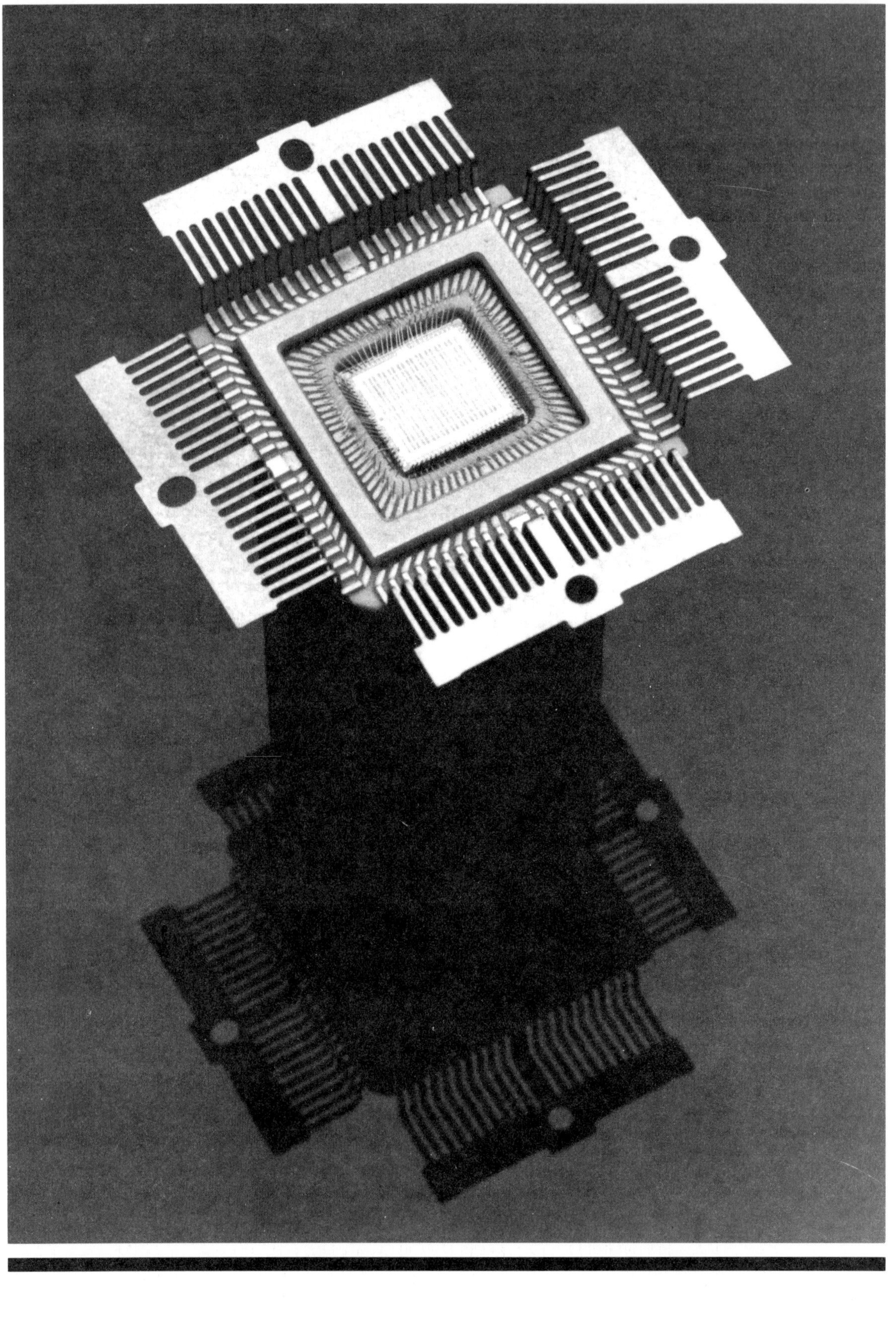

2

Computer Fundamentals —Hardware

CHAPTER PREVIEW

This and the next chapter are intended to provide a quick overview of the manner in which computers are used in data processing. They are intended to provide enough background information so that hands-on-work can begin immediately. A more in-depth treatment of the information will be presented in Part II.

A good computer system requires an artful blend of equipment, programs, procedures, and people. In this chapter we will examine computer **hardware,** those items of equipment which are a necessary part of any computer system. In the next chapter we will examine computer **software,** the sets of instructions which are necessary to guide a computer's work. The study of procedures and personnel will be left for a later chapter (Chapter 14).

To fully understand the manner in which computers are used in data processing requires extensive study, and that is the subject of the entire book. A brief overview, however, can be of great assistance in developing a perspective into which details can be assimilated later. This approach in educational circles is called the spiral approach, and it is useful in teaching not only data processing and computer programming but many other subjects as well. Figure 2–1 provides a visual illustration of a spiral approach to the teaching of data processing. A very similar approach, known as top/down in data processing, provides first for the overall structure (the top) and second for the detail within that structure (down).

This chapter helps us learn about computer hardware. The hardware elements of a computer system are of critical importance, for without them the system will not operate. They allow us to compute in the same way that cars allow us to drive and airplanes allow us to fly. A case study will help us understand the subject matter we will need to know and understand why we might want to know it.

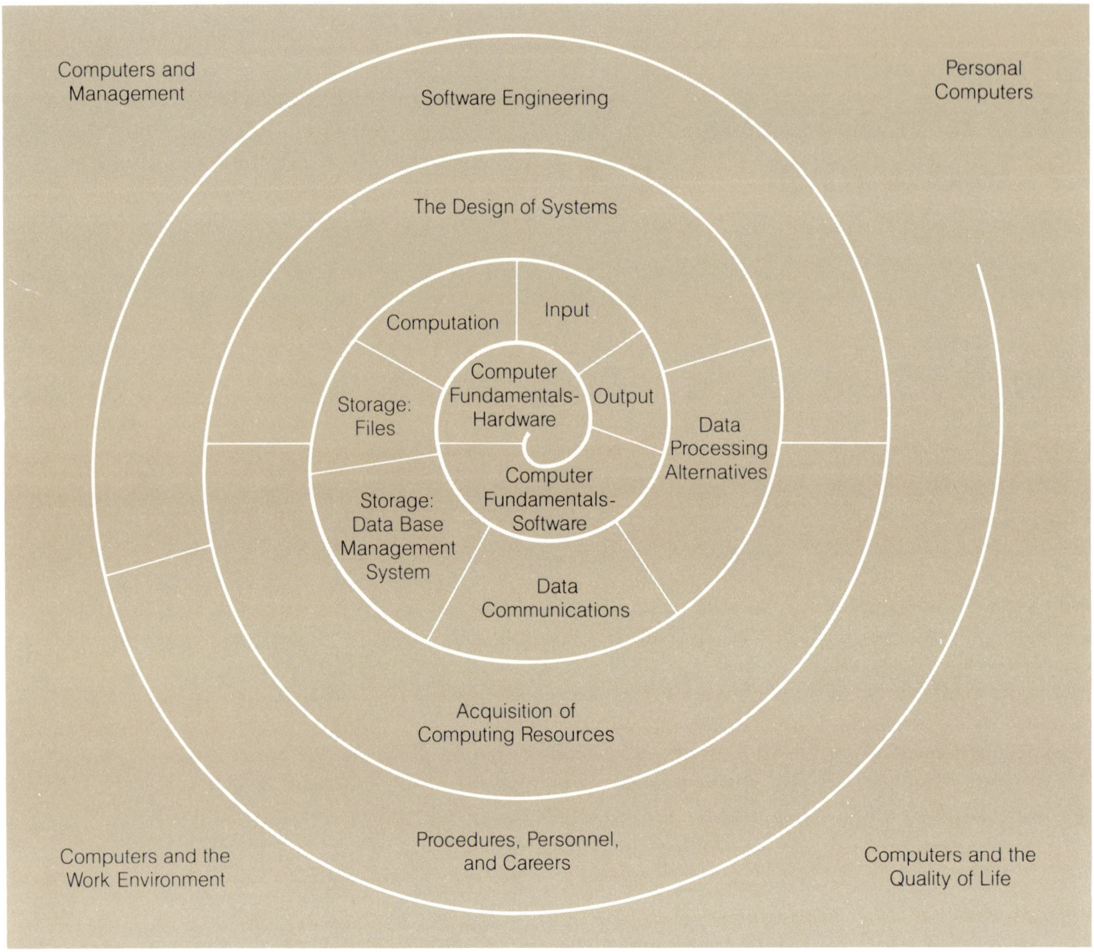

Figure 2–1 Spiral Approach to Teaching Data Processing

COMPUTING CHALLENGE: *A Small System For Work and Play*

Dana Brownell has been selling real estate for two years, since her children entered high school. In their high school course work her children have been introduced to several small computer systems. They have become excited about the use of computers and have encouraged Dana to buy a home computer to help with the record-keeping, property appraisal, and property management tasks which are part of her real estate business. They also know that many computer games are available for some home computer systems, and they hope that their mother will buy such a system.

Although the temptation to buy a work-saving computer device is great, Dana remembers what a difficult time she had when she bought a stereo system. Not liking to have decisions made for her, she refused to buy one of the systems assembled at the stereo store, but chose instead to pick and assemble her own components. As a result she spent six weeks in the library reading about the technology of sound reproduction and component compatibility so that she could buy intelligently.

She visited the computer store with many reservations. The salesperson suggested that she needed a computer, a video display (it looked like a TV to her), a printer, and a small tape cassette. Dana, of course, had no idea which components were necessary and how they might interact to produce a computing system. She was, of course, familiar with televisions and tape cassettes, but what role did they play in a computing system? Dana needed some framework within which to start thinking about her needs in a computer. She needed to understand the roles to be played by each of the pieces of equipment. Additionally, she needed to know whether, for example, the tape cassette is a good or bad choice for the role for which it is intended. Dana discovered, in other words, that she needed an understanding of the framework within which to fit the various elements.

Such a framework is important to any computer novice. Successful completion of this chapter should make it possible for us to:

1. *Represent a computer's primary functions through use of a block diagram.*
2. *Differentiate between the functions of primary and secondary storage.*
3. *Discuss the various sizes of computers which are available.*
4. *Describe some of the important characteristics of a computer's internal representation of data.*

HISTORICAL PERSPECTIVE

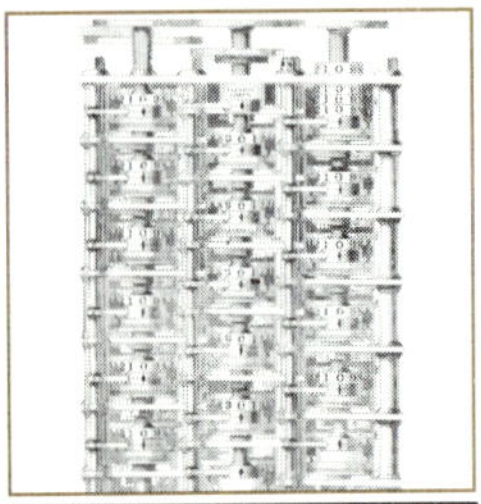

The history of computing machines is rather extensive, but electronic computers have been around for a relatively short period of time. They were first built in the early 1940s. Several developments important to data processing preceded the development of the electronic computer. A review of some of these developments will help us put later materials into proper perspective.

One of the earliest devices to be used to assist in the process of computation was the abacus. As you can see from the picture of the abacus (Figure 2–2), semi-round markers sliding on rods were used to perform addition and subtraction. It is still in use today by Chinese merchants. A mechanical adding machine was built in the 1600s by Blaise Pascal (for whom a programming language has been named). Pascal's numerical wheel calculator is pictured in Figure 2–3. It was followed by the work of Charles Babbage who, in the early 1800s, worked on two mechanical, computational devices: the difference engine and the analytical engine (see Figure 2–4). Modern electronic computers owe some of their conceptual underpinnings to the pioneering work of Mr. Babbage.

In the latter part of the nineteenth century, Herman Hollerith developed electromechanical devices for recording data on punched cards which could later be processed automatically to extract the data. Hollerith's company became part of another company, which eventually became IBM. The Hollerith punched card design was not the first, however; a Frenchman, Joseph Marie Jacquard, developed punched cards to control weaving patterns on a loom many years earlier in 1801.

The first electromechanical calculator was developed in 1944, jointly by

Figure 2–2 The Abacus

Figure 2–3 Pascal's Numerical Wheel Calculator

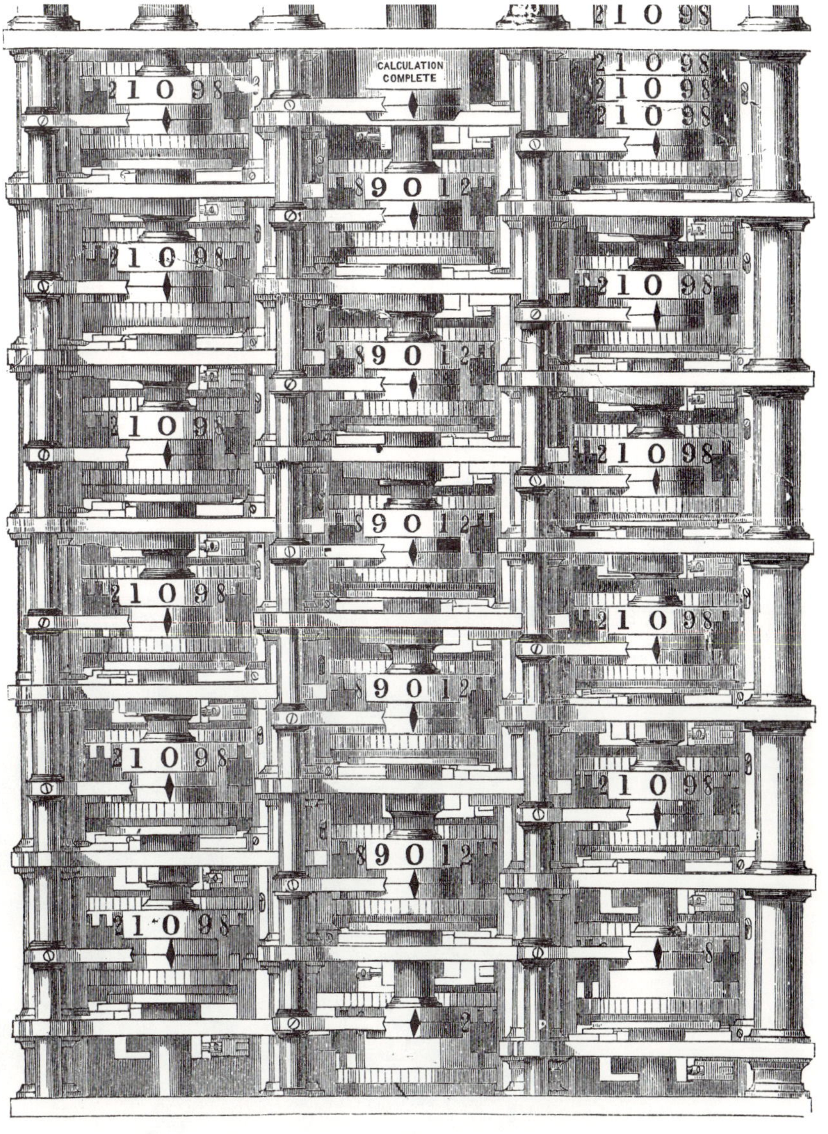

Figure 2–4 Babbage's Difference Engine

Howard Aiken and IBM. It was called the Mark I. John Atanasoff is credited with the development of a working prototype of an electronic computer at Iowa State University in 1939. He and Clifford Berry built the full-scale device in 1942.

Credit for the development of the first electronic computer usually goes to John W. Mauchly and J. Presper Eckert for building, in 1946, the Electronic Numerical Integrator and Calculator, promptly shortened to ENIAC. (Perhaps it was that effort which also sent us irreversibly down the path of acronyms.) See Figure 2–5 for a photograph of ENIAC.

The early machines were built to work from hand-set toggle switches and programs which were implemented in hardware as wired panels. Changing a program required changing some of the wiring. The first machine to use programs stored internally were the Electronic Delayed Storage Automatic Computer (EDSAC) in 1949 and the Electrical Discrete Variable Automatic Computer (EDVAC) built in 1949 and 1950.

The first generation computers were built with vacuum tubes (Figure 2–6). Power consumption and reliability were serious problems. The first commercial computer was sold in 1951 and was known as the UNIVAC I (short for UNIVersal Automatic Computer). The original UNIVAC is at the Smithsonian in Washington, D.C. The computing power of the UNIVAC I hardware can now be duplicated (exceeded really) on a single microprocessor chip. An interesting contrast in the size of computing components is illustrated in Figure 2–8. A microscope is necessary to see the computer memory chip which replaces the huge rack of vacuum tubes shown.

Second generation hardware, based upon transistors instead of vacuum tubes, began appearing in the late 1950s. The most popular computer of the second generation was the IBM 1400 series. Integrated circuits began replacing transistors in the early 1960s, and the *third generation* was un-

Figure 2–5 ENIAC

Figure 2–6 Vacuum Tubes in First Generation Computer

Figure 2–7 UNIVAC 1100

derway. The IBM 360 series pioneered the use of third generation technology. Efforts to make smaller yet more powerful hardware continue. The *fourth generation* machines are characterized by an extension of the concept of integrated circuits on a large scale, as was discussed earlier. The fourth generation machines seem to have begun with the IBM 370 in 1972. Interestingly enough, in late 1983 IBM announced a *microcomputer*, the

Figure 2–8 Four Generations of Computer Circuitry

XT/370, with the same basic instruction set as the original mainframe 370. The computing power of a large mainframe is now available in a machine that fits on a typing table. The computer's processing logic may be contained on a single electronic element known as a **chip.** A comparison of the building blocks of the four generations can be seen in Figure 2–8.

The brilliance of computing pioneers has given us remarkable improvements in computer capability in an incredibly short period of time. Their efforts have dramatically changed the nature of data processing in virtually all organizations.

Concepts: The Basic Functions of Hardware

In the previous chapter we began to see how computers might be useful in an organization to support the decision-making activities of its managers and to process the routine transactions which are necessary to the health of the organization. Here we will see that the coordination of a number of elements is required in order for the computer to be able to accomplish its work. One set of these elements is discussed in this chapter, and the discussion of the other elements is continued later.

A productive computer system requires the coordination of a collection of machines, instructions for the machines, people, and instructions for the people. Computers, storage devices, input and output devices, operators, data clerks, computer programs, and a set of guidelines must all be integrated into a functioning system.

Just as instructions are required to direct the activities of people so that their effort contributes in an efficient manner to the goals of an organization, so, too, are instructions required to direct the activities of the machines so that their efforts contribute efficiently to the goals of a computer system. A set of instructions which directs the efforts of the machines is known as a **program.** A very simple program is shown in Figure 2–9. The collection of programs which direct the activities of the hardware is referred to as software (the subject of the next chapter).

Computer Block Diagram

The four data-processing functions of output, input, computation, and storage were identified in the previous chapter. Virtually every computer system contains specific units of hardware to accomplish these four functions. The block diagram in Figure 2–10 will help us visualize them.

Of the four functions represented in the diagram, notice that the com-

Figure 2–9
Example Program

```
10 REM   PROGRAM TO GREET USER
20 REM   PROGRAMMER: W.L. HARRISON
30 REM   DATE 1 JANUARY 1983
40 PRINT  "HELLO"
50 PRINT  "I AM A COMPUTER"
60 PRINT  "MY NAME IS WART"
70 PRINT  "WHAT IS YOUR NAME?"
80 INPUT  N$
90 PRINT  "HOW CAN I HELP YOU,";N$
.
.
.
.
900 END
```

Figure 2–10
Computer Block Diagram

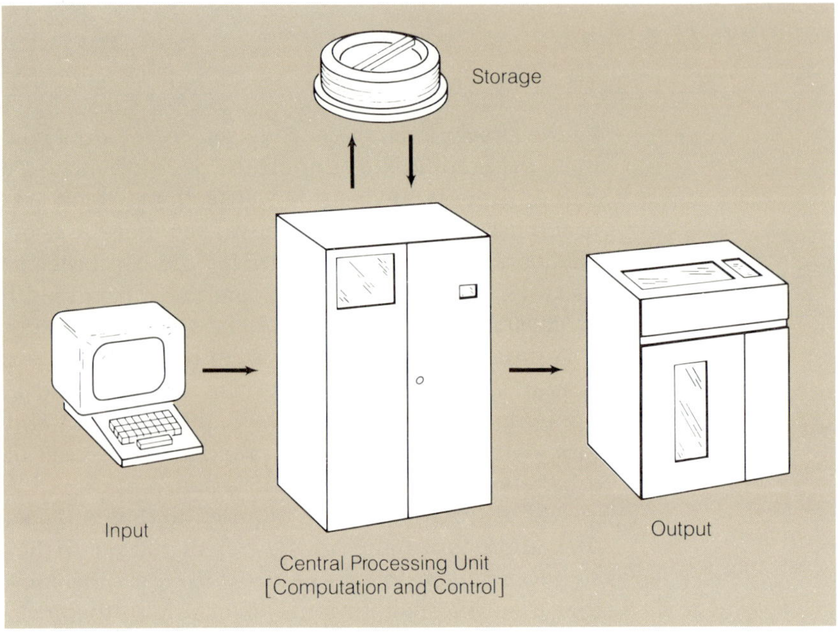

putation function and the control function are contained in a device called the **central processing unit (CPU).** Through the first three generations the phrase *central processing unit* was used to refer to the cabinet which contained the electronics of the processing logic itself and the primary storage electronics as well. In new machines, the processor itself has become a single chip, and the primary storage is contained in a series of chips, all mounted in a circuit board referred to, in some cases, as the **mother board.**

Challenge Update

Dana Brownell has now seen the computer block diagram and can determine how each of the four functions might be represented in a home computer.

Much of the time when people refer to a computer, they are actually referring to the CPU. We will use the phrase **computer system** to refer to the CPU and the various output, input, and storage devices connected directly to it. Such a system is shown in Figure 2–11.

Output. In the previous chapter we learned that during the design of a system, it was useful to discuss the *output* first. Let us continue that approach and discuss further the rationale. In designing any system, the first order of business is to determine what the output of that system is to be. This important, common-sense concept is frequently overlooked in system design, oddly enough. Perhaps an example will illustrate the point.

An impulse purchase is sometimes made just because we happened to have money in our pocket when the temptation presented itself. Sometimes we drive indiscriminately in the car, only because the car was available and we had nothing else to do. We may have taken those actions giving consideration only to the availability of inputs (time, money, and the car) and not to a specific output. Did we have a clear picture of the object we wanted to own before we spent the money in the first case, or a clear idea of a place we wanted to visit before we pressed the car and our time into service in the second case? If not, then we designed a system that was, in each case, designed to accommodate the inputs that were available, not to produce specific outputs.

When we regret the impulse purchase or the ill-defined use of time and car, we begin to understand why a proper system design requires the careful consideration of the output as the first step in the design process. We put together social organizations to accomplish certain purposes (outputs). We start up a business to produce goods and services (outputs). Government agencies are established to deliver certain services (outputs). It is a concept that is equally true in the design of computer systems. The output must be determined first. We must figure out what the system is to produce before we begin considering the resources necessary to produce it.

Suppose, for example, a teacher wanted to design a system through which the students learned as much as possible about a particular subject. The primary concern is: what will the students be able to demonstrate that they know at the end of the course? That is an output! The teacher designs readings, lectures, and homework assignments (inputs) necessary to achieve the desired output. They sometimes believe they are entitled to a good grade because of the effort they put into a class (input) instead of the grade they received on the basis of their performance on graded work (output).

In system design, one of the problems which of course arises is that we seldom have a completely free hand in determining the inputs, computation, and storage functions. Very often the system design question is: "Can we produce such and such an output *given* the system's current inputs and computation and storage capability?" Even here the output is the first consideration. How strange it would be to hear the order reversed and have

Figure 2–11 Layout of Computer System

Output Device (Printer)

CPU

Secondary Memory (Disk Drives)

Input Device (Card Reader)

someone say: "it matters not what the system produces as long as the input, computation, and storage functions are used."

How do we determine which computer output is "correct"? We must, of course, look at the larger organizational activity that is being supported by the computer in order to determine what is "correct" and what is not. If we are trying to accommodate a passenger's purchase of an airline ticket, then the correct output is the ticket, plus some entries in our records to secure the passenger's reservation and to accomplish the task of collecting the payment. If the purpose is to help the sales manager analyze the performance of the sales people, then the correct output might be a graph comparing the performances of the sales people to each other or to a competitor's sales people. The output which is "correct" is the one which best supports the organization's goals. Figure 2–12 shows some examples of possible outputs.

A large number of different types of devices are available for the production of computer output. Television screens, typewriter-like devices called terminals, printers, plotters, voice generation devices, and microfilm devices are all used for computer output. We will discuss these components in detail in Chapter 4. At this point, it is enough to understand that output is one of the four main elements of a computer system, and different hardware can produce different types of output from the system.

The design problem with respect to output is, then, what output should the system produce and in what form should it be produced? Only when those questions are answered can we begin to identify the hardware which is needed. The design problem becomes even more difficult as we design

Figure 2–12 Output Samples

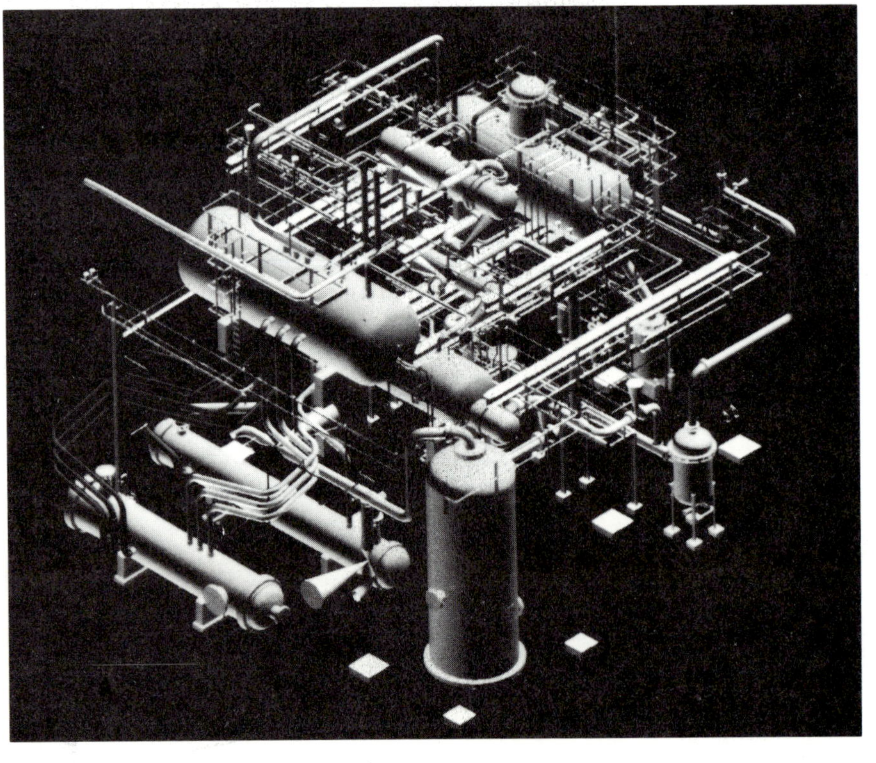

Figure 2-12 Continued

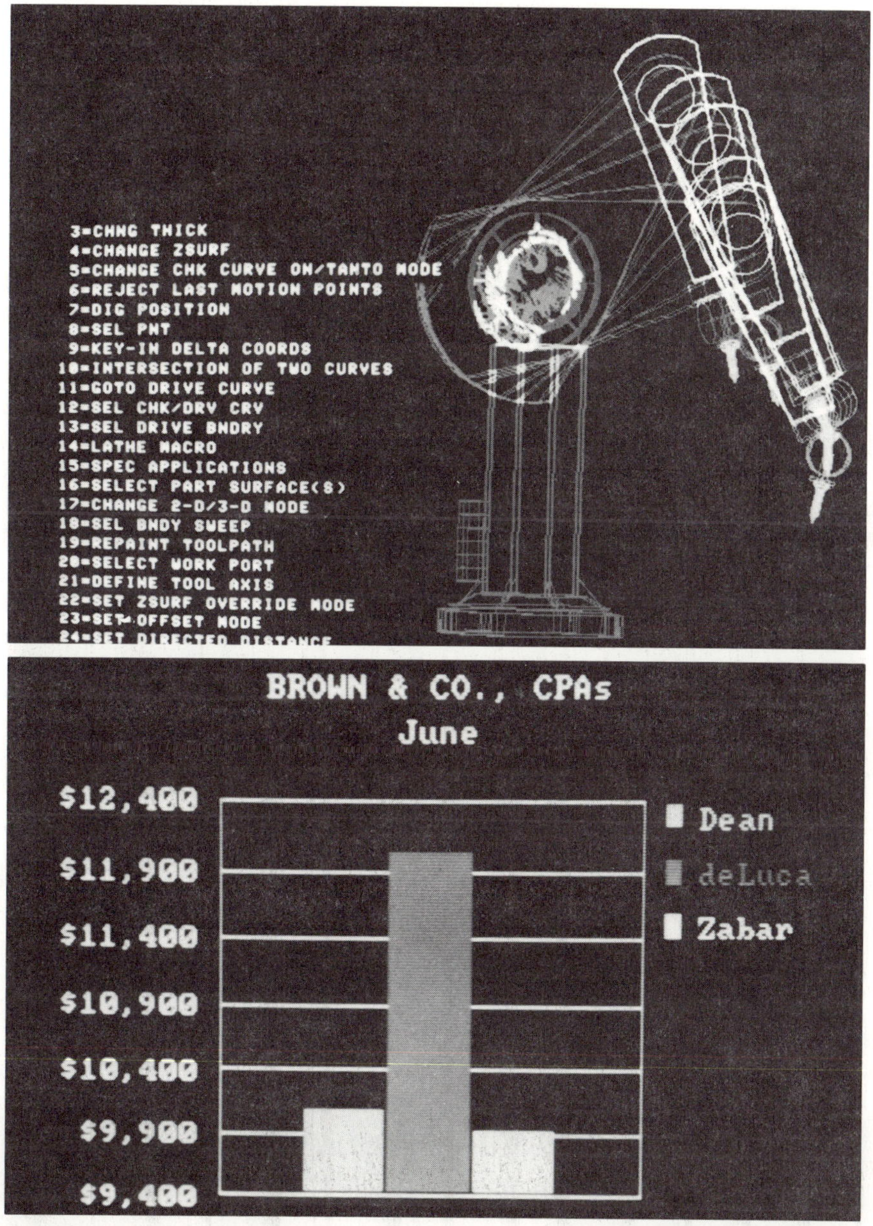

systems which are to be useful not only now, but for some time into the future as well.

Input. The second important element of a computer system is the *input* function. As with output, many different types of equipment are available for accomplishing computer input, the operation which causes data to enter the system. Examples of computer input devices include punched card readers, terminals with keyboards, cash registers as point-of-sale terminals, optical character readers, digitizers, and voice input devices (see Figure 2-13). These devices will be discussed in detail in Chapter 5. An analysis of the outputs required from the system helps us identify the inputs which are needed. We must then devise ways to ensure that all the necessary data is captured and put in a form which allows it to become input for the system.

A few examples of system inputs and outputs will help our understanding. A payroll system has paychecks (plus some entries in the accounting ledgers) as output and time cards as input. A computer-graded testing scheme has test scores (plus some testing statistics) as an output and student answer sheets (plus, of course, the approved solutions) as inputs. A computer game has video pictures and sounds as outputs with player positioning of a set of controls as the inputs.

Computation. The hardware which accomplishes computation, is the CPU Remember that we distinguish between a computer *system*, which incorporates all of the four functions with which we have been dealing in this chapter, and the element of primary importance in the system, the CPU.

In fact, throughout the text when we speak of a computer itself, we will be including only the CPU. When we speak of a computer system, we will include, with the CPU, all of the input, output, and storage devices. The computer itself (the CPU) utilizes a vast array of electronic circuitry to perform the mathematical and logical functions of computation.

The CPU is the hardware component which controls the operation of all the other machines in the computer system. It was historically the case that only the CPU had the capability to store and follow a set of stored instructions. Other machines were without any such "intelligence." As the system's activities have become more complex, and as design abilities have improved, we have found it advantageous to build intelligence into other machines in the system. For now, to keep our task relatively simple, we will consider the CPU as containing all of the system's intelligence.

The intelligence contained in the CPU gives it the capability to perform all the computations which might be necessary, to interpret and perform the actions described in the instructions it receives, and to coordinate the activities of the other machines. The computations performed by the CPU include the full set of arithmetic and logical (true/false) operations necessary for the operation of a calculating device. The operations are performed in a part of the CPU known as the arithmetic/logic unit (ALU).

The CPU also interprets each of the instructions in a computer program and initiates the actions necessary to execute those instructions. These activities are carried out in an area of processing logic known as the **control unit.** Each program is designed to provide the CPU with the instructions necessary to accomplish specific tasks. We will have a great deal more to learn about the CPU's instructions in the next chapter.

Storage. In order for the CPU to be able to carry out its duties, it must have an area in which it can store data and instructions while they are being used by the CPU. This storage area is known as **primary storage.** Other terms which are used to refer to the primary storage are primary memory, main memory, main storage, core memory, and core storage. The primary storage is built of very fast, and usually rather expensive, electronic components capable of accommodating the short-term storage of data and

Figure 2–13 Input Samples

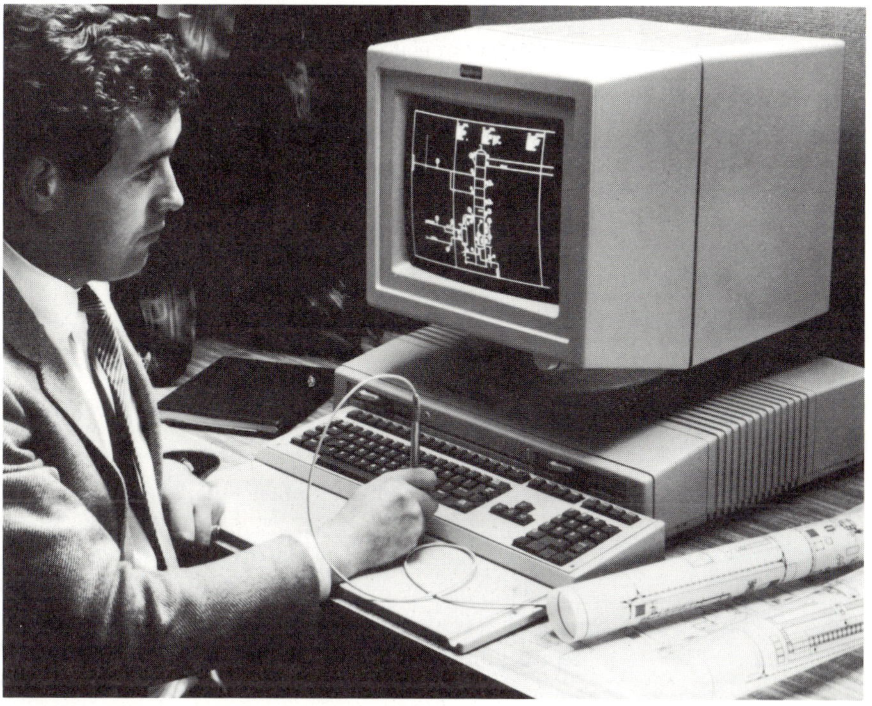

programs for the CPU. Data and programs are moved back and forth between primary storage and other areas as the CPU has need for other data and programs.

The remainder of the storage function is provided by secondary storage devices. The secondary storage devices are located somewhat farther away from the CPU than primary storage and provide vast amounts of storage space by utilizing a number of different technologies. The devices which are used for secondary storage are discussed in detail in Chapter 6. While many such devices exist, magnetic disk drives are the ones most commonly used.

Challenge Update

Dana should now be able to understand that the tape cassette in her system is secondary memory. Primary memory for microcomputers is housed in the same container (box) as the CPU.

Hardware Operations. Let us examine, in very general terms, the typical operations of a collection of computer hardware in accomplishing a data processing task. We will get much more specific later, but it is important to develop an early understanding of the overall scheme of activities as we proceed. To gain that understanding we will compare a computer's memory and program with our own while we play a simple game.

Imagine that we are going to challenge a computer system to a game of tic-tac-toe. We know how to play because long ago someone helped us store the rules in our memory. Similarly, the computer knows how to play only if someone has stored in its memory the instructions it is to follow in playing the game. These instructions would actually be stored in the computer's secondary memory when not being used. When the game itself is to begin, the instructions would be moved into the primary memory.

The game begins. We make a move by filling an appropriate cell on the tic-tac-toe matrix. Our moves become known to the computer through an input device, perhaps as we touch a light pen to a television screen. The computer uses the same television screen to display its moves (output); and, of course, it records our moves in its memory. We alternate moves until a winner is determined or until a draw is indicated. Our choice of moves depends upon our knowledge (stored sets of instructions) of the game. The computer's moves are determined by its program (stored sets of instructions). The logical processes of our minds and the logic of the computer's program compete with each other. If our memory and the computer's both contain a good set of instructions, every game will be a draw.

The person who designed the computer's instructions may have realized that we would not enjoy playing if every game was a draw, so the computer's instructions are probably to let us win occasionally. The computer system for playing tic-tac-toe could be quite simple. The system needs only a CPU, some storage, a television screen output device, and a light pen used in conjunction with a television screen as an input device.

We move now to a discussion of the various sizes of computers which are available. Remember that each size contains the four basic elements. The manner by which the elements' functions are carried out might be quite different, but the concepts remain the same.

Tools: The Range of Hardware Options

Now that we understand the basic functions of computer hardware, let us examine the wide variety of hardware which is available for carrying out those functions. We can gather together a CPU, input devices, output devices, and secondary storage devices for a computer system in somewhat the same way that we might gather together a receiver, a tape deck, a turntable, and speakers for a stereo system. In each case, we would size the components to fit the use we envisioned, and we would make sure that each component was compatible with the rest of the components in the system.

In a computer system, as in a stereo system, we choose the types of equipment we want, the features we need for our data processing purposes and size of the equipment to fit our needs. Computer systems are available in very large and very small sizes. A small one could cost less than $1,000, while a very large one would cost millions of dollars.

The words *large* and *small* used in this context refer not only to physical size, but also to processor speed, primary storage capacity, and overall system complexity. A large computer system could be expected to have a large primary memory and many input, output, and secondary memory devices. In addition, it is expected to have very sophisticated software and be able to execute instructions in the millions-of-instructions-per-second (MIPS) range. Such a system would be physically large as well, occupying a large room in all probability, and would be referred to as a large mainframe.

Only a few years ago we had only large, medium, and small mainframe computers. Small organizations with fewer data processing tasks used small mainframe computer systems.

As companies grew larger, their data processing needs increased, and they moved to larger mainframes. Economists use the phrase *economies of scale* to indicate that certain performance characteristics of a system improve with increasing size. Mainframes exhibit some economies of scale; in particular, the cost of each computation decreases as the size of the machine increases. In addition, a larger mainframe would have more storage and could handle larger programs and more data. A large mainframe is shown in Figure 2–14.

Research efforts to build larger and faster computers continues. The U.S. government continues to stimulate the design of a computer capable of executing a billion instructions per second. Machines capable of executing 800 million instructions per second already exist. Significant other research efforts are directed at making computers smaller. The push toward the miniaturization of computers (and many other devices) began with the space effort. The energy requirements for launching a device into space are so great that the development of miniature devices pays huge dividends in terms of rocket fuel savings. Much of the development of miniature devices carried over into the design of computers.

Partly as a result of that research, we have computer systems now which are quite small. We have minicomputer systems, and even microcomputer systems. The minicomputer systems of today are as powerful as the

Figure 2–14 Large Mainframe Computer System

medium-sized mainframe systems of just a few years ago. The minicomputer pictured in Figure 2–15 is capable of the full range of data processing functions despite it's relatively small size. Microcomputer systems are becoming as powerful as yesterday's minicomputer systems. (see Figure 2–16).

It is virtually impossible to establish a clear-cut classification scheme which would place each computer in its proper category: large mainframe, small mainframe, minicomputer, or microcomputer. The distinguishing characteristics are very technical in nature, and there are more exceptions than rules. Some of the factors used to classify computing systems include the size of the primary storage, the range of capability of the software, the size of an individual storage location, and the amount of hardware under the control of the CPU.

The physical space a computing system occupies can provide an early clue to whether it is a mainframe, a minicomputer, or a microcomputer. Mainframe systems typically occupy entire rooms, sometimes very large rooms. Minicomputer systems tend to occupy a space somewhat less than the size of an office desk, with a few pieces of peripheral equipment scattered nearby. Microcomputers are, for the most part, desktop machines, occupying about the same space as an electric typewriter. Peripherals such as printers and extra secondary storage devices may extend the storage area. For example, the Apple MacIntosh, a microcomputer introduced in early 1984, occupies only a single square foot of desktop space.

Challenge Update

The home computer under consideration by Dana Brownell would be a microcomputer. She can now understand where such a computer fits with the wide range of available options.

Figure 2–15
Minicomputer System

Figure 2–16
Microcomputer System

The uses to which the system will be put determine the particular set of hardware devices required by an organization. A particular set of computer hardware devices is called a **configuration.** An organization's computer system configuration may be built around a small, medium, or large mainframe, or even around a minicomputer or microcomputer.

Technology: Bits and Bytes

We have seen that, at least conceptually, computers are relatively simple devices which accommodate the input of data, its manipulation and storage, and the output of some useful information. These four basic functions are accomplished through special purpose machines, which collectively are called computer hardware.

A data processing system requires not only computer hardware but, in addition, many sets of instructions which control the operation of the hardware. These instructions are discussed in the next chapter on software. Our understanding of the next chapter will be improved, however, if we take a few moments to look into exactly how the computer hardware sends, receives, and stores data.

Internal Representation of Data

In a digital computer system, the basis for all internal representations of data is digital, using two discrete states. In the first chapter, we examined the use of two-state devices to encode data and contrasted that with data in the analog form. All digital computer hardware uses digital techniques to represent data, and most components of hardware in today's data processing computer systems are designed to make use of two-state, digital technology.

Historically, the most common data input medium has been the punched card. In recent years, however, the use of magnetic media has become much more popular. While we will save our examination of punched cards and magnetic media until a more appropriate time, it will be useful to think for a minute about a punched card and the way data is stored there. Data are represented on a punched card as a pattern in binary digital fashion, where the two states which contribute to the pattern are the presence or absence of holes punched into the card. (The location of the holes also has meaning.)

Data inside the various hardware devices are likewise represented by patterns formed by two-state, digital devices. In some cases, the patterns are formed by magnetized spots (North and South poles), while other devices depend upon the presence or absence of an electronic charge, or even the presence or absence of a magnetic domain, known in some cases as a "bubble".

Let us consider a single storage location inside the computer's primary memory. The size of a single storage location varies from machine to machine, depending upon its design. As a matter of fact, the size of a single

Figure 2–17 Bits and Patterns

Bits	Number of Different Patterns
1	2
2	4
3	8
4	16
5	32
6	64
7	128
8	256

location is one of the characteristics formerly used to differentiate microcomputers from minicomputers and both from larger mainframes. Such distinctions are no longer easy to make since the larger microcomputers have storage locations as large as the smaller mainframes.

How large must a single location be in order to store a single character? That is, how many two-state devices do we need at a single location in order to be able to record (and distinguish) each of the twenty-six different letters in turn? Each two-state device is called a binary digit, or **bit.** Figure 2–17 illustrates that 5 bits would give us 32 different patterns, enough for the alphabet, but not enough to include a full set of numerical digits. The number of bits used to represent a single character is known as a **byte.** Most computer systems utilize 8 bits in each storage location (byte) to allow for upper and lower case letters, all the numerical digits (0 to 9), and a bunch of special characters (+ − / * ;, and so on).

Challenge Update

Dana, and the reader, should now understand that bits and bytes are fundamental to the computer's internal representation of data.

Each character is assigned a specified pattern, and all the hardware devices in the system should, of course, interpret each pattern in the same way. Standard schemes have been established for encoding (making a pattern) for each character. Some confusion in the industry is caused by the fact that several different encoding standards exist. Two (or more) pieces of computer hardware designed for different encoding standards would have trouble communicating with each other. Several such encoding schemes are illustrated in Appendix B.

To further our understanding of the computer's manipulation of data, we would need to know binary arithmetic, the basis for all arithmetic operations inside a computer. Binary arithmetic is also discussed in Appendix B.

Computer Chips

A few words about the basic hardware building block are in order. In early computers, the encoded data were transmitted from electronic device to electronic device as electrical impulses along wires. Components were then designed which contained many electronic devices on a single board known

Figure 2–18
Computer Chips on a Silicon Wafer

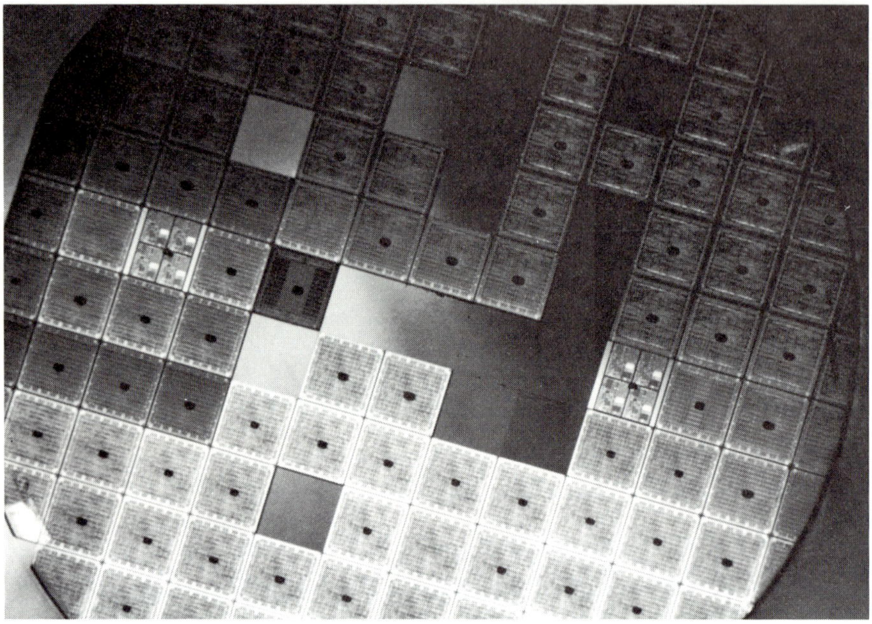

as a **printed circuit board.** Data then traveled along the printed circuits while on the board, and traveled from board to board on wires. The move to miniaturization has seen the complex circuit boards reduced by unbelievable proportions. Hundreds of thousands of electronic devices now reside on a silicon carbide–based chip smaller than a fingernail (see Figure 2–18).

These chips are the building blocks for practically all computer hardware devices. They are responsible for the dramatic improvements which have been made in the ratio of computer price to performance. They also allow distribution of some of the system's intelligence to other machines in the system, **peripherals.** Very similar chips in other settings give us hand-held calculators, programmable microwave ovens, electronic games, and much, much more.

Although the technological advances in computing made over the past decade or two have been dramatic, there really is no indication that the drama is over. We expect even greater improvements in the future.

Newest Developments

We should continue to see great improvement in hardware capabilities, but there are limits beyond which it would seem impossible to go. The process for making chips is a case in point.

The electronic circuitry to be put on a chip is drawn originally on a very large diagram. As a matter of fact, these drawings are done under computer control. The drawings are photo-reduced and light is used to transfer the circuitry to a photo-sensitive layer on the silicon wafer. At some point, the

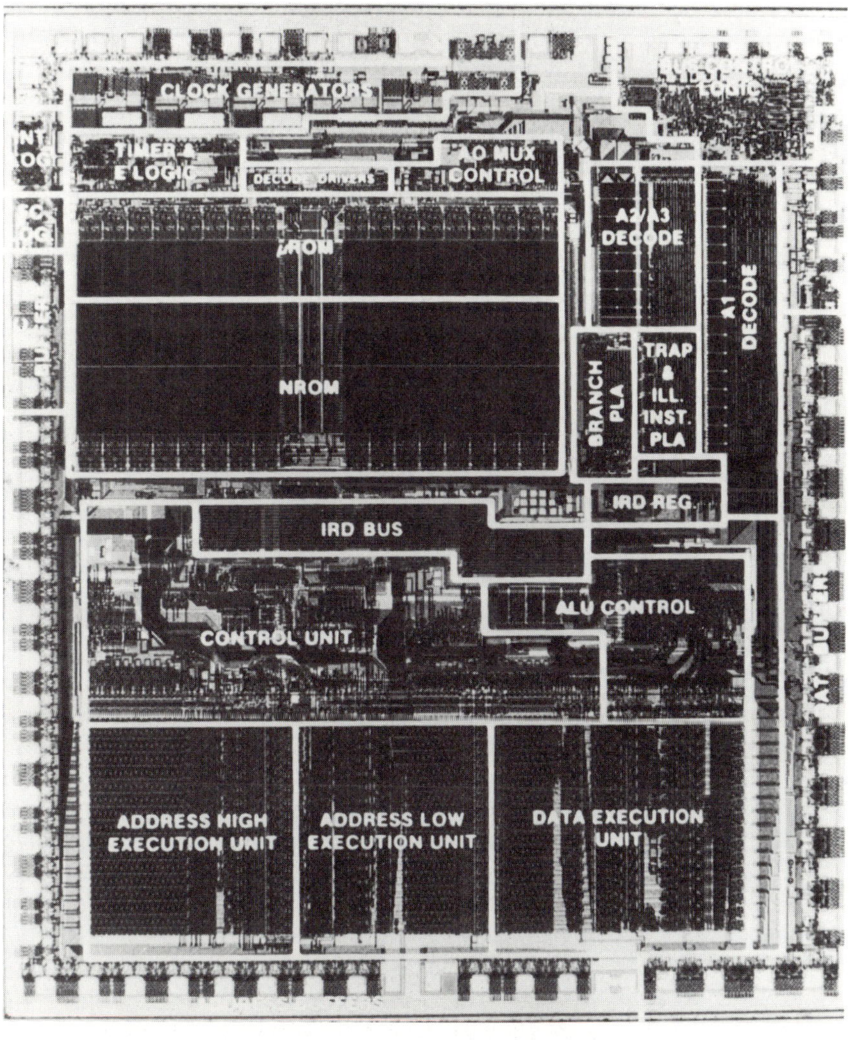

Figure 2–19
Microprocessor Chip

wave length of the light used to expose the circuitry begins to limit how small the lines and spaces between lines can be. The light waves produce "fuzzy" edges, if the edges are inspected under a microscope.

X-rays, with a shorter wave length than visible light, can be substituted, making smaller lines and spaces possible. Eventually, the wave length begins to limit the size reduction, and electron beams are used instead.

Technology has allowed the full logic for a microcomputer to be placed on a chip. Mainframe chip sets with CPU and memory on the same chip are the logical extension of that technology. An entire CPU, including the processor itself, memory, and some communications capability, can exist on a single chip less than a centimeter in width and length (Figure 2–19).

Interesting new technologies continue to be tested in research laboratories. One of these, referred to as the Josephson Junction, uses temperatures near absolute zero to enhance the ease with which electrons can travel in a conducting medium. A computer using this technology could be expected to be many times faster than today's machines and to consume many times less power.

Unfortunately, many technical problems, including one of refrigeration, must be solved before computers based on the Josephson Junction are feasible. Private research efforts in the United States on the Josephson CPU have decreased significantly in recent years as a reflection of the difficulty in solving a problem with seemingly limited application. Research efforts on many other technologies continue; only time and the forces of the market will tell which will be successful.

Integration of electronic components on a very large scale (VLSI) will be extended to very, very large scale. There are, however, physical limits. The Josephson research attempted to circumvent those limits. Other new technologies will appear and challenge as well. Time will eventually provide the answers concerning the feasibility of the new technologies. For now, let us return to the problem with which we began the chapter, the problem of acquiring a computing system for the home.

COMPUTING CHALLENGE: *A Final Note*

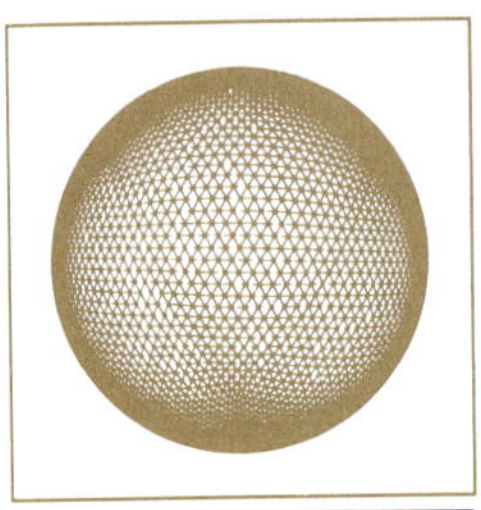

Dana Brownell has become the proud owner of a new personal computer. It consists of a typewriter-like housing with keyboard, a television screen, a small printer and a small tape cassette. Later on she plans to buy a pair of joystick controls so that her children can play computer games, but for now she must put the system to work in supporting her real estate business.

Dana does not know a great deal about computers, but she has seen the block diagram shown in Figure 2–10 used to explain the computer's functions. It might help us to think about Dana's home computer.

1. *In what way(s) is (an) output represented in her system?*
2. *Does she have more than one output device?*
3. *In what way(s) is (an) input represented?*
4. *What function does the tape cassette probably fulfill?*
5. *What function will the joysticks fulfill?*
6. *What must a user know in order to effectively use a personal computer? Bits? Bytes? How to Type?*

SUMMARY

- A productive computer system requires the efficient interaction of people, hardware, and software under the guidance of effective procedures and control activities.

- Computer hardware refers to the machines which accomplish the movement, manipulation, and storage of data.
- The basic functions of a computer system—present in computers of all sizes—are output, input, computation, and storage.
- Proper design of a data processing system requires that the desired outputs be determined first, followed by consideration of the inputs, computations, and storage requirements needed to get those outputs.
- The different types of devices which support the functions of a computer system operate under control of the central processing unit (CPU).
- The internal representation of data and programs depends upon single elements known as bits (short for binary digits) and groups of bits known as bytes.
- Computers are available in many sizes, from very large mainframes to very small microcomputers.
- Computer systems vary in terms of their costs, their capabilities and the amount of physical space they occupy, but the same basic functions are common to all systems.
- Large systems will have more peripherals and a larger variety of peripherals to perform the basic functions than do smaller systems.
- The electronic logic necessary to accomplish processing and primary storage functions can now be built into a single silicon chip.
- Research and development efforts have greatly improved the performance of computer hardware through the years, while computer hardware costs have declined over the same period, and are expected to continue to do so.

CASE: Railroad Company Keeps Track With Computer

Those of us who have trouble keeping track of our car keys, glasses, and umbrellas can easily appreciate what a difficult task it must be for railroad companies to keep track of their rail cars. One such company, the Missouri Pacific must maintain records on over 90,000 freight cars, locomotives, and cabooses which travel over the 12,000 plus miles of track in the system. A sophisticated computing system has proven to be of great benefit in helping the railroad company manage its cars efficiently.

Missouri Pacific Railroad (Mo-Pac) uses a large network of IBM and Memorex computers, display terminals and printers in handling most of their operations. This $1.7-billion-a-year railroad has spent over $45 million on its computerized Transportation Control System to meet two goals: (1) highly reliable railroad service to its shipper-customers, and (2) maximum efficiency in railroad transportation operations without reducing the quality of service. They have data about every railroad car they have on the tracks. They know where every car is, how long it has been there, and where it is going to go next. It is all part of the freight car scheduling system that is to increase productivity and freight car utilization.

Mo-Pac's revenues depend in large part upon the movement of loaded cars from the shipping point to their destinations and the distribution of empty cars to meet future shipping demand. An efficient information processing system can significantly improve the company's performance.

Mo-Pac has a vast number of terminals (with video displays) and printers throughout its extensive network and over 1,250 devices connected to that network. In addition to two large IBM central computers at the main office, Mo-Pac has minicomputers or intelligent terminals at every one of its freight yards. The company also uses Memorex display stations and printers within the St. Louis main office to have information readily available to all who require it.

Their principal use of the system is for making inquiries to locate a specific car. Printers provide documentation to appropriate departments whenever necessary. Mo-Pac management is quick to credit this large system with helping them achieve the best possible service to their shipper-customers.

Source: "Railroad Tracks Freight Cars with CRT's," *Infosystems*, May 1981, part 2, p. 20. Copyright © 1981 Hitchcock Publishing Company.

Questions for the Case

1. What input devices are mentioned in the Mo-Pac system description?
2. What output devices are mentioned?
3. Is there mention of the storage function? What does it contain?
4. Does Mo-Pac's data processing task seem small or large? Are its computers small or large?
5. How does such a system improve the way in which Mo-Pac manages its railroad?

DISCUSSION QUESTIONS AND EXERCISES

1. Generate a list of computer equipment which you have seen or perhaps used. Determine which of the four basic functions each piece of equipment serves.
2. Discuss the historical relationship between computing system performance and the cost of computers.
3. A data processing system must bring together hardware, software, people, and of instructions. Which element is most important? Why?
4. Some people claim that most decisions made in organizations are made on the basis of politics, not facts. If that is true, what will be the impact of increased computer usage in an organization?
5. Explain the concept of computer intelligence. In your answer, explain in what sense a computer has intelligence. What does it mean to say that the intelligence is distributed?
6. How much should an organization manager know about computers?
7. Some of our money we carry with us while some is kept in interest earning accounts. In what way is this analogous to a computer's access to primary and secondary storage?
8. If a computer is used to control an assembly-line robot, what are the outputs? What are the inputs?

9. Organizational information systems should produce accurate output in a timely fashion so that the organization operates more effectively. Could an organization with a good information system still be ineffective? How? Are there examples of effective organizations which have poor information systems? Discuss.
10. Intelligence in computing devices requires memory and the ability to execute programs. How does that compare to human intelligence?
11. Using a two-character alphabet—* and !—develop an encoding scheme for the digits 0 to 9 and the letters A to Z. Compare it to the ASCII and EBCDIC schemes in Appendix B.
12. Visit a nearby computer center. List the different types of peripheral devices you see there.
13. Can people be viewed as information processing systems? If so, what constitutes their "hardware"? Their "software"?
14. In what ways is information similar to an organization's manufactured products? In what ways is it different?
15. In what ways do computers have an impact on our day-to-day activities? How will this change?

ADDITIONAL READINGS

Bender, Roger, Jack Carsten, David Crockett, and Bernie List. "The Chip Revolution, a Candid Conversation." *Datamation*, June 1979, pp. 98–108.

Boraiko, Allen A. "The Chip." *National Geographic*, October 1982, pp. 421–456.

Carstens, Don. "Joy of Hacking." *Science 82*, November 1982, p. 58.

Ceruzzi, Paul E. *Reckoners: the Prehistory of the Digital Computer from Relays to the Stored Program Concept, 1935–1945*. Westport, Conn.: Greenwood Press, 1983.

Lu, Cary. "Microcomputers: The Second Wave." *High Technology*, September/October 1982, pp. 36–52.

Metropolis, A. *A History of Computing in the Twentieth Century*. New York: Academic Press, 1980.

Rogers, Michael. "How Computer Salesmen Size You Up." *Personal Computing*, December 1982, p. 48.

Scientific American, September 1977. The entire issue is devoted to microelectronics. Though somewhat dated, it remains an excellent reference.

Stein, David L. "Price/Performance, Semiconductors and the Future." *Datamation*, November 1979, pp. 14–20.

"Superconducting Supercomputer; Built of Josephson Junction Device." *Scientific American*, June 1979, p. 104.

The, Lee. "Self Improvement: Computers, The Good Life and You," in *Personal Computing*, Vol. 6, No. 7, (July, 1982), p. 89.

Toong, Hoo-min, and Amar Gupta. "Personal Computer." *Scientific American*, December 1982, pp. 86–107.

RM/COBOL
DataStar
DataStar
DataStar
DataStar
TARGET
MasterPlanner
VisiCalc
Languages
C Compiler
microplan
MILESTONE
the wedge
SuperCalc
WordStar WordStar
WordStar WordStar
WordStar WordStar
WordStar WordStar
WordStar
WordStar
WordStar
WordStar
WordStar
dBASE II
Assembly-Language
Relational Database Management
System
SPELLGUARD
FILESHARE
FOR USE WITH CIS COBOL

3

Computer Fundamentals —Software

CHAPTER PREVIEW

Computer hardware by itself is not adequate to bring about the proper completion of data processing tasks. A computer system also requires software, people, and a set of procedures to guide the people's efforts. In the previous chapter we discussed the role of hardware. In this chapter we will discuss the role of software, which is to guide the hardware in the completion of useful tasks.

Many different computer programs are necessary to make any particular set of hardware useful. Some give the hardware the capability of performing specific data processing tasks such as report writing, sales summaries, or accounting for money and goods. Others are necessary for the operation of the system itself so that the activities of the various pieces of equipment can be coordinated by the central processing unit (CPU).

Organizations must buy or develop software specifically suited to their hardware and specifically designed to accomplish the desired data processing tasks. The task of evaluating and selecting software is a difficult one, as we shall see later in the text.

COMPUTING CHALLENGE: *Software for the Home Computer*

A second visit with Dana Brownell (the realtor from Chapter Two) may help us understand why software is important. Dana has selected a microprocessor-based personal computer to help with her real estate business. She selected a microcomputer with keyboard input, a tape cassette secondary memory, and both a printer and a television monitor for output. She has already learned that the tape cassette causes many delays as information is retrieved from the tape. She hopes to move up to something called a floppy disk drive very soon. Her children are still hoping for another input device, the joy sticks which will make it possible for them to use the microcomputer for video games.

Dana learned something about hardware compatibility during her selection of the system, and she understands how the various components must cooperate with each other in order for the system to work properly. In particular, she learned to buy all the system's components from the same dealer so that servicing the system would be a simpler task. Having

"So long, Mr. Schwartz. I'm leaving. Nowadays, software's where it's at."

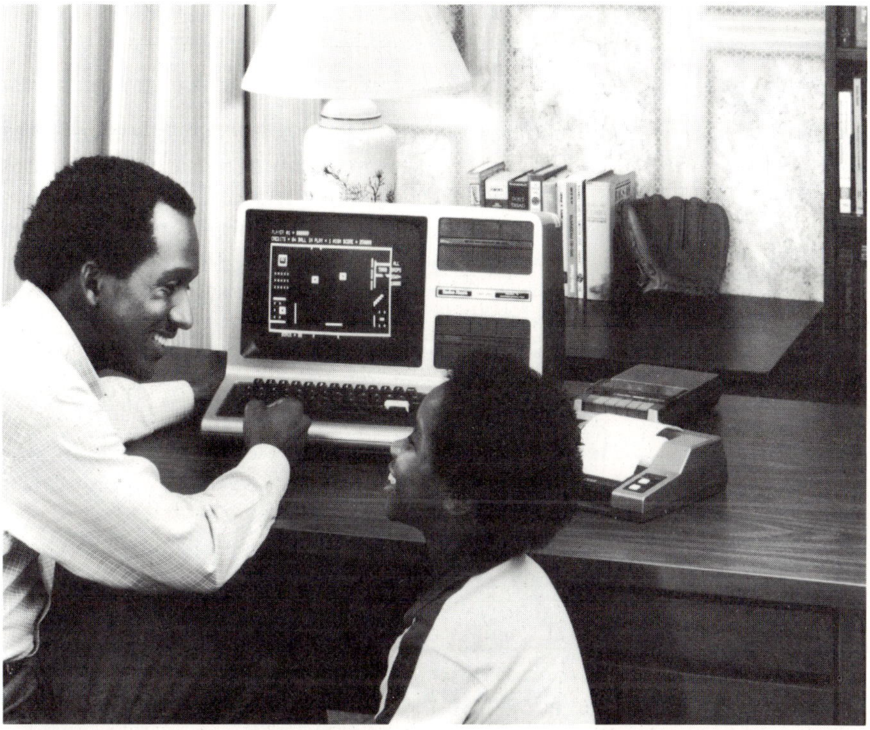

Figure 3–1 Video Games on a Personal Computer

learned from her prior purchase of stereo components, she was clever enough to require that the salesperson unpack and connect all the components, then try them all out before she paid for them and took them home.

Two large issues remain unresolved in her mind. The first is: How are the various hardware devices controlled so that the necessary cooperation among them is achieved? The second is: How can the computer be directed to do the specific tasks which are necessary in order to keep real estate records, do property appraisals, and assist in property management tasks?

Many other questions will arise later. As her business expands, she will become concerned about performing other business functions, such as word processing, and connecting her computer with a multiple-listing network.

This chapter is designed to help us understand the role of software in a computing system. After successful completion of this chapter, the reader should be able to:

1. *Explain how software makes the resources of hardware available to a user.*
2. *Differentiate between user programs and systems programs.*
3. *Describe the role of system (job) control language.*
4. *Discuss the translation and execution phases of user programs written in one of the higher-level languages.*

HISTORICAL PERSPECTIVE

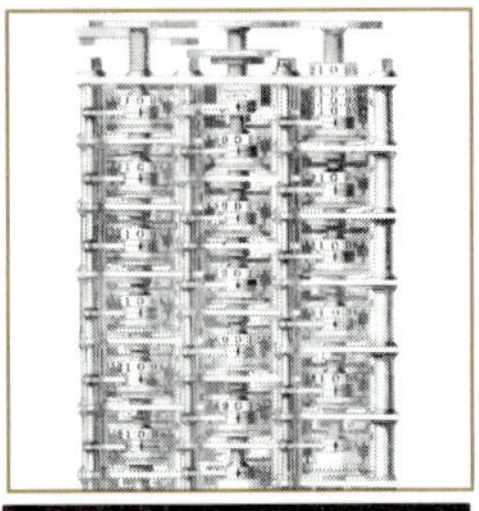

Controlling and directing the activities of a computing system have always been difficult and time-consuming tasks. Even today, many knowledgeable computer experts believe that the costs associated with developing the computer programs which control and direct the computer's actions are greater than those of any other single category. Although hardware costs have been falling, the costs associated with the development of software have been rising.

The first programmer appears to have been Augusta Ada Byron, Countess of Lovelace and daughter of the poet, Lord Byron. She contributed significantly to the development of Babbage's differential machine in the nineteenth century. As a matter of fact, in recognition of her efforts, the Department of Defense has named its new computer programming language Ada.

Programming of the earliest computers was a laborious task. The ENIAC, for example, was programmed by actually changing the wiring and setting thousands of electrical switches to particular positions. John von Neumann, J. Presper Eckert, and Maurice Wilkes all contributed to the development of the EDSAC, one of the first computers to use a stored program during the early 1950s. Von Neumann is shown with one of the early machines in Figure 3–2.

Many computing devices—more correctly, automatic calculating machines—used wired panels to control their operations. For each specific computing task, called an **application,** a specially-wired panel which controlled the machine's activities had to be developed. Early programmers

Figure 3–2 John Von Neumann with Stored Program ENIAC

Figure 3–3 Wiring Panel

developed the complex wiring diagrams necessary to complete the wired panels (see Figure 3–3). When the machine was to process the payroll, the wired panel of payroll processing instructions was used. This panel was replaced by another when the accounts receivable were processed. Employees in the data processing department maintained a set of wired panels for each application. Changing a program required changing the wired panels.

Eventually, it became possible to write a program and to use one of the input devices to enter the program into the system. The program could then be stored in the computer's memory until it was needed. These capabilities are now commonplace.

Computer programs can be written in many different computer programming languages. The most elemental form of programming language is **machine language,** a language in which the individual instructions are identified through a set of numerical codes known as **operation codes.** Each computer is designed to operate in accordance with a particular instruction set, and each instruction is identified through the corresponding operation code. In addition to the operation code, most machine language instructions also contain a reference to a particular storage location referred to as a **numerical address.** The numerical address specifies the location of data to be processed or the location in the memory of the next instruction. Early machines were programmable only in machine language. Machine language programming is still in use today, though its importance as a programming language has diminished. An example of machine language is contained in Figure 3–4.

Programming in a machine language is a difficult and tedious task. A significant improvement became available through the development of **assembly language.** Each instruction in assembly language corresponds ex-

Figure 3–4 Programming Language Examples

Sample Machine Language Instructions:
```
5300100
5300101
2000100
2100101
1000200
5400200
```

Sample Assembly Language Instructions:
```
R    A
R    B
F    A
A    B
S    C
P    C
```

Sample Higher-Level Language Instructions:
```
READ A, B
C = A + B
PRINT C
```

actly with a specific machine language instruction. The big advantages of assembly language programming over machine language programming are:

1. Mnemonic codes (essentially alphabetic codes to help the programmer remember the instructions) replace the numerical codes.
2. Variable names, something like variables in algebra, allow the programmer to associate names with data items instead of having to remember the numerical addresses of the data values. Variable names correspond with storage locations in their use in programming. A computer maintains a table of variable names and their corresponding storage locations so that the proper operations are performed on the correct values in storage.
3. Statement labels are used to identify strategic locations in a program so that programmers do not have to remember the actual, numerical addresses of those storage locations. A programmer can then attach labels to the strategic locations in the program, and the computer maintains a table to translate these labels into the appropriate locations in the program.

The improvements in programming made possible by assembly language illustrate the continuing effort to shift the workload from humans to the computer. While the programmer's work became easier, the computer acquired the added responsibility of *translating* assembly language instructions into machine language and keeping track of the storage locations associated with the various statement labels and variable names. Figure 3–4 also contains an example of assembly language.

The next big improvement came with the development in the 1950s of programming languages, called **higher-level languages.** These languages shifted more of the work from the programmer to the computer system itself. A programmer, by programming in the higher-level languages, can write instructions which look much more like English sentences and algebraic statements. The computing system translates these into machine language, as we shall see later in this chapter. Figure 3–4 contains an example of a higher-level language.

Computer designers create the computer's machine language (and assembly language) as they design the logic of the machine itself. Each elemental action of which the computer is capable will have an operation code associated with it. Machine languages (and assembly languages) are, therefore, **machine dependent;** that is, the language is unique to (and dependent on) a particular hardware design and cannot be transferred to hardware of a different design.

The higher-level languages are described as being **machine independent;** they are not unique to (nor dependent upon) a particular hardware design. For example, COBOL programs may run on computers manufactured by IBM, Honeywell, Control Data, and other firms, but a program written in COMPASS (a Control Data assembly language) will not run on either IBM or Honeywell hardware.

Concepts: The Role of Programs

Programming

A computer program is *executed* by the computer system and causes the computer to perform certain operations. Computers perform only those operations for which they have been programmed, and every instant of a CPU's operational lifetime is spent in the execution of some program. Even when waiting for the next operation to take place, it is executing a program which directs it to wait.

We can perhaps better understand what programming is if we investigate human behavior. Consider the many activities we know how to do. We have had to learn most of the activities we know how to do; they are not activities in which we engage instinctively.

We have learned how to add, subtract, multiply, and divide by memorizing a set of instructions which we follow whenever we want to perform those arithmetic operations. Computers can also, if given an appropriate set of instructions (a program), make use of built-in logic to add, subtract, multiply, and divide figures as necessary. Humans and computers can be programmed to accomplish many other tasks. The basic instruction set for a computer will include instructions for accomplishing the arithmetic operations, data movement operations, comparison operations, and transfer of control operations. Computer programming languages contain statements which cause these basic instructions to be executed in a particular order so that a precise computational sequence is established.

Similarly, we, as humans, have a basic instruction set—those activities we know how to perform because our "programming" has provided the necessary training. We are able to perform (execute) complex tasks (programs) because we can translate those tasks into an appropriate sequence of basic activities.

Occasionally, we see a story in the newspaper about attempts to deprogram someone who had been intimately involved with a cult, religious sect, or other group. Is *deprogram* the correct word? If deprogrammed, a computer becomes inoperable. Imagine the status of a deprogrammed human being. The change required probably is better described as *reprogrammed*, that is, programmed to follow a different set of instructions.

Challenge Update

Dana can now see how computer software (programs) direct the actions of computer hardware in causing useful activities to be performed.

User Programs

When a computer is operating normally, it is, without exception, following the instructions in a program. People, like ourselves, who want to use a computer to accomplish a particular data processing task must write a program to direct its efforts. These programs are called **user programs.**

Some—perhaps most—user programs are intended to process data to accomplish the application of computer technology to a particular data processing task. These programs are called **applications programs.** Applications programs are available to handle inventory control, personnel record-keeping, order entry, scheduling, and a host of accounting functions. In general, applications programs are either written by programmers (as shown in Figure 3–5) within the organization, or they are purchased as **software packages** from outside suppliers. The relative advantages and disadvantages of these alternatives are discussed in greater detail later in the text.

Systems Programs

User programs by themselves are inadequate to totally control the computer's efforts. For example, a computer needs a program to tell it when to quit running one program and start on another. In addition, programs are available to perform many other tasks necessary to the proper function of the system. An executive or supervisor program directs the system's overall activities. Memory management programs control the allocation of memory.

The computer also needs programs to direct its efforts to collect and store accounting information so that users can be correctly charged for their use, to manage the translation of assembly language and higher-level language programs, to maintain a library of programs, and to perform many other tasks. These programs are known collectively as **systems programs** in that they are provided as part of the system itself, and their function is to control the system. They provide for the allocation of the system's resources to data processing tasks. Figure 3–6 shows a system programmer at work, finishing up a modification to one of the systems. The basic set of systems programs necessary to control operation of the computer and permit self-management of the system's resources is known as the **operating system.**

Figure 3–5 Applications Programmers at Work

Figure 3–6 Systems Programmer at Work

Challenge Update

The distinction between user programs and systems programs should now be clear to Dana and to the reader.

Interaction of Software and Hardware

A CPU contains a very fundamental set of instructions which it uses to bring itself from shutdown into active operation. These instructions are often provided in a special segment of the memory known as **read only memory (ROM).** [Note: Two of the fundamental activities of computers are *reading* (looking at but not changing) the contents of storage locations and *writing* (destroying the previous contents by entering new information).] ROM is protected from write operations so that a user will not inadvertently destroy these basic instructions and, thereby, the CPU's ability to operate. The basic startup procedure for a computer system, where it returns to these basic instructions to build itself into operational form, is known as *bootstrapping, booting,* or *initial program load (IPL)*. It draws the first name from the idiomatic expression "pulling oneself up by one's bootstraps."

Most of a computer's capability comes to it in the form of programs (both systems and user programs) which it can execute. The systems programs are stored within the computer system itself, a few perhaps in the primary memory and the remainder in secondary memory. That portion of the program which is being executed by the computer must reside in the primary memory. Other parts of that program, or other programs, are stored in the secondary memory and brought into the CPU as they are needed.

Suppose a user has written a program to calculate the sum of two numbers. The user enters the program and its data (in this case the two numbers which are to be added) through the input device. At that time, the CPU is executing a systems program which causes the user program and its data to enter and be stored, in the primary memory if space is available. If space is not available in the primary memory, the user program and its data will be stored temporarily in the secondary memory. At the appropriate time the user program will be brought into the primary memory for translation and execution. During execution, control shifts to the user program, and its instructions are carried out, causing the two numbers to be added together and the sum sent to the output device. Control then returns to a systems program which schedules the CPU's next activity. This sequence of steps is illustrated in Figure 3–7.

Tools: Programming Aids and Languages

A number of tools exist to help us use a computing system to solve a particular data processing problem. The development of an applications program, for example, first requires an extensive analysis of the application itself. A user must, first and foremost, understand what the computer is supposed to do in order to accomplish a particular data processing task. Only then can the gradual development of the program itself begin.

Some of the available tools focus the programmer's attention on the development of an applications program. In Figure 3–8 we see a programmer working with a client to make sure that the program will serve the "client's" needs. In particular, we will discuss system (job) control language, flowcharting, and pseudocode and take a brief look at some of the more popular programming languages. Additional material is provided in Chapter 13, and the problem-solving/program preparation process is discussed more fully in Appendix A. Readers whose introduction to data processing will include the learning of a computer programming language will want to study Appendix A to prepare themselves for writing programs.

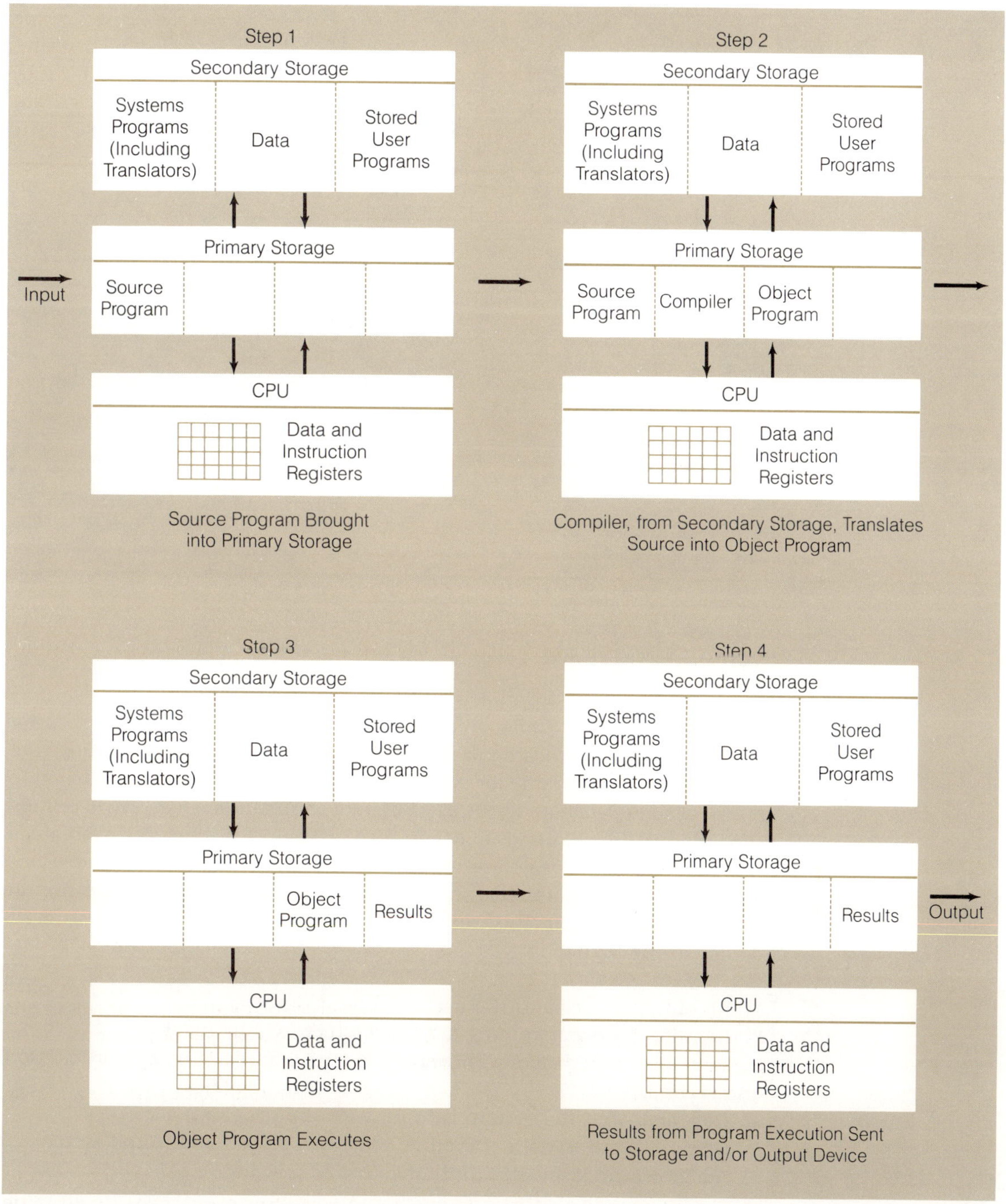

Figure 3–7 Steps in the Execution of a Program

The next topic to which we turn our attention covers a part of the systems software used for system control. System control languages vary so much from one computing system to another that a detailed treatment is best found in the manuals provided by the supplier (or manufacturer) of the computer system itself. A brief introduction to the role of system control languages is provided here. It is a topic of great importance when dealing with mainframe computer systems.

Figure 3–8
Programmer Consulting with User/Client

System (Job) Control Languages

The user of a large computer system is faced with a vast array of resources which can be made available to accomplish the necessary data processing tasks. The key to unlocking these resources is the system control language. The most common name for system control language is one established by IBM—job control language (JCL). The set of commands necessary to request allocation of the resources of the system make up the job control language. One of the systems programs, the job control progam, reads the command written in JCL and initiates the steps necessary to make the appropriate resources available to the user. For example, JCL commands exist to accomplish the following:

1. Identify the user and the user's account number.
2. Identify the programming language which will be used.
3. Set system parameters with respect to time limits, size of memory needed, and so on.
4. Describe what the system is to do with the program.
5. Obtain access to data and other programs stored within the system.
6. Allocate a program run to the necessary devices.

The form and content of these statements vary from one manufacturer's computer to another's. On some systems they are referred to as *control cards* (a holdover from the early, exclusive use of punched cards) or *control statements*. Every programmer who works on a large system needs to know how to use some part of the system's control language in order to gain access to the appropriate resources. Figure 3–9 provides an example of JCL statements.

Figure 3–9 Example System (Job) Control Statements

```
USER,ABCXYZ,LMNPQ.
CHARGE,999111,ABCXYZ.
JOBJR,,50000,25.
DAYFILE,,$11.21.$,T.
        or
*USER NUMBER: BA131AXX
*PASSWORD: ZORRO
*BASIC
```

Challenge Update

Dana and the reader should now be able to describe the role of the system (job) control language.

Programming/Problem-Solving Aids

Not only must a user master the system's control language in order to gain access to and utilize the system's resources, but a user who intends to write programs must develop an ability to think logically and give close attention to details. Programs must contain the instructions essential to the correct processing of the data, with no unnecessary or extraneous steps. The instructions in a program must also be in the correct order and written to comply with a strict set of language rules called the **syntax** of the programming language. The programmer's problem is humorously characterized in the poem which follows.

Programmer's Lament
How I hate this damn machine,
I wish that they would sell it;
It never does quite what I want,
But only what I tell it![1]

The poem is quite true. The computer does an excellent job of following instructions, but it has no means for figuring out what we might have intended it to do, if that is different from what we told it to do. The programmer must, therefore, be very careful to employ the programming aids necessary to the writing of a correct program.

In particular, the programmer must be able to generate a logical statement of the steps necessary to accomplish the required data processing task. This statement is called an **algorithm** and is discussed more completely in Appendix A. Several common methods are useful for displaying the logic of an algorithm: the two most common are flowcharts and pseudocode. Often the two are used in combination.

Flowcharts are graphical representations of the steps contained in the algorithm. A standardized set of flowchart symbols is used to represent the common data processing operations of input, output, computation, and so on. These symbols are reproduced in Appendix A. A sample flowchart is illustrated in Figure 3–10.

---

1. From *The Compleat Computer* by Dennie L. Van Tassel and Cynthia L. Van Tassel. Copyright © Science Research Associates, Inc. 1983, 1976. Adapted and reprinted by permission of the publisher.

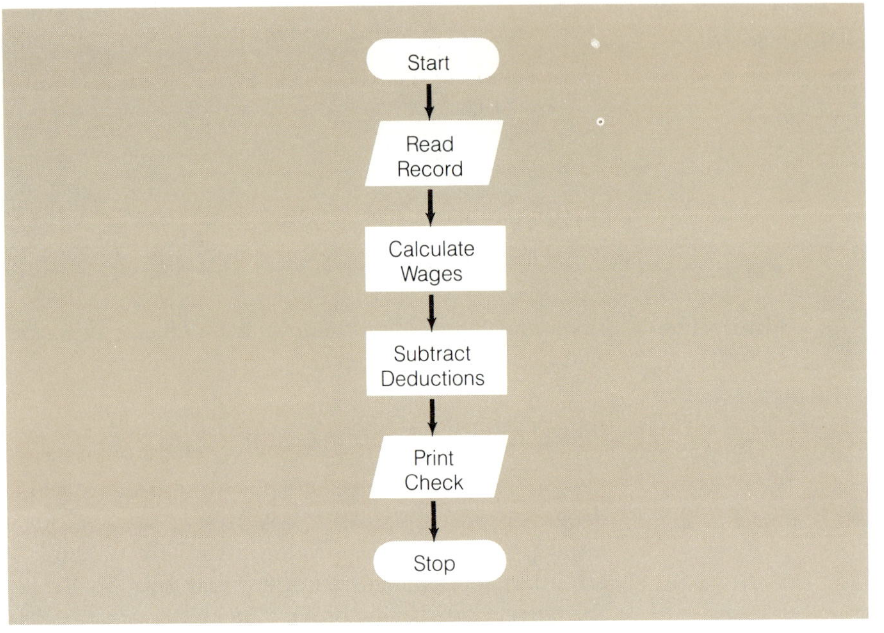

Figure 3–10
Example Flowchart

The second popular method of representation of an algorithm is known as pseudocode. If taken literally, *pseudocode* means "false code." The programming language statements in a computer program are called code; therefore, *pseudocode* would literally be "false programming language statements."

Pseudocode statements are statements, very close to English, which accurately describe the intended logic of a program. Since they are not statements in a programming language they are not code, but they are intended to suggest the appropriate code. Figure 3–11 provides an example of pseudocode.

Yet another technique is useful in representing the processing steps in a user program. This technique is known as *HIPO* (for Hierarchical Input-Processing-Output). It too is discussed in Appendix A.

Programming Languages

Literally hundreds of computer programming languages exist, although many are special purpose languages of very limited use. The languages most commonly used in the United States are COBOL, FORTRAN, PL/I, RPG, BASIC, and Pascal.

The acronym **COBOL** is derived from **COmmon Business-Oriented Language**. Most studies in recent years have indicated that COBOL is the language in which most programmers spend their time. There are indications that most of the programming time spent by professional programmers in businesses in this country is spent in COBOL. Programming languages are constantly being revised, and a revision results in a version identified by a suffix to the language name. COBOL-XX, for example, refers to a revision of COBOL which occurred in 19XX.

COBOL is a language which uses statements which are very English-like in appearance. It is a good language for accomplishing input and output

Figure 3–11
Example Pseudocode

```
DO
      WHILE (test condition is false)
      Add value to accumulator
      Increment counter
ENDDO

IF ID number < last number
  THEN copy old record to new record
ELSE
    IF ID number ≥ last record
      THEN add record to update list
```

operations and file handling manipulations. It does not perform arithmetic and algebraic manipulations very conveniently or very efficiently, and its overall structure is somewhat cumbersome.

FORTRAN, an acronym derived from **FORMula TRANslator,** was one of the earliest higher-level languages to be developed. As its name suggests, it is a convenient language for accomplishing arithmetic and algebraic manipulations, which accounts for its popularity in the scientific community. The numbering of FORTRAN versions changed when FORTRAN-77 (revised in 1977), superseded FORTRAN-IV (fourth revision). As a matter of fact, some people refer to the revision as FORTRAN-V. The capabilities of FORTRAN to process the large files typical of a business organization are not nearly as efficient as those of COBOL.

PL/I was designed to take advantage of the strong points of COBOL and FORTRAN. Although not particularly popular, it is a very useful language because it does combine the file handling capabilities of COBOL with the computational efficiency of FORTRAN.

RPG (Report Program Generator), as its name suggests, is a language for use in generating reports. Its mathematical capabilities are quite limited. Its most recent version is known as RPG-III.

BASIC (for Beginners' All-Purpose Symbolic Instruction Code) is a very popular language for informal users. It is not used by professional programmers as much as COBOL or FORTRAN, but its use by novices is unsurpassed. It is sometimes the only higher-level language available on the smaller microcomputer systems. A detailed description of BASIC is provided in Appendix C.

Pascal is a somewhat newer language than either COBOL or FORTRAN, and the extent to which its popularity will rise is unknown. Its structure requires the student to develop good programming habits, which makes it a popular teaching language for computer science courses.

Another language worth mentioning was developed to be the standard language for applications within the U.S. Department of Defense. It is known as **Ada**, having been named for the first programmer, Augusta Ada Byron. It is difficult to assess the extent to which Ada will influence the civilian world. However, many advances in computer technology have been developed under Department of Defense research contracts.

Technology: The Specific Nature of Program Control

This section extends the previous discussion of the interaction of software and hardware to provide a few more details concerning the "running" of a program on a computer. In particular we will take note of the translation, storage, and execution of the user program. An understanding of each of these phases is important to anyone intending to write and run a computer program. First, we will discuss the translation phase.

Program Translation

In the "Historical Perspective" section of this chapter, the concepts of machine language, assembly language, and higher-level language were discussed. A program written in a language other than machine language will pass through two distinct phases. The first phase is the translation of the statements in the program into a set of equivalent machine language statements, usually in binary form. The second phase is the execution or carrying out of those instructions by the system.

The computer is unable to directly execute any instruction except machine language statements. Statements in assembly language are translated into machine language by a systems program known as an *assembler.* Statements in a higher-level language (such as COBOL) are translated into machine language by a systems program known as a *compiler* (see Figure 3–12). COBOL, PL/I, and FORTRAN are each translated by their respective compilers.

The execution of BASIC and Pascal programs takes place in a slightly different way, through *interpreters* which are able to carry out the interpretation (translation) of these programs one statement at a time. The distinction, to the user, between a compiled language and an interpreted language is not great, and many users do not know (or care about) the difference. As a matter of fact, BASIC is sometimes implemented as a compiled language and sometimes as an interpreted language.

The impact of the difference between compiled and interpreted language is in the time it takes to run a program. Interpreted language programs usually consume more computer time than do compiled language programs. That distinction becomes less important as we become less concerned with strictly hardware efficiencies and more concerned with overall system efficiencies.

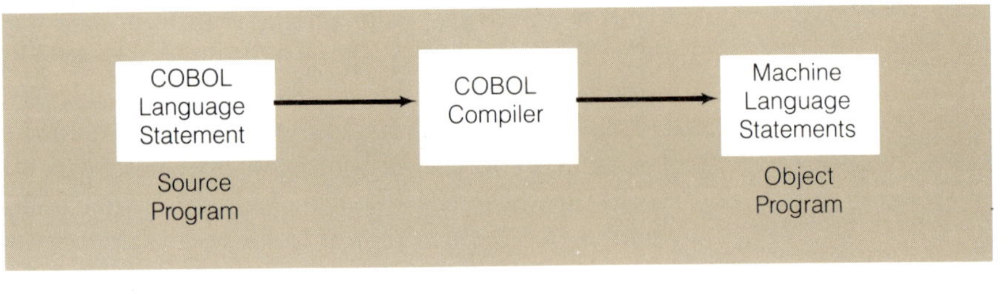

Figure 3–12 Translation of Program From Higher Level Language Into Machine Language

Program Storage

In an earlier example we discussed a user who entered a program through an input device at the time the user wanted the program to run. The program could have been previously entered into the system and stored on a secondary memory device until it was ready to be run. A program written in a higher-level language can be entered and stored in its original, untranslated state; or, it can be entered and translated, and the translated version can be stored for later execution. A program in its original form is known as a **source program,** and the translated version is known as an **object program.** If necessary, the object program can be copied through an output device so that the programmer has copies of both the source program and the object program. The advantage of the object program is that further translation is not required for a subsequent running of the program. Many of the programs which are run in the daily operation of a data processing center are stored as object programs on the secondary memory devices of the system.

Program Execution

In order for a computer to execute a program, it must bring that program and its data into the primary memory. (It is not absolutely necessary that *all* of the data, nor for that matter *all* of the program, be in the primary memory.) The program is compiled and executed, or interpreted and executed, as is applicable to the language in which it has been written. Statements within the program direct the input, manipulation, and output of the data streams.

Small, unsophisticated systems may devote their entire attention to one program at a time, while a larger, more sophisticated system will be capable of distributing its attention to several programs at the same time. The computer's work is managed in these efforts by the system's software.

Challenge Update

The two, distinct phases of running a program in a higher-level language—translation and execution—should now be understood.

Newest Developments

The development of user programs continues to be a costly, labor-intensive, time-consuming process. While higher-level languages offer great improvements over machine language, greater improvement is needed. A great deal of research effort is devoted to improving the applications development process. Surveys indicate that programmers may have applications backlogs of two to three years. Many organizations are abandoning the development of many types of user programs in favor of the purchase of packages of software written by others.

A variety of software development aids are in use to improve the applications development process. Some allow the programmer to employ a "shorthand" method of indicating processing operations, which are then used by a pre-compiler to generate a source program. Others provide the opportunity to link together standard modules of prewritten instructions, while still others require the programmer to describe the desired processing in a table, which is then processed by an interpreter. All offer improvements to the normal programming process at some cost in computer resources, and, of course, in the cost of the package itself.

There is hope that a new level of programming language will make it easier to accomplish data processing tasks. These new languages are called **fourth-generation languages,** following the first three generations of machine, assembly, and higher-level languages. They are also referred to as **non-procedural languages.** Unlike the higher-level languages, in which exact procedures must be written, non-procedural languages specify only a description of the desired results and leave the construction of the procedure by which the results are to be computed to the system itself. These languages are also referred to as **natural languages**—natural in the sense that they are much closer to our English (or some other natural language) than are the higher-level languages.

Software is, then, one of the primary building blocks from which we are able to construct a computer system. Both systems software and user programs are essential to any effective use of the system. A return to the case with which we opened this chapter should help us gauge our progress in learning.

COMPUTING CHALLENGE: *A Final Note*

Of what help can we now be to Dana Brownell in her efforts to use a microcomputer to perform data processing tasks connected with her real estate business? We know that, by itself, the hardware will not function; it must at least have systems software associated with it. We also know that each application to which she wants to apply the computer will require a user program.

Consider the CPU's function of controlling the other hardware devices. In what way does the systems software affect the potential compatibility problem between a CPU and one of its peripherals? If the systems software enables the CPU to control the operation of the peripheral devices, will not the systems software have to know how the peripherals operate?

What programming language or languages will Dana most likely have on her system?

In what ways might she acquire the necessary user programs? (Hint: Is she the first person in the world to need these programs?)

Could she use a copy of a BASIC program she might find advertised in the Real Estate Journal? If the program were in flowcharts or in pseudocode would it be more helpful?

Could she use a copy of a machine language program advertised in the Real Estate Journal?

SUMMARY

- A collection of computer hardware is essentially inoperable without an accompanying collection of software, the sets of instructions necessary to the proper functioning of the system.
- A set of instructions, written in a language the computer hardware can "understand," is called a program, and programs are of two general types: systems programs and user programs.
- Systems programs are essential to control and coordinate the various pieces of hardware, while user programs enable us to make effective use of the hardware/software combination.
- Systems programs interact with the CPU and the peripherals to provide the system with a basic set of data processing capabilities.
- User (or application) programs are necessary in order that the system can be directed to perform specific data processing tasks, for example, payroll, mailing lists, inventory control, sales analysis, and accounting.
- There are four different levels of computer programming languages: machine language, assembly language, higher-level (procedural) language, and fourth-generation (non-procedural or natural) language.
- Machine and assembly languages are machine dependent, while higher-level and fourth-generation languages enjoy some degree of machine independence.
- A computer user must combine an appropriate set of job control language (JCL) commands with a well-written program in order to bring about the correct processing of data.
- A number of different higher-level programming languages are available, including COBOL, the most popular one for professional applications, and BASIC, the most popular personal computer language.
- Higher-level languages must be translated (compiled or interpreted) prior to execution.
- Software development costs are increasing, a trend which runs counter to the rapidly decreasing costs of computer hardware, so many users are buying software packages rather than developing their own software.
- Software development aids are becoming increasingly available to assist the programmer in the development of applications programs.
- Software development aids, together with the increased use of packages and the desire of some users to do their own data processing, may eventually reduce the overwhelming backlog of applications programs.

CASE: A State Department's Use of a Computer

It is not unusual in large organizations for a separate department of administrative services to be established to provide the rest of the organization with essential services. Such is the case with the Wisconsin Department of Administration which actually bills the other state agencies for their services.

Wisconsin's Department of Administration is responsible for providing general services such as telecommunications, systems analysis, fleet vehicles, central mail, and printing to other state agencies. The department is also in charge of the statewide accounting and budgeting processes. With so many activities the department has a large task in keeping on top of its revenues and expenditures and in keeping up with the management information reporting requirements. To help them keep better track of the $65 million that the department processes each year, they have installed a computerized system which they have named the Local Government Financial System (LGFS).

The system has a large collection of programs designed exclusively for the financial accounting, control, and reporting requirements of state and local government agencies. These programs make it possible for the department to correctly bill the other agencies for costs incurred in printing and photocopying as well as appropriately charging out telecommunications and motor pool expenses. Many different types of documents are required to keep track of expenditures, receipts, and transfers, but the flexible programming of the LGFS enables it to accommodate these differences without undue difficulty. The system has helped the department to provide timely and accurate billing to other state departments.

One of the most critical processes of any organization is the preparation of the budget, the financial plan for the coming year. The quality of the budget preparation process has been generally improved through the use of LGFS. The system provides a historical base for the budget process, which helps the budget to be more accurate both now and in the future. The LGFS is very important to Wisconsin and the Department of Administration, particularly when difficult economic times cut deeply into state agency budgets. The high initial cost of developing the computer programs has been recovered through more efficient operating procedures. Managers within the department have been quite pleased with the results obtained so far and are constantly looking for new ways to make even more effective use of the system.

"State Agency Installs Financial Management System," *Infosystems* May 1981, pp. 106–108.

Questions for the Case

1. Are the programs which perform accounting, purchasing, and payroll functions properly called *systems programs*? If not, what are they?
2. Are these programs likely to be in machine language?
3. If these programs are in a higher-level language, could they be moved to another set of hardware?
4. Is it more likely that these programs were written in FORTRAN or COBOL?

DISCUSSION QUESTIONS

1. How do user programs differ from systems programs?
2. Compare the running of a machine language program with the running of an assembly language program. Which uses the computer more efficiently

in terms of CPU utilization and memory space? Which uses the programmer more efficiently?

3. Compare the running of an assembly language program with the running of a higher-level language program. Which uses the computer more efficiently in terms of CPU utilization and memory space? Which uses the programmer more efficiently?

4. Based upon questions 2 and 3 above, what can be said of the relative machine and programmer efficiencies of software development aids?

5. Why do system (job) control languages differ from one manufacturer's computer system to another's?

6. Describe the steps necessary for the system to run a program in a higher-level language.

7. In what sense are the fourth-generation languages non-procedural? In what sense are they natural?

8. Of what use are flowcharts and pseudocode? How are they different? How are they alike?

9. What advantages does assembly language have over machine language?

10. In what ways are higher-level languages superior to assembly language?

11. What is machine dependence? Which language levels are machine dependent?

12. What is machine independence? Which language levels are machine independent? How machine independent are they really?

13. Discuss: "Computers cannot think, they can only perform the functions for which they have been programmed."

14. Some errors in computer programs would make it impossible for the translation process to translate the program, while other errors might keep the program from executing. Discuss and provide examples.

15. Can a program which can be translated and executed be presumed to be free of errors? Why or why not?

ADDITIONAL READINGS

Arms, W. Y.; Backer, J. E.; and Pengelly, R. M. *A Practical Approach to Computing*. New York: John Wiley & Sons, 1976.

Aron, Joel D. *The Program Development Process*. Reading, Mass.: Addison-Wesley, 1981.

Bird, Richard. *Programs and Machines*. New York: John Wiley & Sons, 1976.

Brooks, Frederick P., Jr. *The Mythical Man-Month*. Reading, Mass: Addison-Wesley, 1975.

Frank, Werner L. *Critical Issues in Software*. New York: John Wiley & Sons, 1983.

Gear, C. William. *Programming and Languages*. Chicago: Science Research Associates, 1978.

Pattis, Richard E. *Karel the Robot: A Gentle Introduction to the Art of Programming*. New York: John Wiley & Sons, 1981.

Vallee, Jacques. *The Network Revolution: Confessions of a Computer Scientist*. Berkeley, CA: An/Dor Press, 1982.

The Government are very keen on amassing statistics. They collect them, add them, raise them to the nth power, take the cube root and prepare wonderful diagrams. But you must never forget that every one of these figures comes in the first instance from the village watchman, who just puts down what he damn pleases.

Sir Josiah Stamp
Inland Revenue Dept.
England 1896–1919

Part II

Data Processing Functions

PART PREFACE

Part I of the text was designed to be brief but, at the same time, present the student with an understanding of the fundamentals of computer operation that would be sufficient to begin hands-on exercises. We begin now to build upon that basic understanding.

In this, Part II, we undertake an in-depth study of the four basic data processing functions: output, input, computation, and storage. We will examine the issues which are important to the user in each of these areas. Many diagrams and pictures are included to help the reader visualize the various devices and understand something of their operations.

After completing this part, the reader should have a thorough understanding of the four basic functions and their various implementations.

Chapters in this part are:

- Chapter 4: *The Production of Information: Output*
- Chapter 5: *The Entry of Data: Input*
- Chapter 6: *Computation: CPUs and Operating Systems*
- Chapter 7: *Data Storage: Files*
- Chapter 8: *Data Storage: Data Base Management Systems*
- Chapter 9: *Data Communications*

4

The Production Of Information: Output

CHAPTER PREVIEW

One of the earliest considerations in the design of any system is the determination of its output. The purpose of the system is most often reflected in the system's output. For example, we judge the economy of the United States by looking at the gross national product, an output measure. We judge educational systems by the achievements of their graduates and the quality of the new knowledge which their research generates, both measures of output. We judge restaurants by the meals they produce, another output measure. It is difficult to think of a system for which the output is not the basis for the system's performance evaluation.

We should not be surprised, therefore, to learn that data processing systems are also judged on the basis of the output they produce. A data processing system is expected to produce accurate, useful, and timely information in an efficient manner. Each of these measures derives from output considerations. **Accuracy** implies that the output is a correct representation of reality. **Usefulness** implies that the organization can benefit from the output. **Timeliness** recognizes that the value of the output varies with time, and **efficiency** measures the consumption of organizational resources in the generation of the output.

In this chapter we will consider the output from data processing systems. We will study the important considerations in the design and use of output, the tools which are available for its production, and some glimpses of the technologies underlying those tools.

COMPUTING CHALLENGE: *The Stock Broker's Office*

Perhaps an example will help illustrate the role of output in data processing system design. Consider the plight of Marion Boyd, a newly graduated MBA (Masters in Business Administration) from prestigious Eastern University. Marion has just joined a large stock brokerage and investment firm in Philadelphia. Johnson, Jones, Jackson and Doobenheimer, an old and very reputable firm, has hired Marion specifically to develop a plan to improve services to its customers. Many of the firm's competitors have recently acquired computerized systems, and the senior partners of Johnson, Jones, Jackson and Doobenheimer believe some electronic data processing capability is necessary to keep up with the competition.

The firm's customers expect to receive the following kinds of service from the firm:

1. *Stock price quotes; up-to-the-minute information about the most recent stock prices.*
2. *Statements; a complete listing of the transactions completed for the customer during the month; and a month-end listing of the stocks, bonds, and cash reserves in the customer's account.*
3. *Transaction handling; including a statement describing each transaction undertaken for a customer showing the date, quantity, and price of any stocks bought or sold.*
4. *Research reports; brief descriptions of the financial condition of various companies in which the customers might wish to buy stock.*

Stock brokerage houses certainly provide other services, but the four listed above are sufficient for our purposes. Marion must consider each type of service in turn. Answers to the following questions must be sought:

1. *What outputs must be generated to provide the required services?*
2. *In what form should that output be to best serve the interests of the firm and its customers?*
3. *What do we need to know about a data processing system in order to make intelligent decisions in designing the output?*

In order to study data processing system output, we need to know the different types of output which are possible, the kinds of hardware which are available for producing output and, in some cases, how that hardware works. After successful completion of this chapter the reader should be able to:

1. *Develop a brief set of criteria to guide an analysis of the output from a data processing system.*
2. *List one or more output device(s) which warrant further investigation in terms of meeting the criteria established above.*
3. *Provide a general evaluation of the relative merits of the output devices identified above.*

Figure 4–1 Stock Brokers Use Computer Systems

HISTORICAL PERSPECTIVE

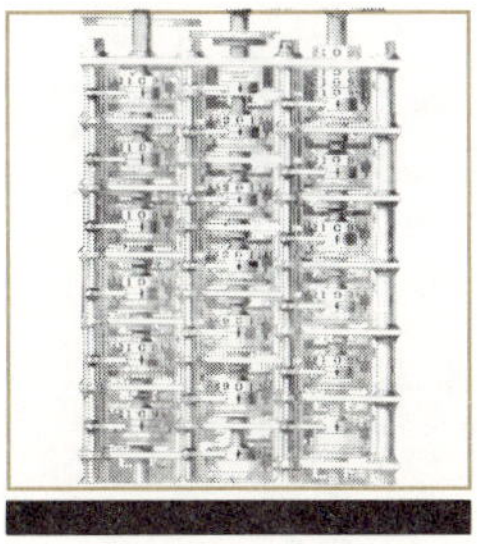

The earliest computing systems had a very limited range of output devices, often only a printer. It is only in recent years that we have begun to see a wide range of output possibilities. The design of computer system output has become more complex as the number of possible alternatives to consider has increased, as we shall see.

Another important factor has contributed to the increasing complexity of output design. Early computing machines seemed wondrous and awe-inspiring, and the users of those machines were willing to go to great lengths to accommodate the machine's shortcomings. Today's users, on the other hand, demand that computer output conform to their needs.

Furthermore, even though programming was a tedious task, it was eagerly undertaken as the key to unlocking the machine's vast power. More recently, we have seen a lot of effort devoted to easing the programming burden.

Historically, input was most often restricted to punched cards or keyboard entry through the operator's typewriter-like console, and very few design alternatives existed. By the same token, output was restricted to data displayed on the operator's console or sent to a printing device. The IBM 650, a first-generation machine, used punched cards. Occasionally, punched paper tape input and output were available, and quite often punched cards were produced on an output device known as the card punch; but the possibilities were limited, and users had to adapt to the form of output which was available.

In spite of the limited range of output devices available and the necessity for the user to adapt to the machine's peculiar ways, users were relatively happy. In point of fact, the user often was also the systems designer, programmer, data entry operator, and computer operator all at the same time. Manual data processing operations were converted to computer applications primarily because users were willing and able to perform those various functions.

Through the years, computers have become more complex by several orders of magnitude. Magnetic tape and magnetic disk input and output were popular with the second-generation machines. Many new types of output have become possible since that time.

The functions of systems analysis, programming, data entry, and computer operating are now performed by different specialists, and the user rarely even visits the data processing center itself. The computer's image has changed from that of a wondrous machine which enables users to do magnificent new data processing activities to something more like a demanding, institutionalized beast that has forced unwanted changes into our working lives.

In particular, the design of computer system output has undergone great change. Not only have there been significant changes in the technology, giving us an impressive array of new output devices, but there have also been great changes in organizations in a social sense. Large numbers of

people now have jobs which are defined in terms of data processing functions. Computing systems have taken on a predominant role in the organization. As a result, people's roles, expectations, and attitudes have changed greatly, and these changes have influenced the output design process.

Concepts: Output Gives Purpose to the Processing of Data

Systems Design Overview

Systems design and output design have been previously mentioned, but now we should develop a more rigorous understanding of the design process. A **system** is defined as a collection of related components which work together to produce a desired result. We can consider committees, religious groups, schools, businesses, clubs, and government agencies as systems. Systems are designed and implemented to produce some desired end result; a system has a purpose (or goal).

The purpose of data processing systems is to process data, but the processing of data, it must be remembered, is not an end in itself. Data are processed to serve some organizational need, and that larger need must be kept in mind as we proceed.

The Role of Output. I have referred previously to many of the *events* which take place in the routine operation of the organization as **transactions.** The checking out of a book from the public lending library is a transaction, as is the purchase of a ticket to a movie. Leaving one's shoes at the shoe repair shop, placing an order with a catalog store, making a payment on a car, turning in accounting homework, and giving an employee a raise are all transactions.

Organizations devote a large portion of their data processing effort to the processing of transactions. Satisfactory processing of the transaction often requires the production of output, such as a cash register receipt to acknowledge a sale. Satisfactory processing might also require that data or information about the transaction be stored for use later to generate output useful in the support of decision making. For example, sales analysis data are generated by the sales transaction processing system. In a similar vein, a university's enrollment statistics are derived from the transactions of students registering for classes.

Data processing systems serve the transaction processing needs of an organization and support the decision-making activities of managers and other members of the organization. A data processing system must produce, in a usable way, the information needed to support the manager's decision making. Again, notice that the focus is on the output of the data processing system.

A brief review is in order.

1. All systems have purposes.
2. The purposes of most systems can be defined in terms of desired output.
3. The purposes of most, if not all, data processing systems can be explained in terms of desired output.

We will therefore focus our attention first on data processing system outputs and the considerations important in output design. Once outputs have been designed, attention can be shifted to consideration of the input, computation, and storage requirements.

System Life Cycle

A brief introduction to the life cycle of a system is important to developing the correct perspective of the design process. The concept of a system life cycle characterizes systems in terms of their birth (design), lifetime (operation), and death (discontinued use). Many somewhat different listings of the steps in a systems life cycle have been published. The number of steps in the cycle varies from three to more than nine. For our purposes, the important steps in a system's life cycle can be captured in the following list. They are represented in brief form in Figure 4–2.

1. Recognition of the fact that an opportunity for improvement exists in a system and a brief investigation of the feasibility of developing an improved system.
2. Development of the system requirements, a detailed description of the purpose of the system.
3. Identification of alternative ways by which the necessary purposes could be achieved.
4. Evaluation of the alternatives and selection of the one which appears to best serve the objectives and needs of the organization.
5. Detailed design of the system to include specification of new components (hardware, software, people, or procedures).
6. Development of the system according to its design and testing it to develop confidence that it works.
7. Implementation—putting the system into operation.

Figure 4–2 System Life Cycle

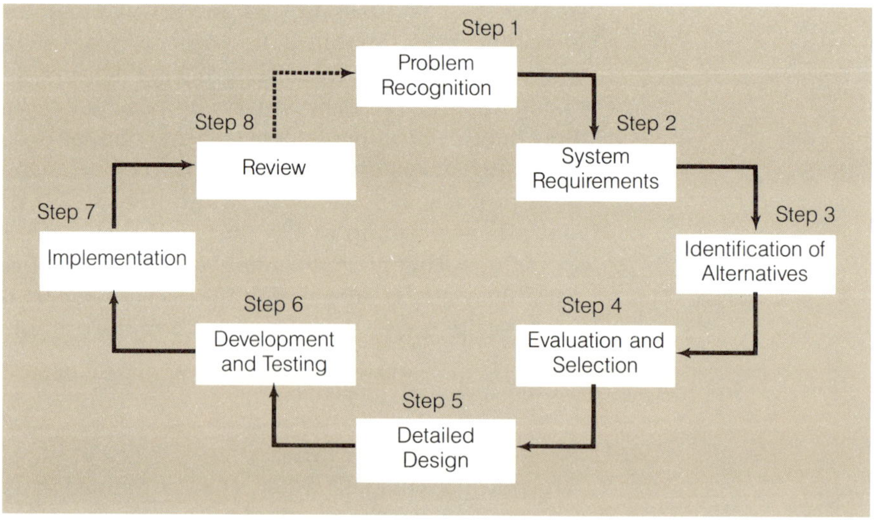

8. Review of the system's operation to see if it serves the organization's purposes. (The last step in this system's life cycle is often the first step in the next system's life cycle.)

The degree of formality with which an organization pursues a system design is a function, among other things, of the size of the system being designed. Some system designs are done quite routinely in a few days' time. For example, a system to generate a report of summary statistics based upon data currently stored in the system could be quickly designed. As another example, a hospice or illness support group could develop a mailing list on a small computer very easily if the appropriate software were available.

Additionally, a small change in an existing system would not warrant a full-scale investigation into a large number of possible alternatives. The alternatives to be considered would be constrained by the fact that most of the system must remain unchanged. That is, much of a systems designer's work deals with small changes in which the designer must accomplish the task using the existing hardware, software, and personnel resources.

Other systems designs may require years to effect and entail the replacement of large quantities of hardware and software. Often the displacement of people is a major consideration. For example, an inventory control or materials requirement system for a large manufacturing firm could require several years of development and consume large quantities of other organizational resources such as labor and money. In circumstances which require large design changes and the displacement of people, the designer's task is more complicated. The people who are to be displaced must move to other jobs or be retrained for other work. (The issues related to job displacement will be discussed in greater detail in Chapter 18.)

The design of output for a data processing system is a procedure which takes place in system life cycle steps 2 through 5 essentially. In step 2 the designer must ask what output is required of the system. The various means by which the output can be produced must be investigated in step 3. The evaluation of the various output alternatives takes place in step 4, while a detailed specification of the output devices is accomplished in step 5.

Output Design Considerations

Now that the role of output in systems design has been established and we have seen the system life cycle for perspective, it is time to discuss output in greater detail. In particular, we must determine the characteristics of output to which consideration must be given in the design process.

Content. An obvious candidate for the most important characteristic of the output of data processing operations is the **content** of that output, that is, what information it should contain. To be useful in the support of organizational activities, the output must contain the appropriate information. The appropriateness must, of course, be determined in terms of the purposes of the system itself.

Consider, for example, the transaction processing system which issues an airlines ticket to a passenger-to-be. What purposes must that system

Figure 4–3
Managers Confer to Determine Appropriate System Outputs

serve? In the first place, it must provide the passenger with admission to each of the flights on which passage has been booked. The ticket must also contain information about carriers, flight numbers, departure times, and destinations so that the passenger can know these details. The passenger must also be provided with a receipt for the price of the ticket and a copy of some of the numerous legal restrictions and airlines rules which are operative.

The system which generates the ticket also serves other purposes, so information about the passenger, the flights' schedules, the method of payment, and the like, are stored for output at a later time as part of other systems for either transaction processing or decision support applications.

While the specification of output contents in most transaction processing systems is relatively straightforward, the specification of output in support of decision making can be much more difficult.

For some decision-making activities, it is relatively easy to identify the information needed by the decision maker as well as the relationships between certain information and the actions to be taken by the decision maker. Under such circumstances it is useful to construct **decision tables** wherein specific actions to be taken are related to the existence of certain predetermined conditions. An example is provided in Figure 4–4. A decision table allows a decision maker to determine which action is most appropriate. From Figure 4–4 we can determine that studying is an appropriate action to take if the snow in the mountains is poor, river conditions are not good, and sunshine is lacking.

In many other decision situations the problem is more complex. Quite often, we do not know how the information should be related to the actions to be taken. In fact, we often do not know how the actions taken are related to the results we wish to achieve.

Consider, for example, the decision an individual must make with respect to buying corporate stock in the stock market. Which parts of the large volume of information about a company are important in determining whether

Recreation Guide

Conditions \ Possible Combinations	1	2	3	4	5	6	7	8
Good Mountain Snow	Y	Y	Y	N	Y	N	N	N
Good River Conditions	Y	Y	N	Y	N	Y	N	N
Sunshine	Y	N	Y	Y	N	N	Y	N
Actions								
Go Skiing	X	X	X		X			
Go Fishing				X		X		
Sit in the Sun							X	
Study								X

Y = Yes; N = No; X = Action to Be Taken

Figure 4–4 Sample Decision Table

or not to invest in that company's stock? Sophisticated research studies of the decision-making activities of investment executives have failed to provide a good answer to that question. Some analysts look at a certain set of performance data, while other analysts rely on entirely different data.

Another interesting question is: How will the potential investor's financial position be affected, in the long run, by the purchase of any particular stock? The uncertainties of free enterprise and the stock market preclude developing any reliable measures to answer that question. What data should be collected to support decision making for common stock investments?

Specification of the contents of the output from a data processing system is sometimes very easy, but often very difficult. A formal study, called a **user requirements analysis** (or detailed investigation), is frequently used to determine the output contents. To complete a requirements analysis, a designer will use interviews of users, detailed logs kept by users, historical records, and sometimes an in-depth analysis by an expert in decision-making research.

Format. In some cases the **format** of the output from information processing systems is almost as important as the contents of that output. A number of choices exist with respect to the format of computer output. Here again, the design problem for transaction processing systems seems to be less severe than that for those systems which support decision making. Once the contents have been correctly specified, the particular form of the output for a transaction processing system would seem like a minor problem. The format of many outputs—for example, that of cash register receipts, class enrollment cards, airlines tickets, and credit card receipts—is of relatively minor importance compared to the importance of the contents themselves. The format of output generated in support of decision-making activities is another matter.

Many studies have shown that the effectiveness of computer system output is a function of the format in which it is presented. Some decision makers are most capable of extracting the meaning from the output if it is presented in the form of graphs, while others prefer statistical representations. Some even seem to perform more effectively when the output is in raw, tabular form. Some managers grasp the understanding of information better if they are presented with the information in narrative form. Another possible form is to present only the exceptional (abnormal) information.

Consider, for example, the case of a production manager for a business firm which manufactures machine parts for the automobile industry. The production manager would like to know which machines are producing well and which are not. One measure of a machine's ability is the number of defective parts produced by that machine. Once that information is computed, there are a number of different formats by which the information could be presented to the production manager. Example formats for the presentation of this data are presented in Figure 4–5 parts a through e. Part e employs a technique known as **exception reporting** to display only the most unusual or unexpected information.

Systems designers must be aware of the different formats in which the output can be presented. Quite possibly, if the project is large and important enough, some preliminary experimentation should be conducted to determine the most effective format. In this experimentation, different formats could be presented to the users to determine which appears to be the most useful. "Most useful" must of course be judged in the context of the application itself.

Media. Closely related to the format of the output is the consideration of the particular **medium** (or media) with which the presentation of the output will be made. The choice of media is part of a larger design decision which determines the particular type of hardware which will be used to generate the output.

The most common medium has historically been paper, and output has most often been put on paper through the use of printing devices. The devices themselves will be discussed in the next section. The various media are:

1. Paper: Output is printed or drawn.
2. Magnetic surface: Output is represented magnetically for intermediate storage prior to presentation to users.
3. Film: Output is photographed and presented in strip, microfiche, or aperture card form.
4. Visual display: Output is presented through the use of television or plasma display devices.
5. Voice: Output is presented through the generation of a voice message or the selection of a prerecorded audio message.
6. Cards and paper tape: Although mostly of historical interest at this point, punched cards and punched paper tape representations of output have been found useful.

Figure 4–5 Sample Formats for Presentation of Data on Defective Parts Produced by Each Machine

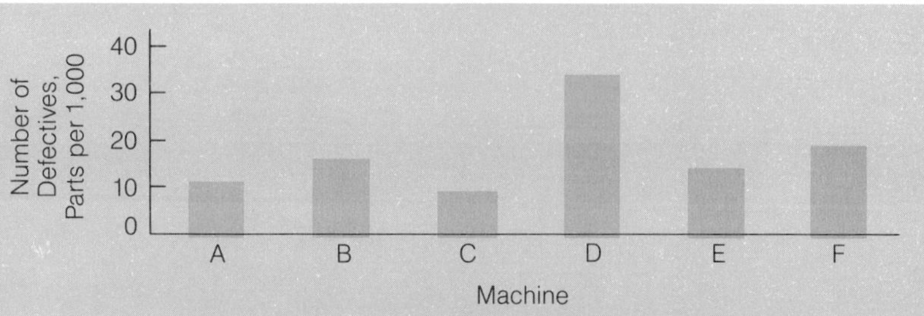

(a) Graphical Representation

Machine	Average Number of Defects/1000	Standard Deviation
A	12.2	2.4
B	16.3	1.9
C	8.1	0.9
D	34.5	6.5
E	13.7	2.8
F	19.8	2.3

(b) Statistical Representation

Machine D continues to be plagued with a high rate of defects and should be scheduled for overhaul as soon as production schedules permit. Machine F has been used to train the new operators, but its rate of defects has improved during the period. The remaining machines are performing within limits.

(c) Narrative Representation

↓ Machine / Batch →	1	2	3	etc. . . .
A	10	13	11	. . .
B	17	17	16	. . .
C	7	7	9	. . .
D	30	35	37	. . .
E	12	12	15	. . .
F	21	20	18	. . .

(d) Tabular Representation

Machines Exhibiting Unsatisfactory Performance	Rate of Defects	Corrective Action to Be Taken
D	34.5/1,000	Schedule for overhaul
F	19.8/1,000	None—operator in training

(e) Management-by-Exception Representation

Figure 4–5d
Tabular Representation

↓ Machine \ Batch →	1	2	3	etc . .
A	10	13	11	. . .
B	17	17	16	. . .
C	7	7	9	. . .
D	30	35	37	. . .
E	12	12	15	. . .
F	21	20	18	. . .

Figure 4–5e
Management-by-Exception Representation

Machines Exhibiting Unsatisfactory Performance	Rate of Defects	Corrective Action to Be Taken
D	34.5/1,000	Schedule for overhaul
F	19.8/1,000	None—operator in training

Designers must choose the output medium which is most suitable for the particular application. Selection of the medium is a function of (1) the needs of the user, (2) the existing capabilities of the present system (if any), and (3) the cost of the medium itself as well as the devices which produce it.

Frequency, Timeliness, and Permanence. It is likely that the **frequency** of output generation, the **timeliness** of that generation, and the **degree of permanence** of the media are considered by the designer in the specification of contents, format, and media, for they are all interrelated. They are listed here in the interest of completeness, so that they will not be overlooked.

The frequency with which output must be generated, the time frame within which that generation must take place, and the extent to which that output must be captured in some permanent form are all factors which must be resolved in terms of the nature of the application itself. These characteristics also influence selection of particular output hardware devices.

Many organizations have data processing activities which must be performed on a regular basis. The frequency with which these activities must be performed varies from application to application. Organizations in an economically competitive society must always be concerned with *costs*. Cost summaries in a manufacturing plant might need to be done monthly, while the payroll for hourly employees might have to be done weekly. Most large banks compute their financial position daily in order to comply with banking regulations. A professional organization might update its membership list annually.

Some applications require a virtually instant update as new data are generated. The aircraft under the control of an air traffic controller must be represented instantly on the output device. Stock market transactions are also displayed with very little time delay. On the other hand, a monthly summary of unit costs does not require such timely display, though frequency itself might be an important consideration in such applications.

It is easy to confuse frequency and timeliness. A simple story will help the reader bring the difference into focus. If your house catches fire and your neighbor *writes a letter* to the fire department, the frequency of reporting is fine (one report per fire), but the timeliness leaves something to be desired.

The degree to which the output must be captured in some permanent form is also important. Regulations of the Internal Revenue Service, for example, require that tax records be kept for several years. Companies which manufacture pharmaceuticals must keep research results and production records for extended periods of time. Many other applications have output requirements where permanence is short-lived. For example, television monitors are used to display the output for computing applications in stock prices, airline flight status, and so on, where frequency and timeliness are important but permanence is not.

Challenge Update

The various characteristics of output from information systems have now been presented. Marion Boyd could review the needs of the systems in the stock brokerage office and determine the relative importance of each characteristic for each application. Output criteria for each application could then be developed.

Now that we have identified the important characteristics of output—its contents, format, medium, frequency, timeliness, and permanence—we turn our attention to the tools which are available for the generation of computer system output. Many such devices already exist, and research leading to the design of new output devices continues.

Figure 4–6
Summary of Output Characteristics

Output Design Considerations
Content
Format
Medium
Frequency
Timeliness
Permanence

Tools: Devices Which Generate Output

As the proper output for a computer system is determined, consideration must be given to the selection of the particular output device which will be used. There are many possibilities. Even in the circumstance where the designer has been asked to stay within the constraint of using the existing hardware, most systems would still offer several possibilities. So, whether the designer is working with the existing hardware or allowed the freedom of choosing from the vast array of available hardware, several alternatives must be compared.

It is important to realize that the output devices must be compatible with the other hardware devices in the system, and that factors such as cost, speed, reliability, and maintenance are important considerations in the selection of all output devices. These particular topics are more properly covered in detail in Chapter 12.

Printers

The most popular computer output device has been the printer, which produces output printed on paper using any one of a large number of technologies. Some printers provide one-character-at-a-time printing, much like a typewriter's mode of operation, and are, therefore, called **character printers.** Others provide line-at-a-time printing, which has led to their being called **line printers.** A line printer is pictured in Figure 4–7. More

Figure 4–7 IBM System/38 Printer

Figure 4–8 A Bit-Mapping Dot Matrix Printer

recently, printers have been designed which proceed a page at a time, so they are called **page printers.** Printer speeds vary from about one page per minute at the slow end to 175 to 200 pages per minute for the largest, fastest machines.

A new type of printer, known as a **graphics printer,** has been designed for personal computers. These printers form characters and draw lines by using an extremely dense matrix of dot printing capability. These printers, with the appropriate software executing on the microcomputers, can print material exactly as it appears on the display screen. They put a dot on the paper to correspond with each tiny **picture element** (known as a **pixel**) on the screen. Their printing is sometimes known as **bit-mapping** since the bits which turn pixels on to illuminate the screen are sent directly to the corresponding position (mapped) on the printer paper. A bit-mapping, graphics printer is shown in Figure 4–8.

Output generated by printers has been readily accepted by users. As a matter of fact, most of the transaction processing systems with which we interact generate printed output. We are all familiar with, and readily accept, printed cash register receipts, airline tickets, grade cards, and class lists. Managers and other organizational users are very comfortable with printed sales summaries, production schedules, and inventory reports.

Printed output is easy to read directly if properly designed, as illustrated in Figure 4–9 and provides permanent copies for long-term storage and reference. The primary disadvantages of printer output are:

1. An excessive amount of it becomes bulky, difficult to carry, and requires a great deal of storage space.
2. It is not easily indexed and stored to provide for quick access in response to nonroutine inquiries.
3. It is costly.

Figure 4–9 Printed Output is Easy to Read

Although many different kinds of printers are in use, or headed for the market, most are still based on essentially mechanical principles. The greatest strides in printer design for the next few years are expected to depend more upon the use of electronic rather than mechanical devices. Reliability and print quality are characteristics of utmost importance to users, and both are expected to improve with new designs.

Terminals

Strictly speaking, terminals are those hardware devices which exist at the end of a communications line through which users obtain access to the capabilities of the computer system. Since this is a chapter on computer system output, our interest here is in terminals which function as computer output devices, although many, if not most, terminals operate both as input and output devices. Discussion of terminals as input devices will be postponed until the next chapter. Two general types of terminals exist: typewriter-like terminals (teleprinters) and visual display terminals.

Terminals can be built with great differences in their capabilities. Some terminals are described as being slow and dumb, while others are described as being intelligent. A slow, dumb terminal is only capable of transmitting one character at a time from the user to the computer system. An intelligent terminal, on the other hand, is **programmable** in its own right, and is equipped with its own memory. In addition, intelligent terminals generally have communications capability and can operate at faster data transmission speeds than can dumb terminals.

Initially, slow, dumb terminals were the most common for many activities which did not require the speed, memory, and programmability of intelligent ones. The primary advantage of the slow, dumb terminals was cost; they were much cheaper. The costs of intelligence (programmability and memory) have declined dramatically, and intelligent terminals have become correspondingly more popular. Computer terminals are the hardware devices with which users most often interact, hence, in their design, consideration must be given to the ease with which someone can use the device.

Typewriter-Like Terminals (Teleprinters). "Typewriter-like" is a good descriptive term for one variety of computer terminal because it does, in fact, look like a typewriter, with a keyboard and paper threaded around a roller. These terminals usually operate at speeds of either ten or thirty characters per second using character-at-a-time printing. Newer designs are making faster printing speeds possible. Many different brands of typewriter-like terminals are available.

These terminals are either connected directly to the computer system (**hard-wired**) or they are built with **acoustic couplers** into which a telephone receiver is placed to provide access through the telephone system. Some have built-in devices called **modems** to accommodate the conversion from computer signals (digital) to telephone transmissions (analog). Details of this type of access will be provided in Chapter 9, "Data Communications."

Visual (or Video) Display Terminals. Many terminals do not produce printed output but instead show a visual display on a screen. The television picture tube, known technically as a cathode ray tube (CRT), forms the display portion of most visual display terminals. Terminals based on CRTs were introduced by IBM in 1965, and their popularity has increased steadily since that time. A CRT terminal is pictured in Figure 4–10.

Visual display terminals enjoy several advantages over their teleprinter counterparts. The first advantage is in initial cost; CRT terminals are cheaper than teleprinter terminals. CRT terminals can be purchased for less than $800, while the cheapest teleprinter costs over $1,000.

A second advantage enjoyed by visual display devices is the ease of use. Visual display terminals provide the operator with commands which make it easier to make corrections during data entry operations, as we shall see in the next chapter.

Visual display terminals are more quiet than teleprinters (no noisy printing mechanism) and operate at higher data transmission rates than do teleprinters. Normal data transmission rates are in the range of 10 to 1,920 characters per second for CRT terminals. Visual display terminals which project images on a large screen are also available.

The major disadvantage of visual display terminals is their inability to produce permanent (hard copy) output. Remote printers are often used in conjunction with a set of visual display devices so that hard copy output can be generated if needed.

A second disadvantage of visual display devices is the size of the screen. The output desired for a particular application is often much larger than can be displayed on a screen. The most common screen size allows a

Figure 4–10 CRT Terminal

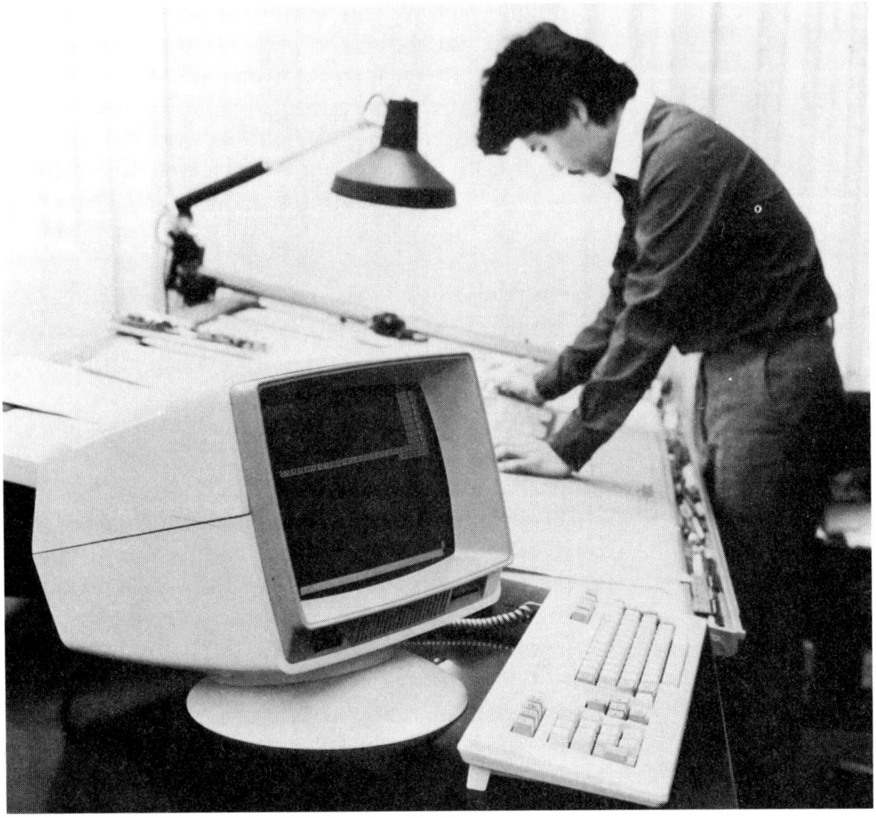

maximum of twenty-four lines of data, each of eighty columns, to be displayed. CRT terminals with intelligence—that is, built to include a microprocessor in their design—have sufficient memory to allow the user to move forwards or backwards (scroll) through the output display. Less sophisticated (slow, dumb) terminals provide the user with only one view; no memory is available to store the data which has moved off the screen.

Yet another disadvantage of the visual display class of terminals is associated with the difficulty of reading the information displayed on the screen. Operators can experience eye strain if the cathode ray tube is not well focused, if the tube has poor resolution, or if overhead lighting is too bright. Manufacturers are beginning to place more emphasis on "human engineering" to make terminal operation a more pleasant (less painful) experience.

Teleprinters and visual display terminals are both very popular. Teleprinters are a good choice for some applications, while visual display terminals are better for others. The nature of the application itself determines which type of terminal will be more satisfactory.

Let us now explore the various types of visual display terminals which are available. The following categories will be discussed in turn: CRT alphanumeric displays, CRT graphics displays, plasma displays, and flat panel displays.

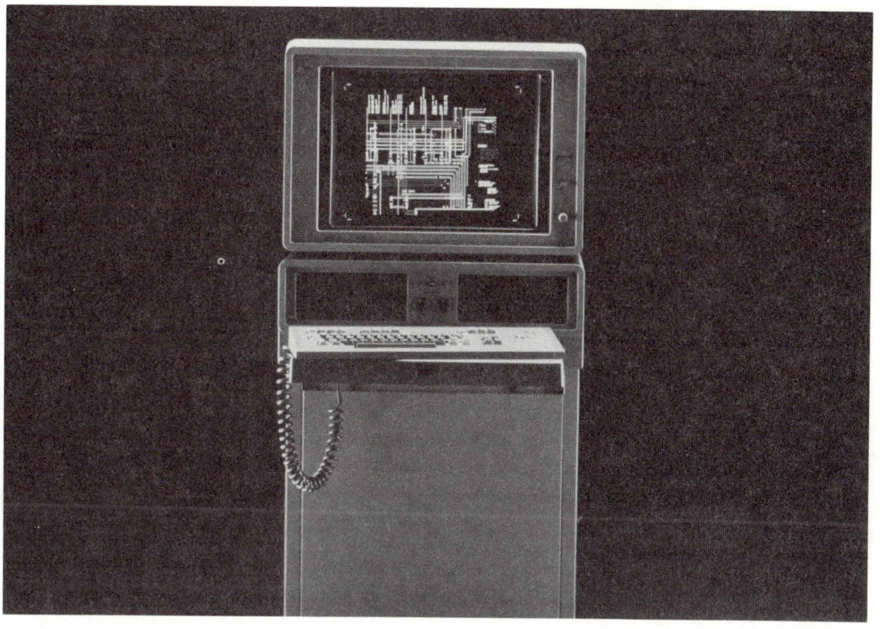

Figure 4–11
Graphics Terminal

CRT Alphanumeric Displays. This, the most common of the visual display terminals, consists of a cathode ray tube, a keyboard, and some associated electronics in an appropriate housing. The CRT will produce a single-color (using either white, green, or amber with black) or multicolored display of alphanumeric data (no pictures) on a screen whose size varies from five to twenty-five inches across the diagonal. Numeric, alphabetic, and special characters are displayed on the screen as a representation of output from the computer system.

As mentioned above, these terminals may be equipped with intelligence to allow the user to scan forwards and backwards through the output. Other features of these terminals will be discussed when their role as input devices is explored in the next chapter.

CRT Graphics Displays. One of the most exciting areas of computer use is the area of computer-generated graphics. Here we rely on the premise that pictures (or more literally, graphic displays) can present, much more concisely than words or numbers, the relationships contained in the data. Research with managers in decision-making situations supports the claim that managers can determine trends and data relationships more quickly and accurately if presented with graphical displays. Color CRTs are used in sophisticated terminals to provide a graphics output capability.

CRT graphics terminals are also used to assist designers, production schedulers, educators, cartographers (map makers), and analysts. If equipped with the appropriate hardware and software, these terminals can present objects in apparent three-dimensional display using up to sixteen different colors. The first graphics terminals were produced in 1970 by Tektronix (see Figure 4–11).

Graphics terminals are reasonably expensive, with only a few models available for less than $3,000. They do provide for exciting presentations of computer output as evidenced by the illustrations of this type of output shown in Figure 4–12.

Plasma Displays. This type of terminal uses a neon gas plasma and the same basic principle as the neon sign to produce either alphanumeric or graphics displays. Its most common use is in PLATO terminals, a joint, computer-assisted educational effort of Control Data and the University of Illinois.

From a PLATO terminal a student can access a large number of interactive, educational programs. The student can respond to questions asked by a PLATO program by either entering data through the keyboard or, where prompted to do so, by touching the PLATO screen itself (see Figure 4–13).

Flat Panel Displays. We are beginning to see examples of this new display which produces graphics displays (and television pictures) without the inherent cabinet depth required for the cathode ray tube in the more usual television format. Terminals and portable microcomputers using flat panel

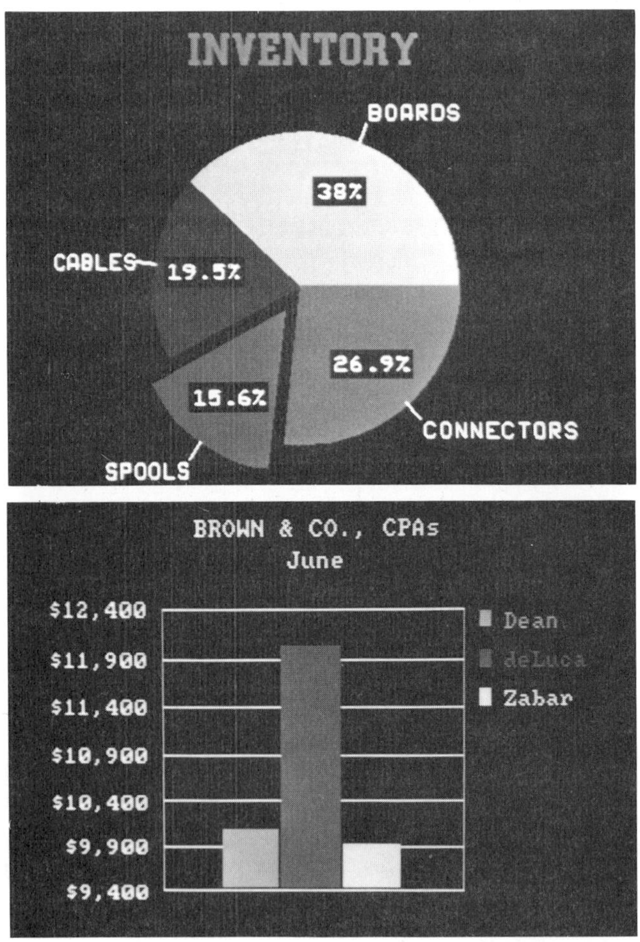

Figure 4–12 Examples of Computer Graphics

Figure 4–13 Plasma Display in a PLATO Terminal

displays began to appear in the market in 1982. A portable microcomputer with a flat panel display is shown in Figure 4–14. If the economic and technological problems can be resolved, flat panel displays will revolutionize terminal design as the bulky CRT gives way to a thin display panel.

Flat panel displays can be quite large. The one pictured in Figure 4–15 is used to provide flight information to air travelers. These large displays

Figure 4–14 Flat Panel Display on Personal Computer

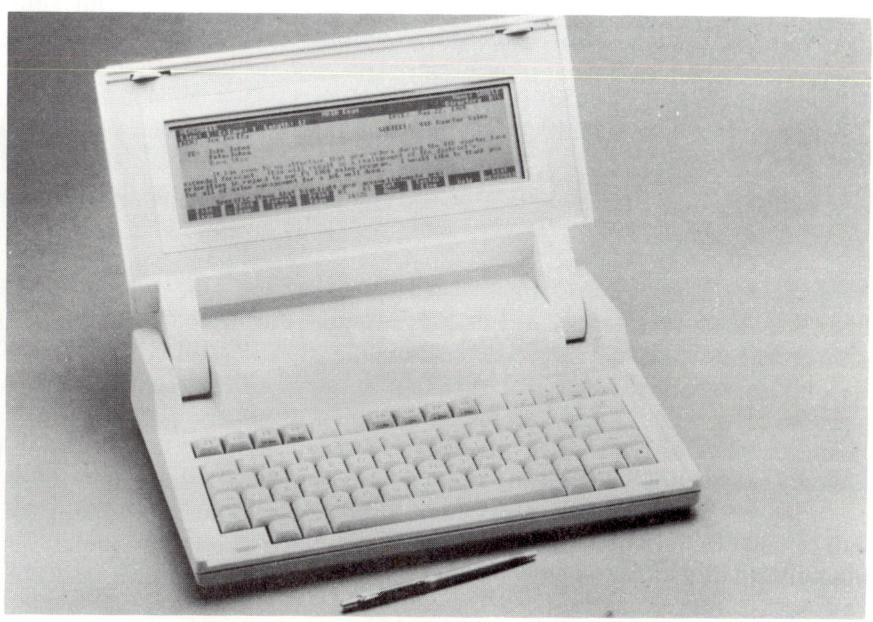

Figure 4–15 Flat Panel Display

represent a great improvement over their electro-mechanical predecessors, in which small signs were mechanically manipulated to form the display.

Several different technologies are currently competing for the flat panel display market. These include the electrochromic display, the thin-film electroluminescent display, the electrophoretic display, and the liquid crystal display (used in digital watches). One of the flat panel displays uses a liquid suspension of iodides which block light when the suspended particles are in disarray but allow it to pass if a low voltage is applied to align the particles (see Figure 4–16). Imagine, an electronic window shade!

Plotters

A plotter is a computer-driven device for performing drafting (drawing). When connected to a computing system and equipped with the appropriate software, it makes many types of drawings possible. Landscape architects use plotters to produce landscape drawings to help visualize the effects on the visual landscape of tree cutting, road building, mining, and other activities. Computer designers use them to produce circuit drawings which are reduced and used in computer chip manufacture. Engineers use plotters to generate engineering drawings in many industries, including the automobile industry. A plotter which produces color drawings is shown in Figure 4–17.

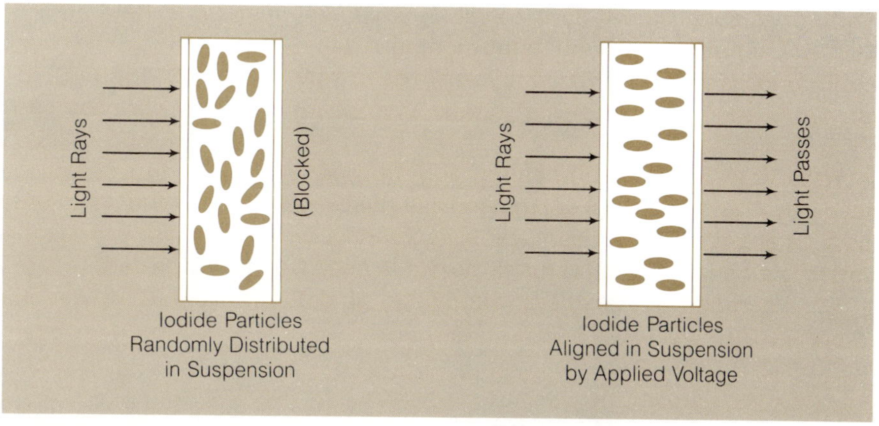

Figure 4–16 Working Principle of Light Valve Flat Panel Display

Two general types of plotters exist: drum plotters and table-top (flatbed) plotters. A flatbed plotter is built so that the pen movement is controlled along two axes while the paper remains stationary. In a variation on the theme of the flatbed plotter, a beltbed plotter uses a vertical surface (see Figure 4–18). In each case one or more pens must be guided over the paper by a program in exactly the desired way to produce the drawing. In a drum plotter the pen(s) move along one axis, while movement of the paper wrapped around the drum provides movement along the other axis.

Color plotters are very popular. Some provide only one or two pen positions and require the user to change colors when necessary. Others provide a wide variety of built-in pens, which are changed under software

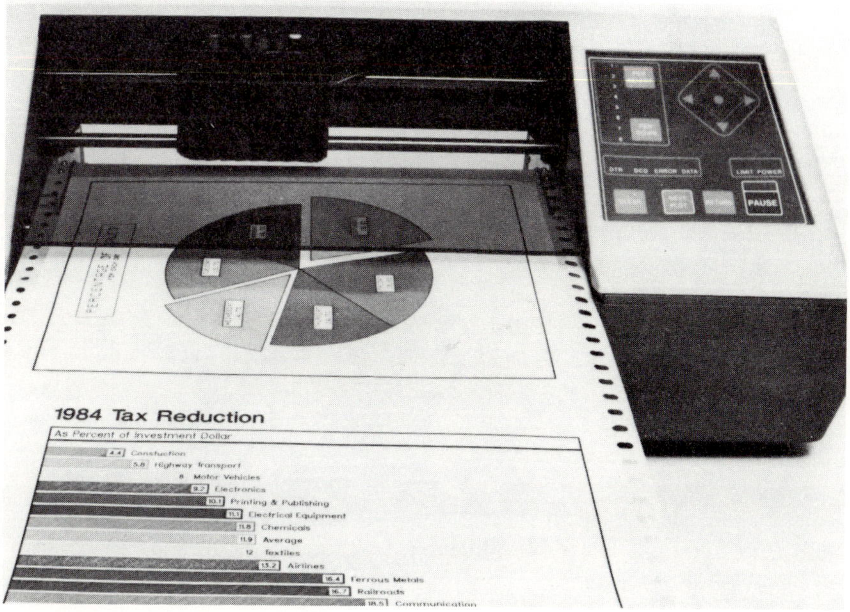

Figure 4–17 Color Plotter

Figure 4–18 Beltbed Plotter

control. Color plotters have become a popular addition to many microcomputer systems (see Figure 4–19).

Microfilm

An increasingly large number of computer installations are generating microfilm as output, a capability known as computer output microfilm (COM). The somewhat older method for producing COM was to store the output

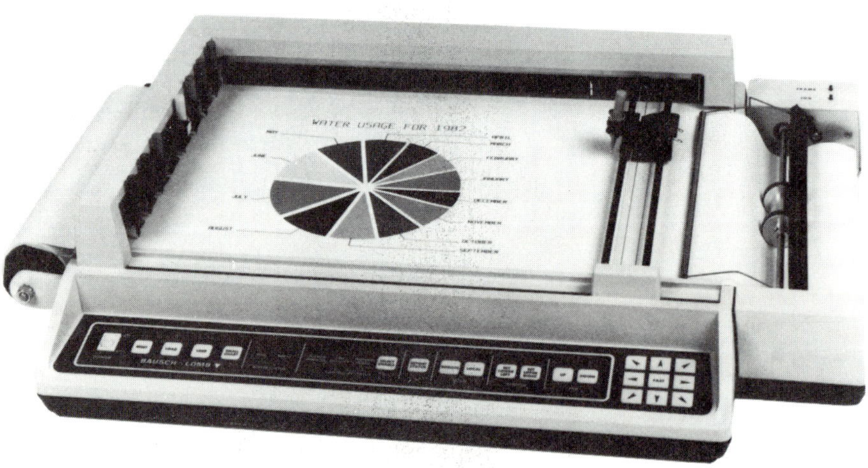

Figure 4–19 Color Plotter for Microcomputer

Computers in Action 2

Meeting the Challenge

1. The timely processing of information is essential to the success of stock brokerage firms such as Johnson, Jones, Jackson, and Doobenheimer. **2.** Stock brokers use microcomputers to gain access to current information on stock prices, customer portfolios and the performance of companies whose stocks are traded.

1

2

3. When a client calls, Marion Boyd must be able to respond to questions and initiate the transactions desired by the client.

4. Marion's computer system provides a visual display of current stock prices and summaries of industry and company performance figures. **5.** This punched paper tape device produced stock exchange information on the famous "ticker tape" before the days of electronic information display.

3

4

5

6

6. Large visual displays in the office complex of Johnson, Jones, Jackson, and Doobenheimer provide up-to-date information for both clients and brokers. **7.** Monthly statements and transaction reports can be prepared for Marion Boyd's clients on a printer connected to the system. **8.** This view of the stock exchange floor provides only a glimpse of the electronic information processing facilities there.

7

8

9. Stock transactions take place quickly and both parties to the transaction must have accurate information on which to base their activities. **10.** The Dow Jones Company markets software for microcomputers which gives individuals access to stock market information. **11.** Facsimile transmitters are used in the back office of Johnson, Jones, Jackson and Doobenheimer to send copies of important documents over a nationwide network for instant delivery.

9

10

11

Figure 4–20
Automated Apeture Card Retrieval

temporarily on magnetic tape, then use the tape as input to a microcomputer-controlled device which generated the microfilm. Organizations not wanting to do their own microfilming sent tapes to a microfilming service bureau. Early microfilming units were capable of handling only alphanumeric output, but newer systems can handle graphics output as well.

In some cases the microfilming unit is directly connected to the computer system, in which case the intermediate step of temporary storage on magnetic tape is not used. The newer microfilm processes allow microfilm to be generated directly. These machines are connected to the system in the same way any other output peripheral might be. One problem with this type of system is that a failure in the microfilming process will necessitate shutting the computer system down or switching to other forms of output.

Microfilm output can take place via several different formats. Since microfilm comes in rolls like movie film, computer output can be stored on the film in this format. Data stored on microfilm are made readable to human beings by either projecting them onto a screen as in a microfilm reader in the library, or by producing an enlarged, hard-copy version. A single frame (to use the same terminology as for a motion picture film) can be mounted in a small hole cut in a data processing card, which gives a format known as an aperture card. Cards can be inserted into an appropriately designed instrument for viewing. Devices are available which provide for the automatic storage and retrieval of aperture cards as seen in Figure 4–20. One such device allows computer terminal–type access to over 200,000 cards for viewing, copying, or file maintenance.

A very popular format for microfilm output is the **microfiche,** a four-by-six-inch segment of film which contains hundreds (even thousands) of frames. The lower right hand frame is typically used as an index to assist the user in finding the correct data. The index yields a frame number in much the same way that map coordinates are used to locate particular streets on a city map.The rows of frames on the microfiche are lettered alphabetically, and the columns are numbered so that each individual frame has a row (letter) and column (number) designation. A user finds the frame designation in the index, then moves a locating pointer on the viewer to that designation which projects the appropriate frame for viewing.

COM has several advantages over the more normal printed output. These advantages include:

1. Microfilm output is cheaper.
2. Microfilm output is faster.
3. Microfilm output requires dramatically less storage space. (A file cabinet full of documents can be reduced to a small card file of microfiche.)
4. Microfilm files can be maintained at a higher level of security than paper output.

At the same time, several disadvantages work to restrict the use of microfilm. They include:

1. Microfilm output requires special equipment for human viewing or printing.
2. Changes can be made only by producing a completely new original, the old microfilm cannot be modified.
3. Microfilming equipment is rather expensive.

Card Punches

One of the interesting characteristics of fields which experience rapid technological growth is the wide disparity between the technologies which are *possible* and those found to be in *common use*. As a practical matter, we hear about innovations long before they are available in the market place, and we continue to use older technologies long after newer ones are available.

Punched cards are an excellent example of this disparity. Knowledgeable computer people are almost embarrassed to talk about punched cards because that technology is so old. Certainly the use of cards is on the decline, but many card-using systems are still in operation.

A card punch is a computer output device which records data on punched cards at a relatively high speed (for cards). They are useful in those situations where information generated by one program will later be used as input for another. For most applications this use of cards has been replaced by the use of magnetic tape or magnetic disk. Many colleges and universities still distribute to students class cards punched by a class scheduling program, which are later used to generate class lists and enrollment data.

Voice Output

The era of talking computers is at hand. Computers are able to produce voice output in at least two somewhat different ways. The simplest, and historically the earliest, voice output devices used a computer program to select an appropriate, recorded message from a set of messages previously recorded and stored in the system.

Recent advances in the technology have allowed voice messages to be synthesized from stored versions of digitized words. The digital output from the computer is fed to a computer chip which synthesizes words selected from a limited vocabulary.

Voice response systems are used to respond to inquiries from the customers of banks (regarding account balances), stock brokers (regarding stock quotes), and telephone companies (for telephone numbers). The related development of a voice store and forward system will be discussed in Chapter 17. The ultimate test for digitized and reconstructed voice messages is referred to as transparency. In this context, transparency refers to the user's perception. If the synthesized speech is so natural that the user cannot "see" the synthesis, the use of automation is described as being transparent to the user.

Optical Disks

Large volumes of computer output seem destined to be stored on optical disks. This technology should provide an effective alternative to microfilm for output which is likely to be stored for long periods of time. As many as 15,000 pages can be stored on a single eight inch disk.

Optical disks should provide efficient, computer-assisted retrieval of documents from long-term, permanent files. The factor which seems to limit widespread use of this technology is the difficulty in erasing the disks and re-using them.

Challenge Update

Marion should now be able to list the output tools which seem to best meet the output criteria established for each of the stock brokerage applications.

Technology: The Inner Workings of Output Devices

Printers

Perhaps nowhere else are there as many competing technologies as in printer design. A reasonably elaborate classification scheme is necessary just to talk about them. This section will discuss two general categories of line printers—those which rely upon impact to generate an image and those which do not.

While the distinction between impact and nonimpact printers is itself not particularly interesting to the user, many parameters which do concern the user are in many cases a function of the impact/nonimpact classification. Noise, for example, might be an important consideration to some users;

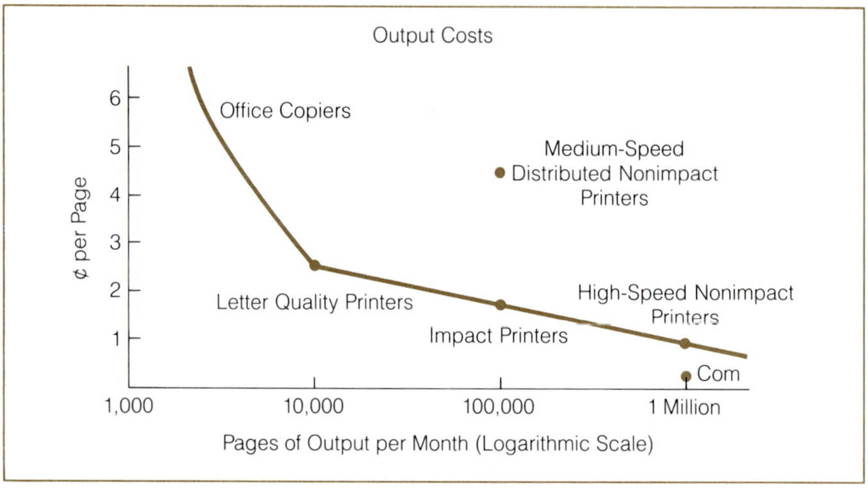

Figure 4–21 Costs of Various Types of Printed Output

and nonimpact printers are, in general, much more quiet than are impact printers. Speed is another important consideration to many users. Although many high-speed impact printers exist and are in service, the highest speed printer is a nonimpact printer. Cost relationships between the two can be seen in Figure 4–21.

Print quality varies greatly from one type of printer to another. The quality of printing tends to worsen as printer speeds increase. A new dimension to computer output printing has arisen as data processing systems merge with word processing systems. Word processing systems require **letter quality printing**—a print quality which would be satisfactory for business letters.

Printing costs are important and include not only the initial cost of the printer but the cost of paper and maintenance as well. Impact printers use

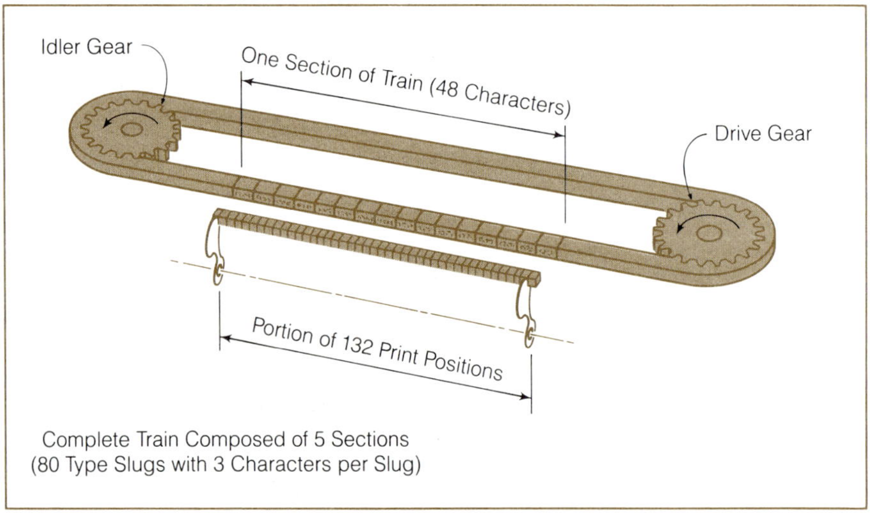

Figure 4–22 Chain/Printer Mechanism

Figure 4–23 Drum Printer Mechanism

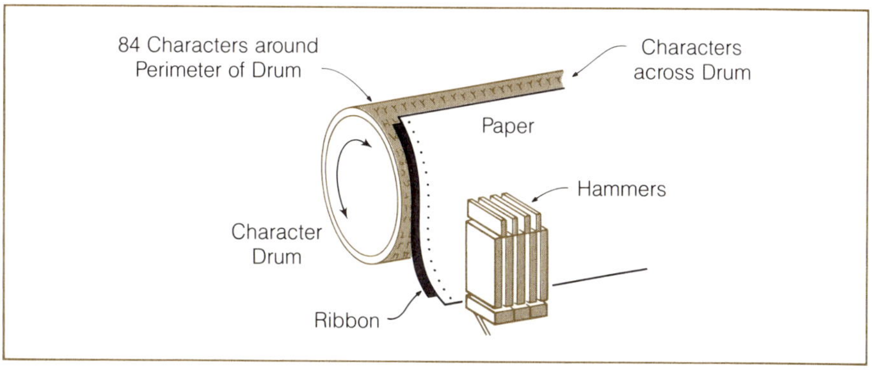

standard paper but some of the nonimpact printers use special types of paper which are more expensive. All printers have many mechanical parts which are subject to breakdown and result in high maintenance costs. Some technologies seem to suffer more than others in that regard.

Impact Printers. Impact printers cause the image of a particular character to be produced by the joint impact of a typeface element, paper, and inked ribbon. The impact is produced either by the typeface element itself striking the ribbon which strikes the paper (as in a typewriter) or by a small hammer which forces the paper against the ribbon to strike the typeface.

Impact printers differ in the manner in which the typeface is presented to the location of impact. A brief note about each of the current technologies will be provided.

- *Chain:* The type is all connected (linked together) as a chain which moves until the correct character is positioned for impact, as in Figure 4–22.
- *Drum:* Complete sets of type exist on a drum at each print position. As the drum is rotated, the impact is timed to strike characters as they rotate into position, and the line is printed (see Figure 4–23).
- *Train:* Type is linked together (as in a train) and moved into position for impact, much as it is for chain printers.
- *Band:* Type exists on a metal band and is moved into position for impact. Bands are more easily replaced than chains or trains. A band printer mechanism is shown in Figure 4–24.
- *Dot Matrix:* Characters are formed as patterns of dots in a matrix which has the capability of producing a five-by-seven (or seven-by-eight) dot matrix. Very small rods strike the ribbon to generate the image of any character. Graphics characters are also possible with dot matrix printers, such a printer is pictured in Figure 4–25.
- *Daisy Wheel:* This device acquires its name because the typeface/font exists on spokes around a center just as petals of a daisy extend from the center. The wheel rotates around the center and impact is timed to strike the correct character. A print wheel mechanism for a daisy wheel printer is shown in Figure 4–26.
- *Thimble:* Much like the daisy wheel, the thimble printer presents its typeface in a form resembling a thimble (see Figure 4–27).

Figure 4–24 Band Printer Mechanism

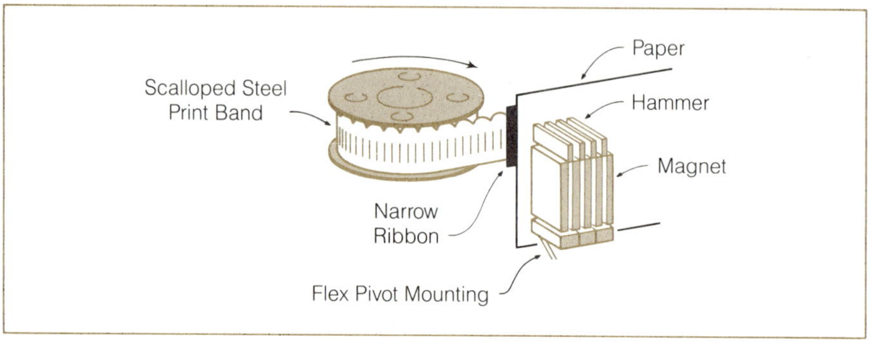

Nonimpact Printers. In recent years the design of printers using mechanisms other than impact to produce images has been emphasized. By the mid-1980s these printers are expected to account for 40 percent of the printer market.

Nonimpact printers, in general, have fewer mechanical parts than the impact printers and should, therefore, encounter fewer mechanical problems. Many of these printers use technologies which originated with office copying machines and, therefore, experience similar maintenance problems.

While most of the nonimpact printers use standard paper, the thermal printers and some of the electrostatic printers require a more expensive, special paper. The operation of nonimpact printers is, in general, more quiet than that of impact printers.

It is difficult to characterize in general terms the relative speeds of impact versus nonimpact printers. Both technologies provide production-grade printers at the low end of the range of speeds, about 100 lines per minute.

Figure 4–25 Dot Matrix Printer

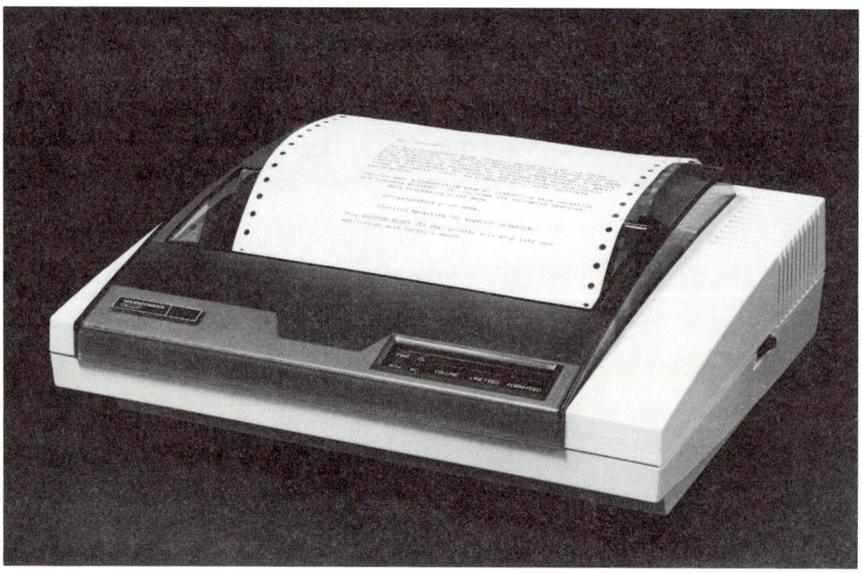

Figure 4–26 Print Wheel Mechanism Used in Daisy Wheel Printers

(Personal computer printers usually operate at somewhat slower speeds.) The highest speed impact printers provide only about 3,500 lines per minute maximum, while a nonimpact printer using a laser technology is reported to achieve speeds in access of 30,000 lines per minute.

A brief description of the nonimpact printer technologies is provided.

- *Thermal:* The thermal printers use a heated roller and special, heat sensitive paper. These printers are relatively slow but relatively cheap if one considers only initial cost of the printer itself. The cost of the paper and the relatively high cost of print head replacement make this an expensive alternative if a high volume of printing is required.
- *Electrostatic:* Electrostatic printers also use expensive, special paper. Images are formed by placing static charges on the paper, then causing ink

Figure 4–27 Print Thimble Used in Thimble Printers

particles of an opposite charge to be deposited onto the paper (see Figure 4–28).

- *Ink Jet:* The ink jet printer is an analog of the dot matrix impact printer. It uses either a set of very small nozzles through which ink is sprayed to form the character images (see Figure 4–29) or electrostatic manipulation of ink droplets. These printers are of relatively high speed. Ink jet printers which produce full color printing are also available.
- *Xerographic:* Xerographic printers use a technology developed by the

Figure 4–28 Electrostatic Printer

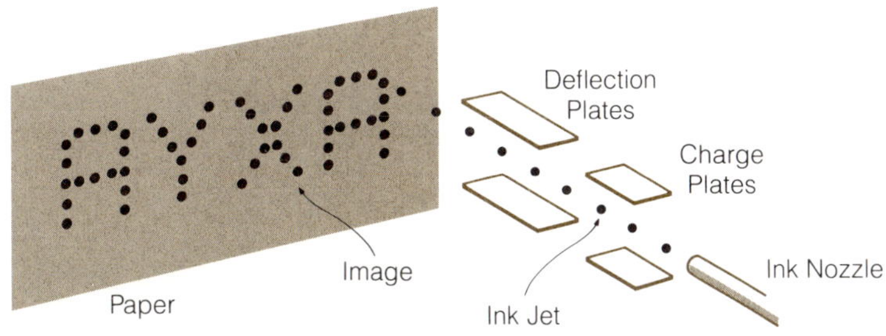

Figure 4–29 Ink Jet Printer

Xerox Corporation for its office copying machines. They rely on a drum which has negative images of the characters on its surface and a source of light inside the drum. The images are projected onto a light sensitive, metal drum. Toner is applied and sticks to the sensitized areas of the drum, from which it is transferred to the paper. A very fast, but very expensive version of the xerographic printer, which uses a laser light source, is available as seen in Figure 4–30.

- *Electrophotographic:* The xerographic printer technology just discussed is a specific case of a larger class of printers known as electrophotographic, which belong to this class by virtue of the photoconductor drum which is used. The surface of the photoconductor drum is charged electrostatically, then the image of a character projected by light onto the surface of the drum causes the electrostatic charges to be discharged to form negative character images on the drum's surface. Charged toner particles are applied to the drum and transferred to the paper as illustrated in Figure 4–31.
- *Laser:* One version of the electrophotographic printer uses a laser light source to achieve printing speeds in excess of 20,000 lines per minute. Laser printers offer high-speed printing of multiple type fonts and graphics at high speeds and low cost, with quiet operation (see Figure 4-32).
- *Ion Deposition:* The ion deposition technology is somewhat similar to the electrophotographic, though its manufacturers claim it is less expensive and more reliable. It relies on the deposit of ions to form images rather than the bombardment of light to discharge electrostatic images.
- *Electro-erosion:* In 1983 IBM began marketing a nonimpact printer which

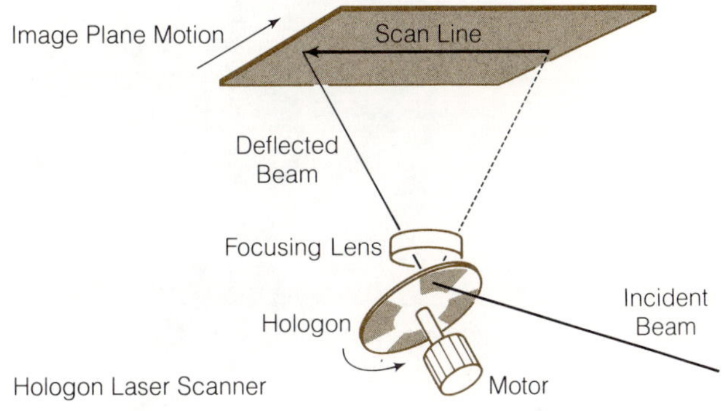

Figure 4–30 Xerographic Printer with Lasar Light Source

Figure 4–31 Electro-Photographic Printer

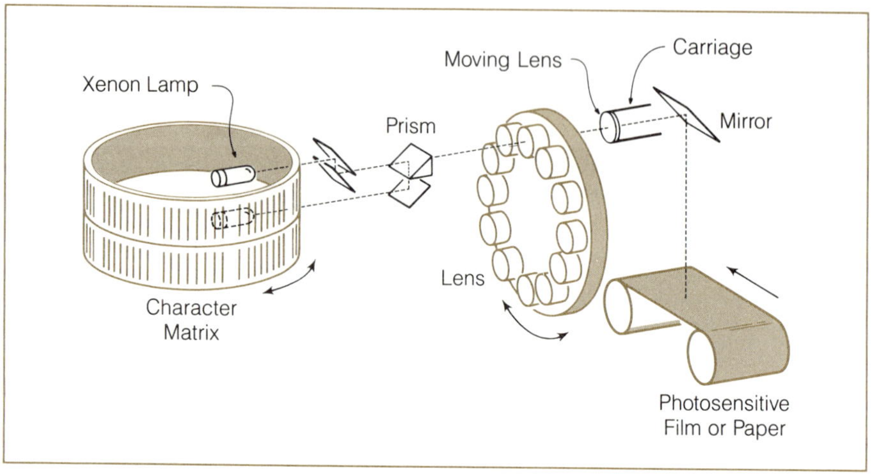

produces a high-resolution output by eroding away an aluminum coating to expose a black undercoating. It is expected that this technology will be utilized in producing camera-ready copy for the publishing industry.

The printer market is large, and it continues to grow faster than any other segment of the computer peripheral market. Such markets tend to attract significant investments in research and development, so we should continue to see interesting new technologies in future printers.

Graphics Terminals

Computer graphics via visual display terminal is a new enough field that the competing technologies warrant some investigation. The typical graphics terminal integrates a microprocessor; a reasonably large, inexpensive

Figure 4–32 Lasers in Electronic Printing

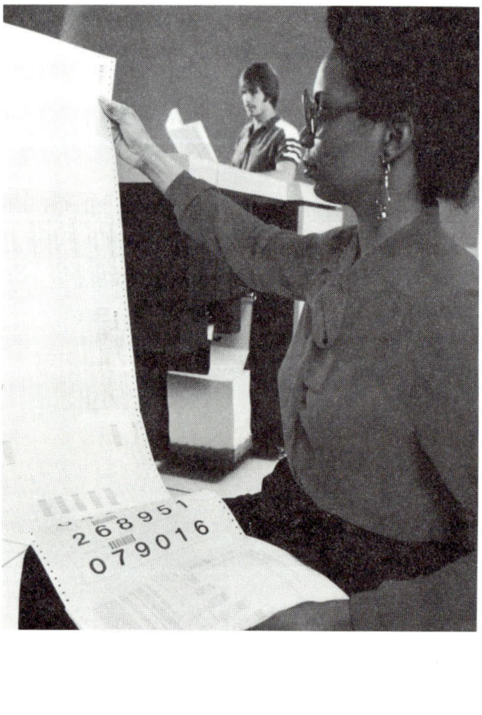

memory; and improved graphics software into an extremely useful system. The computer graphics terminal user provides a description; and the terminal, through its memory, computing, and software capabilities, transforms that description into an image displayed on the screen. Three different technologies are in use to produce the image: refresh, storage tube, and raster.

Refresh. With refresh technology, the image is produced by a directed electron beam which causes the phosphors coating the inside face of a CRT to glow. The picture is produced by directing the beam to trace the appropriate image onto the phosphors. The picture must be refreshed (retraced) forty to sixty times per second as the phosphors fade quickly. The refresh graphics terminal is the most expensive of the three versions.

A refresh graphics terminal requires a memory in which the image is stored electronically, a processor to convert the electronic data into a correctly directed electron beam, and a CRT. Changes in the image in memory are reflected in the image on the screen, which can be used to give the effect of motion, hence animation.

Storage Tube. The storage tube technology uses a directed electron beam to trace the image, as does the refresh technology, except in the case of the storage tube display the image is formed on a fine mesh grid mounted just behind the phosphor-coated screen. The grid is then flooded with electrons from another source, which results in the image being transferred to the phosphors themselves. The phosphors in the storage tube design do not lend themselves to quick fade, hence the image, once projected, cannot be as readily changed as in the refresh technology. The main advantages of storage tube displays are low price and high resolution with less flicker than the refresh display.

Raster Scan. Color graphics displays are available through use of the raster scan technology, which divides the CRT screen into very small areas known as pixels. An electron beam scans each line of the screen and colors and intensifies each pixel according to data stored in an area of the terminal's memory known as a frame buffer. Changes made in the data in a display file cause corresponding changes in the frame buffer and, subsequently, changes in the display itself.

Although the early standard allowed resolutions in the range of 512 scan lines of 512 pixels each, newer technologies promise 2,000 scan lines with a correspondingly improved resolution.

Some of the graphics display terminals available attempt to use combinations of the three technologies mentioned above. They have not, in general, been as successful as the original versions.

Voice Output

Some people believe that the use of voice output will increase to the point that commands to accomplish it will have to be added to the common programming languages. They suggest a TALK command will be added to COBOL, FORTRAN, BASIC, Pascal, and other programming languages.

The computer controlled generation of voice output can be accom-

Figure 4–33 A Voice Generation Module

plished through four different technologies, each of which relies on the storing of digital representations of voice for playback at appropriate times. A voice generation module is pictured in Figure 4–33.

- *Digital Recording and Compression:* This method takes voice message wave forms and converts them to a digital form for later playback.
- *Linear Predictive Coding:* A mathematical model to represent the voice box is used to generate sounds of rather poor quality.
- *Phoneme:* A library of all possible language sounds is generated and then combined to construct a voice message. Quality is also rather low.
- *Parameterized Wave-Form:* This technology combines mathematical modeling with digitized, recorded speech to produce high-quality output.

It is uncertain whether or not voice output will become a predominant form of computer output, although there are some applications for which it might be quite useful. We will perhaps see some greater use of voice *input* systems if technical problems associated with them can be resolved.

Challenge Update

The reader should now be in a position to suggest output technologies which might be best suited for accomplishing the outputs needed in Marion Boyd's firm.

Newest Developments

New developments in the format, nature, or technology of computer output occur (literally) daily. We will doubtless continue to see the use of microprocessors, memory, and dedicated software to improve the functioning of terminals, printers, plotters, and other output devices. We can expect that terminals will increase in capability and that printer speeds will increase. Flat panel displays may dramatically change the appearance of visual display devices. A new technology which produces thin CRTs may also compete for that market.

Perhaps the most exciting developments will be in the area of automated responses. We, as humans, spend far too much time initiating predictable responses to information received from a computer. The current method of providing computer output to a human being who in turn initiates some action will gradually change. Computers will be programmed to initiate the action directly.

Early examples of this movement already exist. For example, manual inventory control systems for raw materials require that a worker physically count the items in inventory and notify a purchasing agent when it is necessary to order additional goods. When the inventory management process becomes computerized, it produces a list of goods which need to be ordered. From this advance, it is only a small step to the point where the purchase orders are printed by the system itself. The next obvious step is to have the computer transmit an order directly to the supplier's computer.

Banking provides another example of this progression. We now have automatic teller machines to deliver cash to consumers, electronic funds transfers so that we can pay bills without handling either cash or checks, and automatic deposits, are also handled electronically.

Computerized systems now perform design, testing, and manufacturing operations in many industries. We also see the computer's control extended to the actual direction of effort in an assemblage, as intelligent robots engage in manufacturing operations. Perhaps we will shop via TV cable systems with delivery accomplished by robots.

Though the rate of technological change seems to be accelerating, people's behavior, in contrast, seems slow to change. People in business seem to encounter the same old problems with regularity. So, although many of our daily activities will be drastically changed by automated processes, life in the business world will still be characterized by meetings, cost consciousness, productivity struggles, coffee breaks, and lunches with clients and customers.

COMPUTING CHALLENGE: *A Final Note*

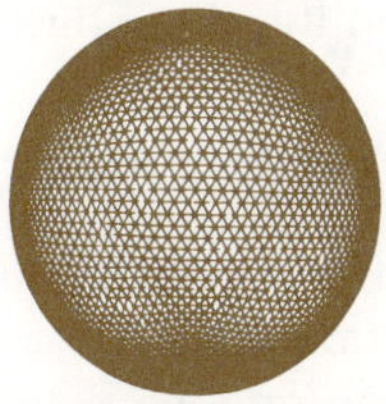

This chapter opened with a problem encountered by a stock brokerage firm with respect to the determination of computer outputs. Marion Boyd had been asked to develop plans to improve customer service with respect to stock price quotes, statements of account, transaction reporting, and research.

Can we now be of some help to Marion in the determination of the outputs necessary to support the activities of brokers in the firm of Johnson, Jones, Jackson and Doobenheimer?

Figure 4–34 A Useful Matrix for Analyzing Outputs for Stock Brokerage Example

Characteristics \ Applications	Stock Quotes	Statements	Transactions	Research Reports
Contents				
Format				
Medium				
Frequency				
Timeliness				
Permanence				

Consider first the four basic types of service which are provided for clients of the firm: stock quotations, monthly statements, transaction records, and research reports. What characteristics of each application are important in determining the proper selection of output? In what ways are content, format, media, frequency, timeliness, and permanence important in each application?

Perhaps one appropriate way to proceed would be to form a matrix (table) of applications and characteristics seen in Figure 4–34.

The matrix can then be filled by entering, in each cell, the data for each application/output characteristic. When that is complete, the characteristics of each application can be analyzed, and lists of one or more output tools which would seem to satisfy the requirements of the application can be generated. The various output tools can then be compared in terms of their cost and relative performance in each application area. Such an analysis would be of great help to someone in Marion's position.

SUMMARY

- Systems have purposes, and the output of a data processing system is closely related to its purpose.
- The design of information systems in organizations requires that we give early consideration to the output requirements and allow the design of the other data processing functions to follow.
- The system life cycle characterizes a system as a living entity whose birth, life, and death evolve in eight significant phases.
- An analysis of the content, format, media, frequency, timeliness, and permanence of the output is necessary.
- Perhaps unexpectedly, the format of computer output is almost as important as its contents in providing effective communication.
- The output requirements of a particular application can only be determined by considering the nature of the application itself.

- A wide variety of output devices exist.
- Output can be printed via line printers or typewriter-like terminals, visually displayed via alphanumeric or graphics terminals, drawn via plotters, photographed on microfilm, punched into cards, used to generate voice messages, or stored on optical disks.
- Output tools vary greatly in terms of cost and their ability to satisfy particular needs.
- The designs of many of the newer output devices incorporate intelligence in the form of a microprocessor and memory to improve their performance.
- Given the choice of a particular form of output, in most cases a variety of technologies exists by which that output can be produced.
- Some output technologies are well tested and known to be reliable, while others are new and their reliability is yet to be established.
- While printed paper has historically been the most common form of output, microfilm and video display terminals seem to be gaining in importance.
- Output devices undergo continuous research and development efforts to improve their performance and to guarantee that we will doubtless see more, rather than fewer, alternatives in the future.

CASE: Computer Answers Oil Drilling Questions On-Site

As the world's known energy supplies dwindle under the pressure of increasing consumption, the search for new sources and new supplies of old energy sources becomes more important. As existing oil fields are being developed and drained, oil companies search for new fields and new techniques. One of these companies, Phillips Petroleum Company, casts their computing capabilities into the fray.

Phillips uses a computer system to forecast oil well production and profitability. The Series 80 MANTIS system allows the development of applications such as oil reserve forecasting and economic evaluations to take place in a fraction of the time that would have been required by traditional methods. These applications have, in turn, reduced the time required to determine whether or not to drill a particular well from hours to minutes. There have been significant productivity improvements for both the data processing department and for end-users in the oil fields.

The information system provides engineers and geologists at remote sites with access to corporate information and programs. Additionally, the system's use is simple enough to allow inexperienced users to be immediately productive with it. The system has caused other important improvements. The MANTIS has made it possible for users, worldwide, to have instant access to drilling information instead of a long wait for batch reports. Before MANTIS, Phillips had very few programmers experienced in developing quick-response applications. Users, therefore, did not have access to needed programs.

The new system is a versatile one that can be used for scientific and technical applications as well as business applications. Outputs generated by the system are made available to users promptly so that operational delays can be kept to a minimum. Output is distributed via a network from the main data processing center in Bartlesville, Oklahoma. Phillips hopes to expand the system in coming years to develop additional applications. Care is taken in the development of each new application to ensure that the users' need for accurate reporting in a usable format is provided in a timely fashion.

"Applications Development System Improves Oil Forecasting," *Infosystems*, December 1982, p. 56.

Questions for the Case

1. The emphasis in this case appears to be on the development of systems which reduce the normal delays in the generation of output. Why might this be important?
2. Give other examples where output delays might be critical.
3. Are quick-response systems likely to be more or less costly than normal batch operations?
4. If we ask a manager if his or her information need requires a quick response, what is the most likely answer? Why?

DISCUSSION QUESTIONS AND EXCERCISES

1. Most descriptions of the operating steps involved in data processing application begin with input. Why?
2. Most descriptions of the design steps involved in data processing applications begin with output. Why?
3. Think of a computer system in support of decision making within a college or university. For this use, describe the importance of output accuracy, usefulness, and timeliness.
4. Discuss the relative advantages and disadvantages of visual display versus typewriter-like terminals.
5. Discuss the relative merits of printed versus microfilmed output.
6. The systems designer and the user must both understand the computer output requirements of a system and the tools which are available for generating it. How might they go about reaching a common understanding?
7. Describe several examples of information processing in which the content of output is the most critical consideration.
8. Develop a short list of processing outputs with which you come in contact during the day. In which of those outputs is format very important?
9. Newspapers, television, and news magazines all compete for our attention as providers of the news. Compare them in terms of content, format, frequency, timeliness, and permanence. Which is a "better" source for the news? (How is *better* defined?)
10. Managers seem to acquire a great deal of information from meetings and conversations with others. Critique verbal information flows as an output in terms of the considerations presented in this chapter.

11. Figure 4–5 provides information in several different formats. As a manager, which would you prefer to receive? Why?
12. Consider a human being as an information processing system. Describe a human's information outputs. Discuss both content and format.
13. A business can be studied as a system. The data processing department can be studied as one of a business's subsystems. What are some of the other subsystems? How are they different from the data processing department? How are they like the data processing department?
14. Consider a student as an information processing system and think about the student's performance on an examination as an output. What are the important characteristics of that output? What kind of examinations would seem to be the best format? Why?
15. The addition of a microprocessor and memory to a terminal gives us an intelligent terminal. Give other examples of devices to which similar intelligence has been added.
16. Discuss the following: Good decisions depend upon good information; good information cannot guarantee good decisions.
17. List the types of data processing output devices you have seen. Where could you go to see a new one?

ADDITIONAL READINGS

Computerworld, a weekly newspaper published by C. W. Communications, Box 880, 375 Cochituate Road, Framingham, MA 01701, provides excellent coverage of new output devices.

Datamation, a monthly magazine published by Technical Publishing, 875 Third Ave., New York, NY 10022, provides excellent discussions of output technologies.

Foley, J. D., and Van Dam, A. *Fundamentals of Interactive Computer Graphics.* Reading, MA: Addison-Wesley, 1982.

Freedman, David. "Inkjets Aim at Color Printing." *High Technology,* October 1983, pp. 23–25.

Harvard Business Review frequently contains articles relating to the use of computers in business.

Infosystems, a monthly magazine published by Hitchcock Publishing, Wheaton, IL 60188, provides excellent discussions of output technologies.

Logsdon, Tom. "High Speed Printer." *Technology Illustrated,* January 1983, pp. 101–104.

Lucas, Henry C., Jr. "An Experimental Investigation of the Use of Computer-Based Graphics in Decision Making." *Management Science,* July 1981, pp. 757–768.

Meyer, Franklin. "Picture Brightens for Flat-Panel Display." *High Technology,* March/April 1983, pp. 33–40.

Miller, Frederick W. "COM's New Role: Out of the Darkroom and On-Line," *Infosystems,* April 1982, pp. 48–56.

Myers, Edith. "If We Could Talk to Terminals." *Datamation,* October 1983, pp. 181–184.

B:DAILY PAGE 1 LINE 15 COL 35
GOOD MORNING!
CAN I HELP YOU?
ENTER YOUR NEXT COMMAND:

5

The Entry of Data: Input

CHAPTER PREVIEW

In Chapter 4 we saw how the design of the output for a data processing application forms the basis from which the design of the other major components (input, computation, and storage) can proceed. Once the output has been specified in terms of content, format, media, frequency, timeliness, and permanence, the manager and the designer can begin to analyze the entry of data into the system. Differences in form and content between the desired outputs and the available inputs must be overcome through computation and other manipulations. Differences in time between the available inputs and the desired outputs must be overcome through the use of storage.

We now turn our attention to the design of the input. Recall the discussion in Chapter 1 of data as signals given off by the various events which take place within an organization. Data entry for the information processing activities of these organizations takes place in three steps. The first, **data capture,** occurs as the data are recorded by some means so that they will be available to the system when needed. For example, data are captured in many instances by writing them on original records known as *source documents.* The second step in the data entry process is the *conversion into a machine-readable format* of the data on the source documents. This is followed by the final step, the actual *reading into the system* of the data.

An example will help illustrate the various phases of the data entry process and give some insight into the ways in which the process is changing. Think first of a retail store in which the clerk writes a sales ticket (source document) to record the items purchased by a customer. (Some of us may have difficulty remembering such a store.) Data are captured in this system by recording sales on the tickets. Data from these tickets could then be converted into machine-readable form and read into a computer for an analysis of sales, computation of sales commissions, or adjustments to inventory.

In more modern systems, the cash registers themselves provide data capture (entry through the cash register keyboard) and encoding of the data in a machine-readable format (recording on magnetic tape). Further integration, and shortening of the data entry process takes place when direct reading of codes on the products substitutes for part of the data capture. Eventually, this integration may lead to direct connections from the cash register to the customer's bank and the store's bank, through which immediate transfers of funds will complete the sales transaction.

The data entry process has a number of characteristics which make it one of the most important steps in the overall processing of data. For one thing, errors introduced into the system during data entry are difficult to detect and costly to correct. Even more serious, of course, is the potential hazard of not

(continued next page)

detecting an error, in which case subsequent processing will result in output which will be in error.

It is also true that the data entry process usually requires an extensive amount of human effort. It is, therefore, a likely source of error. It has historically been a time-consuming and costly operation. One goal of modern data entry operations is to capture the data as close as possible to their source. This eliminates the more costly, more time-consuming, more error-prone processes of encoding in machine-readable form followed by input to the system.

To gain a better understanding of some of the important characteristics of data entry, consider the data entry problems of a retailer planning a change to automated retailing outlets.

COMPUTING CHALLENGE: *Automatic Movie Outlets*

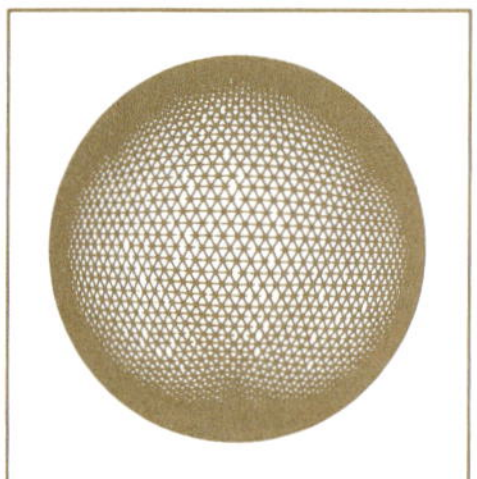

Movie Mint produces and sells movies recorded on either magnetic tape cassettes or video disks. Their products are currently available through record outlets and video stores, but their marketing operations are about to undergo major revision. At the first of the year they are planning to move to automatic retailing through small, fully automated units placed in the center of shopping malls, on street corners, in bus and train stations, in public libraries, and in numerous other high traffic areas.

Under their current operating conditions, Movie Mint's retail outlets are provided with an ordinary, hard copy order blank which lists the available movie titles and provides a space for the retailer to order specific quantities in either the disk or tape format. Retailers mail the order blanks to Movie Mint's production and warehouse facility in Pittsburgh. These orders are received in the Order Entry Department of Movie Mint, where they are entered onto punched cards for processing by the company's computer system. This processing results in the production of picking tickets for the warehouse employees, who will "pick" the goods for the orders from the existing warehouse stock and prepare them for shipping. An invoice is also prepared for the purpose of billing the retailer who has placed the order.

A new warehouse which uses microprocessor-controlled robots to pick orders will soon be in operation. Company officials are interested in automating the order entry operation at the same time the move to automatic retail outlets is completed.

Each of the new retail outlets will operate without human intervention; computer-controlled robots will perform all the necessary functions. Data entry devices will be provided around the outside of the retail unit. Customers hoping to buy movie tapes or disks will make their wishes known through the data entry devices. They may also request a brief viewing of a segment of the movie in order to help them decide whether or not to make a purchase. Robots will direct the preview screenings, dispense any purchased movies (having gift wrapped them if requested), and complete whatever other transactions are necessary.

The automatic retail units will be open twenty-four hours every day. Restocking of the retail units will be accomplished by jobbers who travel, in large trucks filled with movie disks and tapes, out of one of twenty-eight regional warehouses. Jobbers will place orders with Movie Mint to replenish their in-truck inventories at frequent intervals during their travels through their territories.

Some of the interesting data entry questions posed in this case are:

1. *By what means should customers be able to communicate with the robots in order to specify purchases, request screenings, and handle the other necessary transactions?*
2. *By what means should jobbers be able to place their orders with Movie Mint while on the road and while at the regional center?*
3. *Which of the data entry characteristics are important in 1 and 2 above?*
4. *How important would ease of use be?*
5. *Does data entry by the customer represent the ultimate outcome of the decentralization of data entry?*

The study of this chapter on data entry will help give proper consideration to these questions and others as well. After careful study of this chapter the reader should also be able to:

1. *List the important characteristics of data entry.*
2. *Discuss the changing nature of centralized data entry and decentralized data entry.*
3. *Describe and compare several different means for accomplishing data entry.*
4. *Explain the role of standardization in further improvements in data entry.*

HISTORICAL PERSPECTIVE

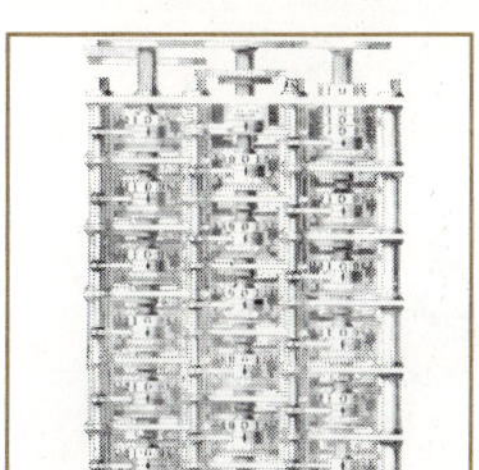

We have previously characterized the processing of information as an activity which is absolutely essential to the well-being of an organization. Information processing has an obvious dependence upon the data entry operation, whether the information processing is accomplished by manual or automatic means. Most automatic systems had manual beginnings, so it is not surprising to consider that large amounts of data have historically been captured through relatively unsophisticated, manual means.

The significant transactions of most organizations have in the past been captured on paper, using pencils, pens, or typewriters to record the necessary facts. Manual systems have by no means disappeared; we will continue to find them in use for many years. In the transaction processing of most early computing systems, data were captured in some handwritten or typed form before they were to be converted into a machine-readable format for introduction into the computing system itself.

The device most often used to accomplish the transformation to machine-readable format was the keypunch, a device in which data were entered through a keyboard and punched into cards. Operators sat for long hours at the keyboard punching cards while reading from the original handwritten or typed documents on which the data had been recorded. The data had been generated by the many different transactions which were occurring throughout the organization. These source documents were carried (or mailed) to a central facility near the data processing center for conversion into machine-readable form.

Another trend is worth noting in order to more fully understand the dynamic nature of the data entry process. Early systems provided only for data entry by personnel associated with the data processing department, and only at a central location within the data processing department. The more recent trend is toward the *decentralization* of data entry operations, moving the responsibility for data entry into the various functional departments within the organization. As the data entry task becomes distributed throughout the organization, it is also being done on more capable, intelligent hardware, as we shall see. A typical data entry operation is shown in Figure 5–1.

Let us turn now to a discussion of the important characteristics of data entry so that later, in the tools segment of this chapter, we can begin to understand how the important characteristics of various data input devices compare. The technology section of the chapter will discuss some of the interesting details of the various input technologies.

Figure 5–1 Large, Centralized Data Entry Operation

Concepts: The Capturing of Data

An analysis of the various means by which data processing is accomplished shows that those processing steps which are accomplished manually are likely to be the slowest, most error-prone steps. A general guideline, therefore, for the design of data processing systems is to keep the number of steps requiring human intervention to a minimum.

An effective data entry operation requires an efficient blend of hardware, software, people, and procedures—as is the case in most other areas of data processing. We will examine the traditional, centralized data entry operation and then discuss some general principles within which data entry systems are designed.

Traditional, Centralized Data Entry

Traditional data entry operations have consisted of the following steps:

1. Capturing the original data on a source document.
2. Conversion of the data to a machine-readable format.
3. Editing the data to detect and correct errors contained therein.
4. Processing the corrected data.
5. Identifying additional errors, if any, and returning to step 3, or quitting after successful completion of the task.

As an example of the traditional steps, let us review the means by which Movie Mint was processing incoming orders. Orders for tape cassettes and video disks from the retail outlets were received by phone or mail and entered by hand (or typed) by salespeople, customers, or clerks at the Movie Mint order desk. The orders (the source documents) were delivered to the data processing department for conversion to punched cards, a machine-readable format. The cards were checked for accuracy and fed to the computer for processing.

In general, in large organizations, source documents are completed by a variety of people throughout the organization during the normal course of operations. For example, retail store clerks produced cash register receipts or handwritten receipts as a by-product of the sale itself. The source documents were traditionally sent, then, to large, centralized data entry departments for conversion to a machine-readable format (see Figure 5-1).

Such a system gave the central data processing people early control of the data, which was of some help in scheduling computer processing runs. The centralized data entry operation also made it possible for the department to be staffed with highly-trained operators. The users, on the other hand, retained little or no control over the input process, the documents themselves, or the scheduling of computer processing runs which produced outputs needed by the managers. Users, in those circumstances, were frequently frustrated by the lack of control they felt that they had over information processing operations critical to the managing of their departments.

As an example, consider an engineer working on a road design where most of the computations and drawings are generated by a computer after the data describing elevations, soil types, loads, and so on have been determined by the engineering staff. In a centralized data entry environment the engineers must determine the data values and submit them to data entry personnel. They must then wait until the data are entered and the road design program run before they can review the results. Errors introduced during data entry operations may cause the entire design to be in error.

Data Capture at the Source

An even more troublesome problem was, and is still, characteristic of traditional data entry operations. Problems arise when the people who convert data into machine-readable form do not know what meaning should be associated with the data. People who continuously operate a data entry device in a central data entry facility view the data only as collections of characters, without meaning. They cannot be expected to place them in any context within which correctness or incorrectness can be judged.

Steps taken at the central facility to verify the accuracy of the data being entered can, therefore, only focus on whether or not the data entered is an accurate representation of the data appearing on the source documents. Some additional checks can be made through software edit routines which check (among other things) to see that data types are correct for each field (no letters in numeric fields nor numbers in alphabetic fields) and that numeric values are within the correct range of values.

Centralized data entry personnel cannot be expected to fill in missing data items or catch other errors which might be obvious to someone familiar with the context within which the data are used. This shortcoming of centralized data entry operations is one of the reasons the recent impetus has been to move the capturing of data as close as possible to the source of the data. Wherever possible, the effort is to combine these two steps in the traditional data entry process and to capture data in machine-readable form at their source. In terms of the road design example above, data entry responsibility would be given to members of the engineering staff who could enter the data as they become available.

Data entry at the source has become possible through the development of more capable data entry hardware and the increased utilization of remote communications. There are many examples of this transfer of data entry responsibility. Admissions clerks in hospitals now have data entry responsibility, as do laboratory technicians, sales clerks, and travel agents. The first principle, therefore, to which attention must be given in the design of data entry operations is the *capture of the data in machine-readable form as close to the data source as possible.*

Timeliness

A second principle to which attention must be given is **timeliness.** Data entry operations must be designed to capture the data in a timely fashion, though timely does not always mean as quickly as possible. Timeliness for an application which generates monthly statistics is different from one which guides an interplanetary missile or does the payroll or processes requests for passenger space on a commercial aircraft. The data entry system must provide for the entering of data within a timeframe which is adequate to support the particular application for which it is being designed.

Error Detection and Correction

The third principle deals with the detection and correction of errors. The data entry system must provide an adequate means for detecting and correcting errors. **Edit checks** support the data entry operator's work by checking that numeric fields contain numbers and that alphabetic fields contain letters. **Range** and **limit checks** can be used to see if data values are within the correct range or reasonable limits. **Validity checks** can be performed to insure that values like account numbers and part numbers do belong to the set of possible account or part numbers.

Other types of checking are also used. **Ascendancy checks** check the number of each record as it is processed to make sure that records are processed in order. **Batch totals** represent an attempt to catch errors by comparing these totals before and after data entry operations. For example, in entering data for a payroll application, the total number of hours worked by all employees could be used as a batch total. A similar type of checking mechanism, called a **hash total,** computes the total value of the numbers in a particular field for each record processed. The hash total uses a field which is not normally used in computations, such as an account number.

Extension checks can be performed to make sure rows of an invoice or purchase order are properly extended. **Cross-footing checks** are used to check arithmetic operations performed on tabular sets of data. The rows and columns are separately summed, then the row and column sums are themselves added. The sums should, of course, be equal.

The general rule is that errors cost more to correct the longer they remain in the system. At the time of data entry it may only cost a few cents to catch and correct an error; but by the time the data has found its way into a file or data base, it may cost several dollars to correct. An error which goes undetected and uncorrected could, of course, be responsible for the making of an incorrect managerial decision, which could be very costly.

Ease of Use

A very important consideration in the design of a data entry system is the attention which must be given to its *ease of use.* Some people in the organization will be spending large portions of their time performing data entry operations. Care should be taken to ensure that the hardware is easy to use and allows worker comfort. The data entry process should be easy to monitor (perhaps on a television screen), and the entire layout should be arranged in an efficient format. The software which controls data entry should be "friendly," that is, easy to use efficiently without it presenting a threatening environment to the operator.

Flexibility

Another factor of some importance is *flexibility,* the ease with which the system can be adapted to different uses. Change occurs continuously in the field of data entry. A flexible system might be able to accommodate change without the necessity of making drastic revisions in the existing system. A flexible system might reduce the inefficiencies which result from large changes later.

Challenge Update

The reader should now understand the important characteristics of data entry.

Approximately 10 to 25 percent of an organization's total data processing budget will be spent in data entry operations, so it is an important component solely in terms of its cost. Add to that the fact that all subsequent operations—computation, storage, and output—will be incorrect if the data entry is incorrect, and we begin to understand its importance to the organization. We turn our attention now to some of the tools of data entry, the various types of hardware which are used to accomplish the data entry task.

Tools: Data Capturing Devices

The user's frustration with a centralized data entry operation together with the availability of improved equipment and communications have resulted in a movement toward decentralized data entry. The character of data entry operations is changing as a result of its movement out of the central data processing facility to a position closer to the source of the data. Approximately 80 percent of the data entry operations characteristic of data processing in the 1970s were located centrally, near the data processing center itself. Only 20 percent of data entry operations are expected to be centrally located by the end of the 1980s. This will cause a basic change in the mix of equipment which is used for data entry operations. Indeed, some of the processing itself is being dispersed as well, as we shall discuss later.

Challenge Update

At this point in the chapter, the reader should be able to discuss the changing nature of centralized and decentralized data entry.

Punched Cards

The punching of data into cards began with Herman Hollerith in 1890 as he attempted to ease the computations associated with the Census of the United States. Punched cards have changed somewhat. They are, however, still in use, though their popularity is declining as they are being replaced by other technologies. Data are punched into the card through use of a machine called a **keypunch** (see Figure 5–2). Keypunch operators, reading from source documents, enter the data through a keyboard, and the machine punches the appropriate patterns of punched holes into the cards. A punched card is shown in Figure 5–3.

Punched cards exist in two principal formats, the most popular of which is a (roughly) 7-by-3-inch card which has eighty columns with room in each column for a single character. A smaller card, approximately 3 inches square,

Figure 5–2
Keypunch

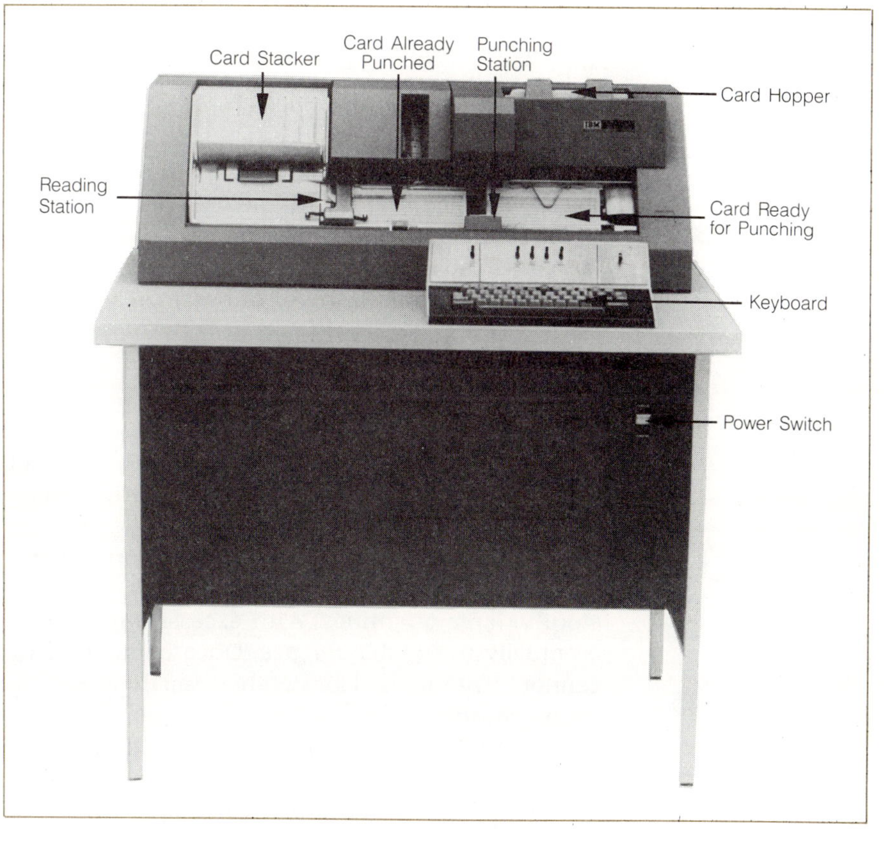

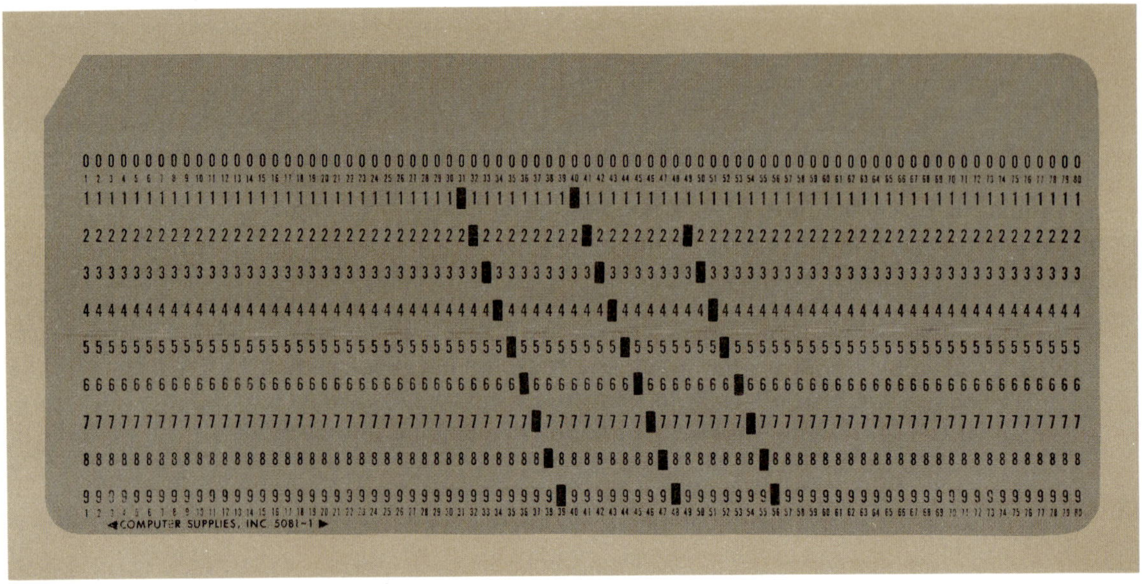

Figure 5–3 80 Column Punched Card

wherein small circular holes were used to record data in three rows of thirty-two columns (characters) each, was designed for use in some IBM systems (see Figure 5–4). Use of the smaller card has been very limited.

Full-scale, punched card data entry stations used **verifying machines** to help detect errors in punched cards. A verifier operator sat at a machine almost identical in appearance to the keypunch, and performed the data entry keystrokes dictated by the source documents. Unlike the keypunch, however, the verifier merely checked the already-punched cards to see if the patterns punched in the cards corresponded with those indicated by the verifier operator's keystrokes. A discrepancy caused the keyboard to lock, whereupon the operator could check the accuracy of the entry and cause a small notch to be cut in the card if the data were in error.

Cards containing information punched from the source documents are read into the data processing system through use of a computer input device called a **card reader.** Card readers operate in the range of 150 to 1,000 cards per minute, which is, at 80 characters per card, approximately 200 to 1500 characters per second, a relatively slow data transfer rate compared to other media.

Punched cards provide a relatively convenient medium for data entry. Cards are relatively inexpensive, though somewhat bulky to handle and store in large quantities. With excessive use, the cards become worn and eventually unsuitable for use. Once committed to a particular use, cards cannot be repunched for another use; they can only be recycled with other paper products or discarded.

One of the problems of punched card data entry operations is the difficulty in detecting and correcting errors. The keypunch effort is essentially doubled by using the verifier to check cards for errors. Once an error is

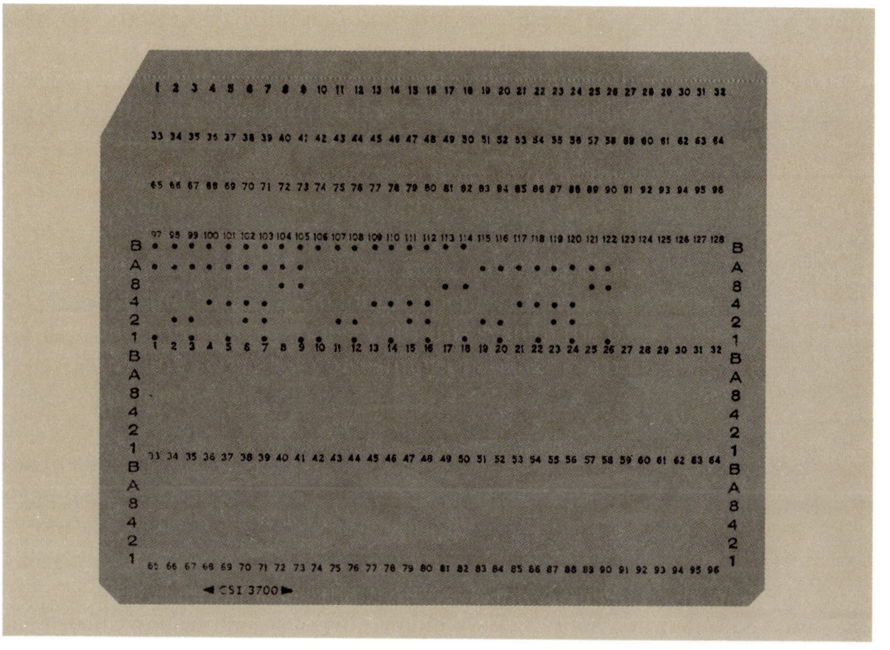

Figure 5–4 96 Column Punched Card

found, the card cannot be corrected; a new one must be punched. Errors may be made in punching the corrected card, and yet another correction must be attempted. Significant improvements can be accomplished through use of the devices to be discussed next.

Key-to-Tape and Key-to-Disk Machines

If a keypunch were to be called a key-to-card machine, we would have no trouble understanding what **key-to-tape** and **key-to-disk** machines do. They simply provide an opportunity for data entered through a keyboard to be stored onto magnetic tape or magnetic disk. These machines provide several improvements over the keypunching of data onto cards.

Many key-to-tape and key-to-disk machines are equipped with television screens to enable the operator to monitor the data as they are entered. Errors detected during the monitoring process can be easily corrected through commands which allow data to be added, deleted, or modified easily. The entering of data through the keyboard is, thereby, more efficiently accomplished.

Most key-to-tape and key-to-disk machines provide data editing software which allow the operator to browse through the data for proofreading purposes, and which provide for validity and range checking. Once the data have been reviewed and found to be correct, an additional advantage of these devices allows the data to be transferred into the computing system at a higher rate of speed than does the card reader. While the upper bound on the rate of transfer of data from cards is around 5,000 characters per second, data transfer from tapes and disks can be as high as 1 million characters per second.

Magnetic tape and magnetic disks both provide for a greater amount of data storage in a smaller physical space than do cards. Both tape and disks can be reused, data are easily erased and new data easily recorded. Additional discussion of magnetic tape and disks in Chapter 7 elaborates their roles in data storage.

Terminals

As data entry operations become more commonly done at work stations dispersed or distributed throughout the organization, and less commonly done in large, centralized facilities, the use of **terminals** as data entry devices increases. The previous chapter discussed the use of terminals as output devices and categorized terminals as either typewriter-like or visual (video) display. We find the same two categories of terminals on the input side, though the visual display terminal (see Figure 5–5) is much more frequently used as an input device than the typewriter-like terminal.

As input devices, visual display terminals have several advantages over their typewriter-like counterparts. Visual display terminals are cheaper than typewriter-like terminals, and they typically operate at faster data transfer speeds. In addition, the visual display provides a much more satisfactory means of monitoring and proofreading the data during the keyboard entry operation itself. The visual display terminal's lack of hard copy is much less important on the input side than on the output side.

Visual display terminals make use of several user friendly mechanisms for accomplishing data entry. A **menu** of possible data entry operations can be displayed for the user, and the system asks the user to select the proper item from the menu. A selection from the menu may lead to a screen display wherein the data items to be entered are highlighted in reverse

Figure 5–5 A Visual Display Terminal Used for Input

video (dark letters on a lighted background) or in color, or the selection may lead to another menu of alternatives. Airlines use this *menu-driven* approach to make it easier for their agents to process the transactions common to passenger service. Hotel registration clerks use menu-driven systems for registering guests and assigning them to rooms. Software written to support these data entry operations presents a series of rigorously-developed screens to the operator to make data entry as convenient, quick, and error-free as possible.

General Purpose Terminals. We can also categorize terminals according to their use. Many terminals are designed for general purpose use, with typewriter-like keyboards and numeric pads so that they can be used across a broad spectrum of applications requiring the entering of alphanumeric data. These terminals may be capable of executing software which provides menu-driven data entry for a variety of applications. They might also be used for interactive programming tasks. They are, quite simply, useful for general purposes as opposed to the quite specific tasks for which the terminals in the following section have been designed.

Dedicated Use Terminals. Wherever the pattern of use on a terminal reveals a limited set of purposes, a terminal designed specifically for that purpose provides an efficient alternative to the standard alphanumeric terminal. The design may cause the screen, the printing mechanism, the keyboard, and the software to be modified. There are simply too many dedicated-use terminals to discuss them all, but we will take a brief look at a few of the more common applications.

Point-of-Sale Terminals. Data generated by the sales transactions in retail outlets can be captured at the source by a device called a point-of-sale (POS) terminal, which doubles as a cash register and computer data entry terminal (see Figure 5–6). A POS terminal may be directly connected to the computer, in which case transactions are captured instantaneously and can be used immediately for data processing tasks. More often, the terminals generate magnetic tape recordings of the transactions which are then used for an overnight updating of information stored in secondary memory. Data collected by these terminals are used in sales analysis, salesperson workload analysis, and inventory control applications.

Many different types of POS terminals exist. A fast-food restaurant will typically have a keyboard for the terminal which has pictures of the various food items which are available. When the clerk presses the key with the picture of a large portion of french fries, the cost of french fries is automatically recorded on the customer receipt, and other data are recorded on tape for later computer processing applications. The number of products available in a department store make it impossible for the same approach to work.

A department store POS terminal is usually equipped with a cash register keyboard, to which a few special function keys have been added (see Figure 5–7). Sales data are entered through the keyboard, or read directly from the ticket on the items(s) being sold, or both. A light pen is sometimes used

Figure 5–6 Point-of-Sale Terminal

Figure 5–7 A Department Store POS Terminal with Cash Register Keyboard

in conjunction with the keyboard entry to improve the efficiency of the process. In order for the light pen to work correctly, the tickets must have been printed using special optical character recognition fonts, which are discussed later in this section.

Grocery stores have utilized a slightly different technology to facilitate the generation of a cash register total and receipt. Most of the products available in the grocery store have had a small area of alternating black and

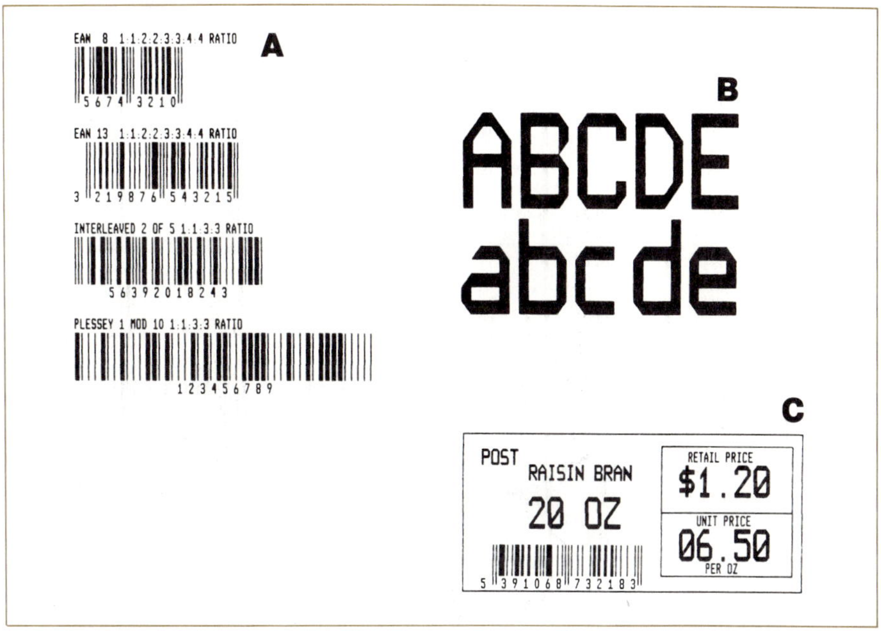

Figure 5–8 The Universal Product Code Commonly Used on Supermarket Items

white stripes, called a bar code, added to their packaging. The **universal product code (UPC),** the most frequently used bar code, has a unique representation for each product in the store, which is scanned by a laser and recognized; then the appropriate data items are collected for use in generating the cash register receipt and making entries in the sales analysis, inventory control files, and other files (see Figure 5–8).

After a slow start in the grocery store market, scanners capable of reading bar codes have become increasingly popular in many other areas. Bar codes and scanners have been used to sort outbound baggage in an airline terminal, to validate vehicle stickers on toll bridges, to keep track of railroad cars, to sort case goods coming from a conveyor belt into a warehouse, and to automate the book circulation process in a library. Some details of bar code scanners are provided later in the technology section of this chapter. Figure 5–9 shows a typical grocery store application.

Automatic Teller Machines. Banks use a special purpose POS terminal known as an **automatic teller machine (ATM).** This terminal allows a bank customer to complete a limited set of transactions without having to enter the bank itself. Automatic tellers are located so that customers have access to the bank's services twenty-four hours a day, seven days a week, often from the sidewalk adjacent to the bank (see Figure 5–10). Although most ATMs are dedicated to a particular bank and installed on its premises, newer versions service a collection of banks from a single terminal installed in shopping centers, race tracks, gambling casinos, and other high traffic areas.

Factory Input Terminals. Many operations in manufacturing, warehousing, and service industries lend themselves to data entry through the use of

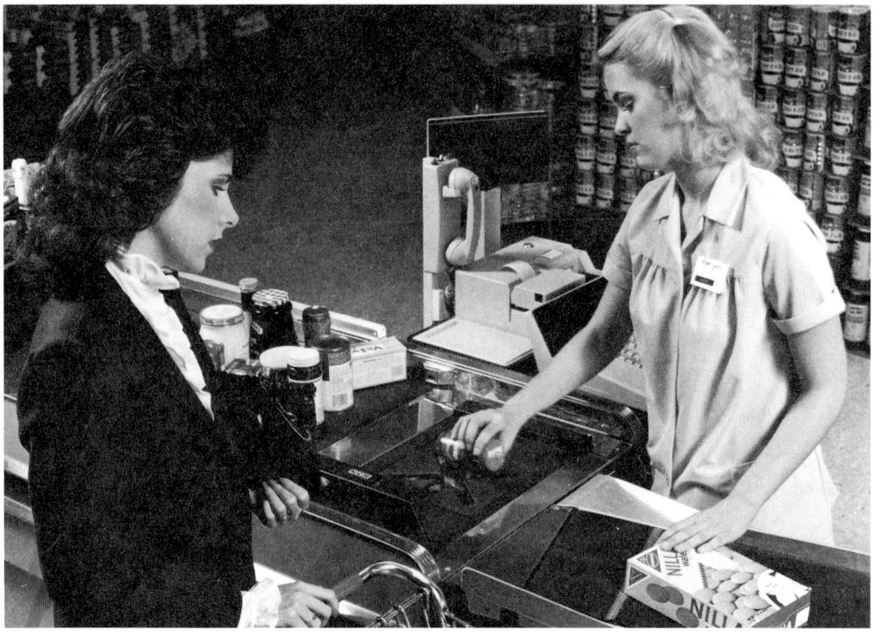

Figure 5–9 Scanner in Use at a Supermarket Checkout Counter

Figure 5–10 An Automatic Teller Machine

dedicated terminals. Custom manufacturing operations, for example, must provide some means for keeping track of the labor, materials, and supplies committed to each job in the shop. Terminals located on the shop floor allow workers to enter such data directly without going through the intermediate step of recording the data on a job ticket, which is later used as a source document for a keyboarding data entry operation (see Figure 5–11).

Figure 5–11 A Factory Input Terminal

Dedicated terminals in warehouses capture the data necessary to record the loading and unloading of trucks and rail cars.

One variety of the factory input terminals is designed to recognize handwritten characters. Instead of using a keyboard or other input mechanism, the operator writes the input on paper which rests on a special, pressure sensitive surface. The handwritten characters are entered into the system as they are recognized.

The volume of data entered through POS and factory input terminals is on the rise. The increased use of these dedicated terminals for data entry at the source is consistent with the move toward *decentralized data entry*. The relative popularity of these devices is illustrated in Figure 5–12.

Transaction Phones

Touch-tone telephone sets form the basis for another, somewhat limited-purpose, data entry operation. For a number of years industrial customers

Figure 5–12
Forecast of the Market for Data Entry Devices

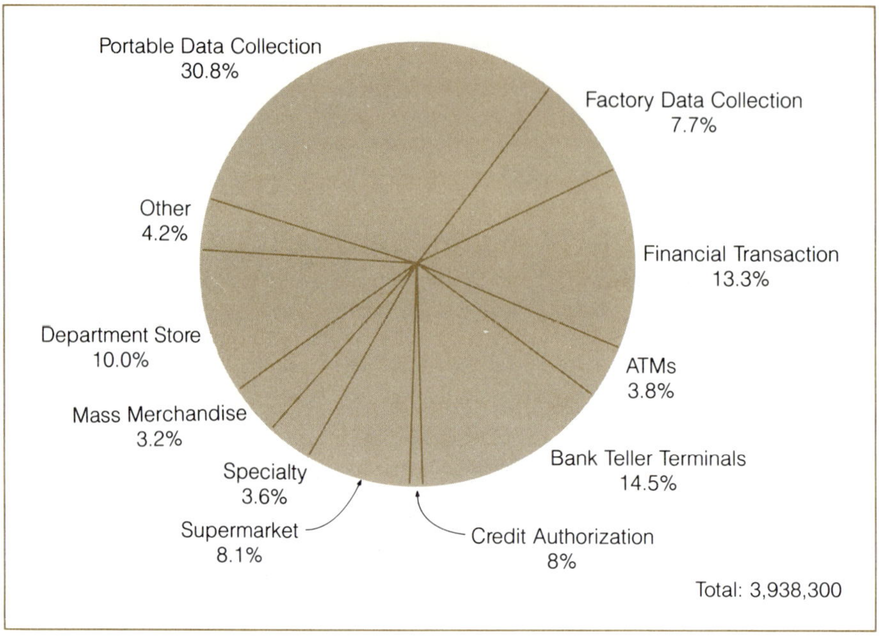

The study is available for $2,500 from IDC, 5 Speen Street, Framingham, Mass. 01701.

have been able to enter orders through special-purpose telephone sets, into which essentially numerical data could be entered by depressing the appropriate keys on the telephone.

Credit card purchases are frequently approved through a similar use of the telephone. One application requires a special modification to the telephone set so that data recorded on the magnetic strip on the back of the credit card can be read by a reader built into the telephone. A computer system at the other end of the line approves (or disapproves) the transaction by activating a signal light on the retailer's telephone-terminal.

Optical Mark Recognition/ Optical Character Recognition

Very early in their academic careers, students are introduced to the concept of **optical mark recognition (OMR)** (see Figure 5–13). Most computer-graded multiple choice and true/false examinations are graded through the use of OMR equipment. Students are asked to darken, with a number 2 pencil, the area between a pair of dotted lines under the answer of their choice. Optical mark recognition equipment is then used to recognize the answer which has been chosen and to compare that answer to the one correctly identified by the answer key.

Optical character recognition (OCR) is a somewhat more difficult task. An OCR input device relies on the optical scanning of an input document, wherein the system must be able to accurately identify the handwritten or typed characters. The system must be able to recognize each character in the character set being used and differentiate it from all other characters.

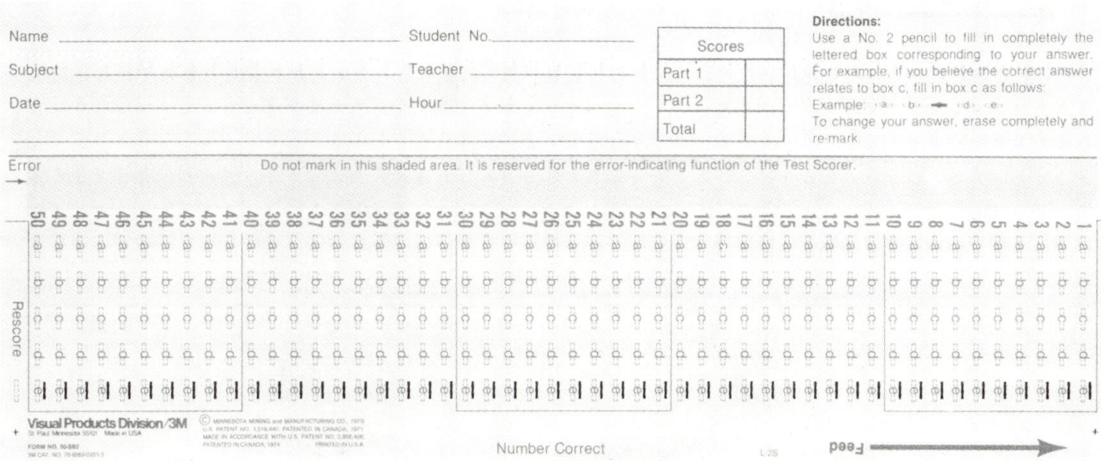

Figure 5–13 Optical Mark Recognition Form

The character set can be controlled in the case of typewritten or printed characters because the typewriter and typesetter can be constrained to a particular set of type, except of course for strikeovers (see Figure 5–14). Handwritten characters provide a more challenging environment.

Unfortunately for OCR equipment, we have not all learned a standard set of characters to represent the numbers and letters. For example, people write the numeral 4 differently. Some computer users slash zeroes in order to differentiate them from the letter *O*. (Unfortunately, there are computer users who slash the letter *O* to differentiate it from a zero.) These idiosyncracies are easily overlooked by humans in the reading of data, but they cause great difficulty to an OCR system.

OCR has been quite successfully used in combination with POS terminals in retail outlets. A light pen connected to the terminal can be used to scan the tickets on each item being purchased. The tickets have been prepared in advance using one of the standard OCR type fonts so that recognition of the characters representing the item and its price is quite reliable. Some improvement in pattern recognition may lead to OCR systems which operate at a higher rate of speed with higher reliability. An OCR device used in library circulation data capture is pictured in Figure 5–15.

Page Scanners

Under carefully controlled conditions, where the character set is a standard, identifiable one, machines called **page scanners** are capable of entering

Figure 5–14 OCR Font

Figure 5–15 An Optical Character Recognition Device

data directly from typed documents. The scanner uses digital techniques to form and enter an image of the document which can then be processed using normal electronic means (see Figure 5–16). Some page scanners can read text which contains several different type fonts. One such machine, for example, is able to read 250 pages per hour and up to eight different typefaces. Page scanners might, then, be able to do the work of some fifty data entry clerks using keyboard entry techniques. Page scanners are used extensively in offices where extensive text processing is done. In lawyer's offices, for example, they are used to read and store legal contracts.

Scanners can be combined with microprocessors and voice output devices to make reading machines. Such a machine can read printed materials such as books, magazines, and reports to people whose eyesight does not allow them to read for themselves.

Magnetic Ink Character Recognition

One of the more successful attempts to automate the data entry process has taken place in the banking industry. A limited number of characters in a special alphabet can be printed with a special magnetic ink on the checks used to disperse funds from checking accounts. The **magnetic ink character recognition (MICR)** characters can be used to encode the bank number, the customer's account number, and the amount for which the check has been written, so that the checks can be cleared through the banking system more efficiently (see Figure 5-17).

Figure 5–16 A Page Scanner

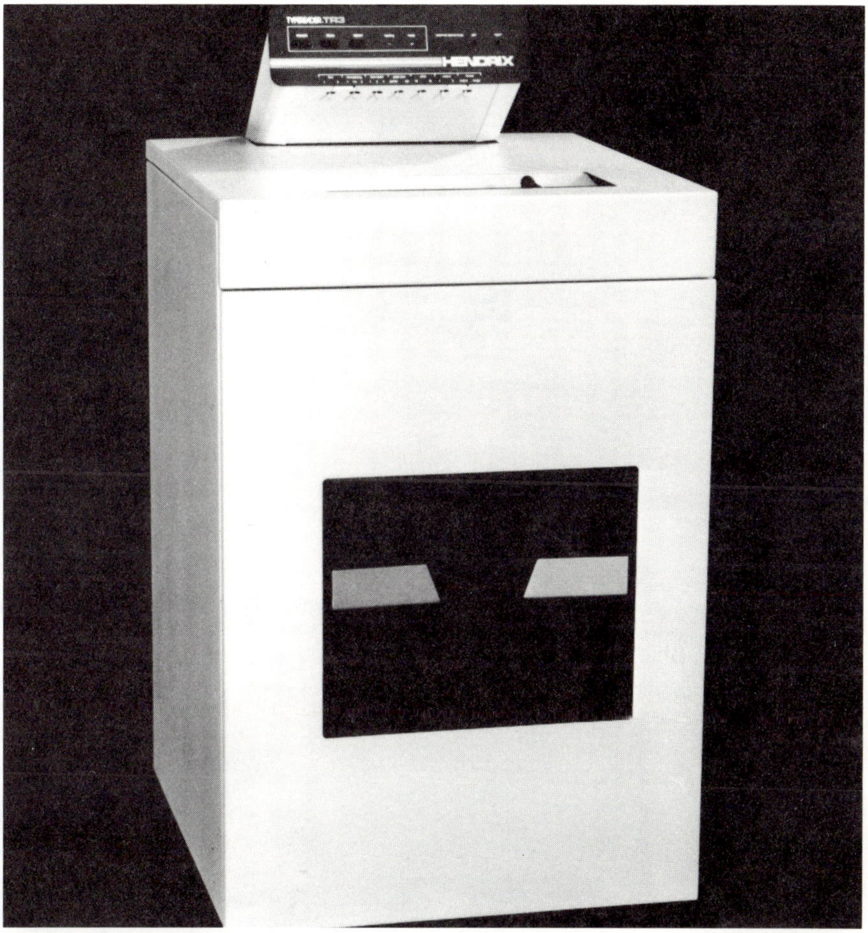

Still, the clearing of checks is an overwhelming data processing task. A later chapter will tell about the attempts to provide for the electronic transfer of funds, a means to eliminate the necessity for writing many of the checks which are written today.

MICR has found practically no use outside the banking industry. Only fourteen characters exist in the standard MICR alphabet, an insufficient number to make it more widely useful.

Digitizers

Not all of the data we wish to capture in a data processing system can be readily characterized as strings of alphanumeric data. Consider, for example, the vast array of data displayed on a map. The map shows the routes for roads, railroads, streams, and lines of elevation, while at the same time illustrating the location of lakes, ponds, schools, churches, trails, and shelterhouses. A large volume of alphanumeric data would be required to describe the information contained in graphical form on a map, yet the map

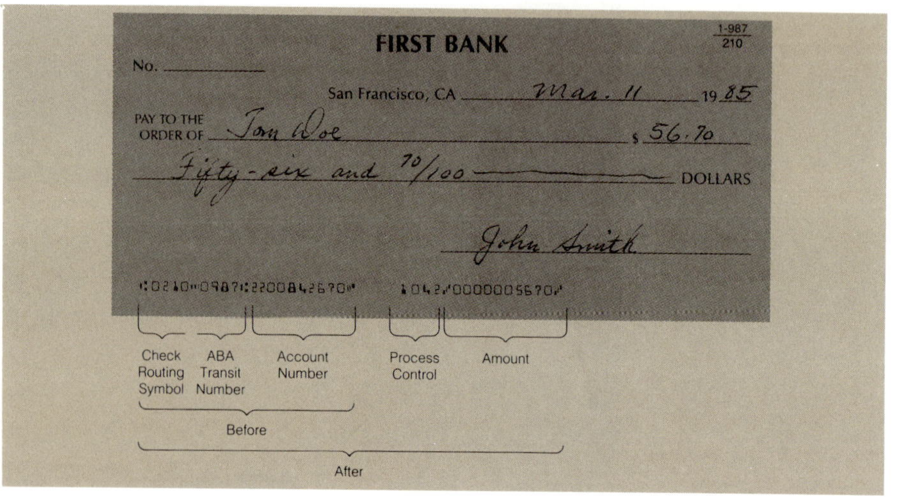

Figure 5–17 MICR Characters on a Check

allows the user to very quickly and efficiently assimilate the information presented.

A **digitizer** allows us to store the information on a map in the computer's memory so that it can be reproduced later. A digitizer usually looks like a drafting table (see Figure 5–18). It is equipped with a small instrument connected by wiring to a computing system so that it can operate as an

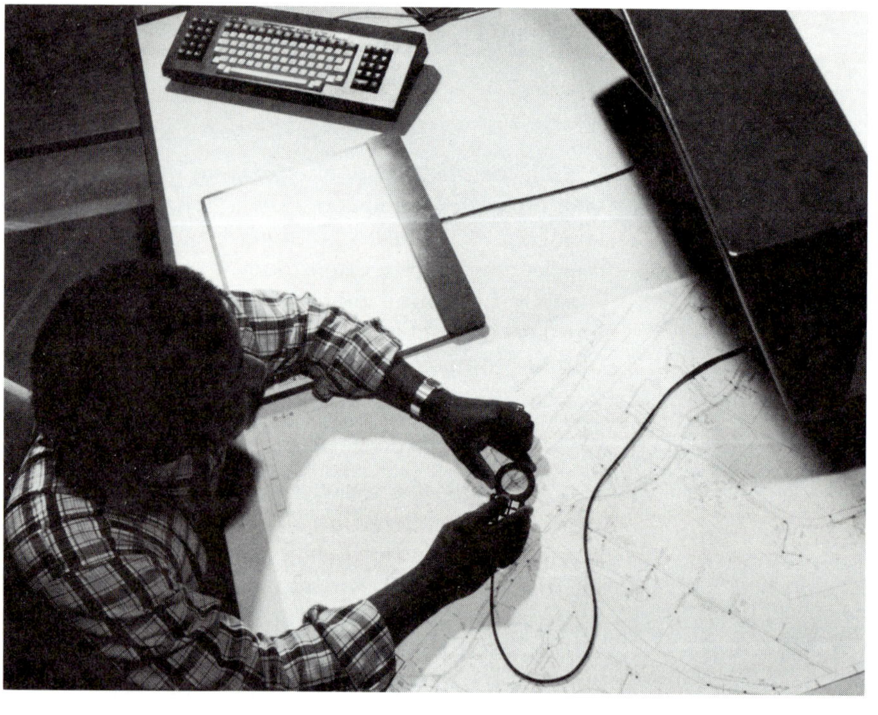

Figure 5–18 Digitizer

input device. The instrument resembles a hand-held calculator; it contains a keyboard for data entry. The instrument also contains a set of crosshairs (like the crosshairs in a war movie submarine periscope) which is used to locate precise positions on the map.

Data are entered by moving the crosshairs to the exact location of an essential characteristic on the map, pressing a key on the keyboard so that the X and Y coordinates of that location are entered into the system, then entering data through the keyboard which identify the nature of the object at that location. The crosshairs are moved along roads, streams, and lines of elevation, and entries are made at critical points so that the entire route is traced and stored in the computer's memory. Figure 5–19 shows a digitizer in use.

Graphics Tablets

The **graphics tablet** is a special form of the digitizer which allows the user to draw with a stylus on a digitizer tablet (see Figure 5–20). The drawing is digitized and can be displayed on a CRT screen. Many versions of the graphics tablet are capable of color graphics.

Two other versions of digitizers are becoming popular. The first, the **mouse,** is an input device initially used on the Xerox Star system to allow the user to provide input more easily than through the keyboard. The mouse is a mouse-sized unit with data entry keys (see Figure 5–21). A user can control the position and movement of a cursor on a CRT by moving the mouse. Cursor (mouse) movements can be used to select processing functions and position inputs on the screen.

Figure 5–19 Using a Digitizer

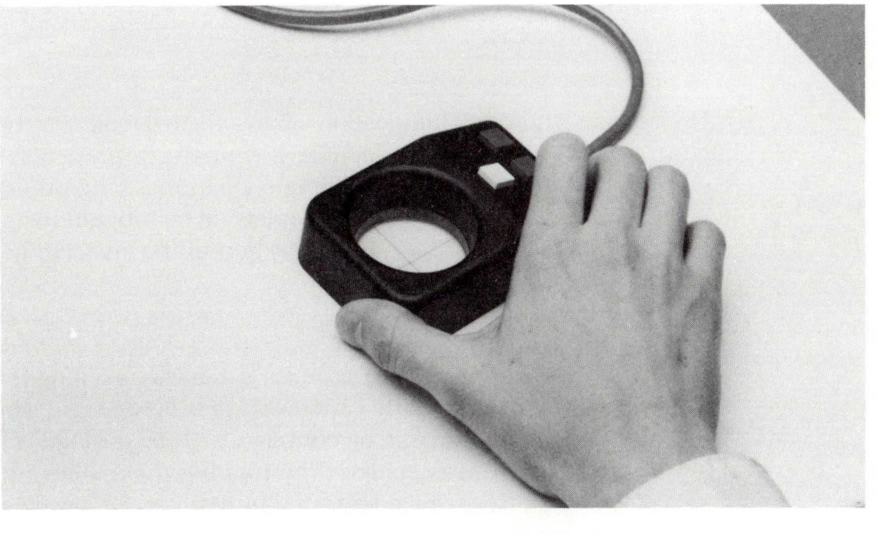

Figure 5–20 A Graphics Tablet

Another modification of the digitizer allows the user to enter data in tabular form by touching a stylus to a particular location on the tablet. Product numbers, customers, quantities, and other information printed on forms lying on top of the tablet can be brought instantly to the screen. Refer to Figure 5–22 for an illustration of the stylus.

Voice Recognition

The future seems to promise some very exciting developments in the area of voice input. Early systems were of limited use. They could recognize only a very limited set of commands from a single user. Recognition of the command was achieved by training the system through many repetitions of the user's voice pattern. More advanced systems have been able to recognize a limited vocabulary from several users. The computer has somewhat

Figure 5–21 The Mouse, a Special Form of the Digitizer

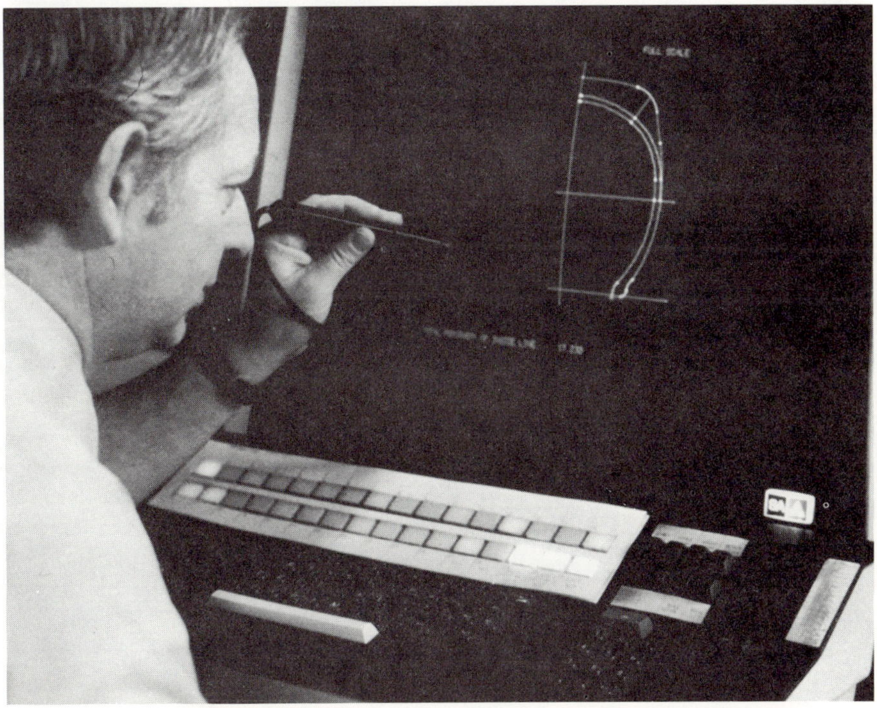

Figure 5–22 The Stylus, Another Modification of the Digitizer

the same trouble in recognizing different people's voices as it has in recognizing different people's handwriting for OCR devices.

The U.S. Postal Service has experimented with voice data entry devices to speed up the sorting of mail by zip code area. An operator would read aloud the zip codes on envelopes passing the sorting station, and voice recognition equipment would direct the envelope into the appropriate mail sack. Standardization of the shape and size of envelopes as well as zip code location might allow that job to be accomplished with OCR equipment. On the other hand, when everyone has a computer terminal and access to a communications network, people will be able to send messages electronically, a procedure known as **electronic mail.** (Additional material on electronic mail is included in Chapter 15.)

Voice data entry has many potential uses. Designers anticipate being able to build units into houses to allow voice control of virtually all electrical appliances in the house. No longer will we have to get out of bed to turn off the lights, or to turn up the television volume, or to let in the cat. Voice commands which activate the proper servomechanisms will be able to control all these activities. A voice recognition input device is pictured in Figure 5–23.

Imagine a voice-driven typing machine, built by adding voice recognition equipment to an electric typewriter or a computer terminal. As we speak to the machine our speech is recognized and displayed on a CRT. Edit commands allow us to correct any errors before the final copy is whisked

Figure 5–23 A Voice Recognition Input Device

off electronically for delivery. We might someday be able to program computers with voice commands so as to avoid long hours at the keyboard entering and correcting program statements.

In voice data entry, as in many other high-technology areas, great differences exist between that which can be demonstrated in the research laboratory and that which can be mass-produced on a cost effective basis. Robots existed for many years in the laboratory before they could be produced for use in manufacturing operations. Only recently have lab robots been able to "see"—to recognize and differentiate among objects. A voice input, data entry terminal capable of capturing human speech at 95 percent accuracy with a vocabulary of 2,500 words may be possible in the laboratory, but it will be some time before we all throw away our keyboard machines.

Portable Data Recorder

Portable data recorders have been available for a number of years. They are similar in appearance, but somewhat larger than, hand-held calculators (see Figure 5–24). They provide a keyboard for data entry to an internal memory medium within the device. Early versions used small tape cassettes for memory, but newer models use more advanced memory devices.

Data are also entered through other means—for example, a light pen—and saved in the memory until the device can be connected to a computer for transfer of the data into the computer. The data transfer can be accomplished over the telephone in many cases.

Portable data recorders have been frequently used by small building contractors who travel among several building sites recording the hours of work of each of the employees. This data can be transmitted over the telephone to the bank to provide the basis for completing the contractor's payroll.

Foresters, for example, can use portable data recorders as they cruise a stand of timber, entering data from which the amount of available timber can later be calculated. Special applications software plug-in modules allow many computations to be easily completed before transmission to a host computer. Grocery clerks and warehouse workers use portable data recorders for the taking of inventory.

Laser Cards

Earlier in this chapter we investigated the use of transaction telephones in conjunction with credit cards which had data stored on a strip of magnetic tape on the back of the card. A card, developed by Drexler Technology Corporation, offers promise of extending the storage capabilities of credit cards. Their card, termed the **laser card,** is capable of storing more than a million characters.

The laser card could be used to record medical histories, personal computer software, purchase histories, dictionaries, training information, or maintenance information. Small, low-cost readers are available to provide data entry of the large volumes of information stored on the card.

Figure 5–24 A Portable Data Recorder

Challenge Update

The reader should now be able to describe and compare several different means for accomplishing data entry.

Technology: Some Input Device Details

Punched Cards and Card Readers

The standard eighty-column card has twelve rows across, in which punches can be made. While the numbering system for the rows is not easily intuited by the beginner, it is not without reason. The cards were primarily intended for the encoding of numeric data, hence the rows most obvious on the card are for the encoding of the numerical digits 0 through 9 in rows of the same designation. Alphabetic characters are encoded through the combination of a punch in one of the numeric rows and an additional punch in either the 11 or 12 or 0 row at the top of the card. Special characters also require a multiple punch pattern. The punched card represented in Figure 5–25 illustrates the punching rows and the punching patterns for numbers, letters, and a few of the special characters.

The ninety-six-column card has, in reality, three tiers of thirty-two columns each. Characters are encoded into the card using small round holes to form patterns in a different way than that used on the eighty-column card. Each punching position on the ninety-six-column card has a column of six possible hole positions. The top two positions of each are used for alphabetic characters in fashion similar to the use of the 11, 12, and 0 rows on the larger card. The bottom four positions have numeric values—specifically, the values 8, 4, 2, and 1. From these values any of the numeric digits can be represented by a single or combination punch. For example, a 3 can be represented by a punch in both the 2 and 1 positions. Special characters again require multiple punches in both the alphabetic and numeric zones. Figure 5–26 illustrates the punching patterns on the ninety-six-column card.

Punched cards are prepared on a keypunch, a self-contained unit not connected to the computing system itself. Card readers are used to read data from the cards and transmit them to the computer's memory. Stacks of punched cards are placed on the card reader, and they proceed one at

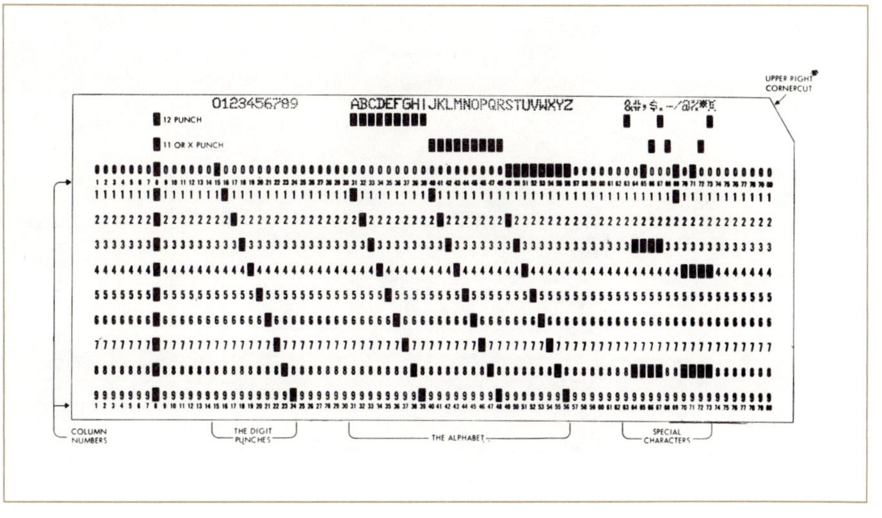

Figure 5–25 Standard Eighty-Column Data Card with Alphabet Punched

Figure 5–26 Ninety-six-Column Data Card

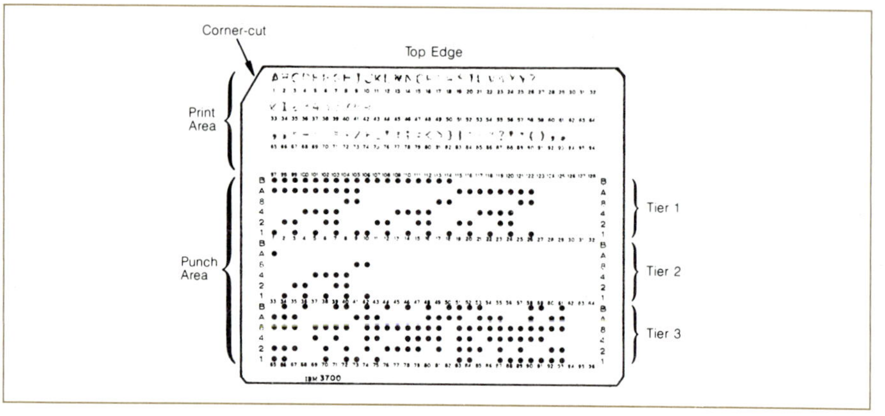

Figure 5–27 Supermarket Product Code Scanner Operation

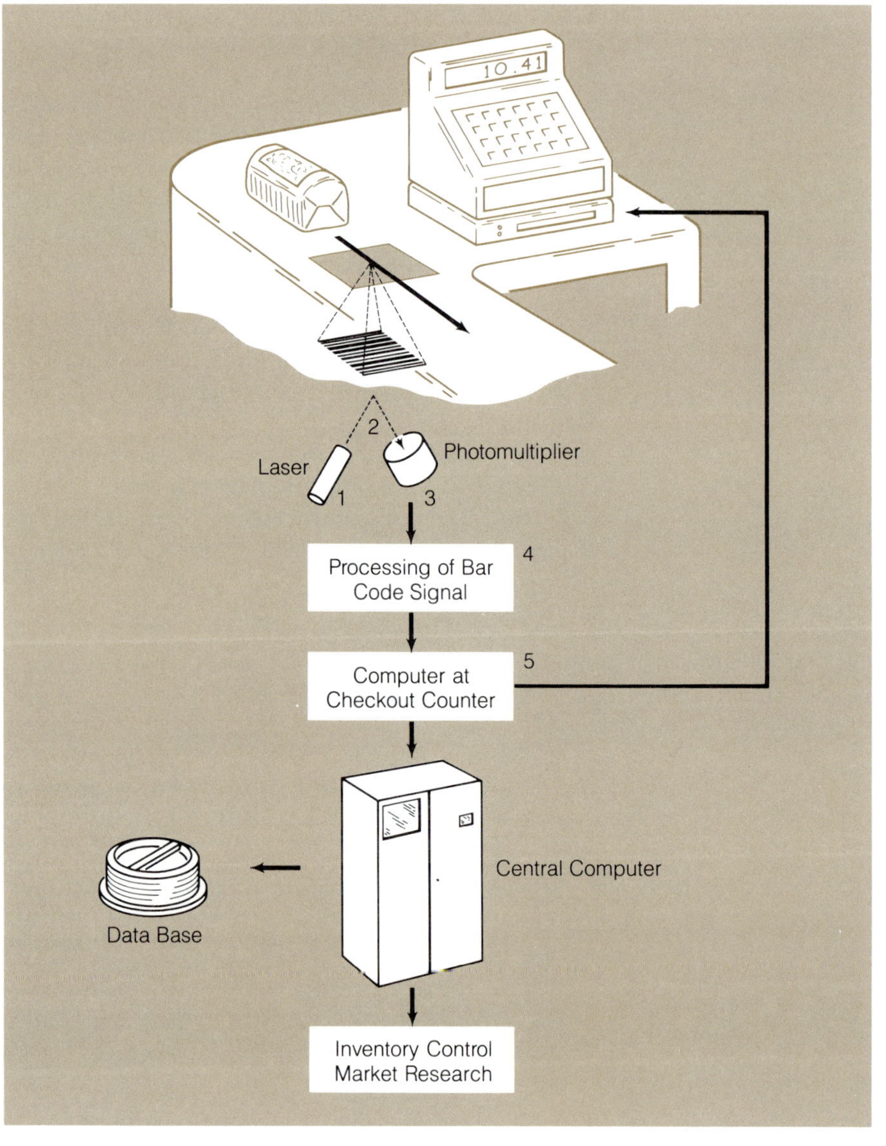

a time past a reading station. Holes in the cards are detected by photoelectric cells or electrically-charged wire brushes so that the data punched into the card can be transmitted to the system. Cards are read by the card reader either a column at a time (known as *serially*) or a row at a time (known as *in-parallel*).

Bar Codes and Scanners

The common bar codes consist of alternating light and dark vertical bars. Information is encoded by varying the widths of the light and dark areas. The bar codes are read by a scanner which consists of a light source, usually provided by a light-emitting diode (LED), and a light detector which measures the relative time the detector "sees" each light or dark bar. See Figure 5–27 for an illustration of the steps in the bar code reading process.

Quite a number of different bar codes exist today. Some of the more popular ones in use are the MSI barcode,[1] the UPC (Universal Product Code) bar code, the EAN (European Article Number) bar code, the CODABAR bar code,[2] the 2 of 5 bar code,[3] and the Code 39 bar code.[4] Differences in the bar codes arise as a result of the manner in which they each treat the light and dark areas, the bars and spaces. Some use narrow bars versus wide bars to differentiate 0 bits and 1 bits. Others use both the bars and the spaces to encode bits. Still others interweave spaces and bars in the overlapped encoding of two characters at the same time. The bit patterns represented by the spaces and bars, by whichever convention, are translatable into numerical codes to represent data.

Optical Character Recognition

Optical character recognition depends, as does the reading of bar codes, upon an optical scanning of the characters to be entered. Optical scanning can be accomplished on a full-page basis, as it is in the larger machines, or it can be accomplished character by character through the use of a handheld wand. Characters are viewed by the scanning mechanism and compared to a standard set of patterns stored in the machine's memory.

Optical character readers are capable of reading a number of different type fonts. The most widely used type font is known as OCR-A, an example of which is provided in Figure 5–28. Another type font designed for optical character recognition applications is OCR-B. The success of OCR is not completely dependent upon these two OCR fonts. OCR readers capable of reading a number of the common electric typewriter fonts are available.

1. Trademark of MSI Data Corporation.
2. Trademark of Welch-Allyn.
3. Trademark of Identicon, Inc.
4. Trademark of Interface Mechanisms.

The technology of OCR can also be used to read handwritten characters, but in applications where handwritten characters are read, the error rate increases significantly. OCR techniques can lead to significant savings in data entry costs. Research on improved methods of pattern recognition provide hope that even faster speeds in OCR input can be achieved.

Page Scanners

The technology of page scanning has become quite complex. The scanners recognize characters on the basis of character height, character width, number and length of vertical strokes, number and length of horizontal strokes, positioning of strokes, loops, and so on. Some are built with software which allows them to learn as they proceed through a document by interacting with the machine operator.

Mistakes in character recognition usually arise as a result of the machine's inability to match an image being processed with that of a known character. Special characters signalling the machine's inability to recognize a character are inserted into the document as necessary. These characters can be identified later by the operator.

Magnetic Ink Character Recognition

Although the limited character set available in MICR has restricted its use to the banking industry, the savings in data entry costs in that industry alone have made the technology well worth the investment. The fourteen characters available in the MICR alphabet are illustrated in Figure 5–29. As the bank customer's checks are printed, MICR characters are printed on the checks to encode the bank's identification and the customer's account number. After the check is written, and it enters the check clearing process, additional MICR characters are added to the check to indicate the amount for which the check has been written. The information thereby contained on the check in MICR form is sufficient to allow automated clearing of the checks through the system and their eventual return to the customer.

Digitizer Data Entry

Earlier in this chapter, the use of digitizers to encode the data normally represented on a map was discussed. Two other applications of this technology are worth mentioning. Scientists engaged in research in the field of particle physics have used digitizers extensively in their efforts to identify subatomic particles and determine their characteristics. Typical of the experiments in this area are the bombardment of some particles by others and a photographing of the paths of products of the collision. The photographs are enlarged, and digitizers are used to capture the paths for hundreds, even thousands, of collisions. Mathematical analysis of the information helps scientists identify old particles and discover new ones.

The other significant application of digitizers occurs within computer design itself. Huge circuit drawings of the electronic circuits of a computer are produced and recorded through the use of scanning digitizers to locate

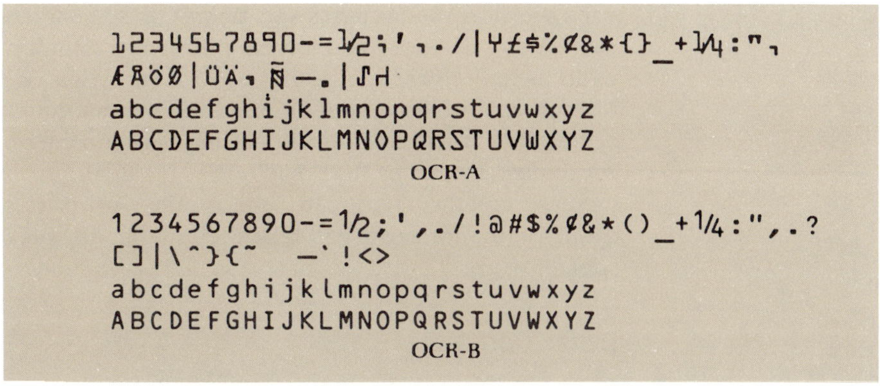

Figure 5–28 Comparison of 1OCR-A & OCR-B Fonts

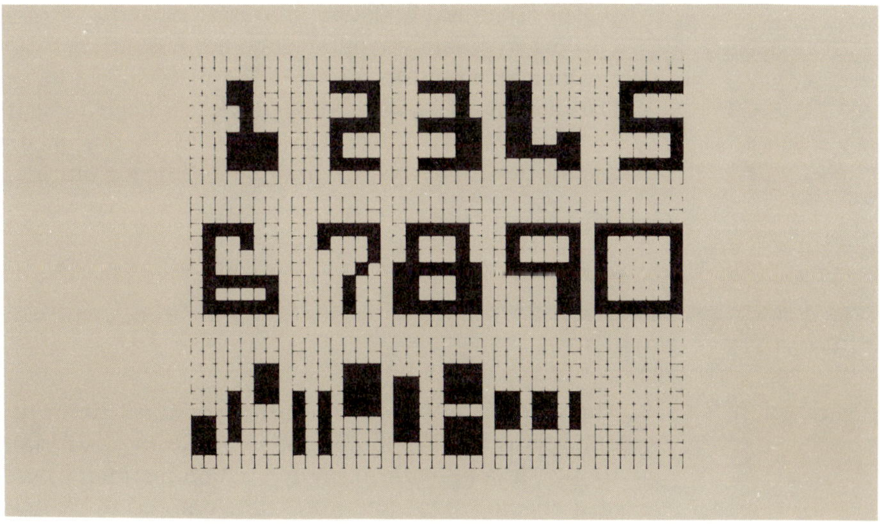

Figure 5–29 MICR Character Set

circuits, transistor junctions, and so on. These drawings, once converted to digital storage, can be modified through the use of a computer terminal by the draftsperson, and finished drawings can then be produced on large table-top plotters. These circuit drawings are eventually photo-reduced and used as masks in the production of computer logic chips approximately one-quarter inch on a side.

Voice Recognition

The technology is such that voice recognition systems require extensive processing and large memories to extend beyond the current capabilities of few speakers and small vocabularies. Systems available in 1983 for a few thousand dollars had vocabularies of approximately 200 words.

Users of voice recognition equipment train the equipment to recognize each word in the system's vocabulary by speaking each word in turn. The system stores each word (or the phonemes which make each word up) so as to be able to recognize that word later, when used in data input.

Each user of the system must train the system to recognize words in his or her own voice. As the number of users increases, and the recognizable vocabulary increases, the machine's workload and memory requirements increase greatly. The greater the number of users and the larger the vocabulary, the longer it will take the system, on the average, to recognize a spoken word.

Laser Cards

Data are recorded on (in, actually) laser cards by a laser beam which burns a microscopic hole in a thin metallic field encased between two layers of plastic. Data are encoded as digital patterns of holes and solid areas according to a data encoding scheme.

Once burned into the card, the data cannot be erased and re-recorded. Data stored on a laser card is much less likely to be destroyed inadvertently or as a result of abuse than are data on the magnetic strip of the usual credit card. Laser cards may be useful for storing medical histories, for example.

Newest Developments

The amount of research effort devoted to the improvement of data entry operations will undoubtedly continue to yield interesting improvements, though it is difficult to predict which techniques will be found to be most cost effective. The amount of data entered to on-line files in real time, that is, entered directly to storage as the transaction itself is completed, is increasing. We can expect those efforts to continue as the price/performance ratio of data entry hardware continues to show improvement.

Data entry operations seem destined to continue to be distributed throughout the organization in order to capture the data as close to the source as possible. This will mean less and less reliance on centralized data entry operations.

Until very recently, the efforts to capture data at the source were restricted by any individual company to locations within that company's borders. Think for a minute about the data which become input for one company after having been produced as output by another. Consider, for example, the many purchase orders for supplies and raw materials which travel between companies. Purchase orders are generated by one company to order raw materials, subassemblies, and supplies from another. These purchase orders may have been produced by a computerized inventory control system which identified several items which were in short supply. These purchase orders become the basis for a data entry operation when received by the supplier.

The net effect has been that we have converted the data stored in the first company's computer into a form readable by humans which could be transmitted through the mail and entered into the other company's computer system. Efforts are underway which will lead to a direct connection between the two computers so that unnecessary output and input operations can be eliminated. There are, of course, many problems of security and standardization which must be worked out before these transfers become commonplace, but the initial trials have been encouraging.

We might also see another example of the combination of several data processing tasks into a single, integrated operation. POS terminal systems may be extended so that payment is accomplished by an electronic signal to the customer's bank which causes the necessary funds to be immediately transferred from the customer's account into the store's account. The integration of systems such as these requires a greater degree of standardization than is currently the case, but there is hope that the technological stumbling blocks to integrated systems will be solved.

Challenge Update

The reader can now see that some of the further improvements in data entry depend upon a greater degree of standardization among organizations.

COMPUTING CHALLENGE: *A Final Note*

We should now be somewhat better prepared to consider the type of input devices which might be useful to Movie Mint. Their retail outlets were to be converted to automated outlets which would require that customers enter their orders through computer input devices for processing by computer-controlled robots. Let us consider a few possibilities in turn.

The first choice we might consider is a terminal. Consider how a typewriter-like terminal would work in that service. In what ways would it provide a good interface between the customer and the robot? In what ways would it be a poor interface?

Consider next a visual display terminal. In what ways would it provide a good interface? In what ways would it be less than ideal? Would it be better or worse than the typewriter-like terminal? Would a menu displayed on a touch-sensitive display screen have possibilities?

Are there other alternatives which might work? How about voice input? What problems might we expect with voice input?

How shall we provide for the entering of orders by the jobber? Would a handwritten order sent through the mail work? Would a voice order over the telephone work? How about a portable data recorder? Could OMR work? How about OCR?

SUMMARY

- The fact that data entry operations account, in many cases, for 25 to 30 percent of the total data processing budget explains why data entry receives careful attention from the managers of an organization.
- The three steps of data entry are data capture, conversion into machine-readable form, and reading into the system, although many data entry applications combine steps to improve the efficiency of the process.
- Data entry operations tend to be time consuming and costly, and are often the source of a significant number of errors.
- Data entry software should provide checking mechanisms to check the accuracy of the data as it is entered.
- The traditional role of data entry has, in the past, been carried out in large, centralized operations in the data processing center itself.
- The trend in recent years has been to decentralize or distribute the responsibility for data entry throughout the organization in an effort to transfer the capture of the data as close as possible to its origin.
- Data entry operations should be designed to capture data in a timely fashion, as close to the source as is practical.
- Care should be taken in the selection of data entry hardware and software to ensure that both are easy for the operator to use and that error detection and correction can be effectively accomplished.
- The nature of the data entry operations changes over time, hence care should be taken to provide some flexibility in the system so that it can accommodate changes in the data entry requirements themselves.
- Numerous different hardware devices exist for the entry of data, many of which provide for the keyboard entry of data and the recording of that data on punched cards, magnetic tape, or magnetic disk.
- Moving the keyboards to the point of origin of the data has given us point-of-sale (POS) terminals, automatic tellers, and factory data entry terminals.
- Other technologies, such as optical character recognition (OCR), page scanners, optical mark recognition (OMR), magnetic ink character recognition (MICR), digitizers, and voice recognition, attempt to reduce the amount of human effort required in the data entry operation.
- Further reductions in the effort necessary to provide data entry will be accomplished through computer-to-computer communications between companies, which will eliminate some output operations for the sending company and some data entry operations for the receiving company. Improvements in data entry operations will require a degree of cooperation and standardization which has previously been difficult to achieve.

CASE: Data Entry at Central Power and Light

A public utility company typically serves a large customer base, which means that their data processing tasks involve large volumes of data. A power and light company, such as Central Power and Light (CPL) in Corpus Christi, Texas, has two major data entry problems. The first is concerned with the entry of meter readings so that customer's bills can be computed, and the second is concerned with the payment of bills themselves.

Portable data records might be very useful in improving the meter reading problem, but a different approach is necessary in the case of bill payments. CPL has about 500,000 customers who are spread over a large geographical area. CPL's old data entry system was a centralized one which required that local offices bundle up the bill payments and send them by messenger to the main office in Corpus Christi. The new system allows customers to pay their bills at any one of CPL's thirty field offices. The new system requires that each field office be equipped with efficient data entry equipment and operators skilled in its use.

CPL's new system uses OCR equipment to improve the productivity of the data entry process. The new system makes use of something known as a turnaround document, a section of the original bill which must be "turned around" by the customer and returned to the company with the customer's payment. The returned section is read automatically by CPL's OCR equipment, causing the account number and billing amount to enter the system. Additional information can be entered through the keyboard of a terminal by the customer accounts clerk.

The new system has resulted in many improvements. The productivity of customer account clerks has been increased; they can now complete each bill payment more quickly. In addition, the new system makes it easier for the clerks to summarize the day's payments and balance their cash receipts. It provides a printed summary of all transactions within a few minutes.

The new system also makes it easier for CPL to manage the flow of cash within the firm. Bank deposits can be made more quickly, allowing the money on deposit (a sizeable sum) to earn more interest. Other improvements which have resulted from the new system include reduced paperwork, improved auditing, and better customer relations.

Infosystems, "Scanner Speeds Cash Entry," January 1984, p. 76.

Questions for the Case

1. Why might CPL's customers be happier as a result of the new system?
2. Why might the customers be less happy?
3. How has the customer accounts clerk's job changed as a result of the new system?
4. Do you suppose the customer accounts clerk is happier or less happy with the job? Why?

DISCUSSION QUESTIONS AND EXERCISES

1. Discuss the developments which have made it possible for the burden of data entry operations to be shifted closer to the origin of the data.

2. What will be the impact of the shift in data entry operations on the people in the data processing department? On the people in the operating departments?

3. Consider the design of data entry hardware. Should the designers involve the users in the design process? In what ways might the users contribute to the design process?

4. Within a few years, we could have commercially available typewriters to which we talk rather than strike keys. Would that be good? In what ways might it be bad? How would such a development be received by someone who earns a living by typing?

5. Describe the data entry task faced by each of the following types of organizations:

a. Public school.
b. Airline.
c. Hospital.
d. Lawyer.
e. Retail store.

6. Both OCR and voice recognition technologies suffer from the variety that exists in human beings. Explain that difficulty. What can be done to make the variety less of a problem?

7. List a number of ways in which we interact with data entry devices in conducting our everyday affairs. Using one of the data entry alternatives suggested in this chapter, describe new ways in which these data entry interactions might take place. Be creative!

8. In what ways is centralized data entry better than decentralized? In what ways is decentralized data entry better than centralized?

9. In what ways is voice recognition better than keyboard data entry? In what ways is it worse?

10. List several of the familiar data entry applications which use keyboard entry. Suggest other mechanisms to replace the keyboards and describe their impact on the system.

11. Is it likely that the bar codes on supermarket products contain pricing information? Why or why not?

12. What are the data entry components of a point-of-sale terminal? An automatic teller machine?

13. We, as humans, are information processors. In what ways do our bodies accomplish data entry?

14. University registration systems have large data entry components. If you were designing a data entry system for university registration, what type of data entry device would you use? Why?

15. What are the characteristics of data entry which make it prone to errors? What can be done to reduce the error rate?

ADDITIONAL READINGS

Buzby, Beth Moorer. *Data Entry: Concepts and Applications.* Chicago: Science Research Associates, 1981.

Cakir, A.; Hart, D. J., and Stewart, T. F. M., *Visual Display Terminals.* New York: John Wiley, 1980.

Computerworld, published by CW Communications, Inc., is an excellent reference for coverage of input devices on a continuing basis.

Datamation, published by Technical Publishing Co., is an excellent reference for coverage of input devices on a continuing basis.

Giulano, Vincent E. "The Mechanization of Office Work." *Scientific American,* September 1982, pp. 148–164.

Infosystems, published by Hitchcock Publishing Co., is an excellent reference for coverage of input devices on a continuing basis.

Ramsgard, William C. *Making Systems Work: the Psychology of Business Systems.* New York: John Wiley, 1977.

Lu, Cary. "Computer Pointing Devices: Living with Mice." *High Technology,* January 1984, pp. 61–65.

Riley, Wallace B. "Data Entry," *Systems and Software,* August 1983, pp. 121–124.

Teja, Edward R. and Gonnella, Gary W. *Voice Technology.* Reston, Virginia: Reston Publishing Co., 1983.

TANDEM
TANDEM

6

Computation: Central Processing Units And Operating Systems

CHAPTER PREVIEW

The third of the four basic data processing functions is computation, used here to include not only arithmetic operations, but data movement, comparison, and ordering operations as well. In this chapter we will concern ourselves with the central processing unit (CPU) and the operations which take place within it. In the previous two chapters we have focused our attention on the role of the peripheral devices which effect input and output operations.

Once the outputs have been designed and the available inputs have been specified, the next task is to bring about the transformation of the inputs into the desired outputs. This transformation may require arithmetic operations, logical operations, and data movement operations on the data which enter as input. The transformations may be relatively trivial or quite complex, depending upon the application itself.

Managers, and other users, interact on a regular basis with the input and output phases of data processing, but they have traditionally had relatively less contact with the computation and storage phases. They routinely see computer terminals, input forms, and printer output, for example, but they rarely visit an operating computer center. Computer center operations have traditionally been the responsibility of data processing managers.

Interaction between users and the CPU has taken place, but it has been less obvious than the interactions with the input and output phases. As a matter of fact, one of the ultimate tests of a computing system is the extent to which the necessary interactions can take place without the system's involvement or role being obvious to the user. The test reveals the system's degree of **transparency;** a system which is considered to be transparent to the user is thought superior.

Perhaps an analogy will help make the last point more clear. If we think for a minute of the systems with which we interact regularly, the ones which seem to serve us well without making that service obvious should receive superior ratings. A good heating and air conditioning system is one which performs satisfactorily without requiring attention. A good university registration system is one which schedules classes and assigns students to classes without focusing the attention of students, faculty, or administrators on itself. A good computing system is one which functions well without our obvious attention to it.

Computing systems are rarely completely transparent to the user. They perform without human attention as long as they are meeting the requirements placed upon them. Once they fail to perform adequately, however, they receive lots of attention. The once obvious mainframe systems seem to be much less obtrusive in modern organizations.

Microcomputers, on the other hand, are currently the focus of a great deal of attention because they represent new capabilities and offer new promise. They seem to be revolutionizing the

(continued next page)

interaction between managers and the information managers need. Eventually, microcomputers will fade into the office surroundings as telephones and calculators have and become just another one of the manager's tools. Someday soon managers will work on microcomputing systems and through them on mainframe systems without giving the process much thought; transparency of the tools themselves will have been achieved.

Most of the subjects discussed in this chapter have meaning both in the world of microcomputing and the world of mainframe computing. Computers in both cases, for example, have CPUs and operating systems. Great differences exist, however, in the sophistication of mainframes and microcomputers. Features which are now commonplace in the mainframe environment are unavailable or only partially developed in the microcomputer environment. As microcomputers evolve, their level of sophistication increases. The announcement by IBM in late 1983 of a personal computer built to operate from the same instruction set as their mainframe 370 series is indicative of the evolution which continues to take place.

Nevertheless, as users of computing systems, we continue to be constrained by the capabilities of the CPUs on which our data processing tasks are performed. Those constraints are significant in both the microcomputer and mainframe environments. In this chapter we will explore some of the more common capabilities of existing computing systems. A brief case study will help us put the problem into a proper perspective.

COMPUTING CHALLENGE: *Construction Project Management*

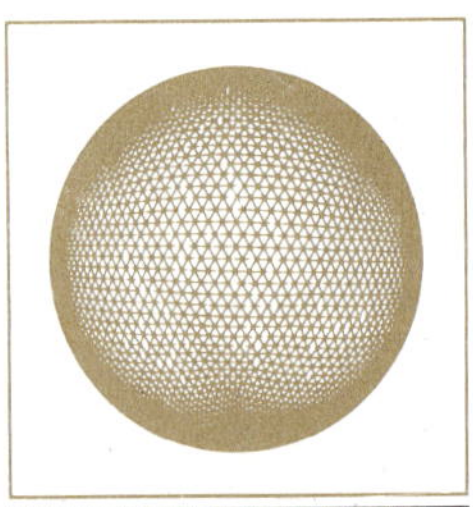

Buckeye Building Contractors, Inc. (BBC), is a small company in Renton, Ohio, which specializes in the management of construction projects. BBC employs sixteen professional construction engineers, four clerks, two secretaries, and a janitor. Each of the construction engineers is a competent project manager in a particular area of building construction. The engineers have developed a computerized project management package useful in the supervision of construction projects.

BBC supplies project management expertise for a fee to those companies or individuals faced with construction projects. The project management software currently runs on a computer owned by an architect in a nearby office, but the amount of that computer's time which is being used by BBC has become a problem. Some of the engineering calculations seem to take a very long time to compute. The architect and the engineers have decided that BBC should acquire a computing system for its own use.

Several sales representatives from computer manufacturers were invited to make sales presentations to the BBC engineers, but those meetings left many unanswered questions. While the engineers understood the role of the input and output devices which had been available on the architect's system, they knew very little about the system itself. Three of them did not know which brand of computer was represented in the architect's system they had been using.

BBC is now in a position requiring its employees to select a computing system—primarily a CPU and the I/O devices necessary to use the project management software. They know very little about the role the CPU plays in the operation of the entire system. They need to learn about primary memory and program execution. They have other questions as well.

What, for example, is an operating system, and what does it have to do with the capabilities provided by a computing system? One of the vendor representatives has suggested that engineering calculations tend to overload the CPU and cause the system to be compute bound. *What is* compute bound? *What is* input/output bound? *How does a program running on the computer affect the CPU? Before they can reasonably select a system, they need to know more about the role of the CPU and more about the characteristics of operating systems. There is much to learn.*

This chapter has been designed to help the reader understand more about the functioning of the CPU and the role of the operating system. It will also explain how computation works with the other basic data processing operations to form a viable system. After completion of this chapter the reader should be able to:

1. *Explain what* compute bound *and* input/output bound *mean in terms of a computer system, and provide example applications which could be expected to be one or the other.*
2. *Describe the role of the CPU in a computing system, and the function of the operating system.*
3. *Describe the range of functions performed by the sets of programs which make up the operating system.*
4. *Discuss operating system features common to modern computing systems.*

HISTORICAL PERSPECTIVE

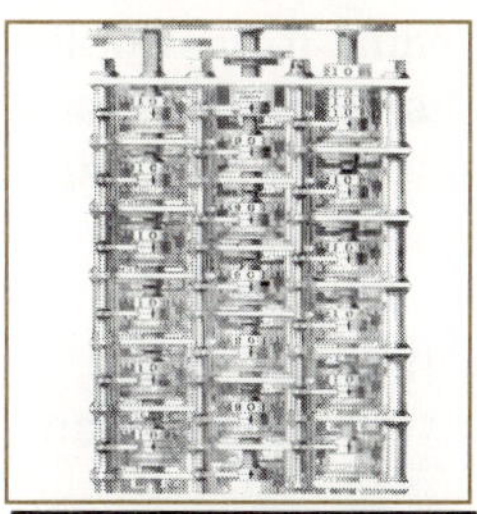

Many people have contributed to the development of the computer. Chapter 2 discussed some of the contributions of Pascal, Babbage, Jacquard, Hollerith, Aiken, Atanasoff, Berry, Mauchly, and Eckert. Others have also played important roles.

Working in the latter part of the seventeenth century, Gottfried Wilhelm von Leibnitz designed a machine which was capable of addition, subtraction, multiplication, and division. The work of Babbage and Lovelace, mentioned previously, followed that of Leibnitz.

William Burroughs, a contemporary of Herman Hollerith, developed the first automatic adding and printing machine which was put into production

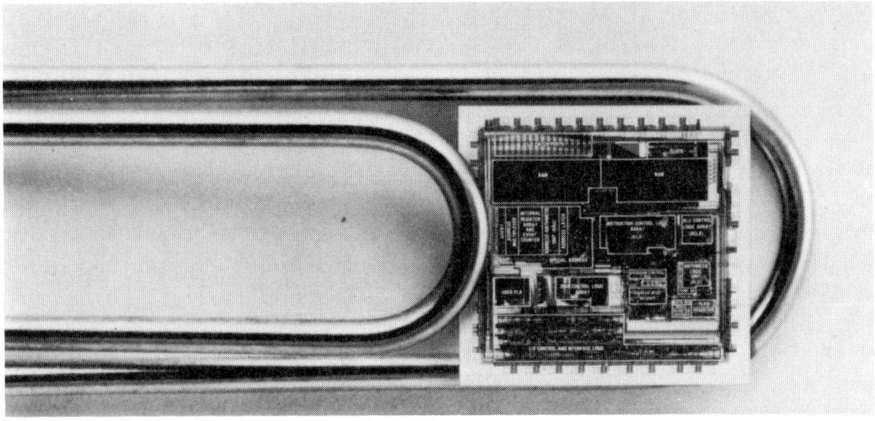

Figure 6–1 A Microprocessor chip

in 1890. The Burroughs Company today is one of the major computing companies in the United States. Herman Hollerith's company, the Tabulating Machine Co., eventually became IBM. An effort parallel to that of Hollerith, by James Powers, led to the Sperry-Rand Corporation, makers of the UNIVAC line of computers.

There is some controversy surrounding the development of the first modern computer. John Atanasoff at Iowa State University, Howard Aiken of Harvard, and Konrad Zuse of Germany all worked on separate projects at roughly the same time. It is not clear whose work should be credited as first, although all appear to have made significant, original contributions. Aiken's machine, called the Mark I, was completed in 1944 and was capable of doing roughly three additions per second. Zuse's work was, of course, unknown to the Western World until the end of World War II.

John Mauchly and J. Presper Eckert, Jr., completed the first electronic computer in 1946. Their machine, called the ENIAC, was the first machine to use vacuum tubes, the basic building block of first generation machines, instead of electrical relays. John von Neumann, a distinguished mathematician, joined the effort, and the EDVAC, BINAC, and finally the UNIVAC I were completed. Most modern computers utilize the basic architecture which resulted from von Neumann's efforts.

The history of microcomputers, on the other hand, has been quite brief but full of excitement. The first commercial microprocessor chip, the Intel 4004, was designed by M. E. Hoff and made available by Intel in 1971. The computing power of the Intel 4004 was approximately equal to that of the ENIAC, but it was twenty times as fast, thousands of times more reliable and cost only one–ten thousandth as much.[1] The Intel 4004 had a meager 2,250 transistors on the chip. Current capabilities allow over 256,000 transistors to be put on a single chip.

Microprocessor-based personal computers reached the marketplace in 1975. Since then, they have dramatically changed the way we work and play. A microprocessor chip is shown in Figure 6–1.

1. Robert Noyce, "Microelectronics," *Scientific American*, September 1977, p. 65.

The Mark I, a largely mechanical device, took five seconds to multiply two ten-digit numbers. A new supercomputer, the Cray 2, designed in 1982, can multiply 2.8 billion pairs of sixteen-digit numbers in one second. Thus, one second's work on the Cray 2 would have taken over one thousand years on the Mark I.

The era of electronic computing is quite young, around forty years at the most, but the progress which has been made is astounding. It has been suggested that the rate of technological advance in computing is so great that, if the same rate had been achieved in aircraft design, the time period from Kitty Hawk to the Boeing 747 would have been six months!

Concepts: The Computational Needs of Applications

We learned in Chapter 2 that the CPU (which contains the arithmetic/logic unit and the control unit) and the primary memory form the most important and complex piece of hardware in the entire system. In this chapter we will see how the combination of hardware and software features of the CPU interact to provide the computing capabilities needed by users.

We will discuss some of the important CPU features, such as processor speed and primary memory size, before discussing the role of the operating system, the set of systems programs which effect the allocation of resources to user programs. We will then discuss the extent to which applications have an impact on the system's resources.

CPU Features

To a certain extent, features of the CPU can be provided through either hardware or software, and it is becoming increasingly difficult for the user to know whether a particular feature is provided through hardware or software. As a matter of fact, users would probably prefer that the exact manner in which features are provided be transparent. For example, users usually do not care to know where a collection of data is stored as long as the system can find it when needed. Features provided through hardware are, however, processed more quickly than are features provided through software. For example, multiplication and division, when performed by hardware, are much faster than the same functions performed in software.

Control. One function of the CPU is the control of the other devices in the computing system. Through control by the CPU, the efforts of all the peripheral devices in the system are coordinated. The CPU accesses the instructions of the program which is executing, decodes them, and initiates whatever activity is required by the instruction.

The CPUs in early computing systems were the only devices in the system capable of decoding and executing instructions. This capability, virtually always combined with memory, is referred to as **intelligence.**[2] The CPU was the only device in the early systems to have any intelligence.

Control of the overall operation of the system was, therefore, left to the CPU. Control consisted of the execution of a systems program to control and direct the activities of the other devices. As systems have become more sophisticated, and the cost of intelligence has declined, intelligence has become common to many of the peripheral devices. These devices may operate independently from the CPU for a limited range of activities, though overall coordination and control is still the responsibility of the CPU.

Increasingly, we find computing systems which have two or more CPUs, illustrating a concept called **multiprocessing.** The ILLIAC IV, for example, had 64 independent processors and the ability to perform, in some circumstances, as if there were 512 processors. A new machine, NASA's Massively Parallel Processor (MPP) has 16,384 individual processors.

Any in-depth discussion of multiprocessing becomes very complex rather quickly. Many systems use separate processors only to perform support functions, but they are not true multiprocessor systems. They may, for example, incorporate separate processors for memory management or input/output control. True multiprocessing requires two or more independent processors which work together to execute program instructions. Control in a multiprocessing environment is very complex, and competition for resources must eventually be resolved by giving a single processor ultimate control over the others. Control in this case is realized through the execution of an appropriate control program by the controlling processor.

It is not at all unusual to find mainframe systems which have been designed to accommodate multiple users and multiple tasks. A large main-

2. The word *intelligence* is used in several different ways in connection with computing. To describe intelligent terminals and peripheral devices it is used to indicate that the device contains some memory (storage) and is programmable; that is, has the ability to execute a very limited range of instructions independent of the CPU. This usage is not to be confused with the use of the word in **artificial intelligence,** an important area of study of a computer's ability to exhibit reasoning, more human-like intelligence.

Computers in Action 3

Meeting the Challenge

1

1. Designers of the Cray 1 fashioned a unique configuration for that supercomputer to provide convenient access and efficient heat transfer. **2.** The system required by Buckeye Building Contractors is likely to be of this general size, though modern design techniques continue to shrink the physical size of all computers. **3.** The inner workings and hidden mechanisms of a CPU are complex and confusing, even to the engineers of BBC.

3

2

4

5

6

4. Computer system operators have access to terminals dedicated to their use for entering and receiving information important to the proper operation of the system. **5.** BBC's engineers use computers to design and build very impressive structures. **6.** Within BBC, engineers and information processing specialists work together to make sure that the computer system serves the engineer's needs. **7.** The computational work of BBC's computer will be done within a tiny semiconductor chip such as this.

7

8

9

8. The question of compatibility between computing devices within BBC, indeed within any company, includes the fundamental requirement that plug-in cables must fit their intended receptacles. **9.** BBC engineers should be familiar with fire protection schemes and they must remember to make provisions for them within their computer center. **10.** The vast array of electronic devices which make up an operating computer center have stringent requirements for the supply of electrical power. **11.** Power supply is an important function in the realm of microcomputers as well.

11

10

12

13

12. Distribution of the electrical power and dissipate of the heat it generates within the CPU and the memory is a problem which designers must overcome. **13.** All electronic systems will eventually experience failure in one or more of the components and BBC must provide for the maintenance and repair of its system. **14.** The more sophisticated the computing device, the more sophisticated the testing equipment must be to provide an adequate analysis.

14

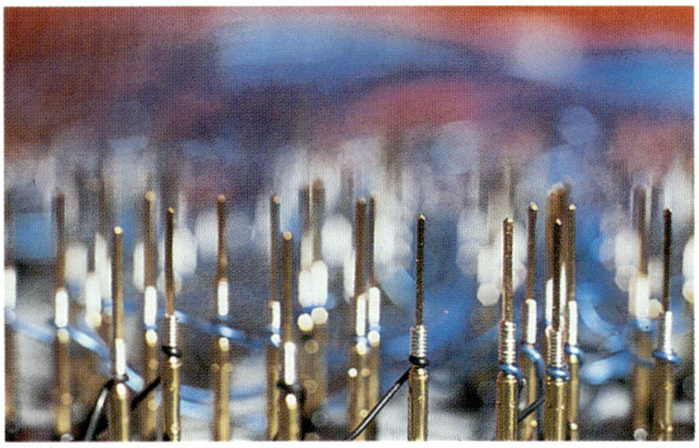

Figure 6–2 Large Mainframe System

frame system is pictured in Figure 6–2. Minicomputers are only slightly less capable in general. Microcomputers, however, are for the most part single-user, single-task machines. Newer designs will undoubtedly make them more capable.

Primary Memory Size. The size (and cost) of the primary memory is much less of a constraint in modern systems than in the systems of earlier days. When the primary memory was built of small, doughnut-shaped, ferrite storage elements (called cores) it was outrageously expensive. Now it is much less so.

The primary memories for mainframe computing systems range from 1 million bytes (1 MB) to 64 million bytes (64 MB). Minicomputer primary memories range from 256,000 (256K) bytes to about 16 million bytes (16 MB). IBM has an experimental chip which contains 512K bits of memory, an extravagant amount for an entire system by the standards of the "good old days." The primary memories of microcomputers now reach 3M bytes in the largest systems, while the minimum remains 2K bytes for a very limited-purpose system. A microcomputer system is pictured in Figure 6–3.

The size of the primary memory contributes to an upper bound on the size of program which can be run on the system efficiently. There are several techniques which make it possible to break large programs into segments and store each in turn in a small primary memory. One such technique allows segments of a program to **overlay** (be written over the top of) other (unused) program segments in the primary memory. Some program execution speed is lost in the process, however. Speed and cost seem always to be traded off, one against the other. A larger, more expensive primary memory always seems to make faster processing possible.

Figure 6–3
Microcomputer

Processor Speed. Several different measures are used to report the speed of CPUs. One method measures the time it takes the CPU to complete one processing cycle and is, therefore, called the **cycle time.** Another measures the number of floating point operations per second (FLOPS)—essentially, arithmetic operations using scientific notation—which can be completed per second. A third, and the one to be used here, reports the number of instructions the CPU can execute per second. The measure has progressed with time to millions of instructions per second (MIPS).

Several machines have exceeded 20 MIPS and have earned the title of supercomputers (see Figure 6–4). The ILLIAC IV (now defunct), the Cray 1, and the Cyber 205 belong to that class. The Cray 2 is expected to operate at 100 to 200 MIPS. Research and development efforts are underway to create a processor which operates at speeds in excess of 1 billion instructions per second (1 BIPS).

Mainframe CPUs currently operate in the range of 1 to 20 MIPS. Minicomputers are available with processing speeds of 0.4 to 5 MIPS, with some systems exceeding that. A minicomputer system is pictured in Figure 6–5. Microcomputer processing speeds range, for the most part, between 0.2 and 0.5 MIPS, but the newer systems will exceed that range.

Overall Performance. While processor speeds, and to some extent primary memory sizes, make interesting topics for conversations between real computer buffs, their importance to the user/manager can be easily overemphasized. More important is the overall performance of the system.

Overall system performance depends not only on the hardware capabilities of the CPU, but also on the operating system which makes the various capabilities available to the user and on the performance of the peripheral

Figure 6–4 Cray Supercomputer

devices which are included in the system. Overall performance must also be evaluated in terms of the types of applications programs which will be run on the system, as we shall see in the next section.

The Impact of Applications on the System's Resources

For illustrative purposes, let us consider a very simple computer system with a single input device, a CPU, primary memory, some secondary storage, and a single output device. Of these devices, the one with the fastest operating speed is the CPU, which is usually capable of several million operations per second. Data and program transfers between the CPU and the memory are usually restricted to something less than a million characters per second, significantly less than the speed of the CPU. By comparison,

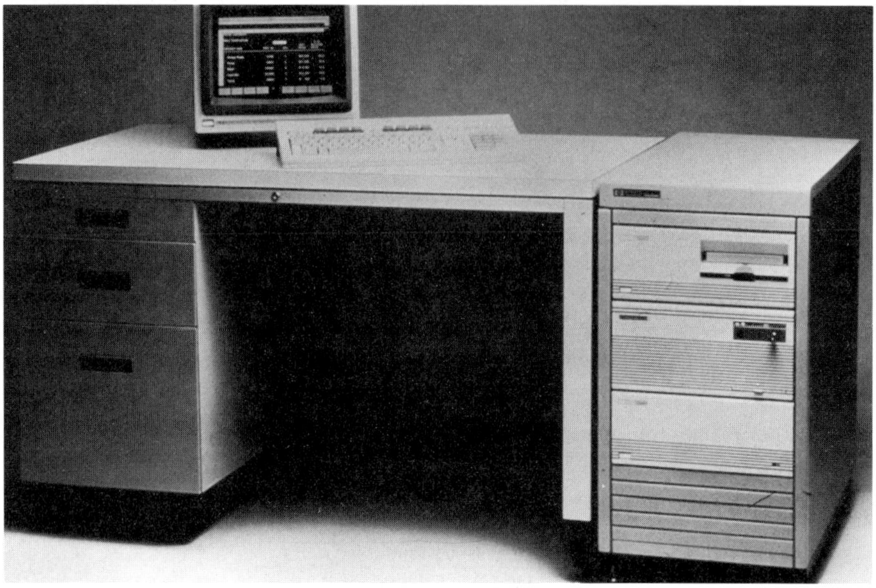

Figure 6–5 Minicomputer System

input and output devices might operate at speeds less than 2,000 characters per second.

It is, therefore, obvious that a great mismatch in speed exists between the respective parts; the CPU is capable of performing at speeds far in excess of that which the other devices are capable of operating. We try to alleviate this mismatch by designing a system which has a collection of input and output devices and the capability within the operating system of allowing work to be done on several programs at the same time. Each input or output device would then consume a relatively small part of the CPU's resources. Here, again, we find an example of great disparity in the sophistication of mainframes compared to that of microcomputers. Microcomputer operating systems have not yet reached the level of sophistication of mainframe operating systems, and few are capable of dealing with a collection of input and output devices.

Input/Output Bound Applications. Applications themselves have differing needs for the various resources of the system. Consider, for example, an elementary payroll application. Time card data are read into the computer; pay rates and withholding information are brought in from the secondary storage; the payroll is computed; the various totals which are kept are sent to secondary memory; and paychecks are printed out. The computation required, in this case, is trivial, and the CPU would operate for only a small fraction of the time it took to complete the total job (assuming no other jobs are being processed at the same time).

In this example it is clear that the speed with which the total job can be accomplished is limited by the speeds of the input and output devices. When the rate at which a given application can be completed is limited by

Figure 6–6 Input/Output Bound Application

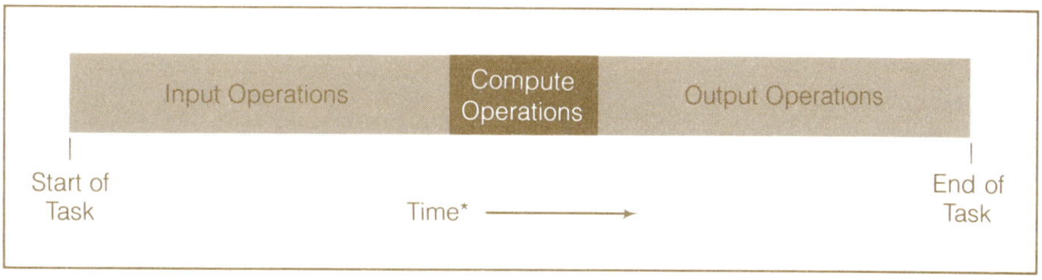

Overall completion time dominated by I/O operations.

the speeds of the input and output devices, that application is said to be *input/output bound* (Figure 6–6).

Anyone who has written a program on a microcomputer has experienced the phenomenon of input/output bound. Entering the program through the keyboard takes a long time compared to the time it then takes for the program to run. The same is true of the output. Output displayed on the screen takes place relatively quickly, but still much more slowly than the computer's execution speed. Output sent to a printer takes even more time.

Compute Bound Applications. Consider a different type of application, say a complex production scheduling application which uses complicated mathematical procedures to determine the most efficient production schedule. The mathematics required to solve such a problem are so extensive that they might require several full minutes or more of CPU time. Some problems are so large that the CPU could be tied up for days, even weeks in completing the computations. When the rate at which a given application can be completed is limited by the speed of the CPU, that application is said to be *compute bound.* Figure 6–7 illustrates an application which is compute bound.

Scientific applications on mainframe computers provide the most significant opportunities for the system to become compute bound. Business applications are much more frequently input/output bound. One can experience compute bound in the microcomputer environment by using graphics routines which require a lot of CPU time.

Application Mix. Part of the problem associated with the great mismatch of speeds between the CPU and the input and output devices is solved by providing a collection of such devices and upgrading the capability of the operating system to allow several different applications to proceed at the same time. We can then provide a mix of applications and a collection of input and output devices so that the overall system works more efficiently. The CPU directs the overall effort and contributes effectively and efficiently to each application in turn.

If we were to arrange applications along a spectrum from heavily compute bound applications at one extreme to heavily input/output bound applications at the other, we would find applications of all types across the spectrum. Figure 6–8 provides us with a glimpse of such an array. Sophis-

Figure 6–7 Compute Bound Application

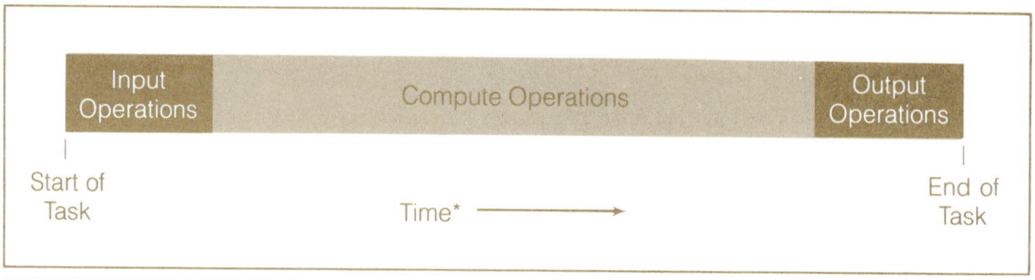

Overall completion time dominated by compute operations.

Figure 6–8 Typical Applications as They Might Be Ordered on the Spectrum from I/O Bound to Compute Bound

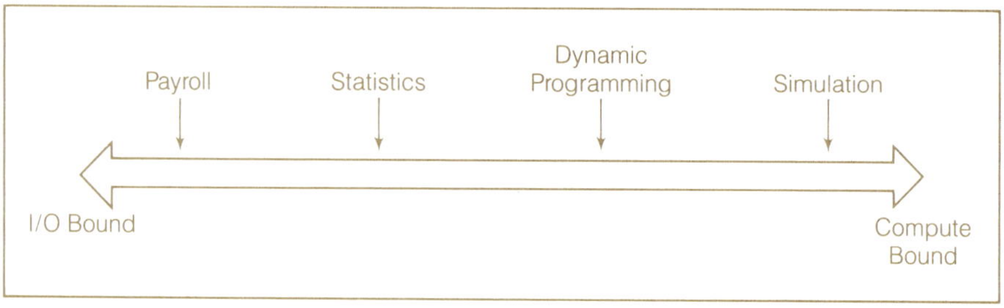

ticated operating systems will blend together a mix of applications so that the CPU's time is used as efficiently as possible.

As we will see later in the chapters on hardware and software selection, the members of an organization have a difficult task in trying to determine how any particular set of applications will run on a particular configuration of hardware. As it turns out, the best way to attack that problem is to find, if possible, another organization which has the same hardware configuration and actually run the programs as a test.

Challenge Update

The engineers of BBC should now be able to differentiate compute bound applications from input/output bound applications. They should also be able to suggest which of their intended applications would tend to be compute bound and which would be input/output bound.

The Impact of the Operating System on the Computer System's Capabilities

The success of the computational phase of data processing is dependent upon an effective blend of hardware, applications software, and systems software. In order for any particular operation to be carried out on a given computing system, the system must have the hardware capability of performing that operation and the operating system capability to effect it. The operating system can provide only that which the hardware allows, and the hardware can only accomplish that which the operating system directs.

An effective blend of applications which makes efficient use of the CPU can only be provided by the combined efforts of the hardware and the operating system. Together they can provide many types of data processing functions. The next section discusses some of the functions served by the operating system.

Tools: The Operating System

Many different systems programs work together to make up the set known as the operating system. The operating systems of early computers were quite limited in function. Most of the workload was borne by the programmer/user.

Through the years, much of this workload has been transferred from the programmer to the system itself. Systems programs were created and made part of the operating system in order to accommodate the shift in work.

The use of acronyms is perhaps greater in the subject area of operating systems than in any other area. The most popular operating systems for microcomputers are DOS (Disk Operating System) by Apple Computer, CP/M (Control Program for Microcomputers) by Digital Research, and PC/DOS (Personal Computer/Disk Operating System), a version of MS/DOS (MicroSoft/Disk Operating System) developed by MicroSoft for the IBM PC.

Digital Equipment Corporation's operating system for the very popular VAX line of minicomputers is known by VAX/VMS (Virtual Memory System). An operating system developed by Bell Laboratories known as UNIX has been accepted as the standard by many users. A microcomputer version of UNIX written by MicroSoft is known as XENIX.

Mainframe operating systems are dominated by IBM, which sells more mainframes than all the other suppliers combined. The two most noteworthy are MVS (Multiple Virtual Storage) and VM (Virtual Memory). The latter is an operating system which allows a computer to execute several operating systems simultaneously.[3]

The operating system has become that part of the computer which the user "sees," that is, that part with which the user interacts. The operating system manages the processor(s), storage, data, and input and output devices. It is responsible for allowing the users to:

1. Interact with the system.
2. Share the system with other users.
3. Accomplish input and output.
4. Maintain the system's operation.

In addition, the operating system makes features such as multiprogramming, timesharing, and networking possible. Some of the programs included in an operating system are described below.

3. Harvey M. Deitel, *An Introduction to Operating Systems* (Reading, MA: Addison-Wesley, 1982), p. xv. Deitel's text provides a comprehensive look at operating systems, a subject we can only introduce in a beginning text.

Challenge Update

The reader should now be able to describe the role of the CPU and the function of the operating system.

The Supervisor, Monitor, or Executive

Control is accomplished in the CPU through the execution of a program called, variously, the supervisor, the monitor, or the executive. Control resides with this program until it is given over to the execution of some other system program or a user program. When the user or system program is complete, or when it can no longer execute, control is returned to the supervisor. At least part of the supervisor program is always resident in the primary memory, thereby reducing the space available for other programs.

System/Job Control Program

Chapter 3 discussed the role of job control language (JCL) in the allocation of the system's resources to a user program. Statements in JCL are read and interpreted by a program known as the system/job control program, which causes the system's resources, if available, to be allocated as needed. For example, if a program executing within the system has need for the line printer to prepare output, the requisite statement in the user's JCL will request the use of the line printer and the job control program will, if possible, allocate it to the program.

Memory Management Programs

The task of managing the allocation of the computer's memory is now performed by system software, though much of the work was formerly the duty of the programmer. Some of the more specific capabilities provided will be discussed in the technology section of this chapter.

Memory management programs must perform the functions necessary to store many programs in the memory at the same time without causing them to become mixed, to move those programs as necessary between the primary memory and the secondary storage, and to maintain connections between the various parts of a program and the data needed by that program.

Input/Output Control

One portion of the set of systems programs which make up the operating system is dedicated to the task of providing control over the input and output devices. This set of programs (known as IOCS, for Input/Output Control System or BIOS for Basic Input Output System) supervises the activities of the various input and output devices and coordinates their activities with those of the CPU.

Communications

The capability of the computing system to communicate with other computing systems, or with other intelligent devices, must be provided through the operating system. A set of communications programs usually works in conjunction with a piece of hardware dedicated to the communications tasks.

Library Maintenance Programs

Practically all computing systems provide for relatively long-term storage of data and programs within the system. The library maintenance programs take care of keeping track of those programs (and data), giving users access to them as needed, and modifying or deleting them as required.

Standard programs are available for doing common data processing operations like statistics, data analysis, mathematical programming, and so on. These programs are maintained within the library for use by the entire community of users of the system. The library maintenance programs make it possible for programs and files to be stored, retrieved, modified, and deleted.

Utility Programs

Conversion of data from one medium of storage to another is a common data processing operation. Data on cards frequently must be converted to magnetic tape; data on seven-track tape must be converted to nine-track tape; and so on. These operations are so common that standard routines are provided as part of the set of utility programs for accomplishing them.

The utility programs become very familiar to the user of a microcomputer system. Programs are provided to copy files, initialize disks, rename files, delete files, and list file contents.

Sort/Merge Routines

Another extremely common data processing operation is the sorting of data into numerical or alphabetical order. Standard routines are available and stored in the system's library for accomplishing these sorting operations. Merging, which refers to the combination of two or more ordered sets of data into a single, ordered set of data, is also accommodated through standard routines which may be stored in the library.

Challenge Update

The range of functions provided by the operating system should now be apparent to the reader and the engineers of BBC.

Technology: The Building Blocks of the CPU

This section explores some of the details of the CPU, both of hardware and of software features, in order to improve understanding of the operation of the system.

Hardware Features

It would be impossible in this type of text to describe, fully and in detail, the hardware features of a CPU. We will restrict our attention to four common features: the instruction decoder, registers, accumulators, and adders. The manner in which these features are implemented varies from machine to machine, so the focus here will be brief and general.

Instruction Decoder. The CPU contains a hardware device, the **instruction decoder,** into which the instructions of a program are brought for decoding. The instructions brought here are machine language instructions, consisting typically of an operation code and the address(es) of one or two operands. The operation code identifies a basic operation which is to be performed, dictated by the design of the system; and the addresses provide the operands for the operation (refer to Figure 6–9). For example, the operation code may specify an addition operation, and the address might give the location of the addends.

The instruction decoder works in tandem with a **register,** which keeps track of the address of the next instruction to be decoded. Assume that the register contains the address of the instruction currently being decoded. That instruction was brought into the decoder by placing the address of the instruction in the register. The addition of one to the register will cause it to contain the address of the next instruction, and cause that instruction to be brought into the decoder for decoding and execution.

Registers. We have just seen how a single hardware location functions as a register to bring instructions into the instruction decoder. Other registers are included in the CPU to provide storage locations wherein other operations can take place. These registers often work in pairs, as did the instruction decoder and its register. Some pairs will be dedicated to the movement of data into memory, called **store registers.** Into one of the pair of registers we put a value, perhaps the value of a variable, and into the other we put the address where we would like to store that value. As the address is put into the address register, the value in the other register is sent to memory at that address.

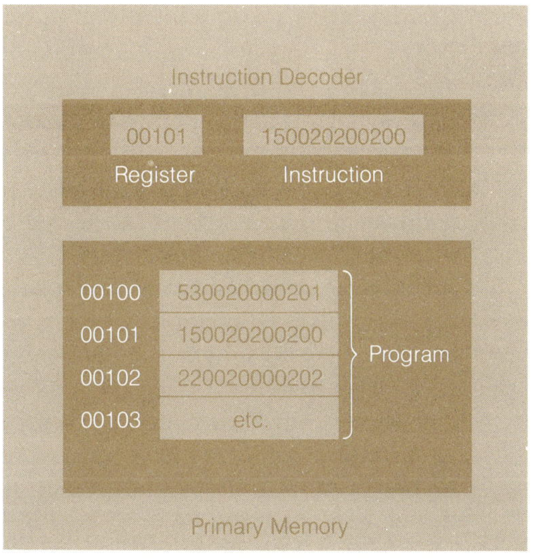

Figure 6–9
Individual Instructions Are Brought into the CPU for Decoding and Execution

A **fetch register** pair works in a similar fashion. If we want to retrieve a data value from memory, we put the address of that value in the address register, and the contents of that address are brought immediately into the CPU. These registers are basic to our being able to manipulate data through the CPU for computational purposes.

Accumulators and Adders. Certain registers are used for the accumulation of totals, subtotals, and so on. These registers are called **accumulators.** An operation characteristic of many machine languages is one which calls for the contents of a particular storage location to be retrieved from storage (through a fetch register) and added to the contents of the accumulator.

The hardware device which accomplishes addition is called an **adder.** Adders are very simple hardware devices when used only for the addition of whole numbers, called *fixed point numbers*. The operation becomes more complex for values with decimal representations, called *floating point numbers.* Most arithmetic operations make use of the adder, and most arithmetic operations now take place in floating point mode.

Software Features

The features to be discussed in this section were previously introduced in general terms earlier in this chapter. This section will provide the names given to each of the features, a topic avoided in the earlier discussion to make it less cumbersome.

Overlapped Processing. As was discussed earlier in this chapter, inefficiencies would result from a system which combined a CPU with a single set of input and output devices. In such a system, the CPU would spend a lot of its time waiting for the operation of the input and output devices.

One way to reduce that inefficiency is to overlap some of the processing steps. For example, a system could allow the input for the second program to proceed at the same time as the output for the first program, as illustrated in Figure 6–10. By extending the overlapping of operations to a number of different input and output devices and a number of programs, the system achieves a more efficient mode, called **overlapped processing.**

Buffering. Another technique useful in improving the efficiency of the CPU is known as **buffering,** which is accomplished by providing a segment of memory into which the input devices can put data without the CPU's constant supervision. The CPU sets aside space in the memory for the buffer and directs the input device to put data into it. The CPU can then direct its attention elsewhere, perhaps to other buffered input devices, returning to the original buffer occasionally to empty it so that the original input device can continue its work without interruption.

Figure 6–10 A Simplified Illustration of the Use of Overlapped Processing to Reduce Overall Execution Time

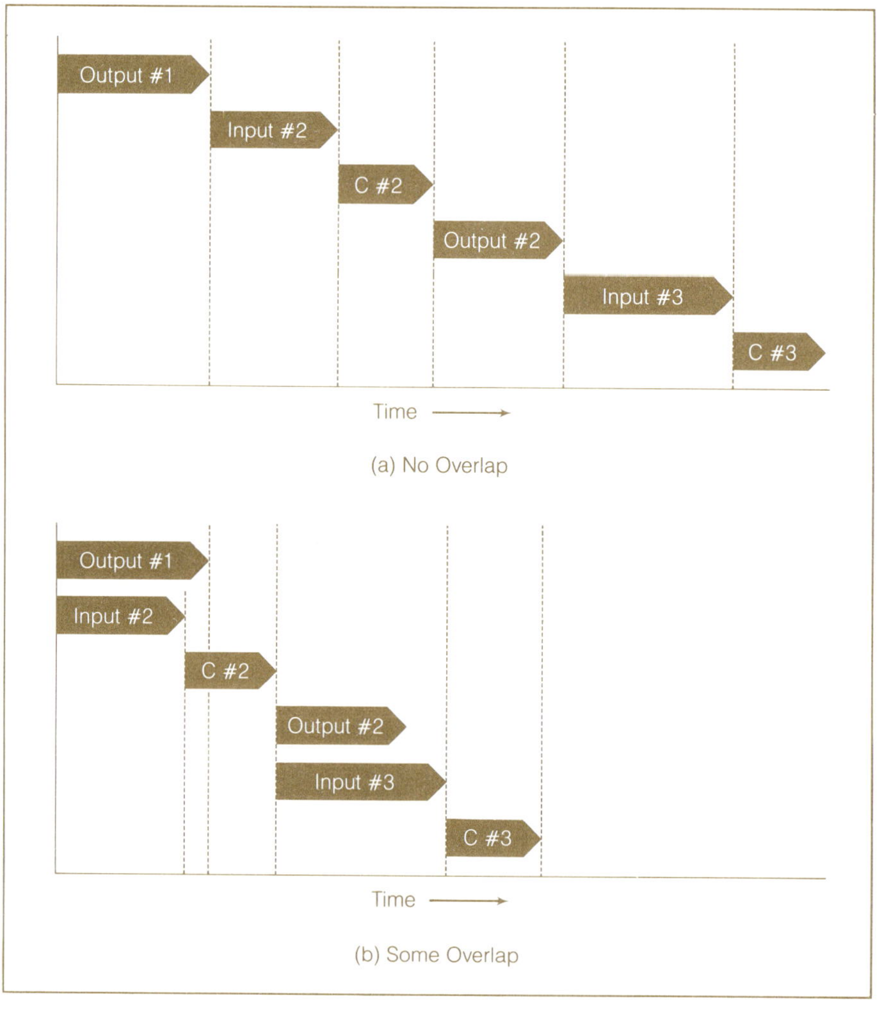

Buffering is a technique used not only in computing systems, but in many other organizational processes as well. Inventories of in-process goods between work stations act as buffers between two operations which might take place at different speeds. Queues and waiting lines of all types act as buffers to accommodate the different rates at which clients are served in banks, at the registrar's office, in doctors' offices, and so on.

Spooling. A particular use of buffering on the output side to accommodate the speed mismatch between the CPU and the output device is called **spooling** (short for **simultaneous peripheral operation on line).** As a program runs and the results are generated by the CPU, they are stored temporarily in an output buffer. The CPU then alerts the output device, which begins to empty the buffer by moving its contents to an output medium. Again the CPU can direct its attention elsewhere, returning to replenish the output buffer whenever necessary.

Students in classes where the instructor lectures at a speed too fast for accurate note-taking experience a relationship analogous to the CPU/printer example. The student could record the lecture on tape (either audio or video) and play it back later so as to listen to the lecture at a more reasonable note-taking speed. The professor's output—the lecture—has been "spooled" to the tape for later processing (by the student) at speeds which can be accommodated.

Multiprogramming. In order to be able to fully take advantage of the increased efficiency possible through the overlapping of processes, it is necessary to have the capability to work on many programs at the same time, a concept called **multiprogramming.** Although a single CPU can direct its attention to only one execution step at a time, a large number of programs can be resident in the memory at the same time, and work on many of them can be overlapped to the point that several programs can be worked toward completion in concert with one another. This capability is increased as intelligence is distributed throughout the devices in the system so that they work more independently of the CPU.

Partitioning. To accommodate multiprogramming, the memory management set of programs must be capable of **partitioning** the memory so that the various programs resident in it will not interfere with each other. Although static (unchanging) partitioning (wherein each of *n* users is given 1/*n*th of the memory) is possible, large computers use allocations that are made dynamically, with programs being allocated larger or smaller partitions as necessary.

Swapping. As the CPU directs its attention to each program in the multiprogrammed environment in turn, that program will need to be brought into the primary memory and into the CPU itself for execution. Other programs, currently in primary memory, may have to be moved out of the primary memory in order to provide space for the incoming program. This continual movement of programs into and out of the primary memory is known as **swapping.**

The workload of swapping is lessened by dividing the primary memory, and the programs and data which occupy it, into segments of a constant size, called pages. **Paging** thus gives the system the capability of dealing with segments of programs and segments of data as it swaps them into and out of the primary memory, which increases the efficiency of swapping movements of data and programs.

Virtual Memory. **Virtual memory** is a phrase coined to represent a perception on the part of the user that the primary memory of a computing system can be virtually unlimited. A system which has virtual memory has software necessary to accomplish paging, swapping, and partitioning in a multiprogrammed environment which is transparent to the user.

Virtual memory software (or a hardware/software combination) manages the memory of the system, moving programs and data back and forth from the primary to the secondary storage as needed by the applications programs which are executing. The primary memory appears to be unlimited because memory management programs take care of moving data and programs into and out of secondary storage in order to make room in the primary memory.

Challenge Update

The reader should now be able to discuss the underlying features common to most modern operation systems.

Newest Developments

Research efforts to improve the capabilities and speeds at which CPUs are able to operate continue. The U.S. Government, through the Department of Defense, is funding efforts to develop a processor capable of a billion instructions per second.

Japan invited computer scientists from around the world to a conference in 1981 to consider the architecture of fifth-generation computers. Their concept of the fifth-generation machine is one which includes a large array of intelligent processors, with dedicated data handling processors in the background and intelligent front-end processors capable of natural language interaction with users.

The Japanese effort relies heavily on advances in the field of **artificial intelligence (AI),** the capability of nonhuman devices to perform intelligent functions normally attributed to humans. Much of the research done in the field of artificial intelligence has been directed toward the development in machines of the human capabilities of reasoning and learning. Early efforts resulted in the development of theorem-proving programs and programs which played checkers or chess. Japan's fifth-generation machine will use artificial intelligence techniques to provide query access to a large body of stored information.

The United States and Britain have each reacted to the Japanese announcement by increasing their own research efforts. The Defense Advanced Research Projects Agency (DARPA) has moved to speed up the development of even more powerful supercomputers in an effort called the Strategic Computing Initiative. The National Laboratories of Lawrence Livermore and Los Alamos have joined with the Stanford Research Institute International to sponsor a research project to be known by the acronym SPREAD, for Supercomputer Project Research Experiment for Access and Development.

Yet another effort has been launched in the United States to counter the Japanese threat to become foremost in computer design. An unusual nonprofit, research cooperative known as the Microelectronics and Computer Technology Corporation was formed in 1982 through the united efforts of Control Data Corporation, Honeywell, Motorola, RCA, and others. These companies will jointly provide staff and financial resources and share in the research results.

The effort in the United Kingdom has resulted in the establishment of the Advanced Information Technology program. Academic institutions, government agencies, and industry will all join the research effort.

The United States has held the leadership in computer technology since the beginning of the industry. The Japanese program signals a substantial threat to that leadership. The escalation of research efforts on a worldwide basis should stimulate an even more rapid rate of technological advance. The structure of the Japanese machine is represented in Figure 6–11.

The supercomputers of the fourth generation are the Cray 2 and the CYBER 205. The CYBER 205 can be configured with up to 16 trillion bytes of virtual memory and is capable of 800 million FLOPS (floating point operations per second). A machine capable of 10 billion FLOPS is expected by 1986. The work to make smaller, faster, and denser chips has been hampered by some interesting physical constraints.

The time it takes for an electron to travel along a conductor limits the speed at which operations can take place within the CPU. A processor capable of a billion instructions per second must overcome the limitation that an electronic impulse travels only a few inches in a billionth of a second, a **nanosecond.** Either the distances must be shortened, or the physical characteristics of the wire must be changed. Increased miniaturization speaks to the former issue, while interesting research continues on the latter.

One area of research, mentioned earlier, has explored the use of the Josephson Junction, which reduces the resistance to the flow of electrons in a conductor subjected to extremely low temperatures. Research in this area has indicated that commercial applications for a Josephson Junction CPU are not likely. There may, however, be military reasons for continuing to develop such a technology.

Another development is taking place, which may be of some significance. Most of the computer chips used today are built on a base of silicon semiconductors. The most common chip technology is referred to as MOS, for metal oxide semiconductor. A faster, but still silicon-based, technology is known as CMOS, for complementary metal oxide semiconductor. CMOS chips consume significantly less electrical power than MOS chips, which makes them more suitable for portable machines.

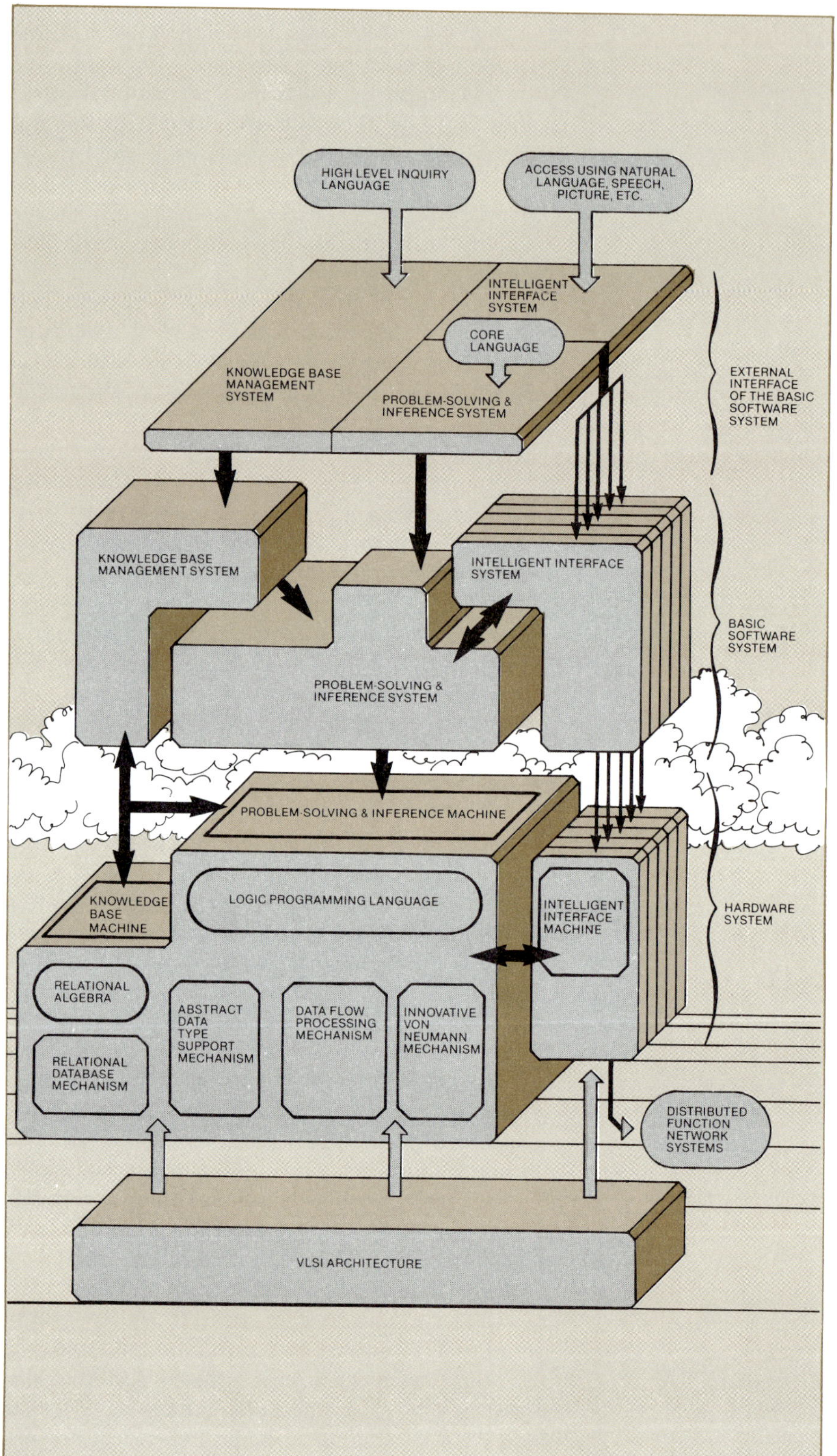

Figure 6–11 Basic Concept of the Fifth-Generation Computer System

Another technology with great promise has found use. Gallium arsenide semiconductors first became commercially available in early 1984. Their use may eventually supplant the use of silicon, because gallium arsenide may be as much as 100 times faster than silicon. They are, unfortunately, about 100 times more expensive as well. If they displace silicon, will the area of the San Francisco Peninsula known as Silicon Valley, where most of the world's silicon semiconductors are manufactured, be renamed?

There are continuing efforts to increase the density of transistors on a single chip. National Semiconductor's NS32032 chip with 70,000 transistors is capable of 1 MIPS, and the 500,000 transistor NS32C132 should be much faster. Inmos Ltd's T-424 chip combines a 10 MIPS processor on the same chip with the logic for memory and communications capability. The technology can be extended to the point that the entire silicon wafer is used to house the integration of many logical chips. This **wafer technology** will increase processing speeds by reducing the distances electrons formerly had to travel between chips.

In yet another area of research, scientists at Heriot-Watt University have been experimenting with an optical analog of a transistor, the basic switching device used in virtually all computers. The optical switch, called a *transphasor,* can be switched up to 1,000 times faster than a transistor. Thus, with transphasor switches we might be able to build computers which operate at speeds much greater than the speeds we can attain today.

Research is also underway in yet another area, which combines microprocessor chip design with genetic engineering, yielding **biochips.** Scientists are working on a biophysical molecular switch in order to increase even further the number of binary switching elements which can be put on a single chip. Current flow in the new switches is accomplished by enzymes which transport electrons in a electro-active polymer.

Scientists at M.I.T. are working on a computer architecture which relies on large numbers of small, cheap parallel processors operating simultaneously. Testing of the conceptual model of this architecture is being conducted on a special purpose system called the Cellular Automata Machine (CAM). A similar design is being studied at Thinking Machines Corporation. Their machine is called the Connection Machine.

Newer, improved operating systems continue to evolve. Efforts are underway to make relatively standard interfaces between the user and the operating system so that more of a user's knowledge is transferable from one computing system to another. For example, the University of California–San Diego has done extensive work in operating system standardization with its UCSD p-system. The trend toward friendlier, more standard operating systems will undoubtedly continue.

Exciting developments are also taking place in the refinement of the interface between microcomputer users and their machines. Rather than require the users to deal directly with the operating system, the new software, called an **operating environment,** provides a user-friendly interface among the user, the microcomputer, and the set of applications available. The operating environment will allow users to switch from application to application easily and will allow data to be moved from one application to another.

COMPUTING CHALLENGE: *A Final Note*

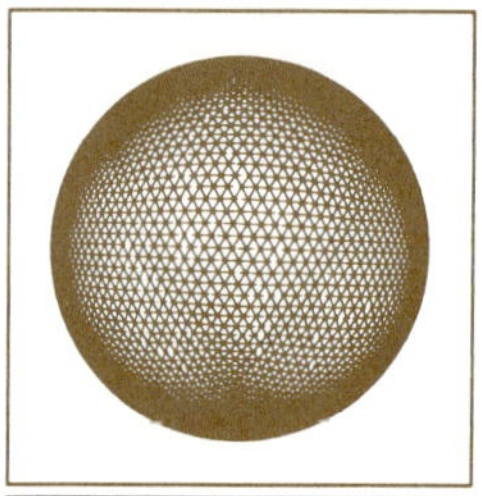

Let us return now to consider the problems faced by the management of Buckeye Building Contractors, Inc., as the company considers the acquisition of a computing system.

BBC would like to use the computer to perform the extensive computations inherent in advanced project management techniques. Such applications would appear to require an extensive amount of computation but a relatively minor amount of input and output. For this application alone, BBC would like to have a relatively fast CPU.

What other applications can we expect that they have? Surely they have the applications of purchasing, billing, accounts receivable, and payroll common to most business organizations. These applications are typically heavy users of the input and output devices, but require a minimum amount of CPU involvement.

They could buy a small, relatively unsophisticated computing system without the capability of multiprogramming and let the system be compute bound during the critical path runs and input/output bound during the other applications. They could buy a somewhat larger, more sophisticated system which would allow the applications to be mixed in a multiprogrammed environment. How will they decide?

If we assume they are already running most of these applications on other equipment, what might they be able to do in order to get a better idea just how a new system might perform?

SUMMARY

- Although it is by no means easy for a user or manager to make intelligent decisions in the areas of input and output, it is decidedly more difficult to make informed decisions with respect to computation.
- For input and output decisions, the user can visualize the impact that different pieces of equipment and methodologies might have on the organization, but it is extremely difficult to make that visualization work for an object which is to most users a "black box" of unknown capability.
- The computations necessary to transform the system's inputs into the desired outputs are accomplished through the coordinated efforts of hardware and software, and an enormous amount of potential capability exists.
- Firms often find that a consultant's technical assistance is necessary in order to understand how processing capability can be transformed into productive data processing operations.
- The impact a particular application has on the resources of a computing system differs from application to application, with some applications requiring heavy use of the CPU, while others place heavy burdens on the input and output devices.

- A properly designed system provides the resources necessary to efficiently process the available mix of applications.
- The operating system for a computing system controls the operation of the hardware and makes the resources of the system available to the user.
- Systems programs are necessary to provide job control, peripheral device control, memory management, data conversions, library maintenance, and other resource allocations.
- Systems programs contribute to the operation of the system by making effective use of the particular set of hardware and software features which have been provided by the manufacturer.
- A large, modern computing system employs overlapped processing, buffering, spooling, partitioning, swapping, paging, and virtual memory to provide a multiprogramming environment which makes efficient use of the system's resources.
- A new era of the worldwide competition in computer design was launched by Japan with their 1981 announcement of an effort to develop a fifth-generation computer, and the United States and the United Kingdom were quick to respond with research efforts of their own.
- The research effort to make faster and more capable computing machines continues with new technologies which give hope for a billion-instructions-per-second machine and, in the longer term, a new generation of machines with which we might be able to communicate in natural language.
- Gallium arsenide chips, commercially available for the first time in 1984, may eventually displace silicon chips; they are about 100 times faster than silicon chips.
- Two technologies, the biochip and the optical computer, offer a somewhat longer-range potential for even faster computers.
- Complete chip sets can be integrated on a single silicon wafer, offering a technology which makes even faster processing speeds possible.

CASE: Computers Ease Complexity of Freight Bills

When we think for a few minutes about the goods we consume, we begin to realize the magnitude of the distribution problem in this country. Vegetables from the fertile valleys of California must be shipped throughout the nation, while untold quantities of manufactured goods must be shipped from factories to retail outlets. Trucking and railroad companies issue freight bills to charge shippers for the movement of these goods. Shipping charges are computed through the application of an extremely complex set of rules and tariffs.

The complexities of tariffs give rise to frequent overpayment, payment in error, or double-payment of freight bills. Only very large companies can afford to employ experts to accurately check their freight bills. A company in Columbus, Ohio, called Comtrac, Inc., has come up with a computerized system that will help many companies detect and correct payment errors. For a fee, Comtrac will review a company's freight bill payments and compare the actual payments against the correct ones. Comtrac's system provides their clients with freight bill auditing and payment control as well as other, related transportation administration functions nationwide.

Frank G. Curran, senior vice president of Comtrac, says that the new computer system can efficiently handle the complexity of tariffs, with their numerous deletions and changes, and the high volume of transactions. The auditing and payment process involves literally millions of applicable freight rates levied by thousands of carriers in every transportation mode. Still, the system maintains tight, positive control over every freight bill paid for every one of Comtrac's clients. The computer record identifies the bill, the carrier, the payment amount, and specifics of the applicable tariffs. This information is always available via terminal inquiry for fast response to any client or carrier.

Comtrac's computerized system enables the company to react faster to new information and automatically update all affected freight rates. Comtrac serves over 500 companies in eighty different industries with the new system. They expect the future to bring improved service to their customers, greater operating efficiencies, and better control.

Questions for the Case

1. Are the computations necessary to calculate a freight bill likely to require a complex arithmetical scheme?
2. Would maintenance of the large collection of tariff information require a fast CPU? A large secondary storage? A fast means for searching through storage?
3. Is Comtrac selling computing power or computerized access to tariff information?

DISCUSSION QUESTIONS AND EXERCISES

1. In what ways does the operating system make the computer system's resources available to the users?
2. Discuss the relative sophistication of mainframe computers and microcomputers. Is it reasonable to expect that the gap will narrow? Why or why not?
3. Consider the following applications and form an opinion about the extent to which they might tend to be input/output bound or compute bound.
   a. Statistical analysis program.
   b. Optimization program to assign students to classes.
   c. Mailing list program.
   d. Aircraft wing design program.
4. Increasingly, we find that work formerly the responsibility of the programmer is made the responsibility of the operating system. Could the

operating system take over the writing of programs? Could it do more than it now does?

5. Discuss the concept of transparency in computing. List examples of transparency in other areas, say in the design of automobiles or home appliances.

6. Describe the nature of the great mismatch in speed between the CPU and the peripheral devices. How does the addition of intelligence to the peripheral devices help?

7. How does a mixture of input/output bound applications and compute bound applications contribute to a more efficient computing system?

8. List the types of tasks normally performed by the operating system.

9. What tasks might be performed by the utilities programs in a microcomputer's operating system?

10. What has been the impact on computer research in the United States of the announcement of the fifth-generation computer project by Japan?

11. Discuss multiprogramming. Explain the role of buffering, spooling, swapping, partitioning and paging in a multiprogrammed system.

12. Differentiate the role of multiple processors in support functions from that of true multiprocessing.

13. Look up the meaning of the word *intelligence* in a dictionary. How does the dictionary definition differ from the use of the word to describe terminals or peripherals? What about artificial "intelligence"?

14. List some of the new technologies under development with respect to CPU design. Which appear to be most promising in the short run? In the long run?

15. This chapter focuses on improvements inside the computer itself. Discuss these improvements in terms of overall system performance and extend that discussion to the performance of an organization.

ADDITIONAL READINGS

Abraham, Eitan; Seaton, Colin T., and Smith, S. Desmond. "The Optical Computer". *Scientific American,* February, 1983 pp. 85–93.

Dahmke, Mark. *Microcomputer Operating Systems.* Peterborough, N.H.: Byte Books, 1982.

Davis, Dwight B. "Super Computers: A Strategic Imperative?" *High Technology,* May 1984, pp. 44–52.

Davis, William S. *Operating Systems: A Systematic View,* 2d edition. Reading, Mass.: Addison-Wesley, 1983.

Deitel, Harvey M. *An Introduction to Operating Systems.* Reading, Mass.: Addison-Wesley, 1983.

Feigenbaum, Edward A., and McCorduck, Pamela. *The Fifth Generation.* Reading, Mass.: Addison-Wesley, 1983.

Hanson, Dirk. *The New Alchemists: Silicon Valley and the Microelectronics Revolution.* Boston: Little, Brown and Co., 1982.

Kidder, Tracy. *The Soul of a New Machine.* Boston: Atlantic/Little, Brown and Co., 1981.

Laurie, Peter. *The Micro Revolution: Living with Computers.* New York: Universe Books, 1981.

Lorin, Harold. *Introduction to Computer Architecture and Organization.* New York: John Wiley, 1982.

Lorin, Harold, and Deitel, Harvey M. *Operating Systems.* Reading, Mass.: Addison-Wesley, 1981.

Metropolis, A. *A History of Computing in the Twentieth Century.* New York: Academic Press, 1980.

Myers, Glenford J. *Advances in Computer Architecture.* New York: John Wiley, 1982.

Rus, Teodor. *Data Structures and Operating Systems.* New York: John Wiley, 1979.

Shapiro, Ehud Y. "The Fifth Generation Project: A Trip Report." *Communications of the ACM,* Vol. 26, No. 9 (September 1983), pp. 637–641.

Smolin, C. Roger. *How to Buy the Right, Small Business Computer System.* New York: John Wiley, 1981.

7

Data Storage: Files

CHAPTER PREVIEW

The fourth of the basic data processing functions is storage. In general, we need to provide storage when a time delay exists between our acquisition of something and our final expected use of it. Manufacturers provide warehouses for the storage of goods from their time of manufacture until their time of use (sale). Libraries provide stacks in which books are stored, awaiting use. Computer systems must provide for the storage of data and programs for later use in the processing of an organization's data.

A computerized transaction processing system typically collects a large amount of data, some of which are processed immediately and some of which are stored for later processing. The time span over which the data are stored is a function of the application itself and varies greatly. Some systems might require storage of data for only a shift, or a day, while others might require that the data be stored for several years.

Several types of storage exist, and the choice of a particular type is determined by the application itself. The speed of access, type of access, storage capacity, length of time the data are to be stored, and cost are all important factors in the selection of storage type. An organization's need for data storage is illustrated in the following case.

COMPUTING CHALLENGE: *University Alumni Relations*

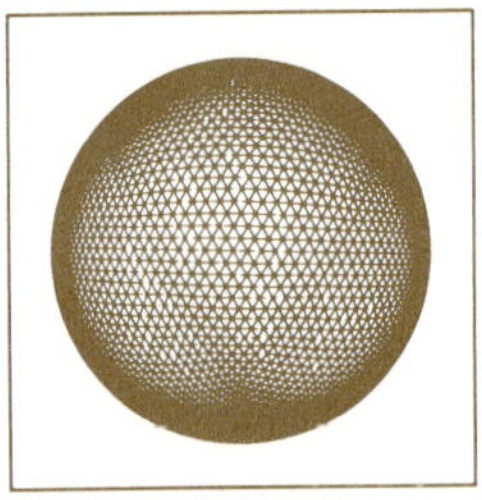

The Alumni Relations Office of Pragmatic State University has asked the director of fund-raising to work on a data storage problem. PSU is a small liberal arts college. The student body numbers a modest 7,500 undergraduates and 1,230 graduate students. PSU is one of the nation's oldest private universities and has approximately 138,000 alumni.

Approximately half of the operating funds for PSU come from the tuition charged its students. The remainder of the budget must be covered by funds derived from federal support and alumni contributions. Federal support varies widely depending on who is President of the United States and how politically popular it is to support higher education. At the present time, federal funds appear to be shrinking, so a renewed effort to increase alumni contributions must be made.

The names, addresses, and contribution records of the alumni are currently maintained on 3-by-5-inch cards in the office of Ms. Ann Grender, the director of fund-raising. She believes these records might be computerized in order to improve fund-raising activities.

The PSU computer center provides access to a modern computing system. The director has pointed out that the center has the capacity to handle a system which might be designed to use punched cards, magnetic tape, or magnetic disks. The computer center has agreed to help with the project and will charge the Alumni Relations Office for whatever service is required, based upon their usual charge for each service.

Ms. Grender needs to determine how the following data processing operations might take place in each of the three environments (punched card, magnetic tape, and magnetic disk):

1. *Sending a funds solicitation to all the alumni in the file.*
2. *Changing the address of an alumnus or alumna.*
3. *Recording a contribution made by an alumnus or alumna.*
4. *Sending an announcement to all alumni living in a particular geographic location, telling them of an upcoming visit by the university's president.*
5. *Generating a list of contributors who have donated more than $100 to PSU within the past year.*

Ms. Grender needs to learn a great deal more than she currently knows about data storage in order to help design the new system. She might very well need to hire a consultant, but first she must become knowledgeable enough to guide a consultant. Some of the questions to which she needs answers are:

1. *In what ways do the needs of an application affect the choice of a file structure?*
2. *What file structures can most efficiently be accommodated by which storage devices?*
3. *How do the various storage media compare with respect to speed, capacity, and price?*

Her problem is not an unusual one. Many managers have been faced with similar problems.

This chapter has been designed to introduce the reader to the types of data storage which are available and to some of the compromises which must be made in order to fit a particular type of storage to a particular application. After successful completion of this chapter, the reader should be able to:

1. *Describe the role that data storage plays in the information processing activities of an organization.*
2. *Discuss the relative merits of sequential files, random files, indexed sequential files, and inverted files as file structures.*
3. *List the advantages and disadvantages of computerized data processing systems where the files are "owned" by specific computer applications.*
4. *List the advantages and disadvantages of the various data storage devices or media: magnetic tape, magnetic disk, and the mass storage devices.*

HISTORICAL PERSPECTIVE

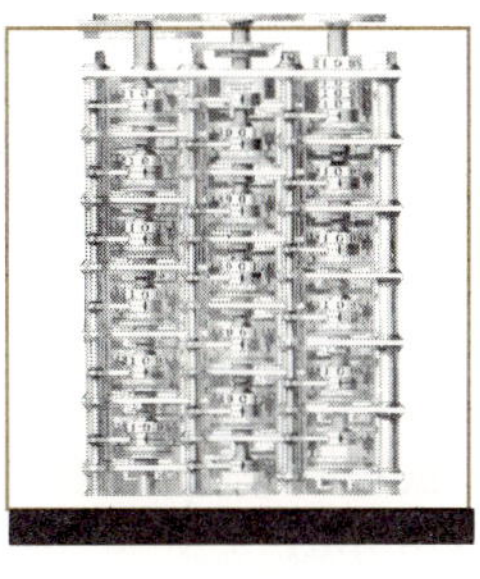

It is hard to imagine a formal organization which does not have need to store data. Governments need to maintain files which reveal who owns which parcels of real estate, who lives in which jurisdiction, and who pays (or does not pay) taxes; social organizations need to maintain membership lists; schools need to maintain the academic records of their students; and business firms need to maintain records of sales, purchases, shipments, production levels, inspections, and so on.

Over the years, these records have predominantly been stored as hand-written or printed entries with paper as the medium. As organizations become older and larger, the amount of paper required to record and store data becomes very large. Large paper (hard copy) files have several serious problems:

1. They occupy a great deal of physical space.
2. Keeping the files current requires a lot of work.
3. Finding a particular record in the file takes a long time.

As organizations acquired the use of computer processing systems, many files were changed so that they could be read directly by machine. For example, many data files were converted to punched cards from which the data could be read by a card reader. Information about customers, suppliers, employees, and stockholders could then be punched into cards with a keypunch or produced on a card punch by a prior computer run. The cards were then stored until needed for additional processing.

Computer programs must also be stored from one use to another. They might be stored within the system or stored on some output medium between uses. Early in the nineteenth century the Frenchman Joseph Marie Jacquard designed a loom which used punched cards to control the loom's actions in order to produce woven patterns. This is directly analogous to our current use of stored programs to control the data processing activities of modern computers.

We learned somewhat later (about 1955) how data could be stored on magnetic tape, represented there by patterns of magnetization. The use of a magnetized representation was then extended to magnetic disks, opening up interesting new possibilities for data storage. When extremely short retrieval times were required, files could be put on magnetic disk and stored so as to be instantaneously available to an executing computer program, as we shall see in this chapter.

Concepts: Applications and Their Uses of Files

It is easy to understand that organizations find it necessary to store information for varying periods of time. Religious and social organizations would like to maintain records for their members, schools would like to record the grades of their students, and businesses would like to record their sales activities with each client.

Data processing applications have need for different types of data storage to fulfill the differing needs of the applications themselves. Information generated by the receipt of orders, sales, shipments, production, and the other business functions must be stored for varying lengths of time. Information about orders which have been received certainly must be stored until the shipment has been made. Sales and production figures are used in monthly and annual summaries, so they must be stored for extended periods. Information in support of tax returns must be stored for years.

A variety of different types of storage are available for computing systems. They represent attempts to design storage devices to meet the various needs of particular applications. They are part of a computer system's secondary storage.

The Role of Secondary Storage

Recall, from the discussion of the fundamentals of computer hardware, that computer systems have storage areas known as primary memory and secondary storage, and that computer programs must reside in the primary memory while their instructions are being executed. That portion of the data files on which the program is operating must also be in the primary memory at the time of processing, although the remainder of the data files may be stored elsewhere (refer to Figure 7–1 for a graphical representation of this data movement).

The size of the primary memory is, however, limited by several factors. One of these factors has to do with the size of an address of a location in primary memory. Each elemental location has a numerical address. The

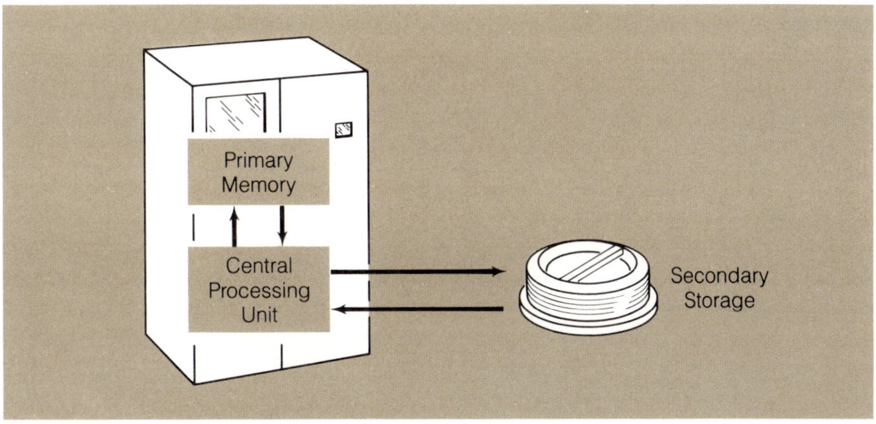

Figure 7–1
Movement of Data and Programs between Secondary Storage and Primary Memory

architecture of the system is such that an individual instruction can contain this numerical address. If the primary memory were unrestricted in size, the value of the numerical address would eventually grow to be too large to fit within an instruction, although indirect addressing schemes are possible.

Another factor which limits the size of a computer system's primary memory is its cost. It is the most expensive type of memory used in the computer system, and we can almost never afford as much of it as we would like.

Computer manufacturers, therefore, provide additional secondary storage. This storage is used to store those data files and programs which are used regularly, during the time they are not actually being used. Both user programs and systems programs may be stored there. Later in this chapter the types of devices used for secondary storage are discussed. Storage devices differ greatly in size and in the time it takes for data to be found and moved into the primary memory. In general, the devices which provide faster access to the data cost more than those devices which allow slower access.

Program and Data Files

Collections of related data are known as **files** in data processing. Data required by the application and the information generated by the application may both need to be stored as data files, either within the system itself or elsewhere. For example, information about current orders might be stored within the system, while information about last year's taxes might not be. Again, when stored in the system, these files and the programs which use them are stored in the computer system's secondary storage until they are actually needed for processing (see Figure 7–2). To accomplish the processing itself, the files and programs must be moved into the primary memory.

Data files stored within the computer system itself—and thus instantaneously available to an applications program—are referred to as being **on-line.** Data files stored outside the system, so that some human inter-

Figure 7–2 Use of Secondary Storage to Store Programs and Files

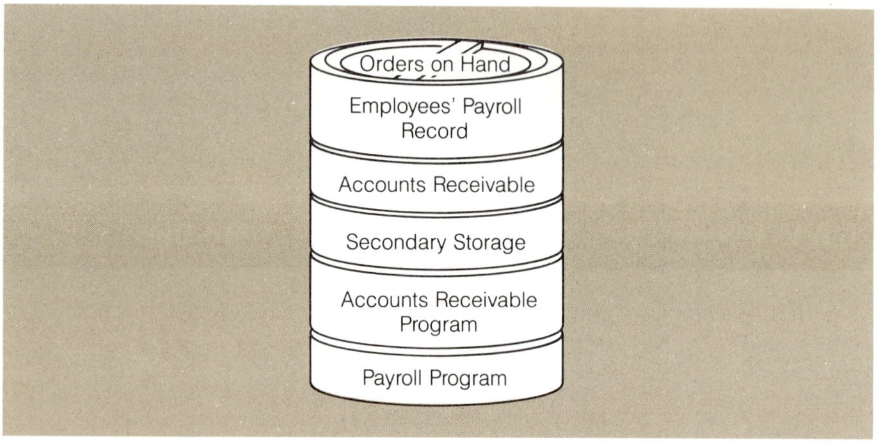

vention is required to make them available, are referred to as **off-line.** Access to on-line files is quicker than the access to off-line files, but on-line capability is more expensive. Both types of storage are illustrated in Figure 7–3.

Much of the added expense of on-line files is easy to understand. If the system is to be designed for off-line files, we could have a large collection of files but have need for only a few (maybe only one) secondary storage devices on which those files could be placed for access. A system designed for on-line files must have enough storage devices so that all the necessary files are ready for access at the same time. A large number of devices would be required for a large collection of files, making the system much more expensive. A large collection of secondary storage devices is shown in Figure 7–4.

Not only are the data files required by an application (input) and the information generated by that application (output) stored within the system, but often the computer program which controls the processing is itself stored within the system. Chapter 3 discussed very briefly the programming languages in which these programs might be written. (The reader will recall that a computer applications program written in one of these languages is called a source program.)

A program stored within the computer system itself may be stored in its original form, as a source program, or it may be stored in its translated (or compiled) form. (Recall that the compiled program is known as an object program.) The advantage of storing the object version of the program is, of course, that it may then be executed directly by the computer without any delay for translation.

Thus we may find virtually any combination of input files, output files, and applications programs stored within the system (on-line). Those which are not stored within the system are stored off-line in some machine-readable form so that they can rather quickly be read into the system. They might, for example, be stored on punched cards or magnetic tape. Figure 7–5 indicates the on-line/off-line choices.

Figure 7–3 Off-Line and On-Line Storage

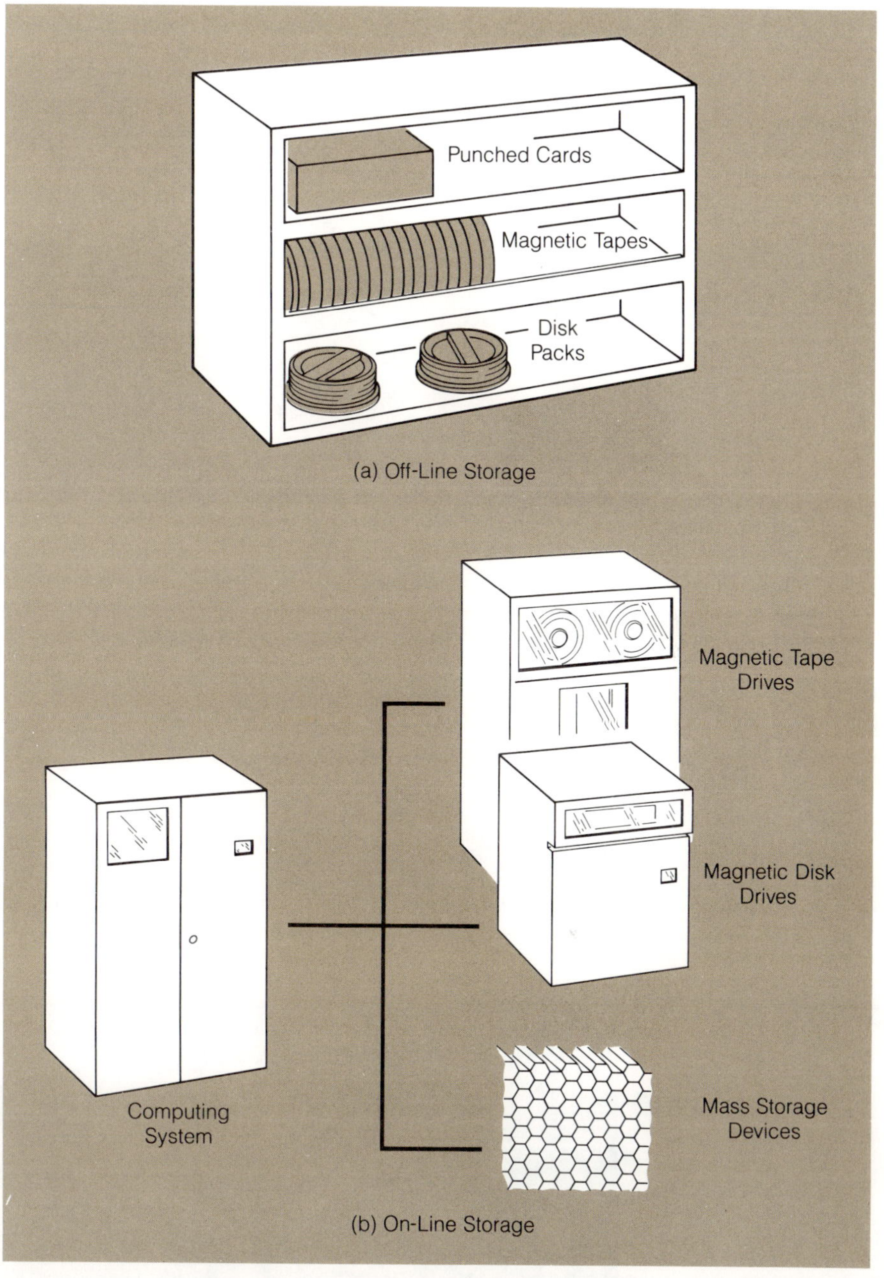

How does a manager or analyst determine the relative merits of on-line versus off-line storage of input files, application programs, or output files? The answer to the on-line/off-line question can only be derived from the nature of the application itself. Some applications require very fast access to programs and data, while others can endure some delay. We see here that, once again, speed is traded off against cost. Data storage devices which

Figure 7–4 A Large Bank of Secondary Storage Devices

Figure 7–5 The Needs of Applications Determine On-Line/Off-Line Choices

Application: ______________________________

Input Files
- ☐ On-line
- ☐ Off-line

Program
- ☐ On-line
- ☐ Off-line

Output Files
- ☐ On-line
- ☐ Off-line

Figure 7–6 Off-Line Storage Facility

Figure 7–7 A Large Amount of On-Line Storage Is Necessary to Support a Designer at a Graphics Terminal

yield faster access to the data almost always cost more money than those which allow for slower retrieval. A system using on-line storage would be more expensive than a system using off-line storage. An off-line storage facility is shown in Figure 7–6.

The question is, would the on-line system be worth the extra money? We decide how much speed we want to buy by analyzing the nature of the particular application itself. A little later we will examine a few hypothetical applications to see just how the application itself dictates the data storage requirements. A graphics application is illustrated in Figure 7–7 as an example. First, let us examine a few file structures to understand the different ways in which the data can be stored.

Challenge Update

Ann Grender should now have an understanding of the role that data storage plays in the information processing activities of an organization.

File Structures

Files can be designed with different file structures to accommodate some types of data processing more efficiently than others. We will explore four structures and the types of activities for which each is most efficient. Efficiency in this context refers to accomplishing the required processing with a minimum consumption of the system's resources.

File Definitions. Some of the file vocabulary terms discussed here are illustrated graphically in Figure 7–8. A *file* is a collection of individual **records,** and each record is made up of a number of **data items.** A data item can be viewed as a single fact. A record can be viewed as a collection of related facts. Records are often associated with people, and the data items in a person's record refer to facts that are known about that person. For example, a professor maintains a file for his classes which contains records for each student. The data items in each record include the student's name, identification number, and test scores. An elections commission would maintain files of eligible voters for which each record would contain the relevant facts pertaining to the voter's name, address, political party, and voting record as data items.

The location within a record in which an individual data item is stored is called a **field.** We might, for example, allocate twenty columns of a record as the field in which a person's last name is to be stored. Data items of standard length—for example, a social security number— are easily accommodated in **fixed length fields.** Data items like previous jobs, courses completed, and schools attended might require **variable length fields** to accommodate a variety of information of different lengths.

We would expect the files of business firms to have records associated with the people and other firms with which they do business. The firm's customers would be found in a customer file, and the firms from whom goods and services are purchased in a supplier file. The data items stored within these records typically include company name, address, shipments made, credit terms, and so on.

Figure 7–8
Illustration of File Vocabulary

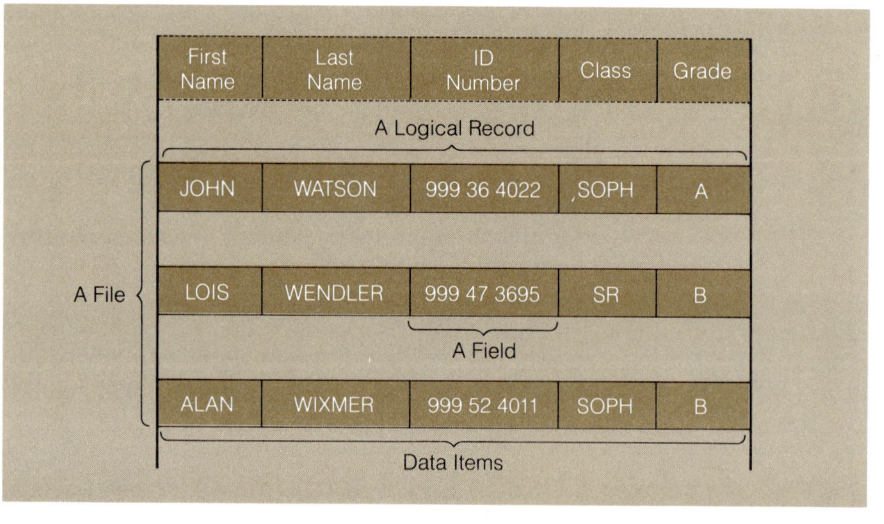

"I'd like a word with your computer"

One means for describing the data relationships in a record is known as the **entity/attribute method.** In formal terms, we say that a record belongs to a particular data item known as an **entity,** and the other data items are **attributes** of that entity. For example, in a customer file the data items in a record are all related to the particular customer. Therefore, the customer is the entity, and the other data items in the record (such as address, purchases, shipments, and terms of sale) are all attributes.

Certain attributes are used in the overall file design to identify and access the records in the file, and when they are used in that way, they are known as **keys.** Since the key is used to identify the record, it must be unique for each record. Social security numbers, student identification numbers, account numbers, part numbers, and customer numbers are all examples of keys. The entity/attribute concept is illustrated in Figure 7–9.

Sequential Files. Some files are stored so that access to their records can only be accomplished in the same sequence in which the data have been stored. For example, in the case of a college class, the professor's class file may be stored in alphabetical order by student name. A file whose records are maintained in sequence so that access to any individual record can only be obtained by proceeding through the sequence is called a **sequential file** (see Figure 7–10 for an illustration). A stereo cassette of music constitutes a sequential file of the various pieces of music on the tape. Each piece of music can only be accessed in sequence, even though the system might

Figure 7–9 Illustration of Entity/ Attribute Definition

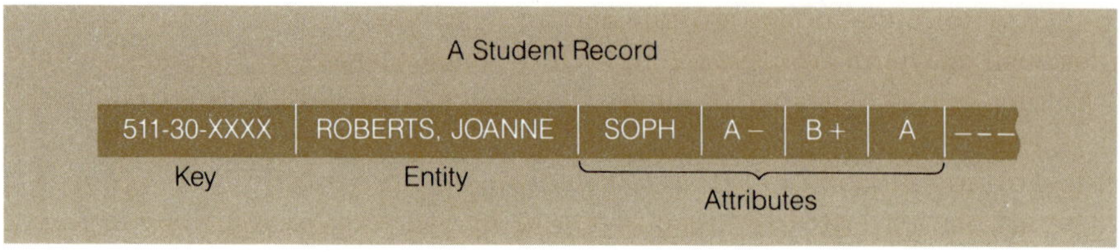

Figure 7–10 A Sequential File

File Entry Here Only →

Student ID # (Key)	Student Name	Course Grade
100 732	Applebaum, C.	A
159 674	Baker, S.	B
203 725	Cochran, F.	A
:	Dixon, M.	C
	Engle, A.	C
	Fox, L.	B
	Gaston, C.	F
	Henry, B.	A
	⋮	⋮
987 466	Zindel, Z.	B

Figure 7–11 A Direct Access File

Access Any Record Directly by Key →

Address	Student ID #	Student Name	Grade
	356931	Engle, A.	C
	201771	Cochran, F.	A
	983644	Zindel, Z.	B
	219639	Dixon, M.	C
	483221	Gaston, C.	F
	312715	Henry, B.	A
	109346	Baker, S.	B
	100424	Applebaum, C.	A
		⋮	
	455461	Fox, L.	B

provide a fast forward setting to minimize the delay in reaching a particular location in the "file" of music.

Direct Access Files. While many computer applications make use of sequential files, other file structures are necessary in some circumstances. If the application's use of a file starts at the beginning and processes the records in order until it reaches the end, a sequential file is quite adequate. On the other hand, an application may require modification of a single record in the file, and such an instance makes the process of working through the entire file cumbersome. To do this a file which has direct, or random, access is preferable. A **direct access file** allows one to go directly to the location of a particular record in the file without having to access other records. The records in such a file appear not to be in any particular order, but instead randomly distributed. The random distribution gives rise to approximately equal access times for all records and the alternative name **random access file** (see Figure 7–11 for an illustration).

There is always some logical pattern to the sequencing of the file, even though the logic might be unknown (even uninteresting) to the user of the file. In a direct access file the location of a particular record can be determined, sometimes computed, from the record key, and the user has access to that record directly, without having to move through the other records.

Loosely speaking, if a reel-to-reel audio tape is analagous to a sequential access file, a phonograph album is analagous to a direct access file. We can check the location of a particular song on the label of the album and move the stylus directly to that song without having to listen to the other songs on the album. Manual movement of the tone arm allows us to enter at any point. (If the analogy were more nearly perfect, we would be able to move the stylus to an exact location within the song.) Direct access files on computer systems allow us to determine the record's location from an index or directory and go directly to that record.

In many cases, records in a direct access file are stored at a physical address which is computed from the record key. A complex numerical algorithm is used to convert the key to an actual address by a process known as **hashing.** Research efforts have developed sets of rules for locating records (called hashing algorithms) that distribute the records relatively evenly throughout the physical address space yet minimize the number of collisions caused by two (or more) records which yield the same address.

Indexed Sequential Files. A compromise between the sequential and direct access files exists for those applications which sometimes require a complete processing of the entire file in sequence and other times require quick access to individual records. The compromise file is called an **indexed sequential file,** essentially a sequential file with an index of record locations to allow quick access to individual records (see Figure 7–12).

Is there a commonplace analog for an indexed sequential file? Perhaps this text will serve the purpose. The information in the text is provided in a particular, logical sequence; but, if we want to find the discussion of a particular topic quickly, we could use the table of contents or index to give us the approximate location.

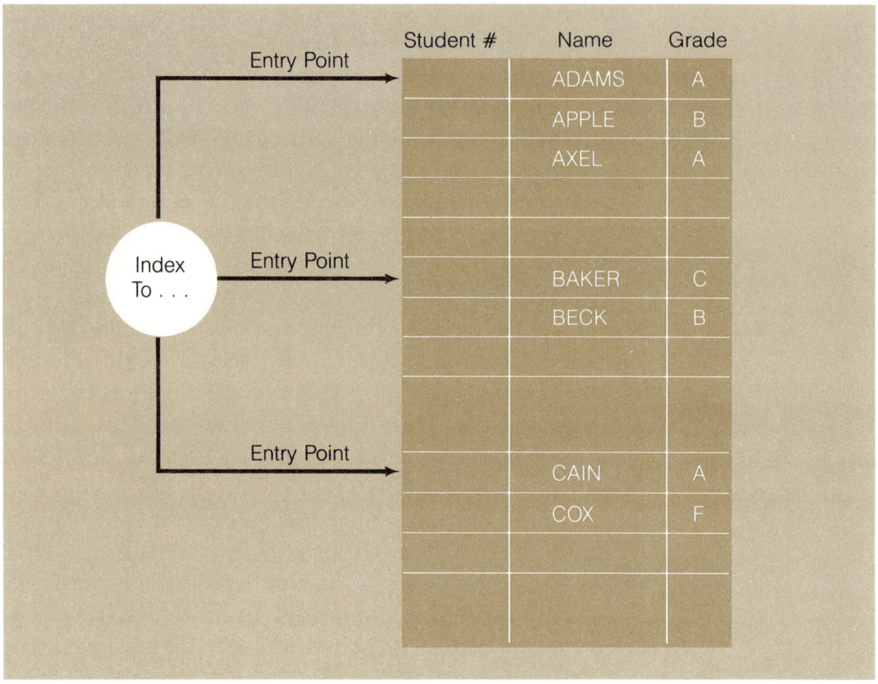

Figure 7–12 An Indexed Sequential File

Inverted Files. Sometimes it is appropriate to list, in an index, all the records which have a particular value for one of the attributes. The file could, for example, provide access through such an index to those students who received A's in a course. Perhaps, as another example, a student file for a university contains an index to specifically identify physically disadvantaged students. Such a file organization concept is called an **inverted file** because the contents of the file can, in part, be inferred by the index (see Figure 7–13). An inverted file would enable us to efficiently access all entities which have the desired value for the particular attribute.

An inverted file gets its name from the fact that the role of the record key and a record attribute are reversed in order to create the file. A file of employees might use the employee number as a key with additional information listed within the record as attributes. One such attribute might be an indication of whether or not the employee had received advanced training in first aid. An inverted file extracted from this file would use first-aid training as the key in order, perhaps, to be able to quickly find the employees who had received that training. The employee number is no longer a key in the inverted file but is, instead, an attribute.

Challenge Update

Ms. Grender and the reader should now be able to discuss the relative merits of sequential, direct, indexed sequential, and inverted files.

Let us now examine how the characteristics of particular types of applications determine the type of file structure to be used and the relative merit of on-line versus off-line storage.

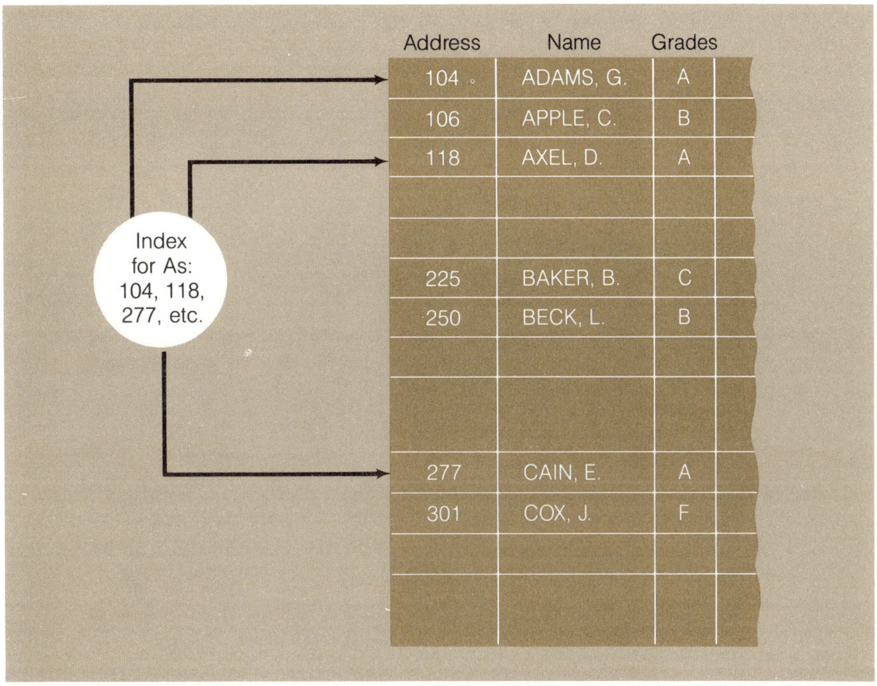

Figure 7–13
Structure of an Inverted File

The Interaction of a Program and Its Files

Computer programs are written to work closely with particular sets of files. The file structure used depends upon the needs of the application, within the limits imposed by the capabilities provided by the system. The intimate working relationship between a program and its files can be a very efficient one. A few examples will illustrate how file types, file structures, and their program interactions are determined by the nature of the application itself.

Routine, but Infrequent, Report Generation. Consider, for example, an application wherein county officials for a rural county in the Midwest must send out the annual real estate tax statements. Owners of real estate are required to pay an amount of taxes to the county based upon the tax rate and the assessed value of the property. We will assume that real property in this particular county rarely undergoes any ownership changes, but tax rates and assessed values do change annually.

Such an application would require routine processing of the entire file in order to send the annual tax statements and would require infrequent changes as properties were bought and sold. Quick access to individual records in the file does not seem to be necessary in this case. This application would probably require only a sequential, off-line file, as illustrated in Figure 7–14. We could, of course, design this system to use direct access, on-line files so that title transfers could be recorded in real time, as they occur, and so that tax status inquiries could be answered quickly. Data processing costs can be expected to be greater for systems with on-line files.

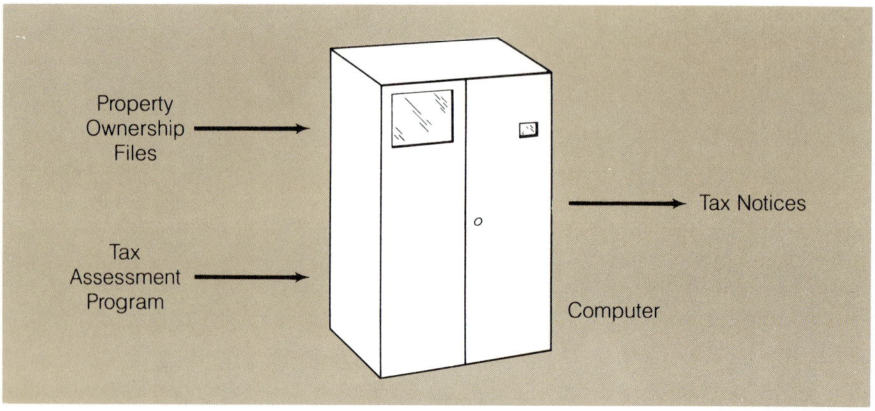

Figure 7–14 Routine and Infrequent Report Application (Program and Files Stored Off-Line)

Would we, as county officials, feel justified in spending the money to have the ownership records, the tax calculation program, or the generated tax statements stored on-line? Probably not.

Routine, but Frequent, Report Generation. Consider an application wherein employees' wages are calculated and their paychecks are generated on a weekly basis in a large company. For such a system, we might expect to find the payroll programs themselves stored on-line to be always available to generate paychecks. Some of the data used by the program comes from the time cards, an off-line source, while other data—for example, withholding rate and fringe benefits—might be found in the employees' permanent records, perhaps also stored on-line. Paychecks, as generated, are dispersed (off-line) but payroll summaries may be stored on-line for future use. The files could be sequential, direct, or indexed sequential, depending upon the frequency and type of access necessary. This application is illustrated in Figure 7–15.

Inquiries Requiring Quick Response. Consider an application which keeps track of passenger reservations for an airline. Customers of the airline require immediate answers to questions about the availability of space on flights, and they need to be able to make, change, and cancel reservations quickly. We would expect the entire system to be on-line, with direct or indexed sequential files. See Figure 7–16 for an illustrative application.

The nature of the application is one of the primary factors in determining the type of data storage and file structure required. Managers must analyze each application and ask themselves:

1. How quickly and in what manner must this application have access to its data and programs?
2. Does the application's need for access to its data, programs, or generated information justify the added expense of on-line storage?

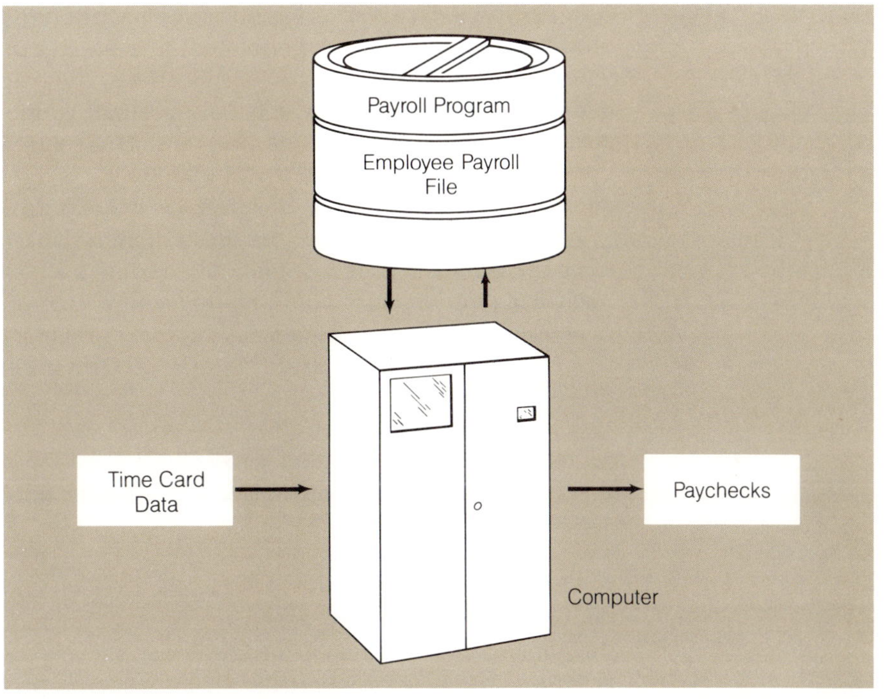

Figure 7–15 Routine and Frequent Report Application (Mix of On-Line and Off-Line Files)

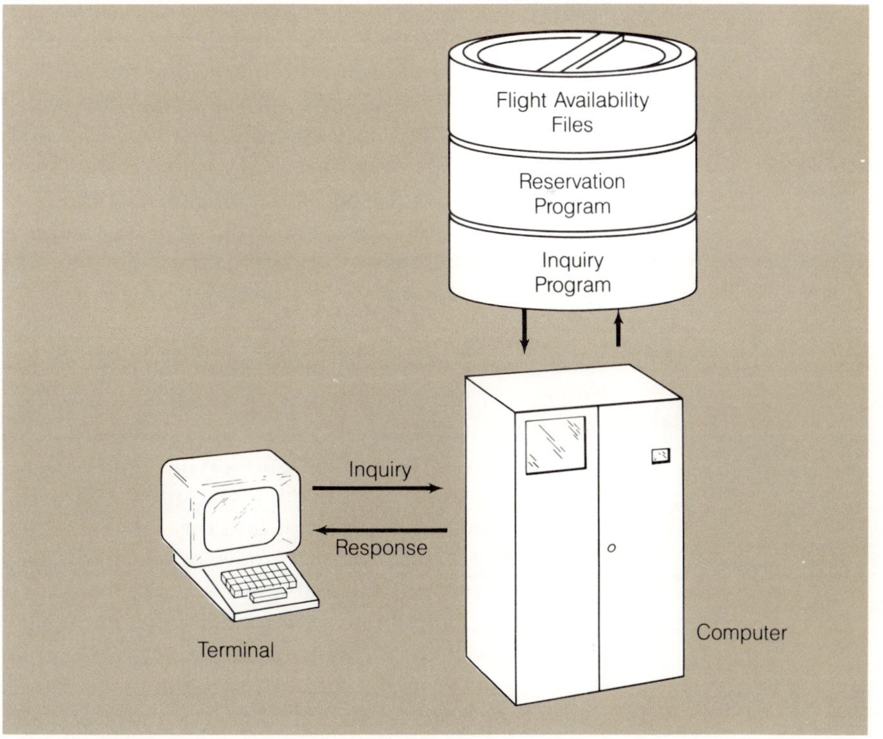

Figure 7–16 Application with Inquiries Requiring Quick Response (Everything On-Line)

File Processing. Often an application is written to provide for the routine modification of somewhat permanent files based upon a set of transactions which have occurred. In such applications, the somewhat permanent file contains information of which only a small proportion changes on any given run of the applications program. The semipermanent file is called the **master file.** The collection of data which is a record of the changes to be made to the master file is called the **transaction file.**

As an example, consider the files which a bank must maintain to keep track of the balances in customer demand deposit (checking) accounts. The master file in this case would be the semipermanent collection of records which contain customer names, account numbers, account balances, and so on. Remember, the master file may be stored either on-line or off-line, depending upon:

1. The bank's need for quick access to this information.
2. The amount of money they are willing to spend to provide on-line capability.

The bank's customers need to be able to open and close accounts, make deposits, make withdrawals, write checks, and inquire into the status of their accounts. The bank on any given day collects the data describing these activities into a transaction file. Then, at appropriate intervals, the bank uses a computer program to bring the master file (account balances) up-to-date on the basis of the activities described in the transaction file. This generates a new master file, and the collecting of transactions begins again.

Some banks operate with an on-line master file which is brought up-to-date electronically as each transaction is completed by the teller. Thus, the master file always contains the most current information, as deposits and withdrawals are recorded instantaneously. The instantaneous electronic capture and processing of data in this fashion is referred to as being done within **real time.** Thus, real time, on-line systems are those systems which provide instantaneous update to data files stored so that they are instantaneously available to the computer program.

File Design. Any given application will require that one or more programs and one or more files be jointly designed to work properly with each other. Programs need to know which data items are in which files, where in the file the data items can be found, what type of data is in each field, and so on. The program, in a sense, "owns" the file in what amounts to an efficient combination of the program and file.

As many applications are developed, many programs and files are designed. We often find that some data items are common to many of the files developed for different applications. Identical data, stored in different files, result in duplication of data entry, maintenance, and storage space. This duplication of effort can sometimes be reduced by redesigning files so that they can be shared by two or more applications.

If two files are to be combined to save storage space, changes will have to be made to the programs which use those files. The amount of work necessary to change the programs and the fear that changing the programs will cause other, unforeseen problems are sometimes sufficient to cause the effort to be abandoned. In Chapter 8 an attractive alternative called data base management is presented.

The Needs of Applications for Storage Summarized

The type of storage needed by an application depends, as we have seen, upon the nature of the application itself. The factors important to an organization in determining the type and amount of storage to provide are illustrated below.

- Access Speed: How quickly can an individual record be accessed?
- Access Method: What types of file structures can be efficiently implemented?
- Duration of Storage: How long will files be retained?
- Capacity: How much storage space is allowed?
- Cost: What does it cost to provide the storage?

The optimum combination of factors is not always available. Compromises frequently have to be made. Costs, for example, almost always cause compromise in the selection of storage devices of high capacity and fast access. As a matter of fact, capacity and fast access affect each other when files become so large that extended periods are necessary to locate particular records within them.

Challenge Update

The relative advantages and disadvantages of computerized data processing systems where tiles are "owned" by specific applications could now be listed, to help administrators at PSU visualize that option more effectively.

The next section points out a variety of secondary storage devices available, which present a user with a hierarchy of choices. Each device represents an attempt to provide a particular blend of benefits.

Tools: File Storage Media and Devices

Data are stored in computer systems in a variety of ways. The two most common media on which the data are stored are **magnetic tape** and **magnetic disk.** In the discussion of storage media, we will consider several different aspects of their performance.

We will be concerned with the type of access to the data files that each media provides, and the ease with which we can make use of the media for data entry and editing. In addition, we will be concerned with the speed by which the data can be transferred from the media to other computer system devices. Other considerations include the degree of permanence of the data on the media and, of course, its cost and the cost of the devices which make it available to the system.

Punched Cards

Throughout the relatively short history of computing, punched cards have received a great deal of use in the service of storing data input files, data output files, and applications programs. There are several advantages to storing data files or application programs on punched cards.

1. Cards have been a relatively inexpensive medium.
2. Corrections to sets of data stored on cards can be relatively easily made by punching corrected cards.
3. When printed during punching operations, cards can be read by a human as well as by the machine.
4. Cards have been used extensively in the past and are well understood by many users.

On the other hand, cards are not an ideal medium. Their disadvantages include the following:

1. They are bulky and require a great deal of physical space to store.
2. They become worn and unusable through repeated use and deteriorate with age.
3. Errors cannot be corrected on the same card; corrected data must be entered on a new card.
4. Two different card formats exist.
5. Punched cards provide only sequential access.
6. Punched cards provide only off-line storage.

Magnetic Tapes

We are perhaps all familiar with magnetic tape as a medium for storing data. Most of us have used, or at least seen, audio tapes in cassette, eight-track, or reel-to-reel versions. Video tape recorders use magnetic tape to record and play video programs. Magnetic tape for computing systems uses a different technology for storing information on the tape, that is, a digital rather than an analog representation, but their usage is otherwise very similar. Magnetic tape is shown in Figure 7–17.

Data elements are recorded on computer system magnetic tapes as patterns of magnetized spots. The data on magnetic tapes are represented by the pattern generated by small magnets oriented in one of two directions. Recall, from Chapter 1, that a two-state representation is common to all digital computers.

The advantages of storing data files and applications programs on magnetic tape are:

1. A great deal of data can be stored in a small physical volume. (If all the data on a single magnetic tape were transferred to punched cards, the cards would occupy a space as large as a file cabinet.)

Figure 7–17
Magnetic Tape

2. Magnetic tapes can be erased and reused.
3. Magnetic tapes are very inexpensive.
4. Data entered onto magnetic tapes can be relatively easily corrected (re-recorded), given that one has the correct equipment (a change which results in longer records could potentially be a problem.)
5. Data on magnetic tape can be transferred to other devices in the system at a much higher rate than can data on punched cards.
6. Data can be stored on magnetic tape for a relatively long period of time and used frequently without serious deterioration.

Magnetic tapes are not without some disadvantages. These include:

1. Only sequential access can be reasonably provided by magnetic tape.
2. Changes to be made to data stored on magnetic tape most often require that the entire tape be rewritten.
3. Data stored on magnetic tape can be destroyed by natural or transient magnetic fields.
4. Magnetic tape is most efficiently used for off-line storage.
5. The data transfer rate for magnetic tape, while faster than cards, is slower than magnetic disks (discussed next).
6. Data stored on magnetic tape are not directly readable by the human eye.

Magnetic Disks

Just as there are some similarities between computer system magnetic tape and reel-to-reel audio tape, there are some similarities between magnetic disks and phonograph records (and more recently, video disks). Information is stored on each in tracks such that any portion of any track can be directly accessed. Magnetic disks have an electromagnetic surface which allows data to be represented as patterns of magnetized spots, just as on magnetic tape. Although the tracks on a phonograph record spiral to the center, the tracks on a magnetic disk are separate, concentric circles. A magnetic disk is pictured in Figure 7–18.

Magnetic disks are often available as sets of disks on a common spindle. Corresponding tracks on the set of disks form (conceptual) **cylinders,** a useful strategy in the distribution of a large volume of data over a set of disks. If, for example, the read/write heads of a disk drive are all positioned above track number 44 on each of the disk surfaces, the entire collection of information in track 44 of all disks is available without further head movement. Read/write heads positioned above track 44 provide access to the data stored in that track on all disk surfaces. From top to bottom we have, in effect, a cylinder of track 44s. The details of magnetic disk storage are covered later, in the technology section of this chapter.

Figure 7–18
Magnetic Disk

The advantages of using magnetic disks for the storage of data files or computer application programs are:

1. Either on-line or off-line storage can be easily accommodated.
2. Although sequential access files are certainly possible, direct access files, indexed sequential files, and inverted files take better advantage of the magnetic disk's capability.
3. The data transfer rate for magnetic disks is greater than that for either magnetic tape or punched cards.
4. Magnetic disks can be erased and reused.
5. Data entered onto magnetic disks can be easily corrected.

The disadvantages of magnetic disks include:

1. Disk systems are more expensive than either punched card or magnetic tape systems.
2. The data files on magnetic disks are more likely to be destroyed by mechanical failures than is the case for either punched cards or magnetic tape.
3. Less standardization exists for magnetic disks than for punched cards and magnetic tape, making the physical movement of data from one system to another more difficult.
4. Data stored on the disk are not directly readable by humans

Other Secondary Storage Devices

Magnetic Drums. The storage of data files for applications programs on magnetic drums is uncommon, but some computer systems contain magnetic drums to provide an extension to primary storage. Drums are both faster and more costly than magnetic disk storage devices. In some computer configurations, drums provide storage with excellent retrieval characteristics for frequently used systems programs. Data elements are stored as patterns of magnetized spots on the electromagnetic surface of the drum cylinder in essentially the same manner as on magnetic disks. Drums are permanently mounted and are not removable.

Data Cells and Mass Storage Devices. Several different technologies exist to provide large-scale data storage. In one version the data are actually stored on segments of magnetic tapes, and the segments of tape themselves are stored in cylinders in a large honeycomb or as hanging strips in data cells (see Figure 7–19). While they provide very large storage areas at a relatively low cost, access to the data is quite slow due to the mechanical actions which are necessary to select and prepare to read the appropriate segment of tape. (Cost comparisons of secondary storage media appear in Table 7–1 later in the chapter.) Files on data cells and mass storage devices are moved to disks when they are needed, which improves the access characteristics.

Figure 7–19 A Mass Storage Device

Technology: Data Storage Details

Magnetic Tape

The device which enables a computer system to make use of magnetic tape is called a **tape drive.** The primary components of a magnetic tape drive are shown on the schematic in Figure 7–20. Data are written onto the tape or read from the tape by the read/write head. Often the reading and writing operations are checked for accuracy by performing a second read operation with another read head placed just after the original head. This provides some protection from errors in the reading and writing operations. Photoelectric cells or microswitches are provided to control the operation of the supply and take-up reels so that an optimum amount of slack is maintained in the tape to buffer the starting and stopping of the tape. Vacuum columns are also used to improve tape handling operations.

Magnetic tape comes in seven- and nine-track versions, with the tracks running the long axis of the tape. Seven-track tape systems preceded the development of nine-track systems, and seven-track is being replaced by the newer format. In each case, one of the tracks is given up for **parity checking,** an error detection mechanism.

Since it is cumbersome to continue to describe the direction of magnetization of the spots, I will instead adopt the usual convention and refer to the bits as either OFF or ON. The representation in Figure 7–21 goes one

Figure 7–20
Schematic of Tape Drive

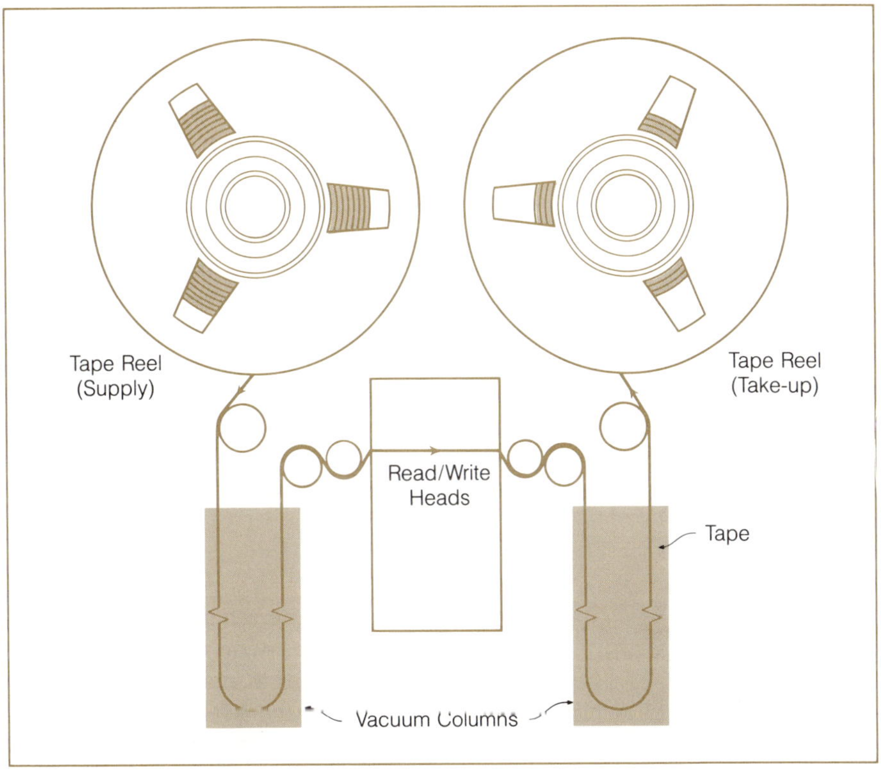

step further and uses the symbols 0 and 1 to represent a bit which is turned OFF and one which is turned ON, respectively.

The mathematics are such that a seven-track tape, which uses six bits for data and one for parity, can be used to record only 2^6 or 64 different bit patterns. That would be enough to represent all twenty-six letters of the alphabet (upper-case only), the ten numerical digits (0 through 9), and a few special characters such as +, −, /, and so on. If we want to be able to

Figure 7–21
Representation of Data on Nine-Track Tape with Even Parity

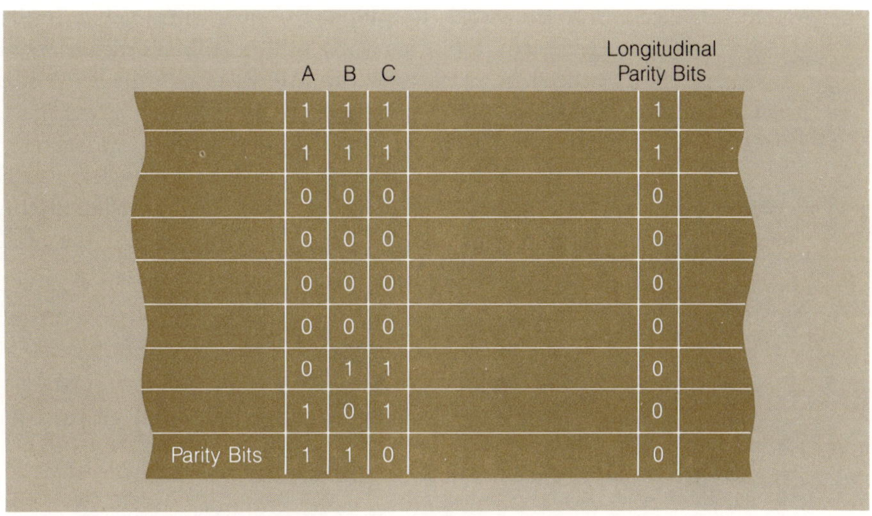

use upper and lower-case letters, we must expand to the nine-track tape version, which can accommodate a character set of 2^8 or 256 different characters.

Parity. The "extra" bits used as parity bits are used in the following way. Let us assume we are working with a machine that has been designed under the convention of *even parity.* (Note: there are also machines designed for *odd parity.*) Our even parity tape drive expects always to find an even number of bits turned on in each cross-sectional column (frame) on the tape and in each longitudinal row (track) if longitudinal parity checking is provided. If the representation of a character in a given column results in an odd number of bits being turned on, the parity bit will be turned on to make the total number of ON bits an even number (see Figure 7–21).

The parity bit at the end of a row is similarly used to ensure that an even number of ON bits exists in every row. If any bit reverses from ON to OFF (or vice versa) during storage of the tape or exposure to a magnetic field, the parity checking mechanism will signal when the tape is read that errors might be present in the data.

Blocking. Most programmers began their careers writing programs in a punched card environment, where a record were the size of the punched card (eighty characters). If that record size were maintained in using magnetic tape, we would find that we have very small slices of data on the tape separated by a segment of blank tape to allow the tape drive room to start and stop between records. The blank segments are gaps in the tape as seen in Figure 7–22. In fact, if we use eighty-character data segments separated by gaps, most of the tape will be blank. To increase the density of data on the tape, we group together several eighty-character records called blocks. Now the tape shows (refer to Figure 7–23) blocks of data and **interblock gaps (IBGs),** sometimes referred to as **inter-record gaps (IRGs).**

With magnetic tape there is no particular reason why the size of a record should be restricted to eighty characters. Instead, the record size is to be determined by the amount of data to be stored there. A single, complete record as it is known to the programmer is a **logical record,** a record the program logic has been written to accommodate. The actual, physical parameters of storage on any particular device defines a **physical record.** Blocking of data on the tape, for example, gives rise to several logical records stored in a single physical record, the data stored between two IBGs.

While the advantage of blocking is the increased density of data on the tape, there is a disadvantage. The records in the data file will need to

Figure 7–22
Unblocked Tape

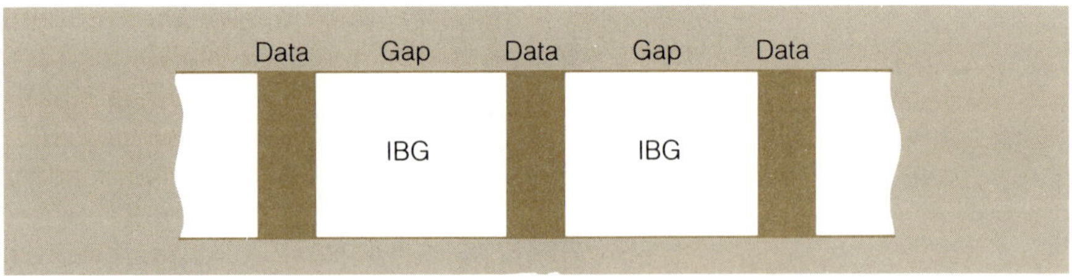

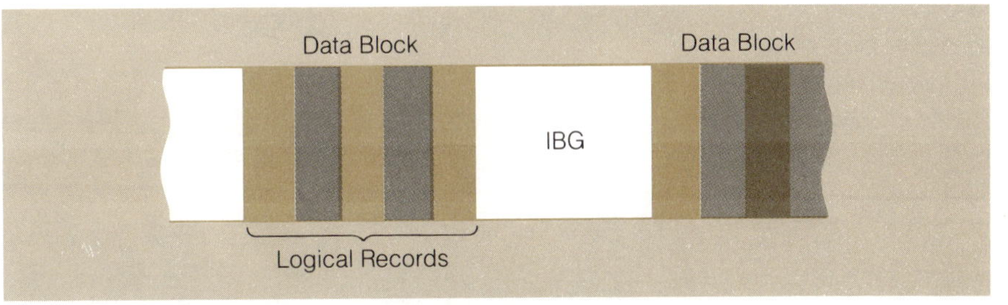

Figure 7–23
Blocked Tape

undergo blocking (into physical records) when written onto the tape and unblocking (into logical records) when read from the tape. The blocking and unblocking operations are performed by utility programs designed for that purpose and provided as part of the system's software. Blocking and unblocking operations result in a slight loss in processing efficiency in order to make better use of the storage medium. The common data densities for magnetic tape are 1,600 and 6,250 bits per inch (per track). Since the tape has enough tracks to record a byte in each frame, 6,250 bits per inch (per track) is effectively 6,250 bytes per inch. New developments in magnetic tape drives will allow tapes to be read completely, without stopping, increasing even further the density of data on the tape as IBGs are eliminated. The rates of transfer of data from magnetic tape can be as high as several hundred thousand characters per second.

Magnetic Disks

The technologies of magnetic disks and magnetic tapes are very similar as far as encoding and storing the data is concerned. The medium itself has a vastly different physical appearance, and the hardware itself is quite different. The machine which allows the computer system to use magnetic disk files for secondary storage is called a **disk drive.**

Disks and disk drives are available in a wide range of sizes. Disks may be as small as three inches in diameter or as large as thirty-six inches, perhaps even larger. They are available as very thin, single disks called **floppy disks** (or **diskettes**) or as assemblies of several rigid disks on a common axis (spindle) called **disk packs.** Disk drives may be designed to allow for routine removal and insertion of the disk packs or the disk pack may be fixed in place. A disk drive with removable disks (shown in Figure 7–24) would allow a user to use many different files of data stored on different disk packs in the same disk drive, although no two could be used at the same time. As you might imagine, however, the design tolerances are such that more trouble-free performance can be expected from disk drives with fixed disks.

Data are written onto the disks or read from them with a read/write head. The disks rotate at a high rate of speed with the read/write head suspended on a thin film of air just off the disk surface. Figure 7–25 illustrates just how clean the disk environment must be. The cleanliness of the disk environment is so important that it has spawned the development of a new

Figure 7–24 Magnetic Disk Drive with Removable Disk Packs

concept in disk drives known as the Winchester Disk, which features disks and read/write heads in a factory-sealed disk pack (see Figure 7–26). The clearance between the disk surface and the read/write head is so very small that even very small particles could cause the head to scratch the surface of the disk and destroy its storage capabilities. Data on the disks are contained in tracks. Most disk drives are built with movable heads so that they can be moved to each track as needed (see Figures 7–27). A few disk drives are built with a set of fixed heads, one for each track.

Data are stored on magnetic disks using VTOC (Volume Table of Contents) directories or indexes which list the actual, physical location of the data files. It is this feature in conjunction with the ability to locate a read/write head above the appropriate track quickly which supports direct (random) access files. Data storage is illustrated in Figure 7–28.

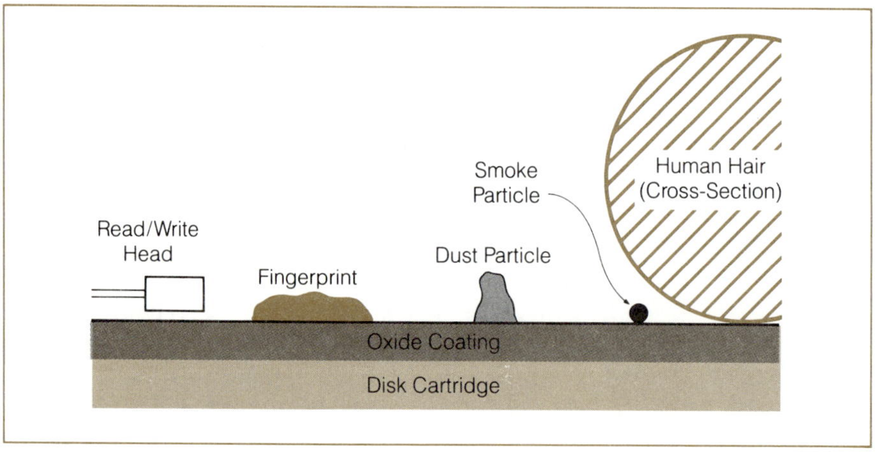

Figure 7–25 Particle Sizes in the Disk Environment

Figure 7–26 Winchester Disk Drive Unit

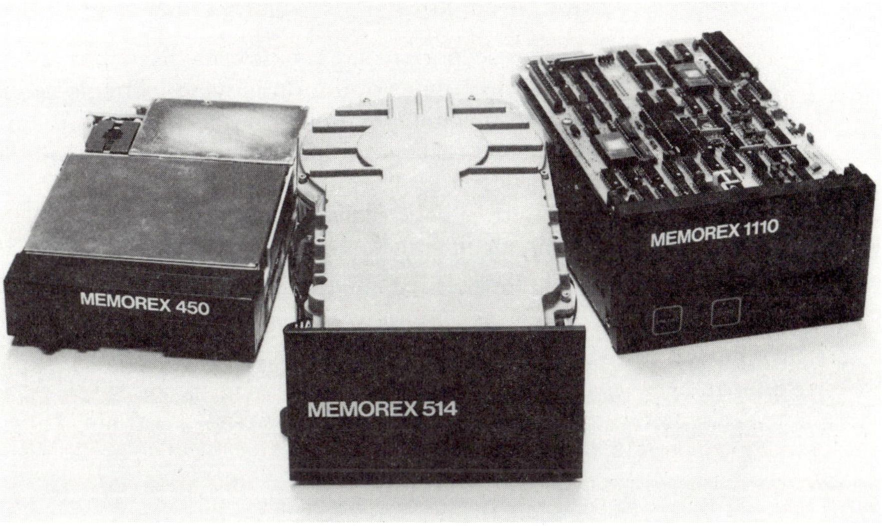

Figure 7–27 Magnetic Disks

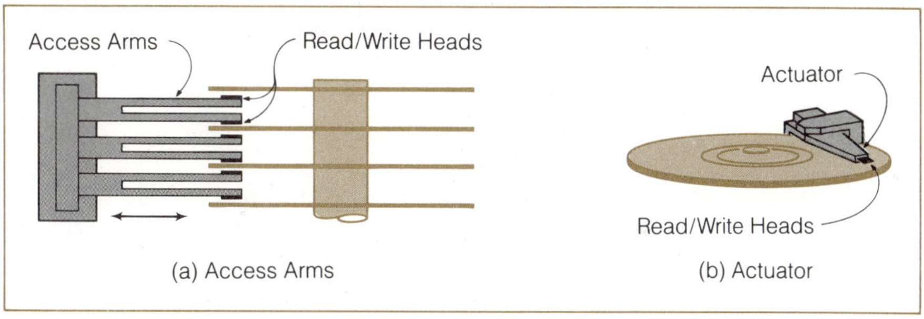

Figure 7–28 Data Storage on Magnetic Disk

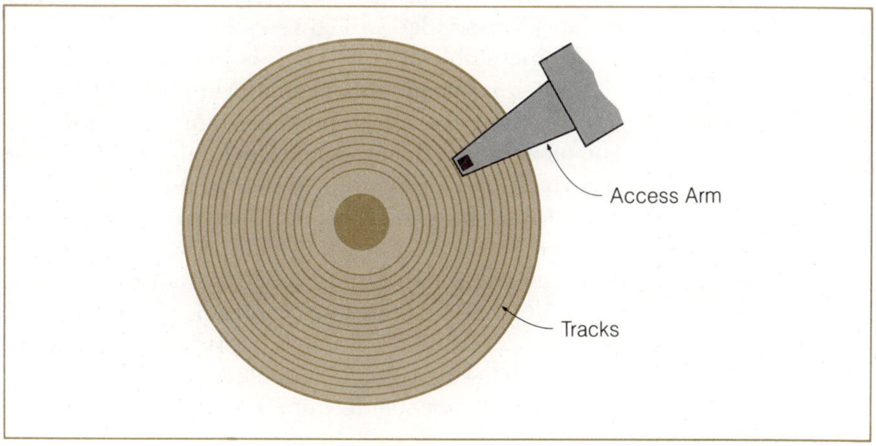

Other Devices

The other secondary storage devices discussed are not so prevalent that a thorough treatment of the underlying technologies is important. Data are stored on magnetic drums in much the same manner as they are stored on magnetic disks. Magnetic drum drives virtually always have fixed, rotating drums and fixed read/write heads.

The data cell and mass storage devices utilize the technology of magnetic tape enhanced with some additional mechanical devices to allow for mechanized access to a large volume of tape.

Challenge Update

The advantages and disadvantages of various data storage devices and media could now be listed.

Newest Developments

There is perhaps more exciting research and development work being done in the field of secondary storage devices than in any other. It is impossible to predict which devices will survive the rigors of cost-effective performance demanded by the market for secondary storage devices. A few of the competing developments are examined next. Comparison data are provided in Table 7–1.

Magnetic Bubbles

Virtually any explanation of the technology of magnetic bubbles will lead the student to disbelieve that such a device actually exists. A "bubble" is really a magnetic domain which is forced into circular form by a magnetic field. It is a lot like the magnetized spots we have discussed on magnetic tape. The difference is, these bubbles are generated in patterns, bubbles and non-bubbles, giving us ON bits and OFF bits. These bubbles are generated to form a particular pattern and are moved around a closed loop to preserve that pattern, which is detected by a reading device. Thus data can be stored in each bubble memory unit. A highly magnified view of bubble memory is provided in Figure 7–29.

The incredible characteristic is that designers are able to store 25 million bits per square inch on a magnetic bubble chip. That means we could store about 100 pages of a telephone directory on a chip smaller than a thumbnail. The technology of magnetic bubbles also offers no moving parts and memory which retains the data stored in it even if the electric power supply is interrupted. Bubble memories also have very good mechanical shock resistance, so they make good memories for portable terminals. Although at one time it appeared that bubble memories were headed for a large share of the market in computer memories, current estimates are much less optimistic. A number of manufacturers have abandoned their bubble memory products as too costly. Bubble memories do, however, seem well-suited for service in portable terminals.

Table 7–1 *Comparison of Data Storage Systems*

Type	Capacity (Bits)	Cost/Bit (Cents)	Media Cost	System Cost	Data Rate (bits/s)	Mean Retrieval Time (Seconds)	Lifetime	Erasable
Bubble Memory	8×10^6	5×10^{-2}	$4000	None	8×10^5	0.040	Long	Yes
Paper Card	640	6×10^{-4}	0.4¢/card	$13,000	1600	Slow	Depends on handling	No
Magnetic Disk (Winchester type, fixed)	4.5×10^9	3×10^{-5} (approx.)	$1500 (approx.)	$27,000	1.5×10^7	0.03	2–3 years	Yes
Magnetic Disk, Rigid, Removable (Single 8-Inch Disk)	1.28×10^8	5×10^{-5}	$60	$6000	9.6×10^6	0.055	2–3 years	Yes
Magnetic Tape, IBM 3850 Mass Storage System	3.7×10^{12}	5×10^{-6}	$188,000	$2.4 million	7×10^6	16	2–3 years	Yes
Magnetic tape, 2400-foot reel at 6250 Bits/Inch	1.4×10^9	1×10^{-6}	$16	$20,000	10×10^7	60	2–3 years	Yes
Microfiche (Digital Equivalent)	10^7	2×10^{-6}	20¢	Over $50,000	Not applicable	Slow	Long	No
Philips Optical Disc*	2×10^{10}	5×10^{-8}	$10	$10,000	$5–10 \times 10^6$	0.1–0.5	Over 10 years	No
Philips Optical Disc Pack*	10^{12}	1.5×10^{-8}	$150	$200,000	$2–5 \times 10^7$	0.05–0.1	Over 10 years	No
Philips Optical Jukebox*	2×10^{14}	5×10^{-9}	1000 discs @ $10 each	$200,000	$2–5 \times 10^7$	3	Over 10 years	No
RCA Optical Disc*	10^{11}	10^{-8}	$10	?	5×10^7	0.5	Over 10 years	No
RCA Optical Jukebox*	10^{14}	10^{-8}	1000 discs @ $10 each	?	5×10^7	3	Over 10 Years	No

*Data for these systems are projected.

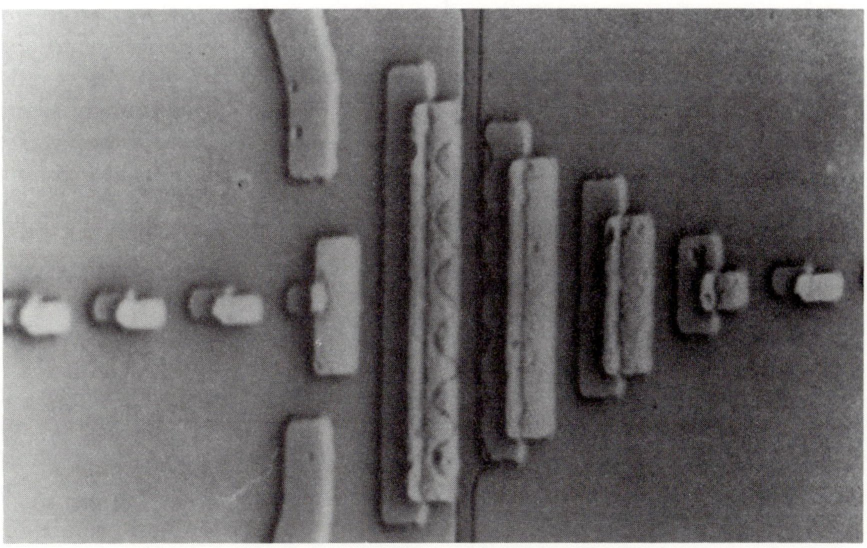

Figure 7–29
Magnified View of Bubble Memory

Semiconductor Memories

The vacuum tubes of days gone by have given way to transistors, the basis for solid-state electronic design. The transistor is a semiconductor device. Integrated circuits contain numerous transistor circuits, and the integration of these circuits has become very large in scale. Very large scale integration (VLSI) techniques are currently the basis for the design of many of the computer's logic circuits.

This technology can also be used to produce semiconductor memories. The 64,000 bit chip was popular in the early 1980s. At the same time, 256,000 bit chips were working their way from the research and development laboratory into production, and 512,000 bit chips were under development. IBM produced an experimental version of a 1 million bit random-access memory chip in 1984. Although there are physical limits to the number of circuits which can reside on a single chip, we seem not yet to be constrained by those limits. One disadvantage of semiconductor memories is that a loss of electrical power causes the data in the memory to be lost.

Optical Disk/Laser Memories

The technology of optical disk/laser memories is essentially the same technology which gives us videodiscs. A videodisc player has information, for example, a movie, embedded in tracks on the disks prior to its sale. A laser beam in the home videodisc player reads the information and generates the pictures we are able to see on the accompanying television screen. The information-storing capacity of a single videodisc is impressive. Under laboratory conditions a storage density sufficient to store the entire Encyclopaedia Brittannica on a single disk has been demonstrated. An optical disk is pictured in Figure 7–30.

The optical disk storage system uses a disk on which the laser records information for long-term storage. Disks cannot, in their most common implementation, be erased and reused; they will allow only one recording of data and will be thereafter used in read-only mode. The recording process uses a laser to change the reflective characteristics of a metallic layer (tellurium) sandwiched between two plastic outer disks. The laser either burns a hole, causes bubbles to form, or otherwise alters the metallic surface to form binary patterns for the recording of data. An erasable optical disk has been announced by Matsushita Electric Industrial Company, Ltd., but little is known of the commercial viability of such a product. Optical Data Inc., of the United States is working on an erasable optical disk which uses dyes and polymers instead of a metallic substrate.

As long-term storage devices, they will be much less expensive than the magnetic media. They can be used to store images and voice as well as data. The optical disk offers extremely high recording densities; for example, a single optical disk can store as much information as 12,500 floppy disks. An optical disk unit made by Storage Technology can store approximately 2 million typed, double-spaced pages of information on a single fourteen-

Figure 7–30 An Optical Data Disk

inch disk.[1] Optical disks also offer a much longer shelf life than magnetic media.

The Library of Congress in Washington, D. C., uses an optical disk system supplied by Xerox Electro-Optical Systems to provide archival storage from which convenient document retrieval is possible. Optical disk systems provide a very efficient means of long-term, archival storage, and their popularity in that service should increase significantly in the future.

Charge-Coupled Devices

The charge-coupled device, to the layman, is a lot like the semiconductor device. The charges are in the form of electrons (for one state) and "holes" (for the other). The charges are moved about to form the patterns necessary to record data. This technology provides potentially high storage densities and low cost per bit stored. Television cameras in space probes will integrate charge-coupled devices with the technology of light sensing to produce digital signals to be sent to earth for decoding and reconstruction.

Electron-Beam Accessed Memory

Electron-beam accessed memory technology may push the storage density to values even greater than those attained with videodiscs. One of the factors

1. "Optical Memory Units Boost Computer Storage," *High Technology*, February 1984, p. 12.

limiting the density of data stored on a videodisc is the wavelength of the light used to detect it. That is, the wavelength of the light used to "read" or store the positions of two bits eventually limits how close together those two bits can be. The shorter the wavelength, the closer together the bits can be placed. Electron beams will give greater densities than lasers.

Recent advances in the technology of storing data on magnetic media indicate that competition will continue to provide alternatives in the hierarchy of secondary storage devices. Magnetic disks, under the conventional technology, use ferro-magnetic coatings which contain slivers of iron oxide oriented in a horizontal plane to form the tiny magnets by which data patterns are formed. The coating material contains epoxy binders, to bind the coating to the aluminum substrate, so the effective volume of magnetic material is reduced significantly. The result is a lowering of the density of data which can be stored on the disk.

A computing technology known as **thin film** yields a disk with a ferro-magnetic surface applied by plating or sputtering techniques. The result is a surface with more magnets, which leads to higher data densities. Thin film read/write heads allow closer tolerances between the head and the surface of the disk so that even greater data densities are possible. The thin film principle can be used in the design of the head, the disk, or both. Recording densities as great as 1,200 tracks per inch and 25,000 bits per inch have been achieved in the laboratory with thin-film techniques.

In an even newer development, known as **vertical** or **perpendicular recording,** the tiny magnets are formed so that they, in effect, stand on end in a crystalline structure made of cobalt and chrome. This technology is expected to yield, for example, a 5¼-inch floppy disk capable of storing 10 million characters. This technology has yielded, in the laboratory, storage densities as great as 100,000 bits per inch. A comparative illustration of horizontal versus vertical magnetic recording is shown in Figure 7–31.

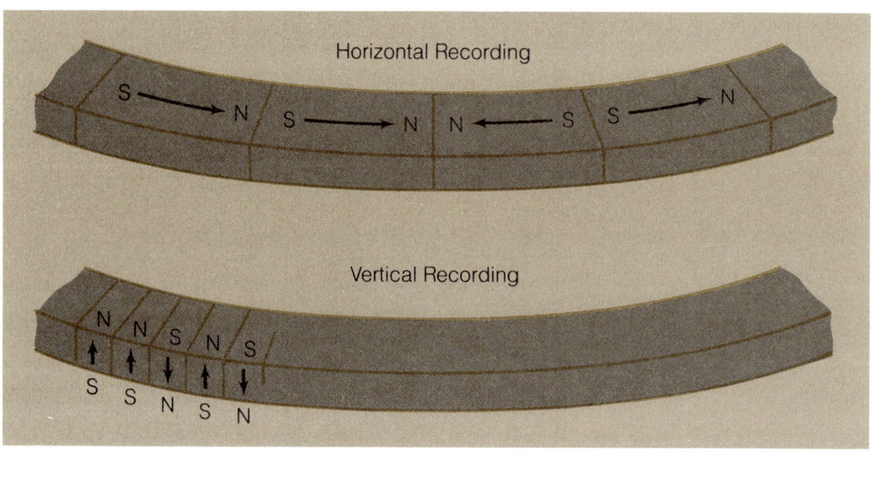

Figure 7–31
Comparison of Horizontal v. Vertical Magnetic Recording

COMPUTING CHALLENGE: *A Final Note*

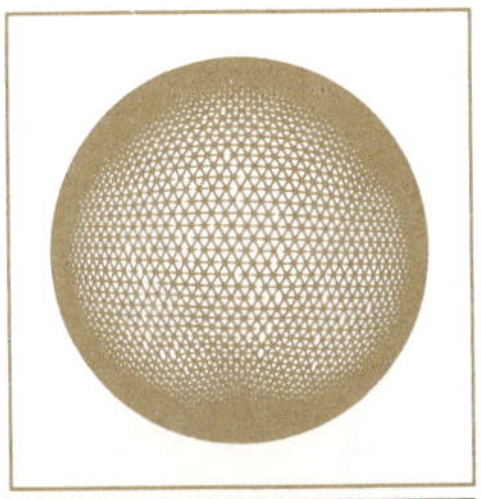

We return now to the problem facing Ms. Grender in the Alumni Relations Office of PSU. She wants to convert her manual files to computerized files, a process which is definitely made easier by the fact that computing services are currently available to her from the university's computer center. She is currently considering the conversion of these four applications:

1. *Sending a funds solicitation to all the alumni in the file.*
2. *Changing the address of an alumnus or alumna.*
3. *Recording a contribution made by an alumnus or alumna.*
4. *Sending an announcement to all alumni living in a particular geographic location, telling them of an upcoming visit by the university's president.*

How would each of these operations be carried out using punched cards, magnetic tape, and magnetic disks?

What data items are likely to be in each record in the alumni file?

Categorize each of the above applications according to its need for on-line data entry, program storage, and output files.

What can we say about the influence of file structure on each of the above operations?

SUMMARY

- Organizations have rather obvious needs for storing data and information over time, and there are many means for accomplishing these needs.
- While many collections of records are currently recorded on paper and stored in file cabinets, an increasing number are stored within computer systems where they can be quickly retrieved when needed.
- Computer programs are written to process a specific set of data into information using particular data files custom-designed to fit particular applications.
- Input files, programs, and output files may be stored either on-line, where they are immediately accessible, or off-line, where human intervention is necessary to accessibility.
- Routine, infrequent processing tasks would most efficiently have off-line programs and files.
- Applications requiring frequent, quick responses are most efficiently processed through the use of on-line programs and files.
- A program and its owned, custom-designed files provide a very efficient combination.

- Data files are stored according to one of several structures, either in sequential, random (direct), indexed sequential, or inverted files.
- The factors which determine the storage method used for a particular application are a function of the nature of the application itself, for example, the type and frequency of access desired, the speed of the data retrieval required, and cost.
- The most common file storage media for computer systems are magnetic tape and magnetic disk.
- Magnetic tape is used most efficiently only for sequential files, while magnetic disks allow any of the data storage methods to be used.
- Large, mass storage devices provide large storage capacities but are primarily used in support of magnetic disk units.
- The hierarchy of secondary storage devices offers many choices in which speed of access is, in general, traded off against the cost of the device.
- Significant improvements in data storage densities for magnetic media have been realized through thin-film and vertical recording techniques.
- Research on new technologies indicates that users will continue to have a variety of storage devices from which to choose, while costs will continue to decline.
- Videodiscs offer impressive capabilities for the long-term storage of data, including voice and graphics.

CASE: Computers and Stock Transactions

The world of corporate finance is a complex and exciting one. On the one hand, corporate financial officers are trying to bring together enough capital to sustain the activities of the business plan. Two important sources of funds for corporate investment are investment bankers and the individual buyers and sellers of corporate stock. One of the functions of an investment banker is to buy corporate stocks and bonds in large quantities and sell them to individual investors in smaller lots.

Chicago's Harris Trust and Savings Bank acts as a liaison between investment bankers and the buyers and sellers of stock. The bank handles approximately $20 million of stock transfers on any normal day of business. These transfers must be processed rapidly because a delay affects both the seller and the investor's monetary return. Additionally, strict laws govern the amount of time that can elapse before stock transfers are recorded.

Many corporations also use Harris to handle the various details associated with stocks that they prefer not to handle themselves. The Corporate Agencies Administration Division of Harris Bank provides stock acquisition and transfer services for 137 major corporations. There are significant information flows between a corporation and its stockholders which must be properly managed. For example, dividends must be paid, financial statements must be distributed, and ballots which exercise the stockholders' voting rights must be distributed and collected. The division also counts proxy votes for corporate elections.

These data processing chores are accomplished on two Hewlett-Packard HP3000 minicomputers. The HPs store about 400,000 stock owners' records. Many stockholders choose to automatically reinvest their dividends, which results in the maintenance by Harris of approximately 25,000 dividend reinvestment holders' records. The computer systems also produce dividend checks and proxy voting cards, which are sent to investors.

James Rouch, vice president of the division, gives the computers credit for the bank's ability to meet the government's time requirement on transfers and, at the same time, reduce operating costs. Customers are provided with timely data, and the bank no longer spends excessive overtime hours trying to meet government deadlines. With this system the bank provides valuable data processing services to investment bankers, corporations, and individual stockholders.

"Computers in Banking; Aid to Corporations," *Infosystems*, February 1982, p. 78.

Questions for the Case

1. What information does the bank probably keep in each stock owner's record?
2. How many characters per record are required for the information specified in question 1?
3. How many characters would be in the entire file of 400,000 records?
4. For quick response to individual inquiries would the stock owners' file be a sequential file or a direct access file?

DISCUSSION QUESTIONS AND EXERCISES

1. List several common data processing tasks which take place within organizations. If those tasks were to be done by a computer system, for which would the input files need to be stored on-line? For which would the programs need to be stored on-line? For which would the output files need to be stored on-line?
2. List several data processing tasks which are common to large organizations. For which would sequential files seem to be adequate? Which would seem to require direct access files?
3. Discuss the manner in which a manager must decide which file structure is appropriate for a given application.
4. Explain the shortcomings of a sequential file on magnetic tape as a secondary storage choice to support an airlines reservation system.
5. Compare the off-line storage capabilities provided by punched cards with those provided by magnetic tape.
6. Compare the on-line storage capabilities provided by magnetic disk with those provided by mass storage devices.
7. Discuss the manner in which a manager must decide which file storage medium is appropriate for a given application.

8. Discuss the efficiency of an environment in which each program owns its separate set of files.

9. Discuss the inefficiencies associated with the environment in which each program owns its separate set of files.

10. Describe an application for which an inverted file structure would be a good choice. Identify the key and attributes of the original file. Identify the key and attributes of the inverted file.

11. For what types of storage will optical disks be best utilized? Give some examples.

12. Discuss the trends in magnetic storage media with respect to data densities and cost.

13. How does real time differ from on-line?

14. When interviewed with respect to the needs of a particular data processing application, managers almost always indicate the application would be better served by on-line files. Why do you suppose they respond this way? What counterarguments could be made?

15. An old master file is *not* usually erased immediately after a transaction file has been used to update it. Why?

ADDITIONAL READINGS

Baron, Robert J., and Shapiro, Linda G. *Data Structures and Their Implementation.* New York: Van Nostrand Reinhold, 1980.

Eadie, Donald. *A User's Guide to Computer Peripherals.* Englewood Cliffs, N.J.: Prentice-Hall, 1982.

Flores, Ivan. *Data Structure and Management.* Englewood Cliffs, N.J.: Prentice-Hall, 1970.

Free, G. "Magnetic Bubbles—New Designs Shrink Computer Memories." *Popular Science,* October 1979, pp. 49–50ff.

Givonè, Donald D., and Roesser, Robert P. *Microprocessors/Microcomputers: An Introduction.* New York: McGraw-Hill, 1980.

Goldstein, Charles M. "Optical Disk Technology and Information." *Science,* February 1982, pp. 862–868.

Hecht, Jeff. "Lasers Store a Wealth of Data." *High Technology,* May/June, 1982, pp. 60–67.

Horowitz, Ellis, and Sahni, Sarta J. *Fundamentals of Data Structures.* Potomac, Maryland: Computer Science Press, 1978.

Posa, John G. "Memory Makers Try Crossbreeding." *High Technology,* August 1983, pp. 43–50.

Solomon, Les, and Veit, Stan, "Data Storage in a Nutshell." *Computers and Electronics,* July 1983, pp. 36–46.

Trifari, John. "Computer Disks: Capacity Soars, Costs Plummet." *High Technology,* January 1983, pp. 47–53.

"Videodisc." *Business Week,* July 7, 1980, pp. 78–81.

8

Data Storage: Data Base Management Systems

CHAPTER PREVIEW

As seen in Chapter 7, an applications program or set of applications programs and the file of data used by those programs make an efficient data processing combination. However, as more and more applications programs are developed, each with its own data file, the potential for several problems arises. Large amounts of data may be common to several files, and multiple copies of the same data lead to excessive data entry, storage, and maintenance costs.

Several other problems arise. Numerous versions of essentially the same information present problems of consistency; that is, how can it be assured that all versions are the same? Does an activity which changes a data item in one version provide for the same change in all versions?

Security and control are also important. With numerous files and versions of files on the system, security is potentially a problem. All versions of the file must be protected and use of them must be controlled in order to provide comprehensive security.

The efficient combination of a program with its "owned" files may eventually lead to the inefficiencies associated with duplication, lack of consistency, poor security, and lack of control. Improved data management techniques are necessary to minimize the negative effects of these problems. This chapter will discuss an approach to data management known as data base management. Some of the problems associated with data management are illustrated in the case of the mail order western wear business described in the Computing Challenge below.

COMPUTING CHALLENGE: *Data Management in a Mail Order Setting*

Webster's Western Wear, Inc. (WWW), has been in the business of selling western wear and accessories by mail order for about fifteen years and has recently expanded its retail outlets from its original location in Dry Canyon, Arizona, to a current twelve locations nationwide. Each year the company mails catalogs to approximately a million potential customers.

Each year WWW processes about 500,000 mail orders for consumer goods, from shoestrings at 50 cents to silver belt buckles at $1,000. Nationwide it employs about 700 people, approximately 150 of whom work in the mail-order department in Dry Canyon.

Early in the firm's history, the processing of mail orders was handled manually. The orders were few enough and the warehouse small enough that an order picker could quickly tell whether or not the desired order was in stock. As the business grew, one function after another was gradually moved to a computer. The first application converted to the computer was the accounts receivable system so that close track could be kept of the payments made by or expected from customers.

Gradually, the processing of the arriving orders became too large a job to handle manually, so the order entry application and its files were next converted to computerized form. Just recently, the purchasing people converted the purchase order/warehouse receipt application to the computer, and additional files were created.

The data processing manager is currently reviewing a proposal to implement a computerized inventory control system. If an inventory control system is designed with its own set of files, he believes some problems might arise.

In addition, middle- and upper-level managers at WWW are beginning to look to the data processing system as a source of information in support of their decision-making activities. They would like to have management reports generated from the huge collection of data. In addition, they would like to be able to gain inquiry access to the data maintained within the system.

The problems faced by WWW's data processing manager are typical of those faced by many such managers. A point is reached where the data entry, storage, data integrity, and maintenance costs cause people to explore alternatives to the environment in which data files are "owned" by their applications. Perhaps improvements can be gained by consolidating the files into a larger collection of data; one which would serve many applications. Questions do, however, arise. For example, what functions can be provided by a data base management system (DBMS)? What are the relative advantages and disadvantages of a DBMS? Which type of DBMS data structure would best serve the organization's applications?

We thus arrive at the subject matter of this chapter—the management of data through data base management systems (DBMSs). After successful completion of this chapter, the student should be able to:

1. *Discuss the comparative advantages and disadvantages of the data base management environment comparative to those of data files "owned" by application programs.*

2. *List the data processing capabilities made available through a DBMS.*
3. *Describe the most common data structures used by DBMSs.*
4. *Explain how a data base processor might improve the operation of a DBMS.*

HISTORICAL PERSPECTIVE

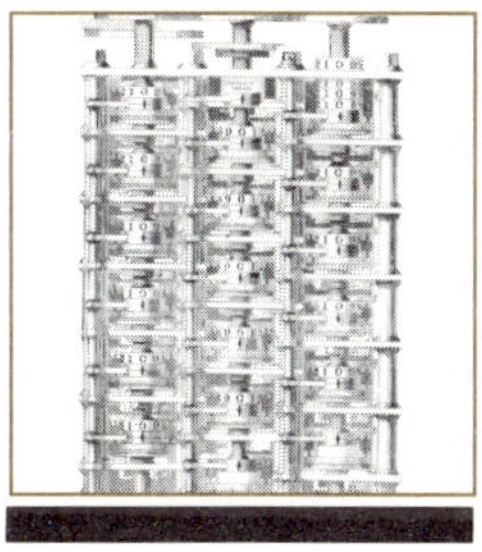

In a sense, Chapter 7 itself provides the historical perspective for this chapter. Applications program/data file combinations preceded the development of DBMSs and are, therefore, part of their history.

Computer applications experts were quick to recognize that the ownership of unique files by each applications program could lead to an excessive amount of duplication of data storage. Efforts were then quickly undertaken to combine the data needed by an organization into large data bases in order to save storage space and duplicated effort in data entry and data maintenance operations. As we shall see in this chapter, data base management software provides, among other benefits, potential savings of storage space and reduced duplication in data entry and data maintenance operations.

The first DBMS of any significance was I-D-S, developed at General Electric in 1964 by a group led by Charles Bachman. Efforts to develop standards for DBMSs began with CODASYL (*CO*nferences of *DA*ta *SY*stems *L*anguages) in 1968. Commercial DBMS software was first available in the early 1970s.

The move to incorporate very large collections of the firm's data into a totally integrated data base led, in many cases, to disaster. The job was too big; it could not be accomplished. If it had been accomplished, the demands on the system's resources to manage that large a collection of data would have been excessive.

We do not know a lot about the optimum size for a data base. Too small (separate files for each application) and too large (a totally integrated data base) have, by trial and error, been found to be less than optimum. We are still working in the middle ground, which is the subject of this chapter.

Concepts: Data Bases and Files Compared

Application Programs and Files

Chapter 7 discussed data input files which were used by applications programs. The files were designed as the applications programs using them were written, or the applications programs were written to use a data file which already existed. In either case, the programs were written with full

"The machine then selects the likely equations from a complicated pattern of theoretical probables. It calculates these, and the correct answer is printed on a card. Then our Miss Swenson files them God knows where, and we can never find the damn things again."

recognition of the manner in which the file was structured. The programs "knew" what kind of records were in the file, which data items were contained in each record, and in which field the data items were stored. The data file was described as being "owned" by the particular programs which used it.

To illustrate, consider the payroll application shown in Figure 8–1. The payroll program knows where in the record to find each data item. If the order of data items in the data file were changed, or if data items were added to or deleted from the record, the program itself would have to be changed to reflect the change in the record.

Consider another application which provides managers with information about the types of skills possessed by the employees, or the jobs within the organization on which individual employees have been trained. This program and a record from its data file are shown in Figure 8–2. Again, any change in the contents of a record, or the order of the data items in the record, will require a change in the applications program itself.

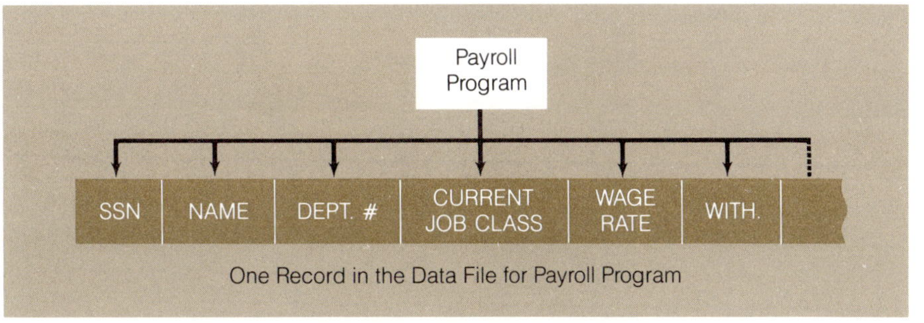

Figure 8–1 One Applications Program and Its Data File

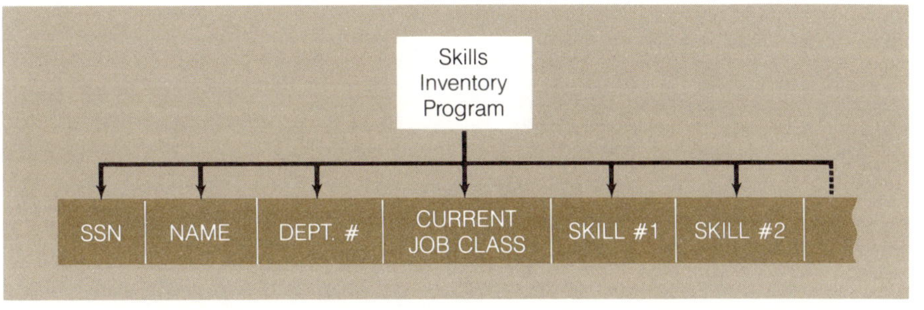

Figure 8–2 Another Applications Program and Its Data File

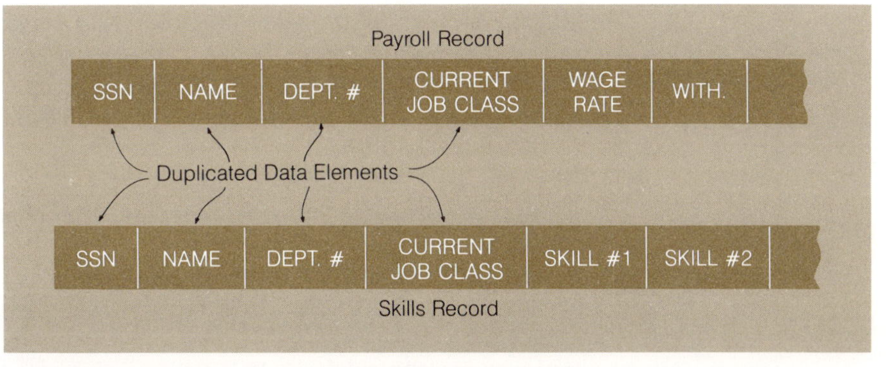

Figure 8–3 Comparison of Payroll Record and Skills Inventory Record

At some point, a bright programmer/analyst will compare the two data files and discover that a significant duplication exists between them (see Figure 8–3). This duplication, or redundancy, occurs not only in terms of space occupied on the data storage medium (e.g., magnetic tape or magnetic disk) but also in terms of the entry of the data into the systems and the maintenance of that data. A good programmer/analyst would be tempted to take steps to reduce this redundancy. The programmer might combine the two data files into one new, larger data file which would be shared by the two applications programs, as shown in Figure 8–4.

Since a record in the newly created file contains data items which did not appear in either of the original files, each of the applications programs will have to be modified to account for the changes. The modifications

Figure 8–4 A Record in the New, Shared Data File

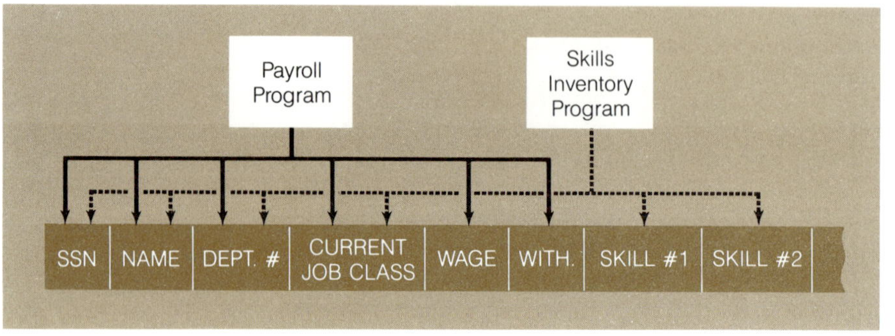

which must be made to the existing programs may be very slight or quite extensive, depending upon the program itself. Experience has shown that even slight changes in programs can yield unexpected results. Slight changes often lead to a great deal of program maintenance work.

Someone interested in saving file space may then find another applications program whose data file duplicates a portion of the data stored in the newly combined payroll/skills inventory data file. Or it could be that someone wants to develop a new application which could use the payroll/skills inventory data file if only a few data items could be changed or added to the records now in the file. Another consolidation would result in changing the data file by adding the new data items to the records, and then modifying once again the payroll program and the skills inventory program to reflect the changes.

Notice, in this example and quite often in practice, as new applications are developed to share existing data files, two events occur:

1. The data files themselves are changed.
2. The programs using those data files must be changed.

The alternative to making these two sets of changes is to design a new data file for the new application, which has the disadvantages of the redundancies discussed earlier.

In the environment in which applications programs "own" data files, the cost of developing a new application is significantly increased by the necessity of either making the required changes or developing a new file. DBMSs offer capabilities which make it easier to develop new applications and offer many other advantages as well. We turn now to a discussion of data base management systems.

The Role of a DBMS

It is easy to conceptualize a DBMS by extending the preceding discussion about applications programs and their files. What we would like to do is provide an integration of the data in several data files, which we will call a **data base,** in such a way that the integrated collection of data is made available to a variety of applications programs. Availability must be accom-

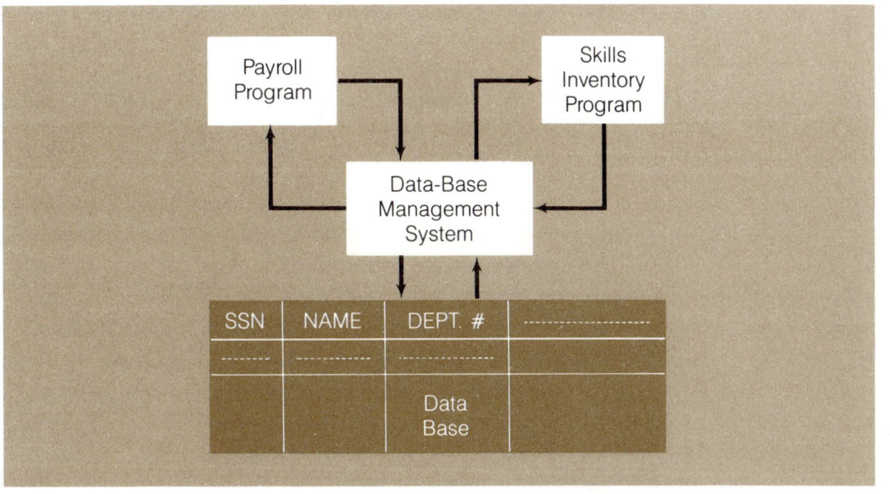

Figure 8–5 DBMS Software

plished without the problems associated with rewriting each applications program that uses the data when the contents of the data base change.

We accomplish this by providing a set of programs which will stand between the applications programs and the data base, as represented in Figure 8–5. These programs will manage the data base. In a sense, an applications program will request that the DBMS provide it with the data it requires to do its work. The DBMS fulfills this request, providing, of course, the data is in the data base and the applications program has correctly issued its request. The development of a new application means that the DBMS will see a new request for data, and it may have to add new data items to the data base in order to honor the new request. The system must be designed so that existing applications are unaffected by this new addition.

If new application programs can be developed in a DBMS environment without causing changes to be made in existing programs, the total work required to develop new applications will have been significantly reduced. This is one of the benefits of a DBMS. It offers a variety of other services, as we shall see in the next section.

The Advantages of a DBMS Environment

The software which is required to implement a DBMS is reasonably expensive in itself, to say nothing of the sizeable organizational effort which is needed in order to define and enter the data to put the system into operation. A number of DBMSs are available commercially for a wide variety of computer systems. A thorough analysis of the costs and benefits of the system should be undertaken in support of the decision to acquire a DBMS. Let us identify some of the benefits a company would expect to gain by moving to the DBMS environment.

Reduced Duplication. One of the potential benefits, which is relatively easy to measure, is the *reduced data storage space requirements* which result from a reduction in data redundancy. Elimination or reduction of the duplicated data will reduce data storage requirements. Space is required for storage of the DBMS software itself, and this space should not be overlooked in the analysis.

A DBMS also uses a significant amount of storage space to maintain the numerous relationships needed between the various data elements. In ordinary files these relationships are represented by the location of fields and the intimate knowledge a program has of its files. The nature of this relationship between a program and its files contributes to favorable processing efficiencies. These same efficiencies are not, in general, available to a DBMS because the DBMS must maintain and store the data relationships required of all programs which use the data base. The savings in reduced storage space are, therefore, somewhat less than expected from a cursory analysis of file duplication.

We can also expect a *reduced load in data entry operations* and *data maintenance operations* as a result of the reduction in data redundancy. The data entry operation, as was discussed, is time consuming, costly, and a significant source of error. A reduction in the amount of data to be entered will reduce the costs associated with that activity. Costs associated with maintaining that data will also be reduced.

Consistency. The next benefit is not nearly as obvious as the previous two. We need a brief note from the short history of computing to help us understand the phenomenon of *consistency.*

Throughout the history of computing we have seen a multitude of manual data processing activities converted to computerized data processing activities. Many activities formerly performed by hand are now done through the use of computers. The transition from a manual to a computerized system raises many complex issues. The working environments of many people are often changed as a result of the introduction of computerized data processing.

Although it is not always the best thing to do, the "computerization" of a particular task is frequently accomplished by strictly automating the former manual process without regard for other, perhaps better, ways in which the same results could be achieved. Analysts typically study a particular part of someone's data processing activities and design a computerized system to accomplish the same functions. (Note: Often, as we shall see later, the analyst fails to make sufficient use of the workers', or users', expertise in completing the design.)

This particular design approach leads temporarily to two systems which perform the same task—one by manual means, the other by computerized means. Unless the old system was very bad, users tend to regard it as the *standard,* the minimum level to which the new system must be able to perform. In addition, the user of the system lacks the analyst's confidence in the ability of the new system to perform satisfactorily the functions of the old system. The manual system is, therefore, usually continued until any initial errors of the computerized system can be corrected. The user may be disturbed at the outset if the answers generated by the two systems are different. Analysts must understand that it is the user's perception of the performance of the new system which is important. The new system may, in fact, outperform the old one from the outset. It will not be accepted by the user until the user's perception changes to coincide with the facts.

As soon as any errors in the computerized version are found and corrected, use of the manual system is to be discontinued. The user—charged always with getting the job done with or without the computer—will often continue to keep data files manually, just in case. The result is that two sets of data often exist, one kept manually (secretly by the user) and the other generated by the computer. A request made by upper management for information in this kind of situation may lead to two different answers, one derived from the old data and one from the new. Many people simply do not trust the computer's ability to respond quickly and accurately because of problems in the past or their belief that the new system will not work correctly.

To further complicate matters, let us now imagine we have two different users in different parts of the organization. Now we might have two different computerized data files and two different manual data files. How can we expect to generate consistent answers to inquiries for information? Only when everyone shares a common database can we expect consistent answers. Workers at all levels can share access as illustrated in Figure 8–6.

The problems caused by the lack of consistent information in an organization are not to be written off as a fairy tale. When, for example, the marketing and production departments of a business get together to discuss past performances and future schedules, much will be said about the quality of each department's data if they were derived from separate data bases. The consistency gained by relying on a single source of data is an important benefit to be derived from a DBMS.

Figure 8–6
Managers Throughout the Organization Share Access to a Common Data Base

That is not to say that data in a files environment are always poor and that data in a DBMS are always good. In either environment there is ample opportunity for error.

Applications Development. We have already discussed the relative ease with which new applications can be developed under a DBMS as compared to the environment of data files owned by applications. When the data files are owned by application programs, the development of new applications often leads to the development of new files or modifications to existing files and existing programs. Such changes can be expensive and troublesome.

Even with a DBMS, the implementation of a new application may cause changes to the data base; for example, new data items may need to be added. These additions, however, would not interfere with existing applications. The data in a DBMS are independent from the individual applications. A new application will require only that the logic for a new program or a new set of programs be developed. The applications programmer can work on the program logic with full attention to it without having to develop a new file concurrently.

Centralized Control. There are other intangible benefits from using a DBMS. Some, for example, derive from the common practice in large organizations of appointing a person to fill the position of **data base administrator** or **data administrator,** someone who is responsible for the data base. The data base administrator helps decide which data will be contained in the data base and how that data will be related to other data in the data base. Centralization of this responsibility to the data base administrator's position yields improved data quality, security, and integrity.

Figure 8–7 Managers Gain Access to the Data Base Through the Use of Inquiry Languages

Many small organizations also make extensive use of DBMS software. The functions of data base administrator are usually assumed on a part-time basis by one of the managers of a small organization when the staff is not large enough to accommodate a full-time position. The administrator's role, however, is still to improve data quality, security, and integrity.

Availability to Users. Another benefit to be derived from a DBMS is the increased availability of an integrated collection of data to a wide variety of users. Provision is usually made in a DBMS for users to construct inquiries in a natural language so that many informational questions can be answered without the necessity of writing a program (see Figure 8–7). These inquiry languages are often **nonprocedural languages** because the user specifies only the type of answer desired, not the procedure by which the answer is to be determined. They are also referred to as **query languages.**

Data Security. Not all users who have access to the data in a DBMS are entitled to unrestrained access. Some data are confidential, and access to those data must be restricted to authorized users. The personal data of employees provide a good example of data to which access must be restricted.

Another security consideration surrounds the act of changing data items stored in the data base. Some people—managers making inquiries perhaps—should be entitled to see data but not allowed to change it. For example, the popularity of microcomputers in organizations allows users to retrieve data from the DBMS and analyze it with software which runs on the microcomputer. The DBMS can allow a copy to be moved to the smaller machine without allowing the user to change any of the values stored under control of the system itself.

The DBMS must, therefore, provide for the security of the data so that protection against unauthorized access and unauthorized modifications are provided. In some extreme cases, the threat to the integrity of the data arises as a result of a determined effort by an individual to destroy the data. The DBMS must provide a level of security adequate to prevent such abuses.

The Disadvantages of a Data Base Management Environment

Unfortunately, it cannot (truthfully) be said that the DBMS environment is the best solution for everyone's data management problems. There are some serious disadvantages to that environment, two of which are discussed here.

Cost. The first and most obvious disadvantage is cost. DBMSs are very expensive. There is, for example, a report that a government agency spent several million dollars toward, and then abandoned, an effort to provide a DBMS for management of their personnel records.

An organization has virtually the same choices with respect to the acquisition of a DBMS as it does with any computer software. Commercial packages are available which may be utilized, sometimes with modification, to provide the functions desired in the DBMS. Another alternative is to develop the software within the organization's own staff. This second strategy is rarely the better choice. Most, if not all, organizations would be much better off buying a commercially available DBMS package, which costs $30,000 to $150,000. An in-house design is likely to take longer, cost more, and perform less satisfactorily than a package from an outside vendor.

Another very significant cost is the cost of implementing the DBMS. The effort to move the data from individual files into the DBMS is a large one. Huge numbers of data elements must be defined and the logical relationships between data elements must be established as the data are entered.

In addition, extensive training of operators, programmers, and users is required so that the system can be used effectively. Training costs will add a significant amount to the overall cost of the DBMS.

System Overhead. The second major disadvantage of data base management software is its impact on the computer hardware itself. The set of programs which make up the DBMS must be executed by the hardware in order to perform the data management functions required by the users. As the data base grows in size, and as the range of functions performed by the DBMS increases, the amount of time the hardware must devote to executing the DBMS software itself becomes large. We can imagine, though it does not happen in practice, the system becoming so large that it spends all of its time maintaining the data base and has no time left for productive work. Execution of DBMS software could amount to 20 to 50 percent of the system's capacity, however.

The time the hardware must devote to maintenance of the system itself is known as **system overhead.** System overhead increases the larger the data base grows, the more complicated the data relationships become, and the more functions the DBMS software is expected to perform. The system overhead caused by the DBMS could require a move to larger hardware.

Challenge Update

The managers at Webster's Western Wear should now be able to discuss the relative advantages and disadvantages of DBMSs.

Data as a Managed Resource

As this book is being written, many organizations are beginning new attempts to improve the management of the organization's data. Some of these attempts are designed to improve the visibility of that part of the organization charged with collecting, processing, and storing the organization's information. Improved visibility is believed to lead to a more efficient and effective data processing department.

The focus of some of these attempts is to improve the productivity of the information processing departments. Productivity improvement efforts usually include attempts to increase the number of lines of program instructions written per day, attempts to decrease the amount of time correcting programming errors, and attempts to improve the ease with which programs can be maintained. Information management is becoming a function of increased importance to the organization.

We are without a clear set of principles which relate to the management of information as a resource. The philosophy is relatively simple. An organization should treat data (information) as any other resource. The money expended in the acquisition and processing of information should be treated as an investment. That investment should be maintained. All managers in an organization have a responsibility to protect the organization's investment in information as well as the organization's investment in other resources.

Only a few organizations have made significant progress into the era of information resource management. We shall have to be patient to see the progress which results.

Tools: Functions of a DBMS

The management of data in a DBMS is accomplished through a collection of programs and facilities. The functions which are provided by a given DBMS vary from system to system. The development of data base management capability is relatively young, and we should continue to see improvement in this area. Without talking about specific systems, let us examine the types of functions provided by a DBMS.

DBMS Functions

The functions to be discussed are included in most commercial DBMS packages for mainframe computer systems. They are available to a lesser extent on minicomputer systems. Data base software for microcomputers is discussed at the end of this section.

Organized Data Storage. The first, and perhaps most important, function is to *provide access* for a wide variety of applications programs *to an integrated collection of data.* The concept of a request made by an applications program for data to be supplied by the DBMS was discussed earlier in the chapter. This request must adhere to some formal requirements. The form of the request in some models is described in logical fashion in a **schema** which identifies the entities and attributes in the data base and establishes the logical relationships among them.

The word *logical* here is used in a slightly different context than that with which the reader might be familiar. Data base designers differentiate between a **logical description,** which describes how entities and attributes are logically related to each other, and a **physical description,** which describes where the entities and attributes are stored and how they are connected. A schema, for example, is a logical description of the entities and attributes and their relationships.

A DBMS provides an environment within which the applications program makes use of the logical relationships without needing to know the physical description. For example, an applications program can count on the fact that an employee's name is logically connected with the employee's current wage rate without knowing whether or not they are stored physically close to each other.

For each individual applications program, a subschema is developed which provides a view of the data items used by the program. A formal list of the names of all the data items in the data base is maintained in a **data dictionary.** An applications programmer uses the data dictionary to determine the correct names of the data items to be used in the subschema.

The important part of all this is that an applications program simply specifies the data it needs from the data base, and it is the function of the DBMS to provide that data to the program.

The manner in which the data are made available is also critical. It is important that the data base be managed in such a way that data are independent from any applications program and that independence is accomplished in a way which is *transparent* to the user. That is, the user cannot see, and does not need to see, just how the data are managed. Data management is independent of, and transparent to, any particular applications program.

Having said that, it is now necessary to point out that the world is not always ideal. The designers of the data base have many difficult decisions to make about relationships between entities and attributes. More numerous and complex relationships lead to a greater number of possible manipulations of the data in the data base, but also lead to greater system overhead and a lower overall average performance.

The relationships established by the schema do influence the relative efficiency with which data can be made available to a given applications program. Applications programs can be written with efficient subschemas and with inefficient subschemas. Data management by the DBMS is not entirely transparent to the user, and perhaps it should not be. The data base administrator should assist users of the data base in constructing efficient subschemas.

Data Validation and Editing. The second function of a DBMS is to provide the capability of *reviewing and editing data* during data entry and update operations. We have already mentioned the role of the DBMS in reducing the overall data entry workload by elimination of duplicate copies of data items. The data entry operation is also the source of a large proportion of the errors which are contained in data files.

Most data are entered manually by an operator through a keyboard. Even the exceptionally competent, professional data entry clerks make errors. Efficient routines are provided by a DBMS to help minimize the errors which result from data input operations by allowing the operator an opportunity to verify entries and by automatically checking the data against reasonable limits to ensure the data items are valid.

Report Generation. Another common function provided by a DBMS is *report generation.* A DBMS should provide a set of routines which make it easy for a user to develop a report and specify its contents and format. This capability, one of the most common, is provided by most DBMSs. For example, a production manager might want to generate a report which provides the total production generated by each manufacturing unit, by product and by month for the most recent twelve months. The report generation capability of a DBMS ought to make such a report easy to do.

The report generation software should allow the user to specify the content and format of the report as conveniently as possible. Column headings, row headings, and data values (either from storage or newly computed) are specified by the user. The system then assumes the responsibility of generating the report itself.

Data Security. The role of the DBMS in *providing data security* has been previously mentioned. The sharing of a data base certainly provides an opportunity for someone in the community of users to gain unauthorized access to certain data. Mechanisms to prevent both intended and unintended abuses of access must be included as one of the functions of a DBMS.

Security is most often provided through either keys or passwords. Only those people who have authorized user numbers and passwords are allowed access to any confidential information. Most systems provide only a "reasonable" level of security. The cost of additional security is basically paid by authorized users. As additional security measures are built into the system, obstacles to access are put in front of both authorized and unauthorized users. Authorized users must be willing to tolerate the additional security-checking procedures designed to prevent unauthorized access.

The magnitude of the threat of unauthorized access and the potential cost of a breach of security must be balanced against the cost of more difficult security-checking procedures which must be borne by all users. A clever and persistent person can usually penetrate the system's security. Users should understand that security measures can be breached by someone dedicated to that task.

Inquiries. One of the most useful functions of a data base management system is to provide a *means for users to get relatively quick answers to nonroutine questions with a minimum of programming effort.* A DBMS should provide a language in which users can construct nonroutine inquiries.

A regional sales manager could, for example, construct inquiries to learn the monthly sales by territory and product for the sales people in the region. This inquiry can be constructed in a nonprocedural or query language, much like English, in which it is not necessary to specify the procedure through which the computer must go to derive the answer. Examples from two commercially available DBMSs are illustrated in Figures 8–8 and 8–9.

The high-level, nonprocedural language query capability is designed to allow managers to extract information in a relatively easy, unstructured way. If a DBMS is to allow such inquiries, some relatively sticky issues must be resolved.

If we allow inquiries to be formed in real time, and simultaneously allow the data base to receive updates in real time, we must consider several possible, undesirable consequences. In the first place, we must prevent data processing "collisions" between the update and query routines. Sec-

Figure 8–8
Sample Data Base Query—INTELLECT

WHICH PEOPLE HAVE THE HIGHEST PERCENT OF QUOTA IN EACH REGION?

REGION	LAST NAME	FIRST NAME	1980 YTD % OF QUOTA
EAST	SMITH	MARY	92.57
MIDWEST	KATZ	MARY	92.71
NORTHEAST	JOHNSON	JAMES	88.09
SOUTHEAST	HIXSON	BRAD	146.91
SOUTHWEST	HASTINGS	STEPHEN	93.49
WEST	ARNETT	ROBERT	90.52

NEXT REQUEST.
FOR THOSE IN THE EASTERN AND WESTERN REGIONS, SHOW ME THEIR SALES FOR THIS YEAR AND LAST YEAR.

REGION	LAST NAME	1980 YTD % OF QUOTA	1980 YTD SALES	1979 ANNUAL SALES
EAST	SMITH	92.57	$647,974	$820,710
WEST	ARNETT	90.52	$633,630	$763,506

Figure 8–9
Sample Data Base Query—FOCUS

FOCUS:
"PROFITABILITY REPORT"
SUM SALES AND COST AND COMPUTE
MARGIN = 1 – (COST/SALES);
BY REGION BY CUSTOMER

PROFITABILITY REPORT

REGION	CUSTOMER	SALES	COST	MARGIN
SOUTHWEST	ABC COMP	1,000,000	600,000	.40
	DELTA INC	750,000	397,500	.47
	ZETA CORP	1,350,000	877,500	.35

Computers in Action 4

Meeting the Challenge

1. Activities within the information processing center support the mail order business of Webster's Western Wear. **2.** Orders are "picked" and packed for shipment in the WWW warehouse and information in support of those activities is available through terminals located there.

1

2

3

3. Order entry personnel for WWW receive orders on the telephone and enter them into the system through a visual display terminal. **4.** WWW's important records can be stored for long periods of time on magnetic tape in the tape library. **5.** WWW's new system with direct access devices in support of their data base management software will be a large one.

4

5

6

7

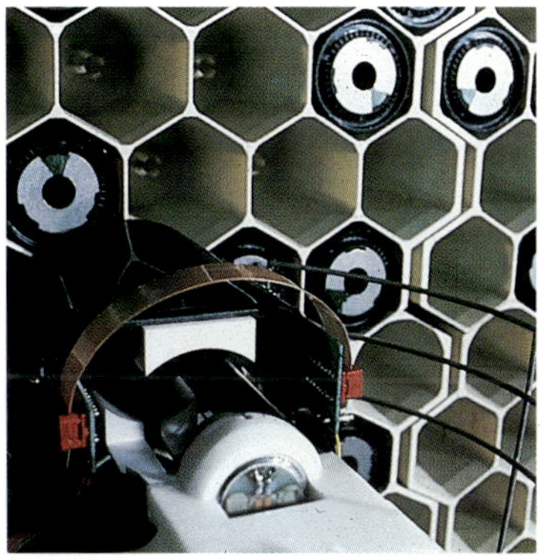

8

6. Each magnetic disk drive in the new system represents an effective marriage of mechanical and electronic devices for information storage and retrieval. **7.** Extremely large files can be economically stored on mass storage devices. **8.** Magnetic tape drives support WWW's routine information processing tasks where quick access is not important. **9.** Webster's Western Wear hopes to implement a new system which will allow customers with home computers to place orders directly.

9

10

10. Somewhere in WWW's future is a completely automated warehouse which will support its mail order business effectively and economically.

ondly, we must decide whether or not to let the query be processed while the data base is undergoing change. The DBMS must provide, as one of its functions, a centralized control of these potential interactions between query and update procedures.

Backup and Recovery. All data storage schemes of any significance should provide for *backup and recovery*, whether the scheme is a collection of applications programs and files or a full-blown DBMS. Backup copies of files and recovery routines are necessary in order to restore the system to its prior status following some unforeseen system failure or error. Backup and recovery are accomplished by providing for the copying of all data files on a regular basis and the storing of the backup copies in a secure place—but not on the same site as the original copy.

Should some disastrous event then destroy the data on the system, the backup data can be retrieved for recovery purposes. Most data processing centers routinely copy important data onto magnetic tape for backup purposes and store those tapes in vaults or other secure places.

Auditability. Another important function of any data processing operation is to provide for the *auditing of the system*. This is particularly true when the data being processed are financial data. Audits must be performed to ensure that financial (and other) transactions are properly and correctly processed.

Manual systems, based on the use of hard copies to verify all transactions, are much easier to audit than are computerized systems, for which the copies are electronic. An effective audit will provide the management of the organization with assurances that the data processing system is working as it should. A DBMS should provide for the auditing of all financial transactions.

Challenge Update

The data processing manager of WWW should now be able to list the data processing capabilities enhanced by a DBMS and explore what those capabilities might mean for WWW.

Microcomputers and DBMSs

DBMSs are such heavy consumers of a computer system's resources that we most often find their implementation on mainframe systems. They are utilized to a lesser extent on minicomputer systems. A few comments relative to their usefulness on microcomputer systems are in order.

A number of software packages are marketed as data base management packages. In comparison with mainframe DBMS software, the microcomputer packages are quite limited in capability. On the other hand, their power and usefulness to the user are very impressive.

For the most part, these systems provide interesting file processing and report generating capabilities. They provide for the creation, modification, and deletion of files. Reports can be generated from the files. The user can employ functions within the software to select particular records or particular fields in order to construct the necessary reports. A limited amount of computation is also allowed in order to generate proportions and row and column sums.

Data base software can be used to create and maintain data files used by other software packages available for the microcomputer. It can, for example, be used to generate mailing labels and form letters in conjunction with software designed to process text. Although data base software for microcomputers at its current stage of development falls short of its mainframe counterpart, if expected improvements in hardware are matched by software improvements, the gap should continue to narrow.

Technology: Several DBMS Structures

It would, unfortunately, be very easy for us to get in over our heads in a discussion of the technical details of DBMSs. While the technology supporting many areas of data processing is relatively easy to understand once an explanation is secured, the same is not true for DBMSs.

The precision required to accurately describe a particular model of data which supports a DBMS and to differentiate one data model from another makes mathematics the best language to use. Few of us have a background in mathematics sufficient to fully understand the discussion.

The next few pages will describe the general process through which an organization goes in adopting a DBMS. Then the three most common data models will be introduced: network, hierarchical, and relational.

If this section leaves the reader less than totally satisfied because of the effort to be brief and nonmathematical, the reader is encouraged to seek the more complete treatments provided in the list of additional readings at the end of the chapter.

Major Steps in the Move to a DBMS

The decision on the part of an organization to move into the data base management environment is a major one. The managers at the top of the organization must understand and support that decision. The path to the successful implementation of a DBMS is full of potential hazards.

Figure 8–10 Data Base System Life Cycle

- Application Development Phase
  1. Requirements formulation and analysis
  2. Logical design
  3. Physical design
- Data Base Operation Phase
  1. Implementation
  2. Operation and monitoring
  3. Modification and adaptation

There are two major efforts in a DBMS project, as there are in most system projects. The first major effort is the **design** of the system, during which analysts and users try to figure out what functions they want the system to perform and just how those functions will be built into the system. The second major effort is the **implementation** effort wherein the analysts, programmers, and operations people put the pieces of the system into operational order.

Both efforts are large, and both are obviously critical to the success of the system. An early part of the implementation step, for example, is the actual loading into the system of the data itself, a major project in most cases. One view of the DBMS life cycle, from an article by Teorey and Fry, is shown in Figure 8–10.[1]

The involvement of the top managers of the organization is most important during the application development phase, so let us examine the three steps in this phase. This phase alone could require a year or more of concentrated effort in a large organization.

The first step in the application development phase is the *determination of the information requirements* of the organization. One of the processes which is involved in this step is the interviewing of users to determine what information they need as they perform their decision-making activities. It is somewhat risky to take the user's word as the only indication of that information which is in fact needed in a decision-making activity; so, in addition to interviewing, a few days may be spent observing the user's decision-making activities. It is also advisable to review the decisions made by the user in the past and analyze the information considered by the user at that time. A study of decision-making activities should not be restricted to the past; the information needs of future decisions must also be considered. These studies of the information requirements should be adequately documented so that their influence on later decisions can be verified.

Once a reasonably accurate model of the information requirements of the users under study is constructed, a determination of the data which need to be collected and stored in the data base can begin. The ever-changing nature of the environment within which the organization operates makes it impossible to ever have "all" the data needed. In fact, it is usually the case in the design of information systems that designers would like to have had more information but could have gotten by with less.

The second step in the application development phase is the *logical design of the data base.* An earlier discussion mentioned how logical design differs from physical design, which, as it happens, is the third step in this phase. Systems designers try to determine, in the logical design step, how the data items are related to each other in terms of their meaning or interpretation.

When files were discussed in Chapter 7, the word *entity* was used to describe the "owner" of data in a record, or the central item of interest in a record. The remainder of the data items in the record were referred to as attributes of that entity. The logical design process is the process of

1. Toby J. Teorey and James P. Fry, "The Logical Record Access Approach to Database Design," *ACM Computing Surveys,* June 1980, pp. 179–212.

determining (1) what the entities and attributes are, (2) how the attributes are related to the entities, and (3) what relationships exist among the various entities. These relationships are determined on the basis of how the data in the data base are likely to be used in support of managerial and other activities.

Analysts, in designing the logical basis for the data base, consider the circumstances under which programs will need access to the data items and the frequency with which that access is likely to be made.

The logical design process determines the relationships between entities and their attributes, the relationships between entities and other entities, the types of access required, and the frequency of access which is probable. These characteristics help in determining which data model would best serve the needs of an organization.

The third step of the applications development phase is the *physical design*. This step sees the conversion of the logical design into a scheme which specifies the actual physical arrangement of the data in storage. The design team must determine how the logical relationships specified in the previous step will be translated into pointers and links between data items.

Three Data Models

The three data models reflected in the DBMSs now available are:

1. Network.
2. Hierarchical.
3. Relational.

We will take a brief look at each in turn.

The **network model** of data belongs to a class of data models known as data-structure-set. The network model can be described using the entity-attribute-relationship terminology with which we have become familiar in this and the previous chapter. The network model uses a data structure diagram to show two general types of logical relationships: (1) attribute relationships and (2) entity relationships.

A data structure diagram is shown in Figure 8–11, an example commonly used in the literature for illustrative purposes, a data base containing data about presidents of the United States. Figure 8–11 is a simplification of the actual examples used in most of the literature.

Figure 8–11 shows three record types (President, Administration, and State), and three relationships between these record types (Administrations Headed, Admitted During and Native Sons). From the data base represented by the data structure diagram we could expect to find out which administrations were headed by which presidents, which states were admitted to the Union during which administrations, and which presidents were native sons (and someday native daughters) of which states. The model represented in Figure 8–11 is a network model because record types and relationships are represented logically by the same symbols, nodes, and directed arcs as are used in the graphical representation of networks.[2]

2. Harvey Wagner, *Principles of Operations Research*, 2d ed. (Englewood Cliffs, NJ: Prentice-Hall, 1979), p. 239.

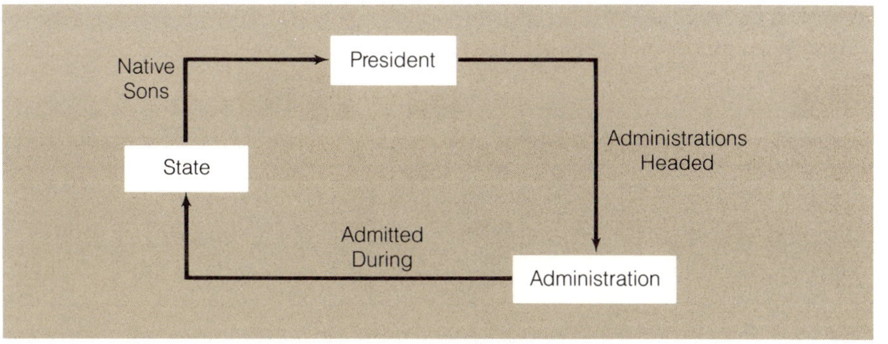

Figure 8–11
Network Model Data Structure

As we follow a relationship arrow in the diagram, we move from a single record at the arrow's tail to perhaps several related records at the arrow's head. For example, a single president would be connected to the one or more administrations he headed. A single administration would be connected to the zero, one, or more states which were admitted during that administration. A single state would be connected to the zero, one, or more presidents who were born in that state.

The fact that the arrows show a directed path which leads back to the starting point after traversing a series of one-to-many relationships is significant. It distinguishes the network data model from the one discussed next, the hierarchical model.

Part of the data shown in Figure 8–11 in the network model form are shown in Figure 8–12 as a hierarchical model. The **hierarchical model** is actually a special case of the network model. In the hierarchical model, record types have parent-child relationships, and closed loop networks are not allowed. Thus, a president is the parent to an administration which he headed; the administration headed is the child. An administration is a parent to the states admitted during the administration.

We have left off the parent-child relationship between states and their native son presidents because such a relationship would make a closed loop in violation of the rules of the hierarchical model. That relationship

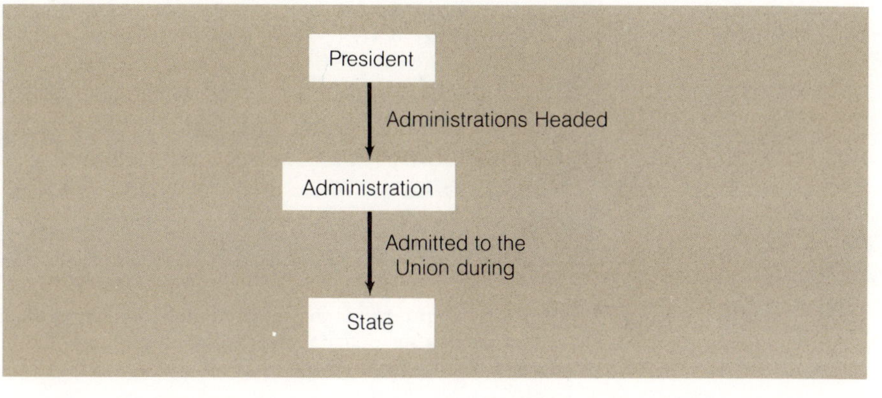

Figure 8–12
Hierarchical Model Data Structure

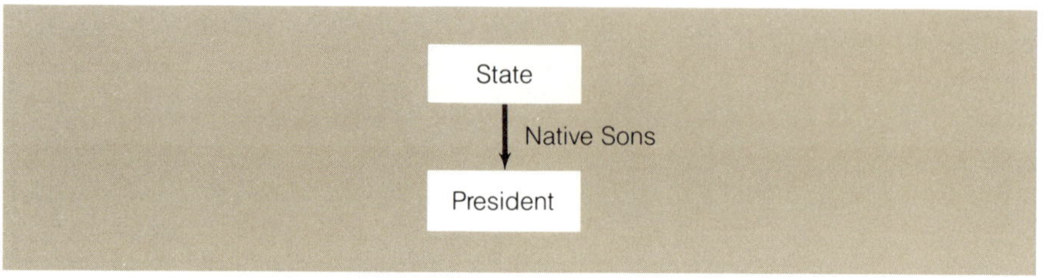

Figure 8–13 Another Hierarchical Model

would be shown as another hierarchy, illustrated in Figure 8–13. Thus we can break a network structure diagram into its component hierarchical diagram(s).

The third data model is the one which currently appears to have a lot of promise as the basis for commercial DBMSs. It is most easily defined mathematically. At the risk of losing some precision, I will attempt a description in lay terms.

A relation, the basis for the relational model, is most easily thought of as a two-dimensional table of data. An example is shown in Table 8–1. The rows of the table correspond to a record, complete with an entity and its attributes. In the relational model the rows are known as **tuples,** while the columns are called **domains.** Both are precise mathematical terms; a domain is an open set, and a tuple is an ordered collection of set members. In mathematical terms a **relation** is a subset of the Cartesian product of the sets called domains.[3] But it is adequate for our purposes to think of relations as tables of data.

The **relational data model** then forms the data base (logically) as a collection of tables or relations. The DBMS extracts the data needed by a particular applications program from the appropriate table(s).

A given set of data can be represented logically as either a network, a collection of hierarchies, or a collection of relations. Of course, a great deal

Table 8–1 A Relation of Presidential Data

Year	President Elected	Party	Home State
1960	Kennedy	Democrat	Massachusetts
1964	Johnson	Democrat	Texas
1968	Nixon	Republican	California
1972	Nixon	Republican	California
1976	Carter	Democrat	Georgia
1980	Reagan	Republican	California

3. The Cartesian product is the set of all tuples such that the first element in the tuple is a member of the first set (domain), the second member of the tuple is a member of the second set (domain), and so on.

of work must go into the actual representation so that the data needed by particular applications can be extracted from the data base in an efficient manner. Of the three types, the relational model seems to offer the greatest flexibility and promise for the future. It does, however, consume more resources of the system, yielding less efficient operation in terms of computer resources.

Challenge Update *The reader could now list the most common data structures used by DBMSs.*

Newest Developments

Since software which is required to provide the capabilities of a DBMS is very expensive in terms of computer overhead, a significant amount of the computer's resources are consumed by the DBMS itself. A DBMS operating with a large and complex data base can bring the overall performance of the computer system down to an unsatisfactory level. While we can hope for performance improvement via a breakthrough in terms of a new data model, there is some improvement to be gained along another avenue.

It is possible to add to the computer system processing units which are specifically designed and dedicated to the service of managing the data base itself. That is to say, we can take part of the load of executing the DBMS software off the main processor and put it on a separate processor—perhaps a microprocessor—specially designed for that purpose. (We will see another example of this design of special processors to ease the work load of the main processor in Chapter 9.)

The concept is relatively simple: reduce the extent to which some of the functions of the DBMS are dependent upon the extension of software by building special purpose, dedicated hardware. Functions performed by hardware features are performed at a much higher speed than are functions performed by software execution. By "off loading" the DBMS functions to the *data base processor,* we can expect to achieve significant improvement in DBMS performance. Figure 8–14 illustrates the use of a data base processor to process casual inquiries directly at the same time as it supports the host processor in more routine operations.

Challenge Update *The data processing manager of Webster's should now be able to explain how data base processors are expected to improve DBMS performance.*

In another development early in the 1970s, content-addressable, or associative, hardware was designed. The principle behind this hardware is that very fast searches of the entire contents of memory are made to find a match between the contents of memory and a particular data value. Data in the memory are thereby located through their contents, not through the more typical mechanism of their addresses.

Figure 8–14
Use of a Data Base Processor

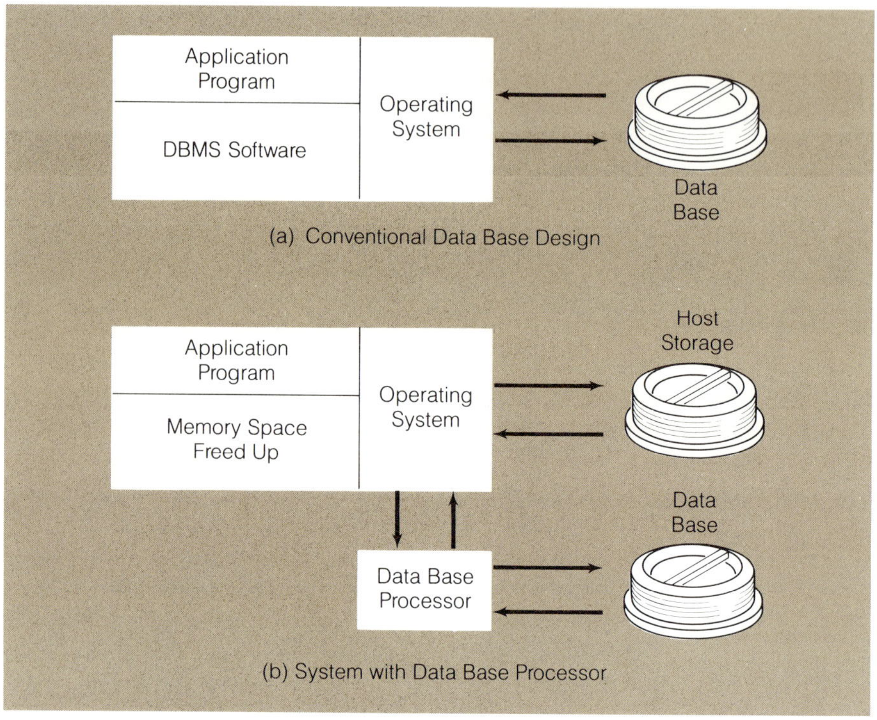

Several commercial implementations of associative memory devices are available. Associative retrieval is accomplished by designing intelligence into memory devices which conduct the search in many segments of the memory at the same time (in parallel).

If, for example, we can divide the memory into 500 segments and conduct a complete search of all segments in parallel, we can search the entire memory in 1/500th of the time it would take a search by normal, sequential means.

As the price of hardware (and therefore intelligence) declines, it becomes economical at some point to provide exhaustive (hardware) searches in parallel rather than software computations of physical addresses. Associative processors may someday make a very significant contribution to data retrieval. The trend of substituting specialized hardware for functions previously achieved via software, as seen in associative processors, is likely to be the basis for major improvements in performance of data base management software.

An intermediate possibility also exists. Instructions (called microcode) can be implemented directly in read only memory during the manufacturing process to yield **firmware,** a technology somewhere between hardware and software. These microcoded instructions can be executed by the system at extremely high processing speeds. Implementing DBMS software as firmware also contributes to improved system performance.

This has been a long chapter, filled with important concepts. A follow-up on the case with which this chapter began should help emphasize the subject matter which has been covered.

COMPUTING CHALLENGE: *A Final Note*

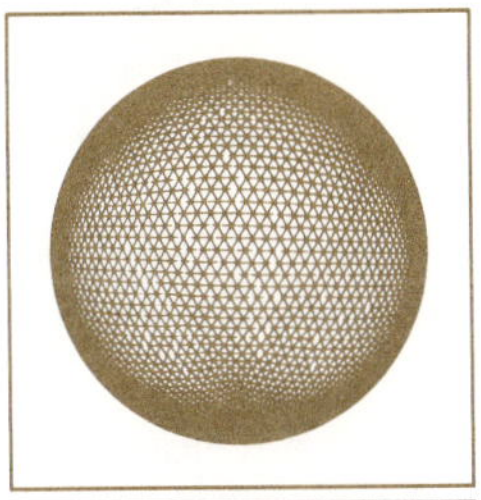

Webster's Western Wear is at a point in the gradual evolution of data processing applications where it makes sense to consider a DBMS. They have a number of applications already in place and can see the development of other, related applications in the near future.

They would like to avoid the duplication inherent to a system in which applications each own a separate set of files. At the same time, they recognize that consistent data retrieval from a secure system is a valuable asset to an organization.

Managers of WWW will have to answer the following questions:

1. *In what ways would the inventory control system interact with the purchase order/warehouse receipt system? With the order entry system? With the accounts receivable system?*
2. *Imagine what a record might look like for each of the above systems. Is redundancy likely to be a significant problem? Is consistency likely to be a significant problem?*
3. *What advantages might the company expect if a DBMS were installed?*
4. *What disadvantages might the company expect if a DBMS were installed?*

SUMMARY

- Somewhere between the data storage environment where each applications program "owns" its own data and the environment where all the data in an organization are stored under one data base management system (DBMS) is an optimum condition.
- Although there are some efficiencies, such as processing efficiency, associated with an applications program's ownership of a set of files, there are also inefficiencies, such as unnecessary duplication, in that environment.
- There are advantages to using a single collection of data under a DBMS to support a group of applications.
- When each application "owns" its own data files, we have too much

duplication of effort, an excessive amount of storage space used, and a difficult time in developing new applications.

- Advantages of a DBMS include improved control, enhanced data security, and better consistency.
- Too large an integrated data base leads to an extreme amount of the system's resources being consumed in system overhead.
- DBMS software is expensive both in initial cost and in implementation effort.
- A DBMS should provide an efficient organization of the data in storage, a query language for the generation of answers to nonroutine inquiries, and an efficient set of routines for accomplishing data editing, data validation, and report generation operations.
- The DBMS must also provide for data security, auditability, and backup and recovery.
- The most common data structures utilized in DBMSs are the network, hierarchical, and relational models, each of which provides a somewhat different set of storage and retrieval capabilities.
- The efficiencies of DBMSs are expected to improve with the development and use of dedicated data base processors. The implementation of DBMS software as firmware could significantly improve its processing characteristics.
- Improved hardware will also improve the performance characteristics of associative memories, which search on the basis of the contents of memory.
- Data base management software performs functions important to all data processing installations, and as its consumption of systems' resources becomes less, the use of DBMSs should become even more widespread.

CASE: DBMS in Market Research

The oil crisis of the middle 1970s caused virtually everyone in the United States to give greater consideration to energy efficiency. Utility companies, especially those with plants operating with fossil fuels, gave a great deal of attention to improving the efficiency of the conversion of oil and gas into electrical power. The nature of the power generation business makes significant change a slow process. Progress, however, is being made.

Westinghouse's Power Systems Company, for example, works with their utility company clients by helping them increase the availability, reliability, and efficiency of existing power plants. Westinghouse maintains and draws from an extremely large collection of information in order to be able to help, for instance, in identifying power generating units which would benefit from equipment upgrades. (Newer technologies achieve more efficient energy conversion.)

Westinghouse had collected and stored information about the operating equipment of over 3,000 electric utilities. Although the information was stored with a computer system, the system was an old one that required that programs be written to generate the reports required by marketing management to identify those clients whose plants were candidates for an equipment upgrade. These programs required extensive programmer effort, and long delays were typical.

Westinghouse implemented a relational DBMS known as Questor, supplied by Comshare Inc., to provide improved information processing capabilities. Over 5 million characters of data are stored in the new system, known as the Utility Information File. Sixteen standard reports are available on the system, but marketing managers familiar with Questor have much broader, more flexible access to information contained in the file as well. Before the new DBMS was installed, the market research group found itself unable to meet important deadlines. The new system has greatly improved the group's ability to respond in a timely fashion to requests for information. Included in the new data base are utility company names, plants, generating units, locations, generating capacities, number of customers, annual sales, peak loads, primary and alternate fuels, and much more.

The DBMS not only provides answers to strategic marketing questions, but it provides support to field personnel working with clients as well. It also helps the company identify new business opportunities and has substantially enhanced the productivity of the headquarters marketing staff.

This case provides a good example of a situation in which a company's overall performance has been improved through an improvement in its information processing capabilities. This performance improvement in turn allows utility companies to improve their energy conversion processes and better serve their customers. The DBMS described has had a positive impact on areas far removed from data processing itself.

"DBMS Supports Marketing Decisions at Power Systems Company," *Infosystems*, January 1983, p. 86. Copyright © 1983 Hitchcock Publishing Company.

Questions for the Case

1. This case emphasizes the positive benefits derived from the DBMS. What can we suspect are the negative impacts?
2. The system stores 5 million characters of information about 3,000 electric utilities. What can we guess about changes in the information in the data base? What fraction of it changes daily? Weekly? Monthly? Annually?

DISCUSSION QUESTIONS AND EXERCISES

1. List the areas of duplication or redundancy which are characteristic of the environment in which each application program owns its own files. How does a DBMS improve upon these areas?
2. What is meant by information consistency? How does a DBMS improve information consistency?
3. How does a DBMS aid the development of new applications?
4. In terms of DBMS software, what is system overhead? Has system overhead increased or decreased as computers have become more complex?

5. Describe the query language function of the DBMS. How is it beneficial to a manager?

6. Tell which of the following would be expected to make more efficient use of the computer's resources during program execution, and why:
a. An application with "owned" files.
b. An application with a DBMS-managed data base.

7. Tell which of the following would be expected to provide more effective support to operating managers, and why:
a. A set of applications with "owned" files.
b. A set of applications with a DBMS-managed data base.

8. Discuss the disadvantages of the DBMS environment.

9. What are the major resources which an organization employs to fulfill its purpose(s)? Is data (or information) included in the list? Why or why not?

10. Of the DBMS functions, which are most likely to be present in microcomputer data base software?

11. List and discuss the cost tradeoffs of acquiring and implementing a DBMS.

12. How will a data base processor improve the overall performance of a computer system which had DBMS software?

13. What is firmware? How can it be expected to improve DBMS performance?

14. What is the impact of expansion of the data base upon system performance? Explain.

15. The claim that "information is a source of power within an organization" is frequently made. If we assume the claim is true, what would we expect the influence of DBMS to be upon that power? Explain.

ADDITIONAL READINGS

ACM Computing Surveys: Special Issue—Data Base Management Systems, March 1976.

Bradley, James. *File and Data Base Techniques.* New York: Holt, Rinehart and Winston, 1982.

———. *Introduction to Data Base Management in Business.* New York: Holt, Rinehart and Winston, 1983.

Date, C. J. "How Relational Systems Perform." *Computerworld,* February 13, 1984, pp. ID15–20.

Epstein, Robert. "Why Database Machines." *Datamation,* July 1983, pp. 139–144.

Kim, Won. "Relational Database Systems." *ACM Computing Surveys,* September 1979, pp. 185–212.

King, Judy M. *Evaluating Database Management Systems.* New York: Van Nostrand Reinhold, 1981.

Kroenke, David. *Database Processing.* 2d ed. Chicago: Science Research Associates, 1983.

Lochovsky, Frederick H., and Tsichritzis, Dionysios C. *Data Models.* Englewood Cliffs, NJ: Prentice-Hall, 1982.

Martin, James. *Managing the Data Base Environment.* Englewood Cliffs, NJ: Prentice-Hall, 1983.

Ozkarahan, E. A., Schuster, S. A., and Smith, K. C. "RAP—An Associative Processor for Data Base Management." AFIPS Conference Proceedings, Vol. 44, 1975.

Ross, Ronald G. *Data Dictionaries and Data Administration: Concepts and Practices for Data Resources Management.* New York: AMACOM, 1981.

Teorey, Toby J., and Fry, James P. "The Logical Record Access Approach to Database Design." *ACM Computing Surveys,* June 1980, pp. 179–212.

Ullman, Jefrey D. *Principles of Database Systems.* Rockville, MD: Computer Science Press, 1982.

OMNIFAX

9

Data Communications

CHAPTER PREVIEW

The usefulness and availability of computers have increased dramatically in recent years as a result of the development of data communication capabilities. Users can now avail themselves of a computer's services from points far removed from the computer's actual location. Data communications links can also be used to allow two or more computers to communicate with each other in order to share data and programs. Data can be transferred between a user and a computer, or from one computer to another, via many different means, as we shall see in this chapter. The distant transfer of data between remote stations is known as **telecommunications.**

This chapter will discuss how computers and users communicate with each other, sometimes over great distances. A collection of interconnected computing devices is called a **network.** Three categories of networks exist to accomplish the necessary connections between users and computers. They differ in terms of the size of the geographical area in which they are capable of operating. One category provides communication within a building or campus, while another operates within a limited metropolitan area. The third provides communications links across vast distances.

A large proportion of the communications among users and computers take place through direct (hardwired) connections between the user's terminal and the computer. Many other common communications links among users and computers take place through the telephone system. In recent years the interest in establishing more communications links through other means, such as private satellites, has increased.

The subject matter of data communications is complex, both technologically and legally. For example, many technological problems must yet be resolved before the various types of networks can be conveniently integrated into an effective system. Learning about the technology in this chapter, we will also discover some of the interesting legal issues which are involved. Court decisions of the early 1980s caused a restructuring of American Telephone and Telegraph (AT&T), the telecommunications giant, and brought about a large-scale reshuffling of the communications market.

This chapter starts with a description of telecommunications concepts and then turns to a discussion of the tools of data communications and some of the underlying technologies. The chapter contains a particularly important set of topics. Timely and effective communications are vital to the success of virtually all large organizations and many small ones as well. An example case will help put data communications into perspective.

COMPUTING CHALLENGE: *Communications in Support of Transportation*

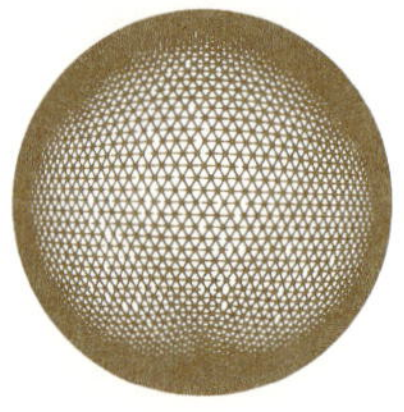

Coast-to-Coast Trucking is a company which provides, as its name implies, trucking services from coast to coast. Businesses and other organizations use Coast-to-Coast to ship goods all over the United States. Coast-to-Coast owns approximately 11,000 trailers in which goods can be shipped in either less than truckload (LTL) or truckload quantities. They contract with drivers (who own their own tractors) to deliver trailers across the U.S. as dictated by the needs of their customers.

Coast-to-Coast maintains truck terminals in each of sixty-five major cities in the United States. Customers call the terminal office to arrange for goods to be shipped or to determine the expected arrival of goods to be received. The terminal work force is responsible for scheduling the pickup of goods to be shipped, the delivery of goods to be received, the accumulation of LTL shipments into truckload shipments for purposes of efficient trailer loading, and the scheduling of tractors to accomplish the movement of trailers.

Coast-to-Coast has several information processing problems. Businesses expecting to receive goods want to know when they will arrive. Businesses shipping goods want to know when they will be delivered. Coast-to-Coast needs to know where the goods are so that they can provide the information needed by their customers. They must also know where the trailers and tractors are located, where they are headed, and when they will arrive so that they can schedule the movement of other goods.

Workers in each of the sixty-five terminals need the capability of entering data concerning the arrival, departure, or loading of each trailer. Drivers need to be able to report their location by telephone so that scheduling of their next load can be accomplished. Drivers also need to be able to report delays due to illness, bad weather, mechanical failures, or accidents. All of this information must be collected at a central location and made available to all terminal offices.

Clearly, the Coast-to-Coast management needs to know something about data communications in order to effectively contribute to the acquisition of a computer system with the information processing capability needed. A study of the technology of data communications will improve our own abilities in this subject area. It is an area of rapid change, one which will require that the reader develop some plan for keeping up-to-date. This chapter will provide a good basis on which to build. After successful completion of this chapter, the reader should be able to:

1. *Explain the role of local area, metropolitan area, and long distance networks in data communications.*
2. *List the fundamental requirements necessary for effective communication.*
3. *Discuss the promising characteristics of microwave, laser, infrared, and fiber optic communications media.*
4. *Describe the role of protocols in data communications.*

Computers in Action 5

Meeting the Challenge

1. Thousands of telephone conversations can be transmitted along hair-thin glass fibers produced by a process which begins with silica tubes like the one being heated on the glass lathe shown here. **2.** Red laser light is used to test the quality of glass fibers used in fiber optic communications lines. **3.** Fiber optic cables could be used within Coast-to-Coast Trucking terminals and within the home office to provide fast data communications capability.

4

5

6

7

SHAREHOLDERS
AT&T
WESTERN ELECTRIC
OPERATING TELEPHONE COMPANIE
BELL LABS

8

9

4. Researchers within Bell Laboratories (part of AT&T) work to develop better computers for switching voice, video and data communications traffic within the telephone system in support of companies like Coast-to-Coast. **5.** Coast-to-Coast dispatchers will benefit from new technologies in microphone design. **6.** New communications technologies enable Coast-to-Coast executives to conduct teleconferences with customers or executives at other Coast-to-Coast locations. **7.** An electronic blackboard would allow Coast-to-Coast to train employees in the corporate office and across the country simultaneously.

8. Automobile telephones allow Coast-to-Coast sales representatives to maintain close contact with the information processing network. **9.** Portable computers with modems allow Coast-to-Coast's professionals to communicate with all Coast-to-Coast locations. **10.** Coast-to-Coast hopes to install video telephones in the offices of important customers so that they can communicate directly with Coast-to-Coast's computing system. **11.** A communications satellite represents a complex array of electronic devices.

10

11

12

13

14

12. Through the use of communications satellites, companies such as Coast-to-Coast can gain access to worldwide information networks. **13.** Private communications companies are participating in the launching of communications satellites to support voice, data, and video communications. **14.** Satellite dish earth stations are a vital link in around-the-world communications networks.

HISTORICAL PERSPECTIVE

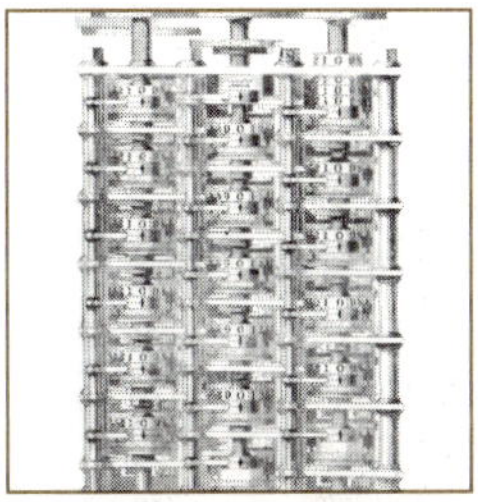

Although we treat telecommunications as a new era of data processing, it is older than the computer era by more than 100 years. The three historically most significant telecommunications devices are the telegraph, invented in 1844, the telephone, invented in 1876, and the teletypewriter, invented in 1915. The first of these, the telegraph, even used a digital code—that is, the dots and dashes of Morse code—to transmit data.

Strictly speaking, a telecommunications system in its simplest form requires only a **transducer,** which converts the signals into a form that can be transmitted, and a **transmission line** over which they will be transmitted. So that we do not need a separate set of transmission lines for each of the many pairs of stations in a telecommunications system, sets of lines which can be shared are provided, and a switching mechanism is established to effect the correct path between any two users.

As an interesting aside, the concept of an automatic switching mechanism to replace the telephone operator's manual duties is credited to an undertaker by the name of Strowger. It seems that Mr. Strowger was the second undertaker in a two-undertaker town. The first undertaker's wife was the telephone operator. As the story goes, Mr. Strowger felt his business was suffering because people calling for an undertaker were connected to the other undertaker. Mr. Strowger invented the automatic switching mechanism to protect his business interests.

The initial efforts to transmit computer system data via the media of telecommunications came at the end of the Second World War, but very little commercial use occurred until the late 1950s. The earliest computers were strictly batch processing machines, and the earliest combined use of telecommunications and computers was to provide for the transmission of batch jobs from remote locations. A remote location would typically be equipped with a medium- to high-speed input device—most often a card reader—and a medium- to high-speed output device—most often a line printer. Microcomputers and minicomputers had not yet been invented, so the need for telecommunications networks was small.

It was very common in those days to transport data from one computing location to another by recording it at one center on punched cards or magnetic tape and physically carrying the cards or tape to the other center. We sometimes see data transferred in the same manner today.

The ability to submit programs and data from a remote location greatly extended the range of computing capability. From such a remote facility, users could enter jobs (programs and data) via the telephone system and receive the results of the processing operations via the same means. A typical configuration would consist of a central computer and a few remote job entry locations.

The first successful commercial marriage of telecommunications and interactive computing occurred in the 1950s with the development of an on-line airlines reservations system by American Airlines. This system connected many geographically remote locations to the central computing facility for reserving space on American's fleet of commercial aircraft.

Timesharing, the sharing of a computer system by many remote users, became popular in the mid 1960s, and the assault on computers via the telephone system began in earnest. Since that time the technologies of computing and telecommunications have become increasingly intertwined. Not only are vast amounts of data shipped routinely all over the country and the world, but the flow of that data is controlled by computing systems dedicated to telecommunications service.

The merging of computing and telecommunications has had a significant impact on today's managers. Managers must not only understand the many capabilities now offered by computers, but they must also understand the capabilities of telecommunications. Each, in itself, is a major task.

Concepts: Connecting Remote Computer Devices

As organizations grow in size, they frequently reach a point where they occupy offices at different geographic locations. Coordination of the efforts of the various organizational units requires the exchange of a lot of information. Communication between the various locations then becomes important. If the size of the information processing task is sufficiently large, and computers are used to assist in that task, then part of the communications problem is a data communications problem.

Network Configurations

The first step in addressing the data communications problem is usually to give people in the various locations terminals so that they can access or communicate with the central data processing computer located in the home office. As the data processing needs of the people in the branch offices grow, they may require more capable, intelligent terminals, perhaps even microcomputers or minicomputers, to be used as terminals. An arrangement of devices which has a large, main computer to which a number of other, smaller computers or terminals are connected is known as a **star network** (see Figure 9–1). Data communications traffic in a star network is controlled by a central computer known as the *host.*

A different pattern of organizational growth might have resulted in a different network configuration. For example, if the nature of the organization's work is such that very little communication with the home office is necessary, but a great deal of communication is necessary between the branch offices themselves, we might see a **ring network** develop (see Figure 9–2). Control of data communications traffic in a ring network is assigned to one (or more) of the computers in the ring.

With time, network configurations become even more complex. A star network may become more complex, and become like a ring and star combined as the branch offices need to be connected to each other. Such a network, shown in Figure 9–3, allows the communication of data to the home office computer as necessary, but also allows the branch offices to share data and programs with each other as desired.

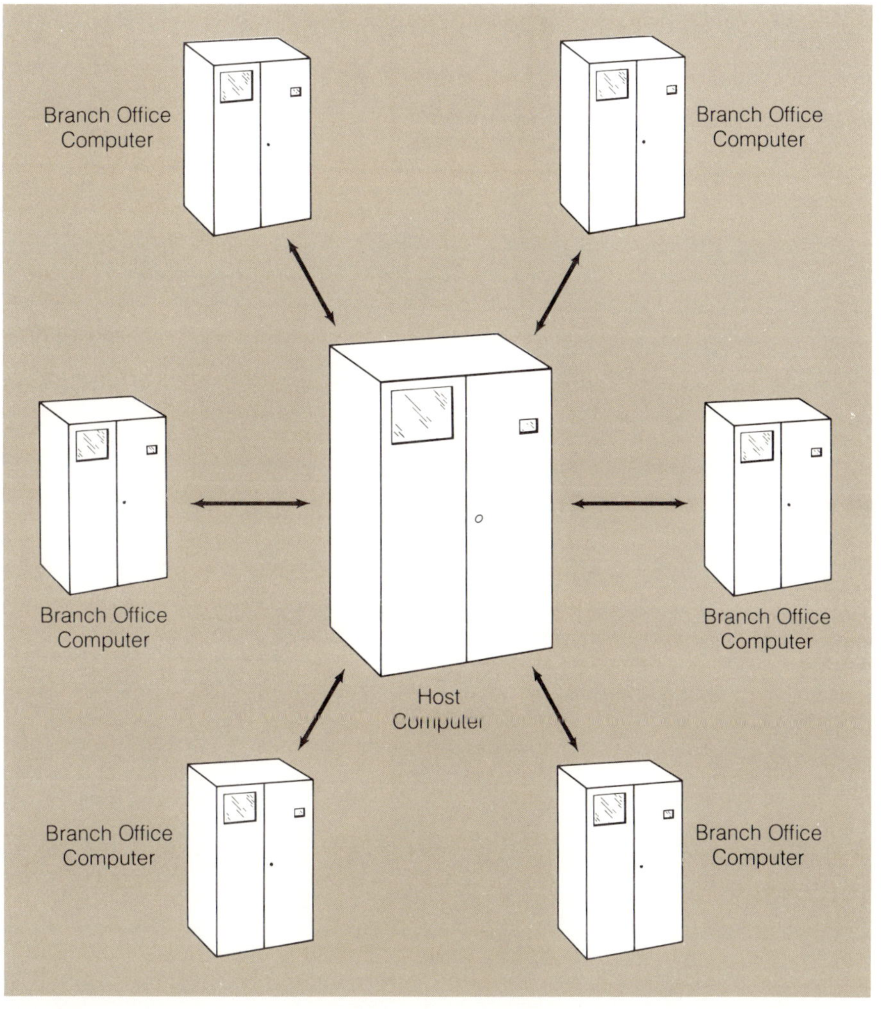

Figure 9–1 Star Network

Another network configuration, called a **bus network,** is used within a limited geographical area. The bus network provides a single transmission line to which all computing devices are connected (see Figure 9–4). The intelligence necessary for network management of a bus network can be centralized in one of the connected devices or distributed among several of them, as it is in a ring.

Hierarchy of Communications Networks

The goal of network management is to make the resources of the network available to the user in as transparent a fashion as possible. (In this, it parallels a computer operating system whose goal is to make the resources of a computing system available to the user in as transparent a fashion as possible.) As more and more computing devices are connected to the network, the configuration becomes quite complex. In turn, the combination of hardware, software, and communications rules necessary to properly manage the network becomes quite complicated (and expensive).

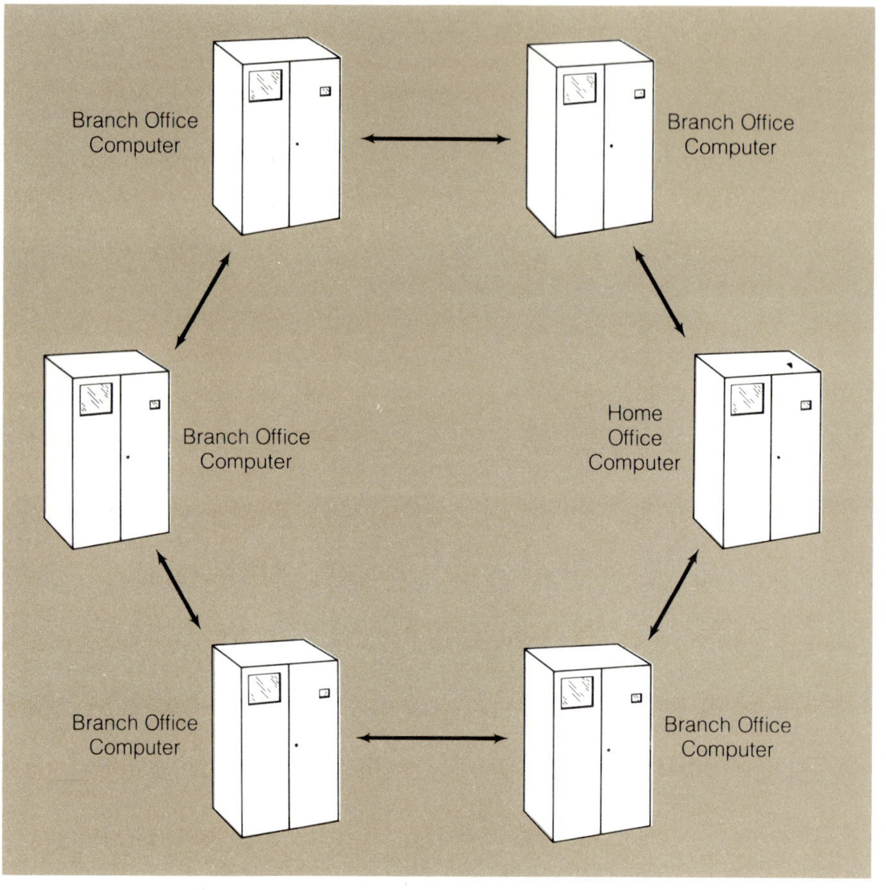

Figure 9–2 Ring Network

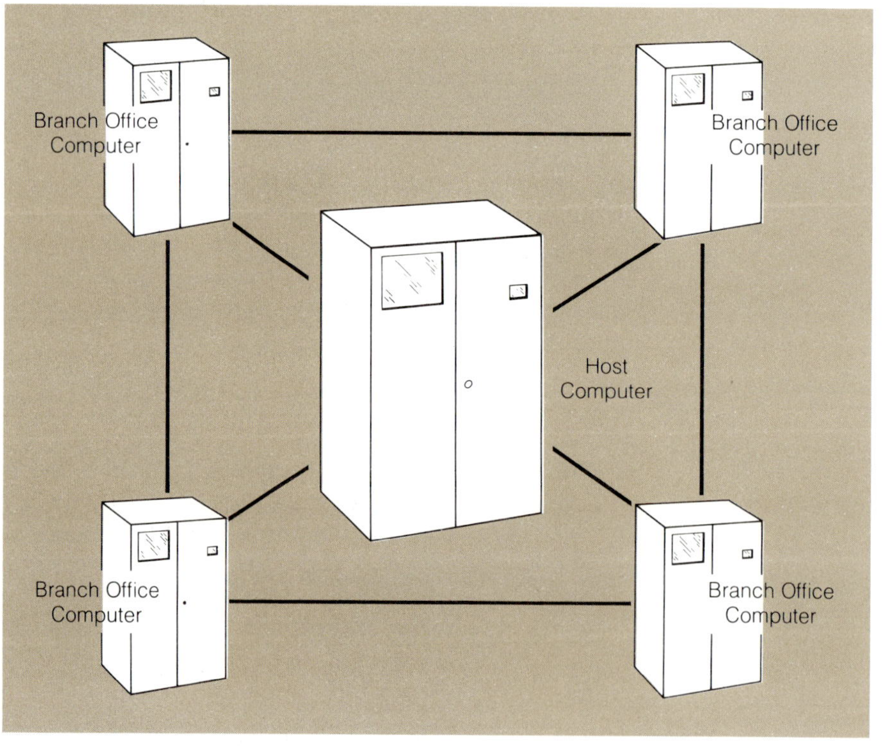

Figure 9–3 Combined Network

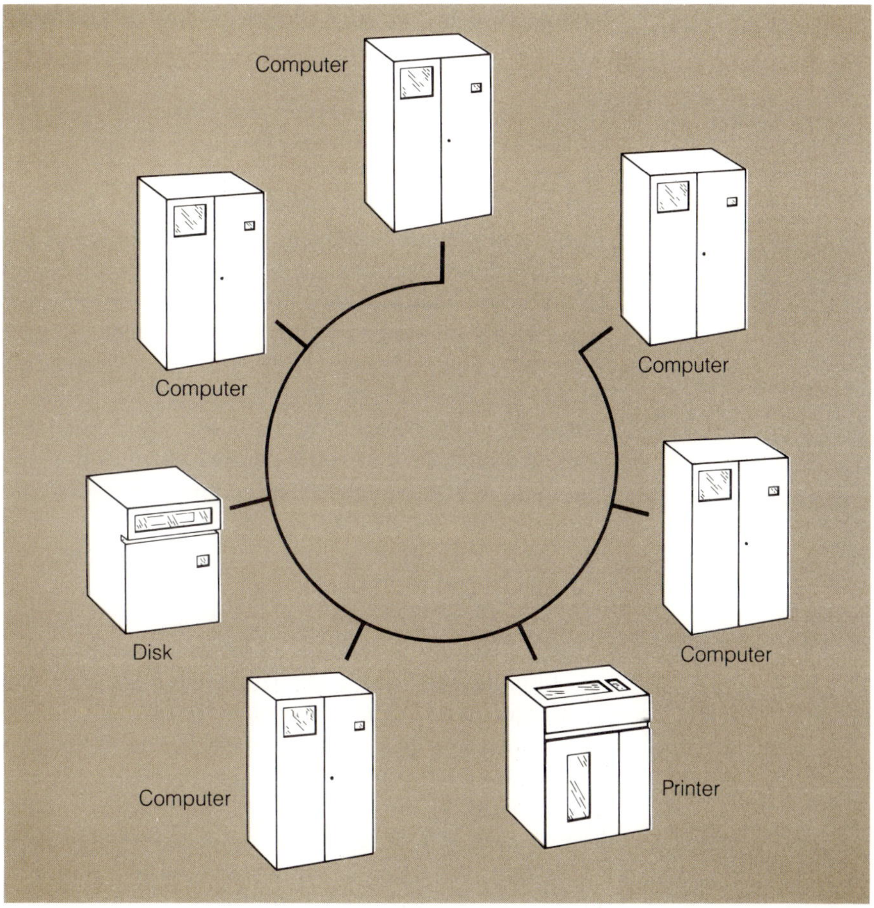

Figure 9–4 Bus Network

Three types of networks have evolved, the long-distance or value-added network, the metropolitan area network, and the local area network. Interconnections among these networks will allow two or more computing devices to communicate effectively, regardless of their respective locations. Each of the three network levels will be discussed in turn, followed by a brief discussion of inter-network connections.

Long-Distance and Value-Added Networks (VANs). Public networks became popular in the late 1970s. These networks provided organizations with a means for communicating with organizational units scattered across a wide geographical area. A company could, for example, have branch sales offices scattered across the country, each of which would be connected via the network with the home office. Today, these networks, in many cases, are capable of handling the transmission of voice, data, and video communications.

Data communication efficiencies can be achieved by combining many separate communications on a single line, a process known as **multiplexing.** One technique for multiplexing is to assign each of the communications to a different frequency range for the transmission, called **frequency di-**

vision multiplexing. A device, called a multiplexor, blends the various communications together for transmission. They are separated at the receiving end. Voice transmissions within the telephone system are multiplexed in this way. Another means for multiplexing several communications onto a single transmission channel is to give each communication the full frequency range for a short time interval, and rotate the time intervals among the users, called **time division multiplexing.** Data transmissions to and from satellites are sometimes multiplexed through this time division.

Telecommunications companies often put together a network by using the existing telephone system but additionally provide improvements in network management to improve the cost and quality of the transmission channels. The network is then referred to as a **value-added network (VAN).** The future potential for this type of network includes the provision of other networking or computing services to enhance the value-added concept. Message storage and retrieval and eventually voice store and forward capabilities will likely be added. Some of these networks require microwave dishes as we see in Figure 9–5.

The Advanced Research Project Agency (ARPA) of the Department of Defense sponsored the development of the first large data communications network, the **Arpanet,** in 1969. The primary use of Arpanet has been to link together the many scientists engaged in critical research areas so that they could collaborate on research projects and share research results.

The original Arpanet grew to permit the interconnection of over 300 computing devices and processed roughly 14 million transmissions per day. Fears that such a large system might not be secure enough caused the network to be split into two separate networks in 1983. Military users now use the Milnet system while civilian researchers have access to R&Dnet.

A number of private companies offer commercial network service. Al-

Figure 9–5 Network Communications Link

though some lease their telecommunications capabilities from AT&T, others have moved to provide independent facilities. Several private satellites have been launched to provide telecommunications service. The use of private facilities to circumvent the telephone system for the transmission of data (and other communications) has become quite popular. The concept is referred to as **bypass technology** in both long-distance networks and the next category to be discussed, metropolitan area networks.

Metropolitan Area Networks (MANs). The second level of communications networking is the **metropolitan area network (MAN).** As the name implies, these networks are designed to transmit data (and sometimes voice and video) between locations within a metropolitan area.

One such service, known as the digital termination system (DTS), uses antennas and computers atop big city skyscrapers to receive transmissions beamed there by satellite. These transmissions are sorted, stored, and redirected via radio frequency transmission to individual customers throughout the city. A MAN which bypasses the (analog) telephone system can provide improved data communications and lower costs. The first downtown satellite communications teleport to support a MAN was built in Washington, D.C., in 1984. It will be used by government agencies, corporations, and news bureaus as an alternative to the telephone network for video, voice, and data communications.

Another means of bypassing the telephone system is provided by the cable television (CATV) system. Cable television transmission already brings video into many of our homes. The same type of cable can be used for data communications as well.

Cellular radio networks provide yet another mechanism for providing networking within a metropolitan area. These networks rely on radio transmission within a given geographical area or cell. Sales people or service workers use this type of network to maintain communications with the home office.

MANs allow transmissions from one company to another or from one location to another within the same company. These transmissions can take place in several different ways. Rooftop devices as part of a MAN, for example, allow communications among the various buildings of an organization in a campus setting or among different organizations (and buildings) in an urban setting.

Local Area Networks (LANs). Private networks in a restricted geographical setting are called **local area networks (LANs),** and they represent another communications possibility. LANs are most often used to connect together a variety of computing devices within the same building. Computer-based office machines, for example, may be connected to a LAN in order to allow users to share files and printers. Late in 1981 the Xerox Corporation installed a local, private network for TransAmerica Corporation. The network consisted initially of fifteen office work stations connected to each other with coaxial cable. Data is transferred between stations at the rate of 10 million bits per second.

Personal computers in managers' offices can also be linked together with a LAN so that data can be shared and electronic mail service provided. The

LAN of the future will have personal computers, word processors, and many other machines sharing a local network with (perhaps) a host computer. Connections between local networks, MANs, and long-distance networks will provide for communications around the world.

Several different technologies are competing for LAN customers. The Xerox Company's version of a LAN is called **Ethernet.** It is one of the top contenders in a very competitive market which has a number of different entries. The lack of standardization in LANs has been a problem and may continue to be so for some time. Ethernet is an example of a network which uses baseband communications, a simpler technology than the other alternative, known as broadband.

Baseband systems use a narrow transmission bandwidth which is capable of maintaining only one communication process at a time. Several different schemes are used by manufacturers to ensure that the communications channel is used by only one user at a time. One scheme uses an electronic **token** which freely travels around the ring network when it is not busy with a communication. The token is removed from the ring by a station to gain permission to transmit and put back into circulation when a transmission is complete. A station must have possession of the token in order to transmit.

Ethernet uses a different scheme called **CSMA/CD,** which stands for **carrier-sense multiple access/collision detection.** This very technical name represents a process analogous to the way in which we make use of a revolving door exit from a busy building. We look to see whether or not the door is in use. If not, we move to enter the revolving slot. If we encounter someone else trying to do the same thing, we back off, wait, and try again.

CSMA/CD networks work the same way. Before transmitting, a station checks to see if the network is in use. If it is not, the station begins to transmit but checks to make sure that its transmission does not "collide" with that of another station trying to do the same thing. If a collision occurs, both stations retreat, wait a random length of time and try again. The random nature of the wait is used to avert successive collisions.

Broadband communications, on the other hand, provide a broader range of transmitted frequencies. This allows communications to be multiplexed so that several stations can use the communications links simultaneously. Their broader wavelength makes it possible to transmit audio and video communications as well as data communications.

Baseband systems, then, are simpler and cheaper, but they provide less capability. Broadband systems can handle more stations and provide greater capability. They are, however, more costly and more difficult to implement and maintain. The common media for local networks include twisted-pair wire, shielded coaxial cable, and fiber optic cable (discussed in the tools section of this chapter).

A LAN using twisted-pairs can handle approximtely 56,000 bits per second (bps). Coaxial cable, on the other hand, can handle 10 million bps with baseband and 20 million bps with broadband. By comparison, a fiber optic cable is capable of transmitting billions of bits per second.

A number of industry, trade, and governmental organizations are working to bring standards to local area networking. One group, the Institute of Electrical and Electronics Engineers (IEEE), published a preliminary set of standards in 1984. The standard, *IEEE 802,* recognizes both CSMA/CD (Ethernet) and token passing (IBM). It does not, however, include the most popular, twisted-pair, personal computer network of Corvus System, Inc. (Omninet) or the network technology preferred by AT&T.

Challenge Update

The reader should now be able to describe the role of long-distance, metropolitan area, and local area networks in data communications.

Inter-Network Connection

Long-distance, VANs, MANs, and LANs will eventually be tied together into an *internet,* a network of networks. For example, one internet, the XTEN (Xerox Telecommunications Network), was designed to accommodate three levels of transmission: (1) within a building, (2) building-to-building, and (3) city-to-city. Unfortunately, it was never implemented.

Arpanet began internet operations in 1983 after implementing TCP (Transmission Control Protocol) and IP (Internet Protocol). Commercial systems are expected to follow by the mid 1980s. These systems are expected to provide the capability for linking together many different varieties of computing devices.

Tools: Data Communications Requirements and Media

The connecting of two or more computing devices so that they can communicate can be a problem. A brief look at a simplified communications diagram will help us understand some of the difficulties which might be encountered. In Figure 9–6 we see a diagram of a very simple communications connection. We see two units, each with the capability of sending or receiving a message. The two units are connected by a transmission line to carry the communication; and between each sender/receiver unit and the transmission line we see the transducer, mentioned earlier, which converts the original message into an energy form which can be transmitted over the line.

Figure 9–6 A Simple Communications Connection

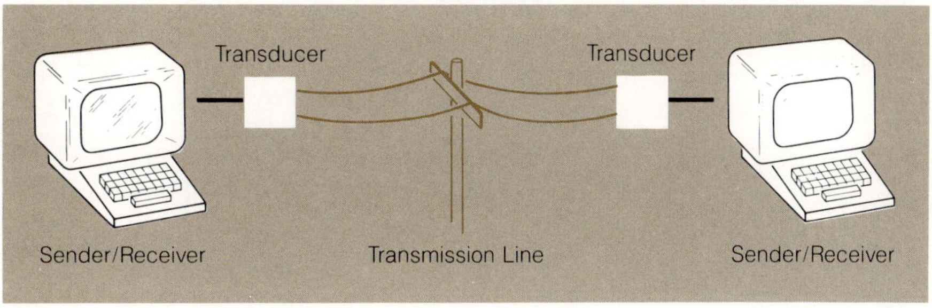

Although the concept of communications between two or more computing devices is relatively easy to visualize, there are many requirements which must be met before effective communication can be accomplished. The next section will set forth those requirements.

Communications Requirements

If we think for a few minutes in general terms about communication, we can derive a set of requirements necessary for effective communication. There must, of course, be at least two participants. In the most simple arrangement, we would expect to have one sender and one receiver. A list of the requirements necessary to allow the two sender/receiver units to communicate directly with each other would have to include these items:

1. The sender/receiver units must share a common language so that each can understand the other's messages.
2. The transducers must be capable of converting the messages into the type of signal which the transmission line requires.
3. The transmission line must be capable of transmitting the messages without causing their content to be appreciably changed.
4. All the devices in the system must be capable of transmitting the messages at a common speed.
5. All devices in the system must be capable of adhering to the same set of rules with respect to the sending of messages, the receiving of messages, and waiting.

Should the communicating units not be able to meet these requirements, interface devices would have to be provided as translators to accommodate differences. Let us investigate each of these requirements in greater detail.

Common Language. The question of whether or not two devices share a common language is dealt with in some detail in Appendix B, which investigates the internal representation of data. Basically, data are stored and moved about inside the electronic components of a computer system as patterns of bits. The exact nature of representation of the bit itself is a function of the particular type of device. For the most part, bits are represented by areas of magnetic flux or logic gates.

Figure 9–7 Digital Signal

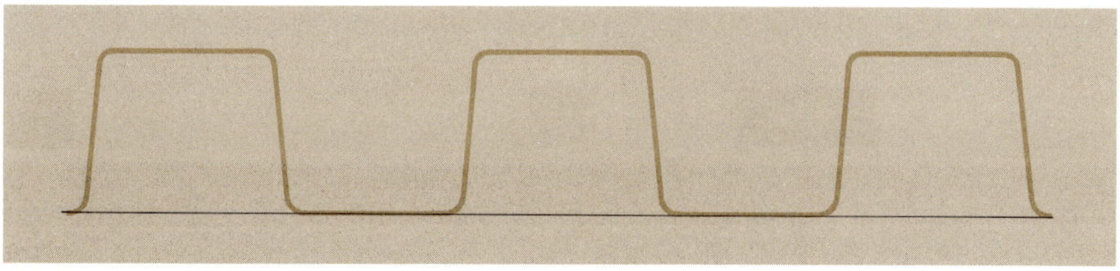

Characters are represented by bit patterns, and several standard encoding schemes exist for determining which pattern of bits represents which individual character. The most common encoding schemes are discussed in Appendix B. Two computing devices designed to use different encoding schemes would have trouble communicating without some mechanism between them to perform a translation. A hardware device known as an interface can be built to perform the translating function between two otherwise dissimilar devices.

Signal Conversion. The concept of signal conversion addresses one of the most basic problems in data communications. Most computing devices are designed on the basis of binary digital techniques, which gives us the two states we have referred to previously as ON bits and OFF bits. Although there are a variety of different ways to represent ON and OFF bits, the one most frequently chosen to transmit data from one computing device to another is based upon voltage differences. The presence of a particular positive voltage is used to represent a bit which is turned on, and the absence of that voltage is used to represent a bit which has been turned off. Figure 9–7 illustrates a binary digital signal.

The telephone system, however, is based upon an entirely different concept. The most common signal transmitted through the telephone system has always been voice, an analog signal. In contrast to the binary digital signal's restriction to two possible states, an analog signal is a continuous function capable of taking on any value between two established extremes.

The telephone system was designed to carry voice messages, and analog signals are very desirable for transmitting the human voice. If it is to be used for data communications, the telephone system must be combined with transducers to accomplish signal conversions. The transducer's problem is to convert the digital signal produced by the computer to an analog signal which can be transmitted via the telephone system. Figure 9–8 illustrates an analog signal.

A device called a **modem** (a contraction of *mo*dulator/*dem*odulator) is used to convert the computer's digital signal to an analog one so that the existing telephone transmission facilities can be utilized. The modulation of the signal can be achieved by changing the analog carrier signal's frequency, as shown in Figure 9–9, by changing the analog carrier signal's amplitude, as shown in Figure 9–10, or by other means. A modem is also used at the receiving end to convert the transmitted signal back to digital form.

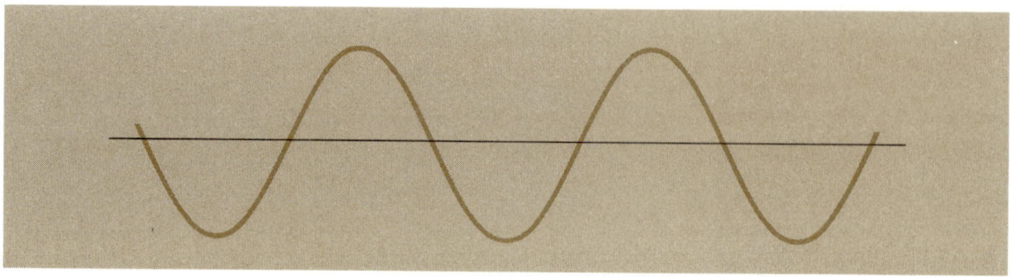

Figure 9–8 Analog Signal

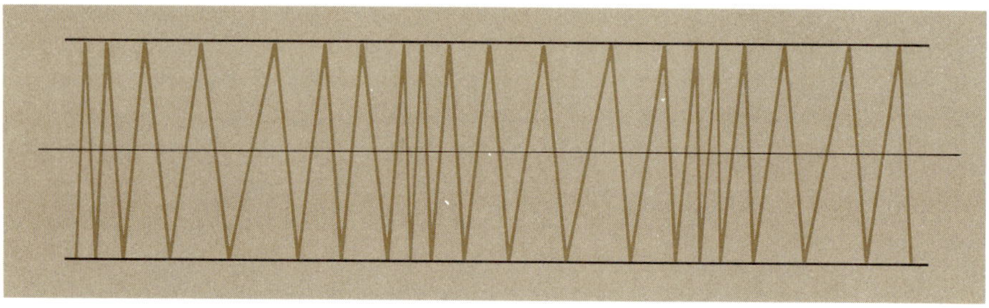

Figure 9–9 Frequency Modulation

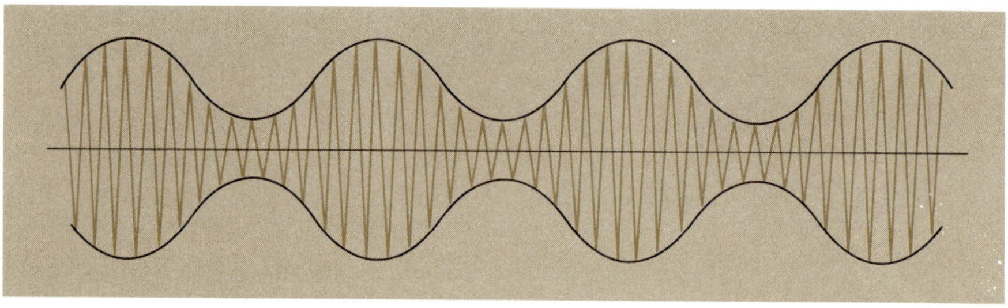

Figure 9–10 Amplitude Modulation

As the demands on the telephone system for the transmission of data increase, the suitability of its analog transmission features decreases. The telephone system's transmission facilities are, therefore, gradually being converted to digital transmission. The largest single provider of telephone service, AT&T, is expected to convert 25 to 40 percent of its long-distance loops to digital transmission by 1990. Approximately 90 percent of local circuits of regional telephone companies are expected to be digital by that time.

If the transmission system itself is to be digital in nature, voice transmissions will have to be converted from analog to digital form at the sending facility and reconstructed at the receiving end. Why, then, convert the telephone system to digital transmission? In part, the answer to that question is provided in the next paragraph.

Transmission Quality. The making of a single long-distance telephone call is sufficient to help us understand that a lot of "noise" coexists with the intended conversation. A telecommunications system which transmits a signal over a long distance must provide for periodic amplification of that signal along the way. If the intended signal is analog, as is the "noise," there is no way to boost the signal without also boosting the "noise."

The transmission of a digital signal, on the other hand, relies on the ability to discriminate between only two states, the peaks and valleys of the signal. Digital signals can be filtered and refreshed to maintain a higher quality transmission. A transmission system based upon digital techniques will, therefore, provide improved data communications and lower error rates.

Speed. We can easily understand why it is important that the sender, receiver, transducer, and transmission line all be capable of operating at the same speed. Any mismatch in speed would result in the loss of part of the message. We have doubtless all experienced a presentation by a lecturer who talked so fast that it was impossible to take accurate notes. A telecommunications system is constrained to operation at the speed of its slowest component, for any faster speed could not be accommodated by all devices in the system.

The speed of transmission of data is reported in terms of the number of bits of data transferred per second. A measurement which amounts to *almost* the same thing is called the **baud rate,** which strictly speaking means the number of discrete changes in the signal per second. If each discrete change represents a single bit, which is most often the case, then baud rate and the number of bits per second result in the same measurement. If a discrete change represented two bits, then the bit per second rate would be double the baud rate. Roughly speaking, a baud rate of 110 will support a data rate of 10 characters per second, while a 300 baud rate translates to 30 characters per second.Some of the common data communication rates are 110, 300, 1,200 and 9,600 baud.

Transmission Rules. The success of data communications depends upon a set of rules which must govern the devices in the system. Some of these rules govern the sequencing of messages, some govern the coordination of messages, and some govern the structure of the messages themselves. The technical nature of these rules will be discussed in detail later, in the technology section of this chapter. First we must turn our attention to the various media which are used in data communications.

Challenge Update

The reader should now be able to list the fundamental requirements necessary for effective communication.

Data Transmission Media Alternatives

A number of alternative media are available in the rapidly changing field of data communications. Managers may choose from telephone-based systems, twisted-pairs, coaxial cable, radio, microwave, fiber optics, and infrared. These media alternatives further complicate the communications choices, as we shall see.

Telephone-Based Systems. The most common medium for the transmission of data has been electrical conductive wire. It has been used for 150 years for the transmission of telegraphic messages and, for a slightly shorter length of time, for the transmission of telephonic messages. Data communications have, of course, taken advantage of the fact that an extensive telephone network exists. The telephone network does, as a matter of fact, carry a great deal of the total data communications traffic. (The telephone system uses transmission media in addition to electrical wire, as we shall see shortly.)

Data communications among computing devices does not, of course, have to involve the telephone system at all. Two computing devices may be directly connected by wire cable giving a connection described as **hardwired.** A hardwired connection is a simple one technologically, and it allows a fast data transfer rate. These connections may be accomplished with twisted pairs of wires, coaxial cables, or fiber optic cables. If the two devices are separated by any significant geographical distance, it becomes uneconomical to provide a simple, hardwired connection.

The next best alternative is to secure a dedicated line through the telephone system, a line wholly committed to that particular service. Dedicated lines can be conditioned to improve transmission so that the data transfer rates are reasonably close to those of hardwired connections. Organizations must pay a monthly fee to the providers of telephone service for the dedicated line.

The next option, and the least desirable one in terms of data transfer rates, is to use the normal dial-up telephone circuits. The advantages of this option are:

1. For low-volume data transmission, it is the least expensive.
2. This type of service is available virtually anywhere there is telephone service.

Many portable terminals are equipped with a particular type of modem called an **acoustic coupler,** which converts acoustic signals to the electrical signals transmitted by the telephone system. The terminals can then utilize the handsets of telephones at home or in hotels and motels across the land to provide access to computing capability. Many modems, particularly those used with microcomputer systems, have receptacles which accommodate the telephone cable modular connector directly. This connection allows access to the telephone network without the need for acoustic couplers. Users are billed at long-distance call rates for this dial-up use of the telephone system for nonlocal calls. The two major problems with dial-up service are:

1. Transmissions facilities can only accommodate data transfer rates at the lower end of the scale.
2. The dial-up lines frequently have an extensive amount of noise, which interferes with the transmission.

Microwave. As the telephone system has become more modern, it has begun to utilize transmission media other than electrical wires. Microwaves, for example, provide an often used alternative to electrical wires as a transmission medium. Microwaves can be beamed across vast distances, either directly from one earth station to another, or from one to the other through a space satellite relay (see Figures 9–11 and 9–12).

Although severe weather occasionally interferes with the microwave transmission of data, such occurrences are relatively rare, and compensation in the form of retransmission can ease the problem. Microwave transmissions are multiplexed to improve the cost/performance ratio through either frequency or time division multiplexing (described earlier). A microwave transmission tower is pictured in Figure 9–13.

Lasers/Fiber Optics. Virtually every day we read about an intriguing new application of laser technology. It, therefore, is not surprising to learn that lasers can be effectively used for the transmission of data. The presence of laser light can be used to represent ON bits, while its absence is used to represent bits which are OFF. Data communications can be beamed from one station to another as long as the distance is not too great and as long as a clear line of sight exists between the stations.

The technology of lasers, when combined with high-quality glass fibers, produces very promising data transmission characteristics. Recent developments in the manufacture of extremely high-quality glass made fiber optics possible. The key to fiber optics as a data communications medium rests with our ability to manufacture glass of sufficiently high quality that very little of the light traveling through the fibers is absorbed by the glass itself. Fiber optics represents an alternative so attractive that it may eventually replace electrical wiring in many applications. A pair of fiber optic

Figure 9–11
Comunications Satellite

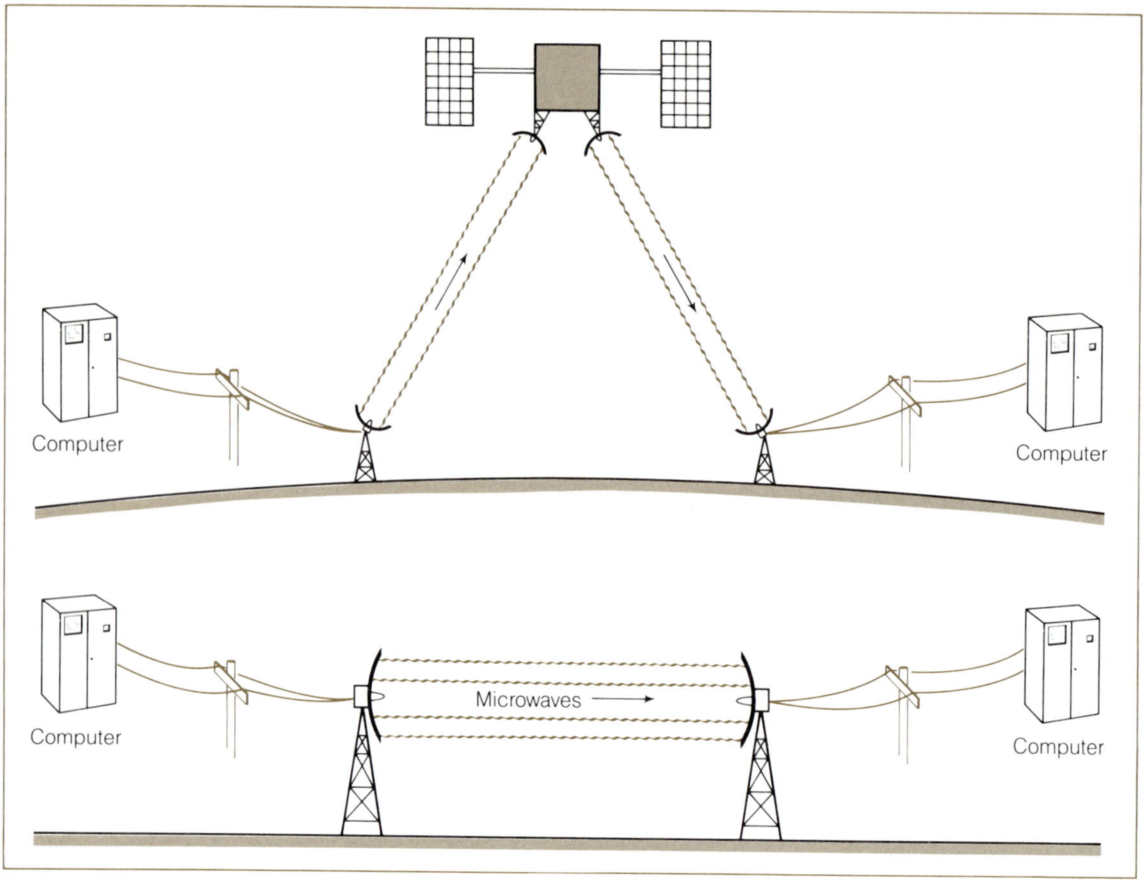

Figure 9–12
Microwave
Transmissions

cables can accommodate 1,300 simultaneous voice transmissions, whereas a twisted-pair electrical cable can handle only twenty-four.

Data are encoded digitally with a laser light source and beamed down the fiber optic cable. A light sensitive receiver converts the message back to an electrical signal for use within the data processing system. Figures 9–14 and 9–15 help provide an understanding of this technology.

The technology of fiber optics offers several advantages over conventional electrical wire. These advantages include:

1. Data transmission can be accomplished with less accompanying noise.
2. The transmission of laser light impulses down a fiber optic cable consumes less power than the transmission of electrical impulses down a wire.
3. Fiber optics allows for transmission over a wider frequency band.
4. Fiber optic strands are smaller and lighter in weight than electrical wires of comparable capacity (see Figure 9–16).

The first large-scale use of fiber optics as a transmission medium resulted in a trunk line, in this case a cable of 144 optical fibers, from Washington, D.C., to Boston. Each fiber is itself capable of the transmission of 672 one-way voice conversations, or the transmission of 45 million bits of data per

Figure 9–13
Microwave
Transmission Tower

second. The fiber optic system is estimated to cost approximately 50 percent less than a comparable electrical wire using coaxial cable.

Fiber optic cable transmission systems are becoming commonplace along both the East and West Coasts. One such cable system around New York City is called FOAM (Fiber Optics Around Manhattan).

Infrared. Effective data communications on a smaller scale can be accomplished through the use of devices which operate in the infrared portion

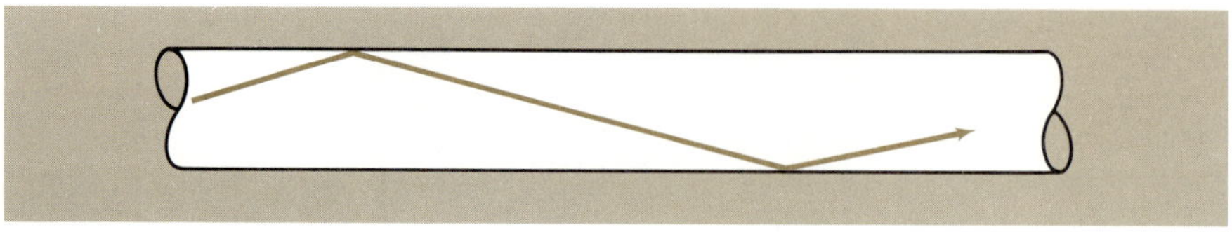

Figure 9–14 Light Beam through Fiber Optic Strand

of the light spectrum. In this technology the sending station computing device is equipped with a light-emitting diode (LED) with which it encodes the data. Photo-sensitive diodes at the receiving station receive the infrared transmissions and convert them to electrical signals for use by the computing equipment at the receiving end.

IBM began selling a personal computer in early 1984, the PCjr, which used infrared to transmit from the keyboard to the CPU. With it, one could sit across the room with the keyboard and still communicate with the system itself. It is, of course, difficult to sit very far away and still read the video display. Incidentally, the same infrared technology is used to provide remote control of televisions and video cassette recorders.

Another potential application for the infrared transmission system lies within offices where a number of different data entry stations might be located. Each data entry station could be equipped with the infrared transmitter; and data from all stations could be collected by a receiving station located overhead, in the ceiling as depicted in Figure 9–17. Without costly rewiring, the data entry stations could be moved about the room as the number of stations changes. Data transfer rates of 64,000 bps can be achieved over short distances.

Infrared transmission can be used over distances of approximately two miles at data transmission speeds of 2,500 bps. Infrared might be a very cost-effective alternative to electrical wiring for building-to-building transmissions.

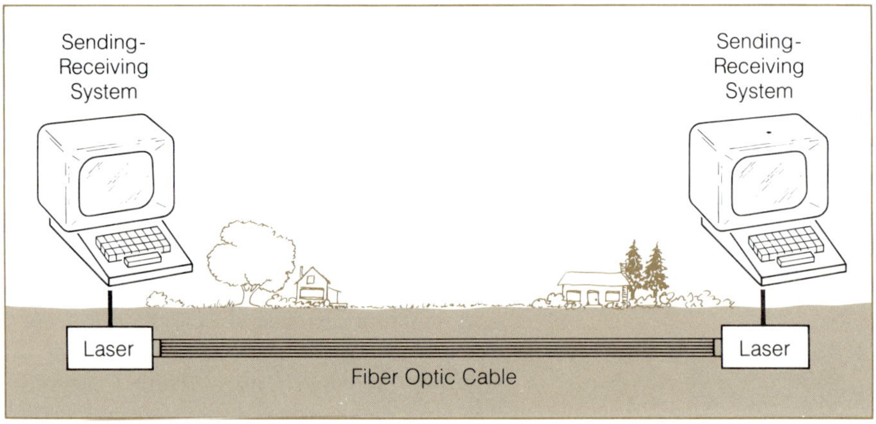

Figure 9–15 Fiber Optics Communications

Figure 9–16 The much smaller fiber optic cable can carry three times as many conversations as the coaxial cable.

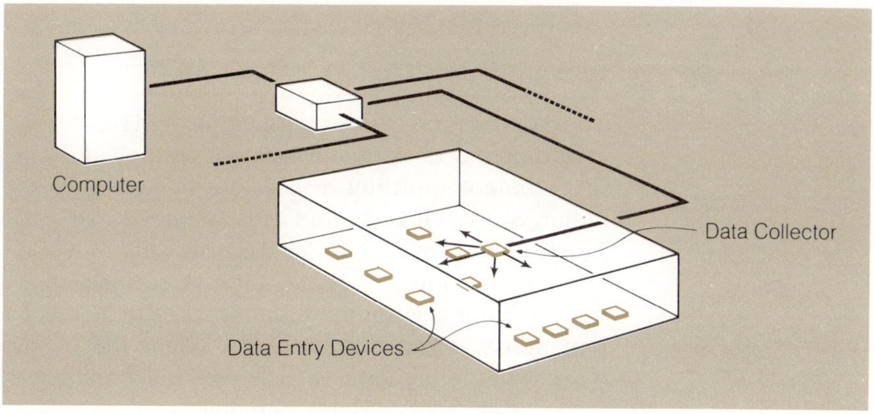

Figure 9–17 Infrared Data Collection System

Challenge Update

The reader and the managers of Coast-to-Coast Trucking should now be able to discuss the promising characteristics of microwave, fiber optic, and infrared communications media.

Technology: Transmission Rules in Detail

Earlier in the chapter the requirements for effective communication were discussed; they include: common language, signal conversion, transmission quality, common speed, and a set of transmission rules. This section will set forth the transmission rules in greater depth, focusing on transmission direction, timing, protocols, and packet switching.

Transmission Direction

A transmission system which permits messages to be sent in only one direction is described as operating in **simplex** mode. Its use would seem to be limited to specialized monitoring situations where data need travel only from a terminal to a data processing device or vice versa. For example, simplex terminals were used in travel agents' offices to receive the transmittal of airline ticket information from the airline's central computer. They have largely been replaced by more capable terminals.

A more common communications approach is to allow messages to move over the transmission medium in both directions but restrict the transmission to only one direction at a time. This mode of transmission is called **half duplex.** Half duplex is a common operating mode for terminals used in interactive computing.

A transmission mode which allows messages to travel in both directions simultaneously is called **full duplex.** Separation of the messages heading in opposite directions is accomplished through separate channels of the transmission medium and, in the case of analog transmissions over the telephone system, separate frequencies. High-speed, intelligent terminals frequently use full duplex transmission.

Transmission Timing

The coordination of message sending and receiving is of utmost importance. Two different design concepts are employed to accomplish the coordination. Some computing devices are designed to rely on timing for coordination of the message and are, therefore, called **synchronous** devices. A synchronous sending device transmits not only the data but also a clocking pulse to provide synchronization. A set of synchronization bits is transmitted at the beginning of the message to alert the receiving station to the impending arrival of a message. When the receiver recognizes the synchronization character, it then presumes that each set of eight bits which follows represents a data character.

Other devices are designed to communicate **asynchronously,** that is, to coordinate message transmission by including a special character or set of bits which act as a flag to indicate the start of the message while another flag indicates the end of the message. Thus, an asynchronous transmission will require more bits than the corresponding synchronous transmission.

Although the general rule of thumb is that synchronous communicating devices are faster than asynchronous devices, it is not a universal truth. Some asynchronous terminals operate at speeds in excess of 36,000 bps.

Transmission Protocols and Packet Switching

One of the most important concepts in the field of data communications is the concept of protocol. A communications **protocol** is a set of rules which governs the sending and receiving of messages throughout the system. The protocol will specify how bits are to be framed into characters and how the characters are to be grouped into messages. The protocol will also specify the sequencing and timing of messages and the means which are to be employed to control errors in transmission.

The role of the communications protocol becomes quite important as we begin to connect large numbers of users together into a network. The switching of data in a network can operate quite differently from the switching of telephone conversations. A telephone conversation is carried out over connections which are established as a circuit through the dialing process, and the circuit remains in effect as long as the conversation is taking place. Although a considerable amount of data is still transmitted by establishing circuits prior to transmission, we find an increasing number of networks which employ a technique known as **packet switching.**

Packet switching networks require that messages be divided into relatively small chunks, called *packets,* as they enter the network. Each packet contains a number of bits required by the protocol as well as some bits to specify the packet's destination, in addition to the bits used to encode that portion of the message being transmitted. At the receiving end of the network, packets are reassembled to provide the original message. Perhaps the best way to gain an understanding of the role of the protocol is to examine several.

One of the most widely used protocols is IBM's BISYNC (Binary Synchronous Communications Protocol), a protocol with which messages encoded in either ASCII or EBCDIC can be transmitted (see Appendix B). The basic structure of a message is illustrated in Figure 9–18. As its name implies, BISYNC is a protocol used for synchronous data transmissions.

Another IBM protocol is SDLC (Synchronous Data Link Control). SDLC is a protocol designed to regulate the transmission of data between stations

Figure 9–18 BISYNC

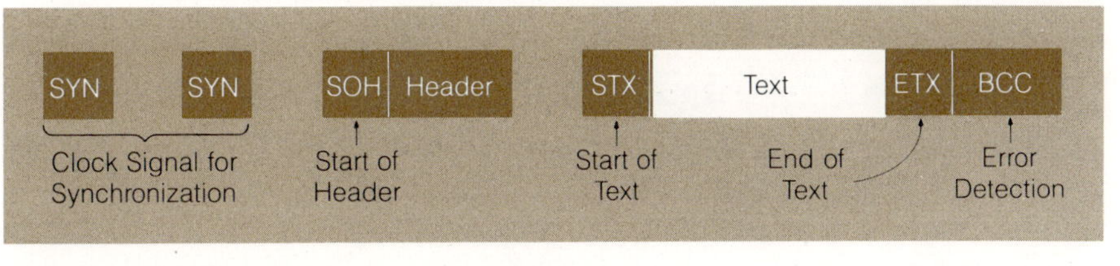

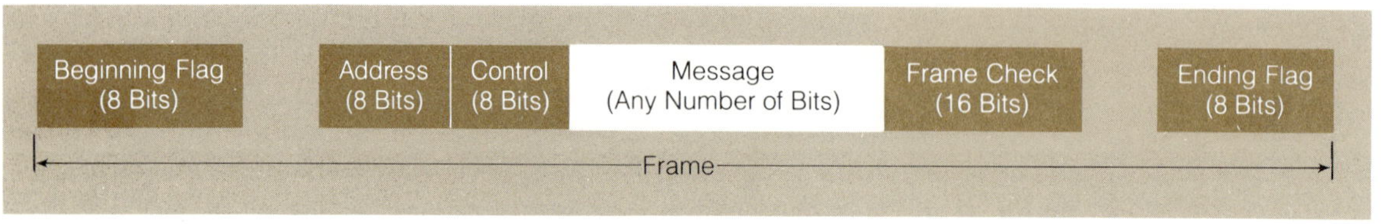

Figure 9–19 SDLC

where one station assumes the role of the primary station while any connected stations are assigned secondary station status. The decision to implement a primary station/secondary station protocol has far-reaching implications for network communications. Some network designers believe that the resulting imposition of primary/secondary roles to the communicating devices seriously limits the flexibility of the network. The SDLC protocol is illustrated in Figure 9–19.

One additional protocol should be sufficient for illustrative purposes. For a non-IBM example, we turn to a protocol developed by Digital Equipment Corporation, called DDCMP (Digital Data Communication Message Protocol). This protocol can be used for either synchronous or asynchronous communication. DDCMP is illustrated in Figure 9–20.

The world would undoubtedly be a tidier place if all communicating devices used a standard protocol. Unfortunately, that is not the case. A number of different protocols exist, and efforts to legislate a standard protocol have largely been thwarted. There is, however, some hope. An interface device called a **protocol converter** has recently begun to have an impact in the market and may eventually solve many of the problems arising from protocol differences. The protocol converter will do whatever protocol translation is necessary to allow two connected devices to communicate with each other.

In an effort to bring order to an otherwise chaotic situation, efforts led by the Consultative Committee on International Telephone and Telegraph (CCITT) are under way to develop a standard model for communications between computing devices. The model, known as the ANSI/ISO Protocol Reference Model, describes seven layers in the communication between stations on a public network. The first three levels, which describe the interface between a user and the network, are known throughout the industry as CCITT Recommendation X.25.

Figure 9–21 depicts the model, which is also known as the Open Systems Architecture for Distributed Processing Systems. No one can predict the extent to which the Protocol Reference Model will cause significant standardization in network protocols. Virtually no one expects the industry to adopt standards which specify all seven levels of the model, but the standardization effort has been helpful. There is, at least, some movement toward increased standardization.

Figure 9–20 DDCMP

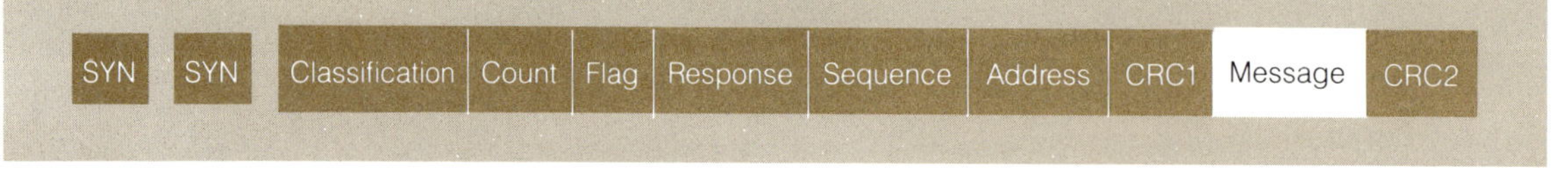

Figure 9–21 Open Systems Architecture for Distributed Systems

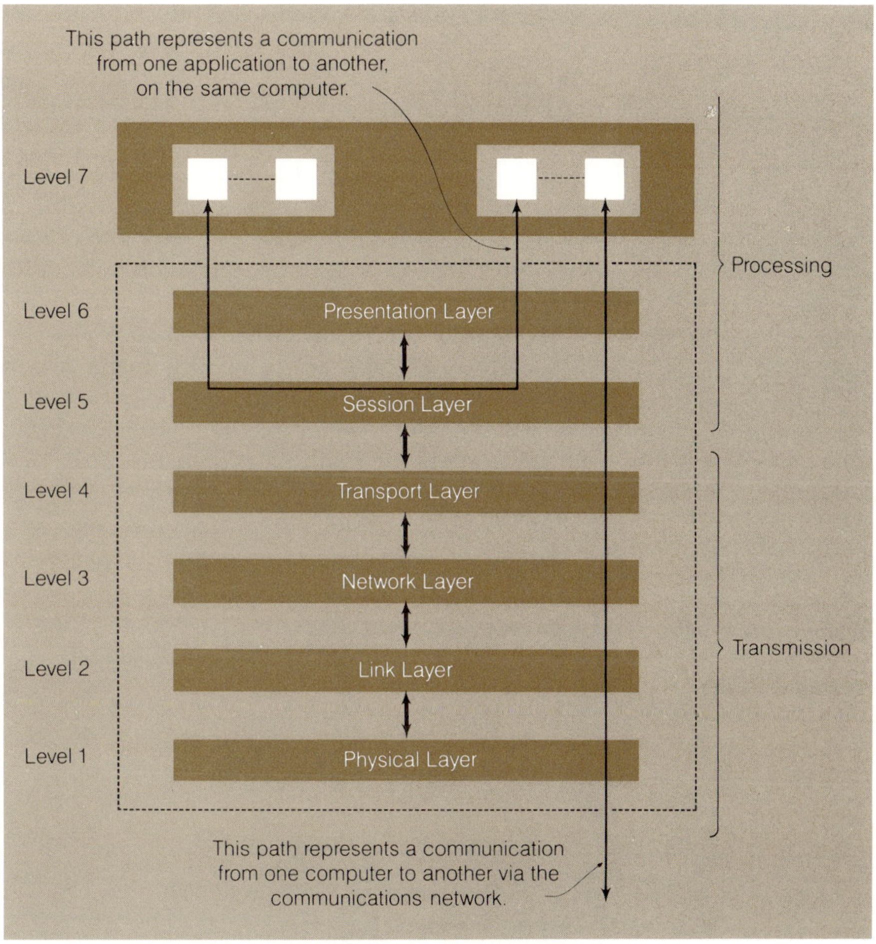

Challenge Update

The role of protocols in data communications should now be clear.

Newest Developments

Although new technologies will undoubtedly emerge for the transmission of data, the really significant gains are expected from the gradual conversion of the telephone and other data networks to digital techniques and the eventual integration of the transmission of voice, data, and video signals. A common network for the transmission of all three types of signals will allow organizations to utilize more fully their data communications facilities. Such a network is called an **integrated services digital network (ISDN).** Video communications, however, consume huge quantities of resources. A communications link capable of 1,200 two-way voice conversations or 50 million bps of data transmission could accommodate only one television video transmission with accompanying sound.

Digital transmission systems will offer a future of transmission with less noise, packet switching, and techniques for compressing data to make transmission more efficient. The conversion to digital transmission will dictate that organizations connected to the network provide digital PBX (*p*rivate *b*ranch e*x*change) systems for the connection. Digital PBX systems became commercially available in the early 1980s. A digital PBX could handle voice, video, and data communications, although it is not clear yet that the economics of such integration are favorable. Figure 9–22 illustrates the integration of the various communication capabilities within an organization.

The integration of the various systems illustrated in Figure 9–22 is a technological possibility yet to be fully realized in a practical system. Integrated systems are expected to be in place by 1985, although fully effective use of an integrated system may not be realized until much later.

Effective integration should eventually result in the network-wide distribution of the information generated by any of the processes illustrated: word processing, personal computing, and host computing. LANs will handle the various communications within the firm with access to other firms

Figure 9–22 Private Branch Exchange–Integrated Digital Communications

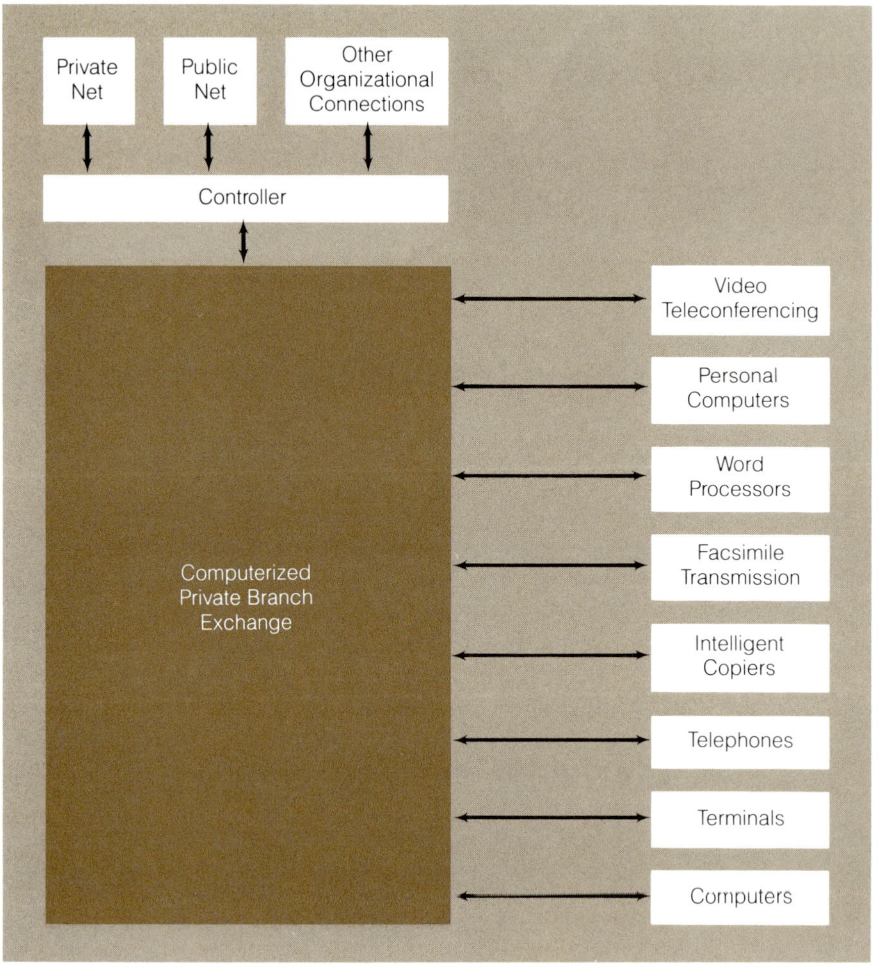

gained through MANs and long-distance, VANs. Information resource management will take on impressive dimensions in such a world. The effective management of these facilities will require managers well versed in computing, communications, and business. A review of the challenge with which we began this chapter will help focus our attention on its contents.

COMPUTING CHALLENGE: *A Final Note*

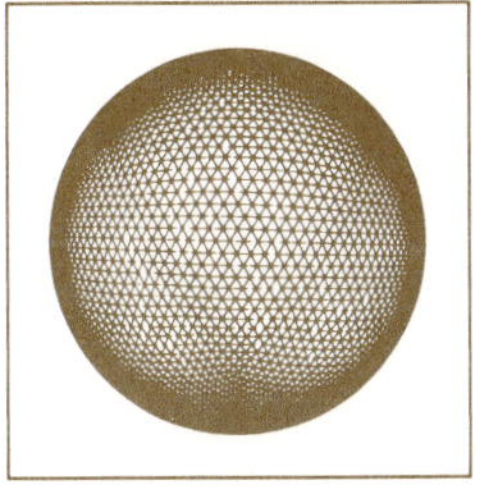

We return briefly to consider the communications problems faced by Coast-to-Coast Trucking. It seems clear that the nature of their business requires the storage of both the current status and the next intended destination of all shipments, trailers, and tractors. Each of the sixty-five terminals must have the capability of entering data into the system to update the status of shipments, trailers, and tractors. In addition, each of the terminals needs to be able to inquire as to the status of any of the three elements of the business.

A long-distance VAN could provide the necessary inter-city connections. The corporate office would probably need a LAN within the building which connects to the long-distance network. Eventually, Coast-to-Coast will be able to communicate with customers via a MAN. Serious problems in compatibility due to differences in encoding schemes and protocols could be avoided by buying hardware from a single manufacturer.

The truck drivers probably do not need computing devices. They can call the nearest terminal to report their progress.

What advantages would connection to a VAN seem to have over a strictly dial-up service?

What types of input devices ought to be considered for installation in the terminal offices?

What types of output devices ought to be considered for installation in the terminal offices?

Would this system use electrical wires, microwaves, lasers, fiber optics, or infrared transmitters? How would the user know? Would the user care?

SUMMARY

- As organizations have become more dispersed geographically, and the use of computing equipment more extensive, the need for means by which computing devices can communicate with each other has become more pronounced.
- Long-distance, value-added networks (VANs) exist to make it possible for businesses to communicate with their widely-dispersed branch offices and to communicate with other businesses.
- Metropolitan area networks (MANs) tie together many different companies for data communications purposes.

- Local area networks (LANs) allow the interconnection of many computer-based devices within a short distance of each other.
- As a result of connection to a LAN, users can share data and programs with other users.
- Networks of networks, or interconnected networks, appear to be possible in the near future.
- Effective communication requires that the sender and receiver share a common language, provide for signal transmission and conversion, operate at the same speed, and adhere to a common set of communications rules.
- The simplest communication connection is the direct, hardwired connection between two devices, but such connections are not economical if the distances separating the devices are sizeable.
- The telephone system provides an already-established network for the communication of data, but a number of disadvantages exist with respect to the speed and quality of data transmission through the telephone system.
- Conversion of the telephone system to digital transmission will alleviate some of the disadvantages now present in the old analog system.
- A number of alternatives exist to electrical wire as a transmission medium, including microwave transmission which has been effectively used for a number of years.
- The use of satellites greatly enlarges the effective area for microwave transmission.
- The technology of infrared light-emitting diodes provides an interesting alternative for short-range data communications.
- The use of lasers in conjunction with small optical fibers offers great promise as a substitute for electrical wire.
- Differences in protocol (the set of rules governing message sending and receiving) will retard progress in data communications until standardization and protocol conversion improve.
- Packet switching networks are available which provide improved services and reduced communications costs.
- Within the next few years, significant movement toward the integration of voice, video, and data communications in integrated services digital networks should take place.
- Telephone systems and private branch exchanges (PBXs) will be converted to the digital technology to make integration possible.
- Managing the various resources necessary to provide information flows and the management of those flows will still be of critical importance.

CASE: Data Communications at Citicorp

Citicorp is one of the giants in the banking industry, with important banking operations located on both coasts and in the Midwest as well. The communications network which links their various sites bypasses the telephone system and uses data transmission rates of 56,000 bps through digital circuits. It also uses microwave transmission rates in excess of a million bps from rooftop to rooftop in an urban setting. Although Citicorp communications costs are over $3 million per month, the costs of the bypass are less than the costs of comparable telephone company communications.

An example of the effectiveness of this communications system is provided by the corporation's mortgage lending business. Citicorp Homeowners offers mortgage money to eligible applicants for real estate investments. The determination of eligibility requires a timely evaluation of an applicant's data and the making of quick decisions, with notification to the applicant as soon as possible regarding the status of the loan. Citicorp's success is the result of qualified people working with the most advanced computerized business equipment available today.

Communications among the main office, the many branch offices, and their customers relies heavily on electronic means. For example, Citicorp utilizes a facsimile machine and computer network that provides the speed and accuracy necessary to conduct nationwide transactions. (A facsimile machine is one which transmits copies of documents from one location to another.) The facsimile machines are compact, desk-top transceivers with microprocessor controls and network connections.

Citicorp uses the computer network in many different tasks, but one of the most important is in conducting the second-mortgage business, which demands a lot of communication among twenty-two offices across the nation. Another important use is, of course, in the first-mortgage market, so each of the branch offices maintains close ties with the builders and sales agents in each area. The computer network has also helped to reduce Citicorp's telephone charges by sending and receiving messages quickly and simultaneously. It allows mortgage applications to be received day or night, even when the office is unattended.

The new system of facsimile machines with access to an extensive communications network is credited with significant increases in both the overall volume of mortgage revenues and in customer satisfaction.

"Fax Network Speeds Transactions . . .," *Infosystems*, April 1981, p. 90. Copyright © 1981 Hitchcock Publishing Company.

Questions for the Case

1. To compete aggressively in the home mortgage market, a firm needs both competitive rates and available funds. How does the communications system described here help Citicorp in each of these areas?
2. This operation indicates the use of a long-distance network. Would a MAN also be useful? A LAN? In what way?

DISCUSSION QUESTIONS AND EXERCISES

1. How do digital signals differ from analog signals? Provide some everyday examples of each. Is a stoplight digital or analog?
2. What value-added services might a communications network provide to data communications?

3. What value-added services might become important as the integration of voice, video, and data communications takes place?

4. Compare the relative advantages and disadvantages of electrical wires and fiber optic cables.

5. Which technologies seem to be most promising for long-range data communications?

6. Which technologies seem to be most promising for short-range data communications?

7. How do baseband and broadband compare? Which is faster? Which is cheaper?

8. What are protocols? How do they affect the transmission of data between two competing devices? How is the word *protocol* used in social or diplomatic circles? Is its meaning there related in any way to its meaning in data communications?

9. List and discuss the basic requirements for effective communications between two people. Compare those requirements to those necessary for the effective communication between two computing devices.

10. What advantages are there to converting the telephone system to digital transmission? What disadvantages?

11. Technology and user acceptance always seem to restrain the rate of change within organizations. Discuss both as restraints to integrated voice, video, and data communications within organizations.

12. Why is it that digital transmissions can be filtered and enhanced while it might be undesirable to do the same to analog transmission?

13. How does CSMA/CD (carrier-sense multiple access/collision detection) differ from token passing? Which is standard?

14. For what reasons might a large organization want to bypass the telephone system and use DTS or CATV?

15. What role will a protocol converter play in network communications?

ADDITIONAL READINGS

Ahuja, Viuay. *Design and Analysis of Computer Communication Networks.* New York: McGraw-Hill, 1982.

Chou, Wushow. *Computer Communications.* Englewood Cliffs, NJ: Prentice-Hall, 1983.

Christie, Bruce. *Face to File Communications.* New York: Van Nostrand Reinhold, 1981.

Gantz, John. *Fiber Optics—An Uncomplicated Guide.* Waltham, MA: International Data Corporation, 1981.

Glossbrenner, Alfred. *The Complete Handbook of Personal Computer Communications.* New York: St. Martin's Press, 1983.

Kreager, Paul. *Practical Aspects of Data Communications.* New York: McGraw-Hill, 1983.

McNamara, John E. *Technical Aspccts of Data Communication.* 2d ed. Bedford, MA: Digital Equipment Corporation, 1982.

"Microbroadcasting." *Scientific American,* May 1980, pp. 84–88.

Nichols, E. A. and J. C. Nichols. *Data Communications for Microcomputers: With Practical Applications and Experiments.* New York: McGraw-Hill, 1982.

Rosner, Roy D. *Packet Switching.* Belmont, CA: Lifelong Learning Publications, 1982.

Thomas, John C., and Carroll, John M. "Human Factors in Communication." *IBM Systems Journal,* Vol. 20, No. 2 (1981), pp. 237–263.

Errors, like straws, upon the surface flow; He who would search for pearls must dive below.

from *All for Love*
John Dryden

No house should ever be on any hill or on anything. It should be of the hill, belonging to it, so hill and house could live together each the happier for the other.

from *An Autobiography*
Frank Loyd Wright

Part III

Information Systems

PART PREFACE

Part 2 was designed to provide the reader with a thorough introduction to the four basic functions of data processing: output, input, computation, and storage. The important fundamentals of data communications were also studied. Concepts important to users and managers have been emphasized; the tools by which these functions are implemented have been discussed; and some of the underlying technologies have been explored.

In this, Part 3, the design and acquisition of information processing systems and their integration with the organization are studied. As the words of John Dryden suggest, the rewards of these efforts are only to be realized through concentrated effort. Frank Lloyd Wright's admonition about house design has a definite analogue in data processing systems design. A data processing system should not merely be in an organization, but of the organization.

Managers and users must accept some of the responsibility for the design of all systems within their organizations, whether those systems process data, manufacture products, develop employees, perform research, secure financing, or generate plans. This part of the text responds to that challenge by looking at the alternatives for data processing and then studying the design and acquisition processes. The chapters in Part 3 are:

- Chapter 10 *Information Systems Alternatives*
- Chapter 11 *The Design of Systems*
- Chapter 12 *Acquisition of Computing Resources*
- Chapter 13 *Software Engineering*
- Chapter 14 *Procedures, Personnel, and Careers*

April
May
June
57,881
60,775
63,814
430
750
700
57,451
60,025
63,114
28,951
30,387
31,912
28,500
29,638
31,202
11,528
11,150
12,496
896
932
941
Load Data
Store Data

10

Information Systems Alternatives

CHAPTER PREVIEW

The first nine chapters have provided a background in the fundamentals of computers. They have provided an examination of the fundamental operations of output, input, computation, storage, and communication as well as the tools which make it possible for users to accomplish these operations in a data processing system. It is time now to explore the overall capabilities of complete systems, to gain some understanding of the alternatives which are available to the user.

While it is necessary to understand the basic elements from which computer systems are built, the elements themselves are insufficient to satisfy the information processing needs of users. Input, output, computation, and storage devices must be combined into an operable system which must, in turn, become an integral part of the organization. Software, people, and control procedures are also very important parts of a successful system.

Users gain access to a computing system in different ways, depending upon the specific needs of any particular application. Some applications require only routine updating of files on a periodic basis. For example, if transcripts of students' academic performance were stored within a computerized system, we would expect that changes would need to be made only once or twice per academic term.

Other types of applications require that files be brought up to date monthly, weekly, or daily. Some require that changes be made instantly, as, for example, they are done in an airlines reservation system.

The choices available to the user are discussed in this chapter. We will explore the three classic alternatives—batch, remote batch, and interactive computing—and some of the more complex issues surrounding the updating of files, stand-alone computing capability, and network computing.

Later in this chapter we will turn our attention to the various types of computing services which are available to users and how they differ from one another. The selection of a particular type of service is a reasonably difficult problem, one which may require a thorough analysis of the costs and benefits of each type of service. On the other hand, the user may be constrained to using the organization's existing data processing service where very little (or no) additional analysis is required. An example will help us understand the potential scope of the problem.

COMPUTING CHALLENGE: *Computing Alternatives for Governmental Agencies*

Let us choose a hypothetical example from the public sector to illustrate the alternatives which are available, though we could just as easily select an example from the private sector. The National Forest System in the United States is charged with the responsibility of managing the forest lands owned by the government. There are about 150 national forests in the United States, each of which is further divided into several districts.

The district ranger is the person in charge of managing the district to see that the various goals of timber harvest, mining, domestic animal forage, wildlife preservation, and recreation (to name only a few) are achieved. The information processing needs of the typical district are rather formidable. A visit with Jan Windstrom, district ranger of the Walden District of the Palambra National Forest in northern Wisconsin, will help us gain the necessary perspective.

The typical district operates, as any business must, to keep track of timber sales, recreational use, payroll, expenses, and the status of every parcel of land under its management. Information must be collected, processed, stored, and eventually shared with the supervisor's office of the national forest to which the district belongs, with the regional office, with the headquarters of the National Forest System in Washington, D.C., and with the U.S. Department of Agriculture. Additional demands for information can be expected from local special interest groups (hikers, campers, skiers, and hunters) and from the offices of government.

In the past, Ms. Windstrom had been able to keep up by mailing the necessary data, recorded on original source documents, to the regional office where the data were changed into machine-readable form for processing by the regional office computer system. Problems in that mode of operation have developed, not the least of which are the delays due to the mail, the errors which required extensive communication between the district clerk and the regional office, and the lack of control felt by the district ranger.

At a recent training session, Ms. Windstrom was introduced to several different schemes for accomplishing the data processing activities common to her organization. She became aware of remote batch processing, interactive processing, minicomputers, microcomputers, and networks, and she wants to explore these alternatives as possible solutions to the district's data processing problems. Some of her questions remained unanswered at the end of the training session.

What are the alternative methods of accomplishing an organization's data processing needs? How are the differing needs of organizations met by the different types of data processing alternatives which are available? What choices does an organization have? These are important questions.

We will explore the answers to these and other questions in this chapter. After careful study of this chapter, the reader should be able to:

1. Differentiate between batch, remote batch, and interactive processing and be able to list some of the desirable characteristics of each.

2. *Describe distributed data processing, stand-alone, and network capabilities.*
3. *Discuss the sizes of computing systems which are available.*
4. *Explain the role of service bureaus, timesharing services, and facilities managers.*

HISTORICAL PERSPECTIVE

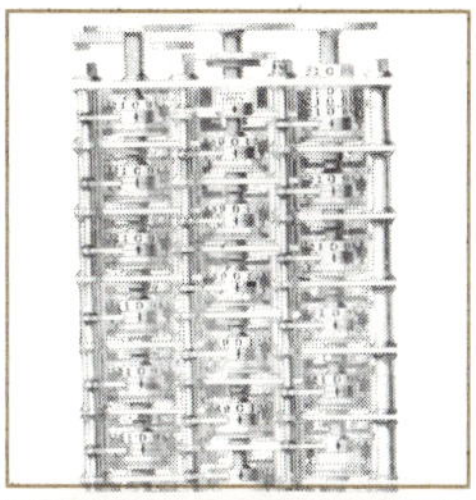

The most straightforward mechanism for providing for an organization's data processing needs has been for the organization to lease or buy a computer mainframe with an appropriate set of peripherals and hire the necessary programmers, systems analysts, and operators to run the system. The result has been a complete **in-house computing facility.**

The earliest type of access provided by computing machines was known as **batch,** and an extensive amount of data processing continues to be done in that mode. The name *batch* was derived from a characteristic of that type of processing in which data to be processed were saved for some period of time and then processed as a batch, as characterized in Figure 10–1. For example, in a batch transaction processing system, the transactions to be processed were collected together in groups, or batches. At the appropriate time, the transaction processing program and the batch of transactions were read into the system, the program was executed, and the results were produced.

Batch processing is still done in basically the same way even today. Since today's computing systems have much greater capacities in secondary storage devices than the older machines, it is now more likely that the transactions are stored in secondary memory during the "batching" period. The program itself, very probably, is also stored on the system, and the entire batch processing run can be initiated by the operator or someone else from a remote terminal. The capability of running batch processing, or any other type of processing, must be provided by the operating system and an appropriate set of hardware. Early computers had, comparatively speaking, very primitive operating systems which allowed only batch processing.

In fact, the earliest of systems did not allow the processing of two or more batch jobs to be overlapped, something discussed in Chapter 6. In these early systems, each batch job was allocated the complete set of system resources while it was being processed. The development of overlapping allowed adjacent jobs in the batch processing sequence to better utilize the system's resources by scheduling certain processing steps of one job to be overlapped with the processing of another. This, as we saw, led eventually to the capability known as multiprogramming. In a multiprogrammed environment, several different batch jobs can reside in the computing system, with each (in turn) being moved toward completion.

The essential characteristics of early batch processing included the requirements that the data and the program be physically delivered to the computing center, that the processing take place on the full collection of data without interaction with the user, and that the output be physically

Figure 10–1 A Characterization of Batch Processing

produced at the computing center. More modern operations, less strict with respect to the source of input and destination of output, are still referred to as batch if only the essential characteristic of collecting transactions over a period of time is maintained.

Only a few years ago, batch processing was the most common mode of operation for students learning to program in an introductory data processing and programming class. Thus, students prepared programs and data on punched cards, turned the cards in at the computer center, and entertained themselves until their programs and output were returned.

Users have often been frustrated by the data processing center's handling of batch jobs. They typically felt as though they had no control over the schedule or any of the details connected with the running of their processing jobs. They were also frustrated when little errors, easily correctable, would thwart an entire run, which then had to be rescheduled.

Fortunately, times have changed, and computing systems now provide more reasonable types of access. Batch is still a popular processing mode, but other types of processing are also being used.

Data Processing Modes

The selection of an appropriate means for providing data processing services to an organization can be a complex problem. Modern computers with their sophisticated operating systems provide an increasingly complicated assortment of data processing possibilities. At the same time, the increasing number of computer applications makes the problem of selecting an optimum system for a particular mix of applications more complex. In this section, we will turn our attention initially to the differing needs of applications and then to the data processing modes available for addressing those needs.

The reader should recall from the discussions of the operating system in Chapter 6, that a computing system acquires its capabilities through the appropriate combination of hardware and software. The operating system must provide and make available to the user the resources necessary to accomplish the different types of data processing tasks.

Some operating systems provide only for batch operations. Others may allow many users to share the system in a timesharing mode. Some operating system capabilities, such as multiprogramming, greatly enhance the efficiency with which a series of batch jobs can be processed. Many operating systems allow the interweaving of both batch and timesharing operations on the same system.

The issue is further complicated by the existence of operating systems which allow the linking together of several computers in a network. Computing systems gain networking capability through the correct combination of hardware and operating system programs. The existence of a network, and the presence in the network of other computers and operating systems, greatly complicates the design problem. The net result is that modern organizations have an increasingly difficult time in identifying the means by which their differing computing needs are to be met.

Differing Computing Needs. If there were no constraints on computing resources, an organization could have a custom-designed system which fits each application perfectly. There are, however, constraints which limit choices. Frequently the constraint is money, but often it is the lack of time or the availability of a skilled person to evaluate other alternatives. Therefore, although the discussion will match an application with an ideal computing system, it is much more frequently the case that matching is a compromise between the needs of several applications.

Applications have differing needs, and addressing those needs is a primary responsibility of a designer. In many cases, systems designers must operate under constraints which require that the application be designed to execute on an existing system, with virtually no modifications permitted. The designer must then adjust the design to fit the available hardware and the existing operating system. The design problem often becomes a problem of compromise, of designing a system which will operate effectively, given the set of constraints. The differing needs of applications are illustrated in the following example.

Consider a system which generates monthly statements for the customers of a bank. For any particular account, a statement is generated monthly (as output), even though the transactions which are processed to generate the statement occur much more frequently. These transactions include the writing of checks, the making of deposits, and the making of withdrawals. Transactions are collected into batches according to some appropriate time period (for example, daily), and the batches are used to update a customer statement stored on tape or disk. At the end of the month, a copy of the statement is generated (as output).

An interesting question to ask is: Is the electronic copy of the customer's statement, which includes the current balance, up-to-date? The answer depends upon what is meant by *up-to-date*. As a matter of fact, the customer's statement could be out-of-date by the length of the time period over which transactions are saved to make up the batch. Is that important? Perhaps.

If we wanted to make sure the customer's account balance was more up-to-date, we would have to provide for a more frequent update. We could design the system to provide for instantaneous update, as each check is cleared or each deposit or withdrawal is made. Such a system would be called a **real time system** and would require that the customer's data be kept on-line, as was discussed in Chapter 7.

The data files which support an application can be kept on-line or off-line, depending upon the needs of the particular application. On-line data can be brought up-to-date through batch means or in real time (instantaneously), again, depending upon the needs of the application. Does it make sense to consider the other possible combination, an application with off-line files and a real time update? Probably not.

If, then, in our banking example it is important to the bank to have customer information which is always up-to-date, the files should be maintained on-line, with updates performed in real time as illustrated in Figure 10–2. Such a system would be more expensive (often greatly so) than one with batch update or off-line files. The trade-off is once again more speed for more money.

An airlines reservation system, which must give quick responses to customer inquiries, requires on-line files with real time updates. An inventory control system could be built with on-line files and real time update, but it could also be built with off-line files and batch update. If inquiry was important in the inventory control system, but the nature of the inventory was such that instantaneous information about shipments and receipts was not necessary, the system could be designed with on-line files for inquiry but with batch update.

Figure 10–2 Bank Teller with Interactive Access to On-Line Files for Real Time Inquiry

Remote Batch and Interactive Computing

The three modes of data processing have always been listed as batch, remote batch, and interactive. While these three categories do not now seem adequate to describe the full range of data processing activities, it is important to understand the meaning of each. Batch processing was explained in the historical perspective section of this chapter. **Remote batch** is a method of processing which allows a user to submit a batch job from a location remote from the computer center. Remote batch is illustrated in Figures 10–3 and 10–4.

Remote batch usually implies that the remote station is provided with relatively high-speed input and output equipment—for example, a high-speed card reader and line printer. The remote station's equipment is connected to the computer itself through a direct wire or some other communications medium. Data processing jobs are submitted to the computing system through the remote input device, and the output is received on the remote output device.

Remote batch offers the processing efficiencies of batch operation with the convenience of remotely entering data and receiving output. For organizational units distant from the data processing center, remote batch is an improvement over regular batch. Transmission of the inputs and output take place at electronic speeds rather than via the mail or messenger service.

Interactive computing receives its name from the interactive effort which takes place between the user and the computing system. An interactive user usually sits at a remote terminal and enters data and programs through the keyboard or through the use of storage devices associated with an intelligent terminal. Output is displayed on the terminal's screen or teleprinter or sent to one of the storage devices.

Figure 10–3 Remote Job Entry Terminal

Figure 10–4 A Characterization of Remote Batch Processing

Figure 10–5 Engineer Using Interactive System for Computer Chip Design

Figure 10–6 A Characterization of Interactive Processing

Interactive computing is illustrated in Figures 10–5 and 10–6. Such a session is interactive in the sense that the user and the system alternate in their communications with each other, with each response influenced by both the actions of the user and the system. Users find the instant (less than 2 to 5 seconds) response of an interactive system to be very rewarding.

Challenge Update

Ms. Windstrom and the reader should now be able to differentiate among batch, remote batch, and interactive processing.

Stand-Alone and Network Computing

The capabilities of computing systems have gone far beyond those represented by the three categories of batch, remote batch, and interactive, all of which focus on a single, central computing system. We have seen how an interactive inquiry can take place with updates that occur in batch mode and how that same application could have been designed to support an interactive inquiry with updates in real time. Perhaps a more complex classification scheme is needed, one which captures the nature (batch or interactive) of the relationship between the user and the system and, in addition, the manner in which updates to the supporting files are accomplished.

We might also need to know something about the generation of the output, which could either be generated in an interactive mode, in small pieces as in a conversation, or spooled temporarily for more complete treatment as a batch output. Alternatively, a user can access the computing system interactively, that is, from a terminal, for the purpose of setting up a batch run.

The classification scheme needs to cover the manner in which the user gains access, the manner in which the inputs are treated, the manner in which the program executes, and the manner in which the outputs are generated. Access traditionally known as batch would be the same as characterized earlier; batch input, a batch program run, followed by batch output. The other extreme is represented by a user entering data from a terminal for processing and the generation of output in real time. Many combinations exist between the two extremes. For example, a user could take advantage of interactive access, via a terminal, for the purpose of setting up a batch run from programs and data already stored within the system.

Distributed Processing

The number of possibilities becomes even greater if the user has a full-fledged computer to use instead of just a terminal or other input device. To this point in the discussion in this chapter, we have assumed that the user was gaining access to the system through an input device which had no intelligence or memory. Consider, now, that the user has a small computer system capable of acting like a terminal. (A computing device which is capable of acting like another computing device is said to be able to **emulate** that device.) It could be that the user's terminal itself has been equipped with a microprocessor to give it greater capability.

The user with a small computer now has additional choices with respect to the manner in which he or she chooses to interact with another computing system. For example, the user can select the location of the processing itself. Small programs might be executed on the user's intelligent terminal, while larger programs are left to the bigger machine. Many data entry operations take place with the user entering and editing the data on a local device, with a later transfer of edited data to the host machine in batch mode.

For example, a large business with many different locations for plants, warehouses, and sales offices could distribute small computers throughout the system so that each location had its own. The local machines could be used for localized data processing tasks as needed, and used as remote stations feeding data into the central computer whenever necessary.

The trend to give users more capable and intelligent input devices connected together or to a central host computer is called **distributed data processing.** It represents an attempt to distribute the processing capabilities throughout an organization, rather than isolate them at one central location. Users gain the ability to develop and execute their own programs on local computers, while maintaining access to the larger system for com-

Figure 10–7
Distributed Data Processing Allows Access to Computing Power Throughout the Organization

puting jobs more efficiently done on a larger machine. Large numbers of computing systems can be connected together into *networks* as was discussed in Chapter 9. An example of distributed processing is shown in Figures 10–7 and 10–8.

Several important factors have contributed to the development of distributed data processing. One such factor, miniaturization and the resultant development of computers on chips, has led to such great improvement in the price-to-performance ratio that organizations can now afford to have computing capability distributed throughout the organization. Miniaturization has also given us desktop computers which do not need special treatment with respect to power supply and air conditioning requirements. Distributed data processing has also benefited greatly from significant improvements in data communications, the topic of the previous chapter.

Improvements in operating system software were also needed in order to be able to coordinate the efforts of many computing systems connected

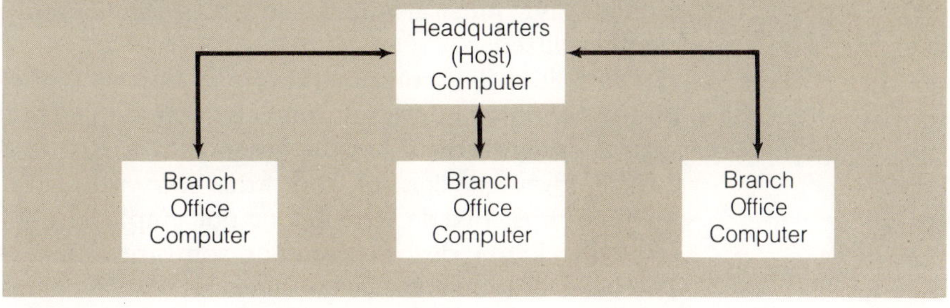

Figure 10–8
Example of Distributed Processing

with each other through a network. Ideally, a distributed data processing system would allow a user to interact with programs and data stored anywhere in the system in such a way that the details of the interaction were transparent to the user. The communications network, in turn, should be smart enough to provide secure (private) interactions for all users, with a built-in capability to recover should any single element of the system fail.

Challenge Update

The concepts of distributed data processing, stand-alone, and network capabilities should now be understood.

Advantages of Distributed Processing. The potential advantages of distributed data processing are impressive. Data entry operations can be significantly improved by moving them closer to the source of data and putting them under local control. Small data processing tasks can be completed on local machines without incurring the communications cost necessary to access a central computer. Many of the frustrations formerly felt by users interacting with a central facility—for example, contention for log-on—are eliminated.

Another apparent advantage of distributed systems concerns the way in which various organizational units are charged for computer use. One very popular method charges out *all* data processing center costs by allocating them as overhead to the various departments using the service. Unit managers generally feel that they have no control over the overhead expenditures within the data processing budget and that they are not getting full value for their allocated data processing costs. Distributed processing, in comparison, gives them visual confirmation and correspondingly greater control over data processing costs.

Disadvantages of Distributed Processing. On the other hand, several interesting managerial problems are brought into focus by the increasing popularity of distributed data processing. First, some *economies of scale* might be lost by allowing processing to take place on smaller systems. In general, the larger the system, the more quickly it can execute instructions. The distribution of processing throughout the system causes programs to be executed on small, rather than large CPUs, which makes the time of execution longer.

Second, upper management could lose control of the data processing resources as they are dispersed throughout the organization. For example, upper management must be certain that security is maintained in the distributed centers so that unauthorized access to sensitive data is prohibited. They must also make sure that the computing resources are efficiently utilized.

Third, sufficient coordination must exist so that each of the local computing operations does not unnecessarily duplicate the programming and system design activities of the others. Most parts of the organization need payroll, inventory control, and order entry programs. The organization as a whole must decide whether or not employees should write their own programs, jointly develop common software, or acquire software packages. There are, of course, hazards associated with allowing users to pursue their own data processing tasks without close supervision. For example, programming standards may be ignored, or data security considerations may be slighted.

Fourth, local managers may not be able to effectively supervise the data processing activities within their part of the organization. Line managers usually have managerial skills developed in other, non–data processing areas of the business. They may not have the managerial talent necessary to supervise data processing activities.

Fifth, data processing personnel in the local organizations may not be able to recognize interesting career paths in the new, distributed environment. In a centralized data processing department, people can see many other jobs (even managerial jobs) to which they might aspire. In a distributed processing environment they may not be able to see a good job to which they might be promoted. There are, for example, far fewer data processing professionals at most remote locations under distributed processing. Will these people have to abandon data processing careers or abandon their current locations in order to be promoted?

Most distributed locations will have only a few data processing employees; some will only have one. A small staff presents other problems. When critical functions are performed by only a few individuals, accommodating absences, vacations, and sick leave is difficult.

Distributed data processing provides an excellent opportunity for the organization to improve the effectiveness of its data processing activities, but it does provide some interesting managerial challenges as well.

Cost/Benefit Analysis

Most well-managed firms perform some type of formal analysis to evaluate a new project which would require a significant expenditure. The particular type of analysis varies from firm to firm. Some, for example, may calculate the cost/benefit ratio by dividing the total projected cost of the project by the total dollar benefits to be derived from the project.

Others may calculate financial quantities such as the net present value, the years to payback, the breakeven point, or the internal rate of return. Each analysis requires that the analyst assign dollar values to the various costs and benefits. Sometimes the assignment of dollar values is an easy task; sometimes it is not. The costs and benefits typical of a data processing system will be studied next.

All managers in an organization have a self-interest in data processing costs and benefits. Costs are usually borne by the various operating units via some chargeout (chargeback) or allocation to overhead scheme and thus become part of each manager's budget. Additionally, the operating departments must usually be able to identify a significant amount of benefits in order to justify data processing expenditures in support of departmental activities.

Costs. The costs of a new computer system can be broken down into several different categories. If the new system requires that new hardware be acquired, then hardware costs will represent one of the categories. (The acquisition process for hardware is covered in Chapter 12.)

Virtually all new data processing systems will require new software, so there will be software costs associated with the new system, whether the new software is developed in-house or purchased from an outside vendor. (Software acquisition is discussed in some detail in Chapter 12.)

The running of new applications on an existing computer will increase the operating costs associated with that system. Additional supplies such as paper, tapes, disks, and so on may be required, as well as increased data entry, operator attention, and system maintenance expenses.

The number of people who will have to undergo training in order to be able to run a new system may be large. Computer operators, data entry clerks, programmers, users, and managers may all have to be trained. Different types of training are, of course, required for each of the different categories of people affected by the new system. Training costs could be as great as 50 percent of the total project costs, so they are not to be overlooked. If training itself is foregone, or poorly done, the resulting inefficiencies in the system could be even more costly.

The analyst must make a concerted effort to identify and evaluate all costs associated with the introduction of a new system. Some costs could be subtle and difficult to evaluate. For example, during the changeover period, both the old and new systems may (and often should) be run in parallel, possibly resulting in significant amounts of overtime. Telephone or other communications costs may also be increased. Employees may incur travel and lodging costs in connection with attendance at training sessions. A proportion of the cost of the new system should be set aside to deal with unforeseen circumstances—a contingency plan.

Benefits. As difficult as it is to identify and evaluate the costs associated with a new data processing system, it is even more difficult to accomplish the same analysis on the benefit side. Some new systems will have obvious cost reduction components, such as reduced communication, data entry, or operating costs. Other benefits will be much more subtle, such as improved customer service, increased inventory accuracy, and more effective presentations of the output to the user. Any dollar benefits associated with such intangible benefits are difficult for an analyst to determine and then defend.

The difficulties of calculating the dollar benefits associated with a new system have caused some firms to abandon the classical cost/benefit computations. Instead, they compute a statement of potential savings at the time the project is undergoing initial justification but delay a thorough analysis of the actual costs and benefits until after the system has been installed. This review of costs and benefits serves as an educational tool to improve the intuition of the analyst and the judgment of managers.

In effect, managers of an organization want to be assured that the system was a good investment in terms of use, efficiency, and effectiveness, even if firm financial figures are difficult to obtain. User satisfaction is often used as one measure, and the amount of voluntary use is often a measure of user satisfaction. An analysis of the relative costs and benefits of data processing projects is essential, whether performed before or after the implementation itself.

Sources of Computing Services

In the computer marketplace of the 1980s, a user has a large number of computing alternatives from which to choose. In this section we will explore some of the more common alternatives. It is important to understand at the outset the many different types of computers which are available. We turn our attention briefly to microcomputers, minicomputers, and mainframes.

Microcomputers, Minicomputers, and Mainframes

The first point which needs to be made in any discussion of computer sizes is that the categories, however well-defined in theory, are hopelessly entangled in fact. There are no clearcut boundaries which separate the micros from the minis, and none which separate the larger minis from the smaller mainframes. There are some general statements which can be made to give the potential buyer some understanding of the general relationships attempted by the categories.

We should not believe that this is a problem which will soon be solved. As a matter of fact, there are attempts to further complicate the categories rather than simplify or more clearly delineate them. For example, some have suggested that new categories be added for supermicros between micros and minis, and midicomputers or super minis between minis and mainframes.

The standard computers produced and sold through the middle to late 1960s were all mainframe machines, and the only categories which existed were small, medium, and large mainframes. In the late 1960s efforts were underway to expand the range of sizes by extending both ends of the range. Supercomputers were developed at the large end of the spectrum, perhaps the largest of which was the ILLIAC 4.

The miniaturization efforts which evolved from the space exploration efforts gave us integrated circuits, large-scale integration (and eventually

Figure 10–9 Large Mainframe System

VLSI), and led to the development of minicomputers. Even smaller machines became known as microcomputers, and the stage was set for confusion.

Initial efforts to distinguish mainframes from minicomputers led analysts to choose word size, software sophistication, the range of available periph-peripherals, site preparation, and cost as the distinguishing characteristics. **Mainframe computers** had larger word sizes (32 or more bits per word), had very sophisticated software (including data base management software), and could be integrated with a large number of peripherals in assembling a computing system. Site preparation for a mainframe computing system was usually extensive, requiring raised flooring to accommodate the connecting cables, a conditioned power supply, and air conditioning with humidity control. The cost of a mainframe system was rarely less than $250,000 and could easily be several million dollars. A mainframe system is pictured in Figure 10–9.

In comparison, **minicomputers** had a word size of 16 bits, very limited software, and few peripherals and required very little site preparation. The cost of a minicomputer system ranged from a minimum of $25,000 to approximately $300,000 for one of the largest, most sophisticated systems. At the bottom end of the scale, **microcomputers** had word sizes of 8 bits and even more limited software and peripherals. Site preparation was essentially nil, as they were designed to sit on a desk and plug into the nearest electrical outlet. Costs ranged downward from $25,000. A minicomputer system is pictured in Figure 10–10.

Figure 10–10 A Minicomputer System by NCR

This rather tidy classification scheme was shaken by the introduction of a 32-bit minicomputer, and then completely destroyed by the introduction of 16-bit and, later, 16/32-bit microcomputers. Additionally, we have seen the arrival of sophisticated software, and an increasingly wide range of peripherals have been developed for both minis and micros. To make matters worse, some of the new systems have both a microcomputer-sized chip and a minicomputer-sized chip housed in the same CPU so that it can execute the software available to either the mini or the micro; hence the new category, supermicro, or minimini, as the case may be. A microcomputer system is pictured in Figure 10–11.

The lesson to be learned is: a buying decision should be based on the demonstrated capabilities of the system, not on the category to which it happens to (or appears to) belong. Attention must be given to the performance of the system in those types of applications for which it will be used. The spectrum of available systems is indeed wide.

Challenge Update

The reader could now help Ms. Windstrom describe the various sizes of computers which are available.

Figure 10–11
Microcomputer
IBM

In-House Computing Facilities

The first alternative which comes to mind, as we consider the means by which an organization can acquire access to computing services, is the alternative of outright purchase or lease of the equipment to be installed on the organization's premises. The resulting data processing center would be staffed with the organization's employees, who would control the operations of the computer, data entry, and software development. An organization typically contracts with the manufacturer for the maintenance necessary to keep the computer equipment operating correctly.

Several advantages, and a few disadvantages, usually accrue to those organizations which manage their own in-house computing facilities. First and foremost is control. An organization with its own facility is always in control of the uses to which the system is put. The system can be operated and maintained so that it can be allocated to jobs according to the organization's changing set of job priorities.

An in-house facility reduces the costs and delays associated with transporting data and information back and forth between the organization and an outside data processing service. Once such a system has been justified on the basis of a particular set of applications, any excess capacity can be used to service marginal applications at very attractive cost. If efficiently managed, the facility can provide the most data processing capability at the lowest cost.

The potential disadvantages to an in-house facility, however, are not to be ignored. Managing a data processing center requires a significant amount of managerial talent, which might not be available. The result could be a poorly managed data processing operation. Managerial costs, operating costs, and maintenance costs must also be considered.

Any installed, in-house system has a very definite capacity limitation because every system has an upper bound to its data processing capabilities.

As new applications are developed and added to the system, the system eventually becomes overloaded. Replacement of the system with a larger one can be a costly, time-consuming proposition. Enlargements of the system must, by their nature, occur in steps. Some systems are designed to accommodate these step-wise enlargements more readily than others.

During the early period of a system's life in an organization, excess capacity will be the norm. Responsible managers would take steps to increase the use of the system to reduce the amount of idle capacity. As a result, new applications will be developed. The workload eventually increases to the point where, in later stages, the system becomes overloaded. As a matter of fact, the system almost never fits exactly. Too large in the beginning, it is too soon inadequate for the load. If, on the other hand, computing services are purchased from an outside vendor, the correct volume of service can be purchased, whatever the volume of applications.

Timesharing

One alternative to an in-house system is to purchase time on someone else's system. **Timesharing,** as we have seen, is the shared use of a computer system by a number of simultaneous users. Recall that it is a capability which must be provided by the computer's operating system. The operating system must provide for multiprogramming and communications so that many users may be on-line at the same time. The operating system directs the computer's attention to each user in turn so that it seems to the users as if they have exclusive use of the system.

An organization might, and often does, provide timesharing service on an in-house machine. Another alternative, however, is to purchase timesharing services from an outside vendor. In such a circumstance, the computing system itself is owned and operated by another party for the purpose of selling time on it to the wide variety of users who access the system from remote terminals installed in the user's place of work.

One of the big advantages of timesharing is that the user can often gain access to a much more sophisticated system than the user's organization could afford to provide as an in-house facility. A timesharing user is charged for use of the system based upon an algorithm which takes into account the amount of time the user is actually connected to the system, the amount of time the CPU and perhaps other resources are allocated to the user's work, and the amount of storage space occupied by the user's files.

Some timesharing vendors provide users with access to data bases or to software specific to their needs. For example, some systems provide access to a computer model of the economy, with its supporting data base, so that the users can apply that information to their strategic planning efforts. This access to software and data bases is a significant advantage in the use of timesharing systems. Timesharing systems maintain logs so that users can be charged an appropriate amount for the use of these systems.

Another advantage of timesharing to the using organization is the manner in which the computing resources are purchased. With timesharing, the user pays only for the usage of the system, with perhaps a small monthly charge for access privileges. In contrast, an in-house facility represents an investment which must be paid for whether it is used or not.

A disadvantage of the timesharing environment is that such a service usually offers less than the full range of computing capabilities. An application which has extensive input or output requirements would be less convenient on a timesharing system than on in-house equipment because of the limited capability of terminals for large-scale input and output.

There is a tendency for usage of a timesharing service to steadily increase with time. As users become more familiar with the capabilities of the system, and as more users in the organization become acquainted with its capabilities, usage increases. Without effective managerial controls, the bill for timesharing services could grow to exceed the cost of an in-house system. A timesharing service is best suited for those applications which have limited input and output requirements and which consume only some fraction of the resources available from a full-fledged system.

Service Bureau

A service bureau is a type of computing service whose capabilities in a sense lie between those of an in-house facility and of timesharing. It is a better alternative than timesharing for those applications which have reasonably large input/output requirements, but it is not as convenient as a computing system installed on the organization's premises.

A **service bureau** is an organization which sells a full range of computing services to client organizations. The service bureau owns (or leases) a computing facility and maintains a full complement of data entry clerks, systems analysts, programmers, and operators. Organizations contract for specific data processing services to be provided by the service bureau. The client's source documents, for example, can be delivered to the service bureau, where they are entered into the system for the appropriate processing. Users may buy other services according to their needs.

Many banks have data processing departments which operate as service bureaus, particularly with respect to certain financial applications. For example, many banks sell a payroll service to their business customers. The customers submit time card data to the bank, which does the payroll processing and deposits the pay of the customer's employees in special accounts established by the bank for each of the employees. The bank is thus able to sell some excess computer time on their in-house computer, perform a valuable function for their customers, and maintain the money for the payroll on deposit within the bank.

Service bureaus fulfill an important need within the full range of data processing alternatives. Businesses can take advantage of a service bureau's offerings until they develop in-house capabilities of their own. They may also use them as a supplement to their own facilities during temporary periods of excessive demand for data processing within the firm. An in-house facility usually provides better control and less opportunity for violation of the security provisions for sensitive data, so firms usually move toward the acquisition of their own systems.

Facilities Management

In the earlier discussion of the acquisition of in-house facilities, I mentioned the problem many organizations have in finding the managerial talent neccessary for the administration of an effective data processing center. Many organizations do not want to remove an effective manager from another area and assign that person to the task of managing the data processing center. The talent of the management group of the operating divisions of the organization is diluted by such a move, and an ineffective data processing manager might be created.

A facilities management firm is a data processing service organization which, for a fee, manages the data processing facilities of another user organization. Employees of the data processing center typically become employees of the facilities manager. In some cases, ownership of the computing equipment itself is transferred to the facilities management firm and leased back to the user organization.

In addition to the advantages of not having to provide the managerial talent, and sometimes not the capital, the user organization often finds that the data processing center is managed much more efficiently by the facilities management firm than it ever was by the firm's own personnel. It is not, however, a solution without some disadvantages. The activities undertaken by the facilities managers must be closely monitored to make sure that they do not engage in tasks which are in conflict with the client organization's goals. They might, for example, be tempted to provide services or staff unnecessary to the central mission of the client.

Challenge Update

It should now be possible for the reader to explain the role of service bureaus, timesharing services, and facilities management firms.

Newest Developments

The future should bring continued erosion of the lines which attempt to divide the various categories of computers. Hand-held computers (see Figure 10–12) will begin to encroach upon the realm of microcomputers. Microcomputers will continue to expand in capability into the area of the minicomputer. Minicomputers will continue to displace the bottom end of the mainframe computer business. Supercomputers of increasing power will continue to be developed.

The effort by the Japan Information Processing Center to define the computer architecture for the 1990s has led to a suggestion that the prevailing configuration will be a federation of special purpose processors with an increased use of artificial intelligence in the system.

The use of timesharing as we have known it may decline as the price/performance ratio of new systems shows continued improvement. Local and geographically dispersed networks linking together processors of widely varying capability, with processing routed to specialized processors, is a likely scenario for the future. Service bureaus and facilities management should, however, continue to be an important part of the array of data processing services available to users.

As the cost and inconvenience of computer downtime increase, we may

Figure 10–12 A Hand-held Computer by Hewlett-Packard

find more and more systems which provide for the duplication of critical elements of the system. At least one manufacturer currently markets a system with duplicate CPUs to provide virtually uninterrupted service in critical application areas.

The newest hardware, cheaper and more powerful than older equipment, will make computer systems an even more attractive investment for an organization. Software packages should make it significantly easier to put together a complete in-house data processing capability. It is an era of hope.

COMPUTING CHALLENGE: *A Final Note*

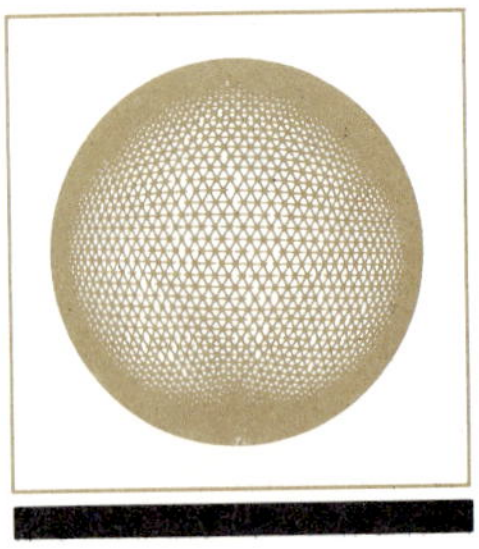

Of what help can we now be to Ms. Windstrom, the district ranger of the Palambra National Forest? We know that many different types of computers exist across a wide spectrum of sizes and capabilities. The number and type of applications will have a big influence on the type of data processing service needed on the district.

If the applications are relatively small and require only local data for the production of information which is used locally, then a microcomputer or minicomputer might be the best choice. If the system has to occasionally interface with a larger data processing center at the supervisor's office, the regional office, or the USDA computing center in Ft. Collins, Colorado, then a microcomputer or minicomputer which can emulate a remote station would be desirable. If large volumes of data will need to be transmitted to one of the other centers, then remote batch equipment or a minicomputer with relatively high-speed peripherals would be desirable.

A government agency is somewhat less likely to contract with a service bureau or facilities management firm than a private organization, although those services are certainly available. Timesharing is a distinct possibility if the expected use of the system is small and the input and output requirements are not excessive. As a matter of fact, for USDA agencies the computing center in Ft. Collins acts as a service bureau with an extensive array of available services.

So a number of possibilities exist. As we will discuss in some detail in a later chapter, compatibility with other Forest Service equipment and the availability of maintenance might be important considerations in any equipment acquisitions for the district.

SUMMARY

- The three classical modes of access to a computing system are batch, remote batch, and interactive, but the complexity of today's information processing applications makes a classification scheme of somewhat greater detail advantageous.
- Any new classification scheme must be able to describe the interaction between the user and the computer (batch or interactive), the mode in which updates are made to existing files (batch or real time), and the mode in which user inquiries secure response (batch or real time).
- Data files may be maintained either on-line or off-line, with real time systems requiring on-line storage of data.
- Computing systems can be configured around a wide variety of CPUs, which exist in size categories known currently as microcomputers, minicomputers, mainframes, and supercomputers.
- The dividing lines between the various classes of computers are rapidly being obscured by technological advance.
- While the most popular means for obtaining computer services seems to be the acquisition of an in-house computing system, several other alternatives do exist.
- Timesharing presents an interesting alternative for applications which do not require excessive compute time or excessive input or output.
- Users may take their data processing tasks to a service bureau, where they can acquire a broad range of computing services in return for payment of the appropriate fees.
- Organizations may contract with others for the management of an in-house facility in a concept known as facilities management.
- Organizations will be able to choose from an increased variety of computing services in the future; the possibilities are virtually limitless.

CASE: Computer Aids Mission Agency

Although computers are used in business organizations very extensively, other organizations can also make very effective use of computerized data processing. Social, religious, and charitable organizations also find it necessary to utilize computers to handle their data processing chores. Sometimes they must work together to share a system as illustrated in this case.

Workers in a missionary agency in Wheaton, Illinois, find the use of an IBM System 38 computer extremely helpful in dealing with their extensive record-keeping, filing, and accounting needs. The Foreign Mission Society (FMS), principal user of this particular IBM system, shares the computer system with three other missionary agencies housed in the same office complex. Installation of the system has resulted in an overhaul of their data processing department, causing it to become more distributed throughout the various offices.

Each of the thirty-five users spread through the four agencies performs his or her own data processing functions, which include adding, deleting, updating, and otherwise maintaining agency records and files. Terminals are available throughout the building shared by the agencies. Beneficial features of the system for the agencies are (1) ease of operation, (2) access to data base management software, and (3) the use of intelligent terminals which permit two different users to work from the same unit. Other potential advantages include the option to increase memory size and disk storage capacity. Data security is also an important feature. The system uses RPG III, which provides sophisticated programming techniques and aids for the programming process.

This system, with all of its features, helps FMS and the other three missionary agencies perform their data processing chores more quickly and accurately. Their data processing tasks include the handling of 100,000 individual receipts a year; the writing of approximately 2,000 checks per month; and maintenance of 1,400 general ledger accounts, 5,000 missionary accounts, and 20,000 constituent accounts.

The computer system does for the four missionary agencies exactly what it would do for any organization. It provides members of their professional staffs with the capability to carry out the tasks necessary to the fulfillment of their organizational goals.

"Mission Agency Supports Others with 'Small' System," *Infosystems*, March 1982, p. 94.

Questions for the Case

1. In what other ways might FMS arrange to have its data processing needs met?
2. Discuss the relative advantages and disadvantages of the ways identified in your answer to question 1.
3. What problems can FMS expect from a shared system?
4. What might be the likely next step for FMS?

DISCUSSION QUESTIONS AND EXERCISES

1. Explain the different types of computer access known as batch, remote batch, and interactive. Name an application for which each seems to be well suited.
2. Choose a typical data processing task of an organization and describe the modes of processing (batch or real time) which would be most suitable for processing the input, handling of inquiries, and generating of the output for that task.
3. Discuss the role of cost/benefit analysis of computer system projects. What are its limitations?
4. Compare an in-house computing system to the use of a service bureau. List the relative advantages and disadvantages.
5. Compare an in-house computing system to the use of a timesharing service. What types of data processing seem to be best for each?
6. Why is it so difficult to accurately define the various categories of computers? Can we expect it to become easier?
7. What are the interesting managerial problems caused by distributed processing?
8. What does it mean to say that a remote computing device has standalone capability? What advantages might this make available to the user?
9. Why might a facilities management contract cost more than the organization managing its own in-house facility? Why might it cost less?
10. Why are the costs associated with computer systems easier to determine than are the benefits?
11. Consider the types of access students have to computing capabilities. What frustrations do students experience from this access? In what ways are those frustrations similar to those experienced by users in large business organizations?
12. Is working on a microcomputer more fun than working on a mainframe? Why or why not?
13. Will managers need to know more about computers in the future? Why or why not?
14. How important is it that we be able to clearly categorize computers by size? What might be a better way to accomplish computer classification?
15. Why might an organization's first experience with data processing take place as timesharing or the use of a service bureau?

ADDITIONAL READINGS

Barton, D. "Distributed Processing in a Small Office." *Software—Practice and Experience*, June 1983, pp. 527–536.

Cooper, James Arlin. *Microprocessor Background for Management Personnel.* Englewood Cliffs, NJ: Prentice-Hall, 1981.

Deitel, Harvey M. *An Introduction to Operating Systems.* Reading, MA: Addison-Wesley, 1983.

Givone, Donald D., and Roesser, Robert P. *Microprocessors/Microcomputers: An Introduction.* New York: McGraw-Hill, 1980.

Harvard Business Review. *Catching Up with the Computer Revolution.* New York: Wiley, 1983.

Lientz, Bennet P. *An Introduction to Distributed Systems.* Reading, MA: Addison-Wesley, 1981.

Long, Larry E. *Design and Strategy for Corporate Information Services.* Englewood Cliffs, NJ: Prentice-Hall, 1982.

Madron, Thomas W. *Microcomputers in Large Organizations.* Englewood Cliffs, NJ: Prentice-Hall, 1983.

Sanders, Norman. *A Manager's Guide to Profitable Computers.* New York: AMACOM, 1979.

Schlueter, Louis, J. *User-Designed Computing.* Lexington, MA: Lexington Books, 1982.

Wetherbe, James C. *Executive's Guide to Computer-Based Information Systems.* Englewood Cliffs, NJ: Prentice-Hall, 1983.

11

The Design of Systems

CHAPTER PREVIEW

This chapter is rather short, somewhat philosophical, but extremely important. It develops one of the most important messages of the entire book: that information systems must ultimately be justified on the basis of their contribution to the overall purposes of the organizations in which they operate. Unless information serves the organization's goals and objectives, its generation and storage will waste valuable resources. We must, therefore, design information systems so that they serve organizational goals and objectives.

Systems design is a topic about which a great deal has been written. People trying to effect change in a transportation system, a social system, or an ecological system are engaging in systems design. Although *systems design* refers to a specific body of knowledge and set of techniques within data processing, it is not, by any means, a subject restricted to computers. For example, an extensive amount of systems design work takes place in social systems: clubs, work groups, churches, schools, agencies, and other organizations.

Systems design is an important area of study for the beginning data processing student. It is important, first, because it plays a major role in any information systems design effort. Secondly, it is important in any effort to bring about purposeful change in any of the systems in which we participate.

It is, however, a subject with great breadth and depth. Enough is known about systems design to fill several complete textbooks. We clearly will only be able to touch some of the highlights here. A preliminary discussion of organizational problem solving will help set the stage.

Problem Solving and Decision Making

Managers earn their salaries by discovering and solving problems, either by deciding on a course of action to avoid a potential problem or by developing some means to correct an existing one. The decision-making process, as described by Herb Simon, consists of four distinct phases, which he has labeled:

1. Intelligence.
2. Design.
3. Choice.
4. Review[1].

Each will be discussed briefly so that the reader will be able to see later how information systems design is related to this characterization of the decision-making process.

Intelligence. The first phase of the decision-making process, the *intelligence phase,* is the activity in which the manager looks for occasions or circumstances which suggest that a decision needs to be made. In problem-solving language, this is the phase within which the problem is identified. A manager may, for example, review either past or current performance levels of a production unit to assess whether production rates, quality control, unit costs, employee attendance, or machine efficiencies present opportunities for improvement. If production rates are down or the number of manufacturing defects up, the manager may need to develop plans (design a system) to correct the problem.

Design. In the next phase, the *design* phase, the manager begins to look for solutions to the problem identified in the intelligence phase. The manager creates, develops, and analyzes the potential results from a number of possible courses of action. A quality control problem, for example, might be solved by the use of better raw materials, improvements in the manufacturing process, or operator retraining. These alternatives are examined in terms of their feasibility, cost, implementation time, possible outcomes, and other criteria in order to evaluate their relative merit.

Choice. In the third phase, one of the alternatives—the "best" one— is identified as the preferred *choice.* Managers try to assess the consequences of implementing each of the alternatives, and compare them in terms of their value to the organization. Value considerations include both tangible and intangible costs and tangible and intangible benefits. In quality control, for example, operator retraining might be easier, faster, and cheaper than changes in the raw materials or manufacturing process. The alternative chosen is then implemented.

Review. This final phase, the *review,* is actually the first phase of the next iteration of the decision-making process. In it, the manager reviews per-

1. Herbert A. Simon, *The New Science of Management Decision* (Englewood Cliffs, NJ: Prentice-Hall, 1977), pp. 39–82.

formance of the system to look for circumstances which suggest that a problem exists. Identification of such a problem leads to another system design effort.

Managers, then, look for problems to solve, and they design systems to solve them. Systems design is one of the activities in which the manager of an organization has a great opportunity to influence the effectiveness of an organization.

Some writers claim that systems design is the most important activity undertaken by a manager. They reason that it is through the design of the various systems which make up an organization that the manager must establish the very means by which the goals of the organization are achieved. If the systems through which the organization seeks to attain its goals are poorly designed, attainment of these goals may be impossible.

Human Factors. Designers must not overlook the impact that changes brought about by systems design have on the people who interact with the system. The success of most systems design projects depends more often on social or human factors than it does on technology. Failure to recognize and plan accordingly has caused many systems to fail.

System changes often have a significant impact on participants' jobs, social interactions, political well-being, self-image, and self-esteem. Systems designers must be clever and sensitive enough to recognize the potential for serious disruptions and develop plans to deal with participants' needs.

System Defined

Perhaps no other word in our language is used in so many different contexts as the word *system.* The space program has given us: "All systems are go". Our teachers tell us: "You can't beat the system." Someone winning in blackjack in the casino is said to have a "system." People who work in data processing are frequently referred to as "systems" people. A definition of the word *system* is obviously necessary if we are going to learn anything at all about systems design.

The best definition of a system is derived from the work of C. West Churchman, one of the most famous scholars and philosophers of our time. Professor Churchman's work in bringing together interdisciplinary teams to work on the problems of management led to the school of thought known as management science. In his work he defines a **system** as a collection of related parts which work together to produce a desired result.[2]

From this definition we can easily see that the space program's use of the word means that all the components of the spacecraft and its controls are in proper working order. Our teachers are trying to tell us that it would be futile for us to rebel against the coordinated set of rules designed to make the school run smoothly, even if not in accordance with our wishes. The blackjack player has a set of rules which try to control risk and produce winnings. And, finally, systems people work with a large collection of sophisticated hardware and software in order to achieve effective processing of an organization's data. Each usage of the word *system* is, then, consistent

2. C. West Churchman, *The Systems Approach* (New York: Delacorte Press, 1968), pp. 42–78.

with the definition, yet the context in which it has been used has made it appear to have many different meanings.

The Importance of Systems

Why do we need to know about systems? It is obvious that if we want to understand the many uses of systems, it helps if we understand the meaning of the word, but a much more important reason exists. We are continuously involved in organizations which have goals, and our efforts within those organizations are frequently (though not exclusively) directed at achieving those goals. For example, the university is a system designed to help students with their education, though it has many other goals as well. One of these is research, a goal the pursuit of which creates new knowledge.

As another example, consider a business organization. Here the goals seem to be those of achieving profit for the stockholders, providing products for the customers, and providing employment for the employees. Religious, social, and recreational organizations also exist as systems to help us achieve other goals. Our participation in these organizations (systems) results in our trying to design and use these systems to attain the appropriate goals. Many of our activities within these organizations are systems design activities. Perhaps a Computing Challenge will help our focus on the extent to which systems design activities are prevalent throughout our lives.

COMPUTING CHALLENGE: *Social System Design*

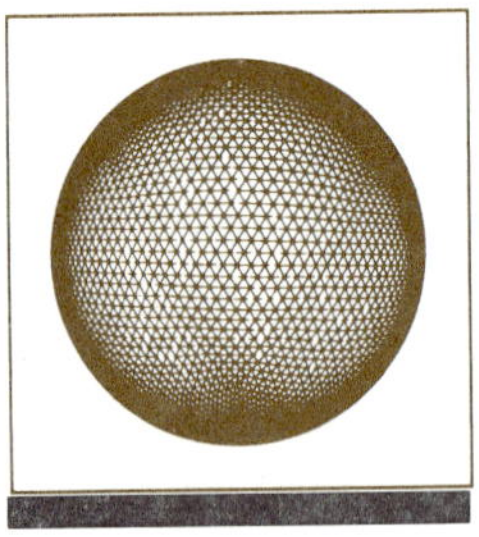

Brett Lindahl was the newly-elected president of his living group at State University. One of his first acts as president had been to convene a meeting of the old and new officers to create a list of objectives for managing the house during the coming year, and to attach priorities to the objectives on the list. He is now reviewing that list, hoping to gain some inspirational flash which would help him deal with the problems they helped identify, most of which had a number one priority attached to them.

1. *Scholarship in the house was down; the grade point average for the house had fallen below 3.00 for the first time in anyone's memory.*
2. *Both the cook and the resident advisor had resigned at the end of the previous term.*
3. *An investigator for the insurance company had recently completed an inspection and had recommended that the house's insurance be cancelled unless a long list of corrections were made within three months.*
4. *The traditional alumni breakfast was only four weeks off, and only the most cursory plans had been made. Brett was to make a presentation to the alumni to secure financial support for a new sleeping porch.*
5. *Solicitation of new members was to begin early in the next term.*

Brett vaguely remembered a lecture he attended as a freshman, in which the lecturer had been trying to convince the students that systems design would play an important role in their lives. It was a long time ago, and he remembers very little of the course. He could not remember the important steps in a systems design effort. How were measures of a system's performance important? In what ways would prototype design be better than a more traditional design approach? What were the benefits of user involvement?

The following material, though new to the reader, is intended to be remedial for Brett, so that he can learn about systems design. If he pays careful attention to this chapter, he should be able to:

1. *Explain the use of goals, clients, and measures of performance in systems design.*
2. *Describe how the overall science of systems design contributes to the design of data processing systems.*
3. *Explain the importance of user involvement in the design process.*
4. *Discuss the concepts of system life cycle and prototype design.*

HISTORICAL PERSPECTIVE

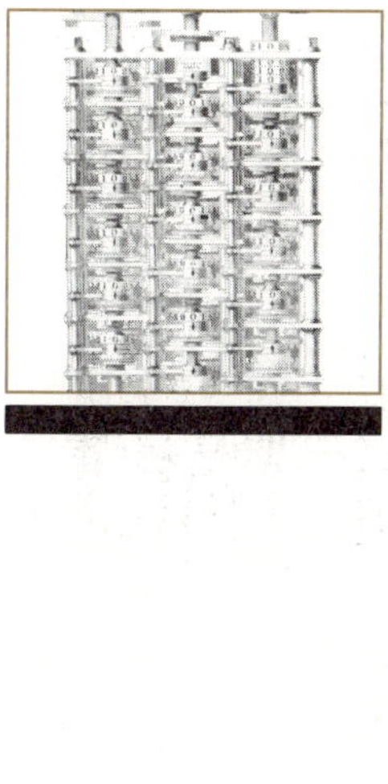

The modern literature on systems begins with the work of Ludwig von Bertalanffy, a biologist who began to make generalizations about the interaction between the components of living systems while studying cells. Because of his insight, it is now easy for us to see how a collection of components, working together, become more than the straightforward sum of their parts. Our bodies are fine examples. They are living systems which serve purposes far beyond that which we could expect from an analysis of the separate parts.

We are indebted to Ludwig von Bertalanffy for his efforts to develop the science we now know as **general systems theory,** which attempts to find the common thread shared by all systems. For example, we know that virtually all systems exhibit growth, have interacting parts, and perform certain control functions. Perhaps there are other characteristics common to all systems.

Most of the literature on systems and their design has appeared since World War II. Two of Professor Churchman's books, *The Systems Approach* and *The Design of Inquiring Systems,* are included in the list of additional readings at the end of this chapter. Much of the systems material in the early part of this chapter has been distilled from Churchman's teachings.

Systems Concepts

Early in the third chapter of *The Design of Inquiring Systems* Professor Churchman describes a set of nine requirements which must be met before

Figure 11–1 The Requirements of a System

1. The system has a goal.
2. The system has a measure of performance.
3. A client exists whose interests are served by the system.
4. System components work together to coproduce the measure of performance.
5. The system has an environment, which also coproduces the measure of performance.
6. A decision maker exists who can change the system's performance.
7. A designer exists who can make it possible for the decision maker to change the system's performance.
8. The designer's intent is to maximize the system's value to the client.
9. The system is stable with respect to the designer.

something can be called a system (see Figure 11-1).

We will use some of the more important characteristics to provide a focus for the discussion of systems design. The discussion will be of systems in general and will be applicable to systems design in virtually any environment. Later, topics more specific to the design of data processing systems will be broached.

Goals

Of primary importance in the design of any system is the specification of the system's **goals,** that is, what the system is to do. For what purpose, or purposes, does the system exist? For example, a business organization is a system whose goals seem to be the pursuit of profit, the provision of employment, and the distribution of a desired product or service. A social organization has a set of goals commensurate with the wishes of its members. Members of these organizations have individual goals as well. Thus, a bridge club may be formed for the purpose of promoting bridge, while individual members join to improve their bridge playing, to get to know other bridge players, or some other, less obvious goal. [Note: For our purposes here, the terms *goals, objectives* and *purposes* are used interchangeably. The literature of management differentiates goals as statements of overall organizational mission from objectives as measurable achievements, but that distinction is not important here.]

It is the system's goal which unifies the efforts of its members and allows them at the same time to work toward their own objectives. Without a goal, nothing serves as a focus for the participants' energies. A system must have a goal.

Client

The system's goals should make it possible to identify those people, the **clients,** whose interests are to be served by the system. A system may, of course, serve several different clients. A business provides a good example. In making a profit, a business organization serves its investors. In providing employment, it serves its employees, their families, and their communities. In distributing a product or service, a business serves its customers. By the same token, a university serves students as clients in its goal to provide education and serves society at large as clients in its efforts to generate new knowledge.

Statements of the system's goals should, explicitly or implicity, specify the client(s) and the interests to be served. Periodic review of a system's performance with respect to its goals is necessary to ensure that the system continues to serve the appropriate client group. One frequently-used indicator of a system's goals is based in the allocation of resources within the system. If no resources are allocated to the service of a particular goal, then it is safe to assume that the system is not actively pursuing that goal.

An example should help make the point more clear. Assume that a government agency adopts as one of its goals a haven for battered women and abused children. If they then allocate no funds and assign no other resources to the project, it is safe to assume that the haven is not an active goal of the agency.

Measure of Performance

A system must not only be in pursuit of a set of goals and in service to a particular set of clients, but a **measure of performance** must also exist so that one can tell when the clients are being better, or less well, served. Some measure must exist which indicates the extent to which the clients' interests are being served such that, the higher the measure the better the clients' interests are being served. In many cases, of course, there are multiple measures of performance.

Some measures of performance are much easier to specify than others. For example, several measures are used to indicate a business organization's profitability. Some of the more common measures are earnings per share, dollars of profit per dollar of invested capital, and profit as a percentage of sales. With all of its shortcomings, a student's grade point average serves as one measure of his or her performance in pursuit of an education.

A review of the first three requirements is in order. A system must have goals and must exist to serve the interests of a client group. The system's performance in the service of the clients must be measurable through the use of a measure of performance.

Challenge Update

Brett Lindahl should now be able to apply the concepts of goals, clients, and measures of performance to the design of systems within his living group.

Systems and Subsystems

One of the most important concepts in all of systems theory is the concept that virtually every system is embedded in some larger system. Collections of systems work together as subsystems within a larger system. An important extension of this concept is the notion that the measure of performance of each of the subsystems is, ultimately, its contribution to the measure of performance of the system in which it is embedded. The subsystems become the components for the next larger system. For example, the performance of subcommittees must be judged in terms of their contribution to the overall committee's task. The performance of departments within a business or government agency must be judged in terms of their contribution to the business or agency's goals.

This concept has a great deal of importance to us as students of data processing systems. A data processing system has subsystems whose goals must be kept in line with the goals of the overall system itself. For example, in the design and purchasing phases of a data processing system acquisition we focus our attention, primarily, on the performance of each *component* of the system. We must not lose sight of the fact that the performance of *all the components working together* is our primary concern.

As we link together the components necessary for a data processing system, another perspective is also important. We must always remember that the ultimate measure of performance for the data processing system is the extent to which it contributes to the achievement of the overall organization's goals. A data processing system that performs well is nice, but, in and of itself, a data processing system that performs well is nothing unless it contributes to attainment of the organization's goals. The performance of a data processing system in a business organization, for example, will ultimately be measured in terms of the business's goals of profitability, employment, and the distribution of goods and services.

To extend the concept further, the measures of performance of the business organization must ultimately be in terms of the performance of the economy (or society) in which it is embedded. An organization does well if, and only if, it contributes to the goals of its society.

What, then, does systems theory contribute to the study of data processing systems? First, a data processing system must have one or more goals. We have seen how data processing serves both transaction processing and decision support roles. We can expect the goals of data processing systems to be in terms of either (or both) of those roles. For example, a data processing system may be designed to record the sales transactions in a department store through a point-of-sale terminal, thereby serving a transaction processing goal. The system could serve sales analysis and inventory control goals at the same time.

Secondly, the goals of a data processing system should, implicitly or explicitly, identify clients whose interests are to be served by the system.

The users of the system are among the client groups, as are the managers whose informational needs are to be served by the system.

In addition, the data processing system must have at least one measure of performance, some means wherein we are able to tell how it is doing. The measures of performance for a data processing system would include items such as timeliness, accuracy, user satisfaction, system availability, and system utilization.

Finally, and most importantly, a data processing system is only a subsystem of the overall organization in which it is embedded, and its measure of performance is the extent to which it contributes to the goals of that organization. Designers must keep their design efforts in perspective so that the data processing system will make valuable contributions to the system in which it is embedded.

Challenge Update

The reader should now be able to describe the manner in which the overall science of systems design contributes to the design of data processing systems.

Hardware/Software Considerations in Systems Design

As a system is designed, the manager in whose area of responsibility the system is to be placed must give careful consideration to the components to be used in that system. Whether that system is a simple one designed to schedule the manager's appointments for a typical business day, or a very complex one designed to effect strategic planning for the manager's department, the correct set of components has to be selected and put into place. Among the components of a data processing system are hardware and software tools, so the design of a data processing system will require the specification of hardware and software items.

Only rarely does the manager/designer team have the opportunity to design a complete computing system. Most often, it is the opportunity to design or redesign a particular data processing operation which presents itself. In these circumstances, the manager/designer team is asked to restrict the design to one that will make use of the existing computing system. That is, when the warehouse manager/designer redesigns the system which prepares picking lists (the list used by workers in the warehouse to "pick" items for an order), the design effort rarely includes permission to redesign the existing data processing center. The manager/designer will normally take the existing data processing system as given and work within its constraints. New hardware and new software may have to be acquired, but rarely is a complete system replaced in those circumstances.

For example, managers and designers may often be faced with the purchase of new terminals, a new printer, a bar code scanner, or an inventory control software package. Much less frequently will they be involved in replacing the CPU, the operating system, or the myriad of other components of the existing system.

To summarize some of the more important concepts presented so far in this chapter:

1. A great deal of a manager's effort will be devoted to problem solving, decision making, and system designing.
2. Data processing systems, like systems in general, must have goals, clients, and measures of performance.
3. Ultimately, the data processing system's performance must be measured in terms of its contribution to the organization's goals.
4. Data processing systems design projects may be very large ones, very small ones, or something in between.

User Involvement in the Design Process

The design of a data processing system requires the close coordination of two important sets of people: *computer specialists* and those people who are specialists in the particular application under study, whom we know as *users.* In organizations which are relatively new to the data processing business, there is a tendency for the users to leave most of the design details to the computer specialists. After all, it is assumed, a data processing system needs computer expertise more than any other. Computer specialists, anxious to demonstrate their abilities, frequently proceed with the design with very little involvement on the part of the users.

In addition, managers often feel as though they have insufficient knowledge of computer systems to participate effectively in the design of systems intended to serve their needs. They, therefore, are reluctant to participate fully in the design process. The result is that computer specialists are then forced to fill the void with their own knowledge of the activity for which the system is being designed. This has often led to the situation in which systems have been designed which did not adequately serve the manager's needs.

It is fair to say that, of data processing failures, more have failed for lack of adequate user participation than for lack of computer specialist participation. Designers must often work, then, to increase the extent to which users are involved in the design process as illustrated in Figure 11–2. Many different techniques are employed to increase the amount of user involvement.

Figure 11–2 Users, Managers, and Designers Share Design Tasks

Encouraging User Involvement. One approach, barely satisfactory, has been to require that managers, or users, "sign-off" on the data processing design project at various, significant points in the process. To *sign-off,* in this context, is to sign one's name to a document agreeing that the goals of the design process have been met and that authority is granted to move to the next phase.

At the other extreme is the technique of assigning a manager, or user, as the director of the system's design project. Such an assignment forces the manager/user to become knowledgeable enough about the system to direct its design. A major deterrent to this approach is the amount of time which the manager/user must commit to the design effort. Most manager/users are very busy with their normal assortment of duties.

Provisions would have to be made, in this latter case, for the manager's workload to be lightened in order that an adequate amount of time can be given to the design process. In some cases it is possible to temporarily assign part of the manager's work to someone else or suspend work on some projects until the manager returns once again to normal duties.

An increased contribution on the part of the users can frequently be secured by integrating data processing goals with the user's normal set of work goals. In this way the user assumes a personal stake in the success of the system, a condition which enhances the likelihood of success.

For example, completion of a data processing project can be made one of the user's goals in a management by objectives program in which users are rewarded on the basis of achieving a set of objectives. Sometimes a data processing goal will be the means to achieving a user goal. If, for example, an organizational goal of increased inventory turnover exists, an automated inventory control system could help achieve that goal.

Benefits of User Involvement. The involvement of the user in the design of the system is important for several reasons. In the first place, the user should be the most knowledgeable person concerning the functioning of the system, and his or her involvement should improve its quality. The user should know best of all what the system is supposed to do. An example will help illustrate the point.

A systems design consultant was in the office of a city manager trying to convince him of the value of user involvement in systems design when the city manager's secretary brought in, for the manager's signature, a purchase order for a new street sweeping machine. The consultant asked if the city employee who drove the current street sweeper and would drive the new one had been asked to participate in the selection of options for the new sweeper.

The city manager failed to see the point, or the connection with user involvement in systems design, but agreed to humor the consultant by taking him to visit with the driver. The driver was very impressed to have the city manager and the out-of-town expert ask his opinion. He reviewed the purchase specifications and suggested that several expensive options not be purchased because they really were not helpful in the process of sweeping the streets. "But", he said, "we really could use a bubble window on the driver's side so I can look out to see the curbing without getting rained on, and a small fan to blow the dust out of my eyes on hot, dusty days."

The requested changes were made in the purchase order; the net savings to the city were about $1,500. The driver of the street sweeper was so proud of the new sweeper that he had helped "design," that it received far better care than any other machine in the city's history. As a result, the city's streets are clean, the city manager became a "believer" in user involvement in systems design, and the consultant went away a happy man.

Another benefit of user involvement in systems design is illustrated by the above example. Not only was there improvement in the design itself, but the user's participation in the design process led to a greater commitment on his part to make the new system work.

If users participate effectively in the design process, they assume a personal interest in the later success of the system. We see examples of this behavior virtually everywhere. Successful programs for young people allow (encourage) the young people to participate in the design of activities. Universities, colleges, and community colleges should pursue the active participation of students, faculty, and staff in program and administrative changes. Similarly, the designers of data processing systems must involve the users in the design process, discussed in the next section.

Challenge Update

Brett Lindahl and the reader should now understand the importance of involving users in the systems design process.

Information Systems Design

In this section we will explore two different design strategies which are regularly used in information systems design. First, we will explore the traditional approach, one which has been used quite successfully over the years. It is an approach which is quite formal and normally occupies a time span of many months of effort.

The second strategy, prototype design, has been used quite successfully in certain circumstances. While the traditional design approach tries to build a finished product in one (rather long) design cycle, prototype design recognizes that information systems are never really "finished." Prototype design, therefore, works toward a gradual evolution of increasingly better systems.

The final part of this section is devoted to one of the very important preliminary steps in any design strategy: the determination of the need for information to support specific managerial activities. That section also explains an approach to information needs analysis known as the critical success factors approach.[3]

Traditional Design: The System Life Cycle

Chapter 4 introduced the concept of system life cycle, which tries to capture the essence of the traditional design cycle for data processing systems. A system's life cycle is a description of its birth, life, and eventual demise. The cycle is repeated here for review and elaboration.

Step 1. Recognition of the fact that an opportunity for improvement in a system exists, and a brief investigation of the feasibility of developing a new system.

Step 2. Development of the system requirements, the purposes of the system in detail.

Step 3. Creation of alternative ways by which the necessary purposes could be achieved.

Step 4. Evaluation of the alternatives and selection of the one which appears to best serve the needs of the organization.

Step 5. Detailed design of the system, including the specification of new components (hardware, software, people, or procedures).

Step 6. Development of the system according to its design, and testing of it to develop confidence that it works.

Step 7. Implementation—putting the system into operation.

Step 8. Review of the system's operation to see if the system serves the organization's purposes. (The last step in this system's life cycle is the first step in the next system's life cycle).

The degree of formality with which the designers treat the design of any particular system is a function of the size of the system, the nature of the

3. John F. Rockart, "Chief Executives Define Their Own Data Needs," *Harvard Business Review*, March/April 1979, pp. 81–93.

organization in which the system is being installed, and the level of experience of the designers. A brief discussion of each step in the process will assist in our understanding of the responsibilities of the user and the designer in each phase.

Problem Recognition. The problem recognition phase is almost always the responsibility of the user. Problem recognition may occur because certain deadlines or goals are not being met, because certain processes seem to inhibit the smooth operation of the organization, or because the amount of manual, clerical work climbs to levels which are considered excessive. Occasionally, recognition that a problem exists comes from the data processing group, through their interaction with the user in other areas of the user's interest. Nevertheless, users must bear the burden of recognizing those circumstances where data processing systems could potentially improve the overall operation of the organization.

The following examples will help illustrate the point. Order entry clerks will probably be first to recognize that the volume of orders is beginning to overload the order entry system. Production managers should first feel the frustration of being unable to retrieve important operating information. Warehouse workers will be able to see when the inventory control system needs to be changed.

Development of Systems Requirements. The bulk of the work connected with development of systems requirements is also the responsibility of the user, who must determine what the system needs to do. A frequent starting place for this phase is an examination of the current system, if one exists. The analysis of the manner in which the current system serves its intended purpose sometimes provides an early list of requirements with which to work. Thus, the design of a new order entry system could reasonably begin with an analysis of the current method of handling orders.

A potential pitfall of basing a new system on an old one is the tendency to perpetuate old practices which may no longer be efficient or effective. [Note: *Efficient* means the organization's resources are converted with a minimum amount of waste. *Effective* means the conversion of resources accomplishes the intended purpose.] A common failing in many systems design efforts is to automate the existing system, without giving consideration to other, more efficient or more effective ways in which the desired results could be accomplished.

An important part of the development of requirements phase is the analysis of the other systems with which the new system will interact. For example, the design of an order entry system would have an impact on an existing inventory control system. Computer specialists can be expected to be helpful in determining the extent to which a system being designed will interact with existing systems.

Creation of Alternatives. This phase of systems design will tax the creative abilities of both users and designers. Once the requirements of the system have been determined in the prior phase, users and designers must turn their attention to the means by which the requirements can be met. Manual alternatives should be considered as well as computer-based alternatives.

Too many times a computer-based system is designed, and it is then discovered that the prior manual system was more suitable.

How many times have people voiced the complaint that computerization has caused some organizational process to be completed more slowly than it was previously? Do paychecks arrive later on a computerized system than when they were done manually? How about utility bills? How about class lists? Although most computerized systems must undergo a period of transition when, in fact, service might be delayed, we have only to consider how the system would work if converted back to manual means to understand that computers have greatly speeded up the processing of most systems.

The point of including a manual alternative in the set of alternatives should not, however, be missed. The manual alternative might be the most cost effective, and that possibility should not be overlooked. For example, consider the home activities which marketers of personal computers describe as wonderful applications for these machines. One such activity is storage and retrieval of recipes. The personal computer would accommodate computerized storage and retrieval of the cook's favorite recipes.

In what ways is the computerized recipe system better than a small file box of recipe cards? In what ways is the card file better? Which will always fit in the kitchen and not be in use when the cook wants a recipe?

Some preliminary design work is necessary while the alternatives are being created in order to be able to later compare the alternative systems, which occurs in the next phase. The design work should not be extensive, for only on the successful alternative will the work have utility.

Evaluation and Selection. Once the alternatives have been created, each must be evaluated in terms of its ability to meet the requirements in a cost effective manner. Frequently it will be the case that some of the alternatives are quickly discarded as too costly. Others may interact with existing systems in such a way that the entire process becomes too complicated or disruptive. Some may not be technologically feasible.

At some point the evaluation process comes down to a comparison of two or more alternatives, each of which seems to be able to meet the requirements. It then becomes a matter of comparing the anticipated costs and expected benefits in order to choose the system which seems to have the most desirable ratio of costs to benefits. Through these comparisons, an alternative is selected.

It is occasionally necessary in this phase to complete more of the design of the two most competitive alternatives in order to have a basis for selecting one over the other. Just how much of the design to do is left to the judgment of the users and designers.

For example, a designer may identify the following alternatives for maintaining the list of customer orders which have been received:

1. Salespeople mail orders to the corporate office, where they are manually entered in the orders-on-hand book.
2. Salespeople mail orders to the corporate office, where they are keypunched into cards for reading into a computer which maintains an orders-on-hand file.

3. Salespeople record orders on OCR forms and mail them to the corporate office, where they are read into a computer which maintains an orders-on-hand file.
4. Salespeople enter orders directly from terminals in sales offices and the central computer maintains an orders-on-hand file.

While some of these alternatives might be dismissed as impractical or too expensive, the final selection might not be possible until preliminary design work is completed.

Detailed Design. During this phase the design effort itself takes place, and the preponderance of the workload falls to the computer specialists. Any hardware to be acquired has to be fully specified during this phase, and the software needs of the system must also be specified in detail.

Some attention should also be given to the impact the new system will have on the working lives of the people whose jobs are affected by the new system. Initial efforts to specify the training which will be required to successfully operate the new system should be undertaken. Training efforts will have to ultimately include users and managers, as well as people in the data processing department. In terms of the order entry example, for instance, the fourth alternative would require the purchase of terminals for sales offices, the training of salespeople in data entry skills, and the specification of hardware and software to process the orders-on-hand files.

Development and Testing. The system itself begins to come together in the development and testing phase. Hardware is acquired and software is written. Both need first to be independently tested; secondly, they need to be tested in conjunction with each other. Testing should be done as extensively as possible, even though there may be great pressure to put the system into operation as quickly as possible.

Most hardware acquisitions are subject to testing before acceptance by the buying organization. Testing and acceptance deadlines should be met, but software should be tested as thoroughly as possible. The remote order entry system would require testing of the terminals, the order entry software, and the hardware/software combinations at the corporate office.

Implementation. This is the phase in which the system is finally put into use. There is a tendency to—sometimes out of necessity—discard the old system one day and start up the new system the next. Disastrous results frequently occur in such circumstances. If at all possible, both the old and the new systems should be run side by side until confidence in the new system reaches the point at which the old one can be discarded. This implementation technique is known as running the systems in **parallel.**

By implementing new systems in parallel with the old, errors detected in the new system can be corrected without the pressure which results from an organizational function which is out of service. Continuing our example, the existing order entry system should be kept in place, if possible, until the new, remote order entry system has demonstrated its ability to work properly.

Review. At some convenient time after the system has been in place and operating, the design team should review the system's status. Several benefits can be expected from such a review.

In the first place, the design team can see whether or not the system is functioning as it was intended. Several types of events could have occurred to prevent that from being the case. It could be, for instance, that the design did not treat some element of the processing as it should have been treated. Say, for example, that the users need a daily summary by salesperson, but the designers built in a daily summary by product line.

It could be that user training was inadequate and that users are not using the system at its most advantageous level. Say, for example, that the daily summary by salesperson is in fact part of the system, but the users do not know how to invoke that part of the analysis. A follow-up on the effectiveness of the training effort will help correct earlier omissions. Good training manuals, for example, are absolutely essential. They do not, however, fulfill the total training obligation.

It could also be the case that the system has changed since the original design was put into place. A few, relatively minor changes in the system might be required to make it more productive. It could even be the case that the users have decided the system is not useful and they have abandoned its use. The review must bring these important matters into view.

The development of computer applications is an expensive proposition. Years ago, hardware costs dominated the overall cost of the development. Through the years, the decline in hardware costs and the increase in software costs have changed the distribution significantly. Costs frequently labelled as "other" have become quite important.

An example will perhaps demonstrate the extent to which "other costs" become significant in the design, development, and implementation of a new system. An executive for a large wood products firm maintained that the costs of developing a new system for his company would be distributed as follows:

- 10 to 15 percent would be spent in the acquisition of hardware.
- 25 to 35 percent would be spent in the development of software.
- 50 to 65 percent would be spent convincing people to use the system.

Although he perhaps exaggerated to make the point, the costs of convincing people to use the system are significant. The review phase of the system life cycle is a good place to begin making such observations.

The review phase is important to the design team in yet another way. It gives the members of the team an opportunity to compare their estimates of the anticipated costs and benefits of the project to the costs and benefits which were actually incurred. This knowledge will help the designers evaluate subsequent design projects.

Prototype Design

The traditional approach to systems design is not well-suited to information systems which must perform in a changing environment. The formal systems design life cycle typically takes so long to complete that the finished product often does not fit the intended use because the environment has changed. The systems requirements established at the beginning of the project may not be appropriate by the time the project is completed.

The **prototype design** strategy recognizes that changes occur continually in the organizations in which we build information systems. It also recognizes that the organizational needs for information are evolving with time and tries to accommodate those changes with an evolutionary design process.

Prototype design is also referred to as **quick-and-dirty design** in acknowledgment of its emphasis on speed; **design-as-you-go design** to acknowledge its appearance to more traditional designers; or **breadboard design,** to allude to the temporary nature of the intermediate design products. A **prototype** is a preliminary version or model of an intended final product. A prototype information system is, then, a preliminary version or model of an information system.

The prototype design strategy calls for the building of a model of an information system which will be tested by the user and the designer to determine its suitability for meeting the system requirements. The prototype gives the user an opportunity to see if the new system would be useful. It also gives the designer and the user an opportunity to see if they have understood each other with regard to the system's capabilities and the user's needs.

As the prototype is tested, corrections and improvements will be identified. These changes will be implemented in a second version of the prototype, and the testing process will be repeated on the new system. The product evolves gradually from one prototype version to another. Each new version provides an opportunity for improvements in the system and changes to accommodate the changing environment.

Another advantage of prototype design derives from its cost compared to the cost of the traditional life cycle approach. The first prototype will virtually always be built at a lower cost than would the system designed by traditional methods. If, therefore, the system (once built) is found to be ineffective, a prototype system could be abandoned with fewer wasted resources than could the more traditionally designed system.

Prototype design is a very appropriate and beneficial strategy for many information systems design projects. It allows the manager's requirements and the system's design to evolve together and reduces the likelihood of very expensive design mistakes. The next section will help us understand how difficult the process of determining the manager's information requirements can be.

Information Needs Analysis

One of the phases of systems design needs further elaboration. For systems which support decision-making activities, an absolutely essential part of the development of system requirements is that the information needed to support the decision be determined. This analysis of information needs is a more difficult process than is initially obvious.

Although in some circumstances the information needed to support a particular decision-making activity is relatively easy to determine, there are many circumstances in which it is very difficult. In addition, managers are not always a good source for specifying their information needs, even though an interview with a manager is a good first step in determining them.

Unfortunately, we find that different managers use different information. For example, investors who buy the stock of publicly-held corporations are moved to make the purchase by a variety of different factors. We also find that some managers do not use the information they say they use. A personnel manager may, for instance, tell a researcher that an applicant's references are used in determining the suitability of that person for employment. The researcher may later find that such checks are made rarely, if ever.

It may also be true that managers do not know what information might be needed. For example, managers might not be aware of certain management science, decision-making techniques which could yield optimum decisions in particular applications. A manager unaware of these sophisticated techniques would not be able to include them in an analysis of information needs.

The difficulty in determining information requirements forces the systems analyst/user design team to exert considerable effort to determine the information needs. A design team is illustrated in Figure 11–3. The techniques which have proven to be helpful in determining information requirements are:

1. Interviews of the decision makers.
2. Logs kept by managers during their decision-making endeavors.
3. Historical reviews of the information which was previously used.
4. Simulations of decision-making processes.
5. Analysis of other systems known to have worked.

Figure 11–3 An Information System Design Team

As we saw earlier, this initial focus on the outputs required from the system is critical. A system designed to produce the incorrect outputs has no hope of success.

The importance of the correct outputs from an information system has been recognized by an MIT research team in their work on **critical success factors.** Through this approach, designers try to identify some three to six factors which are absolutely critical to the success of individual managers in an organization. Interviews are used to determine these factors, which then become the basis for information systems design efforts. The critical success factors approach has gained widespread attention as a means for focusing information systems design efforts on the "correct" set of information needs.

The determination of information needs is fundamental to information systems design. We have seen how the traditional design approach builds on an early determination of those needs and how prototype design tries to accommodate them in a different way. It is time now to see what hope the future might hold for improved design strategies.

Challenge Update

The reader should now be able to discuss the traditional system life cycle and prototype design and help Brett Lindahl select an appropriate design strategy for his systems design projects.

Newest Developments

The data processing systems design effort is a major bottleneck which constrains the rate at which organizations are able to implement new applications. Work yet to be done is referred to as the **backlog.** The backlog of systems analysis and programming work in the average organization is estimated by survey to be anywhere from three to six years. That is, programmers and analysts are three to six years behind in their work!

Another computation of the extent to which there is a shortage of analysts and programmers can be derived from hardware capacity figures. By estimating the average number of instructions a computer of the future will be able to execute, and comparing that with the projected number of instructions that programmers will be able to write, an unbelievable shortfall of programmers is indicated. In any case, many more programs need to be written than we have programmers who can write them.

There are three main thrusts through which improvement in systems design is being pursued. The first effort is concerned with improving the techniques used by systems analysts and programmers. These techniques are aimed primarily at improving the productivity of the data processing staff. These techniques, called *software engineering* are discussed in Chapter 13.

A second set of efforts emphasizes the role of the end users in developing their own applications. These efforts are expected to realize their primary benefits when users are able to use data base inquiry languages, report generators, and fourth-generation languages to generate information which formerly required a formal applications development effort. As distributed processing puts more computing resources into the users' hands, these methodologies enable the users to develop reports and inquiries without the involvement of the systems design staff.

A third effort, *information engineering*, represents an attempt to integrate the efforts of users, managers, and systems design experts to provide an effective system development process. Information engineering starts with the organization's strategic plan and derives a set of data and a set of information processing procedures which support the organization's needs. This approach recognizes an information system's role as that of a purposeful subsystem within a goal-seeking organization along the lines suggested by the work of Churchman (discussed in the early part of this chapter).

These three efforts will all contribute to improvements in the information systems design process, though each contributes in a different way. Further research in information systems design should yield even greater improvements in the design process.

COMPUTING CHALLENGE: *A Final Note*

What does the subject matter of systems design have to offer for the case to which we were introduced earlier? As Brett Lindahl reviews the problems with which he is faced as president of the living group, he begins to see each as an opportunity to practice a little systems design. As a matter of fact, he needs to design a super-system which will cause each of the other necessary systems to be designed.

Such is the essence of managerial work. Many systems need to be designed in order for the administration of an organization to take place properly. The role of the manager is to design an administrative system which causes all of the other systems to be designed and implemented.

Each of the systems will have a goal, a client group, and at least one measure of performance. Each system will be a subsystem to the system in which it is embedded, and its measure of performance should be consistent with the goal of the larger system.

Brett needs a system to improve scholarship in the house, a system to secure a cook, another (perhaps) to secure an advisor, one to deal with the insurance deficiencies, one to put together the fund-raising effort, and one to handle the solicitation of new members. He also needs a system which integrates and manages those systems, as illustrated in Figure 11–4.

Perhaps a version of the system life cycle approach would be helpful in designing the necessary systems. In some cases prototype design might be the preferred approach. Clearly the users must be involved in each design, for none of the systems will be effective unless accepted by the users.

Thus we begin to see the importance of the systems design activity. It can be useful in many aspects of our lives in managing living groups, in designing data processing systems, and in directing the efforts of organizations.

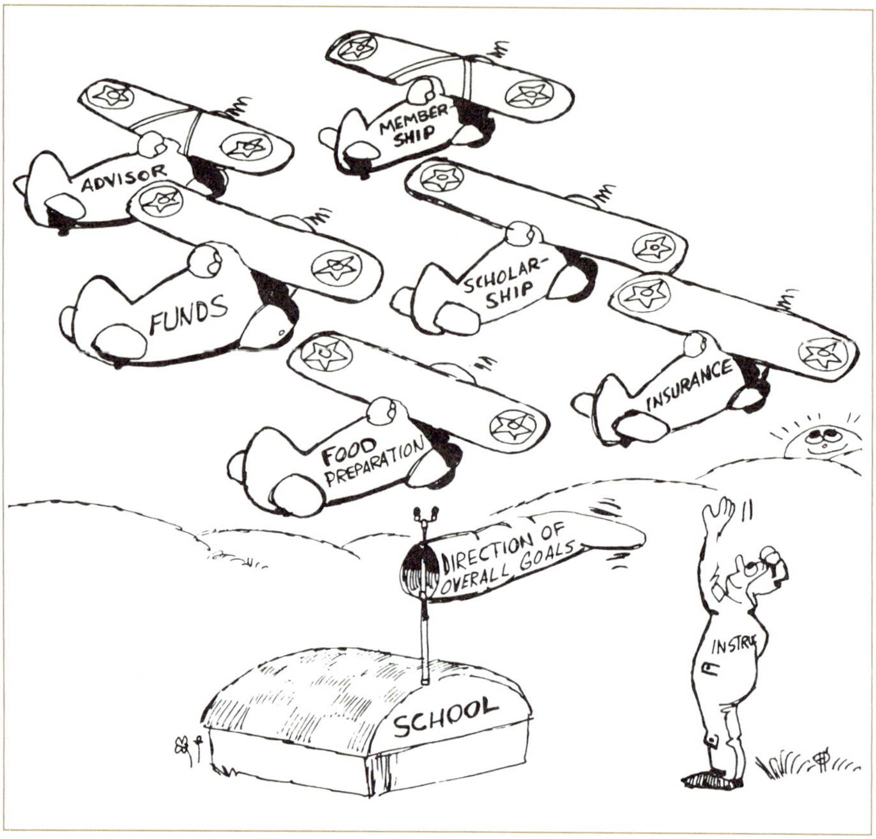

Figure 11–4 Goals of the Individual Subsystems Must Be Aligned with the Overall Goal of the Supersystem and Kept in Line by the Supersystem

SUMMARY

- Systems design is an activity in which we regularly engage, though often we do it rather informally. Systems design is a necessary function within an organization and a necessary skill for a manager.
- The three most critical components of a system, hence three items of interest in systems design, are the goal, the client, and the measure of performance.
- Designers must never lose sight of the fact that each system is embedded in the next larger system and must, therefore, be designed with the goals of that system in mind.
- Ultimately, the performance of any system must be judged in terms of the contribution it makes to the overall system in which it is embedded.
- Although systems design efforts may be large or small, most include both hardware and software considerations.
- An important feature of virtually all successful systems design efforts is the heavy involvement of the user in the design process itself.
- A great deal of effort is devoted to the formal design of data processing systems, but in spite of that (perhaps because of that), the systems design effort has a large backlog of work, with every prospect of falling further behind.

- The concept of a system life cycle has been useful in the development of data processing systems.
- The system design life cycle consists of eight phases: problem recognition, development of system requirements, creation of alternatives, evaluation and selection, detailed design, development and testing, implementation, and review.
- Prototype design offers an evolutionary strategy which allows the systems requirements to be refined as the system itself takes shape.
- The determination of information needs is an activity to which special attention must be paid.
- A particularly useful technique in some circumstances for identifying information needs is the critical success factors approach.
- Further improvement in the productivity of programmers and systems analysts is needed if the backlog of potential applications is ever to be reduced.
- Improvements in the systems design effort are expected to be realized through software engineering, end-user computing, and information engineering.

CASE: A Systems Strategy to Support Business Units

Managers in decentralized business units in most companies are anxious to take advantage of distributed data processing to improve the performance of their units. An effective overall strategy to guide systems design efforts is an important part of the overall management of the firm. Donald Winski, Manager of Management Information System Strategic Planning for Ingersoll-Rand has described a plan which enables the business units to "get on with" their business while control of systems design is centrally managed. The strategy utilizes concepts developed in this chapter.

One of the functions of corporate management in any large, decentralized company is to make the investment decisions which lead to optimum benefits for the corporation as a whole. For example, if managers in Division A and Division B both have projects which require the investment of similar resources, but scarce resources will allow only one investment to be made, corporate management must see that resources are allocated to the project which has the greatest potential return. Investments in information systems must be controlled in the same way.

Winski's strategy requires that members of the management group identify the strategic business units within the overall company and determine the critical success factors for each unit. The set of information processing systems sought for each business unit must then be tied to that unit's critical success factors. Many applications are, of course, related to each other, so the interrelationships must also be considered.

Business units must also provide an analysis of the costs, benefits, and risks associated with the individual applications. Corporate management can then review the applications and consider the total resources needed for the projects. Some applications may be common to several business units, suggesting that a prototype design in one unit could reap multiple benefits.

Ingersoll-Rand's system makes it possible for corporate management to coordinate the information systems design efforts of all units. Corporate resources can be distributed as can the responsibilities for management of the systems design effort. A corporate steering committee plays a vital role in guiding the overall company effort.

"A Systems Strategy: In Search of Excellence," *Infosystems*, January 1984, pp. 62–66.

Questions for the Case

1. This case suggests the existence of a relatively powerful, centralized information systems department. Why?
2. If the centralized information systems department had been weak, how might the corporate strategy have been different?
3. Would you expect that, with time, the information systems expertise within the individual business units will increase? What impact might this have on the existing centralized control?

DISCUSSION QUESTIONS AND EXERCISES

1. Discuss the steps in the system life cycle.
2. Describe how a system's goals and its client(s) are related.
3. Explain the relationship between a system's measure of performance and its client(s).
4. What is the relationship between a system's measure of performance and the next larger system in which the original system is embedded?
5. Why is user involvement in systems design important? What are its expected benefits? What are its expected costs?
6. Why is productivity improvement in data processing systems design important?
7. Identify a decision in local, state, or national government which needs to be made. Discuss it in terms of Simon's four phases of decision making.
8. Identify a personal, local, or national problem for which a systems design effort might need to be made. Discuss the systems requirements and generate some alternatives by which they could be met.
9. Discuss the role of data processing in a business organization. Develop and justify some measures of its performance.
10. Discuss the role of data processing in the state legislative body. How might its performance be measured?
11. Review some systems with which students interact, for example, college registration, institutional food service, or intramural sports. Identify the goal(s), client group(s), and measure(s) of performance for each.
12. In what ways is the traditional approach to systems design better than prototype design? In what ways is prototype design better?

13. What might the critical success factors be for a college president? What might they be for a student?

14. How do information processing professionals and managers differ in terms of their knowledge of an information processing system? Why is it important to blend the different expertise of each together?

15. Consider the various information processing applications within a business organization. List several examples which it would seem best to design through traditional techniques. List several which it would seem best to design through prototype design. What characteristics, in general, distinguish the examples on the first list from those on the second?

ADDITIONAL READINGS

Brooks, F. P. *The Mythical Man-Month.* Reading, MA: Addison-Wesley, 1975.

Churchman, C. West. *The Design of Inquiring Systems.* New York: Basic Books, 1973.

———. *The Systems Approach.* New York: Delacorte Press, 1968.

Ewers, Jack, and Vessey, Iris. "The Systems Development Dilemma—A Programming Perspective." *MIS Quarterly,* June 1981, pp. 33–45.

Finkelstein, Clive. "Information Engineering." *Computerworld,* April-May 1981, pp. 1–8.

Freeman, Peter, and Wasserman, Anthony. *Tutorial on Software Design Techniques.* New York: Institute of Electrical and Electronic Engineers, 1977.

Gehani, N. H. "An Electronic Form System—An Experience in Prototyping." *Software—Practice and Experience,* June 1983, pp. 479–486.

Markus, M. Lynn. *Systems in Organizations: Bugs and Features.* Marshfield, MA: Pitman Publishing, 1984.

Moynihan, John A. "What Users Want." *Datamation,* April 1982, pp. 116–124.

Mumford, Enid, and Henshall, Dan. *A Participative Approach to Computer System Design.* New York: Halsted Press, 1979.

Semprevivo, Phillip C. *System Analysis: Definition, Process, and Design.* Chicago: Science Research Associates, 1982.

Shneiderman, Ben. "How to Design with the User in Mind." *Datamation,* April 1982, pp. 125–132.

Smith, August W. *Management Systems: Analyses and Applications.* Hinsdale, IL: Dryden Press, 1982.

TRS-80
TRS-80

12

Acquisition of Computing Resources

CHAPTER PREVIEW

The previous chapter discussed systems design in general and the design of data processing systems in particular. In most cases, new hardware and software must be acquired as a result of a system design. In this chapter we will concentrate our attention on those new systems which require the acquisition of new computing resources and discuss the proper steps to acquire them.

Figure 12–1 provides an illustration of the relative expenditures for the various categories of computing resources.

There is, of course, no universally accepted set of rules which will apply to all acquisitions. The range of possibilities is simply too great. Some new systems will require only a trivial amount of new resources, while other systems may require the replacement of large quantities of resources. No single set of rules would be found to be adequate to cover acquisitions which vary so widely in scope. Large acquisitions which represent the expenditure of large sums of money and organizational energy will require a formal and complete set of steps to accomplish the task. Small acquisitions may be done less formally.

There are, however, some guidelines which can be used to improve the likelihood that the acquisition of the new resources will be successful. The members of any individual organization must decide just how formally these guidelines should be applied in any given acquisition, depending upon the experience of the organization and the scope of the particular project. An inexperienced organization would want to follow a very formal procedure for the acquisition of a large system. A small acquisition by an experienced organization might require less formality. Shortcuts often lead to trouble, however.

As in previous chapters, a Computing Challenge will be used to help focus the reader's attention on the issues of the chapter. For this case we visit a chemicals manufacturing company along the eastern seaboard.

Figure 12–1 Estimated User Budgets

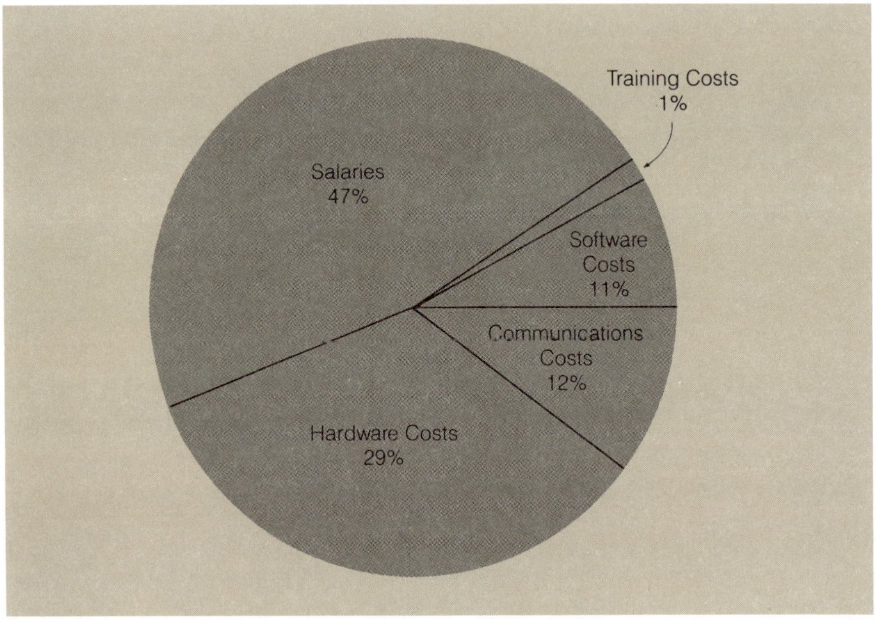

COMPUTING CHALLENGE: *Chemicals Manufacturing*

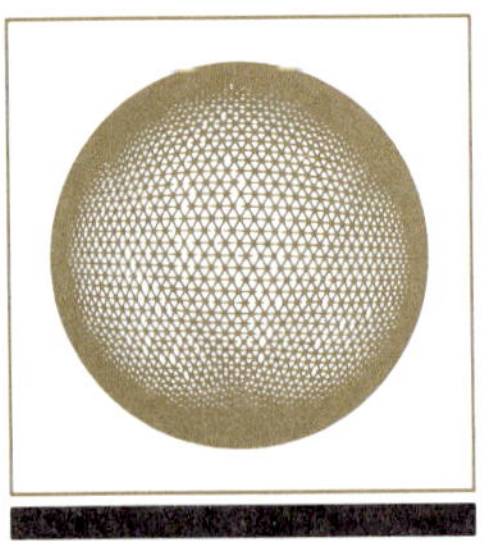

Grass Roots Growers is a small company in Rocky Landing, North Carolina, engaged in the production and distribution of agricultural chemicals such as fertilizers, insecticides, fungicides, and systemics. The chemicals processing plant employs about 1,200 people in the unloading, storing, processing, and finishing of the various products in the company's line. About 145 people work in the packaging facility and warehouse nearby. The corporate office is located just south of the warehouse.

Grass Roots Growers manufactures and sells approximately 260 different items for the care and feeding of all kinds of agricultural products. The president of Grass Roots, Mr. Wilmer Harding, has announced his retirement and the impending sale of the company to a corporate conglomerate in the agricultural chemicals industry, East Chemicals, Inc. A new general manager, Mr. Martin Bauer, has been appointed by East Chemicals and has as one of his first assignments the upgrading of the data processing facilities at Grass Roots.

Until now, virtually all of the data processing at Grass Roots has been done with calculators, adding machines, pencils, and paper. While not a fast system necessarily, it has been adequate to the task, and extremely accurate. In addition, the company almost never ran out of pencils or paper.

But that system will no longer do. As a subsidiary of East Chemicals, Grass Roots Growers must now merge its sales, production, and financial information with those of the parent company. Grass Roots must acquire a computer system which is capable of processing all of the company's data, and one which is compatible with the large system operated by East, so that data can be forwarded to the parent company.

The new system needs to be capable of supporting operations in the plant, the warehouse, and the office. People now unfamiliar with the operation and use of data processing equipment will have to be trained to operate and use it. Mr. Bauer, the new general manager, wants the transition to the new system to go smoothly, for he would like to be promoted to a vice president's position with the parent company.

It is, therefore, essential that the proper procedures be followed in acquiring hardware and software for the new system. What are those procedures? For what pitfalls must Mr. Bauer be alert? What testing can be done? How can software packages help? What is the role of the steering committee? The answers to these questions are important.

Mr. Bauer has requested the services of a small team of analysts from the parent company to assist in the acquisition of the appropriate resources.

This chapter will point out the characteristics of a good scheme for the acquisition of computing resources. This introduction will provide a good basis on which further study of the subject in other courses can be built. After careful reading of this chapter, the student should be able to:

1. *List the appropriate steps of the process to acquire computing hardware.*
2. *Explain the importance of hardware compatibility.*
3. *Discuss the relationship between hardware reliability and maintenance.*
4. *Discuss the relative advantages and disadvantages of in-house software development and software package acquisition.*

HISTORICAL PERSPECTIVE

The growth and diversification which have made decision making difficult in the acquisition of computer systems are a function of developments which have also occurred in the acquisition of many other products. It used to be relatively easy to select a car from among the alternatives, because there were very few alternatives. Henry Ford is credited with stating that car buyers could have a car of any color they wanted, "as long as it was black." Today, in comparison, there are literally thousands, if not tens of thousands, of alternatives available in the purchase of an automobile.

In a similar fashion, deregulation of the airlines industry has made it increasingly difficult to decide among the various fare alternatives for a given trip. As another example, the greater availability of a college education, the increased economic mobility of the citizens in this country, and the large number of new career choices have made it very difficult for young people to choose a major field of study, let alone a career. The difficulty of choosing increases with the number of alternatives from which to choose.

The decision-making problem in the acquisition of computing systems has become almost impossibly complex. Although it has never been an easy decision, the nature of the decision has changed in recent years. In the "good old days," the decision was primarily whether or not to acquire a computing system. Once that decision was made, there were really very few alternatives; because there were only a few manufacturers, and each manufacturer's line of available machines was very restricted.

Then, for each of the mainframes available, only a few peripherals were available. Operating systems allowed only batch processing, so the complications of communications and compatibility with remote equipment did not exist. Most systems processed only punched cards, so many of today's complex processing operations did not exist. Very little was available in terms of applications software. Organizations had to write their own applications programs, so there were fewer purchase decisions to make.

In contrast, today's market offers a complete range of central processing units (CPUs), an extremely wide variety of peripheral devices, and a large number of applications software packages. The user's problem is to select the appropriate combination of hardware and software elements to satisfy the processing requirements. In some cases, software must be acquired to blend with existing hardware, while in others hardware must be selected to run a particular type of previously-selected software. (Personal computer acquisitions, for example, are almost totally software driven.)

The computer mainframe business has been dominated by IBM so extensively that a complete market segment exists for equipment which is *plug-to-plug compatible* with IBM equipment. This equipment is built so like IBM equipment that it can be plugged in as if it were made by IBM. While the bulk of plug-to-plug compatible equipment is peripheral equipment, IBM compatible mainframes are now available. As a matter of fact, in the personal computer market many manufacturers are successfully producing machines which are compatible with IBM's. [In the personal computer market, as we shall see in Chapter 15, "compatibility" usually turns out to be something less than 100 percent compatibility.]

A modern computing system can be built around a mainframe, a minicomputer, or a microcomputer. The number of peripherals available staggers the imagination. *Remote access* and *distributed processing* through a communications network increase the desire to connect together many different systems. Manufacturers have moved to supply hardware and software products to satisfy that desire. Stated another way, the growth and geographical dispersion of organizational units have created a need for a variety of computing products to facilitate communication among the units.

In Chapter 11, we identified stages in the systems design process in which alternatives were identified and evaluated. The diversity of available systems makes the identification and evaluation of alternatives a difficult problem. New systems are being created at such a rate that alternative identification and evaluation might never be completed without some initial ground rules to narrow the field.

This chapter will discuss the selection of hardware and software resources, but by no means will it be able to provide enough material to make anyone an expert. Rather, we will try to reach an understanding of the possibilities and an appreciation of the benefits to be derived from an effective acquisition process. We turn now to the selection of hardware.

Hardware Selection

The goal of the hardware selection process is to select hardware which most suitably meets the needs of the organization. The degree of formality of the process varies with its scope. Some acquisitions are rather simple, while others are very complex.

Microcomputers and terminals may be purchased directly off the shelf, either from a standard set of specifications or on an open purchase agreement. The user, in such a case, needs only to determine the capabilities required before placing the order. In the case of the terminal, the user will need to determine whether or not an intelligent terminal is necessary, whether or not hard copy must be possible, whether or not graphics capability is important, and many other things. Even terminal selection is not a trivial task. Selection of a microcomputer would require an analysis of the uses for which it is intended and the need for compatibility with other systems. Since the cost of microcomputers is small, the potential for great financial error is less.

A large mainframe system, on the other hand, costs a great deal, and the decision to purchase one may take three years of analysis, specification, and evaluation. No single set of rules seems adequate to satisfy both types of acquisition.

Only occasionally are the acquisition of hardware and the acquisition of software separable events. Most often they occur together. In particular, the capabilities of batch processing, remote batch processing, timesharing, and communicating via networks require not only the appropriate hardware but the correct set of operating system capabilities and applications programs as well.

We have previously noted the extent to which different applications need different hardware capabilities. Some applications are heavy users of input/output peripherals, while other applications have extensive computational needs. The concept of "best" hardware inevitably represents a compromise across the set of applications for which it is being acquired. The notion of "best" itself is some combination of such factors as performance, maintenance, reliability, cost, capacity for expansion, and ease of use.

Although the mix of applications and the problem of aggregating many different types of performance features make hardware selection difficult, a good acquisition process can produce good results. The first topic of this section is an examination of the system life cycle as it relates to the hardware selection problem. Next, hardware compatibility and the evaluation of hardware features are discussed. This section will close with some material on reliability and maintenance and the comparison of buy/rent/lease alternatives.

System Life Cycle—Hardware

The steps in the system life cycle are presented for review in Figure 12–2. It seems clear that the first two stages of the system life cycle—problem recognition and systems requirements—can be discussed without reference to hardware. When we get to stage three, the creation of alternatives,

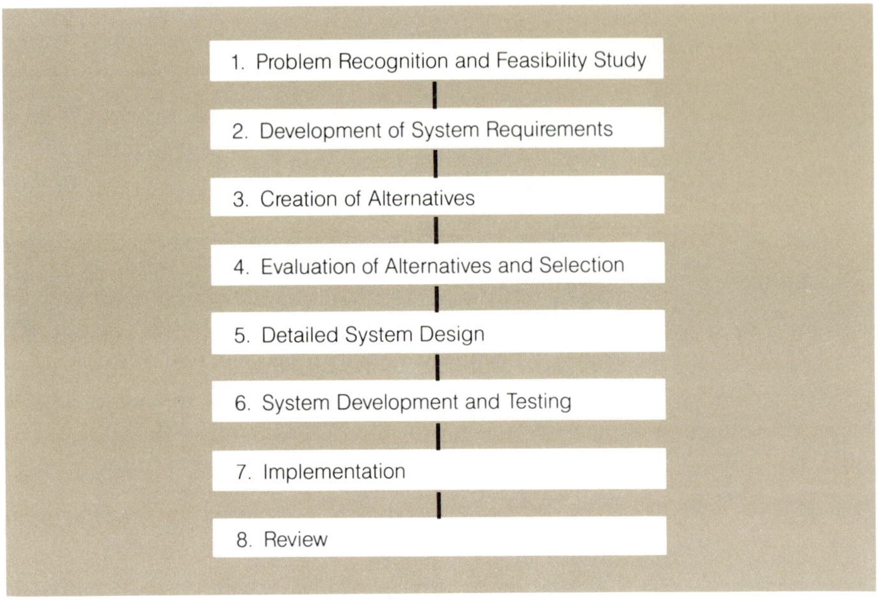

Figure 12–2 Steps in System Life Cycle

however, we must begin to consider the types of hardware which are available. There is an obvious interaction between individual hardware items which are available and the alternatives which can be considered. Some of the alternatives only become viable when specific hardware is considered.

A manager (or user) who knows very little about hardware availability will not be able to be very creative in the identification of alternatives. For example, if we were designing an order entry system, different alternatives are created when we consider issuing to the salespeople, in turn, pencils, OCR forms, terminals, portable data recorders, and microcomputers. Again, the process of identifying alternatives interacts with the range of hardware possibilities to produce a set of viable alternatives.

Consider, as another example, the different possibilities presented by intelligent terminals versus slow, dumb terminals. Different system alternatives are provided by each. For example, data entry through a slow, dumb terminal uses editing software on the host computer and requires full-time use of the communications connection. Intelligent terminals, on the other hand, provide editing by local programs and subsequent high-speed data transfers.

Hardware considerations are clearly involved in each of the next three phases of the system life cycle: evaluation and selection, detailed design, and development and testing. The implementation phase is also heavily hardware oriented and there are significant hardware considerations in the final review phase.

Let us extract a hardware acquisition cycle for further analysis. It is important to remember, in studying this material, that the particular degree of formality with which a given hardware acquisition takes place is a function of the organization and the scope of the project itself. A formal acquisition cycle is presented here, although parts of it can be discarded for any particular application where less formality can be justified.

Development of Specifications. Most of the hardware **specifications** are derived from the system requirements phase of systems design, during which the functions of the system are determined. Preliminary work on the hardware specifications is often done during the creation of alternatives phase because it is occasionally necessary to specify some features in order to completely state the alternative. For example, in the design of an inventory control system for a department store, one alternative is to have cash registers which function as point-of-sale terminals. In creating the alternative, some initial work in the specification of the hardware has been done.

It may also be necessary to do some preliminary specification work during the evaluation of alternatives phase, to see whether or not an alternative is feasible. For example, one alternative for inventory control in the department store might include a proposal to have updates made to on-line files in real time. The implications of that decision on the total set of hardware needed could be so great that an initial assessment of the proposal's feasibility might be necessary.

Accepting, however, that some preliminary work may occur earlier, the really serious work of hardware specification cannot begin until the alternative to be implemented is selected. Only then do the designers begin the very detailed specification of the hardware. The users have decided what the system needs to be able to do, and the designers (with help from the users) have decided which alternative appears to be the best.

The user's needs must be translated into a comprehensive set of specifications against which the offerings of the various hardware vendors will be judged. Hardware suppliers can analyze the specifications to determine which of their equipment would be suitable for the new system.

The hardware specifications must identify the necessary characteristics of each of the input devices, such as type, speed, number required, keyboards, and interfaces to other devices. Similarly, the output devices must be specified in terms of media, number required, speed, character sets, and so on. Secondary memory devices must be fully specified with respect to number and type, total storage volume, access type, and other features.

Hardware specifications must also be written for the computer itself and any other peripheral devices which may be necessary. Communication links, transfer speeds, and computational speeds are all important, but where possible the potential buyers should write hardware specifications in functional terms. It is far more important to require that the system be able to process a given volume of work through the machine per unit of time than it is to specify that the instruction fetch time be less than 120 nanoseconds.

The buyer's interest is in the ends which the hardware can accomplish, not necessarily the means which are employed. A personnel manager, for example, wants to know that the payroll for 1,200 people can be run in thirty minutes and could care less that the memory cycle time is one ten-thousandth of a second. The user is interested in the net result, which the supplier might be able to supply in a variety of ways. Functional specifications serve the user and give the supplier somewhat more freedom in suggesting appropriate equipment. They also place on the vendor the responsibility to demonstrate that the hardware will function properly in the intended service.

Preparation of the Request for Proposals. Unless the amount of hardware to be purchased is quite small, the step which follows the development of specifications is the preparation of the request for proposals. The purchase of a microcomputer or a terminal might not require a request, but any significant expenditure of funds for hardware should make use of one.

The **request for proposal (RFP)** is a formal document which presents in detail the specifications developed earlier. It is sent by the potential buyer to equipment vendors and asks that the vendors submit proposals for equipment which meet, to the best of their ability, the buyer's needs. In other buying/selling situations in other industries, vendors are notified of an opportunity through a similar document known as a request for bid.

In each case the buyer expresses the need to acquire some goods or services, and sellers are asked to quote prices and other conditions for the sale of goods and services which they offer. The RFP gives the buyer an opportunity to tell the various sellers that a purchase is intended. If the sellers want to compete for the business, they are invited to submit a proposal.

The RFP is often prepared with two sets of specifications. The first set is a **mandatory** set, which specifies the functions which must be provided. Any vendor whose equipment does not satisfy the mandatory requirements will not be considered for purchase. An alternate set of specifications of **optional** requirements is used to describe those functions which would be nice to have, but which, in and of themselves, are not essential to the purchase. Both types of requirements are illustrated in Figure 12–3.

There are several reasons for including both mandatory and optional requirements. In the first place, the buyers are never quite sure how much each of the various features will cost. Some features might be advantageous to have if their cost is within reason. As an example, consider the purchase of a stereo tape deck. It might be nice to have a tape deck capable of using metal tapes if that capability does not add too much to the cost of the deck itself.

Figure 12–3 Sample Mandatory and Optional Requirements

Hardware Mandatory Requirements
1. System must be able to accommodate ninety simultaneous users.
2. At full load (ninety users), system reponse time must be less than three seconds.
3. Operating systems have been in operation in other user sites for at least six months.
4. Etc.

Hardware Optionals:
1. System expandable beyond ninety simultaneous users is desirable.
2. Ability to add on additional disk units is desirable.
3. Etc.

Another reason for the mandatory/optional requirements split has to do with the nature of the vendor's product line. Some features are bundled together with other features in the way the equipment is offered or priced. Bundled pricing can cause the cost of particular, optional features to vary widely. Sometimes a vendor can supply an optional feature at no additional cost. If so, the buyer would like to know that such is the case.

As an example, consider the purchase of a car. Assume that a prospective buyer has drawn up a list of specifications and included both mandatory and optional features. The mandatory list might include such features as standard shift, radio, and air conditioning. The optional requirements might include steel-belted radial tires. In shopping, the customer might find that some car dealers have included steel-belted radial tires as standard equipment for which no additional charge is applicable. Other car dealers might supply steel-belted radials, but only at additional cost. The buyer must determine the most advantageous combination of additional features and increased cost. We find exactly the same situation in the purchase of computer equipment.

An RFP might also contain some scheme which tells the vendors exactly how the various proposals will be evaluated, which is discussed in more detail in the next section of this chapter. Government agencies are often required to provide this information to assure vendors that each has an equal opportunity to compete for the sale. Private organizations are not required to provide this information, but many do.

The RFP also specifies the closing date, beyond which proposals will not be accepted, and the date by which a purchase decision is expected to be made. A few weeks or a few months may be allowed for each phase, at the discretion of the buyer, depending mostly on the scope of the project.

Evaluation and Selection. In response to the RFP, those vendors who wish to compete for the sale of the equipment submit proposals to the potential buyer. The buyer must then evaluate the proposals and select the best one.

An effective way to proceed with the evaluation and selection phase is by appointing a **selection committee** to evaluate the various proposals. In fact, if the proposals are complex, it might be necessary to form several committees to complete the evaluation. The selection committee should be composed of a combination of users and data processing specialists. Such a committee is pictured in Figure 12–4.

In the first level of analysis of the proposals, the set of mandatory requirements is considered. Each proposal must be carefully scrutinized to make sure that the hardware proposed by the vendors will in fact satisfactorily meet all of the mandatory requirements. Proposals which do not offer hardware meeting the mandatory requirements are excluded from further consideration.

Next, the optional features are evaluated, and complexities arise. The particular set of optional features offered by a single vendor is in all probability unique—no two vendors will propose to supply hardware with exactly the same capabilities. The buyer must decide which set of optional features would be most useful. Usually this is accomplished by devising a scheme for allocating points to optional features. A feature which the buyer

Figure 12–4
Selection Committee at Work

considers to be twice as important as some other feature receives twice as many points. The system whose set of optional features collects the most points is considered to be the best. This process is illustrated in Figure 12–5.

To return to the car buying example, consider that the buyer has looked at many possibilities and must now select the car he or she most wants to buy. The problem is, some have racing stripes, while others do not. Some have more attractive color schemes than others. Some have steel-belted

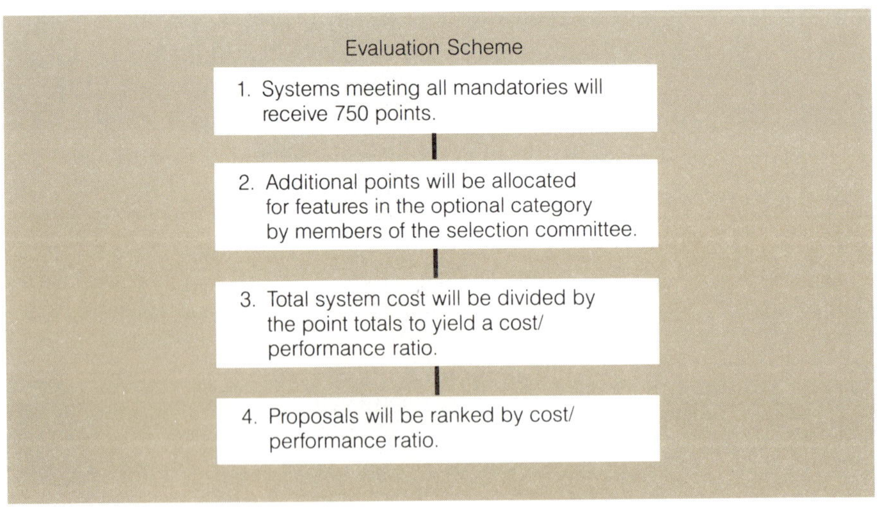

Figure 12–5
Example Evaluation Scheme

Computers in Action 6

Meeting the Challenge

1

2

1. Manufacturing facilities within the chemicals processing industry use process control computers to maintain efficient yields and high quality. **2.** Process control in a large plant requires a sophisticated control panel under the watchful eye of a competent operator. **3.** Information processing computers operate under the watchful eye of an operator who can make adjustments to the CPU's control panel.

3

4

5

4. Departments within a company like Grass Roots may find enough information processing tasks to justify an individual work center. **5.** One of the many tasks for which Grass Roots operators must be trained is the changing of tapes on a magnetic tape drive. **6.** Some information processing operations grow to be quite large and occupy vast areas.

6

7

7. With time, the information stored on secondary storage devices becomes large and many magnetic disk drives could be necessary. **8.** Grass Roots' information processing center will require strict security measures to prohibit access by unauthorized people. **9.** Supervisory personnel within the information processing center will be available to help Grass Roots' employees make the transition to a computerized system. **10.** Employees throughout the Grass Roots organization will require training in order to make the new system a success.

8

9

10

11. Some mainframe computers yield no visible clues on their exteriors to the intense electronic activity which takes place within the cabinet itself. **12.** An information processing manager must check operating logs regularly to ensure that correct procedures are always observed. **13.** Soon, Grass Roots can expect to have a center bustling with the activity of trained professionals.

11

12

13

radial tires, while others do not. We could assign points to each of the desirable optional features and compute the total number of points for each car. The rational buyer would then buy the car with the most points, unless cost considerations dictate a different strategy.

The purchase of computer hardware has proceeded to the point where those proposals which fail to meet the mandatory requirements have been discarded, and a ranking of the proposals according to the total number of points assigned to their optional features has been developed. Several very important considerations remain. One is, can the equipment described by the vendors actually perform as the vendors claim? Another is, which is the most cost-effective purchase to make?

Compatibility, reliability, and maintenance of the hardware are also important considerations, some of which will have been covered by mandatory requirements in the RFP. Each of these important considerations will be discussed in more detail later in the chapter.

The selection committee must ultimately choose from among the proposals the one which most satisfactorily meets the organization's needs. Once the selection has been made, the focus of attention is transferred to the actual implementation of the system.

Implementation. **Implementation** refers to the process of putting the new system in place and making it operational after the selection process has completed the details of the purchase (or rental) and the equipment has been delivered. Sometimes the site where the equipment is to be installed requires rather extensive preparations before the new equipment can be installed.

The most likely site preparations for large systems include the supply of adequate, and adequately conditioned, electrical power and the installation of lighting, air conditioning, and even raised flooring to accommodate the large number of cables between the various pieces of equipment. Fire protection and security precautions might also be necessary.

Site preparations for minicomputer and microcomputer systems require only a minimum of effort. Minicomputers are large enough that their impact on the air-conditioning system needs to be judged, but other site preparation requirements are at a minimum level. Microcomputers require even less—often only space on the top of a desk or table.

Two other considerations are of utmost importance during the implementation phase. One is that, if possible, the old system should continue to be operated until confidence in the capabilities of the new system can be developed. The old and the new systems should be run in parallel, or side by side, until the problems of the new system can be discovered and solved. A changeover to a new system always presents unexpected problems. If the old system can be retained until these problems are discovered and solved, the transition to the new system will be much smoother.

The other consideration of utmost importance during the implementation phase is training. Operators of the new system must be adequately trained in the operational requirements of the new system. Those people who use the system and interact with it must also be trained. Training of a somewhat less detailed nature should also be given to the managers whose work will be changed by the new system. The managers' work is influenced by the new outputs which will be received from the new system, by the new inputs which will be required by the new system, and by the new interactions required of the people who work for the manager. Training costs usually amount to something between 10 and 50 per cent of the total cost of the new system.

Review. An important, though often overlooked, phase of the hardware selection process is the **review,** which should take place several months after the initial implementation has been completed. The purpose of the review is to learn which parts of the hardware selection process worked well and which parts need improvement.

The review process starts with an evaluation of the new system's performance. Any shortcomings in performance should be investigated to determine how the hardware selection process could be changed to prevent the reoccurrence of similar problems in the acquisition of future systems.

A thorough review may point out flaws in the original specifications, errors in the evaluations, mistakes in implementation, or inadequacies in the training. The intent of the review should not be to assess blame for the existing set of problems, but rather to educate members of the organization so that better hardware acquisitions will result in the future. The review phase is simultaneously the last step in one hardware selection project and the first step in the next.

We return now to some topics raised during discussion of the hardware selection process which warrant additional coverage—in particular, testing procedures, hardware compatibility, reliability, maintenance, and financial considerations.

Challenge Update

The reader should now be able to help Mr. Bauer and his Grass Roots staff in listing the steps of the system life cycle appropriate to the acquisition of hardware.

Testing Procedures

One of the problems identified earlier with the evaluation phase was the problem of determining whether or not the hardware offered by the various vendors actually performs as the vendors claim. There is ample evidence to suggest that the cautious buyer should not accept the vendors' untested claims.

Three general classes of procedures exist for judging the ability of hardware to process a given data processing workload. We will discuss a computational approach, a simulation approach, and the use of benchmarks.

Computation. The computational approach attempts to predict the performance of a particular set of hardware in the processing of a particular workload. The computations are based upon such parameters as instruction execution speed, memory access speed, and addition time. The programs to be run on the system are analyzed with respect to the number of instructions they contain, the number of memory accesses needed, the number of additions, and so on. The resulting run time of the program is estimated by computation.

This method is improved slightly by the use of *kernels,* which are small, standard tasks executed on the hardware under evaluation in order to gauge its performance. The complexities of modern systems software which allow such functions as overlapping, multiprogramming, and multiprocessing make the computational approach a relatively unsatisfactory one. These and other operating system capabilities which make it possible for many processing tasks to take place simultaneously and introduce complex interactions between programs make it difficult for the computational approach to be accurate.

The reader must remember that the system's overall performance is a function not only of the hardware but of the software as well. Either an inefficient operating system or inefficient applications program can cause hardware efficiencies to be lost. Consider, once again, the purchase of an automobile. If a customer were to judge a car's performance from its specifications sheet, it is unlikely that satisfactory purchases would be made. As important as piston displacement, weight, and aerodynamic index might be, they rarely predict a driver's satisfaction.

The best that can be said for computational approaches is that they are relatively easy to perform. They require much less effort than the simulation and benchmark approaches discussed below.

Simulation. Management scientists have long used a technique known as **simulation** to gain insight into problems which are too complex to be solved through computational means. In hardware evaluation, a simulation takes the form of a computer program which "acts like" the hardware under evaluation to the extent that estimates of the hardware's performance can be made.

Say, for example, that we are considering the purchase of a hypothetical computer known as the Izzy 5000, and we want to know how it will perform when our accounts receivable package of programs is executed. Assume that we have been able to find a vendor who sells a program which provides a simulation of the Izzy 5000. We acquire the simulation program and submit the accounts receivable package to its analysis. The simulation program predicts how the Izzy 5000 will perform in the running of the accounts receivable programs.

There are some disadvantages associated with using simulation to assess the performance of a particular set of hardware. Simulation programs do not exist for all types of hardware. Even in those circumstances where one does exist, the results are not always very accurate predictors of performance. The writing of a complex simulation program requires that many simplifying assumptions be made. As a result, some accuracy is lost. For example, although flight simulators are used to train airline pilots, the simulator is not the same as the actual experience itself. An advantage of the simulation approach is that it can be used in situations in which the new hardware itself is not available.

Benchmarks. To run a **benchmark** is to actually run a set of programs on the hardware being evaluated to see how it performs. The **standard benchmark** is a set of sample programs which have characteristics common to many of the programs which might be expected to run on the systems in question. Standard benchmarks are used to test the relative performance of one system against a set of others in the same class. The results of these benchmarks, which have been run on a series of computers, are published regularly in data processing periodicals so that people might be able to judge the relative performances of the different machines. An example is provided in Table 12–1.

The set of sample programs which are used for the standard benchmark might include an accounting program, an inventory control program, and a mathematical programming program. Potential buyers of a particular class of systems find the results of the standard benchmark runs helpful in an initial narrowing of the field of potential computer configurations. If the programs to be run by the buyer are principally accounting programs, the system's performance when running the accounting program portion of the standard benchmark would be useful information.

A better benchmark technique, referred to as a **live benchmark,** is to take the actual mix of programs which will be run on the new system and run them on a system identical, or nearly identical, to the one under consideration for possible purchase. Vendors will typically be able to provide this opportunity to potential buyers, unless the hardware under consideration is so new that operating locations do not exist. This live testing of the performance of the system using actual programs is the most reliable of the testing procedures. It is not without some problems, however.

Of course, as was mentioned, an identical system must exist for the test to be possible. Buyers of the newest hardware on the market will probably not be able to find hardware available for benchmark purposes. An additional problem arises when the effort to construct the benchmark set of programs is considered. In general, programs written for one set of hardware are not completely portable to any other set of hardware. Making the programming changes necessary to allow the benchmark set of programs to be run on several different sets of hardware could be very expensive.

Compatibility

One of the problems which continues to be major in the process of acquiring hardware is the problem of equipment compatibility. **Compatibility** of computing hardware means that two or more pieces of equipment are built so that they can be connected to each other in such a way that data can be correctly transmitted between them.

Compatibility problems arise because each of the many manufacturers of computer equipment is free to build products according to standards of the manufacturer's choosing. As a result, computing equipment is built to many different standards. If *no* standardization existed, only equipment made by a single manufacturer could be connected in any given system, since only a few manufacturers make the full range of equipment. There would be no market for manufacturers who concentrated their production efforts on a narrower range of products unless some standards were observed. Thus, there is some incentive for manufacturers to adopt standards. They may resist the adoption of standards in areas in which they feel they have a technological or marketing advantage in the design of their product(s).

Table 12–1 *Example Benchmarks*

32 Bit	IBM	Data General Corp.	Nixdorf Computer Corp.	Honeywell, Inc.
Model	System 38/5	MV/6000	8890/30	6/92
Memory (Bytes)	2M	1M	1M	1M
Operating System	CPF	AOS/VS	Nidos/USE	Gcos/6
Language	RPG-III	Cobol	Cobol	Cobol
Data Base	S/38 DB	Infos	NDB	TPS-6

16 Bit	Digital Equipment Corp.	Microdata Corp.	Hewlett-Packard Co.
Model	PDP-11/44	Reality 2000	3000/40
Operating System	DSM-11	Reality	MPE-IV
Language	Mumps (DEC Standard Mumps)	Basic	Fortran IV
Data Base	DSM-11	Reality	Image 3000

32 Bit	IBM System/38 Model 5 RPG-III	Data General MV/6000 COBOL	Honeywell 6/92 COBOL	Nixdorf 8890/30 COBOL
Data Base Creation	1 hour, 50 min	6 hours	1 hour, 5 min	1 hour, 6 min
Long Query	4 min	4 min, 30 sec	1 min, 25 sec	4 min, 11 sec
Short Query	1 sec	1 sec	1 sec	1 sec
Data Base Occupation (K Bytes)	23.403	22.500	14.799	23.831
Lines of Code	835	1,150	2,219	3,239

16 Bit	DEC PDP-11/44 Mumps	HP 3000 FORTRAN	Microdata Reality 2000 Basic
Data Base Creation	32 min	3 hours, 30 min	48 min
Long Query (17,000 Records)	3 min, 55 sec	2 min, 30 sec	15 min
Short Query (50 Records)	<1 sec	>2 sec	18 sec
Data Base Occupation (K Bytes)	6.073	23.083	3.000
Lines of Code (Source)	183	2,684	391

Government agencies, professional societies, trade associations, and organizations like the American National Standards Institute (ANSI) are all trying to work towards solutions to the standardization problem. Eventually, through negotiation and forces brought about by the marketplace, the extent of standardization should increase. The rapid pace of technological advance will, however, continue to present compatibility problems.

Two computing devices which connect are said to **interface** with each other. If the two devices have been constructed to different standards, an **interface device** is necessary to make the connection possible. In effect, the interface device translates the signal from the first device into the type of signal the second device expects and needs. An interface device is illustrated in Figure 12–6.

We are surrounded by interface devices in our everyday lives. One of the most commonly used interface devices is the telephone. Telephone wires are good conductors of electrical current, but they certainly do not transmit sound very efficiently. When you use the telephone, an interface device must change the sound of your voice into an electrical signal for transmission through the telephone system. The receiver must have a corresponding interface device to convert the electrical signal back to sound.

An interface device is necessary, too, in order for us to enjoy recorded music. Holding a record or tape cassette up to the ear does not produce the sound we want to hear. Several interface devices convert the recorded impressions into sound. One converts the imprint on the record into electrical signals while another converts amplified electrical signals back into sound.

One of the most basic interface problems in computing equipment is the connecting plug. Two computing devices, built to two different plug standards, cannot be directly connected to each other without an interface device to correct the incompatibility of the plugs. (Recall the earlier discussion of plug-to-plug compatible equipment.)

An interface device is also required if the two pieces of equipment use different encoding schemes for data transmission. An **encoding scheme** is a set of rules for translating bit patterns into alphanumeric data. If the two pieces of equipment use different encoding schemes, an interface device is necessary to translate one to the other. (Encoding schemes are discussed in Appendix B.)

The interface device can be physically built into one or the other of the pieces of equipment. If one of the pieces of equipment has intelligence (the ability to execute software), then the interface can be implemented in either

Figure 12–6 An Interface Device Illustrated

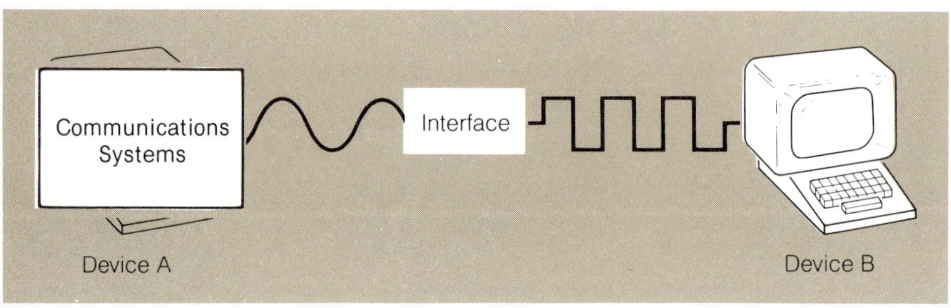

hardware or software. A hardware interface would directly receive a signal of type A and send a signal of type B. A software interface would interpret the meaning of the type A signal, and generate a type B signal of the same meaning. The interface between two dissimilar computing devices, then, can be provided through hardware, software, or a combination of the two. In quite general terms, though, hardware devices are faster than software devices—that is, the signal encounters less delay.

Another point about interfaces is worth making. Although the interface devices are generally quite reliable, an interface does provide yet another set of electronic devices which could fail. Theoretically, two units which require an interface will be slightly less reliable than two units which can operate without one.

Challenge Update

Mr. Bauer and his associates at Grass Roots could now explain the importance of hardware compatibility.

Reliability and Maintenance

The reliability of computers has been the subject of millions of jokes and cartoons. In some instances, the lack of reliability has been the cause of great concern. It would be, for example, discomforting to discover that the computer systems which control our nuclear power generating facilities, or our national defense, are not 100 percent foolproof. (In fact, no electronic device is 100 percent foolproof.)

Most modern computing systems can be relied upon to operate greater than 95 percent of their scheduled operating hours. Most machines are not scheduled for twenty-four-hour service because shutdowns for regularly scheduled maintenance are required. Increased reliability can be gained by providing backup, or redundant, devices. For example, in situations where the loss of the CPU would be disastrous, a backup CPU is provided.

Redundancy of the critical elements has always been an important principle of design in some fields, for example, spacecraft, nuclear reactors, and national defense systems. Several computer manufacturers now offer commercial computing systems which promise 99 percent or greater reliability, made possible through a design which includes device redundancy. Some systems even provide two CPUs in tandem.

A promise of good reliability is not, however, an invitation to ignore

maintenance in the selection of hardware. High reliability is usually achieved through the purchase of reliable equipment and an effective, preventive maintenance program. A program of quick response to unforeseen difficulties is also important.

A regularly scheduled, preventive maintenance program will require that a computer system be periodically removed from operation for testing and repair. Representatives of the manufacturer are frequently on hand to perform the necessary maintenance functions.

It is sometimes important that a malfunction in the system receive immediate attention. A malfunction which causes the system to be inoperable for an extended period cannot usually be tolerated. Some computer systems are large enough that employees of the computer manufacturer are assigned full-time to the site for maintenance purposes. They are available, without delay, to diagnose and repair the problem.

In the case of smaller systems, the costs of such service are too high. Fortunately, the necessity for the service is also somewhat less. To service these locations, manufacturers maintain an on-call service. When problems arise, the manufacturer's representative is called. The time it takes for a maintenance engineer to arrive at the site is important. Delays are costly.

Potential buyers of computing hardware should investigate the availability of maintenance personnel and parts before acquiring a system. Vendors should be willing to sign a contract which guarantees the maximum length of time it would take the manufacturer's representative to respond to a call. The buyer might, for example, require that the repair person be on the customer's premises within three hours of the notifying call 90 percent of the time, and within six hours 100 percent of the time. Replacement parts are sometimes needed in order to complete a repair. The availability of replacement parts is also important to a customer whose computer is down.

Challenge Update

The reader could now discuss with Mr. Bauer the relationship between reliability and maintenance.

Financial Considerations

While the financing of a computer system is a complex enough field to justify a textbook of its own, some treatment of the various alternatives is necessary here so that the potential buyer will know something of the range of alternatives. Selection of the appropriate alternative requires detailed knowledge of the financial affairs of the acquiring organization. The following discussion will differentiate among purchasing, leasing, and leasing-to-buy.

Purchasing. Purchasing requires that the customer pay the manufacturer or other vendor the total purchase price for the hardware. The biggest advantage to an outright purchase is that it is the least expensive alternative in terms of total cash outlay. The disadvantages include the fact that a large sum of money must be brought together at the time of purchase, the possibility that the manufacturer will not be as interested in servicing the system after it has been completely paid for, and the fact that the system will most likely become obsolete during the period of ownership.

Leasing. Leasing, or renting, a system improves the buyer's status with respect to some of the disadvantages of purchasing. The buyer is now faced with a series of smaller lease, or rental, payments spread over time instead of one large sum at the beginning. In addition, the vendor still owns the system and, therefore, has financial and legal interests in maintaining the equipment. The cost of the system's becoming obsolete is borne, ostensibly, by the organization which owns the system.

The other side of the coin, however, is that the owner's risk of obsolescence, cost of money, maintenance, and other risks are built into the lease payment. For this reason, the total cost of leasing will exceed the cost of purchasing. The issue of which is best for the user of the equipment is a complex one, for the treatment of which the reader is directed to a text on finance.

It is not necessary that leasing involve only the acquirer of the system and the manufacturer. Many leasing arrangements occur through a third party, an organization whose business endeavors may be devoted entirely to leasing. Manufacturers sometimes establish subsidiaries for the purpose of managing an aggressive leasing program. Provisions of the tax laws frequently cause buyers to establish subsidiaries, to which they sell their capital assets. The companies then lease them back from the subsidiary. The leasing organization can, however, be an independent organization, not affiliated with either the buyer or the seller.

As a means for comparing the relative costs of purchasing and leasing, consider the acquisition of a microcomputer system. Assume that such a system could be purchased outright for $3,000. The monthly lease payment, which varies with the interest rate, would be approximately $300. The total cost of a ten-month lease is the same as the purchase price, but only with the purchase plan would the user own the machine after ten months.

Lease-to-Buy. A particular type of leasing arrangement, called the lease-to-buy, leads to eventual ownership on the part of the acquiring organization. The leasing contract in such cases will stipulate the number of lease payments which are required, and the transfer price, if any, which accompanies the final transfer of title to the acquiring organization. The lease-to-buy alternative enables the acquiring company the flexibility of less initial capital outlay with a delay in the ownership decision.

We have now seen some of the complexities of hardware selection: the specification process, the RFP, testing procedures, compatibility, reliability, maintenance, and financial considerations. We turn now to an examination of the acquisition of software resources.

Software Selection

This section will discuss the acquisition of both systems software and applications software. Systems software selection is treated first.

Systems Software Selection

Most of the time, the selection of systems software is done in connection with a hardware acquisition. It is, therefore, part of a combined acquisition which follows the process outlined earlier in the chapter.

The selection process will first require that the users be able to specify the functions which the hardware/systems software combination must be able to perform. Some vendors offer relatively standard, fixed, combinations, while others are able to offer considerable variety. In general, the operating system needs to be able to provide the following:

1. Management of the various processes associated with executing a program, that is, moving it from the ready to the running state, allocating the necessary resources to allow it to run, and moving it from running to blocked (and blocked to running).
2. Management of the primary memory to effect partitioning, swapping, paging, and the reconfiguration of memory known as garbage collection.
3. Management of the processor itself, to include its scheduling and error recovery activities.
4. Management of secondary storage, to include the scheduling of access by programs and the normal range of file handling capabilities.
5. Monitoring of system performance.
6. Networking capabilities and the ability to work as a host if necessary.
7. Security, to restrict access to authorized users engaged in authorized activities.

The prospective buyer should include the proper specifications in the RFP for whatever functions are necessary. Upon delivery, systems software should be tested in conjunction with the testing of the hardware. Current users of systems similar to the one under consideration should be interviewed to judge their level of satisfaction with their systems.

Applications Software Selection

Applications software projects come in all sizes. While some are relatively small, many are large enough to require years of effort. Almost all are of significant enough size to require some degree of formalization. The system life cycle concept fits the life cycle of a software project perfectly, as we shall see in the following section.

System Life Cycle—Software. The concept of a system life cycle is a very useful one for software development projects. Most of the steps in the system life cycle have corresponding steps in the life cycle of a software development project. A software version of the system life cycle follows.

Problem Recognition. The recognition that a particular organizational function is a candidate for development into a computerized application is the first step. Users (or managers), as part of their efforts to improve the functioning of the organization, often find that manual data processing tasks can be converted into computerized tasks with a resulting increase in operating efficiency. Data processing personnel frequently recognize and suggest opportunities for software development projects within the various parts of the organization.

Development of System Requirements. The current method for accomplishing the task under study is analyzed, and the requirements which must be met by any new system are developed. In particular, attention must be paid to the output requirements of the system during this phase so that the designers' later efforts will be aligned with the goals of the users and managers. Users, managers, and systems designers must cooperate fully to determine exactly what functions the new software must perform. Many meetings are necessary to achieve full understanding. (See Figure 12–7)

Creation of Alternatives. Once system requirements are determined, an examination begins of the feasible alternatives for acquiring the needed software, to include a search for available packaged software, an analysis of the ability to develop the software through the use of the organization's own programming staff, and a check on the availability of programming contractors or software houses as alternatives. Each of these alternatives will be discussed in detail later in the chapter.

Evaluation and Selection. Next, the decision is made to proceed with the design of one of the alternatives identified above. The three most important criteria in the evaluation of software development projects are usually time,

Figure 12–7
Developing System Requirements

money, and the fit of the resulting software to the task for which it has been designed.

Detailed Design. Once the software alternative is selected, the completion of the logical design of the program, or set of programs, can proceed. A discussion of potentially appropriate design techniques is presented later in this chapter.

Development and Testing. Finally, the actual coding of the programs, their integration into a system, and the testing necessary to increase confidence in the software's ability to operate correctly take place. Most of the work of developing new software systems occurs in this phase, but this phase is heavily influenced by the nature of the work preceding it. A well-prepared logical design, coupled with good development techniques, will make the development and testing phase more productive. A programmer is shown studying the results of a test run in Figure 12–8.

Implementation. Implementation involves putting the new software into place, using the concept of a start-up in parallel with the old system wherever feasible. Training is once again one of the most important activities in any implementation.

Review. A study of the software development project is made in retrospect to learn how the next use of the techniques might be improved. In a sense, continuous review of a software project takes place because software requires almost continuous maintenance. In fact, most of the money spent on software is spent not on development but on maintenance. Estimates of software maintenance costs indicate that organizations can spend 50 to 67 percent of their programming budget on program maintenance. The reliability with which the programs run and the ease with which they are

Figure 12–8
Program Testing

maintained are testimony to the effectiveness of the software development cycle under which they were designed.

Software Trends. A full understanding of software development requires that notice be given to several important software trends. The first is the upward trend of software development costs. While hardware costs have been declining rapidly for years, software costs have been moving in the opposite direction. The proportion of total system costs which must be allocated to software has been increasing, and now amounts to approximately 35 percent of the total cost of a system. Another important trend is the distribution of software costs between developmental costs and maintenance costs. Over a program's lifetime, more than twice as much will be spent to maintain that program than was spent to develop it in the first place. So, though our attention in this chapter is on the development of software, the reader must remember that one of the goals is to develop software which is easier to maintain than has historically been the case.

Another important trend mentioned earlier was the continuing, even worsening, shortage of programmers. Organizations will be even more interested in packaged software in the future simply because the alternative of in-house development may not be available. Small firms would probably not even attempt the development of their own software. To serve these firms, many vendors offer complete hardware/software combination packages ready for operation. These systems are called **turn-key systems** to imply that all the buyer has to do is turn on the key.

In general, two major strategies for acquiring applications software are (1) the in-house development of that software and (2) the acquisition of a software package. We turn our attention now to these two alternatives and then to a brief discussion of some minor variations to the theme.

Software Development Alternatives. Throughout the brief history of computing, the most prevalent strategy for acquiring software was to have the organization's programmers write it. Early in the history of data processing, in-house development of software was the only alternative. In the late 1970s and early 1980s, the availability of software packages became a viable alternative. Contract programming and the use of custom software houses present additional alternatives. Each will be discussed in turn.

In-House Software Development. The in-house development of software proceeds along the lines of the system life cycle discussed earlier. A need for the software is recognized, feasibility is assessed, and the alternatives are considered. Systems analyst/user teams provide diagrams to capture the system's logic, and programmers set to work coding the various program modules.

One obvious advantage of the in-house development of software is that programs can be built to fit the basic organizational process perfectly. In-house development also leads to a feeling of participation on the part of various members of the organization and a corresponding self-interest in making the new system work. Since the programs have been created by the organization's programming staff, when they later require maintenance, it should not be as difficult to find someone in the organization familiar with

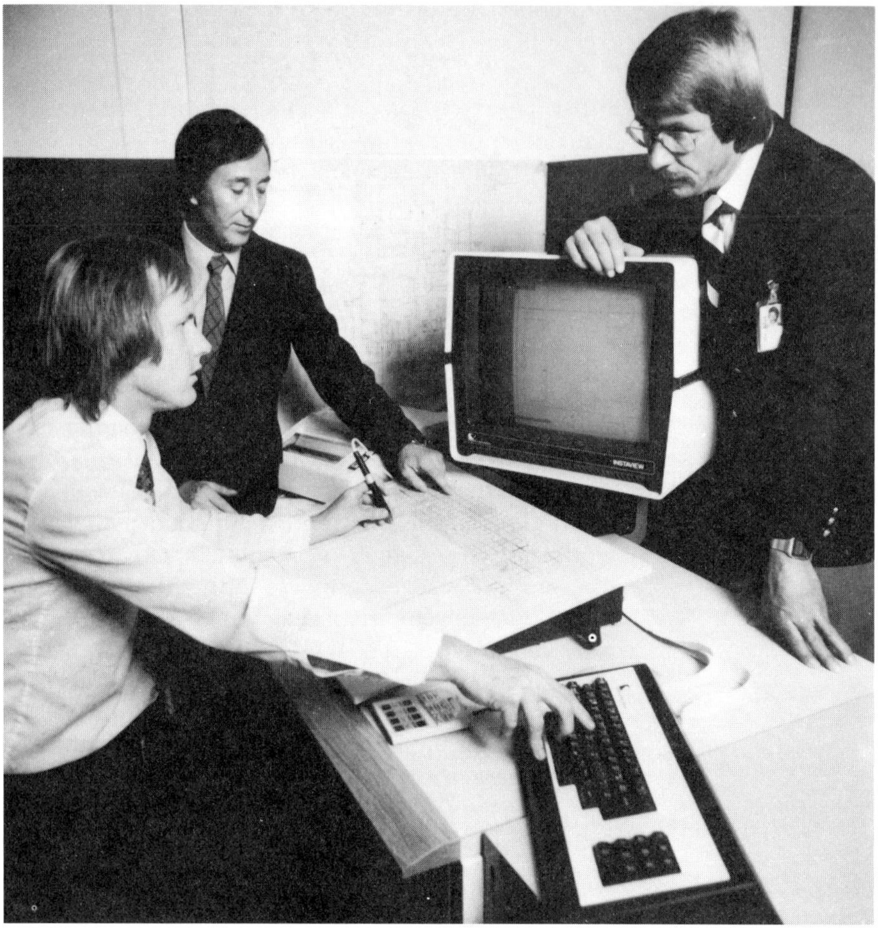

Figure 12–9
In-House Development Requires Extensive Collaborative Effort

the system's logic. Adequate documentation would be, of course, a big help. Programmers working on documentation are shown in Figure 12–9.

The major disadvantages of in-house development of software are the time it takes and the cost of such development. It usually costs more and takes longer to develop software in-house than even the most astute estimators will predict. The history of in-house development of software is one of budgets exceeded and deadlines missed.

The backlog of applications awaiting development and the ever more acute shortage of experienced programmers indicate that the in-house development of software will very likely decline in importance relative to the next alternative, the software package.

Software Packages. A **software package** is a program or set of programs written in somewhat general terms to handle a particular type of data processing task. For example, there are software packages to do payroll processing, inventory control, and accounts receivable. The number of packages available is becoming quite large. As a matter of fact, in 1983 over 200 different packages were available just for handling accounts receivable.

Software packages have been written by manufacturers and software vendors to take advantage of the fact that particular data processing tasks are very similar regardless of the organization in which they are being used. Sometimes a software package is developed by an organization to satisfy its own data processing needs and found to work so well that it is then sold to other organizations with a similar need.

A software vendor which has developed a software package can market it at a fraction of the development cost. It can be sold at a much lower price, for example, than the cost of in-house development of a similar package. The advantage to the software house is that it can sell the package to many buyers and thereby spread the cost of the package's development over many installations.

The primary advantages of the software package are twofold. The cost of the package is much less than the cost of developing the same software through in-house means, and the time it takes to purchase and install a package is much less than the time it takes to develop an in-house application. Packages are available *off the shelf,* for immediate delivery. Some customization might be necessary in order to shape the package to the buyer's particular task, but a software package can be running, in most cases, much more quickly than in-house software can be developed. Figure 12–10 pictures a user working with such a package.

Several notes of caution are necessary with respect to software packages. The buyer must recognize that a software package is written in general terms to make its potential market as large as possible. This generalization means, usually, that a software package will not fit any single application as well as software designed especially for that application. The package

Figure 12–10
Making Use of a Software Package

will probably not run as efficiently on the buyer's system, and the available features of the package will probably not meet the buyer's needs exactly.

A second caution relates to the modification of an acquired package. It is not unusual for a buyer to modify a purchased package in order to customize it to the organization's way of doing business. Such changes are not made without risk.

The making of changes to existing programs is, itself, a risky endeavor, as was discussed earlier. In addition, vendor support of the package may be jeopardized by the buyer's modifications. Wherever possible, modifications should be made the contractual responsibility of the vendor to ensure the continuity of vendor support and minimize the buyer's liability.

A final caution relates to the ability of any particular software package to execute correctly on any particular configuration of hardware. A buyer should make sure that actual experience has demonstrated that the software package in question has satisfactorily run on identical hardware. A buyer might impose a contractual obligation on the seller to ensure that the package can be made to execute properly.

Buyers of software packages should evaluate and compare the available packages before buying. Interviews with other users and benchmarks will help with the evaluation. Actual purchase should take place through a purchase contract which clearly delineates the responsibilities of both the buyer and the seller.

Challenge Update

The staff at Grass Roots should now be able to debate the relative merits of developing software in-house and acquiring it as a package.

Microcomputer software acquisitions present other problems as well. Vendor representatives seldom seem knowledgeable enough about the software they sell to be able to answer questions critical to its use. Buyers should study software reviews published regularly in personal computer periodicals to add to their knowledge of the software. Wherever possible, they should actually read manuals and use the software on the dealer's equipment before buying. The acquisition of microcomputer software packages is treated in more detail in Chapter 15.

Other Software Alternatives. Although most software acquisitions take place through either in-house development or the purchase of a software package, two other significant possibilities do exist. As a replacement for (or supplement to) an organization's in-house capabilities, **contract programmers** can be hired for software development purposes. Contract programmers are usually hired to make it possible to temporarily assign a greater number of people to a software development project or to avoid limitations placed by upper management on the hiring of permanent employees.

Contract programmers work side-by-side with the organization's own programmers to such an extent that they are virtually indistinguishable from each other. After a few months' work, the programmers all seem like regular employees, but the contract programmers receive their paychecks from the contractor.

One advantage of contract programmers is that they can be used to increase the number of people available to work on projects until the workload decreases, at which time they return to the contractor without the normal traumas associated with a reduction in force. Contract programmers can also be added in a much shorter time than the usual hiring process for employees takes.

Custom software houses are available to fill a temporary need for additional personnel in much the same way as contract programmers. The difference is that custom software houses usually contract to complete an entire project, and staffing and supervision become the function of the software house. As a matter of fact, most of the development work usually takes place on the software house's premises, not on those of the buyer of the services.

A custom software house, after successful completion of a software development project, may decide to sell a generalized form of that software as a package. Such arrangements depend upon the generality of the application and contractual arrangements with the original buyer of the custom software house's services.

An important consideration in the development of any software is the language in which the software is to be written. As we have already learned, machine language makes most efficient use of the computer's resources, but it uses more programming resources. In addition, since the machine language of each manufacturer's computer is unique, a machine language program is **machine dependent** because it will only work on the machine for which it was written. Assembly language exhibits virtually the same benefit and constraints.

We turn our attention now to the higher-level languages, which make less efficient use of the machine's resources but better utilize a programmer's time. Higher-level languages are **machine independent** because many different types of machines are capable of running programs written in the higher-level languages.

The reader should be made aware that machine independence is not quite as tidy a concept as the name implies. Although the higher-level languages run on a great number of different machines, there are quite often small differences in the particular way in which each is implemented on the various machines so that some modifications are usually necessary to move programs from one machine to another.

This completes the chapter's treatment of the acquisition of hardware and software resources. It is a complex subject, one which ultimately requires a lot of coordinated organizational effort. A glimpse into the future might be helpful in winding up this chapter.

Newest Developments

Several trends are important enough to justify additional comment. The rate of technological improvement in hardware continues to be very high at a time when prices are declining. While this makes for exciting marketing developments, it is also the cause of some frustration for would-be buyers.

When, for example, is the best time to buy? The buyer knows that, if he or she waits, a better product will be available at a lower cost. The trend to better price/performance ratios for hardware is expected to continue for years. Most buyers cannot delay the purchase forever. When to buy? It is a tough question.

The question of when to buy is made even more confusing by manufacturers who "announce" new products long before they are actually available. The IBM PCjr, for example, was announced in early November of 1983, even though none would be available for purchase until the first quarter of 1984. Such an announcement undoubtedly caused many people to delay purchase decisions, thereby reducing the level of sales of other microcomputers anticipated by retailers during the heavy sales period preceding the holidays.

The impact of hardware compatibility should gradually be lessened. Work to establish interface standards continues, and more widely accepted standards will help. The trend towards improvement in the price/performance ratio for hardware also shows signs of helping with the compatibility problem. As the cost of hardware intelligence declines, it becomes possible to include it in the design of more and more devices. Hardware devices with intelligence can compensate for the lack of a standard interface by being able to accommodate a variety of interface demands.

For example, hardware intelligence in terminals will make it possible for them to be connected to a wider variety of computing systems. Hardware intelligence in the connecting networks will make it possible for a variety of computing devices to communicate with each other.

The trend in overall software costs seem to be in the opposite direction from hardware costs. A large fraction of the costs of software are associated with the maintenance of old programs. These costs are expected to keep increasing, though the software engineering techniques discussed in the next chapter may eventually have a favorable effect.

Software packages are playing an increasingly important role in the acquisition of computing resources. Initially, there were few available, so firms developed their own software in-house. As packages became more readily available, firms were able to purchase them if they fit, or could be made to fit, their existing business functions. Now we are beginning to see firms willing to change their business practices in order to make a package acquisition possible and avoid the in-house development of software or the in-house modification of a package.

The acquisition of computing resources remains an important task in the overall management of an organization. As computing resources are increasingly distributed throughout an organization, every participant in the organization can expect additional responsibility with respect to the acquisition of these important resources.

COMPUTING CHALLENGE: *A Final Note*

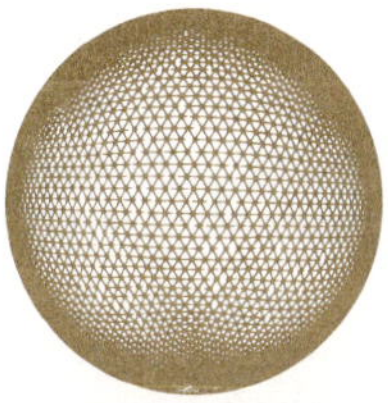

Mr. Bauer recognizes the size of the task to which he has been assigned. He must develop a data processing facility within Grass Roots which will provide local data processing capabilities as well as the capability of transmitting information directly to the corporate computing center of East Chemicals. An overall systems design effort needs to be implemented, within which a complete set of hardware and software must be specified, evaluated, and implemented.

One of his first efforts will be the appointment of a selection committee to oversee the acquisition of the necessary computing resources. Representatives from the manufacturing plant, the warehouse, and the general office will be appointed to the selection committee, which will be chaired by Mr. Bauer.

A study will be initiated to determine the data processing needs of the organization. The information needs of the parent company and the needs of the local subsidiary will both have to be considered. This will eventually lead to a statement of equipment specifications and a formal request for proposal to be distributed to potential vendors.

The selection committee will also develop a scheme for evaluating the proposals and selecting the best system. A few software packages will be selected, tested, and acquired. Software necessary for many other applications will be delayed until a software development group can be put together.

Training will be an important part of the implementation phase since most employees of Grass Roots have no prior exposure to electronic data processing. Efforts must be taken during the training period to pinpoint the uncertainties which might be troubling employees as new procedures are developed.

Consideration will necessarily be given to the interface between the Grass Roots' system and the system at East's corporate headquarters. Reliability and maintenance are also very important because the Grass Roots location is not near any large city where maintenance facilities might be available. Vendors will be asked to substantiate claims of system reliability and demonstrate that maintenance engineers and the spare parts inventory will provide adequate protection against excessive system downtime.

Financial considerations do not seem to be a problem. East owns a leasing subsidiary, through which financing of the system will be arranged. The integration of the various hardware and software resources into a viable and effective system will still, however, require a great deal of effort.

SUMMARY

- Most data processing systems design efforts result in the acquisition of new computing resources, which may range in scope from an acquisition as straightforward as a terminal to one as complex as a complete system.
- The effort and degree of formality necessary to ensure a good acquisition vary with the size of the acquisition, but some degree of formality is suggested for all but trivial acquisitions.
- Most often, acquisitions of hardware and systems software occur together, and in many cases, both new operating system capabilities and applications software are required.
- The successful acquisition is one which integrates the appropriate collection of hardware, systems software, and applications programs.
- The hardware acquisition process begins with the derivation of the system specifications from an analysis of the uses to which the system will be put.
- Hardware specifications should be functional wherever possible and as complete as possible.
- A formal request for proposal (RFP) document is prepared for the acquisition of significant amounts of hardware.
- An RFP contains the system's specifications and initiates a dialogue between the buyer and the various vendors with regard to the suitability of each vendor's equipment.
- Proposals submitted by vendors in response to the RFP are evaluated, and one system is selected for implementation.
- The evaluation of hardware can be done by computational methods, simulation, or benchmarking.
- Two characteristics important to a successful implementation of a data processing system are the parallel operation of the old and new systems and the conducting of sufficient training to enable operators, users, and managers to function in the new environment.
- A review of the acquisition process a few months after its completion will improve an organization's ability to conduct another acquisition.
- Compatibility is an important consideration in any hardware acquisition, although devices which are otherwise incompatible can be made to communicate with each other through an interface device.
- Several financial alternatives exist for the acquisition itself, including purchase, lease, and lease-to-buy.
- The hardware acquisition problem is made more complex by the rapid rate of technological advance in the industry; currently available equipment seems always to be displaced by newer models which are cheaper yet capable of higher levels of performance.
- Although costs associated with hardware for a given level of performance are decreasing, software costs are on the rise.
- To counter the rising cost of the in-house development of software, organizations are increasingly turning to software packages.
- Temporary software development personnel can be acquired from a contract programming agency.

- Custom software development firms provide an alternative to in-house software development.
- Most applications programs have some degree of machine dependence which makes it necessary to modify them when moving them to a new environment.
- The acquisition of computing resources in a distributed processing environment involves many organizational participants.

CASE: Computer Does McCormick's Labeling

McCormick and Company Incorporated, is a worldwide leader in the manufacturing and marketing of seasoning and flavoring products. Its seasoning and spice products are available in the retail market and are used extensively in the institutional and industrial food processing markets. To serve its institutional and industrial customers, McCormick and Company ships bulk seasonings and spices in large drums. The drums have to carry identification labels which identify the product, its date of manufacture, its lot number, the customer, the shipping address, and so on. Often the labeling process, done manually, required four different labels and a considerable amount of employee time.

McCormick decided to investigate a computerized system to speed up the labeling process. Specifications were prepared and several alternatives were evaluated. Management decided to buy an integrated system of hardware and software from the Standard Register Co.

The firm acquired an automated label preparation system (LPS 3002) which utilized a dual disk drive, an intelligent terminal, and a matrix printer with an appropriate set of software. The new system allows employees to enter only the product number and let the system generate all standard labeling information, such as the ingredients list. Variable data can then be added to the label for specific shipments as the operator enters the order number, quantity, and date of manufacture. Label accuracy is checked by the software and the operator before the system prints the pressure-sensitive labels. The new labels are easy to read and can be easily attached to the product drums.

Product quality and safety are always important concerns in any operation involving food additives. McCormick's new system produces an audit trail that can be used to review all labeling transactions. The audit report is reviewed by the appropriate departments to ensure that all orders have been properly executed, labeled, and shipped.

The new system represents a successful acquisition of computing resources for McCormick and Company. It simplifies a process which had been troublesome to them and provides additional benefits in terms of labeling accuracy and record keeping. It has also resulted in an annual savings of over $33,000.

"Labeling Saves Time and Money," *Infosystems*, June 1982, pp. 144–145.

Questions for the Case

1. Does this system seem to be large enough to warrant a full-blown, formal acquisition process? Why or why not?
2. Would the new system have been run in parallel with the old before the old system was discarded? What advantages would be realized from a parallel operation? What disadvantages?

DISCUSSION QUESTIONS AND EXERCISES

1. Explain the role that hardware selection plays in the overall process of systems design.
2. Why is it sometimes necessary to complete some of the hardware specifications during the creation and evaluation of alternatives phases?
3. What purposes are served by the request for proposal? How does it serve the buyer? How does it serve the vendor?
4. Explain the use of benchmarks and the difference between standard and live benchmarks.
5. For what purposes is a new system run in parallel with the old? What are the advantages of implementation in parallel? Disadvantages?
6. What is the purpose of the review phase of hardware selection?
7. How are hardware reliability and maintenance related?
8. What characteristics of the computer industry make the acquisition of equipment more difficult than other industries? In what way can we expect the situation to improve?
9. Compare the acquisition of a large mainframe with that of a microcomputer.
10. What factors in the market for computer equipment stimulate the manufacture of equipment built to different, incompatible standards? Should the government pass and enforce laws to restrict designs? Why or why not?
11. Explain the relative advantages and disadvantages of in-house development of software.
12. In what ways is the purchase of a software package a better alternative than the in-house development of software?
13. Why are software packages becoming the acquisition alternative most frequently chosen?
14. Compare the hardware evaluation methods of computation, simulation, and benchmarking in terms of effectiveness.
15. An applications program developed by a custom software house may be marketable as a software package. How would this be advantageous to the original client? How would it be advantageous to the software house?

ADDITIONAL READINGS

Benwell, Nicholas. *Benchmarking.* Washington, DC: Hemisphere Publishing, 1975.

Blumenthal, Susan. *Understanding and Buying a Small Business Computer.* Indianapolis: Howard W. Sams, 1982.

Clark, Jon D., and Reisman, Arnold. *Computer System Selection.* New York: Praeger, 1981.

Computer Systems Buyer's Guide by *Computerworld,* August 24, 1983.

Davis, Gordon B. *Management Information Systems.* 2d ed. New York: McGraw-Hill, 1982.

Frank, Werner L. *Critical Issues in Software.* New York: Wiley, 1983.

Hedberg, Augustin. "Choosing the Best Computer for You." *Money,* November 1982, pp. 68–116.

Henkel, Tom. "*Computerworld*'s Annual Hardware Roundup." *Computerworld,* August 20, 1984, pp. 29–40.

Kerzner, Harold. *Project Management for Executives.* New York: Van Nostrand Reinhold, 1981.

Lucas, Henry C., Jr. *The Analysis, Design, and Implementation of Information Systems.* 2d ed. New York: McGraw-Hill, 1981.

Martin, James. *Application Development without Programmers.* Englewood Cliffs, NJ: Prentice-Hall, 1982.

Morris, Michael F., and Roth, Paul F. *Computer Performance Evaluation.* New York: Van Nostrand Reinhold, 1982.

Timmreck, E. M. "Computer Selection Methodology." *Computing Surveys,* December 1973, pp. 199–222.

UTS 400

13

Software Engineering

CHAPTER PREVIEW

Software development is a process which has consumed large amounts of scarce organizational resources for years, and it seems likely to continue to do so for many years to come. Increasingly, organizations are turning to the acquisition of software packages, yet applications development efforts within these organizations are far from extinction. It seems that there will be a continuing need for applications programmers and applications development efforts for some time.

An analysis of the programmers' workload in most large organizations with mature data processing departments would show two significant facts. In the first place, we would find a large backog of applications awaiting development. Secondly, we would find that most of the programming effort has to do more with maintaining old programs than with developing new ones. To make matters worse, many of the old programs were poorly written and inadequately documented, so the maintenance effort is characteristically tedious and inefficient.

The continuing need for the development of new applications software and the programming errors of the past suggest that improved methods of software development are extremely desirable and important. We need to make applications development more like a science and less like an art. Many efforts are underway to improve systems analysis, design, and programming. Collectively these efforts are known as **software engineering,** and their principal aim is to add *structure* to the applications development process.

This chapter on software engineering starts with a review of machine and assembly languages and then moves to a discussion of the more popular higher-level languages. We will then examine the issue of software quality before discussing the various techniques designed to improve the productivity of software development efforts. As usual, we begin with a Computing Challenge to direct the material which follows.

COMPUTING CHALLENGE: *Grass Roots Revisited*

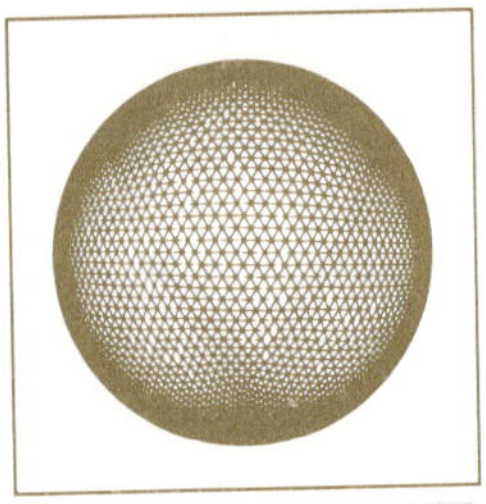

Perhaps a return visit to Grass Roots Growers will help develop some perspective for the challenge of the software development process. Mr. Martin Bauer, the new general manager of Grass Roots, has supervised the selection committee's work in acquiring new data processing resources. The new hardware, with its associated systems software, can accommodate both batch and timesharing, which means both batch and on-line, real time processing can be considered for future applications. Site preparations for the new hardware are almost completed, and Mr. Bauer expects most of the system to be delivered within the next three months.

Start-up and operator training are expected to consume most of the first two months after the system is installed, then the system will be available for the running of applications programs. Mr. Bauer figures that he has a total of six months to put in place a software engineering effort capable of developing and maintaining applications programs.

Acceptance of the change to computerized data processing seems to vary greatly from department to department within Grass Roots. A newly-hired data processing manager seems very eager to hire a large programming staff and begin writing programs. The production scheduling engineer in the manufacturing plant is extremely anxious to work with a computerized production scheduling program, but the comptroller seems very reluctant to begin conversion of any accounting work to a computer-based environment.

Mr. Bauer's superiors at East Chemical are getting impatient for the conversion of financial data to a form compatible with the corporate data processing system. Some additional expertise is clearly needed within the company in order to design a software development strategy which will best move the company towards its business goals. Mr. Bauer, the new data processing manager, and the department heads of Grass Roots must develop a plan for the long-range development of a software engineering capability. But first, they have some questions. What programming language(s) is (are) most commonly used by business organizations? What are the fourth-generation languages? What improved software engineering techniques are available to assist in the development of programs?

The nature of the software engineering task will be discussed in this chapter, which has been designed to help the reader do the following:

1. *Describe the nature of software quality.*
2. *Discuss some of the differences among the common programming languages.*
3. *Explain the techniques of structured programming.*
4. *Explain the importance of documentation.*
5. *Discuss the productivity improvement strategies of software engineering.*

HISTORICAL PERSPECTIVE

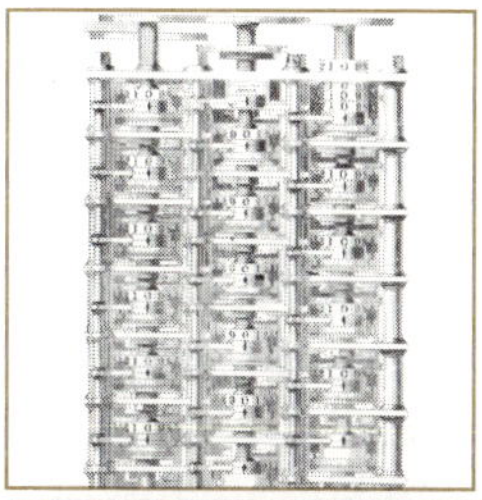

Wired panels controlled the activities of the earliest of the modern calculating machines. The computations of an accounting program would require a particular wired panel, and those of the payroll program would require a different panel. The "writing" of a program in the days of wired panels meant that a complex wiring diagram was used to properly place the wire leads in the panel.

Eventually the capability to enter and store a set of instructions in the computer's internal storage became sufficiently developed to include in commercial machines. Programming became much easier with the development of the stored program concept. Programs could then be entered into the machine by first punching the program into punched cards (or punched paper tape) and having the cards (or tape) read into the machine. Since that time, further improvements have allowed the process of program development to become even better.

As was discussed in an earlier chapter, the lowest level of programming is a numerical language known as machine language. In machine language, each instruction in the language corresponds exactly with one of the elemental instructions in the computer's instruction set. Machine language programs are, therefore, very efficient users of the computer's resources, though not very efficient users of a programmer's abilities.

Assembly language, a level above machine language, has three distinct advantages. Instructions in assembly language are mnemonic; for example, the letter *R* rather than a number might stand for READ. This quality makes them easier for the programmer to use. In addition, the system relieves the programmer of the necessity of remembering actual, physical addresses by allowing the substitution of variable names and statement labels instead. Assembly language instructions are still one-for-one with machine language; that is, there is still an assembly language instruction for each of the machine's elemental instructions.

Assembly language is, therefore, a relatively efficient user of the system's resources, but an assembly language program does require translation into machine language before it can be executed. The translation is accomplished by a program known as an assembler. Assembly language and machine language are unique to each particular computer design. (Examples of each language were given in Chapter 3.)

Languages at the next level are referred to as higher-level languages. Here we find the popular programming languages such as COBOL, FORTRAN, BASIC, PL/I, and Pascal. These languages maintain the advantages of assembly language and extend them even further. Mnemonic instructions become even more like English or algebra. In addition, an instruction in a higher-level language exhibits something known as **power,** the capability of combining many machine-language instructions into a single command. An instruction in a higher-level language might, as a matter of fact, translate into many instructions in machine language, which means the higher-level language has more power.

Higher-level languages must be translated before execution by programs known as compilers, or in some cases interpreters. The translated machine-language version of a program, originally written in a higher-level language, is not usually as efficient a program as the same program written originally in machine language. This means that the higher-level languages use the machine's resources somewhat less efficiently. On the other hand, the programmer's efficiency is greatly increased by the use of the more powerful language.

Most of the languages with a higher-level language designation are *procedural languages.* The programmer must specify exactly the procedure by which the results are to be obtained. *Nonprocedural languages* give the user the ability to specify the results desired without having to specify the procedure by which the results are to be obtained. These nonprocedural languages offer hope that users who do not know how to program will be able to interact with the computer effectively (see Figure 13–1). [Note: Machine, assembly, procedural, and nonprocedural languages are referred to as the first-, second-, third-, and fourth-generation languages, respectively.]

As the level of language with which the user and the machine interact becomes higher, an increased amount of work is shifted from the user to the computing system itself. Machine language is directly executable, but the other levels all require translation before execution, and the higher the level the greater the translation. As a result, the computing system must perform more and more of the work.

Fortunately, the computer *hardware* has gotten more and more powerful so that the increase in its share of the workload has not caused its efficiency to degrade significantly. As a matter of fact, the computer's ability to do the work has increased so dramatically that programmers are now much less concerned about whether or not the machine's resources are used

Figure 13–1 A Nonprogramming User Gains Access to Data Base through Nonprocedural Language

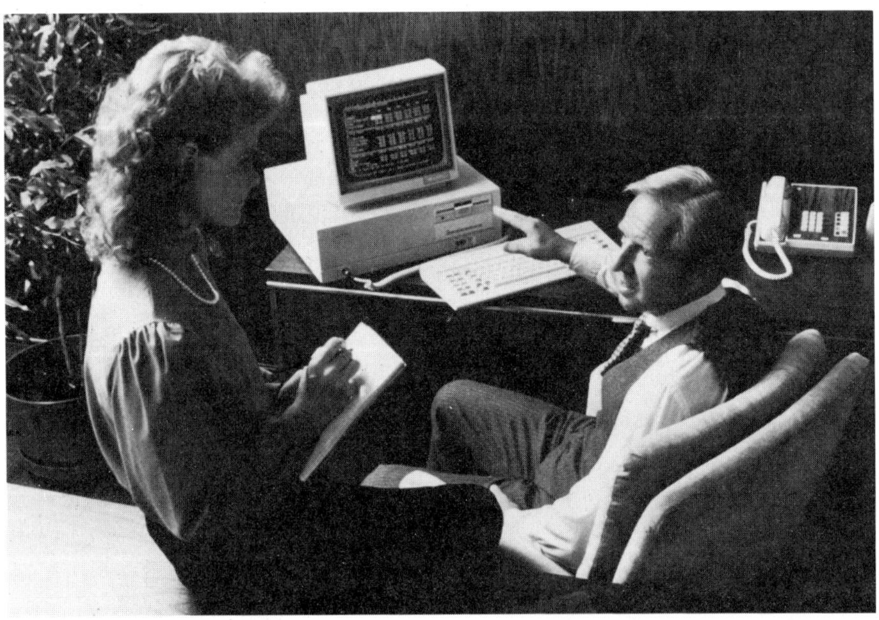

efficiently and are more concerned with the efficient use of programming resources. A continuation of that trend will be apparent from the material in this chapter.

Software Quality

In any purchase decision, the quality of the product under consideration is one of the attributes which deserves serious attention. Software quality is no exception. Buyers should try to determine the level of quality of any software they intend to buy.

Unfortunately, software quality is rather difficult to fully assess. The best test is actual use. Buyers should, therefore, try to arrange for extensive testing before purchase. In some markets, testing is difficult to arrange. In the personal computer market, for example, a buyer cannot usually arrange for a test copy of the software, but must rely on a demonstration.

The National Bureau of Standards has developed a list of attributes of software in an attempt to give definition to software quality. A partial listing is provided here to give the reader an improved understanding of the word *quality* as it applies to software products.

1. *Reliability* is the ability of the software to perform as intended, without errors.
2. *Clarity* means the software is well documented, with modular structure and clearly stated algorithms.
3. *Robustness* means the software is able to recover from unacceptable input or incorrect commands.
4. *Maintainability* is the ability to understand and modify the software when necessary.
5. *Ease of use* means the software presents an interface to the user which is easy to understand and use.
6. *Portability* exists when software is written so it can be easily moved to another processing system.
7. *Documentation* must be provided to facilitate use and maintenance of the software. The documentation must be accurate and complete.

The last category, documentation, is important enough to justify special attention. Software documentation should be complete and clear enough that other programmers, and even the author of the program at a later time, can tell exactly what the program does and how it works. As a minimum it should consist of:

a. Comments within the program itself to explain how each section of instructions interacts with the program-at-large.
b. A flowchart for the overall program and flowcharts for each module.
c. Pictorial layout and examples of all inputs and outputs.
d. A description of each file used by the program.
e. A narrative to describe the algorithm(s) and the overall working of the program.
f. A program run book which contains complete instructions on running the program, including computer setup and restart procedures.

Good documentation is an essential component of quality software. It must accompany software packages acquired on the outside and applications developed within the firm. Without adequate documentation, running the programs is difficult and maintaining them virtually impossible. An interesting article by Gerald Weinberg, described in the next paragraph, indicates just how treacherous making program changes can be.

In his article, Mr. Weinberg describes some program maintenance errors and the costs of those errors to the organizations in which the programs were running. The three most expensive errors involved a change in "a *single character* in a previously correct program." [Emphasis added.][1] The most expensive error cost the organization $1.6 *billion* while the cheapest of the three cost a *mere* $245 million. Weinberg's experience indicates that a change in a single line of a program has a 50 – 50 chance of making the program incorrect.

Is it any wonder then, that efforts to improve program structures in order to improve program maintenance receive a great deal of attention and research? Software quality must be vigorously pursued. Improvements in applications development processes can potentially yield excellent returns.

Challenge Update

The new data processing manager at Grass Roots should now have a new appreciation for the concept of quality in software.

We now turn our attention to the higher-level languages in which most applications software have been written. Following that, we will explore the techniques which provide structure to analysis, design, and programming.

Overview of Programming Languages

Hundreds of computer programming languages exist, but most programming is confined to a relatively small number of languages. The selection

1. Gerald M. Weinberg, "Kill That Code," *Infosytems*, August 1983, pp. 48 – 49.

of a particular language depends upon several factors, not the least of which is the purpose for which that language is intended. If, for example, the choice is for the purpose of writing applications programs in a business organization, the most likely candidate is COBOL. If the application is a scientific one or one in engineering, the most likely choice is FORTRAN.

One factor which frequently conditions the choice of a programming language is its availability. Most computing systems offer only a small subset of the programming languages which are available, perhaps even a single language. Ease of learning and the ease with which programs may be written, understood, and maintained are also important considerations in language selection.

If the choice of the language is for purposes of learning the art of computer programming, the most commonly used languages for this purpose are BASIC and Pascal. PL/I, RPG, and APL are the languages of a somewhat more restricted use but are, nevertheless, popular within certain spheres of use. After an extended period of development, the Department of Defense's new language, Ada, is now available for use. A brief overview of each language follows.

COBOL

Surveys continue to demonstrate that **COBOL,** which stands for **COmmon Business Oriented Language,** is the language in which most professional programmers spend their time, and the one in which most business applications programs are written. One of the earliest higher-level computer programming languages, COBOL has undergone several revisions since its initial development in the late 1950s.

Standards for COBOL were first published by the American National Standards Institute (ANSI) in 1968. A revision and extension of those standards was published by ANSI in 1974. Language versions are frequently identified by the year of the revision, hence the version of COBOL established by the 1974 standards is known as COBOL-74. The most recent revision was initiated in 1980 but was not well received by the community of users because changes proposed for the language caused previously written programs to be in nonconformance. Discussions concerning the new standards continued through 1984 before the revised standard was published.

Compared to programs in other higher-level programming languages, programs written in COBOL are more like English since the commands are full English words and the rules for naming variables allow long, hyphenated English phrases as variable names. For example, the word ADD (instead of a + sign) is used to indicate addition, and GROSS-PAY is an allowable variable name. As a result of COBOL's English-like nature, its programs are longer and require, thereby, more time to write and enter into the system than do most other programming languages.

The structure of a COBOL program is very similar to English. In COBOL we find words, clauses, statements, sentences, paragraphs, sections, and divisions. Reserved words in COBOL, such as ADD, IF, and MOVE, cause specific data processing operations to occur.

Every COBOL program is divided into four divisions. The IDENTIFICA-

Figure 13–2
Sample COBOL Program

```
IDENTIFICATION DIVISION.
PROGRAM-ID. INTEREST.
AUTHOR.

ENVIRONMENT DIVISION.
CONFIGURATION SECTION.
SOURCE-COMPUTER.HONEYWELL.
OBJECT.COMPUTER.HONEYWELL.

INPUT-OUTPUT SECTION.
FILE-CONTROL.
    SELECT IN-FILE ASSIGN TO INPUT.
    SELECT OUT-OF-FILE ASSIGN TO OUTPUT.

DATA DIVISION.
FILE SECTION.

FD IN-FILE
    LABEL RECORDS ARE OMITTED
    DATA RECORD IS IN-RECORD.
01  IN-RECORD.
    05 DEPOSIT       PIC 10(9)V99.
    05 FILLER        PIC XX.
    05 YEARS         PIC 99.
    05 FILLER        PIC XX.
    05 RATE          PIC 99.
    05 FILLER        PIC X(59).

FD  OUT-FILE
    LABEL RECORDS ARE OMITTED
    DATA RECORD IS PRINT-LINE.
01  PRINT-LINE       PIC X(80).

WORKING-STORAGE SECTION.
01  COMPUTATIONAL-VARIABLES.
    05 INT-RATE      PIC V99.
    05 END-BALANCE   PIC 10(9)V99.

01  INPUT-LINE-1.
    05 FILLER        PIC X(80) VALUE
        "INPUT DEPOSIT YEARS AND RATE IN THE FOLLOWING FORM".
01  INPUT-LINE-2
    05 FILLER        PIC X(80) VALUE
        "0000047362.79  04  06".
01  RESULTS-LINE.
    05 FILLER    PIC X(18) VALUE
            "ENDING BALANCE IS".
    05 END-BALANCE  PIC $$$$$$$$$9.99.
                -OUT
PROCEDURE DIVISION
MAIN-LOGIC
    OPEN INPUT IN-FILE.
    OPEN OUTPUT OUT-FILE.
    WRITE PRINT-LINE FROM INPUT-LINE-1 AFTER 1.
    WRITE PRINT-LINE FROM INPUT-LINE-2 AFTER 1.
    READ IN-FILE
    COMPUTE INT-RATE = RATE / 100.
    COMPUTE END-BALANCE = DEPOSIT + DEPOSIT * YEARS * INT-RATE.
    MOVE END-BALANCE TO END-BALANCE-OUT.
    WRITE PRINT-LINE FROM RESULTS-LINE AFTER 2.
    CLOSE INPUT IN-FILE.
    CLOSE OUTPUT OUT-FILE.
    STOP RUN.
```

TION DIVISION is used to identify the program, the programmer, and the purpose of the program. The ENVIRONMENT DIVISION is used to specify the type of computer on which the program has been designed to run. The next division in a COBOL program is the DATA DIVISION, which is used to define the location and format of data to be processed by the program. Finally, the PROCEDURE DIVISION contains the actual encoding of the algorithm designed to process the data. A sample COBOL program is illustrated in Figure 13 – 2.

COBOL is well suited to the processing of files, which accounts for its popularity as a business data processing language where the predominant form of data processing is file manipulation. COBOL does not, however, accomplish basically computational tasks efficiently, which accounts for its lack of popularity in the scientific community.

FORTRAN

FORTRAN, which is a shortening of **FORmula TRANslation,** was developed in 1957, making it the first, higher-level computer programming language. Numerous revisions of the language have taken place, with the earlier versions designated by a revision number, such as FORTRAN IV. The most recent version, however, is known as FORTRAN 77, done in 1977.

As with COBOL, ANSI has published standards for FORTRAN. Several other versions of FORTRAN exist in popular enough forms to warrant their mentioning here. One version, known as WATFOR, developed at the University of Waterloo in Ontario, Canada, has gained significant popularity. An updated version of WATFOR, known as WATFIV, is also popular in university environments. Another version of FORTRAN, useful in teaching, was developed at the University of Minnesota. The newest version of this FORTRAN is known as M77.

FORTRAN appears to be the second most popular programming language in terms of its use by professional programmers. It is a language well suited for the programming of scientific and engineering applications primarily due to its power in accomplishing complex computations. Assignment statements in FORTRAN, where value is assigned to variables, look almost exactly like their algebraic counterparts. This feature makes the language a popular choice for applications requiring extensive mathematics. A sample FORTRAN program is illustrated in Figure 13–3.

FORTRAN has not historically been a good language with which to manipulate strings of alphabetic data, but that capability was enhanced with the 1977 revision. Also improved was the language's ability to support the concepts of structured programming, a topic to be discussed later in the chapter. (Note: **Structured programming** refers to a set of principles which guide the programming effort so that better programs are written.) FORTRAN's ability to accomplish file manipulations is significantly less than that of COBOL.

BASIC

Long a popular computer programming language for beginners, BASIC has enjoyed a resurgence in popularity as the most frequently used language

Figure 13–3
Sample FORTRAN Program

```
      PROGRAM INTEREST
C
C  TITLE: SIMPLE INTEREST PROGRAM
C  AUTHOR:
C  PURPOSES: THIS PROGRAM CALCULATES THE ENDING
C    BALANCE OF A SAVINGS ACCOUNT USING SIMPLE
C    INTEREST CALCULATIONS.
C  INPUT: THE INPUT CONSISTS OF: THE DEPOSIT, THE
C    PERIOD OF TIME IN YEARS, AND THE RATE OF
C    INTEREST (PERCENT).
C
      REAL RATE
C  RATE -- RATE OF INTEREST
      REAL DEPOSIT
C  DEPOSIT -- AMOUNT OF INITIAL DEPOSIT
      REAL PERIOD
C  PERIOD -- TIME OF DEPOSIT
      REAL ENDBAL
C  ENDBAL -- ENDING BALANCE OF ACCOUNT
      PRINT*, 'ENTER AMOUNT OF DEPOSIT'
      READ*, DEPOSIT
      PRINT*, 'ENTER PERIOD OF TIME (YEARS)'
      READ*, PERIOD
      PRINT*, 'ENTER RATE OF INTEREST'
      READ*, RATE
C  CONVERT RATE FOR CALCULATIONS
      RATE = RATE / 100
C  CALCULATION OF ENDING BALANCE
      ENDBAL = (DEPOSIT + (DEPOSIT * RATE * PERIOD))
      PRINT*, 'ENDING BALANCE --', ENDBAL
      STOP
      END

END OF FILE - REQUEST EXECUTED 32 TIMES
```

for microcomputers. **BASIC,** which stands for **Beginners All-Purpose Symbolic Instruction Code,** is perhaps the easiest language to learn; which makes it a common language in introductory data processing courses in high schools and colleges.

BASIC was developed in the early 1960s at Dartmouth University. It has since become the most frequently used timesharing language. BASIC and FORTRAN are very similar languages. For example, the assignment statements for each are practically identical. FORTRAN might offer the programmer more capability, but BASIC presents an easier environment within which to learn to write computer programs. BASIC's ability to manipulate files is also less satisfactory than the capabilities of COBOL. Figure 13–4 provides a look at a sample BASIC program.

One of the most serious shortcomings of BASIC has been the lack of a standard definition of the language. ANSI published a standard for Minimal BASIC in 1978, in an attempt to provide some standardization to the language. Another shortcoming of BASIC is the difficulty of using structured programming concepts. Very few of the available versions of BASIC allow the programmer to utilize the good programming practices of structured programming. A brief treatment of BASIC is provided in Appendix C.

Pascal

Pascal is one of the relatively new languages, having been developed by Niklaus Wirth in the late 1960s. The name of the language is not an acronym, but the last name of a French mathematician of the seventeenth century, Blaise Pascal. As a programming language, Pascal has found extensive use in computer science departments of universities for the teaching of programming principles.

Pascal is a relatively easy language to learn and is a very good language for putting the tenets of structured programming into practice. Assignment statements in Pascal make use of the familiar notation of algebra, just as BASIC and FORTRAN do. Pascal is also an efficient language in terms of its use of system resources. A Pascal program is shown in Figure 13–5.

Two limitations of Pascal need to be mentioned. First, like BASIC, it suffers from the proliferation of many versions and a lack of standardization. As late as 1982, no standard for the language had been published by ANSI, although efforts were underway to establish one. The other limitation is in the language's ability to perform file handling functions. COBOL remains the best language for file manipulations.

Ada

The newest of the major programming languages is **Ada,** named for Lord Byron's daughter, Ada Augusta, the Countess of Lovelace, and (in a sense) the world's first programmer. The work put into the development of the language Ada has been more extensive than that of any previous computer programming language. Development, which began in 1975, was the result of an effort by the United States Department of Defense to establish a standard language for the armed services and the contractors who serve them. The influence of the Department of Defense in the United States is

Figure 13–4
Sample BASIC Program

```
10 REM   PROGRAM
20 REM
30 REM   TITLE: SIMPLE INTEREST PROGRAM
40 REM   AUTHOR:
50 REM   PURPOSE: THIS PROGRAM CALCULATES THE ENDING
60 REM     BALANCE OF A SAVINGS ACCOUNT USING SIMPLE
70 REM     INTEREST CALCULATIONS.
80 REM   INPUT: THE INPUT CONSISTS OF: THE DEPOSIT.
90 REM     THE PERIOD OF TIME IN YEARS, AND THE RATE
100 REM     OF INTEREST (PERCENT).
110 REM   VARIABLES:
120 REM                R -- RATE OF INTEREST
130 REM                D -- AMOUNT OF INITIAL DEPOSIT
140 REM                P -- TIME OF DEPOSIT
150 REM                E -- ENDING BALANCE OF ACCOUNT
160 REM
170 PRINT "ENTER AMOUNT OF DEPOSIT"
180 INPUT D
190 PRINT "ENTER PERIOD OF TIME"
200 INPUT P
210 PRINT "ENTER RATE OF INTEREST"
220 INPUT R
230 REM   CONVERT RATE FOR CALCULATION
240 R = R/100
250 REM  CALCULATION OF ENDING BALANCE
260 E = D + (D * R * P)
270 PRINT "ENDING BALANCE IS --   "; E
280 END
```

Figure 13–5
Sample Pascal Program

```
PROGRAM INTEREST (INPUT,OUTPUT);

(**************************************************)
(*  TITLE: SIMPLE INTEREST PROGRAM                *)
(*  AUTHOR:                                       *)
(*  PURPOSE: THIS PROGRAM CALCULATES THE ENDING   *)
(*    BALANCE OF A SAVINGS ACCOUNT USING SIMPLE   *)
(*    INTEREST CALCULATIONS.                      *)
(*  INPUT: THE INPUT CONSISTS OF: THE DEPOSIT,    *)
(*    THE PERIOD OF TIME IN YEARS, AND THE RATE   *)
(*    OF INTEREST (PERCENT).                      *)
(**************************************************)


VAR
    RATE        : REAL;  (* RATE OF INTEREST *)
    DEPOSIT     : REAL;  (* AMOUNT OF INITIAL DEPOSIT *)
    PERIOD      : REAL;  (* TIME OF DEPOSIT *)
    ENDBAL      : REAL;  (* ENDING BALANCE OF ACCOUNT *)

  BEGIN
    WRITELN ('ENTER AMOUNT OF DEPOSIT');
    READLN ( DEPOSIT );
    WRITELN ('ENTER PERIOD OF TIME (YEARS)');
    READLN ( PERIOD );
    WRITELN ('ENTER RATE OF INTEREST (PERCENT)');
    READLN ( RATE );
    RATE: =  RATE / 100; (* CONVERT RATE FOR CALCULATION *)
    (* CALCULATION OF ENDING BALANCE *)
    ENDBAL: =  DEPOSIT + ( DEPOSIT * RATE * PERIOD );
    WRITELN;
    WRITELN ('ENDING BALANCE IS -- ',ENDBAL:10.2)
  END.


  END OF FILE - REQUEST EXECUTED 32 TIMES
```

Figure 13–6
Example Comparing COBOL to Ada

```
COBOL:
process-code.
                IF code  = 'a'
                THEN  PERFORM process-a-code
                      GOTO finished-code
                ELSE  IF code  = 'b' OR 'c'
                      THEN PERFORM process-bc-code
                           GOTO finished-code
                       ELSE  IF code  = 'd'
                 THEN  PERFORM process-d-code
                       GOTO finished-code
                 PERFORM process-unknown-code.
finished-code.

Ada:
     CASE code IS
 WHEN 'a'                  => process_a_code;
 WHEN 'b' | 'c'            => process_bc_code;
 WHEN 'd'                  => process_d_code;
 WHEN others               => process_unknown_code;
END CASE:
```

probably sufficient to ensure that Ada will become a major programming language.

Built on a Pascal base, Ada goes well beyond the capabilities offered by most programming languages. A programmer working in Ada has a full-fledged programming environment made available through the language. The environment includes a set of sophisticated software tools to assist in program development and to speed up program maintenance. The Ada environment will include an integrated data base to manage program modules, an editor for making changes, a debugger for finding errors, a link loader to tie program segments together and other programmer support tools. An Ada program segment is shown in Figure 13–6.

An interesting note on the development of Ada is the intent to fully develop the language before any Ada compilers were written. The development of the language began in 1975, but compilers did not appear until the early 1980s, and the early compilers dealt only with a subset of the language. Standards have been established for the certification of Ada compilers.

Although the future of Ada is difficult to predict, it will probably be one of the major programming languages. Some people believe it may eventually become even more important than either FORTRAN or COBOL.

PL/I

The development of **PL/I,** for **Programming Language/One,** was undertaken by IBM in the mid-1960s in order to capture in a single language the best features of COBOL and FORTRAN. As such, PL/I was expected to meet the needs of both the business and scientific communities. Unfortunately, the dream was never realized; and although PL/I is a very good programming language, it has never achieved its anticipated level of use.

Any new language faces a great deal of inertia in its attempt to displace languages already in use. For example, the fact that there are thousands and thousands of COBOL programs (and COBOL programmers) means that there is a lot of inertia which will work counter to conversion to PL/I or any other language. Organizations do not want to undertake the huge costs and delays which would accompany any conversion of existing programs, and programmers are basically reluctant to discard old skills for new.

Still, the fact that PL/I is a good programming language for a wide variety of applications provides some temptation for its use. PL/I is also a good language for utilizing the concepts of structured programming. COBOL, however, has not yet been displaced. Some comparisons between COBOL and PL/I are illustrated in Figure 13 – 7.

PL/I is a relatively difficult language to learn, and there is definitely a shortage of experienced programmers who know PL/I. Also, PL/I requires a relatively large computing environment in which to run.

RPG

RPG, which stands for **Report Program Generator,** is a limited-purpose language which has found a relatively extensive group of users within its sphere of applicability. RPG is an easy language to learn and requires a minimum of programming skill for use. As its name implies, it is a language used for the preparation of reports. Its compiler is small, so RPG can be made available on relatively small computing systems.

RPG can perform limited arithmetic, sufficient to do such functions as row and column sums, percentages, and extensions; but it has none of the control structures common to the full-purpose languages. Lack of standardization can also be a problem with RPG.

APL

APL, which stands for **A Programming Language,** is another language which, like BASIC, has been designed for the interactive computing environment. APL was developed by Ken Iverson in the early 1960s, and though it has never been a serious contender for the list of most popular programming languages, it has gained the admiration of a dedicated group of users.

In its simplest form, APL works like a calculator, yielding answers to algebraic expressions directly. At the other extreme, APL can be used to program the most complex mathematical manipulations in the most concise form of any of the programming languages. In terms of computing power, it is unsurpassed. For example, a single character is sufficient to cause the inverse of a matrix to be computed, a complex arithmetical procedure.

An unusual characteristic of APL is its use of Greek symbols as mathematical operators. This limits its use to terminals designed for APL. No ANSI standard exists for APL.

Structured Programming Constructs	Structured COBOL Programming	Structured PL/I Programming
 Execute	ADD, SUBTRACT, MOVE, READ, ETC.	Assignment, GET, PUT, CALL, etc.
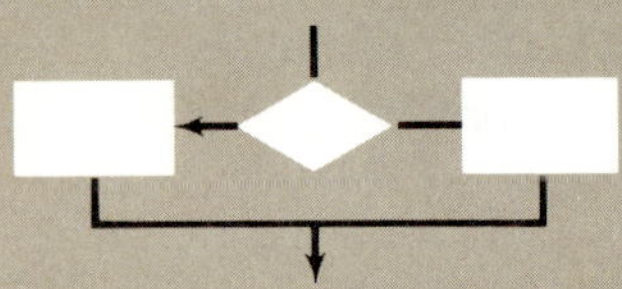 If . . . Then . . . Else	If condition (THEN actions) ELSE (ELSE actions)	IF condition THEN DO; (THEN actions) FND; ELSE DO; (ELSE actions) END;
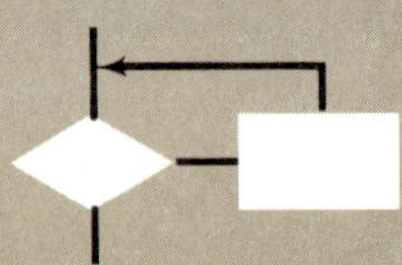 Do While	PERFORM LOOP-BODY UNTIL not condition . . . LOOP-BODY (loop actions)	DO WHILE condition; (loop actions) END;
 Do Until	PERFORM LOOP-BODY. PERFORM LOOP-BODY. UNTIL condition . . . LOOP-BODY (loop actions)	DO UNTIL condition; (loop actions) END;
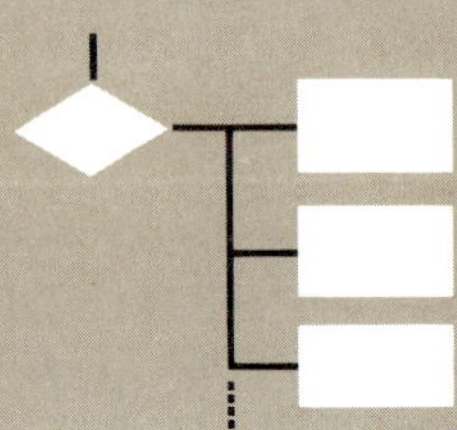 Case	GO TO CASE-1 CASE-2 . . . CASE-n DEPENDING ON variables	IF variable = case[1] THEN DO; (case[1] actions) END; IF variable = case[2] THEN DO: (case[2] actions) END; . . .

Figure 13–7
COBOL and PL/I Compared

One of the handiest features of APL is the immediate execution feature which causes each line of the program to be executed upon entry by the programmer. In an interactive programming environment, immediate execution is of some assistance in finding programming errors. To its disadvantage, APL requires a relatively large computer system for its execution.

Challenge Update

The reader and the data processing manager for Grass Roots should now be able to discuss differences in the common programming languages.

Productivity Improvements in Software Development

During the thirty-plus years of the computer revolution, the hardware costs associated with executing a program have been reduced by a factor of 2,000. This same period of time has seen software costs per line of code produced increase by a factor of two.

The number of programmers has grown to approximately 300,000, yet the backlog of applications waiting to be programmed has gotten longer. More and more powerful computers will cause the shortfall in programming capabilities to become even greater. Clearly something must be done.

A number of programmer productivity improvement techniques are being used to counter the increased cost of software development. One set of these techniques concerns itself with building structure into the software development process, and the other set of techniques is concerned with providing aids to the programming environment. In the next three sections we will explore, in turn, design aids, structured software techniques, and program development aids.

Design Aids

Many aids exist to help in the design of a new system. These aids take on a variety of forms, including techniques or methodologies intended to guide the efforts of the designer. Some of the analysis and design aids are computer-assisted techniques. Although some operate in a batch environment, an increasing number are implemented as on-line, real time systems with which the designer interacts to specify the design of the system. Some of these techniques derive their focus from the structure of the data to be processed. Typical of these is the methodology of Warnier-Orr, which is illustrated in Appendix A.

Other techniques focus the designer's attention on processes and data flows. One of the more successful techniques has been developed by Ed Yourdon, the references for which are in the readings list at the end of this chapter. His *structured life cycle* consists of six activities, any number of which may take place simultaneously. He emphasizes the fact that the focus of the traditional system life cycle is on a sequence of phases which are executed one at a time, not beginning one until the previous phase has been completed. In contrast, the basic activities of the Yourdon method are visited and revisited in order to achieve **step-wise refinement** in the design of the overall system. The six basic activities are:

1. The Survey, during which the user's current system is analyzed, the goals of a new system are formed, and an initial feasibility study is completed.
2. Analysis, during which the product of the survey, known as a project charter, and the policies of the user are used as inputs to form a logical, structured specification of the new system.
3. Design, during which the modules which make up the new system and the hierarchical relationships between the modules are specified.

4. Implementation, during which program coding takes place and the modules are integrated into a skeleton of the eventual system.
5. Generation of Acceptance Tests, during which user acceptance tests, incorporating those features important to the user, are generated.
6. Performance of Quality Assurance, during which final testing is accomplished.

Many other methodologies exist which try to build structure into the analysis and design steps. Data flow diagrams (DFDs), for example are rather extensively used to illustrate the flow of data in a system. Both Yourdon and the Improved Systems Techniques Division of McAuto provide DFD methodologies, which are only slightly different. The additional readings list at the end of the chapter will help the curious reader learn more about these methodologies. The program development process can also benefit from structured techniques, as we shall see in the next section.

Structured Software Techniques

Analyses of the costs of software indicate that several times the original cost of developing a program will be spent in maintaining it. Poorly written programs are much more difficult to maintain than are well written ones. Experience has shown that additional effort in the original development of the program can pay good dividends in the later maintenance of that program.

Good programming practice now includes the use of structured programming techniques, modularity, and top/down design. Efforts such as code reviews and walk-throughs to disconnect the programmer's ego from the program itself have also shown good results in program improvement. Each will be discussed in turn.

Structured Programming. A programming language needs only three basic structures in order to be useful for writing *any* program. These three structures are:

1. **Sequencing,** or the ability to specify a sequence of instructions.
2. **Selection,** the ability of the program to choose between two or more possible paths.
3. **Iteration,** the ability of the program to repeat certain sets of instructions.

Sequencing in most programming languages is accomplished by the assignment of sequence numbers to the statements or the convention of executing the instructions in the sequence in which they are presented to the system. Selection is usually accomplished through use of an IF-THEN-ELSE set of statements, which provides choice between two possible paths depending upon the truth or falsity of the IF statement.

A variety of means are used to accomplish iteration, or loops. The two means acceptable to structured programming are DO-UNTIL and DO-WHILE statements. DO-UNTIL executes until a particular ending condition is satisfied, and DO-WHILE executes as long as a particular condition exists.

Most languages provide a version of the GO TO statement, which causes control of the program to jump from one instruction to another, outside the normal sequence of instructions. Unfortunately, too many GO TO statements can lead to a very confusing program. Good programming technique suggests that the use of GO TO statements be kept to a minimum and that, in particular, no GO TO statements be allowed to direct control back towards the beginning of the sequence of instructions. In general, the more the programmer resorts to GO TO statements, the less readable the program is likely to be.

Modularity. The difficulties in writing, testing, debugging, and modifying programs seem to increase exponentially with program size. A program which is twice as large as another seems to have four times as many difficulties. Large programming tasks are, therefore, much better accomplished in a set of small programs than in a single large one. The concept of dividing a large programming task into a series of small programs, or subprograms, is known as **modularity,** and modularity is good programming practice.

Program modules should each be designed to accomplish a single, logical task. This makes the logic of the program easier to understand. Dividing a program into modules also makes it possible to more efficiently assign a number of programmers to complete a particular program. A number of programmers working on a single, large program get in each other's way, and the length of time it takes to complete the program is unnecessarily long. On the other hand, if the program is divided into modules and different modules assigned to different programmers, the overall program stands a much better chance of being completed in the allotted time.

Modularity, then increases the quality of the program by making it easier to understand, test, and modify, while it decreases the amount of time required to write a program. Subroutines, functions, and procedures are the programming language features that make modularity possible.

Top/Down Design. The structured software technique of top/down design is closely related to that of modularity. As we have just seen, modularity dictates that large programs be broken into smaller subprograms, or modules. Each module is designed to complete a single, straightforward processing task. **Top/down design** is the principle which says that the overall structure of the program, including the specification of the interrelationships between the modules, must be completed before the details of logic of each of the modules themselves are addressed.

Perhaps an explanation of bottom/up design will help make the principle of top/down design more understandable. Imagine that the accounts receivable software for a mail-order business is to be programmed. Programmer Amy is assigned the task of writing the billing program which generates invoices to be sent to those customers in the accounts receivable file who have a balance due. Programmer Bob is working on a program for order entry, so that orders received can generate the necessary entry in the accounts receivable files and produce a picking list for the warehouse employees. Programmer Mark is working on a program which processes the payments received from the firm's customers and reduces their account balance in the accounts receivable file.

A bottom/up design approach would let each of the programmers work on their individual tasks until their programs were completed. Then the three programmers would work together to figure out how the three completed programs would interact with each other. A top/down design, on the other hand, would force the three programmers to decide exactly how the three programs must interact with each other *before* any of the individual programs were written. A top/down design makes the overall integration of a set of programs, or program modules, easier to accomplish.

Many systems have, in the past, been forced into a bottom/up design by the nature of the evolution of the organization's software. Early in the organization's history with a computing system, individual applications were designed and programmed as it made good business sense to do so. Later, when a full set of programs was completed, their interactions were addressed and efforts were begun to integrate them.

Top/down design and modularity specify that large programs will be subdivided into modules, and that the logic of the interactions between modules will be completed before work on the individual modules is begun. Dummy modules are often used to test the overall program structure, and later the dummy modules are replaced with the real ones.

Code Reviews and Walk-Throughs. Programming has historically been an individual challenge, a struggle between a tenacious programmer and an unyielding machine. The product of that effort, the program, has been viewed as the creation of the individual programmer. The artistry and ego of the programmer and the quality of the program have been intertwined. The discovery of errors in programs or attempts by others to modify them have frequently been threats to the programmer's security.

New program development techniques are aimed at uncoupling the programmer's ego from the programmer's product. The belief is that better quality programs will result from the collective efforts of several programmers to review the code produced by each of the programmers individually. Programming teams, headed by a **chief programmer,** provide an excellent program development environment. **Code reviews** and **walk-throughs** are group efforts designed to provide an objective review of a program in an effort to improve it. In them, the programmer who wrote the program presents the program to the review group by walking them through its logic (see Figure 13–8). Suggestions for improvement are made and discussed, and eventually incorporated into the program if they are determined to be worthy of inclusion.

Code reviews and walk-throughs are also excellent training tools for inexperienced programmers who have an opportunity to see how particularly difficult programming tasks can be overcome. These group sessions also provide an excellent opportunity to see that programming standards are observed and that all requirements of the program have been satisfied.

Challenge Update

The reader should now be able to explain the techniques associated with structured programming.

Figure 13–8
A Programming Code Review

Program Development Aids

Structured software techniques seem capable of enabling programmer productivity to be increased by a significant amount, something on the order of 25 to 50 percent. An improvement of that magnitude, however, will not be enough to overcome the impending shortage of programming talent. Additional measures are necessary if an order of magnitude improvement is to be realized. The program development aids to be discussed next offer hope for gaining even greater productivity improvements than those of the structured techniques above.

Program Generators. Several different types of software exist in the category of program generators, but the central purpose is the same—to generate an applications program. Some of the program generators are **precompilers,** which allow the programmer to use shorthand notations for predictable elements of the program. For example, a shorthand notation could be used for the IDENTIFICATION DIVISION of a COBOL program and many other standard parts of the program. The precompiler translates the shorthand into appropriate COBOL statements.

Another program generation approach, called the **link-edit** approach, allows the programmer to edit and link (tie) together standard blocks of executable code to form a complete program. The code blocks themselves can be purchased from the vendor or defined by the programmer.

Some program generators work from tables, in which the programmer has described the numerous parameters of relatively standard data processing tasks, such as report generation or screen formatting. Data in the table are interpreted by the system as the program executes, and the appropriate data processing is accomplished.

The final program generator to be discussed here relies on the fact that most data processing tasks within organizations follow fairly standard routines, and programs can, therefore, be generated by following a standard scheme. These program generators, called **predefined logic systems,** provide skeleton logic for the most common types of programs and allow the programmer to tailor the skeleton to fit the particular needs of the individual application.

Other Work Savers. A number of other work savers are available to automate the programmer's work environment. Very briefly these include:

1. *Librarian* programs to assist in the creation, storage, and retrieval of such items as blocks of code, job control language, and data to ease the programmer's workload.
2. *Data dictionaries,* which contain the names and descriptions of all data items stored in the system.
3. *On-line documentation aids* to help generate the documentation necessary for finished software development projects.
4. *Test data generators,* designed to help the programmer generate the data necessary to adequately test a program.

Documentation

The Achilles' heel of most data processing operations is in the availability and quality of the documentation, the formal descriptions of the how, what, when, where, and why things in the system work. Without adequate documentation, the success of the entire system could be in jeopardy.

There are always good excuses for the lack of documentation. Programmers are often removed from one programming task and assigned another before the necessary documentation is complete. Sometimes employees quit or get transferred or fired before the documentation is produced. The excuse can be lack of time, lack of money, or even lack of ability. It may even be lack of interest. Very few programmers indicate a strong desire to work on documentation.

Most of the excuses can be traced to managerial failures. Managers of the systems development activity must make it clear, in thought and deed, that quality documentation is an essential part of the project development task. Employees must be provided with the necessary time and other resources to generate the necessary documentation. Many of the new online development aids are designed to assist in the generation of documentation concurrent with the system's development.

Adequate documentation is needed in several important areas. These include:

1. Policy manuals, which contain formal statements about management's intentions in conducting business and guidelines to help determine appropriate courses of action.

2. User manuals, which describe in detail the step-by-step functioning of the system from the user's perspective.
3. System manuals, which review the operations and interactions of the various systems.
4. Program documentation, which contains program narrative, flowcharts, listings, input examples, output examples, file descriptions, and so on.
5. Operating manuals, which describe the operational setup and procedures necessary to run the system.
6. Managerial summaries, which provide managers with an understanding of the role of the system without the burden of technical detail.

Documentation is an essential part of the system development effort. The project management team must ensure that it is properly completed. Without it the task is unfinished and probably headed for trouble.

Challenge Update

The importance of good documentation should now be clear to the reader and to the staff of Grass Roots.

Newest Developments

Software development is an expensive process, and it is expected to increase in cost. The applications development backlog, and a continuing shortage of experienced programmers will cause organizations to seek measures which offer relief. Several possibilities appear to have promise.

Fourth-Generation Languages

The continuing distribution of computing power throughout the organization will tempt many users to seek their own software. Users in distributed systems will turn to software packages and to the writing of their own software because the central data processing department will be basically unable to respond to their requests for additional service. The increased sophistication of fourth-generation, nonprocedural languages should allow many users to use them in conjunction with data base management systems (DBMSs) to eliminate the need for some software development projects.

Data processing centers will themselves turn to software packages in order to lessen the pressure for software development in times of declining programming resources. Programmers will increasingly use the structured techniques which encourage good program design. The use of program development aids should continue to increase as more and more sophisticated program generators and work savers are developed.

As each new programming language has appeared on the scene, supporters of its use have boldly predicted the demise of COBOL in favor of the new language. Somehow, COBOL survives. The inertia with respect to rewriting programs and retraining programmers continues to favor the status quo. A new COBOL standard which might make many old COBOL

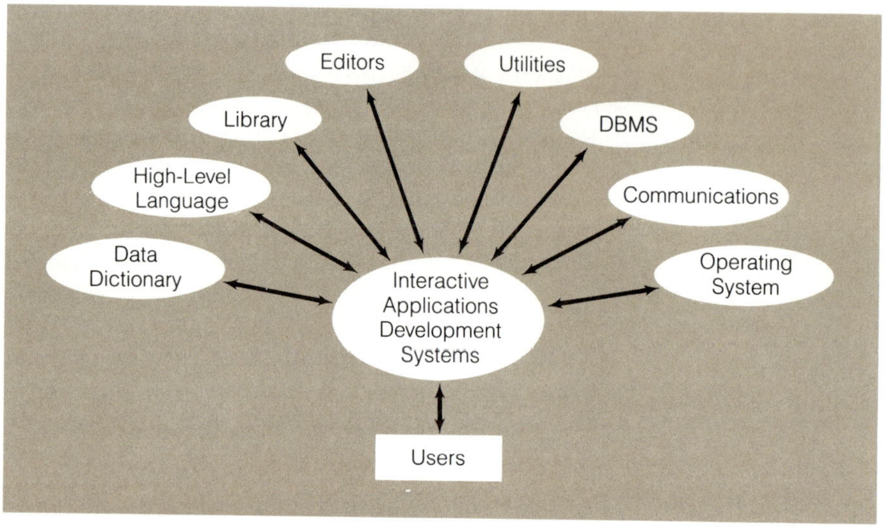

Figure 13–9 A Complete Applications Development Environment

programs obsolete, and the power of the Department of Defense behind Ada, may at last, however, signal the beginning of the decline of COBOL.

There is hope that the fourth-generation languages will ease some of the perennial problems of software development. Fourth-generation applications languages are intended to give *users* inquiry and report generation capability via natural language instructions.

Fourth-generation systems software products will be designed to provide a user interface to the full capabilities of the operating system. The new products are expected to provide centralized data dictionaries to define the status and relationships of all data processing resources of an organization. They should also provide an integrated system of editors, screen creators, graphics management, support for applications development, and the merging of text, data, and word processing. In short, they will offer user access to a complete environment within which to accomplish data processing tasks, as illustrated in Figure 13–9.

Fifth-Generation Languages

Earlier we discussed the efforts to develop fifth-generation hardware which are underway in the United States, Japan, and the United Kingdom. There are parallel efforts to develop fifth-generation languages. One of the candidates for fifth-generation status is a language known as Prolog.

Prolog was originally devised by Alain Colmerauer and associates at the University of Marseilles.[2] It is a language suited to the writing of programs in the field of artificial intelligence. The Japanese are expected to use a language like Prolog in their fifth-generation project.

A great deal of research is being done with **natural languages** in order to make computer system inquiries easy for all users. The problem is, most natural languages rely on the context in which a sentence is uttered in

2. William F. Clocksin and Jon D. Young, "Introduction to Prolog, A 'Fifth Generation' Language," *Computerworld,* August 1, 1983, p. ID/1–16.

order to remove ambiguity, which is quite difficult for a computer to do. A computer must be able to analyze (**parse**) a sentence to derive an unambiguous instruction, or seek additional help from the user. Three examples of natural language systems are Intellect (from Artificial Intelligence Corp.), ASK (from Frederick Thompson at Caltech), and Themis (from Frey Associates). A schematic of an inquiry in Intellect is provided in Figure 13–10.

Figure 13–10
Schematic of Natural Language Processing

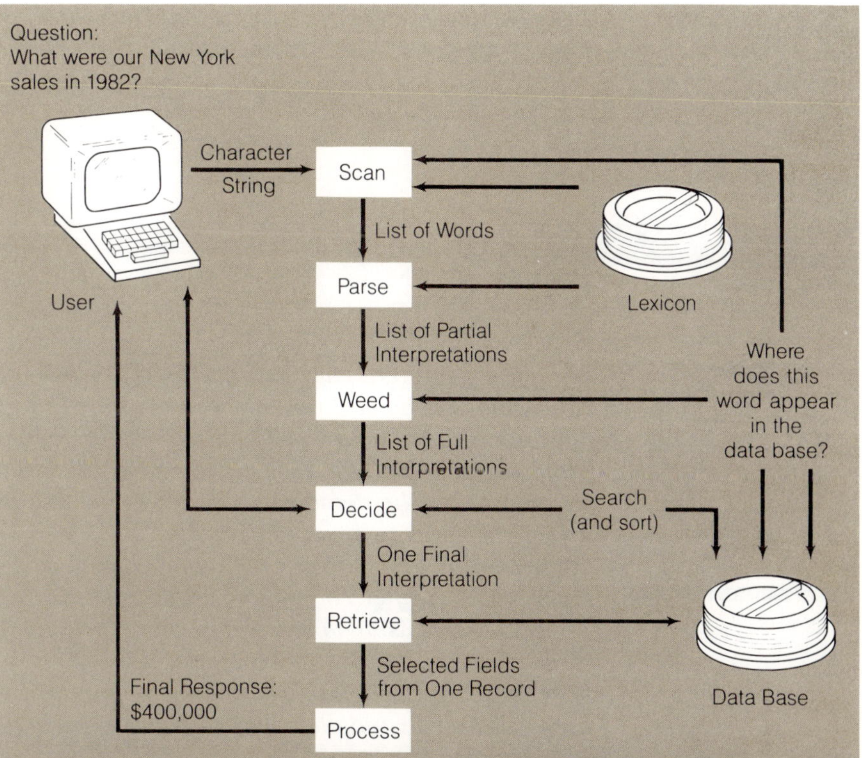

The Intellect natural-language processing system progresses through several steps to interpret and respond to a user's request for information. First, the scan function breaks the request "What were our New York sales in 1982?" into appropriate word entities, using information from both the computer's data base and the system's lexicon (vocabulary). The scanner can't just assume that breaks occur at every space; for instance "New York" should be classified as one, not two, word entities. Next, the parser grammatically diagrams the sentence in as many ways as possible and passes a list of partial interpretations to the weed function. Weed attempts to "fill in the holes" in the partial interpretations, using the data base for guidance. Any complete interpretations that result pass to the decide process. Decide, in part, uses the relative difficulty with which each full interpretation was produced to assign preference values to each. If the system can't clearly choose one final interpretation based on its preference rating and from additional searching of the data base, it may query the user for additional information. For example, it might ask if "New York" refers to the city or the state, a decision it couldn't reach alone if its data base contained sales figures for each. Once the final interpretation is chosen, the system retrieves the requested information, processes and organizes it as necessary, and displays it to the user.

Perhaps the future will, in fact, bring easier, but at the same time more capable, support to both programmers and users. Software engineering may provide significant improvements which would be appreciated by both. A review of the computing challenge with which we began this chapter will help us refocus our attention on some of the problems.

Challenge Update

Grass Roots personnel should now understand the productivity improvement strategies of software engineering.

COMPUTING CHALLENGE: *A Final Note*

What insight have we been able to gain considering the problem of designing a software engineering effort with which Mr. Bauer is faced at Grass Roots? The hardware for a new system is to be delivered in the near future, and Grass Roots has no programmers and no experience in computerized data processing. Mr. Bauer did have the foresight to send six employees who demonstrated an aptitude for programming and systems analysis to a crash course in software development techniques offered by one of the major computer manufacturers. They are to return in a few weeks, after completion of the course.

East Chemicals, the parent company, has agreed to lend Grass Roots three of its regular data processing employees, a senior programmer, a systems analyst, and a software development project leader for a period not to exceed six months. They will be very helpful in demonstrating software engineering techniques to the new employees.

Mr. Bauer has selected a committee of user representatives from the various Grass Roots departments, and with that committee has begun the development of a list of potential software projects. These projects will be ranked according to several criteria so that the data processing manager will know which projects have the highest priority. The criteria for assigning priorities include such considerations as profit potential, time to develop, and eagerness of the user group to have the software.

Relief from the intense pressure to get the data processing operation productive as quickly as possible should derive from the acquisition of software packages. In-house development can take place in those areas where adequate packages do not exist.

In a sense, Mr. Bauer is in an extremely fortunate position. He has the opportunity to start up a new data processing operation without inheriting obsolete programs, obsolete programmers, or the old biases of the user community. He can implement structured software development in a user-friendly environment. Many data processing managers would welcome such an opportunity.

SUMMARY

- Software projects come in all sizes, from relatively small modifications to existing software to enormous projects requiring years of effort and millions of dollars.
- Even with an increased dependence on software packages, many organizations will require an extensive software development efforts.
- Poorly written programs result in high programming maintenance costs.
- Software engineering, which adds structure to the processes of analysis, design, and programming, should lower program maintenance costs.
- Software quality depends upon such factors as reliability, clarity, robustness, maintainability, ease of use, portability, and documentation.
- There are hundreds of computer programming languages, but COBOL remains the one in which most programmers work.
- COBOL is the language best suited for the programming of business applications because of its exceptional file handling capabilities.
- BASIC is the most popular interactive language, while FORTRAN is the most popular language in the scientific community.
- Pascal is a well-structured language, widely used in educational circles for the teaching of programming concepts.
- The language of the future is very likely to be Ada, owing to its adoption by the Department of Defense as the standard programming language for the armed services and the programming environment it provides.
- A shortage of experienced programmers and an increasing number of applications needing programs have stimulated efforts to improve the productivity of programmers.
- The use of program development aids in an improved programming environment is expected to further increase programmer productivity.
- The programming aids in use include librarians, data dictionaries, link-edit packages, test data generators, and applications generators, and use of these aids is expected to increase with time.
- Fourth-generation languages will offer increased productivity to the applications development effort through capabilities which form an integrated, user-friendly environment.

CASE: Productivity Improvement at Equitable Life

This chapter mentions the backlog of applications programming tasks with which most large companies are faced and discusses some of the techniques which are being employed to improve the productivity of the applications development process. This case provides an example of a company which did have such a backlog and the steps they took to reduce it.

Faced with a tremendous backlog of program development tasks and a shortage of technical personnel, Equitable Life Assurance searched for some means to improve the productivity of applications development and reduce program maintenance. They chose Hogan Systems, Inc.'s Umbrella system, a set of integrated applications development tools for very large banking and savings institutions. Umbrella is an on-line system which accommodates development of both on-line and batch applications.

Through the use of Umbrella, an application can be developed by an analyst who chooses the correct system components, supplies the parameters necessary to customize the set of components to the particular application, and, finally, integrates any needed programming into the final package. Umbrella also allows the use of prototype design.

Use of the new system has had an added, unforeseen benefit. Some tasks are so easy with the new system that work which formerly required a technical employee can now be completed by a nontechnical one.

Applications development time has been cut in half by the use of Umbrella. It also allows the user to play a somewhat greater role in the overall development of important applications.

Umbrella also has an effect on program maintenance. Old programs can in many cases be completely rewritten with the new system rather than subjected to the tedious task of repair.

Equitable managers are very happy with the new system. It has contributed greatly to the improvement in programmer productivity and a reduction in program maintenance.

"Prototyping Slashes Insurance Firm's Backlog," *Computerworld*, January 30, 1984, pp. SR/23–24.

Questions for the Case

1. The case tells us that Equitable's managers are very happy with Umbrella. Do you believe their programmers are also happy? Why or why not?
2. Suppose the backlog of programming tasks were to be reduced to near zero. What might then happen to the programming staff? Would they like or dislike the new system? Why or why not?

DISCUSSION QUESTIONS AND EXERCISES

1. What is the relationship between software engineering and program maintenance?
2. Most large organizations in the early 1980s had a sizable backlog in applications development and a shortage of good programming talent. How might that change as a result of software engineering techniques?
3. Will software packages make programmers obsolete?
4. Which is the most commonly used programming language for business applications? What forces are at work to maintain the status quo in programming language popularity? What forces are working to change the status quo?
5. What three programming structures are essential to any complete programming language?
6. What advantages are there to program modularity? Explain the relationship between modularity and top/down design.

7. For what purposes have structured programming concepts been developed? Why are they important?
8. Why have program development aids been developed? What impact will they have on programmer employment?
9. List and discuss the elements of software quality.
10. How do code reviews and walk-throughs improve program quality? How do they improve programmer training?
11. What has happened in the realm of hardware to make it possible for us to consider using fourth- and fifth-generation languages?
12. Why is program documentation important?
13. What arguments suggest that Ada will be the predominant programming language of the future? What arguments suggest that it will not be?
14. What benefits will natural language processing bring?
15. List the various kinds of documentation and explain the importance of each.

ADDITIONAL READINGS

Bruce, Phillip, and Pederson, Sam M. *The Software Development Project: Planning and Management.* New York: Wiley, 1982.

Cassel, Don. *The Structured Alternative: Program Design, Style and Debugging.* Reston, VA: Reston Publishing, 1983.

Daly, Edmund B. "Organizing for Successful Software Development." *Datamation,* December 1979, pp. 106–120.

Davis, Dwight B. "En●glish: The Newest Computer Languages." *High Technology,* February 1984, pp. 59–63.

Fox, Joseph M. *Software and Its Development.* Englewood Cliffs, NJ: Prentice-Hall, 1982.

Frank, Werner L. *Critical Issues in Software.* New York: Wiley, 1983.

Freeman, Peter, and Wasserman, Anthony I., eds. *Software Design Techniques.* Long Beach, CA: Institute of Electrical and Electronic Engineers, 1977.

Hill, I. D., and Meek, B. L., eds. *Programming Language Standardization.* New York: Wiley, 1980.

Martin, James. *Application Development without Programmers.* Englewood Cliffs, NJ: Prentice-Hall, 1982.

Parikh, Girish. *The Guide to Software Maintenance.* New York: Winthrop Publishers, 1982.

Pressman, Roger S. *Software Engineering: A Practitioner's Approach.* New York: McGraw-Hill, 1982.

Stefic, Mark, et al. "The Organization of Expert Systems a Tutorial." *Artificial Intelligence,* Vol. 18, 1982, pp. 135–173.

Wasserman, Anthony I., and Gutz, Steven. "The Future of Programming." *Communications of the ACM,* March 1982, pp. 196–206.

Weinberg, Gerald M. "Kill That Code." *Infosystems,* August 1983, pp. 48–50.

Wexelblat, Richard L. *History of Programming Languages.* Proceedings of the ACM SIGPLAN Conference, Los Angeles, CA, June 1978.

Yourdon, Ed. *Structured Design.* Englewood Cliffs, NJ: Prentice-Hall, 1979.

———. *A Software Development Methodology.* New York: Yourdon, 1979.

1-2-3
MENUS
LOTUS

14

Procedures, Personnel, and Careers

CHAPTER PREVIEW

Although the combination of hardware and software in a data processing system makes the system operable, the system cannot be considered to be effective without a full complement of qualified personnel and a well-designed set of procedures to govern their behavior. People are necessary to perform the various data processing tasks such as data entry, computer operation, systems analysis, and programming. Procedures are necessary to ensure that the work is properly scheduled, that audit trails exist for financial transactions, and that opportunities for fraud and theft are suitably minimized.

In this chapter we will study activities specific to the management of an information processing department. These topics have become important to all managers as distributed processing environments have brought information processing professionals and their activities into all areas of the organization. We will first discuss the project management techniques necessary for control of a systems project, the techniques that managers can use to follow progress of the new system's development. We will then turn our attention to the control procedures needed in the day-to-day operations of a data processing center to provide for efficiency and effectiveness in the center's operation.

A look at the organizational structure of a data processing department and some brief job descriptions for its professionals will help round out our understanding of information processing operations in large organizations. Any study of information processing personnel would be incomplete without some mention of their career paths, motivation and employee development, with which this chapter ends.

COMPUTING CHALLENGE: *Grass Roots, One More Time*

One last visit with Mr. Bauer at Grass Roots Growers should provide motivation for reading the material in this chapter and provide perspective. Mr. Bauer, when last we reviewed his progress, seemed to have set in motion a plan which would cause the appropriate software and hardware to find its way into the data processing department of Grass Roots. That in itself is an accomplishment, the end result of a lot of work. Mr. Bauer understands, however, that it is only the beginning of the design of the system which will ultimately fulfill the day-to-day data processing needs of the company.

A new data processing manager, Laura Boggs, has been hired. She will begin work next week. Ms. Boggs has twelve years of experience in data processing, the last three as an assistant to the data processing manager of a small petroleum products company. She has a bachelor's degree in computer science from a nearby university and an MBA which she acquired while attending night classes at a city university near her previous place of employment.

Mr. Bauer and Ms. Boggs have scheduled a lengthy planning session for the end of next week to begin the task of developing a series of interim organizational charts to move the company gradually toward a full-fledged data processing department over a period of three years. Positions need to be defined and job descriptions need to be written to cover the personnel needs for the next three years.

Procedures must also be established to ensure that the department grows into an effective part of the company. The interests of users in both the development of new applications and in accomplishing data entry tasks must be considered. The treasurer of the parent company, East Chemicals, has expressed concern about the ability of accountants to audit the procedures which process transactions which have an impact on the financial status of the company.

Ms. Boggs and Mr. Bauer must also develop a plan for the hiring and training of the people needed by the data processing department as well as the procedures necessary to ensure its effective operation. They both realize that the development and implementation of a proper plan will save them untold miseries later, so they are committed to an extensive planning effort.

The material presented in this chapter is designed to provide the reader with an understanding of the integration of hardware, software, personnel, and procedures which is necessary to the effectiveness of a data processing organization. It is designed to answer questions such as:

- *What role do the various procedures play in information processing activities?*
- *What career opportunities are available?*
- *What new developments are there in information processing management?*

After careful study of this chapter the reader should be able to:

1. *Discuss the project management of data processing projects.*
2. *Explain the necessity for a comprehensive set of control procedures for a data processing department.*
3. *Discuss the employee development of data processing personnel.*
4. *Describe the various career positions available to data processing professionals within a data processing department.*

HISTORICAL PERSPECTIVE

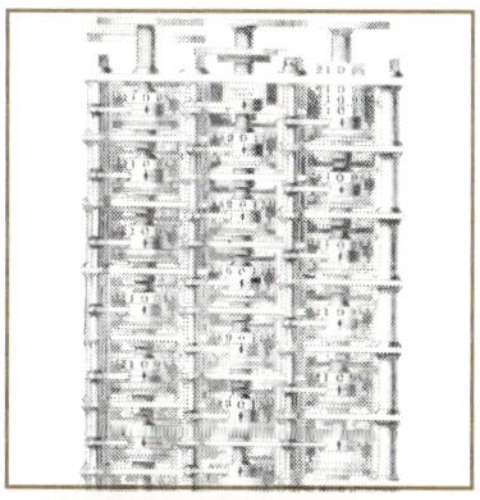

While the "good old days" of data processing were not, in general, better, they were simpler. A computing system's entrance into an organization was usually justified on the basis of a single, well-defined application, and the justification was usually completed by someone who was eager to put the computer to work. As a result, the computing center was located in whatever department the eager user worked. Thus, if the user was an accountant and the application an accounting one, as was frequently the case, the computer's home turned out to be the accounting department. In situations where the computer advocate was an engineer from, say, the manufacturing division of the company, the computer was housed there.

Wherever the computer was located, the eager user generally was systems analyst, programmer, data entry clerk, and computer operator all rolled into one. The user had to perform a variety of duties because no one else was around to perform them. As others in the organization noticed the productivity improvements brought about by the computer and began themselves to use it, it became necessary to formalize the organization surrounding the computer.

The original users were often quite willing to help others develop their computer applications, but the workload of programming and data entry which resulted gradually became unwieldy. First, a full-time programmer was needed; then a data entry clerk became necessary. A computer operator was added as more applications were developed, then more programmers and more data entry clerks.

Soon it was necessary to provide some supervision to the work of programmers, data entry clerks, and computer operators. For example, a higher level of authority was needed to settle disputes over which work was most important, as it clearly could not all be done at the same time. Before long an entirely new department, the data processing department, was born.

Thus, data processing departments have evolved within accounting departments, within manufacturing departments, and even within marketing departments. As the number of applications has grown and the application mix become organization-wide, data processing has become part of an administrative services group, where it is most often found today.

Integration of Hardware, Software, People, and Procedures

Three essential phases of data processing operations require the integration of an appropriate collection of hardware, software, people, and procedures. The first occasion for which that integration is necessary is the management of the acquisition project itself. We have discussed the system life cycle with respect to the acquisition of hardware and the development of software in previous chapters. That discussion will now be enlarged to include a control structure of people and procedures so that the likelihood of success of a project is enhanced.

Secondly, the day-to-day running of the data processing center also requires the integration of hardware, software, people, and procedures. For example, data processing tasks must be scheduled, development projects must be completed, and program maintenance activities must take place in an orderly way.

The third occasion for the integration of hardware, software, people, and procedures occurs during the long-range planning activities which must take place to ensure that the data processing system stays in tune with the organization's needs. Hardware replacement, software acquisition, employee development activities, and the upgrading of procedures are all necessary to maintain an effective data processing center. Each of the three areas will be discussed in somewhat greater detail.

Management Control of Data Processing Projects

A large-scale computing project requires managerial attention just as any large-scale project does. Managerial effort is needed to bring together the acquisition of new hardware and software with the training of operators and users and the development of procedures to govern the operation of the data processing center. A project manager must be appointed to supervise the integration of the various resources needed for a viable operation. Large projects will require a full-time manager, while smaller ones may be managed by someone who has project management responsibility added to other responsibilities.

If possible, a project manager with previous project management experience should be chosen as the senior person in charge. An assistant project manager can be appointed to ease the workload on the senior manager and provide a training position for future project managers. Figure 14–1 illustrates a project manager at work.

Although candidates for the position of project manager might come from any background, it is most likely that they will have considerable business or computer science experience, or both. A data processing project manager has to work at the interface between the business functions of the organization and the technical computer staff. A combination of business experience and computer science skills is desirable.

Three major activities are key to the management of a data processing project. The first of these, development of the specifications for the hardware and software, has been previously discussed. The other two major

Figure 14–1 Project Manager at Work

activities are the development of the project budget and the project schedule.

The project budget begins with the cost/benefit analysis which might have been done to justify the investment in the project itself. Resource constraints such as money, time, and the skills of people critical to the project must be identified. These constraints must be incorporated into the schedule in order to determine the likelihood that the project can be successfully completed.

The schedule must develop a plan for bringing together the various resources in a time frame which makes successful completion of the project possible. Estimates of the length of time required to complete the various phases of design, site preparation, coding, hardware installation, testing of both hardware and software, training, and changeover must be made.

A popular, computer-based technique for generating a schedule is the use of **Program Evaluation Review Technique/Critical Path Method (PERT/CPM).** Using the PERT/CPM technique, a *network* is developed of all significant events and activities of the project, and their relationships to each other are identified. This network displays which activities must be completed before which other activities throughout the life of the project. Estimates of the resources necessary to complete each activity are included in the network. A simple network example is provided in Figure 14–2.

A computer program analyzes the network and identifies the **critical path,** the longest path through the network from project start to project completion. The program also computes an estimate of the total resources needed for successful completion and provides a schedule for the utilization of those resources.

Activities along the critical path are critical in the sense that any delay in the completion of these activities will make the project late, that is, make the critical path longer. By the same token, the allocation of extra resources

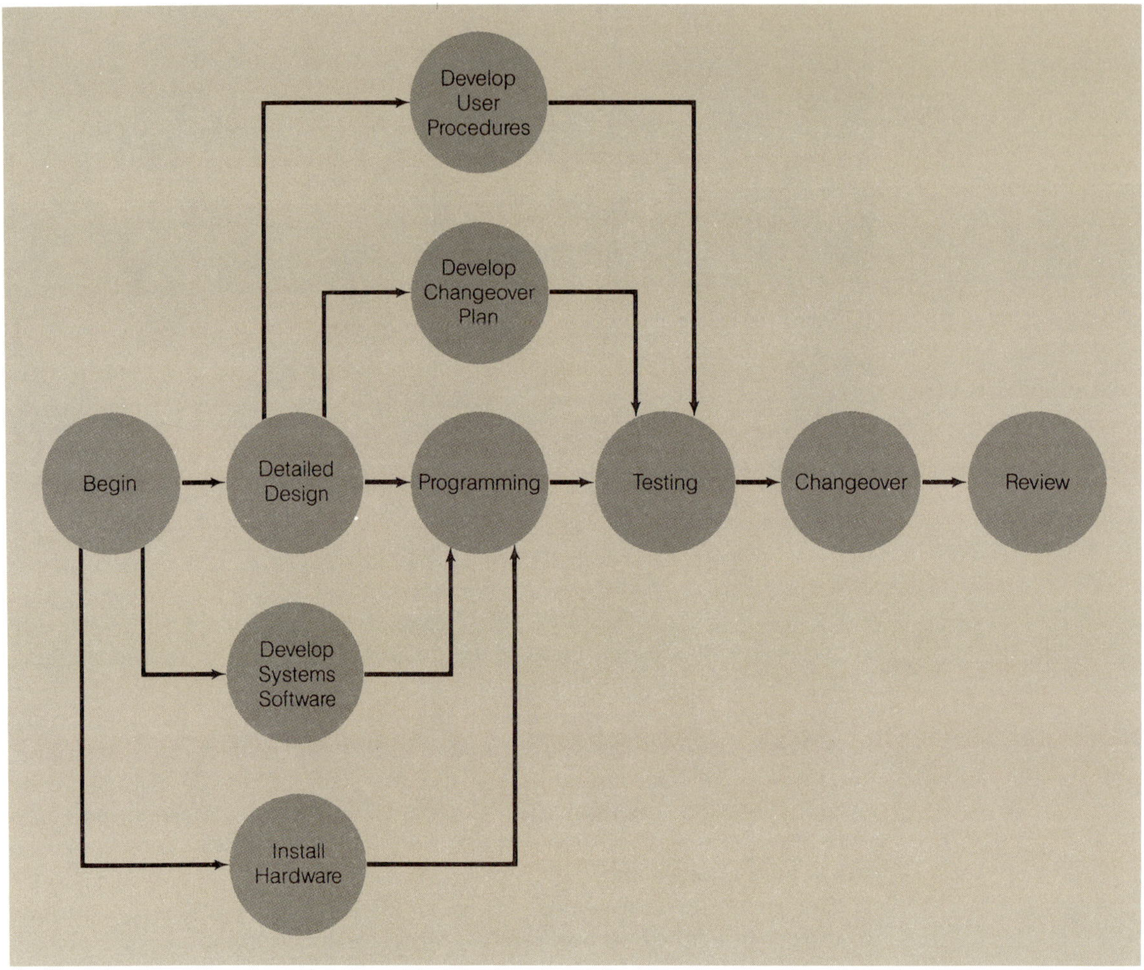

Figure 14–2
Simplified PERT Chart for System Conversion

to shorten any activity on the critical path will result in an improvement in the project completion date. The allocation of resources to any activity not on the critical path does not affect the completion time for the project as a whole. Such an allocation may be wasteful. Students planning the completion of required courses to establish a graduation data are quite familiar with some of the techniques of CPM. Course sequences and prerequisites establish the critical path, while electives are of less importance. A summer term of critical path classes may hasten graduation, while electives taken during the summer may not.

Once the project budget and schedule have been determined, the managerial effort changes to one of control. The project manager's responsibility is to ensure that expenditures are kept as close to budget as possible and that the schedule is maintained. Virtually all projects encounter some unforeseen difficulties, and most project plans include some monetary and time contingencies to facilitate the handling of these difficulties.

Regular meetings between the project management team and the community of users and managers of the organization will help coordinate the other activities in the organization which interact with the startup of the project. In particular, the training of operators and users can be scheduled, as can the changeover itself. Effective planning will minimize the disruption caused by the changeover.

Challenge Update

Mr. Bauer and Ms. Boggs of Grass Roots should now have an understanding of project management for data processing projects.

Operational Control and Security

Once the data processing center is an ongoing operation, controls are necessary to protect the organization's interests from intended or accidental abuse. Some of these controls are implemented to guarantee the physical security of the data processing center and its employees, while others are designed to prevent fraud, theft, or accidental errors.

Students frequently experience firsthand the inconvenience or extra cost of insecure information processing operations. Unsuspecting students in programming classes sometimes have their computer account numbers stolen, their passwords changed, and their allocation of computing resources expended by someone else. Prosecution of the criminals who illegally use someone else's computing resources has been made somewhat easier by clever operating system techniques.

Physical Security. Some years ago, the pride of ownership was often sufficient to cause an organization to locate their data processing center so that customers, stockholders, and passers-by could see that the organization was progressive enough to have one. As a result, data processing centers were located in very visible locations. For example, they might have been on the ground floor at a busy, downtown location, behind only plate glass windows for public viewing. The novelty gradually wore off, and data processing centers moved to more secure surroundings. Some people claim the movement was hastened by the civil unrest of the 1960s when the centers made attractive targets for those wishing to make their protests noticed. Though perhaps not as obvious today, significant threats to the physical security of data processing centers are still a major concern.

In any case, it is now much more common to find (or not to find, as it were) the data processing center hidden in a location where access can be restricted. Several methods are used to control the people who have access to the center. Some entrances are controlled by key, combination, or card locks so that only authorized personnel may enter (see Figure 14–3). Some make use of closed circuit television and two sets of locked doors to cause an unauthorized person to think twice before entering the locked chamber which separates the center from the outside world. In still other circumstances guards are used.

The concerns of physical security are more broad than just restricting access. Protection against fire, wind, and weather are also major concerns. In many situations a power outage is a serious mishap, and precautions are taken to ensure that alternate sources of power are available. Water from broken or malfunctioning plumbing, or even from fire-fighting efforts,

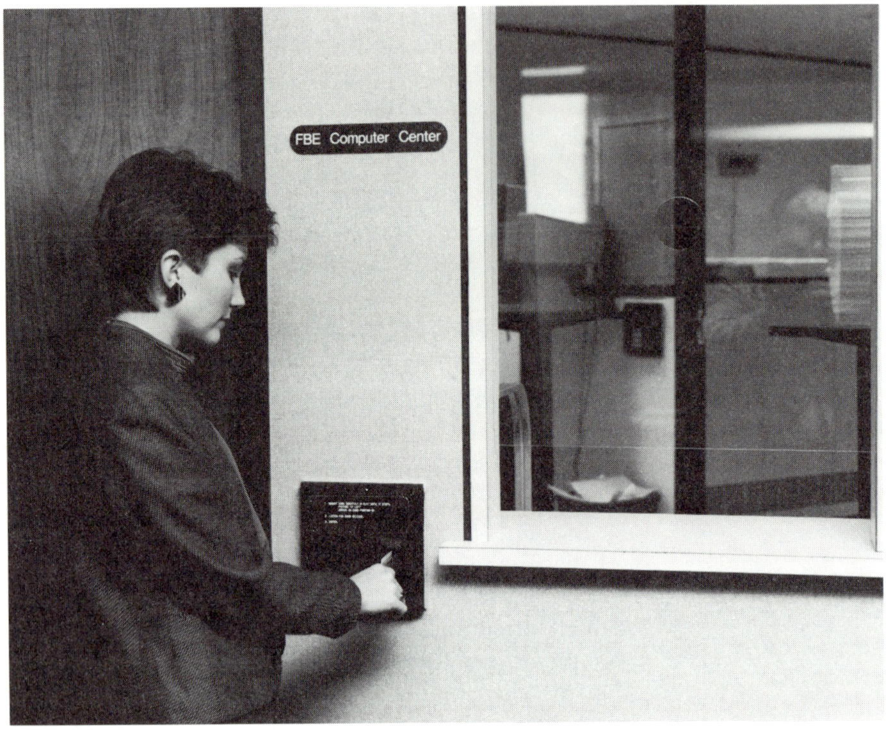

Figure 14–3 Data Processing Center Security

would present a serious hazard in a data processing center. Sabotage is also a potential danger.

Interestingly, a new type of firm has emerged in the industry to help companies recover from some types of disasters. For example, data stored on magnetic disks can sometimes be recovered after a serious malfunction, or even a fire, by these firms. Such recovery can be of great importance to a company which might have lost its customer list, accounts receivable files, or tax records through such a disaster.

Part of the security routine in most centers is the copying of important backup files from time to time and storing the backups in a secure place at another site. These backup files could be used to reconstruct the important files should some mishap cause the original files to be destroyed. The sophisticated computing systems of today have automatic mechanisms for ensuring that backup files are created routinely.

Procedural Controls. A well-managed data processing center has a comprehensive set of rules and procedures designed to guard against both intentional and unintentional abuses. Some of these rules are administrative in nature, and others deal specifically with either inputs, outputs, files, or programming. Some example rules will be discussed as we explore each category.

Administrative. A well understood procedure for determining the scheduling of jobs and the relative priorities of those jobs should exist and be used. Insofar as it is possible to do so, the schedule should be maintained.

Much of the friction that occurs among the employees of the center and those in the rest of the organization arises from either missed schedules or misunderstood scheduling. The schedule should be determined through the combined efforts of the data processing manager and the managers who use the center's services.

A business organization is particularly vulnerable to fraud, theft, sabotage, and espionage through its data processing operations. For this reason, it is important that procedures and programs establish a clear audit trail, a path that an auditor can follow to monitor the processing of all transactions. One element of the audit trail is the computer operating log, the diary in which all interactions between the computer operator and the computing system are recorded. A teleprinter terminal can provide such a log when used as the interface between the operator and the system. The supervisor of computer operations should review the log regularly (see Figure 14–4), and a permanent file of computer operating logs should be kept.

Another administrative rule which helps prevent computer system abuse is the practice of keeping the duties of computer operation and programming separate and distinct. Computer operators should not be allowed to intervene in the execution of a program to modify the programming, and programmers should not be allowed to operate the computer. Neither the programmers nor the computer operators should be allowed to participate in data entry operations.

These tasks are kept separate to reduce the likelihood that someone would be able to change a program, or its data, in order to defraud the company. If the tasks are kept separate, then collusion among a group of people is necessary to perform the fraudulent act. A fraudulent scheme involving a group of people is much more likely to be detected than one in which a single person has been able to perform the fraudulent act singlehandedly.

Figure 14–4
Computer Operator and Supervisor Reviewing Log

Input. The data entry operation is the most error-prone, time-consuming operation in the data processing center. One procedure commonly used in the input phase to reduce the number of errors is the verification of data upon entry. Verification is usually implemented by duplicating some part of the data entry procedure. For example, in a punched card system, the cards produced on the key punch are sent through a very similar machine where the second operator verifies the data punched in the cards. Most read operations performed by card readers, tape drives, and optical character readers provide a redundant second-read operation to check the accuracy of the first. Voice input systems typically display their inputs for operator verification.

Another procedure used to reduce errors is the use of control totals. Control totals are totals, frequently done by hand, which accompany a batch of data to be processed. The control totals for a payroll processing operation, for example, would include the total number of hours worked, the total gross pay, and the total number of employees. These totals would be checked against the computer's totals to ensure that someone has not introduced an extra time card.

Data entry personnel are responsible for keeping track of data and making sure it is available when needed by a scheduled run. Sets of data are formally entered in a log to ensure that careful track of its whereabouts is kept.

Output. Control totals are used for output in much the same way. If, for example, there were 365 time cards to be processed, there should not be 366, or 364, paychecks generated. Checks and other negotiable instruments present additional problems. Checks going to the computer center for printing should be prenumbered, and the number of checks transferred the subject of accounting controls.

Another important consideration on the output side is the distribution of the output, which should go only to those people authorized to receive it. Extra or old copies of sensitive outputs should be destroyed. Control of the output is made more difficult in an environment where the outputs are sent to remote terminals. The computing system must use a series of passwords or other means of identifying the recipient, under such circumstances, before the output is sent to the terminal. The use of terminals by unauthorized personnel must be avoided.

Files. Two problems are worth noting with respect to the security of files. The first, which has been mentioned previously, is the problem of providing backup for those files whose loss would cause great expense or inconvenience. Backup files should be stored in a secure location, different from the location of the computer center itself.

The second concern with respect to files is the prevention of unauthorized access. Passwords and the restriction of terminal use to authorized users will help a great deal, but neither can make the system completely secure. Some deterrent can be provided by an electronic log, implemented in software, which records each access to restricted files.

Programming. Applications programs themselves can be written to include some routines for checking the validity of the data or the transaction to be performed. Edit programs for data entry can check for the reasonableness of the data, to make sure that certain limits have not been exceeded, and to make sure that the transaction code is an allowable one.

A check of the sequence of records is sometimes used to verify that the processing is taking place as it should. Some systems, such as a double-entry accounting system, have balancing entries which can be checked for balance when the processing has been completed. Transaction logs can be maintained to provide the data necessary for an audit trail in some circumstances.

A system which provides on-line, real time updating to files presents an interesting problem when two different applications attempt to change the same data element in the file. Unless the correct precautions are taken, one of the updates will be lost.

For example, assume that a customer is making a withdrawal of $50 from a bank which uses an on-line, real time update for such transactions. The program processing the $50 withdrawal will look up the customer's account balance, say it is $400, subtract the $50, and restore $350 as the ending account balance. If another program, say the check clearing program, were allowed to proceed at the same time, it might retrieve the account balance of $400, subtract a check of $100, and store the new account balance of $300 just before the withdrawal program stores its balance of $350. The $300 balance is replaced with $350, and processing of the check has not caused the customer's balance to be correctly reduced. On-line, real time systems must be programmed to avoid such problems by locking out one program while another is in progress.

Challenge Update

Grass Roots managers and the reader should now be able to explain the necessity for a comprehensive set of control procedures for a data processing department.

Software Checks. The operating system in most computer systems provides many different types of reliability and security checks. Passwords are checked by the operating system to reduce the likelihood that unauthorized users will gain access to the system. In addition, the operating system enforces different types of restraints on the use of programs and files stored on the system. File protection can be set so that files may be read but may not be changed. Programs can be stored so that they can be run but not copied or changed. For example, a user may utilize LOCK or WRITE PROTECT commands to protect files or a PUBLIC command to allow free access.

Some software is sold to users on a royalty basis, whereby the user incurs a charge for each use, or on a rental basis, whereby the user pays a fee for a limited period of use. To prevent abuse, the software can be made to self-destruct, or be made otherwise inoperable by the user unless the royalty or fee is paid.

Software which processes transactions related to the financial condition of most business organizations is subject to audit on a regular basis. Auditors run test data, check particular types of transactions, analyze codes, and study the various logs to ensure that the system operates correctly.

Long-Range Planning

The long-range planning effort must be formally designed to keep the capabilities of the data processing system in line with the needs of the organization. Two major areas will be discussed: systems planning and employee development.

Systems Planning. It is imperative that managers of an organization recognize two important trends which are typical of data processing operations. The first is that the resources needed to serve the current group of users will continue to increase. That is, the resources needed to keep the current users satisfied will become larger with time, even if no new applications are developed.

In part this increase is due to the growth of the business itself. Increased sales lead to an increased requirement for employees, materials, supplies, and productive capacity. The files for personnel, accounts payable, inventory control, production scheduling, and accounts receivable will all increase as a result. This, in turn, causes longer program runs and larger requirements for secondary storage.

The second trend which will increase the demand for computing resources is based in the development of new applications. Current users will develop new applications; and new users, with their applications, will migrate to the system. This migration will require larger equipment and, in some cases, new types of equipment.

Managers must, as part of their long-range planning effort develop long-range plans for data processing. It is an essential ingredient to the maintenance of an effective organization. It is an effort made more difficult by the distribution of data processing to decentralized locations.

Employee Development. Data processing professionals' skills become obsolete at a rapid rate. Last year's skills are seldom satisfactory for this year's problems. New hardware, new software, and new design techniques are constantly appearing. Managers in organizations with data processing staffs must be alert to the training needs of data processing professionals. Unless the skills of these professionals are continuously developed, the quality of the staff will deteriorate.

Since most data processing professionals are in short supply, efforts to improve and upgrade the skills of the current employee group will have additional dividends. An effective employee development effort can help managers retain their current employees.

Rotation of jobs, subscriptions to professional journals, attendance at professional seminars, and educational leaves are all important employee development tools. Many firms are making effective use of personalized instruction and video-assisted instruction systems. An aggressive program of employee development will provide a steady supply of competent, satisfied employees.

Challenge Update

The importance of employee development for data processing personnel should now be clear.

Data Processing Careers

It would be a bit overwhelming (and not very interesting) to present a comprehensive statement of the various job descriptions for data processing personnel. Large organizations, for example, may have forty to sixty different job classifications for data processing personnel. Nonetheless, a few comments about the more common categories could easily aid in the understanding of the various career opportunities within a data processing department. The functions of systems analysis, applications programming, maintenance programming, systems programming, computer operations, data entry, and management will be discussed. Figure 14–5 provides one example of an organization chart which demonstrates how positions based on these functions might be structured.

Systems Analysis

People who work within the **systems analysis** group assume the role of consultants who enter the user's (client's) work environment in order to design a system to serve the user's needs. The systems analyst must be a skilled data processing professional. In addition, the analyst must be able to communicate effectively and understand fully the process of bringing about organizational change.

Systems analysts usually work with the user in determining such things as information needs, data flows, and distribution of output. The product of the interaction between the user and the systems analyst takes the form of a flow chart, data flow diagram, or structured diagram illustrating the system to be designed.

A systems analyst should have a solid background in the development of applications software and usually has prior experience as an applications or maintenance programmer. It is also helpful if the systems analyst knows something about the functioning of the organization and, in particular, knows something about the functions performed by those departments within which the systems analysis is to be performed.

Figure 14–5
Example Organization Chart for Data Processing Group

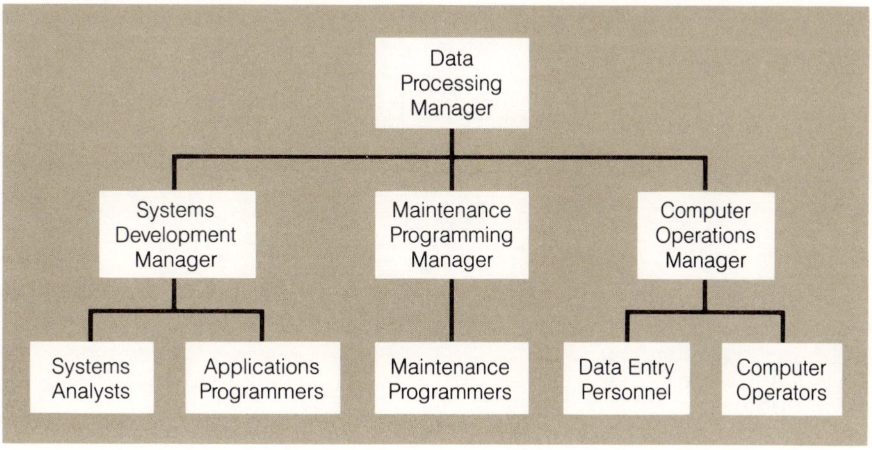

A good systems analyst is one who has the necessary technical and interpersonal skills to bring together the best thinking of users and data processing specialists in the development of a new system. An educational background and work experience in both computer science and business would be advantageous. The career path for systems analysts frequently leads them into the position of project leader, in which they supervise the software development efforts of programmers and analysts.

Applications Programming

Those who work in **applications programming** are responsible for taking the flow diagrams or structure charts from the systems analyst and writing the necessary programs to put the system into production. Programmers are responsible not only for writing the programs, but also for testing them and for providing the documentation necessary for the proper use and maintenance of each program.

An applications programmer needs to have good programming skills in at least one higher-level language and needs to know the principles of good program construction. Programming requires one to think logically and analytically, and people who are good in the quite similar field of mathematics are usually good also in programming. The extent to which interpersonal skills are required of programmers is determined by the organization itself, but sometimes programmers find they can compensate for a lack of interpersonal skills by demonstrating superior programming abilities.

Since the applications programmer writes programs to accomplish or-

"But I don't want to be a computer programmer!"

ganizational tasks, it is helpful if the programmer has some knowledge of the functioning of the organization. The logic of the system, however, is to be provided by the systems analyst, so knowledge of the organization on the part of the programmer is not actually required. People enter the field of programming from a variety of backgrounds. Universities, community colleges, and private institutions all offer programming courses. Entry level positions are sometimes difficult to find because employers always hope to find experienced programmers.

Maintenance Programming

Approximately two-thirds of the programming effort is **maintenance programming,** yet the development of new applications programs seems always to get more outside attention. Programs require maintenance for a variety of reasons. In some cases, programs are found to contain errors which cause them to run incorrectly. Such errors must be found and corrected.

Often a program must be changed because the job it is supposed to do has changed. For example, payroll programs need to be changed as the available fringe benefits or income tax laws change. As the organization grows or changes in other ways the programs which support the data processing activities of the organization must also be changed. It is the function of the maintenance programming group to make the necessary changes.

The maintenance programmer frequently is asked to modify the oldest and most poorly written programs. Sometimes the programs are so poorly written that they should be rewritten, but the demands on the maintenance programmer's time are usually so great that they cannot be. In such cases the programmer postpones the rewriting of the program, does the best that can be done, realizing the program will probably be back later for further modification.

The maintenance programmer needs all the skills of the applications programmer, for the programs which are to be maintained are predominantly applications programs, plus some additional intuition for finding and correcting errors. Maintenance programmers, as a rule, get very little recognition from outsiders for their efforts, so it helps to have a personality which allows satisfaction from knowing that a job has been well done.

Systems Programming

Very early in the text, systems programs were defined as those programs which perform functions necessary to the operation of the computer system itself, as opposed to applications programs which accomplish a particular data processing task for users. Some data processing centers are large and sophisticated enough to maintain a staff of **systems programmers** to create and modify systems programs, while others are not. These programmers make changes to the system software or develop software for new systems functions. They frequently assist applications and maintenance programmers in tasks which require a thorough understanding of the operating system. The more complex the operating system, the greater the

Figure 14–6
Systems and Applications Programmers Work Closely in Applications Program Design

number of systems programmers. A systems programmer is shown at work in Figure 14–6.

A large part of the programming effort of systems programmers is necessarily done in machine or assembly language. Systems programmers, then, need to have good programming skills in the particular languages being used. Their analytical and logical skills should be excellent. They are only rarely required to work with people outside the data processing profession, so the breadth of their training can be significantly less.

Computer Operations

People in the computer operations group are responsible for the actual running of the system itself. Within the computer operations group are found people who control the operation of the various machines in the system, including the printers, tape drives, disc drives, card readers, card punches, and other machines (see Figure 14–7). If the system is small, one person may perform all the operating functions.

The key person in the computer operations group is the **computer operator,** whose responsibilities include the startup, supervision, and shutdown of the equipment. The operator, or an assistant, must mount and remove tapes and disks as required by the processing being done. The computer operator often works at a control console/CRT terminal, making adjustments to the system as necessary to maintain its proper operation. The computer operator needs to enjoy working with high technology devices while serving the needs of others. Knowledge of programming is not required.

Figure 14–7
Operations within a Data Processing Center

Other positions are sometimes staffed in large data processing centers to maintain the library of tapes or disks so that they will be available to programs when needed and to assist in the proper handling of input and output. These jobs require some of the same skills as the computer operator position.

Data Entry

In keeping with the principles of secure operation, the data entry function is usually kept separate from either the programming or computer operations functions. Control personnel associated with data entry operations are responsible for receiving data from users and entering it into the system. A large proportion of user data still arrives at a centralized data entry department in a form which cannot be directly read into the system, so it must first be entered through the keyboard of a terminal, keypunch, key-to-tape, or key-to-disk machine as seen in Figure 14–8. Data entry personnel need to have exceptional keyboarding skills.

Since the data entry operation is costly, time-consuming, and prone to errors, efforts are continuously underway to move data entry closer to its origin and capture it in machine-readable form as early as possible. Point-of-sale terminals and factory terminals were both discussed earlier as examples of efforts to capture data closer to its origin.

Management

The number of levels of management within the data processing department is a function of the size of the department. Small data processing departments might have a single **data processing manager** who directly supervises people in each of the functions. A large department would have separate managers for systems analysis, applications programming, maintenance programming, and so on.

One management position not otherwise obvious from the functions previously discussed is that of **data base administrator** (or **data administrator**). In data processing departments using data base software, it is common to appoint a manager as data base administrator to supervise the activities associated with maintaining the organization's data base operations.

The level in the organization of the manager to whom the data processing manager reports is an important measure of significance of data processing

Figure 14–8 Data Entry Operators at Work

to the organization. In an organization in which data processing is absolutely essential to the firm's goals, the data processing manager might report to the president or a senior vice-president. In an organization to which data processing is less important, the data processing manager might report to one of the lower levels of management. The level is sometimes important in budget negotiations or in resolving disputes between data processing managers and other managers in the organization.

Challenge Update

The reader should now be able to describe some of the positions available to people who pursue careers in data processing.

Information Resource Management (IRM)

The distribution of information processing activities and equipment throughout an organization has increased the managerial challenge. New emphasis and new techniques are necessary in order to effectively manage the information processing effort. One approach to the problem of effective management is discussed here.

A special commission on federal paperwork in the mid-1970s was responsible for coining the phrase, **information resource management (IRM),** and for stimulating government and private enterprise to manage information as a resource. The Paperwork Reduction Act of 1980 established, within the Federal Government, the guidelines of IRM as the planning, budgeting, and controlling of the collection, use, and dissemination of information.

The magnitude of the information management problem within the government is difficult to comprehend. The Internal Revenue Service, for example, must process about 135 million tax returns. The Social Security Administration maintains about 200 million accounts and sends about 40 million checks monthly. IRM within the government is meant to help the government cope with these large information processing systems.

In the private sector, IRM is intended to focus the attention of the management of organizations on the value of information to the organization. IRM could provide the following services:

1. Provide a clearinghouse for all information so that information-seeking activities can be compared with the available information resources to eliminate duplication of effort.
2. Promote the elimination of unnecessary paperwork.
3. Facilitate the planning and budgeting activities for information management systems.
4. Increase organizational awareness of the quality of data and information with respect to accuracy, timeliness, and precision.
5. Assist upper management in capitalizing on the value of the information resource.

It is not at all clear whether IRM will become a viable managerial concept or another in a long line of buzz words associated with information management. It could even become another bureaucratic boondoggle. Good information can be of great value to an organization. Its collection, use, and dissemination should be properly managed as should any valuable resource. Whether this new managerial concept will be accepted, though, is yet to be seen.

Newest Developments

As the use of computer-based systems increases, the need for newer and better techniques for accomplishing project management and operational control will increase. The distribution of processing into user departments will mean that project management and operational control skills will become more necessary.

Applications and maintenance programmers will be needed throughout the organization, not just in the central facility. Training and supervision of these data processing professionals will become more difficult. It will also be more difficult for them to perceive the availability of attractive career paths within an organization. A similar trend will take place with data entry personnel as data entry is moved closer to the origin of the data. These people may have to look to the functional areas of the business for career advancement opportunities.

The role of the applications programmer may change slightly as the use of program generators becomes more common and as organizations turn more and more to the acquisition of packaged software. The role of the systems analyst will expand to include the consideration of software packages as potential solutions to user's problems. Applications programmers, systems programmers, and maintenance programmers will all have to cooperate in the integration of software packages into the system. All are at the top of the list of needed personnel in projections toward 1990. Little change is expected in the roles of people who work in computer operations.

The future of IRM is difficult to predict. It will no doubt be a popular phrase at professional information management seminars for several years, but whether or not it brings about the true management of information as a resource is difficult to foresee.

An indication of the importance of data processing personnel and data processing itself to business organizations can be gleaned from a 1982 survey by *Infosystems,* whose findings are summarized here:

1. The 1982 budgets indicated that approximately 1 percent of a firm's revenues are allocated to data processing expenditures.
2. About 45 percent of the data processing budget goes to personnel costs.
3. The average number of data processing personnel in a firm is about twenty, with large firms having several hundred.
4. In about 30 percent of the firms surveyed, the top manager of the data processing group reports to the president of the firm or the general manager.

Data processing operations are a critical element in the activities of almost all firms. A return to look at the problems encountered in the computing challenge will help wrap up this chapter.

COMPUTING CHALLENGE: *A Final Note*

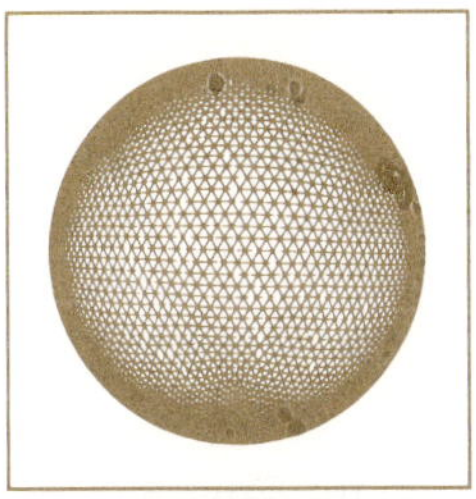

Mr. Bauer has a full set of problems with which to deal as he oversees the installation of a new data processing system at Grass Roots and the building of a data processing department. He is fortunate to have been able to find an experienced data processing manager in Ms. Boggs, who will assume the role of project manager for the installation of the new system.

The parent company, East Chemicals, has agreed to make its computer system available for the generation and maintaining of a project management system. This will greatly facilitate the scheduling activities associated with the installation of the new system.

Boggs and Bauer recognize the need for two computer operators and three data entry clerks in addition to the six programmers who are currently being trained. Most of the programmers will be assigned initially as applications programmers until the need for maintenance programmers develops. Several systems analysts are being made available by East until such time as Grass Roots can develop or hire its own.

A full set of procedures has been sent down from the parent company. These, together with the experience of Ms. Boggs, will enable a preliminary set of procedures to be drawn up for use at Grass Roots. Modifications will be made as necessary as the data processing department gains some maturity.

SUMMARY

- The integration of hardware, software, people, and procedures required by the implementation of a large-scale computing system requires the application of good project management techniques.
- Once the system specifications are completed, a project manager can make use of PERT/CPM software in controlling the scheduling and budgeting operations of the project.
- The project manager must ensure that good communications exist among vendors, users, and the project staff throughout the life of the project, and make sure that the necessary documentation is completed.
- Once the system becomes an ongoing data processing operation, the focus of managerial control is on procedures and personnel.

- Procedures to prevent accidental and intentional abuse of the system must be implemented.
- Procedures must be developed to provide physical security as well as preserve the integrity of the data processing operations themselves.
- Proper administration of a data processing center must include control procedures which describe the proper handling of inputs, outputs, files, and programs.
- Long-range planning efforts are necessary to maintain the ability of an information systems department to meet the information processing needs of the organization.
- An aggressive employee development program is needed to maintain a staff of competent and contented employees.
- The most common functions within the data processing center are those of systems analysis, applications programming, maintenance programming, systems programming, computer operations, and data entry.
- An effective management team must be provided to coordinate and direct the efforts of data processing professionals within the center.
- Information resource management (IRM) recognizes that information has value to an organization and that value can be enhanced through effective planning, budgeting, and controlling activities.
- Without enthusiastic, capable people most organizations would not be able to operate effectively.
- A well-thought-out set of procedures and quality documentation to support them are essential ingredients to the functioning of an information processing operation.

CASE: Computer Benefits Large Motel Chain

Organizations with many offices distributed over vast geographical distances have interesting problems of training, communications, and employee development. These problems are especially difficult when the staff in each office is relatively small, as it might be in the case of a chain of motels. As employees are hired, they must be trained in the normal motel management functions. This case illustrates how a computerized system helped reduce the time required for a new employee to become proficient.

A large Atlanta motel chain recently switched from a service bureau reservations system to an in-house system that utilizes software designed specifically for their system. Days Inn of America Incorporated, the sixth largest motel chain in the nation, reduced the cost of transmitting reservations by 50 percent. In addition, they simplified the system in order to reduce the training time of a clerk from four days to two hours.

The new system eliminates complicated codes and uses instead a fill-in-the-blank technique where the operator needs only to answer questions presented on the CRT. The computer immediately responds to input with a reservation confirmation or cancellation. Input errors have been greatly reduced as a result.

The system handles a daily volume of over 100,000 transactions from 316 motels across the United States and Canada. The system supports a large facility in which 130 reservationists receive telephone calls and use terminals to make or cancel reservations. Once a reservation is made, the computer schedules its transmission to the appropriate motel. It holds non-urgent messages until lower long-distance telephone rates are in effect. This has reduced telephone charges by $10,000 a month.

The system will also be able to process data to support the daily operations for the motels, restaurants, and gas stations across the country. A series of overnight computations at the headquarters in Atlanta will allow managers to know the chain's previous-day performance. The system is flexible enough to support payroll, personnel, accounting, and planning functions. It can also be modified to communicate with airlines and car rental agencies to provide further benefits for Days Inn's customers.

Questions for the Case

1. Many of the economic gains cited in this case resulted from procedural changes which reduced errors and decreased training time. What are the characteristics of the reservation operation which makes it a good candidate for such improvements?

2. Consider the nationwide network of motels (over 300 in number) described here, and think about the introduction of a new, computerized system. Describe, briefly, a plan to guide the training of employees on the new system.

DISCUSSION QUESTIONS AND EXERCISES

1. Discuss the use of PERT/CPM in computer system project management.

2. For what other types of projects might PERT/CPM be useful? Give examples of controls which should be in place in each of the following areas:

a. Input.

b. Output.

c. Files.

d. Programming.

3. Describe the three general types of programming positions and explain how the skills required for each might differ.

4. What are the functions of the computer operator? The data entry clerk?

5. Why are the functions of computer operation, programming, and data entry kept separate?

6. Discuss the goals of information resource management (IRM). Are they likely to be realized? Why or why not?

7. Discuss campus computer security with some classmates. Is it a serious problem? What can students do to improve security?

8. Arrange for a tour of a nearby computer center. Describe the precautions taken to make the center physically secure.

9. Discuss the impact of distributed data processing on the effort to develop long-range plans for information processing.

10. In what ways do employees benefit from their employer's programs for employee development? In what ways does the company benefit?

11. Diagram a university degree program as a critical path network and point out the critical path. Where do elective courses fit in the network?

12. In what way will distributed data processing make control over data processing operations more complex?

13. How does an audit trail help prevent fraud? Why are audit trails more difficult in a computerized system?

14. The demand for computing services always seems to grow. What accounts for this trend?

15. What impact will the productivity improvement aids of Chapter 13 have on a programmer's job? What impact will they have on programmer employment levels?

ADDITIONAL READINGS

Albrecht, Michael J., Jr. "Managing Employee Careers." *Computerworld,* August 15, 1983, pp. ID/21–32.

Block, Robert. *The Politics of Projects.* New York: Yourdon, 1983.

Inmon, W. H. *Management Control of Data Processing.* Englewood Cliffs, NJ: Prentice-Hall, 1982.

Metzger, Philip W. *Managing a Programming Project.* 2d ed. Englewood Cliffs, NJ: Prentice-Hall, 1981.

Smith, C. O., Podell, Harold J., and Knowles, Ben. *Management Auditing of Computer Operations.* Silver Springs, MD: IEEE Computer Society, 1976.

Strauss, Melvin J. *Computer Capacity: A Production Control Approach.* New York: Van Nostrand Reinhold, 1981.

Weiss, Edmond H. *How to Document a Computer System.* Englewood Cliffs, NJ: Prentice-Hall, 1983.

The youth gets together his materials to build a bridge to the moon, or, perchance, a palace or temple on the earth, and, at length, the middle-aged man concludes to build a woodshed with them.

Henry David Thoreau
Journal July 14, 1852

That is the key to history. Terrific energy is expended—civilizations are built up—excellent institutions devised; but each time something goes wrong. Some fatal flaw always brings the selfish and cruel people to the top, and then it all slides back into misery and ruin. In fact, the machine conks. It seems to start up all right and runs a few yards, and then it breaks down.

C. S. Lewis
Mere Christianity

Part IV

Computer-Induced Changes in Our Lives

PREFACE TO PART IV

Simply knowing about computers and the design of computing systems is not enough. Managers and other users must integrate them in productive ways into their daily lives. Productive uses for computers have been developed in virtually all areas. They have been put to use in business and professional offices, not-for-profit organizations, factories, homes, and many other locations.

The first three parts of this text provide the necessary background for the discussion of computer uses which follows in Part IV. The fundamental concepts of data processing and the tools by which it is accomplished have provided a solid base on which to build. The material on the design and acquisition of computing systems of Part III has focused attention on some of the critical aspects of those processes.

This part will provide an examination of personal computers and of the impact of computing on management, on office and factory work, and on other areas of our lives. The chapters in this part are:

- Chapter 15 *Personal Computers*
- Chapter 16 *Computers and Management*
- Chapter 17 *Computers and the Work Environment*
- Chapter 18 *Computers and the Quality of Life: Today and Tomorrow*

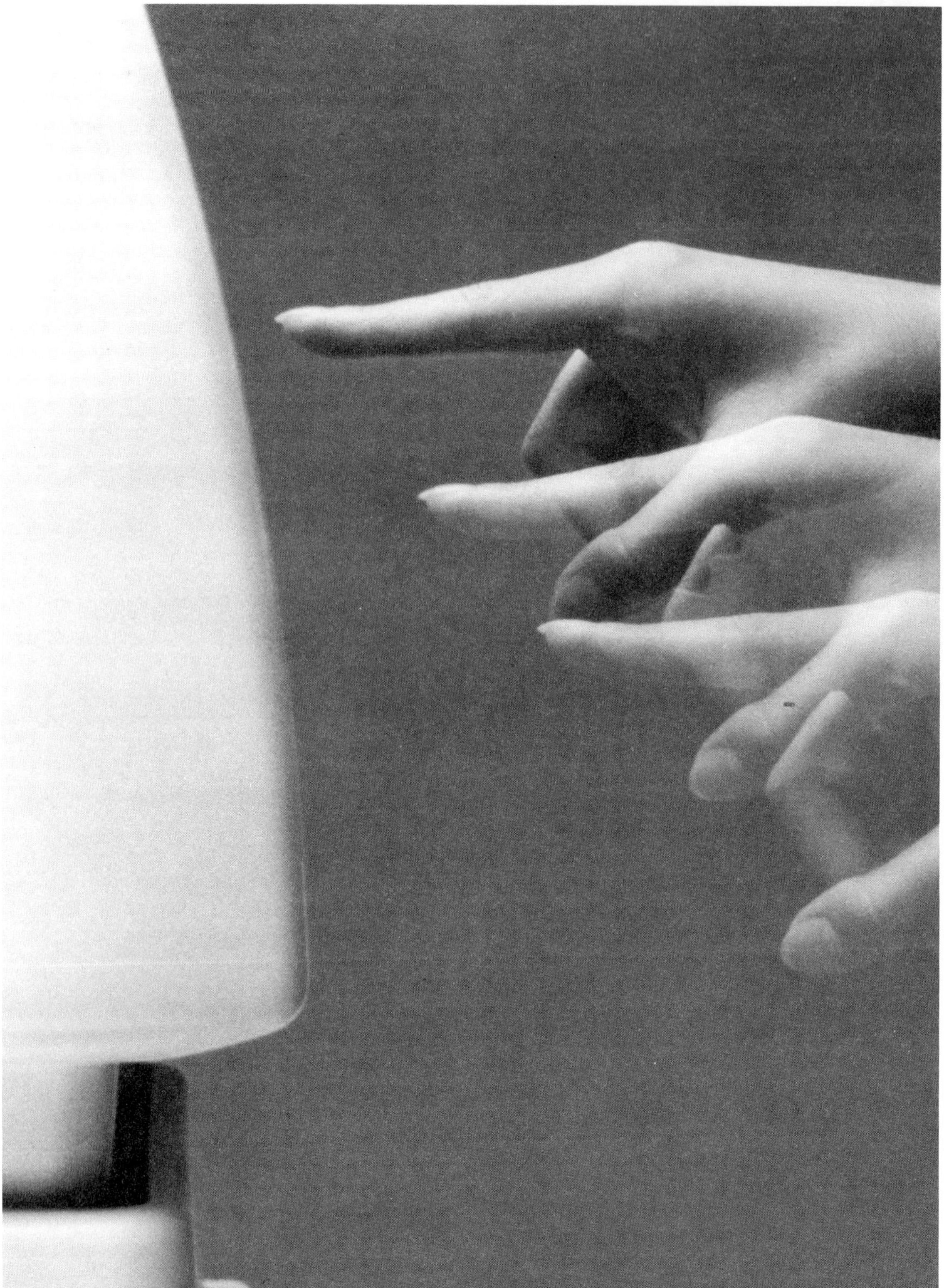

15

Personal Computers

CHAPTER PREVIEW

Microcomputers, as personal computers, have come into our working lives—into the board room, the factory, and the office. They are having a significant impact on the ways in which we work and live. In addition, many machines and appliances make use of microprocessor technology to provide greatly enhanced capabilities. The microprocessor has made it possible for the computer to become a personal machine.

This chapter will discuss the use of personal computer software which makes such activities as record keeping, word processing, spreadsheet analysis, and games possible. It will also discuss the hardware elements of personal computers. Both software and hardware have been discussed earlier in the text and, in a sense, we will not encounter anything new in this chapter. The differences between personal computers and computers in general are only in terms of scale, convenience, and cost. The basic concepts remain, however, the same as those presented earlier.

Personal computers are the rage of the 1980s. They are everywhere around us. Many people are buying them even though, in strictly economic terms, it is a purchase which probably cannot be justified on the basis of costs and tangible benefits. Personal computers can, however, provide many time-saving and educational services, so they are well worth our attention here.

The benefits to be derived from a personal computer are both tangible and intangible. Personal computers are exciting and fun. They allow us to perform many tasks with greater productivity. They are part of the future, the age of computers.

Fortunately, one does not have to know how to write computer programs to make effective use of a personal computer. An incredible amount of software has been, and is being, written so that the user of a personal computer can purchase software to satisfy virtually any need. These programs will be discussed in the early part of the chapter.

Next, we will take a look at the hardware devices which are available to provide the basic data processing functions of output, input, computation, and storage at the personal computer level. We will then discuss the various information services available to personal computer users. People are able to access a large number of information services through the use of terminals or personal computers in combination with communications provided by the telephone and cable television networks. The final major topic of this chapter, security, deals with both software piracy and the unauthorized activities of some over-zealous personal computer users.

Many of the readers of this text will readily be able to imagine the uses to which a personal computer could be put. Some readers will already have access to such a machine.

(continued next page)

Readers should, then, have a clear framework within which to fit the topics of this chapter. The infusion of personal computers into our private lives is well underway. People who cannot remember what life was like before television will have the same trouble with personal computers.

Children are dragging their parents to computer stores only to find out, after the purchase, that their parents monopolize the machines. We may now be in the era of the electrician and the plumber in the sense that our daily lives are dependent upon their services, but the era of the computer repair person is on its way. The personal computer service industry has only begun to grow. A computing challenge will help set the stage for this chapter.

COMPUTING CHALLENGE: *The Personal Machine*

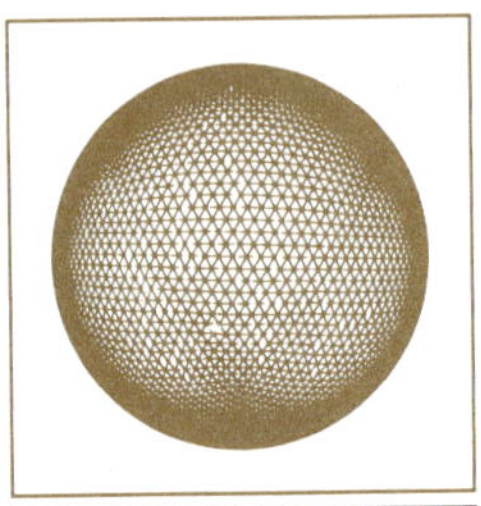

Frances Molton and her husband Charles are much admired by the other residents of Big Sky, Montana. Frances and Charles, who live on a large ranch just west of Big Sky, are parents to nineteen children. Only three are their children by birth; the rest are either adopted or placed with the Moltons for foster care. The children range in age from twenty-one (Tom) to ten (Rachel). Two are students at a nearby university, seven are in high school, six in junior high, and four still in grade school.

The ranch on which the Moltons live is primarily a cattle ranch, but some of the land is used for wheat and other cereal crops. Some of these crops are fed directly to the cattle in fattening pens, while the remainder are sold as cash crops.

The Moltons are convinced that they need a personal computer. They reason that it would be very helpful in maintaining the pedigrees of their registered cattle and in keeping track of revenues and expenses for the ranch. They also believe that a personal computer would be of great assistance to the children in their school work and help them develop the skills necessary to compete for jobs in the tight market for professionals.

The Moltons need to be able to find a comprehensive introduction to the world of personal computers without having to sift through the bits and bytes of the computer hobbyist's literature. They need only a basic understanding of the capabilities of a computer system, not an in-depth treatment of the technical underpinnings. Their questions are very basic ones. What data processing tasks can be effectively done on a personal computer? What equipment is needed? How much will it cost? Where can software be purchased? How do people learn to use the various software packages?

After careful study of this chapter, the reader should be able to:

1. *Describe the various uses to which personal computers, with their software, can be put.*
2. *Describe each of the following home information services: shopping, telephone directory, banking, news, weather, and airline and train schedules.*

3. *Discuss two interesting security issues which arise as a result of personal computing.*

HISTORICAL PERSPECTIVE

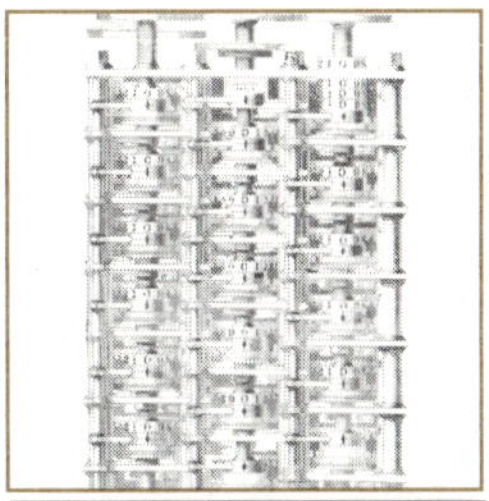

You might expect the history of personal computers to be brief, and indeed it is. Personal computers are small computers built around a microprocessor chip and used by individuals for a variety of computing tasks. Although the first microprocessor chips were available in 1972, and the personal computer industry was born in 1975, it was not until the introduction of the Apple II[1] (by Apple Computer), PET[2] (by Commodore), and the TRS–80[3] (by Tandy) in 1977 that its growth became exciting. Until then, prices were very high and the scarcity of software made it impossible for people to visualize the personal uses of computers. All that changed drastically with the introduction of the Apple II (see Figure 15–1) and a software package known as VISICALC,[4] developed by Software Arts and marketed now by VISICorp. VISICALC allowed people, for the first time, to visualize uses for the small machines.

Figure 15–1
The Apple II from Apple Computer

1. Apple II is a registered trademark of Apple Computer.
2. PET is a registered trademark of Commodore.
3. TRS-80 is a registered trademark of Radio Shack.
4. VISICALC is a registered trademark of Software Arts.

By 1982 the market was filled with options for the potential buyer. Hundreds, if not thousands, of vendors now offer products in the personal computer market. The lower end of the personal computer market was filled with very inexpensive machines of very limited capability. Some of these were dedicated to video games and could not be programmed for other uses.

At the upper end of the market currently, very sophisticated systems can be purchased. These systems can include large primary memories, extensive secondary storage, and a variety of hardware peripherals. Numerous software packages are available to give the systems capabilities which rival those of the smaller mainframes of only a few years ago, for a fraction of the cost. We will understand these capabilities after the discussion of personal computer software, which follows.

Personal Computer Software

In personal computers, as in mainframe computers, the system's ultimate capability is made available to a talented user through the combination of hardware and software which is provided. Perhaps the best way to discuss the uses to which a personal computer can be put is to discuss the types of software which are available. Typically, a software vendor will respond to the recognized needs of users by developing and selling software for which there appears to be a sufficient market. Software is usually provided on floppy disks which can be purchased at any computer store. Prices range from $29.95 to $600, or even more in some cases. We will focus, in turn, on operating systems software and applications software.

Operating Systems

A personal computer's operating system has the same role as the operating systems on larger machines: to make the system's resources available to the user as they are needed. The operating system contains programs to monitor the keyboard, manage the video display, interface with the user, control output and input operations, manage primary memory, and communicate with secondary storage devices. Applications software packages call on the operating system as needed to accept input, generate output, store files, and so on.

Lack of standardization has been a significant problem in personal computer software. Software developed for one manufacturer's machines may not (and probably will not) run on another manufacturer's machines. The potential buyer should make sure that the software is suitable for its intended use. Some manufacturers solve the software compatibility problem by incorporating in their machines one of several standard operating systems. The CP/M[5] (Control Program for Microcomputers) system from Digital Research was the most frequently used standard for the early, 8-bit systems. As a result, thousands of different software packages are available for CP/M machines.

5. CP/M is a registered trademark of Digital Research.

Other operating systems exist for other personal computing systems. The personal computers from Apple Computer tend to use Apple's proprietary operating systems. The IBM personal computer, which became the most popular machine in 1983, used PC/DOS[6] (Personal Computer/Disk Operating System) and MS/DOS[7] (MicroSoft/Disk Operating System). Many companies produced personal computers which used MS/DOS in order to take advantage of the popularity of the IBM PC.[8]

The popularity of an operating system can be judged, to some extent, by the number of applications programs which have been written to run under it. A software locator service in San Antonio, Texas (Sofsearch) reported in early 1984 that 6,428 different software packages were available for Apple machines, 5,047 were available for Tandy/Radio Shack machines, and 4,111 were available for the IBM PC.[9] Virtually everyone expects IBM PC software to take over the top spot before their next survey is published, however.

The IBM PC has forced some standardization in operating systems for the 16-bit computers. Operating systems competing for the 32-bit market are discussed later in the chapter. Operating systems, of course, are not the full story. Applications software is needed in order to be able to put the personal computer to productive use.

Applications Software

The average buyer must be quite confused by the variety of operating systems and the workings of the various applications software packages. Finding the "right" applications software packages for a personal computer is difficult. Unfortunately, most software suppliers do not allow people to take software home for trial. They fear that the customer will copy the software and its documentation without buying it, an illegal act, as is discussed later. Potential buyers are forced, then, to rely on demonstrations and a review of the documentation to judge the suitability of a particular software product. Other sources of information are sometimes available. For example, personal computer magazines publish software reviews and, often, current users of the software can be found at personal computer club or user group meetings.

Interestingly, approximately half of personal computer software purchases occur through mail order. Mail order prices usually reflect attractive discounts from list prices. Personal computing magazines are literally filled with such advertisements for software. Many magazines print program listings themselves as features within their magazines. Subscribers may then enter the program through the keyboard of their machine, and run it.

Several programming languages are available on personal computing systems for those who want to write their own software. BASIC and Pascal are both available on a large number of systems, while FORTRAN and subsets of COBOL are available to a lesser degree. A subset of Ada is available for at least one system. (Languages were discussed in more detail in Chap-

6. PC/DOS is a registered trademark of IBM.
7. MS/DOS is a registered trademark of Microsoft.
8. IBM PC is a registered trademark of IBM.
9. *Infoworld*, April 16, 1984, p. 17.

ter 13.) Personal computer users most often seek applications packages rather than writing their own programs. This section of the chapter will present a description of the types of packaged software which are available for personal computing systems. Seven general areas of use will be discussed:

- Spreadsheet analysis
- Word processing
- Data base
- Graphics
- Games
- Communications
- Integrated packages

Spreadsheet Analysis. One of the most popular types of software packages for the personal computer has been the software which managers use for spreadsheet analysis. The software provides a table of rows and columns, and into each cell formed by the rows and columns the user can put one of several types of entries. For example, a cell may contain text (to provide column and row headings), numerical data, algebraic formulas (which relate that cell to other cells), or functions which automatically compute sums, averages, percentages, and other quantities. A sample use of a spreadsheet is illustrated in Figure 15–2.

A spreadsheet software package can be used to compute profit and loss statements, budgets, students' grades, and many other useful outputs. Some systems enable spreadsheet software and word-processing software to interact so that tables done in the spreadsheet can be incorporated in reports done with the word processor.

Word Processing. Word processing software is one of the most versatile pieces of software available for the personal computer. It can be used for writing reports, letters, articles, and books. In addition to the normal set of text-editing functions for entering, rearranging, and editing text, word processing software can make use of programs which check spelling and grammar and can work with mailing list software to generate form letters. The

Figure 15–2
A Spreadsheet Application—Expense Report

	JAN.	FEB.	MAR.	APR.	MAY
HOUSE PAYMENT	625.00	625.00	625.00		
HEAT	48.72	52.11	46.57		
ELECTRICITY	88.50	92.77	84.36		
WATER	15.23	16.40	17.92		
SEWER	8.50	9.12	9.56		
GARBAGE	11.00	11.00	11.00		
CABLE TV	17.50	17.50	17.50		
TOTAL					

spelling checker reads the document generated and brings to the user's attention any words which it believes are incorrectly spelled. Most spelling checkers have a built-in vocabulary of several thousand words to which the user can add. Thesaurus software is also available to suggest synonyms to a writer who uses word processing software.

The capabilities of word processing software packages vary greatly, and one should try each package out before purchase. Some of the capabilities of MicroPro International's **WordStar,**[10] one of the most popular packages, are illustrated in Figure 15–3.

Word processing software can interact with mailing list software to provide additional capability. Mailing list software itself can be used to select,

Figure 15–3
Menu for Word Processing Program

```
^Q        A:TEST DOC     PAGE 1   LINE 1   COL 01            INSERT ON

                 <<<          Q U I C K  M E N U          >>>

 ---Cursor Movement---          -Delete-     --Miscellaneous--            --Other Menus--
S left side    D right side     Y   line rt  F Find text in file          (from Main only)
E top scrn     X bottom scrn    DEL lin lf   A Find & Replace           ^J Help     ^K Block
R top file     C end file                    L Find Misspelling         ^Q Quick    ^P Print
B top block    K end block                   Q Repeat command or        ^O Onscreen
0-9 marker     Z up      W down                key until space          Space bar returns
P previous     V last Find or Block            bar or other key         you to Main Menu.
                                                                                  ^Q menu

^O        A:TEST DOC     PAGE 1   LINE 1   COL 01            INSERT ON

              <<<          O N S C R E E N  M E N U          >>>

 -Margins & Tabs-        -Line Functions-         --More Toggles--          -Other Menus-
L Set left margin      C Center text            J Justify       off (ON)  (from Main only)
R Set right margin     S Set line spacing       V Variables     off (ON)  ^J Help    ^K Block
X Release margins                               H Hyph help     off (ON)  ^Q Quick   ^P Print
I Set   N Clear tab        ---Toggles---        E Soft hyph     on (OFF)  ^O Onscreen
G Paragraph tab        W Wrd wrap off (ON)      D Prnt disp     off (ON)  Space bar returns
F Ruler from line      T Rlr line off (ON)      P Pge break     off (ON)  you to Main Menu
                                                                                  ^O menu

^P        A:TEST DOC     PAGE 1   LINE 1   COL 01            INSERT ON

                 <<<          P R I N T  M E N U          >>>

     ------Special Effects------             -Printing Changes-          -Other Menus-
 (begin and end)     (one time each)        A Alternate pitch           (from Main only)
B  Bold  D Double    H Overprint char       N Standard pitch          ^J Help     ^K Block
 S Underscore        O Non break space      C Printing pause          ^Q Quick    ^P Print
 X Strikeout         F Phantom space        Y Other ribbon color      ^O Onscreen
 V Subscript         G Phantom rubout         --User Patches--        Space Bar returns
 T Superscript       RET Overprint line     Q(1) W(2) E(3) R(4)       you to Main Menu.
                                                                                  ^P menu
```

from a stored set of names and addresses, a particular subset for use in form-letter mailings. The dedicated user of a personal computer could, for example, keep the names and addresses of friends and relatives to whom correspondence is regularly sent. People who operate small businesses can take advantage of mailing list software to address invoices or promotional literature.

A package known as SAMNA WORD is representative of the state-of-the-art in word processing on a personal computer in 1984. Introduced in the summer of that year, SAMNA WORD III[11] was a full-featured and easy to use package. It included all the normal word processing features of editing, moving, inserting, deleting, searching, replacing, automatic paging, and formatting. In addition, SAMNA WORD offered headers, footers, boldface, underline, super- and subscripts, and hyphenation.

The features which really placed SAMNA WORD III at the top, however, were the inclusion of automatic footnoting (footnotes are typed at the point of reference and placed automatically during printing), proportional spacing, overstriking, and newspaper column printing (columnar text, continuous from bottom left column to top right column). SAMNA WORD presented an environment within which a user could easily exercise control over a complete set of word processing tasks.

Word processing software on a user-friendly system with a quality printer quickly eliminates one's need for a typewriter. The ability to correct errors and revise drafts without retyping is indeed a pleasant one to have. Other packages to supplement word processing software are available. One, for example, provides sets of words that rhyme with a word selected by the user. At least one package is also available, which suggests improvements in grammar. In addition, typesetting software is available which sets type directly from the output of the word processing program.

The reader should not, by the way, confuse these discussions of the capabilities of personal computers with economic justifications for their purchase. Many personal computing systems are purchased for convenience, entertainment, education, or intellectual stimulation. Only in the service of income generation can they be properly justified on the basis of cost/benefit analysis. These discussions are intended to help the reader understand the uses to which the machine might be put after the purchase decision has been made on other grounds.

10. WordStar is a registered trademark of MicroPro International.
11. SAMNA WORD III is a registered trademark of SAMNA Corporation.

Data Base. We are all faced with a number of record-keeping duties which could be aided by a personal computer. Software is available for maintaining a filing system, for accomplishing useful computations, and for maintaining data bases. Data base or filing software gives the user the ability to generate headings and subheadings, retrieve, edit, add, and delete files. People use data base software for maintaining customer lists, supplier lists, inventories, sales and tax records, and for many other uses.

Data base packages have taken on many of the sophisticated characteristics of mainframe data base management systems (DBMSs). Two such packages are **dBase III**[12] from Ashton-Tate and **R:Base**[13] from Microrim. These packages provide for the creation and use of relational data bases, and both include inquiry language access. A newer Microrim product, **CLOUT,**[14] adds artificial intelligence to the user interface to make inquiry even easier.

Two other data base packages are worthy of description here. These products were state-of-the-art as of mid-1984. They each provide very sophisticated software at the microcomputer level. The packages to be discussed here are SALVO[15] (from Software Automation, Inc.) and KnowledgeMan[16] (from Micro Data Base Systems, Inc.).

SALVO provides a relational DBMS within which users can create a set of data files, tie them together as necessary to support inquiry access or report generation, and enter or change data in the data base to meet the needs of applications. Inquiry access is gained through a conversational natural language interpreter which communicates with the user to remove any ambiguities in the inquiry. A powerful set of commands is provided within SALVO to fully support the generation of specific applications without having to resort to higher-level languages. Particularly helpful to the user is a special feature which displays graphically a representation of the files available and the relationships which exist between them.

KnowledgeMan provides a similar set of capabilities. Its relational data base allows "virtual fields," data generated from existing fields through the use of special functions which make it unnecessary to allocate an additional field to accommodate the new data. Inquiry access is provided, which is like IBM's mainframe inquiry language SQL/DS.[17] KnowledgeMan also includes a full-featured spreadsheet capability which allows the user to integrate those functions with the data base package. In addition, graphic representations of data in the data base are available through KGRAPH. Full-color screen design capability for input or output screens is available through another part of the package—KPAINT. KTEXT, the word processing component, rounds out the information management capabilities of the KnowledgeMan series.

Graphics. Software is also available for assisting the user in the generation of graphic images to be produced on a video screen or on a printer. Graphics

12. dBase III is a registered trademark of Ashton-Tate.
13. R:Base is a registered trademark of Microrim.
14. CLOUT is a registered trademark of Microrim.
15. SALVO is a registered trademark of Software Automation.
16. KnowledgeMan is a registered trademark of Micro Data Base Systems, Inc.
17. SQL/DS is a registered trademark of IBM.

Figure 15–4
Sample Graphics

software helps the user construct graphs, bar charts, and pie charts and usually provides for multi-colored formats and the inclusion of text as seen in Figure 15–4. Type fonts of different sizes and type styles make it possible to build slide presentations or tables and drawings for reports. Images generated on the video screen can be photographed or routed to a graphics printer.

Some graphics packages also offer aids for pseudo animation by providing basic geometrical shapes and animating functions. From these basic shapes and functions the user can construct animated images for video games or interactive, educational software. Sequences of images can be programmed to support oral presentations for management or sales conferences.

Games. The fact that software for games is available for personal computers should not be a surprise to anyone. The typical video game presents the user with a competitive, sometimes combative, environment within which to maneuver (see Figure 15–5). The program accepts user input from either the keyboard or a set of "joy sticks" and processes the user's input under control of the game program itself.

Many one-person and two-person games are available, and the use of these games is extensive. A large number are in color and utilize graphics and sound to provide a more exciting experience. Games are also addictive and have been known to interfere with other, normally productive activities.

Figure 15–5
Advertisement for Personal Computer Game

Communications. While personal computers provide a very interesting set of capabilities in their own right, real excitement is possible when they are connected to each other or mainframe machines through networks. These communications have, in the past, been a great source of difficulty, as was discussed in the data communications chapter (Chapter 9). Lack of standardization in personal computer and network design has given us difficult problems to overcome.

There are many software packages available which make communications possible. Some packages allow a personal computer to **emulate** (act like) a particular type of terminal, thus allowing the personal computer to communicate with any mainframe with which that type of terminal could communicate. Other packages allow somewhat more flexibility. Some, like the personal computer cluster program offered by IBM in mid-1984, allow a set of personal computers to form a small network.

Integrated Packages. Early application software packages were each capable of only a rather limited set of functions. Thus, we had word processing packages which processed text handily, but other packages, such as spreadsheets, were necessary for tables of data and worksheets. To the extent that these packages were separately designed, they used sets of commands that were quite different. For example, cursor control might be accomplished quite differently in the word processing package than in the spreadsheet. These differences led to confusion on the part of users and extended the time it took a new user to become proficient.

Combinations of applications packages were designed and marketed as **integrated packages.** In some early examples the integration was at a very minimum level. They might have, for example, used similar sets of commands and allowed the user to move from one use (such as word processing) to another (such as spreadsheet). They often did not, however, allow data to be transferred between the applications.

Newer packages overcame this shortcoming and allowed data transfer between applications, although often the transfer was cumbersome to the user. Eventually we began to see integrated packages in which all applications worked from the same data and changes in the data produced simultaneous changes in each application.

One of the most popular software packages has been **Lotus 1-2-3,**[18] from Lotus Development Corporation. The three applications integrated in this software were data base, spreadsheet analysis, and graphics. A newer product from Lotus, called **Symphony,**[19] added word processing and communications to the three applications of 1-2-3. A competing product from Ashton-Tate is called **Framework.**[20] It integrates word processing, data base, graphics, and spreadsheet analysis. Framework also includes a programming language and an application designed to help users prepare outlines or structure ideas.

18. Lotus 1-2-3 is a registered trademark of Lotus Development Corp.
19. Symphony is a registered trademark of Lotus Development Corp.
20. Framework is a registered trademark of Ashton-Tate.

Figure 15–6
Personal Computer with Screen Partitioned by Windows

The trend toward integration of applications software seems destined to continue. In the early attempts at integration, the individual application pieces might not have been as capable as their single-application counterparts. That difference is, however, becoming smaller as better and better integrated packages are designed.

Windows/Operating Environments. As integrated packages have become popular, two other capabilities have developed. One, the **windows** capability, partitions the video display so that segments of each of several applications can be viewed at the same time as shown in Figure 15–6. The windowing capability for personal computers was first introduced in early 1983 with Apple's **Lisa.**[21] Windowing is now available on other machines.

Another extension to the concept of integrated packages has led to the concept of an **operating environment,** an overall umbrella in which applications packages can run as integrated ones. The operating environment sits, in a sense, above the operating system and provides an environment in which applications packages can be brought together to increase the user's productivity.

These developments in personal computer software have contributed greatly to the appeal of personal machines. The hardware options available are discussed in the next section.

Challenge Update

The reader should now be able to help the Moltons describe the various categories of use of personal computer software.

21. LISA is a registered trademark of Apple Computer.

Personal Computer Hardware

Personal computers come in a variety of sizes. The initial machines, roughly the size of an electric typewriter, were **desktop computers.** They are small enough to be carried by one person, but not conveniently. The monitor, keyboard, and processing unit are sometimes integrated as a single unit on desktop models, but more often implemented as two or three separate pieces. A desktop computer is shown in Figure 15–7.

A step down in size we find the so-called **portables,** more reasonably called **transportables.** They are single, self-contained units that can, with some difficulty, be carried (see Figure 15–8). Even smaller personal computers were introduced in 1983. They are called **lap-size** or **notebook computers** (since *portable* had already been used to describe larger machines). See Figure 15–9 for an illustration.

Personal computers are of a smaller scale than the mainframe machines discussed through most of this text, but they possess the same basic functions of output, input, computation and storage. These functions are, however, incorporated in a smaller scale. They have been reduced in order to provide a closer fit with the needs of the individual user and to reduce the price to a level which can be paid by an individual. We will discuss the hardware options available for each function in turn. A typical microcomputer system is shown in Figure 15–10.

Output

Most of the types of output devices discussed in Chapter 4 are available, in some form, for personal computers. Of these, video displays, printers, and plotters will be discussed here.

Monitors. Most personal computers make use of a video display screen,

Figure 15–7
Desktop Personal Computer

Figure 15–8
Portable (Transportable) Personal Computer

called a *video monitor*. Monitors can be built with a variety of different phosphors, the light-emitting chemical which coats the inside of the screen, and different filters to produce very different visual characteristics. The potential buyer should inspect as many as possible to find the best combination for his or her use. It is a good idea to visit a number of personal computer dealers, or a trade show, in order to find the most desirable monitor combination.

Figure 15–9
Lap-size or Notebook Personal Computer

Figure 15–10
A Complete Personal Computer Sytsem

Single-color (monochrome) monitors are available in either white, green, or amber at prices which range from $100 to $300. Multiple-color monitors are also available. Some personal computing systems use standard color television sets as monitors, though the resolution with a color television screen is not as good as that with a color monitor. Color monitors cost from $300 to several thousand dollars, depending upon size and resolution. High resolution monitors provide text and graphics displays which show more detail and are easier to read.

A user who plans frequent and long use of a video monitor will need to be particularly careful about the flicker of the displayed characters, the glare reflected from overhead lighting, and radiation from the screen. Filters are available to reduce glare, and a special filter containing lead is effective at eliminating the radiation inherent in television viewing.

Printers. Many different printers are available. Those at the lower end of the price scale are impact printers which form characters with a dot matrix. They have higher speeds but lower print quality than the more expensive daisy wheel or thimble printers. Although many printers use standard paper, printers which use thermal paper are also available. Thermal printers offer a low initial cost and quiet operation, but the thermal paper is much more expensive than standard paper. Even moderate volumes of printing would raise the overall cost of a thermal printer above one which uses ordinary paper. (Printer technologies were discussed in greater detail in Chapter 4).

A low-cost, **dot matrix printer** which uses standard, 8½ × 11-inch paper costs approximately $500, while a **letter-quality printer** costs over $1,000, with a few (slow) exceptions. The ever-present trade of money for speed is true of printers. Fast printers cost appreciably more than slow ones. (Slow is ten to fifteen characters per second for letter quality; fast is fifty to eighty characters per second.) Ink jet printers for personal computers became commercially available in 1983. They provide the capability for color printing. An interesting ink jet printer offered by Hewlett-Packard called the ThinkJet,[22] offers disposable jets to avoid a troublesome maintenance problem.

Graphics Printers. One type of printer, the **graphics printer,** is different enough to warrant special mention. This printer uses dots, or in some cases other special characters, to print, dot by dot, the same image as is represented on the video display. Thus, anything represented on the screen by picture elements is mapped directly, bit by bit, to the printer. This mode of operation gives rise to the name **bit mapped printer.**

These printers are capable of printing both graphics and text. In the best cases, the characters formed by such printers approach letter quality. Their versatility makes them an excellent choice for personal computing enthusiasts.

Plotters. An exciting output capability can be provided by a plotter, and several different types of plotters are available for personal computers. These plotters are capable of single-color or multiple-color graphical representations. They can be used to produce either drawings or transparencies. They cost from $1,500 to $4,000.

Input

The keyboard is the most popular input device for personal computers, although there are a number of alternatives available which try to make input operations easier for those users who do not type. The popular alternatives to keyboard entry include touch screens, light pens, touch pads, digitizer tablets, trackballs, joysticks, and mice. In this chapter we will consider touch screens and mice, the two most promising alternatives not covered elsewhere in the text.

Touch Screens. Although touch screen input was an integral part of earlier PLATO terminals, their appearance on Hewlett-Packard's Model 150 personal computer in late 1983 brought new excitement. The Model 150 uses a grid of red light-emitting diodes and phototransistor detectors around the outside edge of the video monitor. When the user touches the screen, the location of the touch can be determined by the coordinates of the light beams interrupted by the touch as shown in Figure 15–11. The system interprets the coordinates of the touch in terms of choices displayed on the screen at the time and an appropriate response is initiated.

Other touch screen technologies exist. Some measure the change in electrical properties where the touch occurs, while others use the pressure of the touch to complete an electrical circuit.

The question of whether touch screen devices are convenient input

22. ThinkJet is a registered trademark of Hewlett-Packard.

Figure 15–11 Touch Screen Input Mechanism

mechanisms or a passing fad has not yet been answered. While possibly convenient for some types of operations, touching the screen can be inconvenient, even tiring for others.

Mice. A **mouse** is an input device which controls movement of the cursor on the video display so that selections from menus or other input operations can take place. Movements of the mouse on its flat surface are translated to cursor movements on the screen. The mouse made its presence known in early 1983 with the introduction of Apple's Lisa.

The purpose of the mouse is to make it easier for users to communicate with the computer. The Lisa, and more recently the Apple MacIntosh, allow the user to display menus, to make selections from the menus, to move text and boundaries, and to "draw" or "paint" on the screen. In conjunction with **icons** (small drawings which represent computer functions and operations), the mouse gives the user control over the system's operation.

The Lisa mouse is an *optomechanical* device which uses mechanical linkages and light emitting diodes (LEDs) to monitor the mouse's movements on virtually any flat surface. Other mice use LEDs in combination with a reflective grid on a special surface on which the mouse must be used. Mice are equipped with one, two, or three buttons (depending upon the manufacturer) so that the user can signal his or her intentions. Single button mice are believed, by those who make them, to allow the most simple interface with the machine.

Joysticks and trackballs are used extensively in computer games, while light pens and digitizer tablets find use with personal computers in the same types of work for which they are useful in computers in general.

The article by Cary Lu listed in the additional readings at the end of this chapter provides a good source of information about each of these technologies. We next turn our attention to the computation function.

Computation

Personal computer CPUs provide a name-dropper's paradise. Those who keep abreast of computer chip developments can easily confuse the novice with information about the vast array of microcomputer chips.

Chips are categorized according to their architecture. Two elements seem important: (1) the number of bits which can simultaneously be sent to the **data bus** (the CPU's connection with the rest of the machine) and (2) the number of bits which can be accommodated in a single word by the internal architecture of the CPU itself.

Personal computer chips are categorized according to three word sizes (8, 16, and 32 bits) for each of the two components (data bus and internal architecture). Table 15–1 shows the more popular chips, their classification, and some of the more popular personal computers in which they reside.

The specific technology of the chip translates into processing speed and size of the primary memory which can be addressed directly. The 16-bit chips can address (directly) a larger memory and transfer data faster than the 8-bit chips. The 32-bit chips are faster still and can address larger memories.

The personal computer enthusiast's interest in microprocessor chips is rivalled only by his or her interest in operating systems. The two most popular 8-bit operating systems have been CP/M (Digital Research's Control Program for Microcomputers) and Apple's DOS (Disk Operating System). The IBM version of MS/DOS (MicroSoft/Disk Operating System), known as PC/DOS, dominates the field for the 8/16-bit 8088-based machines.

Supremacy at the 32-bit level has yet to be determined. AT&T's candidate is UNIX, while PICK (by Dick Pick) and others are also in the competition. As casual users and (perhaps) disinterested standers-by, we can only hope that some degree of standardization will eventually occur so that we can get on with the productive use of the personal machines.

Table 15–1 *Microcomputer Chips and Personal Computers*

Chip	Manufacturer	Data Bus	Internal Architecture	Personal Computer
Z80	Zilog	8	8	CP/M Machines
6502	MOS Tech.	8	8	Apple II
8088	Intel	8	16	IBM PC
80186	Intel	16	16	Tandy 2000
80286	Intel	16	16	IBM PC AT
68010	Motorola	16	32	Apple Lisa
WE3200	AT&T	32	32	AT&T 3B2
HP Focus	Hewlett-Packard	32	32	HP9000
NS32032	National Semi	32	32	
80386	Intel	32	32	

Adapted from "Microprocessors: the heart of the micro revolution" by Peter Bartolik in *Computerworld*, April 4, 1984, p. 15.

Storage. The usual unit of measurement for memories is the byte, which has been described elsewhere in the text. A byte is a memory space large enough to accommodate the storage of a single character. In describing the size of the memory, shorthand notation is used in which *K* is used to represent "thousands." (Note: the precise value of K is 1,024, the tenth power of 2.) Ten thousand bytes of memory are referred to as 10K.

Primary memory capacities for personal computers range from 16K to 512K bytes, although machines are available below and above that range. The size of the primary memory limits, in a sense, the size of program which can be run on the system.

Systems with small primary memories must use programs which have been written in modules. The module which contains the functions currently in use is stored in the primary memory while the other modules reside in secondary storage. When it becomes necessary to change program functions, the appropriate modules must be exchanged in memory. The exchanging of modules causes delay in functioning of the system. A personal computer with a small primary memory will be slowed in its execution of a program by the exchanging of program modules (called overlays).

Several different types of secondary memory are available. A small magnetic tape drive can be used, although its use is usually limited to backing up other devices because it operates so slowly. Miniature floppy disk drives are available as secondary memory, in 3, 3.25, 3.5, 5.25, and 8-inch sizes. (Standardization appears never to be the norm.) Most of the software currently available for personal computers is sold on 5.25 floppy disks, although the future may belong to the 3.5 inch disks.

"Now that's what I call a personal computer!"

The floppy disk provides fast data transfer rates at a relatively low cost. Hard disk drives of the sealed-environment, Winchester variety are also available at a somewhat higher cost. Floppy disk drives cost from $200 to approximately $1,000, and hard disk drives cost from $1,500 to $5,000. The principal advantages of the hard disk devices are (1) a larger capacity and (2) a faster data transfer rate. Floppy disks store from 120,000 to 350,000 bytes, while hard disk systems store from 5 to 20 million bytes. Hard disk systems capable of storing hundreds of millions of bytes are expected by the mid-1980s.

A personal computing system with a full set of components in a very minimum configuration will cost at least $1,000. The IBM PCjr, a home computer first shipped in early 1984, was initially priced at $700 to $1,300, depending upon the exact configuration desired. A high-quality, high-capability personal computer system can, on the other hand, cost as much as $10,000 to $12,000. It is, however, always possible, and sometimes even tempting, to spend even more. In 1984 most buyers acquiring full capability systems were spending $4,000 to $6,000.

The proliferation of personal computers in homes, schools, businesses, and other organizations has given us access to a wide range of information services, to which we turn our attention in the next section.

Information Services

Microcomputers in combination with communications systems promise access to a vast array of information services. The transmissions to provide these services can be accomplished in two different ways. They can either be broadcast, as are radio and television programs, in a development known as **teletext;** or, they can be delivered to the home over existing telephone or cable television circuits, which is called **videotext** (shortened routinely to **videotex**) (see Figure 15–12). The particular information services which will be made available in this way are constrained by people's willingness to pay for the service. A joint venture between IBM, CBS, and Sears, Roebuck & Co. called Trintex was announced in 1984. Such a venture indicates that videotex may be big business.

The first commercial videotex service in the United States began in Miami, Florida, in October of 1983. The service, called Viewtron, was offered by Viewdata Corporation of America, a subsidiary of a newspaper company. One of their services was, of course, electronic news. A terminal for Viewtron cost $400 to $600, and monthly charges were expected to average around $30 per customer. The most commonly used services of videotex are banking, shopping, news, and games.

Banking

Many normal banking transactions can be performed from the home. Actual deposits and withdrawals require the exchange of cash and checks, which still require a visit to the bank or an automatic teller, but payments to the accounts of others and transfers between one's existing accounts could be

Figure 15–12
In-Home Videotex Terminal

handled via videotex. The user needs only a limited-purpose terminal (a push-button telephone will work) and the transactions can be completed from the home.

The electronic transfer of funds (EFT) has had the backing of the banking industry for some time, but consumers have been reluctant to accept it for two reasons. In the first place, consumers worry about the security of their accounts if remote access transfers are allowed. The second disadvantage associated with EFT has to do with float. Float is the advantage one has with respect to having sufficient funds in an account to cover checks due to the fact that it takes several days for the checks to be processed. People who write checks before payday, recognizing that the checks will not be cleared and deducted from their account for several days, are taking advantage of float. EFTs take place in real time, so there is no float.

Many people already use a direct deposit scheme which authorizes employers to send paychecks directly to the employee's bank for deposit to their accounts. In many such cases, notice to the bank is done via electronic means rather than the mailing of an actual check. Both the bank and the employer experience work reductions in their check processing operations when EFT is used.

The Bank of America began offering banking services through videotex terminals in late 1983. Chemical Bank of New York began commercial banking services via videotex the same year. Should banking by EFT appeal to enough people, traffic in the bank lobby should decrease, as should the need for space and personnel.

Shopping

Videotex makes it possible to review items for sale via television and place orders directly through a terminal or telephone. Videotex shopping may also be accompanied by the electronic transfer of funds. Mail-order houses and grocery stores seem to be very interested in providing shop-at-home services. An obvious advantage accrues to physically disadvantaged people, who might be unable to leave their homes to do their shopping. Figure 15–13 illustrates the services which could be made available.

In using a shopping service, the user finds items of interest by working through menus displayed on the television screen. The first menu for a supermarket might give the user the choice among meats, dairy products, produce, bakery items, or general groceries. Successive menus become in-

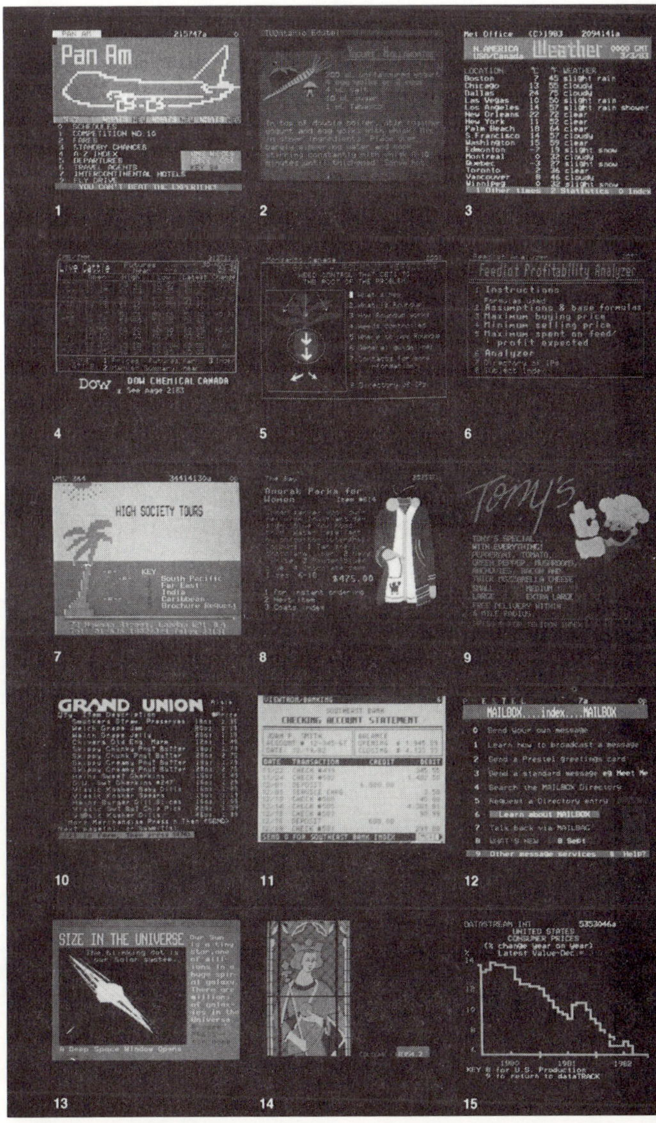

Figure 15–13
Information Services Available Through Videotex

A videotex sampler

1. Airline flight information (Prestel); 2. gourmet tips (Telidon); 3. North American weather report (Prestel).

4-6. The Grassroots service helps farmers run their businesses.

Advertisements show marked difference in graphics quality: 7. (Prestel); 8. (Grassroots); 9. (Telidon).

Conducting errands from home: 10. grocery shopping (CBS/American Bell); 11. banking (Viewtron); 12. sending messages (Prestel).

Videotex as encyclopedia: 13. a lesson in cosmology (Telidon); 14. rendering of stained glass from a Cologne cathedral (Telidon); 15. the declining rate of inflation (Prestel's large pixel size turns smooth line into stairsteps).

creasingly refined until the selection of the specific item is made possible. While shopping via videotex may be a definite advantage to some, it is not clear that everyone will be willing to pay for the privilege.

In France, where videotex shopping has been in use since 1981, some mail-order houses use an intriguing, microprocessor-aided form of delivery. The mail-order house delivers goods ordered by customers to individual lockers which are located in train stations, subway stations, and other public places. The lockers have microprocessor-controlled locks into which the delivery man enters the customer's identification number. When a customer determines from a home terminal that the goods have been delivered to the locker, he or she goes to the locker, inserts a credit card, and enters the identification number in order to obtain the goods.

Telephone Directories

The first automated telephone directories were tested in France in 1981. Telephone service subscribers were given limited-function terminals through which they could gain access to the directory. Telephone customers could search the business and residential listings by name and the "yellow pages" by product or service desired. For example, a customer in search of a restaurant could request the names of restaurants which specialize in Italian food and actually review the menus, prices, and hours of service of each restaurant. Upon making a selection, the customer could arrange a reservation.

A telephone company with an on-line, real time directory system to which its subscribers have access has no need to maintain a large staff of directory assistance operators and no need to publish telephone books. Subscribers are able to obtain up-to-the-minute directory information in much greater detail than was formerly the case.

Financial Information

Access to financial information via special-purpose terminals became a reality in the early 1980s and spread to personal computers via telecommunications in 1982. Through this service people may obtain current information about stock and commodity markets. This service may expand to allow buyers and sellers to enter their orders through their terminals and to utilize EFTs to complete the transactions.

One such service, the Dow Jones News/Retrieval service, offers subscribers access to financial news, stock prices, histories of stock quotations, and surveys of economic indicators. Several years' worth of articles from financial journals can be searched by industry, government agency, or key words.

News

The wire services, network news providers, and telephone companies, to mention a few, are all interested in the use of videotex to provide continuous news service to users upon demand through the use of videotex. Newspaper publishers are understandably reluctant to share the news business in this way for fear that it will mean the decline of the newspaper industry. It is interesting to note that the first commercial videotex service is owned by a newspaper company, Knight-Ridder Newspapers, Inc.

The advantage of the electronic news service is that consumers will be able to purchase access to news broadcasts on television at any time. Menus will enable the users to select only those news items which are of potential interest, and to pursue those interests to whatever depth the user desires.

Libraries

The card catalogues and perhaps even some significant portion of a library's holdings will eventually be available to users via videotex. Numerous abstracting services are now available to researchers, who use key words or phrases to locate abstracts which can then be scanned for usefulness. The appropriate bibliographic references or copies of the books or articles can then be obtained from the library system. Electronic access to libraries via terminals in the home could open the great libraries of the world to more extensive use.

Educational Programming

Although the use of television broadcasting techniques for educational offerings has been common for years, the use of videotex could make broadcast coursework truly interactive. People working on terminals in their homes will be able to select courses and lessons within those courses for study at home, as shown in Figure 15–14. Homework and examinations

Figure 15–14
Sample Educational Software Screens

could be administered electronically through an interactive terminal. Software may even accomplish the grading and direct the student to the next lesson, depending upon his or her performance.

Challenge Update

The reader should now be able to explain the various information services to the Moltons.

In spite of the information services options just described, the apparent utility of the software, and the exciting developments in hardware, personal computers give rise to some difficult issues which must be resolved. It is to two of these that we now turn our attention.

Personal Computer Security Issues

Personal computers and their increasing popularity have brought a number of interesting problems. Two of these problems are concerned with security. The first has to do with the protection of personal computer software, and the second concerns the threat of so-called "hackers" to existing computer networks. First, we consider software protection.

Software Piracy

One has only to imagine the total number of personal computers which have been sold in order to gain some grasp of the size of the market for personal computer software. Sales of the IBM PC in 1984 were expected to be close to two million units. If as many as 25 percent of those buyers additionally choose a particular software package, sales of that software would be around 500,000 units. The programmer(s) who wrote the software could expect to receive millions of dollars in royalties.

The programmers' royalties would, however, be reduced by violations of the laws which make it illegal to copy personal computer programs protected by copyright. Many people ignore the law and make illegal copies. Although many protection schemes exist to make it difficult to copy protected software, an almost equal number of schemes exist to overcome those protections. Some protection schemes actually provide a mechanism by which illegal copies can be traced to the original owner who violated the copyright law initially.

The copyright law prohibits copying, and many software licenses allow software to be used only on the single personal computer for which it has been purchased. An organization purchasing ten personal computers to be used for spreadsheet analysis must buy ten separate copies of the spreadsheet package. This seems like an unnecessary expense to some users and represents a very real financial burden to nonprofit educational institutions. The law, however, is clear—material protected by copyright cannot legally be copied.

Some software vendors offer a compromise. Multiple-CPU licensing arrangements can be used which allow financial relief to the buyer but maintain protection and revenues for the vendor. Serious as the software piracy problem is—and estimates are that it represents $100 million of criminal activity annually—the threat of intrusion by "hackers" is even greater, as we shall see in the next segment.

Illegal Access

The proliferation of personal computers and the growth of communications networks to which they can be attached pose a serious security problem. Serious, but misdirected, computer buffs working with personal computers to gain unauthorized access to other computer systems have become known as **hackers.** [The original hacker was only a computer buff who was trying to learn about computing by "hacking around," trying numerous activities to see which ones worked. More recently the word *hacker* has taken on the connotation of illegality.]

The vast network of computing systems connected to the long distance telephone provide fertile fields in which the hacker can work. Only a little ingenuity has been necessary to allow the hacker unauthorized access to computers exercising important roles in medical care, communications, banking, diplomatic endeavors, and national defense. Although the FBI and the Department of Defense have both stopped up efforts to detect, trace, and prosecute those who gain unauthorized access to sensitive systems, a comprehensive program of protection does not yet exist.

Congress has been rather slow to react to the threat of unauthorized access. A confidential access code to a large national credit data base was found in an electronic bulletin board used by many hackers in mid-1984. Through use of the code many people were able to gain access to the credit files maintained by the information services Division of TRW Inc. This and other breaches of security finally led Congress to consider the Counterfeit Access Device and Computer Fraud and Abuse Act of 1984.

Challenge Update *The reader should now be able to discuss two security issues which result from personal computing.*

Newest Developments

Changes in the field of personal computing are occurring so rapidly that it is virtually impossible to keep abreast of the new technologies. Each new announcement makes someone else's product obsolete, and each, in turn, will be made obsolete by some later development.

Personal computers will become more and more capable, and users will gradually work them into their personal and professional lives with less and less fanfare. Eventually, we might imagine, they will no longer bask in the light of extraordinary attention they now receive. They will be recognized as productive tools with which everyone will be expected to be familiar. They will become second nature to their users, somewhat as telephones have become.

There is, however, hope for those who wish to remain unscathed by the personal computer revolution. At least two organizations have been formed to bring together those who might be characterized as opposed to the computer revolution. Both the Crabapple Anti-Computer Club and the Society for the Prevention of Cruelty to Users seek to bring peace to those who have been disturbed by the growth of personal computer use.

Meanwhile, new models continue to roll off the production line. The Apple IIc brought portability to the company which many view as the technological leader in personal computer design. New IBM models represent counterattacks to the Lisa and MacIntosh[23] lines. Hewlett-Packard's new lap-sized machine, the Model 110, brought new competition to the arena of small machines. The IBM PC AT brought multiuser capabilities into the market. The war goes on.

COMPUTING CHALLENGE: *A Final Note*

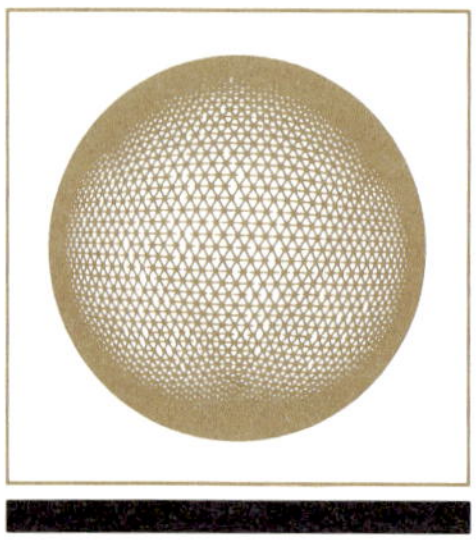

Meanwhile, the Moltons have decided to make the plunge. A quick analysis of the various uses to which personal computers could be put has led them to decide that no single machine will be adequate. Therefore, they have bought two new systems.

To support the business functions on the ranch they have purchased an IBM PC, by far the most popular machine among business users. They acquired spreadsheet, data base, and word processing software packages to give them the capabilities they needed. They also purchased a letter quality printer in order to use the system for business correspondence.

For the children they have purchased an Apple MacIntosh.[24] This system has certainly demonstrated that it is easy to learn to use, for even the ten-year-old (Rachel) has put it to good use. She regularly uses MacPaint software to create drawings which can be easily reproduced on the bit-mapped printer.

The Moltons are seriously considering the purchase of another machine but have decided to wait for the next series of new product announcements before buying anything else.

SUMMARY

- A personal computer gives the user the ability to use software to accomplish programming, word processing, record keeping, spreadsheet computations, games, graphics, and communications.
- A personal computer in combination with a communications link allows

23. MacIntosh is the registered trademark of Apple Computer.
24. Ibid.

a person to communicate with a variety of other computing devices connected to a network.

- Personal computer operating systems have not shown much standardization, but the most common ones have been CP/M, Apple DOS, PC/DOS (MS/DOS), and UNIX.
- The trend in applications software is toward integrated packages and operating environments.
- The four functions of output, input, computation, and storage are all represented in available personal computer hardware.
- Personal computer CPUs have shown a gradual migration from the early 8-bit architectures to 16-bit systems and on toward 32-bit architectures.
- Although keyboard input is provided for virtually all personal computers, new input devices such as mice and touch screens represent attempts to make the systems easier to use.
- Videotex will bring many new information services to the fingertips of the personal computer user.
- People who subscribe to videotex will be able to perform many banking and shopping functions through that service.
- Automated telephone directories and access to financial information, news services, libraries, and educational programs are other possibilities which are provided by the combined use of a personal computer and the communications link provided by the telephone or cable television circuits.
- Only time will tell which of these services will attract enough users to make them financially attractive to the providers.
- New personal computer systems will give way to even newer, more sophisticated systems.
- We may eventually see the personal computer settle into its role of an information processing tool without the media hype which currently accompanies its use.

CASE: New Uses for the Personal Computer

Personal computers initially meant only computer games in our homes. Eventually, they became powerful information processing tools for both the home and the office. We may also, it seems, use personal computers to automatically turn on the lights, monitor the heat, watch for burglars, feed the cat, and get rid of mice! Needed are a standard home microcomputer, an analog-to-digital (A/D) converter, a few contraptions, and a bit of intricate wiring, and the computer can operate the entire house.

A/D conversion is the key. It is the process whereby an electrical current, from a thermostat for example, is changed into a sequence of individual impulses that can be understood and regulated by the computer. The A/D converter, when combined with an appropriate set of hardware and software, can effect all kinds of magic.

Earl Wallace, an engineer from Santa Clara, California, has pioneered such an automated home. His latest scheme is a combination cat-feeding and rat-detection and removal system. It's a very clever gadget. In it, a weight-sensitive mat is placed by the cat's food dish so that when the cat comes to feed, a predetermined amount of food would be dispensed. But if a rodent came instead to snitch from the dish, the mat would register a weight insufficient to be the cat, so a mechanism would swoop up the rat and dispose of it in a nearby garbage can.

Complex programming, costly contraptions, and intricate wiring are, of course, necessary, but once in place, they can control a home to the degree desired. With such a personal computer based system, occupants of the house can be relieved of many unwanted tasks.

"A/D Conversion Brings the Real World to the Personal Computer," *Personal Computing,* June 1982, p. 60.

Questions for the Case

1. In what ways can a homeowner justify a personal computer through cost/benefit analysis?
2. Are most personal computers in the home likely to have been cost justified? What other justifications are there?

DISCUSSION QUESTIONS AND EXERCISES

1. Describe briefly the different types of software available for personal computers.
2. Discuss the advantages of integrated software packages over individual applications packages.
3. Explain how the various information services might be useful to a business professional. To a student.
4. How will suppliers of the home information services decide which ones to include in their offerings?
5. For what data processing tasks in the home would word processing software seem beneficial? Spreadsheet software? Data base software?
6. What factors encourage the use of banking and shopping via videotex terminals? What factors discourage that use?
7. In what ways will electronically delivered news be better than current newspaper and television news? In what ways will it be worse?
8. What are the advantages of purchasing personal computer hardware from a mail-order house? What are the disadvantages?
9. What will operating environments offer that operating systems have not?
10. Compare and contrast Apple Computer's role in the personal computer industry with that of IBM. What gave Apple its early lead in the market? What factors made IBM an instant market success?
11. What advantages are there to personal computer CPUs which have 32-bit architectures compared to those with 16-bit architectures?
12. Visit a retail outlet for personal computers. Ask for a demonstration of some hardware/software combination. What were your impressions?
13. Under what circumstances can personal computer software be legally copied?

14. What elements are necessary for a hacker to be able to gain unauthorized access to a computer system?
15. Why might a student want to have access to word processing in order to do a term paper?

ADDITIONAL READINGS

Blank, Hannah. *Mastering Micros.* Princeton, NJ: Petrocelli Books, 1983.

Computerworld, by C.W. Communications, Inc. Framingham, MA has a microcomputer section.

Cook, Rick. "Operating Systems in Transition." *High Technology,* June 1984, pp. 65–70.

Datamation, by Technical Publishing Co., New York, New York publishes timely articles on the use of microcomputers.

Davis, Dwight B. "Personal Computer Networks Go On-Line." *High Technology,* March 1984, pp. 61–68.

Hecht, Jeff. "Information Services Search for Identity." *High Technology,* May 1983, pp. 58–65.

Infosystems, by Hitchcock Publishing Co., Wheaton, Ill., publishes microcomputer articles.

Infoworld, by Popular Computing, Inc., Framingham, MA is devoted almost entirely to microcomputers.

Lu, Cary. "Computer Pointing Devices: Living with Mice." *High Technology,* January 1984, pp. 61–65.

McGlynn, Daniel R. *Personal Computing.* New York: Wiley, 1982.

McWilliams, Peter A. *The Personal Computer Book.* Los Angeles: Prelude Press, 1982.

Meador, C. Lawrence, Keen, Peter G.W., and Guyote, Martin J. "Personal Computers and Distributed Decision Support." *Computerworld,* May 7, 1984, pp. ID/7–14.

Mosco, Vincent. *Pushbutton Fantasies.* Norwood, NJ; Ablex Publishing, 1982.

Personal Computing, by Hayden Publishing Co., Boulder, Colo., publishes microcomputer articles regularly.

Peterson, Dale. *Big Things From Little Computers: A Layperson's Guide to Personal Computing.* Englewood Cliffs, NJ: Prentice-Hall, 1982.

Shea, Tom. "The FBI Goes After Hackers." *Infoworld,* March 26, 1984, pp. 38–44.

Tydeman, et al. *Teletext and Videotex in the United States.* New York: McGraw-Hill, 1982.

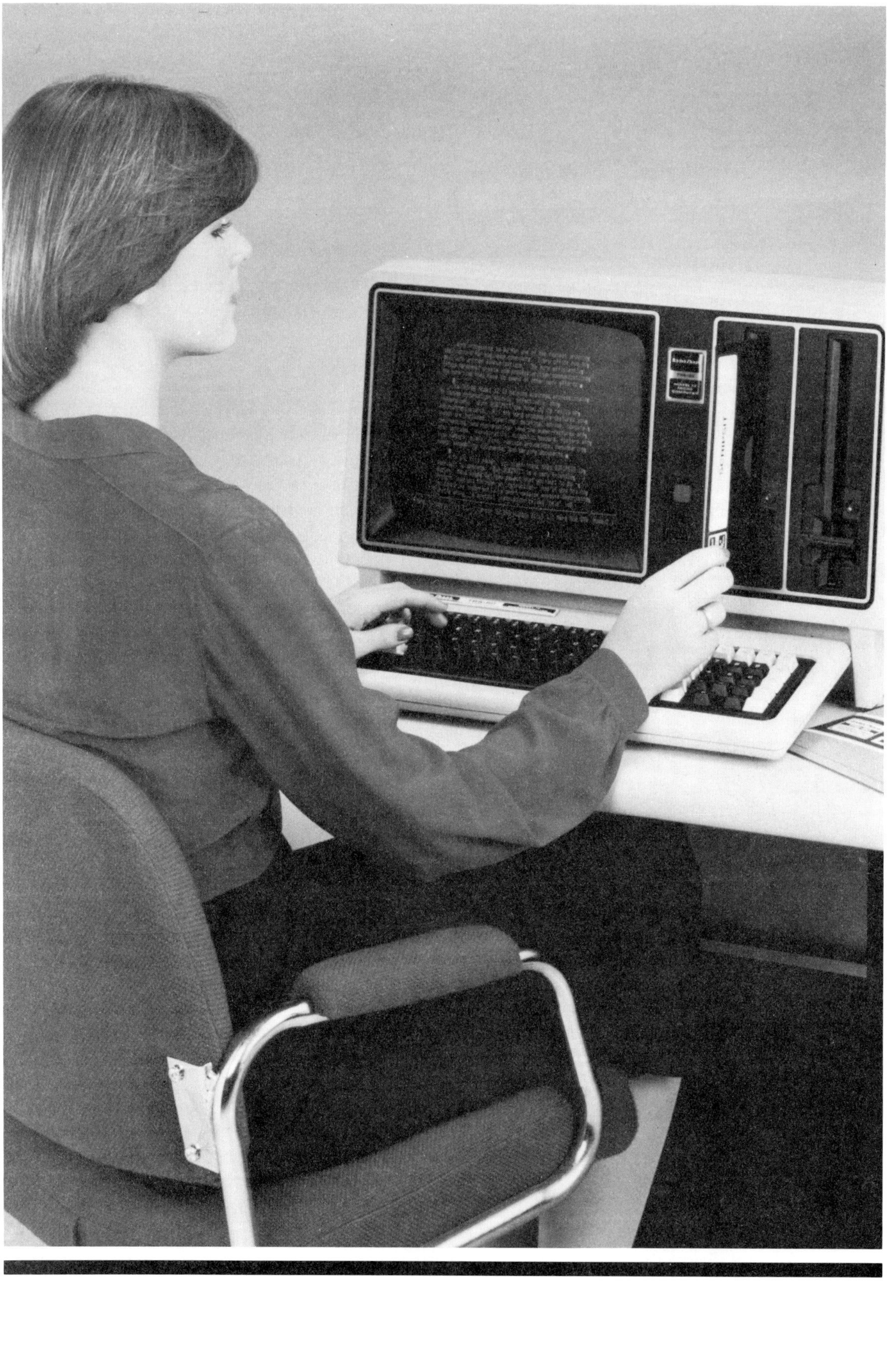

16

Computers and Management

CHAPTER PREVIEW

The focus of this text continues to be on the use of computers to support the transaction processing activities of organizations and the decision-making activities of managers. This chapter deals almost exclusively with the support of managerial decision making.

Organizations are dependent upon their information systems. Unless information can be efficiently and effectively processed, the health of the organization itself will be threatened. Both transaction processing systems and managerial support systems are of critical importance to the organization's well being.

The first part of the chapter is devoted to the topic of management itself. In it, the activities common to management are discussed. The various levels of the management hierarchy are then presented in order to develop an understanding of the different ways in which computerized systems can support managers. Computerized systems in support of managerial activities vary according to the particular activity they support and the level in the organization to which the support is directed.

In general, computer applications which support the decision-making activities of managers fall into one of two categories, the first called management information systems (**MIS**) and the second called decision support systems (**DSS**). A third, and relatively new, category known as expert systems, is treated in the "Newest Developments" section.

There are differences of opinion among professionals concerning the relationship between MIS and DSS. The differences of opinion are of interest to serious researchers in the field but of considerably less interest to managers themselves. The distinction necessary for our purposes is provided by the next paragraph.

MIS is a field of study of the use of computerized data processing systems in support of a variety of managerial functions within organizations. DSS is a field of study of the use of a particular class of computerized data processing systems in support of certain kinds of managerial functions within organizations. DSS is, for our purposes, a subset of MIS. Their similarities and differences may cause considerable academic debate, but the finer points of their differences will not interfere with the substance of this chapter.

Management information systems will be discussed after we have discussed managerial activities and levels. The role of MISs in transaction processing, managerial control, and strategic planning will be explored. Decision support systems will then be discussed so that it will be possible to understand the particular class of problems for which they are useful. Following these discussions, the implications that increased computerization are expected to have for management as an art and a science will be discussed. As always, a computing challenge is provided to stimulate our thinking about the appropriate issues of the chapter.

COMPUTING CHALLENGE: *State Agency Productivity Improvement*

Many people, well into their professional careers, have faced the sudden change brought into their working lives by the installation of a computing system. A manager, upon whose shoulders the burden of managing in the computer age has recently been thrust, is an example of just such a person. Winston Sterling, Director of the State Highway Department in one of the Rocky Mountain States, is a good candidate for further study.

Mr. Sterling has been with the State Highway Department since graduating from the state university with a degree in civil engineering in 1947. Few are the jobs within the department in which he has not worked. As a matter of fact, he could still perform the duties of most jobs without difficulty. A worker's manager, Winston has climbed to the very top of the department. He recognizes, better than most, that everyone's contribution is critical to the success of an organization.

Recently an aggressive, young governor was elected to run the state, and one of her campaign promises was to upgrade the level of management of the state's various agencies and departments. To that end, she has initiated an effort to upgrade the productivity of every department through the increased utilization of computers. To set a good example for the agencies, the executive office will use a computer model this year to bring together the budget planning activities for all agencies and departments.

A computerized personnel system began operation last year in support of the state system of civil service, providing job search and referral services to all state employees wishing to transfer within the state system. Time and attendance reporting for all state employees is scheduled to go on-line next month. Mr. Sterling's own department, the Highway Department, has been asked to convert equipment and materials inventory listings to a computerized system during the next fiscal year.

Mr. Sterling finds his position a difficult one. His college education was completed thirty-five years ago; and, in spite of the fact that he has attended numerous professional development seminars through the years, he feels his ability to manage is threatened by the new technologies. Although he is several years from retirement, he has actually been considering an early retirement just to avoid having to deal with them.

He wonders what impact the computerization of the various department activities will have on the management function. Will he still be able to do the fine job he has done in the past? Will his effectiveness as head of the department become less as computer processing becomes distributed throughout the state system? Will his department, clean of such problems as fraud and theft, continue its good record? Will computerization make it any more difficult to keep corruption at bay?

These are not unusual questions; they are quite normal. Managers face the conversion to computerized management systems with as much uncertainty as a salesperson faces a new order entry system or a department store clerk faces a new point-of-sale terminal. Any significant change in the technology of work has the potential to be disruptive.

Workers at all levels must develop appropriate, constructive responses to the challenges presented by computers. Although most, but certainly not all, technological advances have benefits which accrue to the organization, their effect on workers is not always so obviously beneficial.

Students of management must prepare themselves so that they will be able to:

1. *Explain the use of management information systems (MISs) in support of transaction processing, managerial control, and strategic planning.*
2. *Explain the class of problems for which decision support systems (DSSs) are applicable.*
3. *Discuss the implications that computerized MISs have for the job of manager.*
4. *Discuss the threat to security posed by computerized information processing systems.*

HISTORICAL PERSPECTIVE

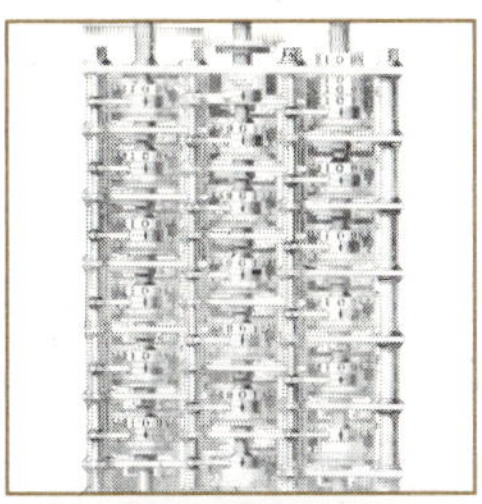

Although the history of management itself is extensive, it is only in the last thirty years or so that management and computing have become intertwined. In this century, management has worked its way through several schools of thought. Early on, through the works of Frederick Winslow Taylor, scientific management represented the application of scientific methods to the practice of management. To this era we owe time and motion studies, piece-rate pay, and early industrial engineering efforts.

The next identifiable school of management thought was that of human relations. The famous Hawthorne studies gave us new insight into the motivation of the working class. The human relations school of thought was followed by management science—the integration of many disciplines into the practice of management. Predominant among management science techniques have been those of quantitative methods. More recently we have been introduced to Theory Z (scientific management was Theory X and human relations was Theory Y) and the Japanese style of management.

Computers began working their way into business organizations in the 1950s. Since that time their role in the organization has changed from that of a specialized tool in a specific area to an ever-present participant in virtually all information processing endeavors. The benefits and challenges they provide form the work of this chapter.

Management

This section examines the various levels of management within a large organization and characterizes the activities which take place at each level.

These discussions will provide the background necessary to understand the discussions of MIS and DSS which follow in the next sections.

The Functions of Management

What is it that managers do? A complete answer to that question would, of course, require far more space than is available here. We will, however, provide a brief overview of management. Readers wanting more information will find many books on the subject in the library or bookstore.

Henry Fayol described a basic set of functions common to management: planning, organizing, staffing, directing, and controlling.[1] A brief description of each is provided.

- *Planning.* The purpose of planning is to provide goals for the organization and develop strategies for achieving them. Overall organizational goals are translated into targets in specific areas, and plans are made to move the organizational units in the direction of the targets.
- *Organizing.* This function describes the many activities necessary to bring together the correct collection of resources to pursue the plan. Included in this function is the determination of an organizational structure which would be appropriate for pursuit of the targets identified in the planning function.
- *Staffing.* The talents of many people must be secured and coordinated in order to move an organization in the direction of the plan. The staffing function includes all those activities necessary to find, attract, hire, train, and coordinate them.
- *Directing.* Coordinated effort in virtually all organizations depends upon the leadership of those in charge. They must direct the efforts of all participants so that targets identified by the plan can be realized.
- *Controlling.* Within this function, managers work to determine the value of the various parameters of performance, to compare them with the desired values, and to initiate activities designed to move the organization closer to its goals. The measurement of actual performance and its comparison with planned performance are fundamental to this function.

While virtually all managers engage in virtually all of these functions, the exact nature of each function varies with the level of the manager in the organization. A look at the levels of management will help clarify this concept.

Management Levels

Most discussions of the levels of management identify them as upper management, middle management, and operations, or lower, management as illustrated in Figure 16–1. These discussions use a triangle to illustrate, among other things, that the smaller numbers of people in upper management are supported by managers at the middle management level. They,

1. Henry Fayol, *General and Industrial Management* (London: Sir Isaac Pitman & Sons, 1949).

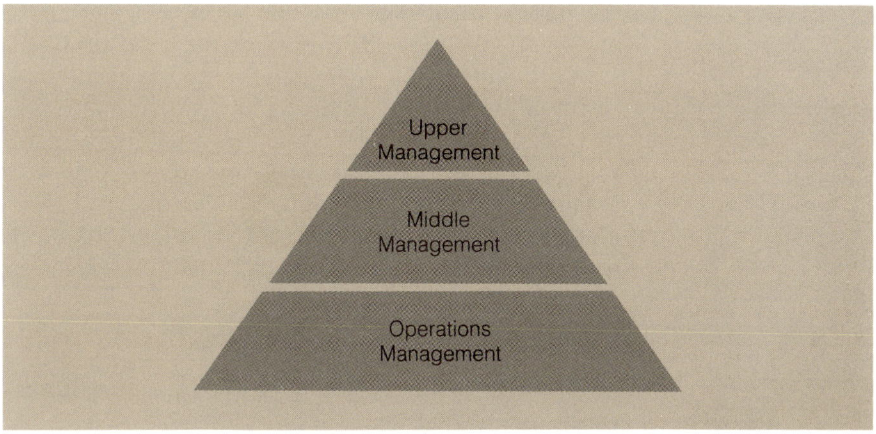

Figure 16–1 Levels of Management

in turn, draw support from the large numbers of managers at the operational level.

The nature of managerial functions changes from level to level. Managers at the upper level work typically on problems with a longer time horizon than do managers at lower levels. They, for example, engage in the formation of strategic, long-range plans for the organization. These plans address issues important to the organization one, two, five, or even ten years in the future. In comparison, managers at the middle level focus more frequently on monthly and annual planning efforts. At the operational level we find the time horizon to be even shorter. Problems at that level frequently require immediate action. Other differences among managerial levels exist. For example, the types of problems faced by managers differ from level to level. Many of the problems faced by operational-level managers are **well-structured.** A well-structured problem has the following characteristics:

1. The problem definition is straightforward.
2. The solutions are well-defined.
3. Relatively simple solution techniques exist.

Consider, for example, the problems faced by the department manager of a manufacturing operation. Problems at this level typically include production scheduling, inventory control, quality control, productivity, and mechanical efficiency. Good algorithms exist to help solve each of these because they are well-structured problems.

In contrast, the problems faced by managers at the upper levels are **unstructured.** The characteristics of unstructured problems are:

1. Problems are difficult to define.
2. Solutions are difficult to identify.
3. Solution techniques are not readily available.

Consider, for example, the problems faced by the vice president in charge of marketing in a large consumer product corporation. Included in the problems faced by the vice president are customer acceptance of the product, advertising effectiveness, long-range trends in the market place, and the threats to market share posed by competitors' actions. Reliable techniques for dealing with these unstructured problems are difficult to find.

The differences in managerial function at the three levels are largely the result of the differences in the time horizon and the degree of structure of the problems encountered at that level. As a result of these differences, managers at the different levels vary in the extent to which their decision making can be effectively supported by computerized information systems. Managers at the lower levels rely heavily on computerized systems, while managers at the upper levels have been much less successful at doing so.

Levels and Functions Combined

An analysis of the nature of the managerial function at the upper level would reveal that:

1. Planning is of the strategic, long-range variety.
2. Organizing is done at the general level for the organization as a whole.
3. Staffing activities deal with upper-level, key people.
4. Directing and controlling have a long-range focus.

On the other hand, the practice of these functions at the lower, operational level illustrates that:

1. Planning is a short-range activity.
2. Organizing is focused on the department or unit level.
3. Staffing is concerned with workers and other important people.
4. Directing and controlling become day-to-day supervision.

As the nature of the function changes from level to level, the nature of the information system to support that function must change as well. Some functions are best supported by traditional MISs, while others receive better support from the newer DSSs. A discussion of each follows.

Management Information Systems (MISs)

A definition for a management information system can be constructed by looking at the definitions of each of the three words which comprise the phrase. *Management* has been defined as "the planning, organizing, directing, staffing, and controlling of an organization." *Information* has been previously defined as "processed data relevant to a particular decision-making situation." A *system* was defined, in Chapter 10, as a collection of related components which work together to achieve a goal. A **management information system (MIS)** is, then, a collection of related components which work together to produce processed data relevant to the decision-making activities of those who engage in organizational planning, organizing, directing, staffing, and controlling.

MISs serve the informational needs of managers at all levels in an organization. The extent to which they have been successful in supporting the activities of managers, however, has been different at each level. Most successes have been achieved at the lower level, that of operating management. The activities of upper management are much more difficult to support through the use of computer systems.

Transaction Processing Systems

Most information processing systems are dependent upon the aggregation of data generated during the completion of the organization's basic activities, which we have called transactions. For example, in a retail business, where one of the basic transactions is the selling of goods to customers, a transaction processing system would record the item sold, the quantity sold, the salesperson doing the selling, the selling price, the conditions of sale (cash or credit), and perhaps the customer's name. These data are used, as illustrated in Figure 16–2, to generate information to support the activities of sales analysis, accounts receivable, inventory control, and, eventually, the profit and loss statement.

For another example, consider the reserving of a campsite at a state campground. The act of making the reservation is itself the transaction, and a transaction processing system for this application would collect, store, and process the reserver's name, address, camping date, campsite, and campground. These data would be used later to compute statistics of use, vacancy rates, and the level of tourist activities for the state.

Transaction processing systems collect and store data to support nearly all managerial activities. They also generate electronic and hard copy records to verify that the transaction has taken place. For example, in the retail example above, a sales receipt would have been generated in addition to the entries which would have been made in the electronic files for retail sales. In the example of the campground reservation system, a notice of

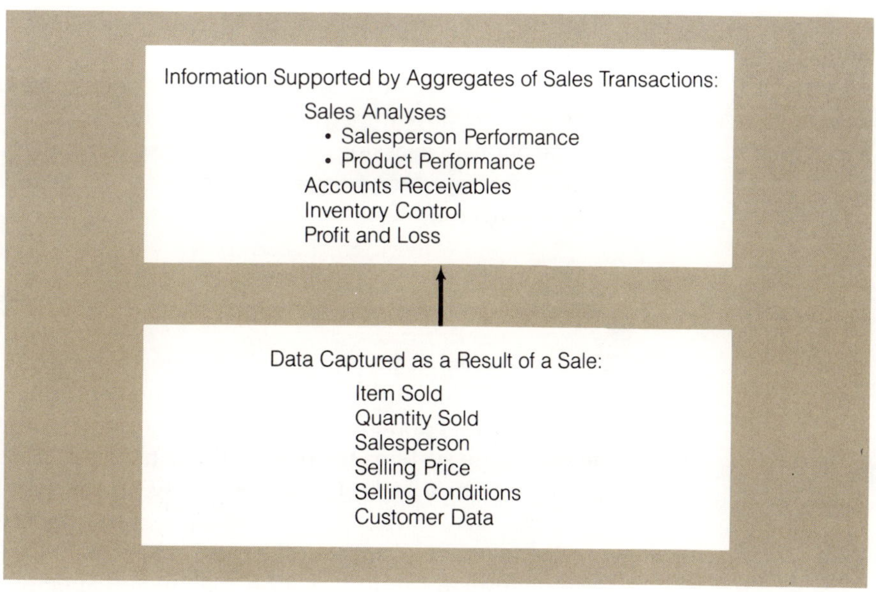

Figure 16–2 Information Collected by a Transaction Processing System Supports Management Decision Making

confirmation would have been mailed to the person making the reservation.

Thus, transaction processing systems serve two different functions. First, they provide tangible evidence of the completion of a transaction. Second, they collect data needed by the managerial systems to be described next.

Managerial Systems

The systems which support the middle level of management differ in some ways from the transaction processing systems just described. For one thing, managerial systems typically deal with the longer-range activities of managers. For another, these systems usually provide summary information and analysis to support the planning, directing, and controlling activities of middle managers. Perhaps an example will help make the distinction.

Consider the job of a manufacturing manager making, say, soap. In trying to schedule production for the coming week, the manager needs to know several important pieces of information. The most helpful piece would, of course, be a listing of the number of cases of each brand which will be ordered by the company's customers next week. Unfortunately, this information is not available in advance, when the manager must decide, so a forecast must be used as an estimate of next week's purchases. Most forecasting methods use historical data to predict future demand. Therefore, data collected by a sales transaction processing system would provide historical data for the forecasting system.

To schedule production effectively, the manager must also find out how many cases of each brand are included in the current inventory. Another transaction processing system, which processes orders received, shipments made, and receipts from producing departments, should provide the necessary inventory information. The manager must then integrate the forecast with the status of inventory information and combine that with other information about the availability of raw materials, equipment, and personnel in order to be able to generate a production schedule for the coming week. The manager uses a managerial data processing system to assist in the integration of this information.

Managers also utilize systems to review costs, quality, manufacturing efficiencies, downtime, and productivity. Most of these systems rely on transaction processing systems for their supporting data. Many different types of computerized systems are in use today to support the activities at the managerial level.

Strategic Planning Systems

The managers at the upper level in most organizations devote a significant amount of their time to the development of long-range plans for the organization. In general, data processing experts have been less successful in designing systems to support the activities at this level. This shortcoming is not due to a lack of effort or ability on the part of the data processing professionals; rather, it is due to the nature of long-range planning itself.

For instance, transaction processing systems and systems at the managerial level are much easier to define and specify than are the systems to support upper-level activities. The extra difficulty is due to the differences in managerial function at the various levels, which were discussed earlier.

In addition, managers at the upper level deal with longer-range activities, for which uncertainty is greater and problem specification is more difficult. For these reasons the successful design of data processing systems in support of managers at the upper levels has been a most difficult task. Some successes have been achieved through the use of DSSs, discussed next.

Challenge Update

The reader should now be able to consult with Mr. Sterling to develop an understanding of the use of MISs in transaction processing, managerial control, and strategic planning.

Decision Support Systems (DSSs)

For the purposes of this text, decision support systems will be treated as a special class of MIS. Their defining characteristics will be discussed first, followed by a few examples of their use.

Defining Characteristics of DSSs

Decision support systems (DSSs) have two essential characteristics: (1) they must be interactive, and (2) they must deal with semistructured problems. Both characteristics need further discussion.

In an earlier chapter, three different data processing modes were described: batch, remote batch, and interactive. DSSs are interactive rather than batch or remote batch. Managers will interact with the system when making decisions. The interaction between the manager and the system, aided by DSS software, extends the capabilities of both the manager and the computer. The computing system contributes a large memory, a collection of computerized problem-solving techniques, and the ability to perform huge computational tasks in a short period of time. In addition, it rarely makes mistakes. DSS software incorporates these strengths into a problem-solving environment.

Managers, on the other hand, are not particularly good at any of these tasks. Managers do have curiosity, intuition, and experience in their repertoire. By taking advantage of the best capabilities of the manager, and combining them with the capabilities of the computer, a DSS brings about better decisions then either could accomplish unilaterally.

The type of problem addressed by DSSs is referred to as semistructured. While a rigorous definition of semistructured problems exists within the field of decision-making theory, it is necessary here only to provide some distinction between them and the two other classes of problems, structured and unstructured.

A structured problem is one wherein the problem solver knows the ends which are achievable and the means which are employable to achieve those ends. A structured problem is one for which there are known techniques which provide optimal solutions. For example, under certain conditions

Figure 16–3
Manager Using Interactive DSS

yields from chemical processing can be accomplished in optimal fashion through the use of mathematical techniques. An unstructured problem confronts the problem solver with no clearly distinguishable means/ends connections. Contract negotiations between labor and management are, for example, unstructured.

Semistructured problems are those which fall somewhere in-between. We know enough about the problem to provide some structure, but our knowledge is incomplete. A semistructured problem may, for example, have means and ends which are identifiable, but have connections between them which are uncertain.

Managers work interactively with DSSs to explore a problem and its possible solutions (see Figure 16–3). The managers are typically allowed to pose a series of "what if" questions and let the computing system demonstrate the consequences of each action. They can try numerous alternatives and select the one which, on the basis of the computations done, looks most promising.

DSSs are designed to integrate three basic resources: the manager's decision-making skills, the organization's data, and a set of management science models. Many different models may be built into the system's capability. Some problems will fit linear programming models, while more difficult mathematical programming techniques are required for others. A number of different types of forecasting models are available for use in problems which require that a forecast be made.

On the other hand, many problems do not have mathematical solutions. For these, computer simulation is used to gather evidence of the system's behavior. A computer **simulation** requires the writing of a computer program to capture the important entities and relationships of a system. The computer program is run to predict how the system will behave. Random events are built into the simulation through random number generators and probability distributions in order to achieve "realistic" representations of actual events.

A simulation program can be run a large number of times to generate statistics intended to help indicate how the system itself would run. It is an extremely useful technique for problems which are difficult or impossible to solve mathematically. For example, computer simulations are used to predict the effects of the meltdown of a nuclear reactor, submarine warfare, nuclear warfare, and other catastrophic events we hope never to experience in reality.

Computer simulations are also useful to predict population growth and determine the effects of timber management techniques on commercial timber stands. Simulation is used in these studies because life cycles are so long that real-life studies are difficult.

DSSs provide managers with powerful access to data, computing power, and modeling techniques. The manager makes use of a special-purpose, DSS language via a computer terminal to bring these resources together, as illustrated in Figure 16–4. Some examples will help the reader understand the types of decision-making support which can be achieved.

DSS Examples

Three example applications in which DSSs might be used will be discussed. The first example addresses the problem of scheduling production in a manufacturing plant, and the second describes planning activities within

Figure 16–4 A DSS Brings Together Data, Models, and Managers

a large bank. The third is a budgeting and enrollment application within a large university.

Manufacturing DSS. Production scheduling is a critical operation in most manufacturing plants, as in the soap manufacturing plant used in an earlier example. Grocery brokers order soap products from the manufacturer according to their beliefs about future sales. Future sales are influenced by the season, the state of the economy, advertising, and any promotional activities which may be underway. The demand experienced by the manufacturer is, therefore, not completely predictable. (Forecasting models in the DSS are used to predict demand.)

Production scheduling activities must take into account the expected demand, the quantity of finished soap products in the warehouse, and the availability of raw materials, personnel, and production facilities. Each production line can be dedicated to the production of only one product at a time, and changeovers are expensive, so extended runs are scheduled as long as shortages do not occur in the warehouse. (Linear programming models are useful in production scheduling activities.)

In order to make production scheduling decisions, a production manager will review the levels of inventory of each of the finished goods, ascertain the availability of resources, and predict the shipments which will be made next week in order to determine whether or not a particular product must be produced. If a DSS were available for this application, a manager would be able to use it in the following way.

Sitting at a terminal, the manager would review the current finished goods inventory levels stored in the perpetual inventory data base. A prediction model could be taken from the models available within the DSS, and expected shipments could be predicted for each product based upon prior shipment histories, promotions, and sales growth curves. The DSS could then highlight on the terminal's screen those products which appeared to be in need of production.

The manager could then call in a minimum-cost, mathematical model to produce a suggested schedule for the manager's review. Some events which have an impact on the schedule may be known to the manager but unknown to the computer. For example, such things as employee vacations or scheduled maintenance activities may make it difficult to produce according to the suggested schedule. In such cases, the manager may reject some part of the computer's schedule and ask it to calculate a new one.

The DSS integrates the computer's data and problem-solving techniques with the manager's expertise to generate solutions which are better than either could achieve alone.

Banking DSS. A second example comes from the banking industry. In the most simplistic terms, a bank attracts funds by offering a combination of interest paid for deposited funds and service to its customers. Funds are then loaned to other customers, who pay interest for the privilege of borrowing the money. The bank must loan money at rates of interest high enough to pay interest on customer deposits and finance bank operations. Fluctuating interest rates and the availability of both short- and long-term loans and deposits makes the problem an interesting one.

Bank managers need to predict the direction in which interest rates will move in the short term and in the long term in order to be able to decide whether to seek short-term loans, long-term loans, or no loans at all. Interest rates, however, are difficult to predict. They depend upon the relationship between the supply of and the demand for money, so they are dependent upon the overall performance of the economy itself.

A bank manager with access to a DSS could use it in the following ways:

1. A model of the economy, called an **econometric model,** could be used to predict interest rates.
2. A forecasting model could then be used to predict the future quantities of savings and demand deposits for the bank in much the same way as the soap shipments were predicted in the example above.
3. Other forecasting models could be used to predict demand for consumer, real estate, and commercial loans.

The bank manager would then use a mathematical model of the bank to predict the future financial condition of the bank. The DSS again allows the manager to make adjustments, and ask "what if" questions to examine other possible combinations. For example, the bank manager might ask:

- What if the rate of interest on savings increases?
- What if the rate of interest on long-term loans declines?
- What if people withdraw 10, 20, or even 50 percent of their savings?

The strengths of the computer and the strengths of the manager are combined by the DSS to improve the manager's ability to make the necessary decisions.

University DSS. As a final example, consider the problems faced by colleges and universities in scheduling classes. If administrators knew in advance which students were going to attend the university, which classes they were going to take, and which faculty members would be available for teaching, the class scheduling problem would be relatively easy. Since this information is not known to administrators, the class scheduling problem is made more difficult. Once the schedule of classes is fixed, the assignment of students to them is a fairly routine computer application. The determination of the schedule itself is another matter.

A university administrator who had access to a DSS might be able to predict enrollments using forecasting models like those previously mentioned and integrate that information with the output from another forecasting model, which predicts the classes students will decide to take. A mathematical model of the university could then compute the faculty and classroom resources which are needed to meet those demands. This information could then be combined with budget information in order to arrive at a schedule which meets the students' needs within the constraints imposed by availability of faculty, classrooms, and money.

The DSS model of the university could then be used to explore the effects of adding sections, cancelling sections, adding students, and reducing faculty. The enormous data manipulating ability of the computer would be used in conjunction with mathematical analysis and the intuition of university administrators to provide an effective schedule.

These three are but a few of the many examples of ways in which decision support systems can be useful in supporting managers. As the uses of such computerized systems increase, the impact upon management will become greater. The next section discusses some of the implications to management of the increased use of computers in organizations.

Challenge Update

Mr. Sterling and the reader should now be able to explain the class of problems for which DSSs are applicable.

Implications to Management

Without doubt, computers have changed what managers do and how they do it. Computer advocates have predicted for years that the manager of the future will have a terminal on his or her desk. The popularity of personal computers makes that prediction now seem more likely. A manager's job will change in interesting ways, and that is the subject of this section of the chapter.

Distributed Processing and Communications

The two areas of computing which seem to have the greatest potential for impact on the nature of managerial work are distributed processing and communications. Greatly improved communications systems will mean that managers can communicate more effectively with colleagues and fellow managers anywhere in the world. Portable—perhaps even hand-held—computers, as shown in Figure 16–5, will give managers access to the organization's data processing system from virtually any place that has telephone service. New capabilities such as voice-store-and-forward (the storing of voice messages), facsimile transmission (the sending of copies of documents electronically), and electronic mail (computer-aided messages) will also extend the abilities of the manager. These are discussed in the next chapter.

Computing power itself is being distributed throughout organizations as hardware becomes better and cheaper and as communications capabilities improve. The distributed processing capability which results provides the manager simultaneously with both increased control over the resources necessary to the job of managing and yet another area of expertise to master. Distributed processing places computing power and the additional burden of managing it in the hands of users. If users and managers can respond favorably to the challenge, organizational units of increased efficiency and effectiveness should result.

The issues surrounding distributed processing are very complex. On one hand, users see the acquisition of computing power as freedom from the frustrations of dealing with a centralized data processing authority. Data

Computers in Action 7

Meeting the Challenge

1. Mr. Sterling works hard to understand how to make effective use of a portable computer system in order to set a good example for other employees of the State Highway System. **2.** Office workers within the State Highway Department adapt easily to their new word processors. **3.** The visual display provides a convenient mechanism to proofread and edit work done on a word processor.

1

3

2

4

5

6

4. Many managers within the State Highway Department have found that spreadsheet software on a desktop computer is a productive combination. **5.** A portable data recorder makes many information gathering tasks at a construction site much easier. **6.** Mr. Sterling expects the offices of the State Highway Department to become very modern in appearance as well as in fact.

7. Telecommunications networks will allow some workers to work at home. **8.** Employees in Mr. Sterling's department are eager to accept the challenge of computing and can regularly be found after hours helping each other learn the intricacies of computer work. **9.** Mr. Sterling's executive assistant makes effective use of a portable personal computer while travelling between the Highway Department offices and the Governor's office.

7

8

9

10

11

10. Even as new Highway Department facilities are being constructed, an eager engineer works on his personal computer to keep abreast of other projects.
11. Highway Department engineers working at remote locations will be able to send data to the main office via telephone connections. **12.** Other state agencies are also working to improve their performance ratings through the utilization of computers. Here, for example, is a state agricultural extension agent who can make effective use of a portable personal computer while visiting some neighborhood hogs.

12

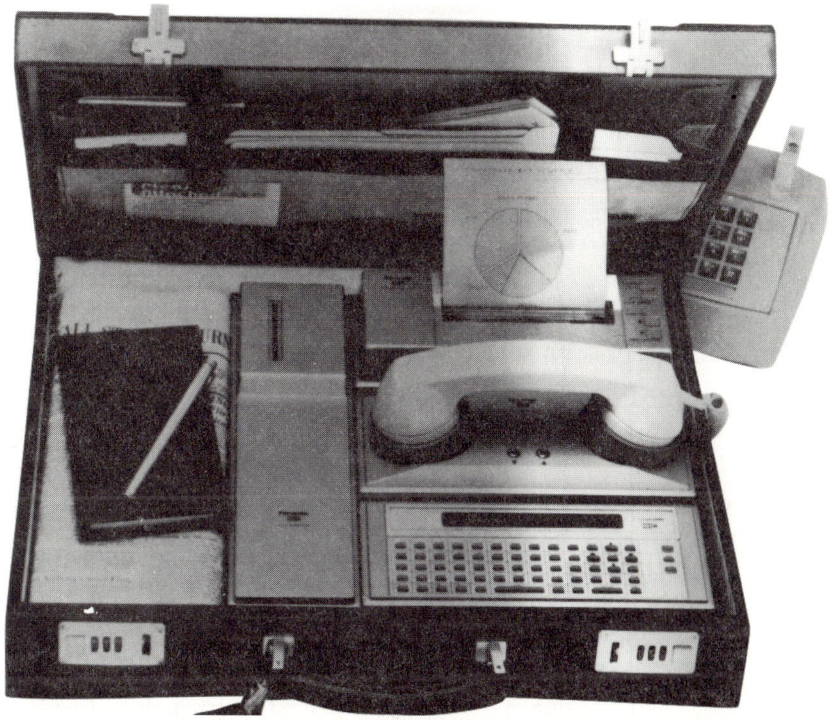

Figure 16–5 Handheld Computer System

processing managers, on the other hand, visualize the decentralization of computing devices as the path to chaos and duplication of effort.

Proponents of centralization argue for increased control, economies of scale, and efficiency. Proponents of decentralization argue for the flexibility of local control, faster turnaround, and greater effectiveness. The extent to which computing resources will be distributed depends upon many things, including the organization's overall philosophy of management.

It appears that the overall trend is toward greater distribution of computing power. Managers must, therefore, develop an ability to manage the data processing functions in branch offices and other distributed centers. Selection, training, and supervision of data processing professionals will then be added to the unit manager's responsibilities. In addition, the issues of data security, system security, standards, and coordination with the central facility become more important. The manager's role in hardware acquisitions, software development, and the professional development of data processing personnel will increase significantly.

All of these issues must be addressed in a distributed environment. Distributed processing offers managers solutions to many of their data processing problems. Unfortunately, the solutions bring new problems as well.

Technological Enhancement of Managerial Work

Two important issues surround the topic of automation with respect to managerial work. The first is: will managers be replaced by computers? The

"they'll never replace Thorndike, there, with a computer . . . because nobody knows what he does."

answer seems to be "no." The second is: will the productivity of managers be improved by computers? The answer to the second seems to be "possibly"; the productivity of some managers might be improved through the use of computers. Upon what considerations are these answers based?

One of the computer's principal strengths is its ability to accurately perform routine tasks at a high rate of speed. These characteristics, however, are not often found in managerial tasks. Managers spend most of their time meeting with the people who work for them, with the people for whom they work, and with other managers. Since a large part of their work depends upon interactions with other people, the likelihood that they will be totally replaced by computers is slight.

Computers are, however, probably responsible for a slight reduction in the number of managers at the middle management level. Citibank, for example, was able to reduce the number of its middle managers by approximately 10 percent by reorganizing and distributing its data processing operations.

The extent to which managers interact with a computerized information system depends upon the level in the organization at which they work. Upper-level managers interact more with other managers and less with computerized information systems than do managers at the lower levels.

Some enhancement of managerial work through technical means has, of course, occurred. For the most part, the tasks which have been technologically enhanced have been those in support functions. For example, we find technologically enhanced production scheduling systems, office procedures, telecommunications, and, to some extent, conferences. Two, somewhat similar efforts, for example, are underway to improve managerial conferences.

The first, **teleconferencing,** allows managers to meet via television. Managers at different geographical locations attend a teleconference by visiting a local conference facility which has television transmitting and receiving capabilities. Via color television they can see and hear the other participants, who can also see and hear them.

Teleconferencing facilities may include systems for transmitting documents and visual aids. Teleconferencing is an attractive alternative to assembling a group of managers from different geographical areas, because travel time and travel expenses are eliminated. Meeting through the medium of television is, however, somewhat less effective than normal, face-to-face meetings.

The other attempt to enhance meetings uses a facility known popularly as a "**war room**" because it resembles the rooms used by the military for directing military activities in time of war. Some corporations have installed "war rooms" which include very sophisticated graphics and communications systems. In these rooms, computer graphics terminals and large, rear-projection screens provide upper-level managers with the ability to review large volumes of conveniently displayed information. Although the high cost of such facilities will keep them from becoming commonplace, a number of large corporations already make use of "war rooms".

Managerial Competence

There are indications that a very subtle change is taking place in management as a result of improved information processing. Managers who rely mostly on "experience," "intuition," and "professional judgment" may find that those attributes are no longer sufficient. Improved information processing will provide better information by which to judge the performance of managers at all levels in the organization. These tools may threaten the existence of managers with inadequate skills.

Managers will not only be more visible in the arena in which they work, but the skills necessary to manage effectively will change—in fact, are changing. The increased use of MISs means that managers at the very least will have to be able to study computer-generated information and extract the appropriate meaning. Distributed processing will mean that managers will have to be effective participants in system development activities. The distribution of data processing personnel will mean that managers will have to supervise these specialists in addition to the other specialists in the decentralized units. DSSs will go even further and require that managers actually interact with computerized systems.

Executive Workstations

Many managers will use desktop microcomputers to interact with DSS software. The microcomputers in this case are called **executive workstations.** They bring exciting new capabilities to the manager's fingertips.

In the first place, executive workstations are full-functioned, stand-alone computers in their own right. Their software enables a manager to compose

"The computer is only a tool. There will always be a place for unbridled avarice."

text, perform analyses, send and receive messages, maintain files, generate reports, keep an appointments calendar, and graphically display important information.

Secondly, the executive workstation can work as an intelligent terminal to provide access to the corporate data center. Managers using them can extract data from corporate sources and bring it into the workstation's memory, where it can be included in the text of a report or letter, used for analysis, or displayed graphically.

Although early versions of many home computers found uses in the office, by 1984 the market seemed dominated by the IBM Personal Computer. Two versions of the IBM machine, the XT/370 and the PC 3270, provide compatibility with IBM mainframe products—the 370 series of mainframes and the 3270 terminal, respectively. They offer interesting capabilities to a user who must connect a desktop microcomputer to a mainframe computing system.

Though the technology was basically in place by the end of 1983, extensive use of workstations by executives was not common. Although some technical problems with microcomputer networks and mainframe-to-microcomputer linkages remained, there was also resistance on the part of many managers to becoming keyboard users. Apple Computer's Lisa and MacIntosh, for example, were designed specifically to make it easier for users to interact with the system.

Although the full impact of executive workstations will not be known for some time, large numbers of managers are using them. As the technology improves, and as new generations of managers graduate from programs where computer utilization is high, the use of executive workstations should increase.

The Workstation at Home

A personal computer equipped with communications capability becomes an intelligent terminal (see Figure 16–6) which a manager or other professional worker can use to work at home, providing that is acceptable to the employer. Work generated at home can be transferred electronically to the office if the two systems are compatible. Journalists, technical writers, programmers, and others may find that working at home gives their productivity a boost.

There are other advantages to working at home. For example, travel time and travel costs are reduced since fewer trips to the office are required. Creative work usually requires long periods of uninterrupted concentration,

Figure 16–6 A Home Workstation

something rarely possible in the typical office environment. A home workstation may provide the creative worker with the tools to support his or her creative efforts at any hour of the day or night. Workers with obligations to care for children or senior family members unable to care for themselves can perhaps manage to work at home without having to hire outside help.

There are some disadvantages, of course. Communications costs for the link between the home and the office computers could be expensive, and the stimulus of working with other professionals could be reduced if one were to work exclusively at home. A proper mix of at-home and at-the-office work experiences could be quite beneficial to productivity and to morale.

Control Data Corporation has been using a system called Homework since 1978 to allow employees to work at home. One of the advantages they have experienced is a reduction in the time employees are not able to work due to medical leave. Many employees have been able to work productively from their homes when otherwise unable to travel to and from the office.

The uses to which personal computers can be put in the home are many and varied. Professional workstations, home management centers, educational tools, and entertainment centers can all be implemented on a microcomputer base.

Computers have, in many cases, caused the manager's job to become more complex, although in others, computers have provided the analytical power to ease a difficult task. Factories and offices, to be discussed in the next chapter, have been greatly changed by the computer, which will, in turn increase the level of complexity with which managers must deal.

Challenge Update

Mr. Sterling, his staff, and the reader should now be able to discuss the implications that a computerized MIS might have to the management of the State Highway Department.

Additional complications arise when security is considered. Computers, though neutral in themselves, have caused the nature of these threats to change significantly.

Security. Security is a sensitive area. Managers of most organizations would be reluctant to admit that their organization had unresolved security problems, but few managers have taken an active enough stance with respect to the problem to be considered experts on the matter. Security has, for the most part, been left to the data processing professionals.

One has only to be a regular reader of the popular press to understand that security problems do exist. Beyond that, they exist to such an extent that managerial attention is required. All managers must share the burden of developing secure systems, it is not just a data processing problem.

The previous chapter examined the problems of software piracy and intrusion by unauthorized users. In this chapter we will consider four other areas: fraud, theft, sabotage, and espionage.

Fraud. *Fraud* is the deceitful conversion of someone else's resources for personal gain. For example, unauthorized use of a computer, changing the credit histories in the data base of a credit bureau, and arranging a loan under false pretenses are all fraudulent acts. There are far too many examples of fraud in data processing operations. A 1984 study in the banking and insurance industry revealed two major fraudulent acts in every 100 companies.[2] Perpetrators were from all areas of company operations, indicating the extent to which management must deal with these activities. Computerized data processing systems have several characteristics which make the organizations which use them more vulnerable to such acts.

In the first place, transaction processing which takes place within a computer system does not take place in full view, as the transaction might in a manual system. As a result, it is more difficult to see the fraudulent act. Secondly, many computerized transaction processing systems do not leave an adequate audit trail, so fraudulent acts are more difficult to detect.

In addition, the large volume of transactions handled by most systems makes it more difficult to find those that are improperly done. One fraudulent transaction hiding among millions of honest transactions will be more difficult to find than one hiding among hundreds. Finally, the ease of remote access via the telephone system, which means that people can engage in fraudulent acts without being anywhere near the organization's premises, makes it more difficult to catch the criminal.

Many different frauds have been perpetrated through improper use of computer systems. People within the data processing department have been caught in the act of issuing illegal checks, causing improper deposits, shipping unauthorized goods, and otherwise converting their employer's resources to their own use. One scheme, carried out by an employee of a credit bureau, involved changing (for a fee) the credit ratings of people who had poor ones. With improved credit ratings, these people were able to get loans otherwise unavailable to them.

One of the biggest frauds involved the management personnel of a large life insurance company. To improve their cash position, many insurance companies sell their previously-issued policies to re-insurance companies. The officials of one insurance company decided that the computer could be used to fabricate false policies, which could then be sold to the reinsurer. The fraud was eventually reported to authorities by a disgruntled ex-employee.

Most fraudulent acts against organizations are carried out by employees or ex-employees. They sometimes have the knowledge, the access, and the motivation to perpetrate fraud. Managers must employ separation of duties for data processing personnel, effective control procedures, and frequent audits to protect against fraud. Duties of the various data processing professionals are separated to reduce access to a complete set of tools to perpetrate fraud. Control procedures are designed to prevent it, and audits are necessary to discover it.

Theft. *Theft* is the unlawful taking of someone else's property. Computer theft occurs when someone steals programs or computing time or uses the computer system to steal other property. Computer systems have been

2. Peter Bartolik, "Study Points to DP Fraud at Banks, Insurers," *Computerworld,* May 28, 1984, pp. 1–4.

known to aid theft either by making it possible or by concealing the fact that a theft has taken place.

The modern banking system is built on a computer-controlled network of electronic funds transfers. One of the biggest thefts in history was accomplished from a pay telephone in the lobby of the bank from which the funds were stolen. A man, with inside knowledge of the bank's computer codes, was able to enter information into the system which caused the transfer of over $10 million to accounts controlled by him personally.

One method employed by the banking system and others to prevent illegal access to funds transfers and other sensitive information is to use data **encryption,** the use of secret encoding schemes to make the data unintelligible unless the decoding scheme is known.

Another type of theft is illustrated by a recent case where the thief was able to penetrate the order entry system of the telephone company's equipment manufacturing subsidiary. He caused millions of dollars of telephone equipment to be delivered to his warehouses. This equipment was then sold and shipped back to the telephone company. The thief caused bogus purchase orders to be issued within the telephone company's own computerized ordering system.

Numerous thefts of computer time have occurred as unauthorized users were able to penetrate an organization's computing system from a remote terminal via a communications hookup. Computer software has also been stolen in this manner. The possibility of theft is greatly increased when remote access to a computing center is possible. One of the first lines of defense is to keep the computer's phone number a closely guarded secret, but, of course, much more is necessary.

Computer system security begins with the operating system, which has the responsibility for monitoring access to all the system's resources. Threats to the system's security may be intended or unintended. Physical access must be restricted, potential threats must be monitored and logs maintained to detect breaches.

Sabotage. *Sabotage* is the destruction of someone else's property, and sabotage with respect to computing systems usually refers to the destruction of programs or data. Sabotage can be directed against the computer system hardware, but such occasions are less likely. Hardware abuse does, however, occur.

The circumstances surrounding acts of sabotage are similar to those which contribute to fraud and theft. The saboteur is most often an unhappy employee or ex-employee. Remote access to the system increases the threat. In one case involving a state civil servant, an employee who had been given notice of his impending termination destroyed large sections of the files maintained by the department of motor vehicles. In another, a programmer who had just been fired made a series of changes in programs he had written as an employee, which caused the programs to be inoperable.

Protections against sabotage are similar to those against fraud and theft. Protection of remote terminals from unauthorized use, secret telephone numbers, passwords (which must sometimes be changed after an employee termination), and file access logs will all help prevent system abuse. Terminated employees are more frequently given severance pay in lieu of two weeks' notice to reduce their opportunity to engage in disruptive acts.

It makes sense for an employer to carefully screen those potential employees who will have the opportunity to commit acts of fraud, theft, and sabotage. (Yes, that's practically everybody.) Careful interviewing procedures and a thorough checking of references from previous employment are important. Adequate training vis-à-vis security procedures is also important.

Espionage. *Espionage,* the theft of secrets, is an act more frequently associated with foreign governments than with data processing, but it does occur in data processing. Trade secrets, pricing information, customer lists, and product information are all likely candidates for espionage efforts.

In 1982, several employees of computer manufacturing companies in another country were apprehended while allegedly stealing computer design secrets from IBM. Court proceedings later indicated the illegal activities had, in fact, taken place.

Software can also be the target of espionage activities. A data base management software vendor has claimed in its advertisements that a foreign power offered a spy $500,000 for theft of its DBMS software. At the time, sales of that particular type of software were prohibited in the interest of national security.

Some espionage efforts seem to be the result of efforts of devoted computer fans, known as hackers, to test their cleverness at breaching the system's security. Many computing systems contain a large amount of sensitive data, which some people seem to view as temptation.

Again, restricted access, passwords, secret telephone numbers, and access logs will help reduce an organization's vulnerability to acts of espionage. Managers who use sensitive, computer-based information must make sure that the system provides an adequate level of protection before using it.

Challenge Update

The reader should now be able to discuss with Mr. Sterling the threat to security posed by computerized information processing systems.

Ethics

Ethics are the rules which attempt to control behavior by identifying certain behaviors as "good" or "bad." Ethics condition behavior in order to make society more tolerable to its citizens. An appropriate response to the increase in acts of fraud, theft, sabotage, and espionage discussed above would be an increased emphasis on ethical behavior.

Managers would be well advised to seek additional training in ethics, just as students in professional schools would be well advised to include courses in ethics in their studies. Professional organizations usually provide short courses in ethical issues of their professions, and the same is true of data processing organizations. Roundtables, seminars, and workshops which cover ethical issues are common.

Employees must be made aware of the ethical implications of their behavior. Unethical acts should not be condoned. Management has the responsibility for setting the tone after which other employees can pattern their own behavior. Unethical behavior at the top of an organization will stimulate the same behavior throughout.

Newest Developments

New theories of management will continue to evolve. Theory Z is not, in fact, the last word we can expect on the subject.

Increasingly capable microcomputers will take on an even more significant role in support of managerial activities. As communications capabilities and micro-mainframe links are improved, the range of support activities for which microcomputers are useful will broaden. Other important developments in computing have led to expert systems, which offer a great deal of promise. They may eventually have great impact on the art (or science) of management.

An **expert system** is a system which combines knowledge, computing power, and a human problem-solver to apply their synergistic (the whole is greater than the sum of the parts) strengths to the solving of problems requiring a specific expertise. An expert system is built to combine facts with rules of inference and search so that the human user of the system is able to generate the solutions which could be expected of an expert in the field. For example, doctors could use an expert system to support their medical diagnoses, attaining diagnostic capabilities far beyond their own individual skills. Such an expert system, available to a network of remote terminals, could greatly enhance the medical diagnostic capabilities of small or understaffed medical facilities across the country, even around the world.

Expert systems first emerged in the mid-1970s. Early systems included DENDRAL, to generate possible molecular structure of unknown chemical compounds, and MYCIN, to diagnose and treat infectious blood diseases.[3] Other expert systems provide problem-solving expertise in legal reasoning, geological exploration, computer system configurations, and analysis of military situations.

Expert systems can be used to enhance planning and other managerial skills to supplement a manager's efforts. They can be used to train new managers, reducing training time and the costs associated with assigning an expert manager to conduct training.

Expert system software, which provides a framework within which an expert system can be built, is also available. A microcomputer package, Expert-Ease, introduced to the market in 1984 by Expert Systems, Inc., provides such an environment. The user needs only to add knowledge about a particular subject and inference rules to build an expert system in any area of expertise.

Knowledge is added in a convenient way, by providing examples. The system uses the examples to build a network of facts. In effect, the system builds a decision tree which can be applied later by the user to make decisions consistent with the earlier examples. Any inconsistencies in the

3. Frederick Hayes-Roth, Donald A. Waterman, and Douglas B. Lenat, *Building Expert Systems* (Reading, MA: Addison-Wesley, 1983), pp. 8–11.

examples are brought to the user's attention, as are any branches of the decision tree which are incomplete.

Once the examples are entered, the user can ask the system to either (1) display the decision rule inferred by the examples or (2) execute the query system to generate decisions. Expert-Ease is very flexible and extremely easy to use. With it, users can build expert systems to perform medical diagnostics, allocation of orders to warehouses, class scheduling, and a whole host of other decision-making tasks. We will undoubtedly see more systems of this type and an increased level of use of expert systems in general.

COMPUTING CHALLENGE: *A Final Note*

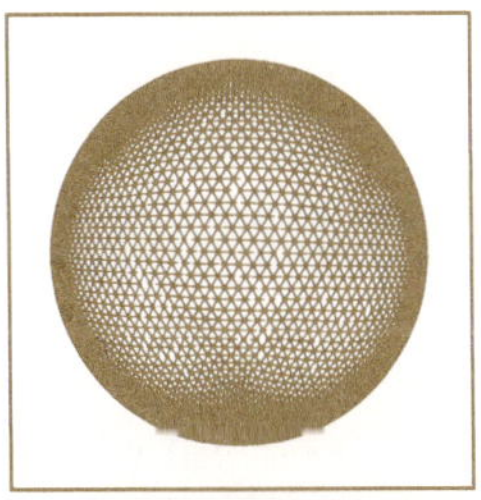

A brief review of the situation in which Mr. Sterling, the Director of the State Highway Department, finds himself is typical of a manager whose skills have not kept pace with the technology of management. His alternatives are relatively easy to identify. He can (1) take early retirement and avoid having to deal with the new technologies, (2) remain in his position and oppose the introduction of new technologies into the Highway Department, or (3) undertake to bring his skills up-to-date and motivate his subordinates to do the same.

Assume that he accepts the greatest challenge and chooses the third option. He should, as soon as possible, seek training for himself and his staff in the use of computers in management. He should make sure that users and managers alike are given the necessary training to enable them to effectively use the new systems. His own personal level of enthusiasm will establish a standard by which others in the department will judge their own efforts. A lack of enthusiasm on his part would quickly be detected by others in the organization, and the entire effort would fail.

He should, of course, understand that his own commitment and enthusiasm may not be enough for everyone. He should be sensitive to others' perceptions of the impact the new era will have on their working lives. As a manager he is obligated to pursue the best interests of the organization. As a person he must do all he can to help others make the necessary adjustment.

Mr. Sterling should be an active participant in the design and development of any new systems. His active participation will enhance his knowledge of the system and improve the system's quality. He must also ensure that adequate protection against fraud, theft, sabotage, and espionage is provided. Attention to ethical issues is also of vital importance. Here, again, the example he sets is critical.

SUMMARY

- The functions of management are planning, organizing, staffing, directing, and controlling.

- The nature of managerial functions differs according to the level within the organization at which they are being performed.
- Upper-level managers engage in the solving of unstructured problems with a long time horizon, while lower-level managers deal more with structured and semistructured problem solving of shorter time horizons. Computer-based support has, to date, been found to be more useful with structured and semi-structured activities.
- The use of computers in organizations is changing the nature of the work of those who manage.
- Transaction processing systems have automated the handling of many of an organization's transactions and provided data with which systems at other managerial levels work.
- While management information systems (MISs) provide managers with access to more information than ever before, decision support systems (DSSs) offer a new level of integration of the skills of managers and the capabilities of computers.
- Managers must actively participate in the design of both MISs and DSSs in order for the design to be as good as possible.
- Distributed processing and communications system improvements place additional demands on the managers of modern organizations, which means that managers in the future must be more knowledgeable about computers and more skilled in the supervision of data processing professionals.
- Computers are unlikely to replace many managerial functions but rather will be used to supplement the manager's abilities.
- An executive workstation can provide an interesting array of capabilities to a manager, allowing a manager to accomplish a number of independent data processing tasks or access a large host computing system.
- For social and political reasons, the actual use of systems such as executive workstations lags somewhat behind their availability.
- The increased use of computing systems, especially those with remote access, has caused security problems to increase.
- Stringent controls, improved selection of personnel, greater security, better training, and thorough audits must be combined with more emphasis on ethical behavior to limit abuses to computer systems, their programs, and their data.
- Expert systems combine knowledge, computing power, and people to provide expertise which can be broadly distributed.

CASE: Computer Manages Marriott Assets

Companies are formed to bring together the assets (resources) necessary to offer a product or service to the market. Some of a company's assets are *fixed,* that is, they do not change very quickly (or easily) with time. Fixed assets usually include land, buildings, plants, and productive equipment. These assets, except for land, are gradually consumed by the production process, that is, they eventually depreciate (wear out). Federal tax laws allow companies to consider this depreciation as a business expense.

Tax laws change from time to time to allow different mechanisms of depreciation, accelerated schemes for charging depreciation to expense, and even credits against taxes for some types of investment (to encourage investment). Companies, as a result, must keep up with the tax laws in order to manage their fixed assets to produce the greatest economic benefit. Fixed asset management is, therefore, a complex but important process.

The Marriott Corporation is well known for its chain of hotels. Few people know, however, that half of Marriott's revenue comes from other companies in the corporation that do not provide lodging. For example, Marriott owns a group of restaurants, including the Roy Rogers chain, Farrell's ice cream parlours, Big Bit Coffee Shops, and Hot Shoppe cafeterias and restaurants. Marriott is also active in airline in-flight kitchens and cafeteria operations for businesses, educational institutions, and health care organizations. There are Marriott airline terminal restaurants and gift shops; the corporation owns the Great America theme parks near Chicago and has an interest in Sun Line Ships cruise company. This diversification has resulted in a great accumulation of fixed assets such as land, buildings, and capital equipment.

Marriott makes extensive use of a computer system to manage its extremely large number of fixed assets. These assets are depreciated, for tax purposes, under federal guidelines. Asset managers must also consider the investment tax credit, proper utilization of assets' depreciable lives, acquisition of new assets, and disposal of assets still possessing book value.

Marriott's computer system maintains a comprehensive fixed asset data base. In it is stored information such as the asset's location, name of its vendor, its acquisition date, purchase order number, and all the appropriate accounting data. The system calculates depreciation and determines the tax advantages of each of several different depreciation methods.

The new system has changed the roles of financial and accounting managers within Marriott. The new tools allow better asset management and tax planning.

"Fixed Asset Package Helps Hotel Meet Tax Regulation," *Infosystems,* July 1981, p. 104. Reprinted from INFOSYSTEMS July 1981.

Questions for the Case

1. Does asset management at Marriott seem to be structured or unstructured, according to the definitions of this chapter?
2. Does the new system require the financial managers to know more or less about taxes and depreciation?
3. Would this area (asset management) seem like a good candidate for an expert system? Why or why not?

DISCUSSION QUESTIONS AND EXERCISES

1. Explain the functions of management and give examples of each.
2. Discuss how the functions of management change with the level of management.

3. Explain the role of transaction processing systems in support of management information systems.
4. Compare and contrast MISs and DSSs.
5. Why are MISs much more successful at the lower levels of an organization than at the upper levels?
6. Explain fraud, theft, sabotage, and espionage and discuss how computer systems make an organization more vulnerable to such acts.
7. In what ways will distributed processing and communications systems change the role of the manager?
8. Why has the computer not replaced the manager to a greater degree? Hint: What do managers do that computers cannot do well?
9. What factors encourage the use of executive workstations? What factors slow down their rate of acceptance?
10. Imagine and then describe a DSS which might be useful to students in the registration process.
11. Review the definition of a well-structured problem. Give examples of well-structured problems. Is "management" likely to be a well-structured activity?
12. In what ways will a workstation at home be advantageous to the worker? To the company? Disadvantageous to either?
13. Imagine and then describe an expert system that might be useful in a university. In a business.
14. Give examples of problems for which simulation might be an attractive tool and explain, for each example, why simulation might be good for that problem.

ADDITIONAL READINGS

Ahituv, Niv, and Neumann, Seev. *Principles of Information Systems for Management.* Dubuque, IA: Wm. C. Brown, 1982.

Alter, Steven. *Decision Support Systems: Current Practices and Continuing Challenges.* Reading, MA: Addison-Wesley, 1980.

Argyris, Chris. "Management Information Systems: The Challenge to Rationality and Emotionality." *Management Science,* February 1971, pp. B-275–292.

Barr, Avron, and Feigenbaum, Edward A. *The Handbook of Artificial Intelligence.* Los Altos, CA: William Kaufman, 1982.

Bennett, John L. *Building Decision Support Systems.* Reading, MA: Addison-Wesley, 1983.

Blank, Hannah I. *Mastering Micros.* Princeton, NJ: Petrocelli Books, 1983.

Clowes, Kenneth W. *The Impact of Computers on Managers.* Ann Arbor, MI: UMI Research Press, 1982.

Connell, Stephen, and Galbraith, Ian A. White Plains, NY: Knowledge Industry Publications, 1982.

Goldberg, R., and Lorin, H., eds. *The Economics of Information Processing. Vol. 1: Management Perspectives.* New York: Wiley, 1982.

Goldstein, Bruce. "Computer Crime and Its Prevention." *Computer Security*, January 1983, pp. 63–66.

Hayes-Roth, Frederick; Waterman, Donald A.; and Lenat, Douglas B. *Building Expert Systems.* Reading, MA: Addison-Wesley, 1983.

Lucas, Henry C., Jr. *Information Systems Concepts for Management.* New York: McGraw-Hill, 1982.

Martin, James. *Design and Strategy for Distributed Data Processing.* Englewood Cliffs, NJ: Prentice-Hall, 1981.

Michie, Donald. *Introductory Readings in Expert Systems.* New York: Gordon and Breach Science Publishers, 1982.

Mintzberg, Henry. "The Manager's Job: Folklore and Fact." *Harvard Business Review*, July–August 1975, pp. 49–61.

Rochester, Jack B., ed. *Perspectives on Information Management.* New York: Wiley-Interscience, 1982.

Salerno, Lynn M. *Catching Up with the Computer Revolution.* New York: Wiley, 1983.

Sprague, Ralph H., Jr., and Carlson, Eric D. *Building Effective Decision Support Systems.* Englewood Cliffs, NJ: Prentice-Hall, 1982.

Stefic, Mark, et al., "The Organization of Expert Systems, A Tutorial." *Artificial Intelligence*, March, 1982, pp. 135–173.

Synnott, William R., and Gruber, William H. *Information Resource Management.* New York: Wiley-Interscience, 1981.

Weil, Ulric. *Information Systems in the 80s.* Englewood Cliffs, NJ: Prentice-Hall, 1982.

E
水
R
口
D
木
S
尸
X

17

Computers and the Work Environment

CHAPTER PREVIEW

Computers have very dramatically changed the environment within which work is done in most organizations. They are used to control individual machines or assembly lines in the factory and entire processes in some industries. Computer-controlled robots are becoming commonplace in work areas that were formerly the exclusive domain of human beings. At the same time, great strides in office worker productivity have been promised as microprocessors find their way into office machines. Already in use are microprocessor-controlled typewriters, copiers, facsimile transmitters, and filing systems.

The topics of this chapter are exciting ones. They relate directly to the means by which individual and organizational goals are achieved in the work environment. The new technologies offer opportunities for better working environments, more challenging work, and a greater degree of personal development.

First, we will discuss the use of computers in process and machine control. In both, computers are used to direct other machines in the accomplishment of routine, predictable work activities. In so doing, they release people from boring, repetitive tasks.

The second topic is the fascinating field of industrial robotics. Robots are gaining widespread acceptance in many industries. They allow workers to be relieved of tedious and dangerous work.

Next, we will examine the ongoing improvements in office equipment and review the capabilities provided by the new office hardware. Most workers in the United States are office workers. They became greater in number than blue-collar workers late in the decade of the 70s. Changes in the office will affect millions of people. To help direct our attention to the crucial issues, a computing challenge will be used.

COMPUTING CHALLENGE: *State Highway Department Revisited*

For this case we return to the State Highway Department for a follow-up visit with Winston Sterling, who is enthusiastically trying to help the governor improve the productivity of state agencies. In particular, he is trying to automate the office functions of the department. He was shocked to find that thirteen of the typists in the department still worked on manual typewriters. The most "state of the art" piece of equipment in the entire office was a magnetic card typewriter, almost a museum piece in itself.

Mr. Sterling has arranged a meeting of several interested parties to investigate means for bringing the office equipment and the skills of the office workers up-to-date. The governor, Ms. Mackell, has established a fund from which state agencies can draw to pursue projects which will improve the productivity of state workers. Mr. Sterling hopes to put together a proposal which will secure allocation of the first funds to be distributed from the governor's office for that purpose.

Attending the meeting are Mr. Larry Speisel, chairperson of the Governor's Commission on Productivity; Ms. Molly O'Donald, dean of the Business Department of the local community college; Mr. Bert Bonwell, president of Pro-Tem Employment Agency; and Ms. Betty Lockwood, office manager of the State Highway Department offices. All are expected to bring their personal expertise to bear on the following agenda for the meeting:

1. *Identify those items of office equipment which will bring about significant productivity improvements in the new office environment.*
2. *Construct job descriptions for new positions in the departmental office, and list the skills needed on the new jobs.*
3. *Inventory the current skills of people now working in the office.*
4. *List the skills identified as needed in item 2, but not currently available.*
5. *Discuss the opportunities for training and hiring to obtain the necessary skills.*

Mr. Sterling is a bit apprehensive as he considers taking on a large project so close to his retirement, but he is determined to bring his own skills and those of his co-workers up to a level sufficient to operate a modern department. Everyone seems eager to help.

This chapter presents an overview of the technologies currently making their way into the work environment. After careful study of this chapter, the reader should be able to:

1. *Describe the use of computers in machine control and process control.*
2. *Discuss the trends in industrial robotics and the impact those trends are expected to have on levels of employment.*
3. *List several microprocessor-controlled machines in the office environment, and describe the productivity improvements expected from each.*

HISTORICAL PERSPECTIVE

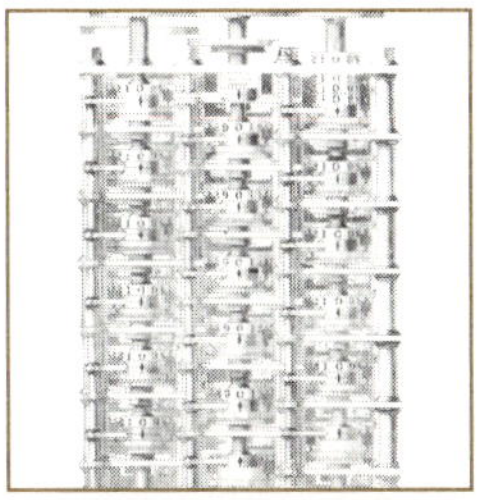

An interesting perspective of our industrial society can be gained from Alvin Toffler's view of the history of man presented in *Future Shock*.[1] He divides the span of human existence into lifetimes, of which there have been a total of 800. The first 650 of these lifetimes were spent in caves. Only in the latest six lifetimes have we had printing, and electric motors have only been around for two lifetimes. Computers appeared on the scene only one-half of a lifetime ago.

Indications are that the Chinese had developed the capability of printing as early as the ninth century, though Johann Guttenberg is credited with inventing the printing press in 1440. The industrial revolution began in the middle 1770s, and in 1784 automation came to the steam engine as James Watt invented the governor.

Typewriters were invented in 1867 by Christopher Sholes. Electric typewriters came on the scene in the 1940s, and the magnetic media typewriter appeared first in 1964.[2] The first video screen word processor appeared in 1969. In spite of the new technologies, approximately 10,000 manual typewriters were sold in 1984. Old machines, though obsolete by technological standards, somehow manage to retain considerable utility.

We turn now to the more modern machines, those that offer new and improved capabilities. We first turn our attention to the machines of the factory and then to the machines of the office.

Machine Control/Process Control

Although our primary concern in this text is with the use of computers to process transactions and support the decision-making activities of managers, computers do have significant other uses. Two of these uses are in the areas of machine control and process control. Computers have been used for many years in both areas.

Machine Control

The manufacturing processes of many products require that the products be milled, drilled, or turned on a lathe. These operations formerly required highly-skilled machinists performing complex operations on finely-tuned machines. Machinists worked from blueprints or engineering drawings to generate the machined parts necessary to sustain an industrialized economy. Each type of part typically required a different machine set-up and a different sequence of machining operations. As the economy grew, the need for highly-skilled machinists increased. Highly-skilled machinists were usually in short supply.

1. Alvin Toffler, *Future Shock* (New York: Random House, 1970), pp. 11–19.
2. Paula B. Cecil, *Office Automation* (Menlo Park, CA: Benjamin/Cummings, 1984), pp. 10–11.

The addition of computerized controls to the machines made it possible to operate them with semi-skilled operators. High quality work could then be produced even though highly-skilled machinists might not be available. Control of these machines is accomplished through numerical commands, so they are called **numerically controlled (N/C) machines** (see Figure 17–1). Semi-skilled workers, operating N/C machines, are capable of producing products of high quality at a faster rate and lower cost than was previously possible.

The earliest computer-controlled machines were capable of reading a series of numerical instructions punched into paper tape and executing the specified machining operations. More recently, machines were designed to read and execute instructions stored on magnetic tape. Microprocessors are now built into the control elements of the machines to determine and execute the necessary control instructions.

The initial cost of developing the machining program is expensive, so machine control has only been profitable in repetitive operations; but in that service their quality of work is impressive. They can even be programmed to make slight adjustments to compensate for the wear of the machine itself.

The number of highly-skilled machinists which would have been required to produce the number of machined parts used in today's industrialized economy would be staggering. N/C machines have undoubtedly resulted in a shift in the skills currently required in industry. Semi-skilled workers have been substituted for more highly skilled ones.

However, other skills are now required in jobs which formerly did not exist. For example, software engineers are needed to generate the programs necessary to control the machines. Technological advance changes the character and composition of the work force and the skills needed to be part of it.

Process Control

Many of the products we use on a daily basis have undergone chemical processing as their manufacturers prepared them for our use. Food products, for example, are weighed, mixed, screened, washed, filtered, and cooked as they are prepared. The accurate control of pressures, temperatures, and flow rates is important to the correct processing of food products. Thousands of other products are processed under similar circumstances.

Proper control of the important variables in a processing operation is essential to the production of a quality product within the bounds of an economic yield. In **process control,** computers are used to monitor the important variables and adjust pressures, temperatures, levels, and flows to maintain an effective and efficient manufacturing process. A process control computer is illustrated in Figure 17–2. It is an important application of computing power; one that has been with us for many years. It will undoubtedly increase in importance as more and more of our manufacturing processes become automated.

Consider, for example, the manufacture of soap products. Soap was formerly made in batches by cooking a mixture of animal fat and lye. The current soap-making process is a continuous one where fats and oils are

FIGURE 17–1
N/C Machine

FIGURE 17–2
Process Control
Computing System

split into fatty acids under conditions of high temperature and high pressure before neutralization by caustic chemicals to make soap. The process runs continuously and the proper control of temperature, pressure levels, flow rates, and pH are critical to the operation's success. Synthetic detergents undergo even more complicated processes. Similar processing takes place in the oil industry, the food processing industry, the cosmetics industry, and the paper industry.

Today microprocessors are built into process control devices. In that service they function as a computer by working under the control of a program to receive inputs, manipulate them, and generate outputs. The inputs are messages from the various sensing devices installed in the processing environment, the manipulation is specified by the program, and the outputs are messages to adjust the various control mechanisms in the process. As a matter of fact, a process control computer and a management information computer seem to be performing somewhat the same functions in different arenas. In process control, however, the adjustments which need to be made are more predictable.

The computerized control of valves, pumps, temperature regulators, and pressure controllers provides for the reliable production of goods of high quality. As a result, the skills required of operating personnel have declined. Semi-skilled operating personnel have replaced the highly-skilled operators of the past. Old jobs have disappeared, and new ones have been created.

Challenge Update

Mr. Sterling, his group of experts, and the reader should now be able to describe the use of computers in machine and process control.

Industrial Robotics

The use of robots (see Figure 17–3) to replace industrial workers is one of the most controversial topics of our time. It is, however, a natural extension of the trend that began with the industrial revolution, the substitution of machines for human labor. Although we have embraced the concept of eliminating human effort on jobs that are tedious, dangerous, and physically demanding to an extreme, people continue to be concerned that replacement of human workers might go too far. The end result could be that an insufficient number of jobs might be left to maintain a high level of employment.

Robot Defined

The Robot Institute of America defines a *robot* as "a programmable, multifunction manipulator designed to move material, parts, tools, or specialized devices through variable programmed motions for the performance of a variety of tasks." The key words in the definition would seem to be *programmable* and *variable.* These words differentiate robots from the vast array of mechanical manipulators which have been used in industry for

FIGURE 17–3
Industrial Robot

years. Mechanization occurs when machines are used to perform tasks previously done by people. Semi-automatic devices require the close interaction of people and machines. Automation takes place when essentially no human intervention is required by a process.

Although industrial robots have been with us since the early 1960s, the 1980s are expected to be the real era of the robot. There are many different types of robots, but an extremely technical discussion is necessary in order to differentiate among the various classes. We will, however, not need a sophisticated classification system for our purposes here.

Robots are classified with a progression similar to the classification of computer terminals from slow and dumb to fast and intelligent. The less capable robots are manual manipulators with a narrow range of functions. The more capable ones have sensory equipment which enables them to "see" their environment and react appropriately to it.

Many scholars work in the field of artificial intelligence, trying to enhance the ability of machines to exhibit human-like intelligence. Extensive research has been done to develop machines which could mimic—or outperform—human beings in tasks requiring intelligence. Robot development has been greatly aided by this research. Robots at work are shown in Figure 17–4.

Artificial intelligence research has also been done in the areas of theorem-proving, problem-solving, and pattern recognition. As was discussed earlier, the next generation of computers is expected to make heavy use of the principles of artificial intelligence.

Production and Use of Robots

Japan leads the world in both the production and use of robots, with the United States a distant second. Several differences in the industrial envi-

FIGURE 17–4
Robot at Work

ronment between the two countries account for the wide gap in the use of robots between the two. There are several significant economic differences and one major cultural difference which has both economic and social consequences. Japan's early interest in industrial robots was stimulated by a shortage of industrial workers, something which has not recently occurred in the United States.

The economic differences arise from the close ties among business, banking, and government in Japan. The Japanese government, for example, has established a leasing company which buys robots for leasing to Japanese companies, saving them the high cost of outright purchase. Japanese companies can, therefore, acquire robots much more easily than can their American counterparts.

In addition, interest rates are kept lower in Japan than has frequently been the case in the United States, because governmental control of the banking industry in Japan has lead to a lower interest policy. With lower rates of interest to be paid for borrowed funds, Japanese companies can borrow more extensively for the purchase of robots and other capital goods. The third economic advantage is in the rate of taxation; Japanese companies have the advantage of lower taxes. The net result of these three differences is that robots are cheaper to a Japanese company than they are to American companies.

The major cultural difference, which enhances Japan's ability to use robots, is the virtually lifelong commitment which exists between an employer and an employee in Japan. The initial screening process for hiring an employee is much more extensive in Japan than in the United States, and once the hiring decision has been made, the employee knows that the job is for life. A Japanese employee may be *displaced* to other work when a robot is introduced into the factory, but he or she will not be *replaced.* An American worker might oppose the introduction of robots into the

American factory because his or her job may be at stake, but a Japanese worker does not have that fear.

It is not surprising, then, that Japan is ahead of the United States and other countries in the use of industrial robots. Japan's lead may translate to economic advantage in world markets. Two tales of the automation of Japanese factories will help illustrate the extensive use of robots in their factories.

A vacuum cleaner factory was converted to robots recently, and 350 workers were displaced to other work. Operation of the factory now requires only about ten workers. The workers who were displaced were transferred to a two-year training program in order to provide them with the skills necessary to become software engineers. Robots do need programs to control their actions, and software engineers are needed to write the programs.

Another company, this one a machinery company in Japan, has a night shift where robots work unattended by human workers. Interestingly, the factory floor is practically dark during this shift because the robots need very little light by which to work. The 200 or so workers displaced by these robots are working in other areas of the company.

Impact on Employment

Many industrial workers will be displaced by robots during the 1980s. An estimate prepared by the United States Congressional Budget Office predicts that 15 percent of current American manufacturing workers will be displaced by robots before 1990. It is difficult to predict whether or not this displacement will result in massive unemployment. Economic growth, new industry, governmental retraining and employment programs, early retirements, and reductions in the work week can all be used to ease the impact of worker displacement.

One prediction which seems safe to make is the prediction that higher levels of skill will be needed in the future to sustain present employment levels. Just as N/C machines displaced highly skilled machinists and process control computers reduced the need for highly trained operators, robots will displace semi-skilled workers in large numbers. The remaining jobs would seem to require either very highly skilled technicians or unskilled laborers.

The accelerating rate of change indicates that lifelong learning and the ability to adapt to new environments will be important personal attributes. Computer-controlled robots will eliminate much of the work which is tedious, dangerous, and physically demanding, leaving work which is more intellectually challenging. Efforts to educate and train the work force will be needed even more extensively in the future. Private enterprise, government, and individuals themselves must all share the education and training burden.

Challenge Update

The reader should now be able to discuss the trends in industrial robotics and the impact those trends are expected to have on levels of employment.

Computer-Aided Design/Computer-Aided Manufacturing (CAD/CAM)

Efforts to mechanize or automate factory work have, by and large, been successful. Another area of success, discussed next, actually bridges the gap between the factory and the office environment.

CAD/CAM (for **computer-aided design/computer-aided manufacturing**) results from the merging of the two fields named in the term. The method brings promise of completely automated processes to move products from creation to completion. Although not exactly a new field (it began in the aerospace industry in the 1950s), CAD/CAM has grown as the hardware and software which support computer graphics have improved (see Figure 17–5). Market surveys indicate that sales of CAD/CAM equipment now exceed $1 billion annually. Robots and N/C machines capable of carrying out automated manufacturing processes have also contributed to the growth.

The design portion of a CAD/CAM system features a designer working at a graphics terminal with other computer peripherals, such as digitizers, plotters, and tape drives, nearby. Design software helps the designer create an image of the product on the terminal screen, often in color and with the perspective of three dimensions. Input to the design process may come from a light pen and a special surface on the terminal display.

If the product is a mechanical part which requires machining, software is available to simulate the machining operations. Control tapes for N/C machines can be produced as a product of the same software. Research at Princeton University's Interactive Computer Graphics Laboratory has demonstrated a robot milling machine which downloads its control program

FIGURE 17–5 Plastic Container Design Graphic

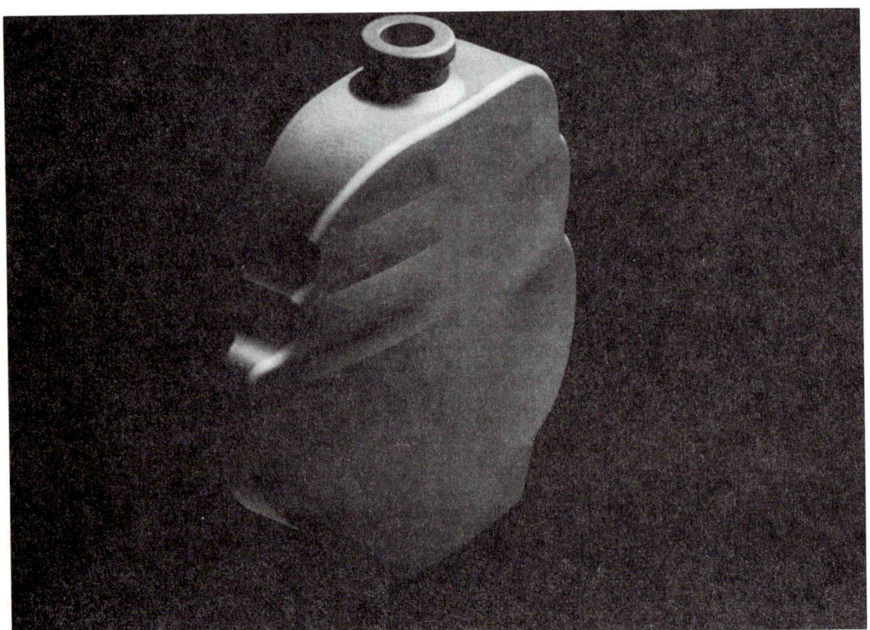

directly from the IBM mainframe on which it was developed.[3] Some CAD/CAM systems allow for simulated testing of the parts after they have been designed. A few examples will help illustrate the capabilities of sophisticated CAD/CAM systems.

In the design of aircraft, designers cause the curved shapes of aircraft bodies to be displayed on their video screens. Design software then converts the curved shapes into flat patterns, which will be used to guide the tools for cutting the various pieces of the aircraft's "skin." The software then fits the patterns for the various pieces together to minimize waste as the pieces are cut. The cutting operation itself utilizes a cutting machine robot with a laser cutter.

IBM uses a CAD/CAM system to automate the production of prototype computer chips. Circuit designers working in various locations around the world transmit designs via satellite to an IBM production facility in New York. There the designs are computer tested, and instructions for their manufacture by automatic equipment are generated. Then, only a few days after the design has been created, the new chips can be produced.

Automobile manufacturers use CAD/CAM systems extensively for the design of the car's exterior, where parameters like wind resistance can be tested, and the car's mechanical parts, where stress and wear can be simulated (see Figure 17–6). Manufacturers of farm implements are also extensive users of automated design and manufacturing systems.

The use of CAD/CAM systems will reduce the length of time between the creation of the design of a product and its appearance in the marketplace. They should enable manufacturers to produce better quality products at lower prices.

The impact of CAD/CAM systems on the work force is very similar to that of machine control, process control, and robotics. Some workers will be displaced. For example, the number of people employed to perform drafting seems certain to decline. Others in the work force will have to acquire different skills. Designers, for example, will have to be proficient at working with a computer terminal.

The impact of technological change will be felt in other areas as well. Office environments, for example, will undergo significant changes, as is discussed in the next section.

Technological Enhancements in the Office

Perhaps the most popular topic in computing today is the "Office of the Future," also known as the "Automated Office" or the "Paperless Office." Whatever the name, the effort is intended to improve the productivity of office workers.

Proponents of the automated office are quick to point out that the average capital investment in support of office workers (about $2,500) is significantly below that of factory workers (about $25,000). This capital investment gap

3. Tom Henkel, "Researchers Working toward Integrated Factory," *Computerworld*, April 25, 1983.

is alleged to result in significantly lower productivity for office workers than should otherwise be the case. A rephrasing of the claim leads to the belief that an increase in capital investment in the office is sure to raise the productivity of office workers. This claim has yet to be proven.

The computer industry, it appears, has fallen prey on many occasions to the "oversell" of its new ideas. Products are announced early, before they have been built, and actual performance often falls below expectations. Rarely have the promises of computer equipment vendors been achieved to the degree and within the time frame advertised. Oversell is a fault common to the field of marketing it seems, and it certainly is not confined to a single industry.

The incorporation of microprocessor-based office equipment will undoubtedly bring many changes to the way of doing business in many offices. Just how great the changes will be cannot yet be determined. Large firms seem much more likely to incorporate large amounts of electronic equipment to enhance the office environment. Since 60 percent of this country's white-collar workers are employed by medium- to large-sized firms, the impact of the new technologies could be great.

The prudent manager should probably continue to be somewhat cautious about the potential impact of the new office technologies. Certainly it makes good sense to become as knowledgeable as possible about a new technology before making a sizeable investment. Let us explore the devel-

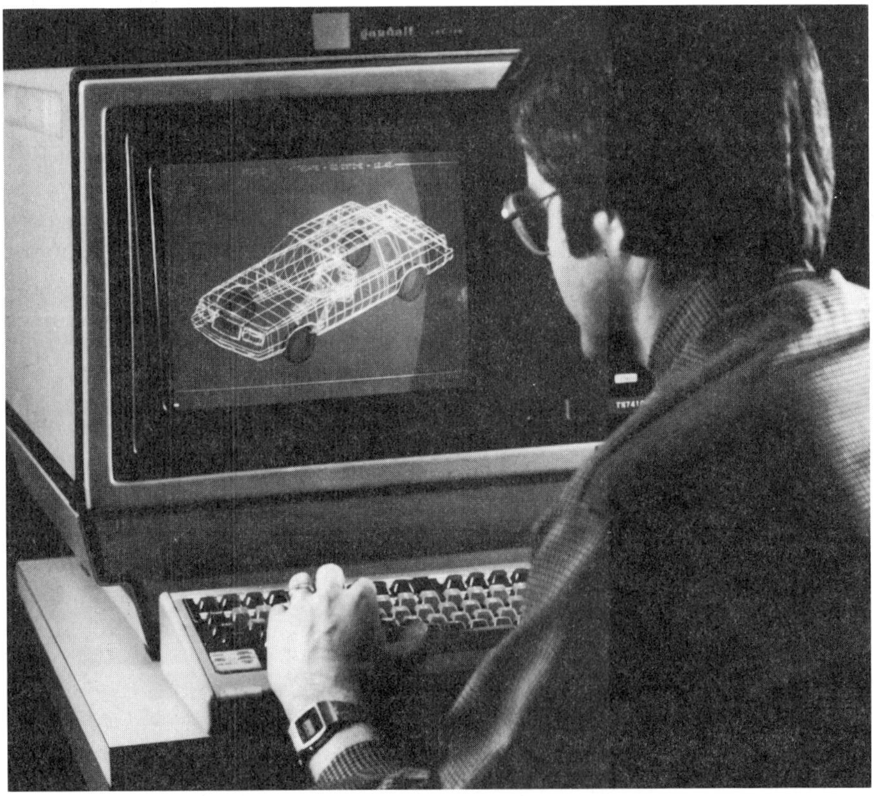

FIGURE 17–6
CAD/CAM System in Use

"As of September 1st, I'm sorry to say, you will all be replaced by a tiny chip of silicon."

opments which are expected to have the greatest impact on the nature of office work.

Word Processing

The cornerstone achievement has been the development of microprocessor-based word processing equipment, which encompasses a variety of enhancements to improve the functioning of the electric typewriter. Formerly used almost exclusively for data processing, microprocessors equipped with special purpose software can greatly expand the productivity of a typist. [A brief description of word processing software for personal computers was presented in Chapter 15.]

Word processors (that is, word processing software operating in a microprocessor environment) allow a user to electronically store and retrieve text and to edit that text through the use of commands to accomplish insertion, deletion, and movement of segments of the text (see Figure 17–7). An on-line spelling program can review the text as it is entered and detect and correct spelling errors. An on-line thesaurus is also possible.

Word processing allows convenient revision of reports, term papers, and

FIGURE 17–7 Personal Computer Serves as a Word Processor

FIGURE 17–8 Word Processing System

other documents without the necessity of retyping. Changes are made to the document while it is contained in the microprocessor's memory. Print parameters can then be selected so that the finished document can be viewed on the screen prior to its actual printing. Embedded commands can be used to change margins, paragraphing, and spacing as printing takes place (see Figure 17–8).

Electronic copies of text can be stored on magnetic tape or magnetic disk and later used to automatically set type. IBM magnetic card typewriters were the earliest version of word processing equipment, but newer machines have many more features.

The features offered by the various word processors differ greatly. A buyer would be well-advised to proceed cautiously. The buyer must analyze the type of work for which the word processing is intended in order to buy one well suited to the specific application. Comparisons of the capabilities of word processors are published regularly in such publications as those listed at the end of the chapter, and they make an excellent reference for the potential user or buyer.

Some computer applications require that information generated by the **data processing system** be merged with text generated on a **word processor.** Although this merging may at times be extensive, it could also be as simple as inserting a table of data into a report. Unfortunately, the integration of data processing and word processing has not yet gone well. It currently suffers from the lack of standardization, but there is hope that improvements will be realized soon.

Different word processing equipment manufacturers produce to different standards, just as data processing equipment manufacturers were found to do in previous discussions. The lack of standardization within each field is made significantly worse by the lack of standards between fields. Improved design may eventually eliminate the problem, but the difficulties associated with the integration of word and data processing systems are currently great.

New developments in word processing will allow voice editing of a stored document. A document stored in the word processor's memory can be displayed on a screen for review, and voice commands used to control the addition, deletion, or modification of text. Voice recognition requires some "learning" on the part of the machine, which is accomplished by having the user pronounce a series of words, prompted by the computer. The microprocessor tunes itself to a particular user's voice in this way in order to reduce the rate of errors.

Voice editing will be followed by full-fledged voice entry. Users might eventually be able to dictate letters and reports directly to a sophisticated word processor which will, in the end, generate the finished document.

Software for Desktop Computers

Analysts at Arthur D. Little, Inc., predict that by 1990 nearly half of all American workers will be making daily use of electronic computing equipment. Software developers are working long hours to be able to offer programs for those machines (see Figure 17–9). Several categories of software were discussed in the earlier chapters.

The desktop computers with the full range of integrated software products discussed earlier are expected to bring about significant improvements in the productivity of professional employees.

Software vendors offer a variety of software packages for desktop machines to support common, organizational activities. Packages are available to handle accounting, property management, patient billing, purchasing, record keeping, project management, and so on. These packages should contribute in a positive way to improvements in productivity across a broad range of professional work.

Of course, productivity improvement is not entirely a technological problem. Many other factors are present in professional employment which contribute to the overall productivity of the professional worker. As a matter of fact, the correct approach to enhancing the effectiveness of professional workers starts with an analysis of areas of inefficiency, not with the technology.

That is, one should focus on business-related problems and then review current technologies to see if they offer any solutions. It would be completely backwards to take a new technology into the office and try to find some use for it.

With this caution in mind, we now turn our attention to other office functions for which new technologies might be useful. First, we consider the needs for long-term storage of information.

FIGURE 17–9
Desktop Computer

Archival Storage

As was discussed earlier, organizations have well-established needs for storing various kinds of information for extended periods of time. Tax records, employment histories, product testing results, and research results must all be stored for several years. These records have historically been stored in their original, hard-copy form.

Alternatives based upon several different technologies are available for the archival, or long-term, storage of files. Many systems currently use microfilm for long-term storage. Information stored on magnetic disks and tapes can be saved for several years, although manufacturers of magnetic media suggest relatively frequent maintenance procedures to prevent deterioration. For example, manufacturers suggest semiannual cleaning of magnetic tape if long-term storage is planned. Videodisc storage provides another excellent alternative for archival storage. Both microfilm (micrographics) and videodisc will be discussed further here.

Microfilm. Microfilm images can be produced either by photographing the original documents or as a direct result of computer output operations as discussed in Chapter 4. The images can be left in the original film strip form, arrayed in microfiche form, or mounted in aperture cards. The speed with which information retrieval can occur in a microfilm storage system is greatly enhanced when microprocessor-based storage and retrieval devices are used.

CRT viewing screens coupled with microprocessor-aided retrieval provide a definite improvement over the older microfilm equipment, and viewers with fiber optic projectors will eventually make color micrographics popular. Printers associated with the storage and retrieval devices provide hard copies when needed. One can imagine that in the not-too-distant future managers will be able to enter requests for retrieval of microfilmed documents in the organization's archives from the terminals in their offices. A personnel manager, for example, could request employment summaries of retired employees to prepare for a company picnic.

Videodisc. The newest form of archival storage is the **videodisc.** Information is stored in digital patterns by a laser which either burns tiny holes in a metallic layer within the plastic disc or causes the reflectivity of the metallic layer to be otherwise changed. Storage is permanent; there are currently no commercially-available, economically feasible means for erasing and recording other information, although laboratory versions of such machines exist. The information stored on the disc is read by another laser device, an example of which is available for the home entertainment market. Although the reading device is quite inexpensive, the recording device is reasonably expensive (about $45,000).

Videodisc storage offers extremely low-cost archival storage on a medium which is practically indestructible. The disc can be dropped, washed, even walked on without destroying the information stored on it. A single videodisc is capable of storing as many as half-a-million pages of text and thousands of pictures. Microprocessor-based retrieval devices with color video screens and printers to produce the desired copies round out an extremely attractive storage system.

Message Systems

Managers spend a great deal of their time in discussions with other managers. Some of these discussions are formal conferences. The role of teleconferencing in reducing the costs of these formal meetings was discussed in the previous chapter. Many of the discussions which take place between managers are, however, much less formal, such as conversations in the hall, during lunch, or over the telephone.

Two significant technologies have been developed to improve the productivity of managerial conversations which take place over the telephone. One additional technology allows the transmission of facsimiles of documents. We turn now to a brief explanation of electronic mail, voice mail, and facsimile transmission.

Electronic Mail. **Electronic mail** is the name given to the exchange of messages which takes place through the communications network connecting several computing machines. Users gain access to the system from terminals, through which they enter messages to be delivered to other people who have terminals connected to the same network. If the receiving person's terminal is connected at the time the message is sent, delivery is instantaneous. If not, the presence of the message is made known to the receiver when he or she connects to the network.

Some companies maintain private networks for the transmission of messages between managers and other employees of the company, while other companies subscribe to public electronic mail systems. Some word processing systems, when connected together, provide electronic mail capability. A large electronic mail system may have thousands of terminals and process hundreds of thousands of messages daily.

Electronic mail systems provide software to effect security for restricted messages, distribution lists for the broadcast of a single message to many recipients, and procedures to notify the sender of the receipt of the message. The two principal advantages of electronic mail are instantaneous delivery and relatively low cost. Electronic mail messages cost about 30 cents, while the normal business letter costs about $7.00.

Managers seem to spend a lot of their time trying to reach each other on the telephone; electronic mail offers an efficient alternative. Effective use of it should increase productivity.

Voice Store-and-Forward. Statistics reveal that more than 60 percent of the time a telephone call does not reach the intended person on the first trial. If the call is not answered, another attempt will have to be made if the call was important. If someone—but not the desired person—answers, a message can be left, which necessitates a return call. It is a very inefficient process. Electronic mail offers one alternative for improvement, and voice store-and-forward systems offer another.

In a **voice store-and-forward** system, a voice message is electronically recorded for later delivery. The caller can cause the message to be recorded for later delivery to the recipient, avoiding the necessity of leaving a message with the person who answers, and avoiding a return call. (Statistics indicate that about half of all telephone calls are for the purpose of one-way communication anyway.)

Copies of the message can be sent to other people whenever it is appropriate. If the person receiving the message on a voice store-and-forward system wishes to reply, the return message can be directed to the sender without having to redial the sender's number. Some systems allow a user, upon returning from an absence, to scan the first few seconds of each message stored in the system to distinguish those which require immediate response from those which do not.

Facsimile Transmission. Facsimile transmission supplements the keyboard message sending of electronic mail and the storing and forwarding of voice messages. **Facsimile transmission** makes it possible to send copies of documents through a communications network. Although facsimile transmitters based upon analog principles have been in use for years, the quality and reliability of the transmission has been poor. New digital techniques offer higher transmission rates, better quality facsimiles, and more reliable operation. A facsimile transmitter is illustrated in Figure 17–10.

For example, analog facsimile transmitters take approximately six minutes to transmit a single page. Long-distance telephone rates provide an incentive to decrease the transmission time. Digital facsimile transmitters take less than a minute to transmit a page. Digital transmission produces a copy of much higher quality than does analog transmission.

Microprocessor-based copy machines, equipped with communications capability and connected to a network, can cause copies of an original document to be distributed worldwide in a matter of seconds. Facsimile transmission devices are often found as part of a teleconferencing facility. They can be used to transmit textual and graphical information to receiving stations. For example, they could be used to transmit copies of legal con-

FIGURE 17–10
Facsimile Transmission Device

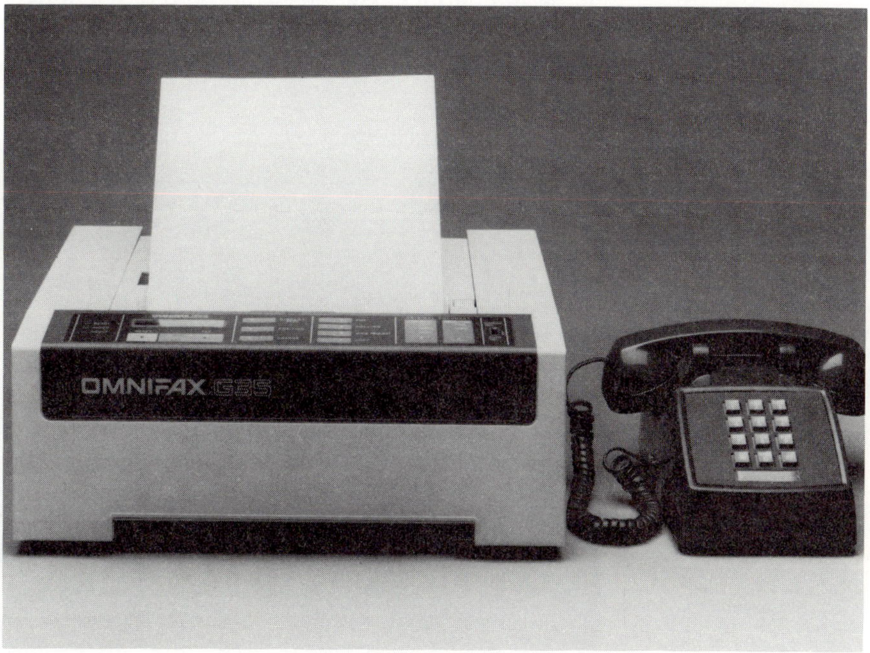

tracts, purchase agreements, engineering drawings, or product specifications.

Communications

Productivity improvements in the office would not be complete without the capability for the various workstations to communicate with each other. We have seen in Chapter 9 how computing systems communicate with each other through metropolitan area and long-distance networks and how local area networks allow office machines to communicate with each other. A brief review is presented here to focus the reader's attention on the office environment.

Local Area Networks (LANs). As word processors and other microprocessor-based machines begin to populate the office environment, the need arises for them to be able to share information. For example, a computer terminal may have data needed within a report being prepared on a word processor, or a word processor may need to retrieve a file from archival storage to incorporate into a document currently being prepared. Local area networks (LANs) make it possible to connect the various office machines to each other. Data, text, and programs can be shared by users connected to the network. See Figure 17–11 for an illustration.

A discussion of the two competing LAN technologies was presented earlier. Approximately fifty different vendors offer LANs, including both baseband and broadband products. Some, led by Ethernet of Xerox, offer carrier sense, multiple access/collision detection access, while others, including IBM, offer token passing.

Data, video, and voice communications will eventually be integrated into a single LAN product. This will provide an effective communications medium among local stations. Internet connections will expand these communications to the global scene. In the interim, managers will have to sort

FIGURE 17–11 Users Conected via Local Area Network

through a variety of potential compatibility problems in order to build an efficient and effective communications scheme.

Digital PBXs. A critical piece of equipment in most offices is the **private branch exchange,** or **PBX,** which allows incoming telephone calls to be switched to the appropriate extension within the office (see Figure 17–12). As was discussed in Chapter 9, the telephone system is basically an analog system, not well suited to the transmission of digital data. The volume of data communications traffic has become so large in comparison with that of voice, that conversion of the telephone transmission system to a digital system appears profitable. The conversion will, of course, take place very gradually.

As users begin to manage their communications efforts, they will consider the integration of voice, data, and facsimile transmissions. Since data and facsimile transmissions are in digital form, but voice is not, voice communications would require an analog to digital conversion before transmission via a digital PBX. Digital PBXs are cheaper than their analog counterparts and are easier to maintain. Higher transmission rates and transmissions of greater quality are also possible with digital PBXs.

If and when the telephone system becomes a digital system, the question of whether or not to install a digital PBX will be answered. Until then, organizations with relatively larger volumes of data communications than voice communications might want to seriously consider the digital device.

FIGURE 17–12
A PBX of the "Good ol' Days"

These new technologies offer promise of significant changes in the office environment. Since approximately 50 million people work in offices, the impact will be great. A discussion of the potential benefits of the new technologies follows.

Benefits of New Office Technologies

Although the new technological enhancements are exciting developments, it is not at all clear that productivity of the office worker will increase. Productivity improvements will be realized only if old work habits can be replaced by new ones. Office workers must learn how to make the most effective use of the new facilities in order to realize productivity gains.

One area in which a significant amount of improvement is expected is the area of information "float." Float in the banking system—that is, the delay between the writing and clearing of a check— is a benefit to the check writer. Banking float allows the user's account to take advantage of the funds' presence for several days after the check to disburse them is actually written. In contrast, the delay caused by transmission of information through normal channels, can be a definite liability. Delays in the delivery of information could cause sales to be lost, meetings to be missed, and incorrect decisions to be made.

Electronic message systems should reduce information float to almost zero. As a result, the following excuses should become almost unnecessary:

"The report is being typed."
"The files are being searched."
"The check is in the mail."

FIGURE 17–13
Executive
Workstation

Electronic message systems should provide almost instant access to information throughout the system.

Redundant work should also be significantly reduced by the new technologies. Retyping will be unnecessary since word processing systems provide editing of electronic files. The manual effort associated with filing and retrieval from files will be reduced. Integration of data and text processing should eliminate efforts which were formerly duplicated.

In general, it is expected that people will be relieved of repetitive, manual tasks so that time can be spent on jobs which better utilize human capabilities. Opportunities to exercise judgment and exhibit initiative should be increased. These in turn should contribute in a positive way to the attainment of individual and organizational goals. The new work environment is shown in Figure 17–13.

Challenge Update

Mr. Sterling and the reader should now be able to list the microprocessor-controlled machines which can be expected to bring productivity improvements into the office environment.

Newest Developments

Fortunately, very few organizations are discarding their old but proven office technologies in order to bring in the new ones. The prudent approach is still to make necessity the mother of invention. Managers must continue to apply available technologies to solve specific problems.

Interesting tales are told of unsuccessful efforts to integrate the new technologies into the office. In one, a manager (who would not type) read his electronic mail messages at his terminal but dictated replies for his secretary to enter. In another, a manager called his secretary into the office to enter information through the keyboard as he gave her instructions.

The new office technologies will, however, be applied in those areas in which true benefits are forthcoming. Their use in these areas will bring improved productivity to office professionals.

In the factory the wave of the future would seem to be robotics. The National Bureau of Standards has designed the Automated Manufacturing Research Facility to stimulate research in the standardization of interfaces between the various types of computing and robotic machinery. The new facility will help manufacturers find automated manufacturing systems that can be connected together to form efficient, integrated systems.

The years ahead will be interesting ones in terms of new technologies for both offices and factories. The new technologies are driven by the necessity to remain competitive in world markets but hindered by the rate at which we, as humans, can adapt to new environments.

Let us see how Mr. Sterling has progressed with his challenge.

COMPUTING CHALLENGE: *A Final Note*

The meeting convened by Sterling to discuss the skills needed in the office group turned out to be very informative. Speisel, of the governor's staff, let Sterling know that the Highway Department's effort would be funded as a pilot project by the governor's office.

The office manager, Lockwood, expressed the opinion that use of a keyboard would be the single most important skill which would be required in a computerized office. Since the office was well staffed with excellent typists, most personnel had the basic skill on which to build.

The dean of the Business Department of the local community college, O'Donald, made two important points. In the first place, the college was eager to work with the Highway Department in the development of several short courses of classroom training to help bring the skills of the department up to the necessary level.

Her second point was even more important. She believed it would be a serious mistake to train the workers without training the supervisors. She suggested a short course on computer fundamentals for everyone, with subsequent, more specialized courses as needed by individual groups.

Bonwell, from the employment agency, agreed with the dean. As a matter of fact, he and the dean had just completed a training program to upgrade the skills of some of his clients who had outdated skills and were having difficulty finding work. Several of the people who had completed the program were now available for either temporary or permanent assignment if needed by the Highway Department.

Sterling was very encouraged by the discussion. He realized that untrained managers have a difficult time determining which types of processes are good candidates for computerization. Therefore, he immediately directed the office manager to work out a schedule for the initial training of all personnel in the department. Managers and workers would then be able to develop a plan for the introduction of the new technologies which could be justified in terms of increased productivity. Speisel would assist in this phase of the work.

The Business Department could provide the necessary training facilities and faculty. The office manager and Sterling have agreed that the employment agency's trained people will be considered for any vacant positions which occur. Productivity improvement within the State Highway Department seems well underway.

SUMMARY

- The use of computers to make work processes more productive is a continuation of the trend established by the industrial revolution.

- Computers are well suited for controlling any repetitive operations whether those operations occur in the factory or in the office.
- In the factory, numerically controlled (N/C) machines, now with embedded microprocessors, provide work of high quality.
- Microprocessors are also used as process control computers in the chemicals and food processing industries.
- In both process and machine control the computer has been used to provide controls which make it possible to make products of uniformly high quality without the necessity for highly-skilled workers.
- The basic role of the computer is the same in both the factory and the office environment—the conversion of inputs to outputs under the control of a program.
- Industrial robots provide yet another step in the progression to automated work as robots with embedded microprocessors become "intelligent" workers with good skills and extreme patience.
- The integration of computer-aided design and computer-aided manufacturing occurs in CAD/CAM systems, which provide automated links between design and production.
- CAD/CAM systems are used extensively in the automobile, aircraft, farm implement, appliance, computer, and other industries.
- Microprocessors have been added to office machines to make intelligent devices capable of greatly improving office worker productivity.
- Great numbers of office workers already utilize desktop computers to executive word processing, spreadsheet, filing, and data base software.
- Communications capabilities and local area networks (LANs) will give word processors, facsimile transmitters, computer terminals, and personal computers the ability to share information and data.
- Message systems and automated retrieval from archival storage systems should enhance the productivity of office workers and managers.
- Advances in productivity through the use of technologically-enhanced equipment in the work environment will not occur without adequate preparation and training, the skill levels of workers and managers alike will need to be improved.
- The impact of automation of the work environment will probably place increased downward pressure on employment levels and will likely raise the average level of skill needed to find employment.

CASE: Computerized Factories at General Electric

General Electric has long been a leader in the manufacture of electrical appliances and many other product areas as well. Their products must compete in worldwide markets, so the company must always be able to offer quality products at competitive prices. To respond to pressures of the competition, they must develop new and improved methods of manufacturing their products.

General Electric has undertaken a project that involves the retooling of its own and other American factories into largely automated "plants of the future." They have committed over $1 billion to the automation of factories which produce dishwashers, jet engines, toaster ovens, and locomotives. They hope to sell the idea of the "factory of the future" to other manufacturers and encourage them to modernize their plants with N/C machines, robots, and computers. These machines can be used for design, manufacturing, automated order entry, and warehousing systems.

GE is relying on the success of its own automation, and a healthy marketing budget, to convince companies that automation is a necessary reaction to competition in the world market. To help make the initial expense less of an issue, GE offers attractive financing plans to interested firms.

GE maintains that automation is something that labor unions will accept as a necessary transition. If companies fail to automate their factories in order to remain competitive in world markets, those markets will be lost and companies will be forced to close. The choices seemingly faced by the unions are difficult ones. Short-term employment gains may be wiped out by long-term losses.

Wherever possible, people displaced by these efforts to automate will be retrained to aid the transition from unskilled to skilled jobs. The improvements to be gained from automating the factories, such as shorter production runs and reliable production rates, should improve a manufacturer's competitive position and stabilize employment in the long run.

Factory automation opportunities may not present a choice at all. Competitive pressures worldwide may dictate that we have no choice except to automate. There are certainly many product areas in which manufacturing capacity has moved from the United States to foreign countries in response to competitive pressures. GE's aggressive stance on this issue may be the only alternative to further loss of manufacturing capacity.

Laura Landro, "GE Promotes Factory Automation but Some Doubt Big Market Exists," *Wall Street Journal,* October 21, 1982.

Questions for the Case

1. Automated factories seem to be the wave of the future. What impact will such automation have on:
(a) The price of manufactured goods?
(b) The ability of U.S. firms to compete in world markets?
(c) Unemployment of unskilled workers?
(d) Employment of skilled workers?

2. Whose responsibility should it be to retrain unskilled workers for more highly-skilled positions?
(a) The company's?
(b) The union's?
(c) The government's?

DISCUSSION QUESTIONS AND EXERCISES

1. Explain the similarities in the role of the computer in N/C machines, process control, and data processing. Discuss inputs, outputs, and processing.
2. Describe the integration sought in CAD/CAM systems.
3. How do the economic and cultural differences in the Japanese and American systems result in an advantage in robotics for Japan?
4. Describe the impact of the addition of a microprocessor to a typewriter, to a microfilm retrieval system, and to a copier.
5. How will the new message systems improve office productivity?
6. What impacts will the automation of factory and office work processes have on the size and composition of the work force?
7. In what ways are people's working lives improved through the use of office equipment enhanced by the addition of microprocessors?
8. In what ways are people's working lives made worse through the use of office equipment enhanced by the addition of microprocessors?
9. What factors are at work which constrain the rate at which productivity improvements can be realized in the office? What can be done to minimize the negative effects of these factors?
10. Will automation of factories and offices increase unemployment? Why? Why not?
11. Contrast changes seemingly driven by the desire to use a new technology with those made necessary by the recognition of a problem.
12. Recall the argument that the office is lacking in capital equipment to support office workers in comparison with factory workers. Extend that argument into higher education and comment on the lack of capital equipment to support students.
13. While videodisc systems for archival storage seem to be increasing in number, the home entertainment videodisc market seems to be shrinking. Contrast these two uses for videodisc systems to explain the difference in popularity.
14. Arrange for an office visit and an interview with an office manager. Discuss the blend of old and new technologies which are present.

ADDITIONAL READINGS

Cecil, Paula B. *Office Automation*. Menlo Park, CA: Benjamin/Cummings, 1984.

Chorafas, Dimitris N. *Office Automation: The Productivity Challenge*. Englewood Cliffs, NJ: Prentice-Hall, 1983.

Computerworld, published by CW Communications, Inc., regularly publishes articles on the topics in this chapter.

Datamation, published by Technical Publishing Co., regularly publishes articles on the topics in this chapter.

Electronic Offices: Management and Technology. Pennsauken, NJ: Auerbach Publishers, 1981.

Engelberger, Joseph F. *Robotics in Practice: Management and Application of Industrial Robots.* New York: Amacom Book Division, 1980.

Fitch, Donald. *Increasing Productivity in the Microcomputer Age.* Reading, MA: Addison-Wesley, 1982.

Giuliano, Vincent E. "The Mechanization of Office Work." *Scientific American,* September 1982, pp. 149 –164.

Hiltz, Starr R. *Online Communities: A Case Study of the Office of the Future.* Norwood, NJ: Ablex Publishing, 1984.

Infosystems, published by Hitchcock Publishing Co., regularly publishes articles on the topics in this chapter.

Krouse, John K. "Automation Revolutionizes Mechanical Design." *High Technology,* March 1984, pp. 36–45.

Lieberman, Mark A.; Selig, Gad J.; and Walsh, John J. *Office Automation.* New York: Wiley, 1982.

McWilliams, Peter A. *The Word Processing Book.* Los Angeles: Prelude Press, 1982.

Werneke, Diane. *Microelectronics and Office Jobs: The Impact of the Chip on Women's Employment.* Geneva, Switzerland: International Labor Office, 1983.

18

Computers and the Quality of Life: Today and Tomorrow

CHAPTER PREVIEW

The relentless advance of technology has had both positive and negative repercussions upon the quality of our lives. Most technological advances, brought about for the purpose of improving some fact of our existence, have demonstrated some negative side effects. It seems, as it is often claimed, that there are in fact two sides to every story. The automobile, for example, has given us great mobility, but it has also given us air pollution, noise, injury, and death. Television has given us the opportunity to view cultural, educational, recreational, and sports events in almost unlimited fashion; but it has also brought violence, boredom, and a reduction in interpersonal communications into our homes.

It is important to remember that it is not the technology itself but the uses to which it is put which must bear the burden of right or wrong. Atomic energy gives us nuclear bombs and electricity, nuclear waste and a treatment against cancer. Technological advance can be either good or bad, depending upon its use.

The computer is another in a long line of technological advances which has the potential for both positive and negative influences on the quality of life. Throughout this text we have seen how computers can enhance our ability to perform information processing, accomplish clerical duties, conduct analyses, improve our productivity, and rid us of tedious or dangerous work. At the same time, computers can contribute to invasions of our privacy, to unemployment, and to crime in our society. As *users* of this new technology, we would like to be able to enhance its positive influence on our lives and, at the same time, minimize any negative impacts.

This chapter will discuss some of the many ways in which computers are used to improve our lives. It will concentrate on the positive influences but note the significant negative possibilities. The areas to be discussed are agriculture, art, economics, education, health care, law, national defense, and urban affairs. The computer has had an impact on each of these areas; and these areas have, in turn, had an influence upon the quality of the life we lead. We first consider a computing challenge to provide a focus for the issues, although articles about them are in the popular press almost daily.

COMPUTING CHALLENGE: *The Jury Is Out*

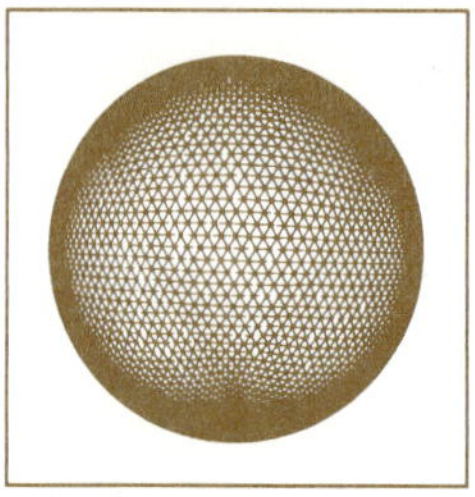

It was earth year 1988, but the earth was gone. The sole survivor among the inhabitants of earth, Thad Watson, had been rescued at the last possible moment. He was taken to Orthon 792 aboard a sleek spacecraft not unlike the ones described by those who, in earlier years, had reported seeing "flying saucers."

His rescuers, the Phelonians, had asked many questions since Thad's arrival on Orthon 792. Their inquiries seemed to be directed at establishing the contributions earth's civilization might have made to Progress and The Good Life. As a matter of fact, Thad had been asked to make a presentation to the Phelonian Assembly on "The Good and the Bad of the Earth."

On earth, Thad Watson had been a business school professor. For years he had preached the virtues of Unbounded Computing to all who would listen. He had supported their use in factories and offices to displace human effort and had taken part in the research effort to pioneer the use of voice-activated (listening), voice-generating (talking) robots to replace clerks and service workers. Thad had even helped persuade the Powers-That-Be that computers were essential to the National Defense. He must assess the value of earth's recently-departed civilization, and he should put forth his best effort.

He needed to review the many arenas in which computers had been found to be useful on earth as a starting point for his presentation to the assembly. It was as if he were on trial. How would the Phelonians find a jury of his peers? Did any of this make any sense? He wondered if those who read the material in this chapter would be able to:

1. *Define productivity and explain the probable impacts on productivity of the substitution of computers for human labor.*
2. *Discuss the impact of the computer on unemployment.*
3. *Describe several potential threats to privacy which have become enhanced by computerization.*
4. *Discuss the characteristics of computing systems which contribute to increased crime.*
5. *Explain some of the positive impacts computers have had on our lives through their use in agriculture, art, economics, education, health care, law, national defense, and urban affairs.*

HISTORICAL PERSPECTIVE

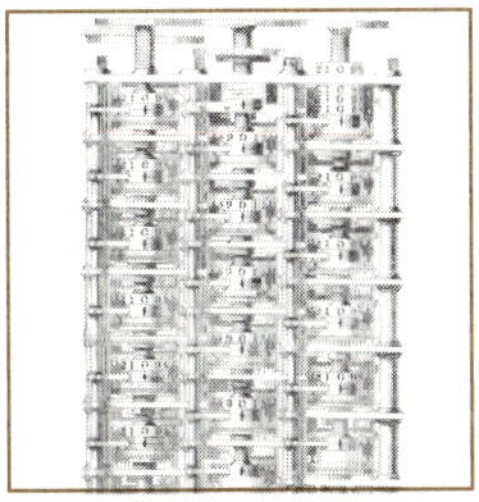

From the abacus of the ancient Chinese through the works of Pascal, Babbage, Ada of Lovelace, Jacquard, Hollerith, and the many others who worked in the field has come the computer as we know it today. Its history has been brief, but its impact on our lives has been great. From easing the burden of the census of 1890 to providing portable computing power for the masses, computers have taken great strides in only a few short years.

Although its early uses were strictly computational, the modern computer now provides wonderful transformations not only numerically, but in graphical and textual manipulations as well. Progress has been great. We will review some of the highlights of that progress in this chapter and speculate a bit on the future.

Agriculture: Today

Perhaps no sector of our society is more important than the agricultural sector which supplies us with food and other products necessary to our survival. Agricultural production is aided in many ways through the use of computers. In the first place, the many organizations which are responsible for agricultural production use computers in the transaction processing and information processing tasks common to those organizations, as has been pointed out throughout the text. Farmers, cooperatives, extension agents, and government agencies within the Department of Agriculture use computers extensively for research, management information, accounting, payroll, purchasing, and so on.

Some other interesting applications exist within agriculture, however, and they are the subject of this section. Four of these applications will be discussed to illustrate some of the uses to which the computer has been put. The four to be discussed are weather forecasting, availability of water, agricultural production, and landscape design. Each of these areas contributes in an important way to the quality of life. The first three are directly related to food production and have, therefore, an obvious connection with the quality of life. The final example, landscape design, contributes to the scenic beauty which surrounds us.

Weather Forecasting

Hardly a day goes by without a news report of the adverse impact of extreme weather conditions upon the yield of one of the agricultural crops of the country. Early and late freezes damage the citrus crops of Florida, excess rain lowers the quality of cherries in the Northwest, and drought continually stalks the cereal crops of the Great Plains. Our timber reserves are depleted by high winds, reduced by lack of rainfall, and destroyed by lightning-caused fires.

Most of our agricultural products are heavily influenced by the weather. Accurate short- and long-range weather forecasts could help farmers take actions to mitigate the impact of adverse weather. For example, fans and water sprays are used in some parts of the country to protect crops from damage due to frost. Additional water supplies can sometimes be secured and water conservation measures can be taken to alleviate a prolonged drought. Improvements in the long-range forecasting of weather would enable farmers to increase their yields by utilizing the appropriate protective actions. An accurate weather forecast is, however, a complex problem.

The forecasting of weather requires the simultaneous solution of thousands of equations, with data to be gathered from thousands of locations. Weather forecasting requires an extremely large and fast computer. The United States Government continues to fund research directed at the development of larger, faster computers in part to improve our ability to forecast the weather (see Figure 18–1). The hope is that new, larger, and faster computers will lead to better forecasts, which in turn will lead to greater agricultural productivity and a world with less hunger.

Availability of Water

One of the essential ingredients in the successful production of most agricultural products is the availability of water at the proper time and in the necessary amounts. Computers are used in several different ways to assist in the measurement and distribution of water for irrigation purposes.

Vast stores of water exist in underground caverns known as aquifers, from which water is pumped for the irrigation of farm products. The heavy use of water from these aquifers has caused their water levels to drop to extremely low levels in recent years. Computers are used to keep track of the water levels in these important storage areas and to monitor the rate at which water is withdrawn to insure that water rights are not exceeded.

Many areas of the country rely on water drawn from surface streams and rivers for the irrigation of farm land. Here the flow of water and its availability for irrigation depend mostly on precipitation in the watershed. In many cases the precipitation takes the form of snow in the mountains;

Figure 18–1
Computer System in Support of Weather Forecasting

hence, the water flow through the producing months is a function of the level of the snow pack. Computers are used to gather data which is beamed via satellite from sensors strategically placed to measure snow levels. Knowledge of the water content of the snow pack can help administrators initiate conservation measure if the water supply appears to be inadequate for the summer season.

Computer simulation is also used to help predict water flows and to adjust the rates of flow through dams in order to maintain adequate stream levels for irrigation, navigation, and maintenance of fisheries while producing electricity for some of our other needs. In some areas of the country, notably the Southwest, water is in extremely short supply. Improved water management techniques based upon accurate water supply information can help lessen the severity of drought conditions.

Agricultural Production

Computers and satellites are used by the government to determine the level of production of agricultural products worldwide. For example, infrared sensors in satellites can be used to gather data which is later enhanced through the use of sophisticated computer programs to determine the type of vegetation growing in an area (see Figure 18–2). Scientists can use information gathered by satellite to determine many things.

For example, through these means our scientists can predict the wheat harvest in Russia, the corn crop in Iowa, and the location of marijuana plantations within our forests. As a matter of fact, satellite sensors can provide information not only on the nature of the vegetation and its area of coverage, but also on its age. Old growth timber, for example, can be distinguished from younger stands.

Information on the worldwide inventory of crops can help economists predict markets and prices well in advance. Unfortunately, political considerations keep this information from being used in the most humane way—to reduce hunger worldwide.

Landscape Design

In another use, the Forest Service employs computers in an interesting way to determine the effect of an anticipated timber harvest on the scenic view from various ground locations. Computer graphics are used to simulate the appearance of the skyline which would be in view from, say, a major highway to determine if a particular harvest would have a negative impact on the scenery. Thus the Forest Service seeks to maintain our visual resources while simultaneously using the forests to meet our other resource needs as well.

Many other instances of computer use by the Forest Service contribute to the public's well-being. For example, timber stand management is improved through the use of timber growth simulators. They also use computers to assess the environmental impact of various activities, design roads, maintain inventories, and administer the mailing lists which keep the public informed.

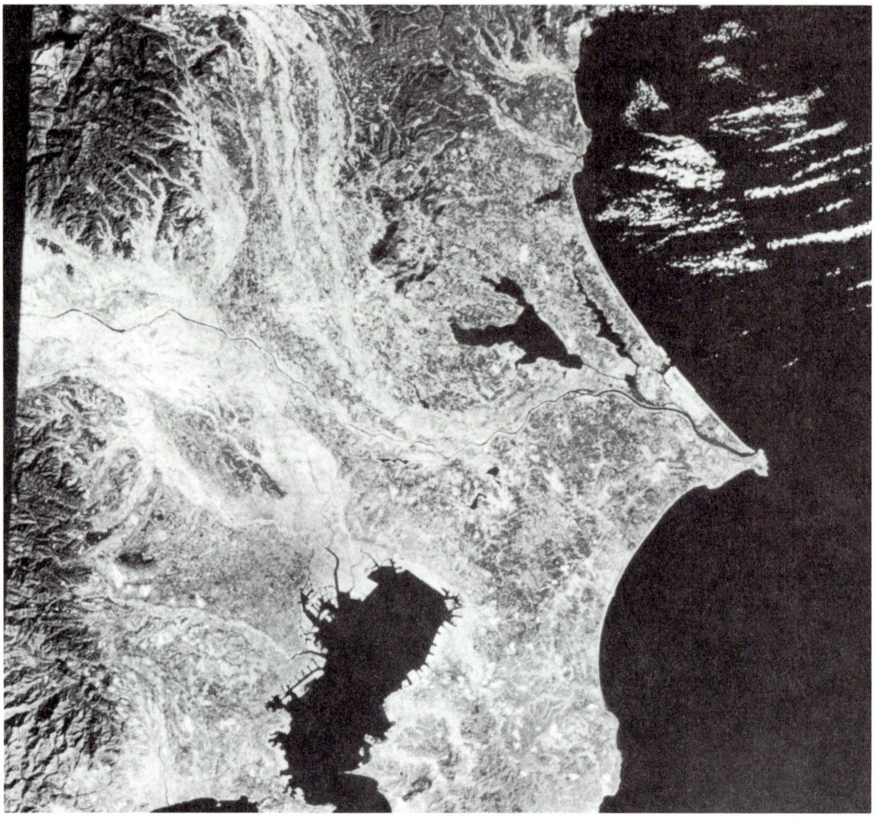

Figure 18–2 Satellite View of Earth

All told, computers are extensively used in agriculture well beyond the categories of use mentioned here. Genealogical histories of superior trees, plants, and animals are maintained and studied to improve production. And, of course, the business side of agriculture is well served by the types of business systems which have been discussed throughout the book.

Agriculture: Tomorrow

Tomorrow's farms will make extensive use of computer technologies. Computer-controlled environments for raising farm animals and the use of personal computers for keeping records, performing analyses and making projections should become commonplace. Large supercomputers will improve our weather forecasting and water management capabilities. Agricultural production can be coordinated on a worldwide basis in order to alleviate hunger and promote peace. Robotics will have an impact not only on the manufacture of farm implements but will become integrated with their use.

Art: Today

The computer is used in many ways to support the arts in addition to the common organizational uses discussed throughout the text. Art inventory management is one of the uses discussed earlier which has particular applicability to art museums where keeping track of the museum's collection of art objects is a critical part of museum management. Extensive use is made of the computer to catalog and keep track of the various objects of art under the museum's control.

Computers have also been found to be useful in the analysis of art objects to determine their authenticity. Numerous forgeries of art objects have been detected with the help of computer-aided analysis. Computers have also been found to be useful in the reclamation or reconstruction of art works which have deteriorated or have been damaged.

Computer-generated art forms have been quite successful in the fields of dance, drawing, music, and the making of films (see Figures 18–3 and 18–4). Computers have been successfully used in dance choreography. To choreograph a dance, for example, a computer must first be taught the basic movements which dancers can perform. By integrating a digitizer with the projection of videotaped sequences on a special screen, it is possible to enter the dancer's movements into the computer's memory. The computer can then be used to select and sequence these movements to choreograph dance sequences.

Computer-generated drawings are everywhere around us. Some have been generated by programmers who have spent the otherwise-boring hours of a late shift at the computer center generating drawings on the plotter. A great deal of serious art has also been generated by artists who have made effective use of the computer. Even robots have been used to generate art, as illustrated by the robot calligrapher pictured in Figure 18–5.

Computers assist artists in other ways. A sculptor, for example, can plot

Figure 18–3
Computer Generated Art

Figure 18–4
Computer Generated Art

the design of a new creation on a graphics terminal, rotate it to check its perspective, and modify it as desired. A computer with a color monitor can be used much more readily than paint itself to assist a painter in the selection of colors. The computer/graphics terminal combination allows the artist to change colors and their locations until the desired effect has been created. Either color video displays or color plotters are used to capture the artist's work.

Figure 18–5
Calligraphy Instruction by Robot

Numerous examples of synthesized music exist as well. A music synthesizer combines the necessary electronic parts with a keyboard to generate sounds of excellent quality to imitate musical instruments. Synthesized versions of many of Bach's works, for example, are widely available. Computers have also been used to compose music. Synthesized music can be stored in the computer's memory for later recall and blending with other stored musical segments. Complete, computer-controlled concerts can be the result.

Late in the 1970s, and extending into the 1980s, computers were used to assist in the making of films. Their use has progressed from the design of backgrounds to that of controlling the sequences of space ship combat and eventually to integrating actors with the electronic imagery itself.

Film making requires a large computer. As a matter of fact, the Hollywood film studio of Digital Productions uses one of the world's largest computers, a Cray X-MP/22. A full-screen movie display requires the setting of about 24 million picture elements, or **pixels,** for each frame of the movie. Assuming that the computer must perform about eight calculations to determine each pixel, each frame will then require 192 million calculations. Movies run at twenty-four frames per second, which leads to the conclusion that about 5 billion computer calculations are needed to produce one second of film.

Although these calculations overstate the case, because every pixel does not change in every frame, they do indicate that the computations necessary for a full-length film could be enormous. The Lorimar Productions film *Starfighters* required months of computation to generate thirty to forty minutes of film.

We find ourselves now in an interesting middle ground between the art of the masters at one extreme and the art of the electronic generation at the other. Each provides a stimulus to enhance our appreciation of the other. Future generations will benefit in exciting ways from computer enhancements to art and its management.

Art: Tomorrow

Computers and art seem, at first, contradictory, but we have seen how the computer can enhance films, art authentication, dance choreography, and music. We have also seen interesting examples of computer-generated art. We should see more of these uses in the future.

It would seem that the techniques of CAD/CAM might be useful in the field of sculpture. A sculptor with full CAD/CAM graphics capacity could design, visualize, and test a sculpture electronically before implementing it in its final medium.

Economics: Today

We have previously considered the role of computers in executing large programs which model the economy and attempt to predict future levels of interest rates, investments, employment, and other economic statistics. These econometric models provide important information to those people who are in charge of the nation's economic policy. Working from equations which try to capture employment levels, money supply, interest rates, and so on, these models compute the growth of the economy. Managers of large banks and large manufacturing firms tie models of their own firms' performance to the larger models of the economy. Business plans are then developed from the use of these models.

Computers have a significant impact on the health of the economy in at least two other ways. One of these is in the area of productivity. We have seen numerous examples in which the productivity of factory, clerical, and managerial workers has been improved through the use of computers.

Productivity improvement leads to the production of more goods by fewer people, which foretells the other significant impact. We have also discussed the threat of computer-caused unemployment. As long as the consumption of goods is growing, productivity improvements can be absorbed without serious worker displacement. When growth in consumption does not occur, workers are displaced by productivity improvement. The impact of the computer on productivity and on unemployment needs further discussion.

Productivity

Productivity is defined as the ratio of outputs generated by a particular process to the inputs consumed by that process. Commonly used productivity measurements include pounds of product per employee, passenger miles flown per gallon of fuel, and sales dollars per dollar of employee wages. To be meaningful, productivity figures should have the effects of inflation removed by computation.

The productivity figures most frequently reported are those associated with the labor inputs. Thus we see productivity figures which measure output in terms of the hours of labor or dollars of wages involved in its production. A substitution of capital for labor will almost always produce a favorable improvement in productivity, if we look only at the productivity of labor.

Perhaps a numerical example will help. Consider a small plant with ten employees which produces $100,000 worth of lawn mower blades per month. The plant's labor productivity is $10,000 per employee. If the plant purchases and installs a robot which makes lawn mower blades and terminates two of the employees, the impact on its labor productivity is startling. The new productivity figure would be $12,500 per employee, a 25 percent increase. If, in the lawn mower blade example, the business grows to $125,000 per year, ten employees at $12,500/employee would again be necessary. Displacement of the two workers would not be necessary if business growth is adequate to absorb the improvements in productivity.

Any analysis based only upon labor productivity fails to measure the impact on the other factors of production such as materials, energy, and capital, and, therefore, gives incomplete information. Improvements in labor productivity might, for example, be accompanied by declines in the productivity of capital.

The installation of a computer system is a substitution of capital for labor in most cases. We could, therefore, expect that a computer acquisition would be reflected in favorable labor productivity figures. Its impact on the productivity of energy, capital, and materials would, however, require more complex analysis.

The many areas of computer use provide the manager with the opportunity to improve labor productivity figures in the factory, in the office, and in professional areas of work. A thorough analysis of the productivity of all factors of production should be considered an integral part of any computer justification. Productivity improvement is *not*, of course, the sole justification for the use of computers. It is also *not* the foremost goal of a manager. Computers can be utilized to relieve people of boring, tedious, or dangerous work (see Figure 18–6). They can also be utilized to provide more challenging work. Their impact on unemployment will be discussed next.

Figure 18–6 Robots at Work

Challenge Update

Thad has, at this point, been able to define productivity and explain the probable impacts on productivity of a substitution of a computer for human labor.

Unemployment

The level of employment in our economy depends upon many factors in the short run. Some of these factors are economic growth, new industry, retraining, retirement policy, and adjustments in the work week. In the long run, however, an economy must be able to consume the goods and services it produces. Production can be increased only as long as consumption increases to remove the surplus goods from the market. Population growth, increased levels of personal consumption, and the opening of new markets all contribute to greater consumption. If there is some limit to the ability to consume, then there is also a limit to the level at which production should occur.

Reductions in population growth, the decline of scarce resources, and a slowing in the rate of growth of our standard of living all place finite limits on consumption, and thereby production. Increases in labor productivity would then contribute to unemployment. Automation, to the extent that it increases productivity, would thereby contribute to unemployment. Many new jobs are created by the computer industry itself, which, of course, lessens its ultimate impact on unemployment. It does seem clear, however, that we would not, for example, use 100 people to build a computer which was capable of performing the work of only 50 people.

Economics: Tomorrow

The impact of computers on economic matters in the future is of utmost importance. The substitution of computers for human effort seems likely to continue in the foreseeable future. These substitutions should cause favorable changes in labor productivity figures.

The impact of computers on unemployment is more controversial. While many believe that computers will ultimately cause employment levels to rise, others counter that the many new jobs created by the computer industry will keep unemployment levels down. On the pessimistic side, economist Gail Garfield Schwartz predicted that only 75 percent of the work force would be needed in the next decade to produce all needed goods and services.[1] That claim, if true, would result in an unemployment level of 25 percent, an unheard of level in modern times. Schwartz recommended that young people prepare themselves for jobs that computers and robots cannot do, such as working *with* those machines or working in the services, care, advice, or information industries.

The potential exists for automation, through the use of computers, to cause significant unemployment. Changes in the length of the work week, the retirement age, the number of holidays and vacations as well as changes

1. Gail Garfield Schwartz and William Neikirk, *The Work Revolution.*

in unemployment, retraining, and welfare programs can be used to mitigate the impact of displacement from jobs.

The composition of the work force has changed and will undoubtedly continue to change as a result of the increased use of computers. New jobs in the computer manufacturing and service areas will, to some extent, offset those lost in other areas. The services area seems destined to grow considerably as the new machines require new, more highly skilled service personnel. As noted earlier, over half of the members of the work force are employed in white-collar positions.

One of the dominant areas of employment in our economy will be in the area of so-called knowledge workers, those who work with information tools instead of mechanical tools. The other area of employment growth, mentioned above, will be in the services industry. Individuals should prepare themselves for the employment opportunities which will be presented by these changes.

Organizations should develop plans to help displaced workers gain the training necessary to be productive in the new era. One of the mechanisms which can be utilized is education, to which the next section is devoted.

Challenge Update

Thad and the reader should now be able to discuss the impact of the computer on unemployment.

Education: Today

Education has been greatly influenced by the development of computing systems. An obvious influence is reflected in the presence of many educational programs which teach computer programming, data processing, systems analysis, data structures, and computer design. In spite of the increased emphasis on computer-related educational programs, the demand for such programs seriously outstrips their supply. Experienced programmers, systems analysts, software engineers and other computer professionals have been scarce. Unfortunately, teaching resources such as faculty, computer time, and state-of-the-art equipment are also in short supply. The facilities of computer-related educational programs will probably be under severe strain for several years.

Schools, as organizations, have found many administrative uses for computers to schedule classes, process registration information and grades, score examinations, and assist researchers in their scholarly tasks. Microcomputers and the many pieces of microprocessor-aided office equipment are being brought into schools for classroom and other uses. To accommodate these uses, teachers, clerical workers, and administrators must all be trained, adding to the strain in existing programs.

School budgets, long-range plans, and enrollment projections are all benefiting from the use of computers in schools and colleges. Three other areas of their use in educational institutions are worthy of note here. These are aids for disadvantaged students, computer aids to instruction, and simulation. Each is discussed in turn.

Aids for Disadvantaged Students

Several devices are in use, and many others are being designed, to help those students who have a physical impairment which hinders their access to the educational system. Students without sight can use microprocessor-aided machines for reading assistance. Two different machines are currently in use. The first, a reading machine, reads printed papers and books and provides voice output for the student. The second type of machine produces a braille version of the text. Both are important aids for those otherwise unable to read.

Another type of device makes it easier for the physically handicapped students to move about campus. This device integrates a microprocessor utilizing voice recognition with a motor-driven wheelchair. The student issues voice commands to direct the wheelchair in an appropriate route around the school grounds.

The development of interactive educational programming delivered to people in their living quarters via telephone or cable television connections is also possible. This should make educational services available to many people who are currently excluded because of physical access limitations or cost.

Computer Aids to instruction

Computers aid instruction in several direct ways. Many different examples of **computer-aided instruction (CAI)** help students learn mathematics, improve their vocabularies, and learn various other subjects. Most CAI systems use a microcomputer, or a terminal, equipped with a video output and keyboard input (see Figure 18–7). Software written for the purpose controls the interaction with the student to teach, test for comprehension, and cover again those topics in which the tests indicate the student is weak.

A lot of software is available for the development of educational programming. Most of it is available for microcomputers so that its cost is within reach for most school systems. These programs use graphics and a requirement for active participation on the part of the learner to effect impressive gains in educational effectiveness.

One of the most successful computer-aided instruction systems is the PLATO system developed by the University of Illinois and Control Data Corporation. Some PLATO implementations use a special-purpose terminal which allows the student to touch the screen to provide input and also allows the integration of 35-mm slides in the instructional presentation.

PLATO uses a special-purpose language for program development to make it easier for educators to develop learning modules. PLATO software is available on floppy disks for home computers. Lessons in math, physics, computer literacy, and foreign languages, to name but a few, are available. All require the student's active participation (see Figure 18–8).

Simulation

Many disciplines in educational circles make use of computer simulations to provide students with experiences somewhat more realistic than the

Figure 18–7
Children Using Computer-Assisted Instruction

Figure 18–8
Computer Assisted Training

standard classroom presentations. Business school students, for example, interact with computer programs whch simulate business organizations. In these simulations, students are asked to make decisions with respect to production schedules, marketing, finance, and management, while the computer simulation projects the consequences of those decisions in terms of sales, profits, and labor unrest. Such simulations help the student integrate classroom experiences from several different fields into the overall management of a business.

Simulations are used in economics to illustrate the principles of macroeconomics; in biology, botany, zoology, and anthropology to demonstrate population growth; in forestry to model timber growth; and in engineering to predict the performance of various equipment designs. Other simulations are helpful in demonstrating the spread of infectious disease, the assimilation of new technologies, and the effectiveness of the football team's offense against a potential opponent's defense.

Simulation is a useful technique for problems which do not have a mathematically determined answer, or which require excessive time or resources in the real world. Timber growth, for example, takes many years. This makes experimentation on timber growth very difficult. Simulators can allow the experimentation to take place in a model environment. Nuclear and germ warfare are also simulated because of the problems of real-world experimentation.

Education: Tomorrow

Future users of computers in education should integrate personal computers, communications networks, and videotex capabilities into an exciting delivery system for educational services. Personal computers are, of course, already extensively used in elementary, secondary, and post-secondary schools. They have been, for some time, the object of computer literacy courses. They are also used as powerful problem-solving tools in many community college and university courses.

In the future we can expect campus computing networks which will give students access to a computerized card catalog at the library, perform bibliographic searches of extensive data bases, offer electronic mail access to professors and fellow students, and broadcast course work. Interactive courses will be possible through teleconferencing, which will allow submission of graded work and grading via computer networks. Many people, unable to participate in today's educational offerings, will be able to participate in future offerings. Educational processes benefit greatly from the use of computers, both directly and indirectly. The same is true of health care.

Health Care: Today

Health care organizations of all sizes use computer systems for transaction processing and to support managerial decision-making activities, just as organizations in other areas do. In fact, the field of health care even has a form of process control. Computers are used extensively in medical laboratories where microprocessor-controlled laboratory equipment is used to analyze the many different types of samples taken for diagnostic purposes (see Figure 18–9). Some of these machines are even capable of dialing the office of the doctor who requested the analysis and generating a voice message describing the results of the analysis.

Many other interesting applications of computers have occurred within the field of health care. Voice-actuated robots are being used to help physically handicapped patients be self-sufficient, as they have helped students move about school campuses. Microprocessor chips have been used in research studies to provide hearing devices for the deaf and aids to sight for the blind. Microprocessors have been embedded in yet other devices to help hospitals monitor the vital signs of critically-ill patients.

Three other very interesting uses have been found for the computer in the delivery of health care. The first of these is the computer-aided tomography *(CAT)* scanner, a device which uses a very large computer in conjunction with a sophisticated X-ray machine to produce cross-sectional images of the human body (see Figure 18–10). An X-ray machine takes low-level radiation pictures completely around the body, and the computer processes the data from these pictures into the cross-sectional images. It is an expensive process, but one which greatly enhances the diagnostic capabilities of the medical staff. Even newer machines use nuclear magnetic resonance *(NMR)* or position emission tomography *(PET)* instead of X-rays to generate cross-sectional images. Both use computer assistance in much the same way as the CAT scanner.

Another example of a diagnostic tool is an interactive program which

Figure 18–9
Computers Aid Medical Diagnosticians

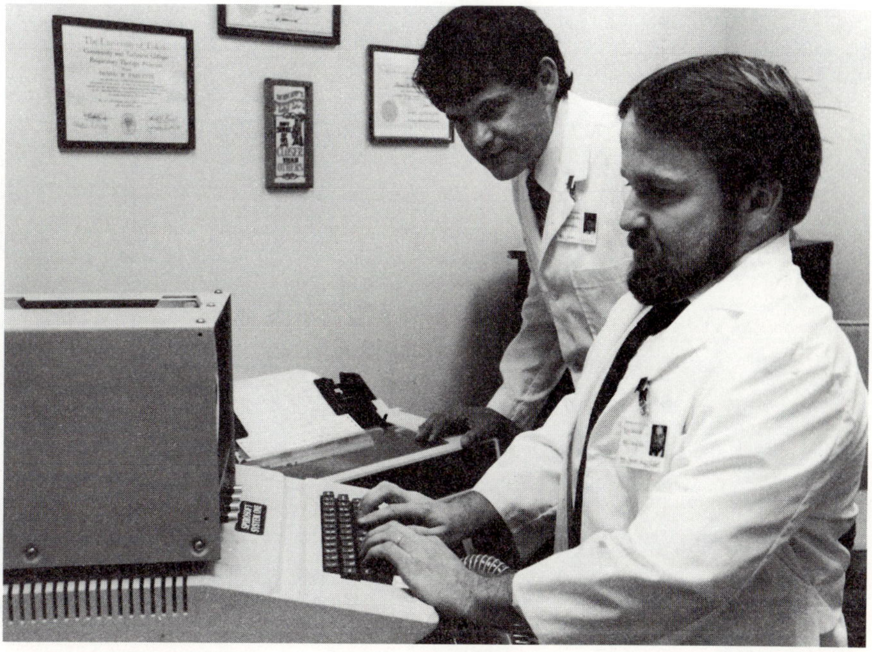

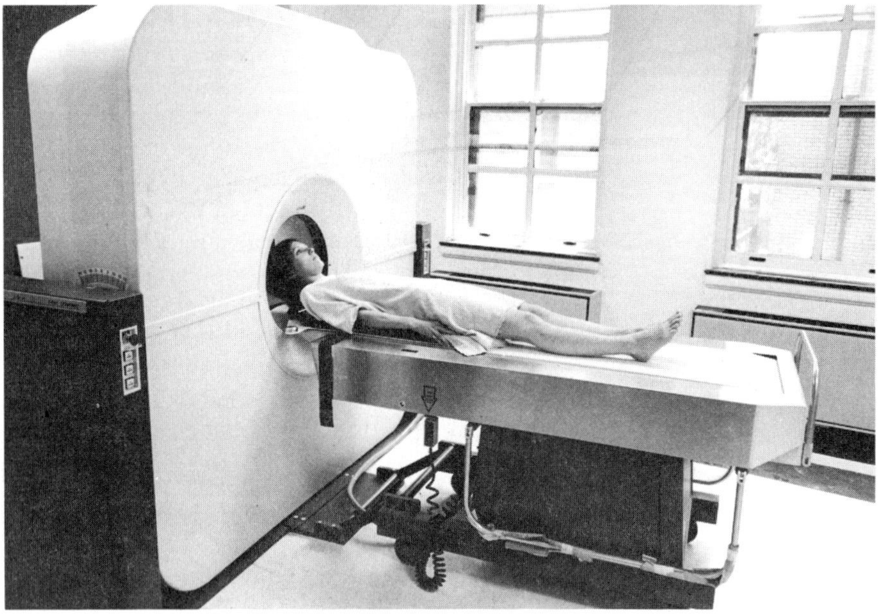

Figure 18–10 C.A.T. Scanner

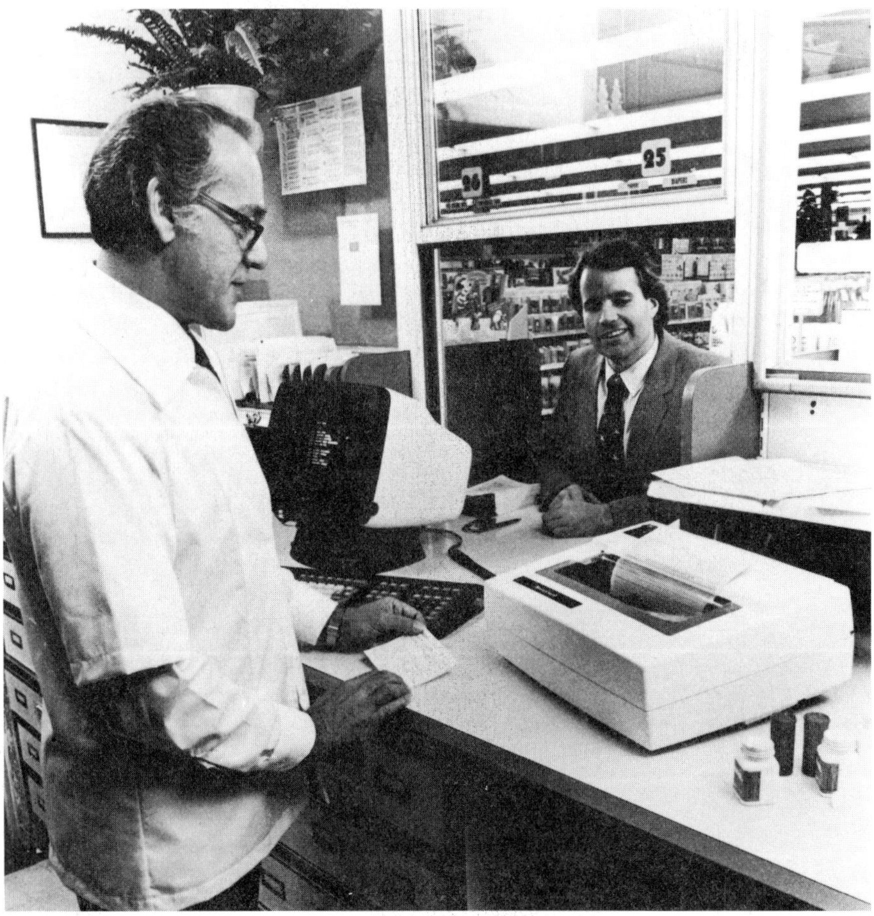

Figure 18–11 Computers Serve Pharmacists and their Customers

Computers in Action 8

Meeting the Challenge

1. Tucked away in the woods of Oregon, an author finds a personal computer to be a warm and loving companion.

1

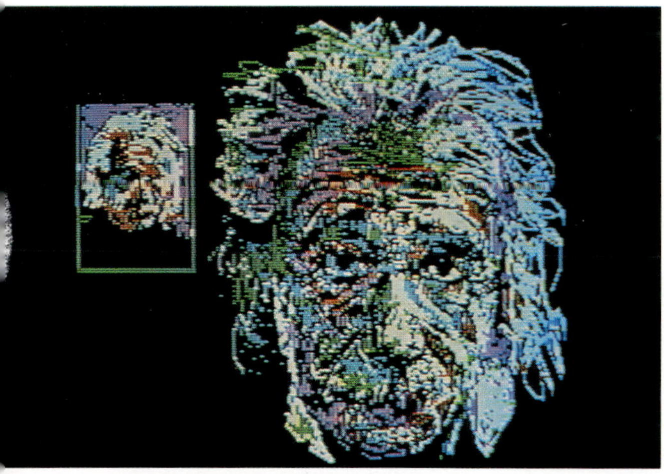

2

2. Some personal computer software packages provide exciting graphics capabilities. **3.** This computer-generated art is exceptionally beautiful. It should help Thad Watson convince his Phelonian captors that computers have contributed positively to the quality of life.

3

4

5

4. Keyboards connected to a computer-controlled synthesizer make beautiful music together, which even the Phelonians could appreciate.
5. Many schools and colleges provide microcomputer laboratories to enhance their educational processes.
6. Computers are essential to the information processing tasks involved in urban planning. **7.** This is a breathtaking view of the surface of the planet Orthon 792, taken from an errant satellite.

6

7

8. Thad will be able to explain to the Phelonians that some of Earth's robots were put to good use.
9. Those with physical impairments which make it impossible to read benefit greatly from a reading machine which combines a page scanner, a computer, and a voice generation unit.
10. Computers with light pens as input devices assist people whose ability to type is hindered by injury or disease.

8

9

10

11. The buying/selling process on Earth was greatly aided by special point-of-sale terminals. **12.** The inhabitants of Earth will be forever in the debt of these automatic teller machines. **13.** Even as Thad suffers through his Phelonian trial, his friends compare notes on personal computer software packages. **14.** When he returns to Earth, Thad will have to return to the task of budgeting his expenses for the coming year, something his parents have asked for repeatedly. His spreadsheet program awaits his return.

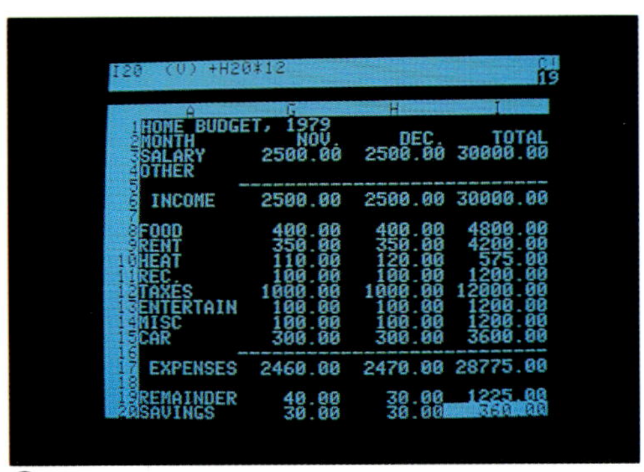

makes use of the results of laboratory tests, the observations of a doctor, and a vast amount of medical information to help the doctor develop diagnoses on an interactive basis. Doctors, or their assistants, enter patient information through the keyboard of a terminal, and the program suggests various possible diagnoses to the doctor and outlines the various procedures necessary to refine the diagnosis. While these programs are not currently as competent as the best specialists in a particular area, they do provide an excellent screening technique and valuable assistance to doctors without training in specific areas of medicine.

The use of computers in pharmacies provides yet another improvement in health care delivery. In addition to handling the routine matters of filing, billing, and inventory control, systems are available to help pharmacists detect errors in the prescription of drugs or the existence of potentially dangerous drug interactions. The pharmacist's computing system maintains a file regarding patients' allergies, drug sensitivities, and their current usages of drugs. Then, when a new drug is prescribed, the program can check that drug for possibly dangerous interactions with the patient's current medication or for possibly negative side effects with the patient's other health problems. See Figure 18–11 for an illustration.

Health Care: Tomorrow

Computers should continue to contribute positively to health care delivery well into the future. The use of expert systems to improve diagnostic procedures and spread expertise throughout the medical community should increase with time. Computer-aided equipment will continue to be used in testing and treatment procedures.

Other computer-related activities include the taking of case histories, the use of computer-aided self-diagnosis, and medical histories implemented in "smart" cards—microprocessor-based cards with large storage capabilities. Even greater improvements should be forthcoming as we learn more about diseases and their cures. Computers are used extensively to support medical research efforts.

Another very interesting area of computer use is within the area of law. A brief look at some uses of computers in professions related to the law is presented next.

Law and Law Enforcement: Today

Several systems are in place to assist in the making of laws, the use of laws in the court system, and the enforcement of laws. Only a few of those systems can be discussed here.

The Making of Laws

Two of the information processing burdens which must be borne by the legislators on both the state and national level have recently been made

Figure 18–12
Computer-Aided Research by Legislative Staff

less burdensome through the use of computerized systems. The first burden is that of keeping track of the status of each of the hundreds of bills which comes before the legislature. An on-line system, to which legislators and their staffs have access, could detail the current status of each bill. Through use of such a system (see Figure 18–12), lawmakers can plan their research more effectively, use their time more efficiently, and respond more adequately to the questions of their constituents.

The second burden for lawmakers is that of staying abreast of the opinions of their constituents on issues which are being discussed in the legislature. Many legislative sessions are now being broadcast via cable television. The advent of two-way videotex systems will enable legislators to poll the voters in their respective districts through the use of home computers and network communications. Limited testing of this concept began in the early 1980s.

The Courts

Cases tried in our courts are judged on their merits with respect to the written laws of the country and the precedents set by prior, similar court cases. Legal staffs often spend countless hours researching historical court records to find cases which might have bearing on current litigations. A computer-based information retrieval system can be used to greatly improve the productivity of the research effort.

Law Enforcement

Large collections of information about citizens exist in the computer-based systems of the government which were built to serve other needs. Personal information about most adult Americans can be found in the files of either the Internal Revenue Service (IRS), the Social Security Administration, the Armed Services, or the Federal Bureau of Investigation (FBI). Many other local, state, and federal agencies are sometimes allowed access to these files (see Figure 18–13). The FBI, for example, maintains an enormous data base in the National Crime Information Center to which law enforcement agencies throughout the United States have access.

Figure 18–13
Computers Aid Law Enforcement and Public Safety Efforts

A rather subtle use of these large collections of data began to be made in the early 1980s. The previously separate data bases maintained by the IRS, the Social Security Administration, and Medicare, among others, became the target of government efforts to catch people who were defrauding the government. Income tax records could be used to find people who had defaulted on the repayment of student loans. For example, files of the IRS were used in 1982 to send notices to those young men of draft age who had failed to register. Similarly, comparisons of the welfare rolls of adjacent counties could be used to identify fraudulent claims.

Efforts to use the previously separate files in combination, for purposes beyond their original intent, brought increased concern about the misuse of data contained in the files. Informational privacy becomes a very important issue when computerized data banks are under discussion. For example, a system was proposed in the early 1980s to help keep problem drivers from obtaining a driver's license. The National Driver Register would be computerized and used to allow states to check the driving records of license applicants before issuing a license. Such a large collection of potentially sensitive information accessed by many states could lead to abuse and invasions of privacy.

Privacy

As citizens, our rights to privacy are protected by law, although laws which guarantee our rights with respect to informational privacy are not as comprehensive as they perhaps should be. Informational privacy issues arise when information about us is shared with people without our permission and access to that information is not adequately controlled. Most people would prefer that information about their school grades, driving infractions, creditworthiness, and legal and social problems not be made available for other than official use.

Our informational privacy rights are much more likely to be violated in a computerized information environment which allows inexpensive sharing of large data banks and access to them from remote terminals. Sometimes the organizations to whom we give personal data to secure a loan, obtain a credit card, or gain membership will sell or otherwise share that information with other organizations. For example, magazine publishers and mail-order houses rely heavily on mailing lists acquired from others. It becomes impossible to know which organizations have copies of our personal data in their files.

Two very sensitive areas within which we would like to see some control exercised are the areas of financial information and law enforcement information. There are several critical questions which cause conflict in attempts to establish effective legislation. Does a potential employer have a right to know a job applicant's criminal record? Does that right extend to both convictions and arrests? Is there any length of time beyond which the applicant's criminal history is unimportant, or does the employer have a right to know about events that happened ten, twenty, or even thirty years ago? Does that mean that people will never be forgiven for their past mistakes?

A similar set of questions can be raised with respect to applications for credit. Does a potential lender have a right to know the applicant's complete financial history? Will a poor credit rating be allowed to follow a person forever? Can we protect both the lender and the borrower at the same time? These questions illustrate that a balance must be achieved between one party's right to know and the other party's right to outlive the past.

In general, business organizations have always expressed an interest in voluntary compliance with a set of guidelines rather than in having state and federal legislatures pass comprehensive privacy laws. Such an approach would certainly be less costly, in general, if an agreeable level of informational privacy can be achieved.

The most significant pieces of privacy legislation have been the Fair Credit Reporting Act of 1970 and the Privacy Act of 1974. Both, however, seem to fall far short of the level of privacy protection which is desirable. The Privacy Protection Study Commission, created by the Privacy Act of 1974, has since identified two major areas in which privacy legislation seems to be lacking.

First, there are inadequate protections for an individual's privacy during routine information-gathering procedures. Videotex services via cable television provide an excellent example. Records of a customer's use of Videotex services are routinely made in order to correctly charge for use of the service. Summaries of this data could provide profiles of the users themselves, information which should be private. A court trial in 1982, for instance, raised the question of a community norm for viewing X-rated television programs. Data collected by the cable television station were used to compute the average viewing of "adult" material by households in the community.

The second major concern expressed by the commission was the lack of control over sharing of informally collected information among organizations. Current laws seem only to restrict the sharing of information which is explicitly confidential. A great deal of work remains before adequate informational privacy becomes the norm.

Challenge Update

The reader should now be able to describe several potential threats to privacy which have become more likely due to computerization efforts.

Fraud and Theft

Chapter 15 discussed the issues of software piracy and unauthorized access. Chapter 16 discussed the responsibility of management with respect to the potential increases in fraud, theft, sabotage, and espionage. So-called **computer crime** presents an interesting challenge to the quality of life. A clever fraudulent act or theft is still a criminal act. A resurgence of interest in the development of moral principles is needed to guarantee that such acts do not become disruptive in a major sense.

Modern computing systems have several characteristics which those people with criminal intentions find useful. They are extremely fast, so they can be used to try telephone numbers and password combinations to gain unauthorized access. There are vast numbers of computing systems connected to the long-distance telephone network, which makes the systems accessible from remote locations. They also provide an electronic environment in which few "footprints" or other clues are left behind by an intruder.

Computers themselves are only neutral devices, but they can be used in unfortunate ways. Computer professionals, managers, and educators all have obligations to exercise good judgment in the use of computers and in the training of those who use them. An introductory data processing or computer literacy class is a good place to begin that effort.

Meanwhile, legislative efforts to develop effective laws to deal with computer crime seem slow to materialize. A report by John Gallant indicated that although there were a number of bills in Congress in the spring of 1984 which dealt with computer crime, very little action seemed to be taking place. The bills, if they became law, would make unauthorized use of a computer to defraud or steal a federal offense.

Law and Law Enforcement: Tomorrow

Legislative bodies and their members can be expected to significantly increase their use of computers in the future. Computers will be found useful by legislative staffs to accomplish research and analysis as well as communication via electronic mail with other offices, government, and constituents. In conjunction with videotex, computers in legislative offices could be used for improving citizen involvement in the legislative process. Law enforcement agencies will improve in their abilities to gain access to information about criminal activities on a nationwide basis. The courts will continue to use computers to keep court calendars and expand their use to jury selection and management.

Legislation to deal effectively with computer crime will eventually be passed, though we should not expect its deterrence or enforcement to be any more effective than laws against other criminal acts.

Predictions of the future seem to indicate that computer security will become even more important as more people access larger data banks over increasingly distributed networks. We could see a decrease in physical control, an increase in errors, and a greater risk from unauthorized use.

Challenge Update

The reader should now be able to help Thad describe the characteristics of computing systems which contribute to computer crime.

National Defense: Today

National security keeps us from knowing the full extent to which computers are used in military applications in support of the defense of the nation, but we can be assured that such uses are extensive. Military applications include intelligence-gathering satellites and far-reaching networks of earth stations. Computers are also integral parts of weapons delivery systems in tanks, airplanes, missiles, and pieces of artillery. Virtually all of the missile systems are computer launched and computer guided (see Figure 18–14).

The military establishment makes extensive use of computer simulations for training and the design of defense strategies. Nuclear war simulations provide indications of the impact of a nuclear attack on this country and its inhabitants. Submarine warfare simulations provide training for the personnel who will be assigned to that service. Flight simulators have been used for many years in the training of pilots. Numerous other simulation programs are used throughout the military services.

Many of the technological developments in computing were funded by the Department of Defense. The first computer network, the ARPANET was funded by the department's Advanced Research Projects Agency (ARPA). Extensive research efforts requiring extremely large budgets are currently underway because most of the technological advances in computing have national defense ramifications.

It is difficult to assess the impact on our lives of activities undertaken in the interest of national defense. These activities have clearly increased the prevailing level of employment. They have also led to significant technological advance, particularly in the area of computing. Their social, political, and economic impacts are much more difficult to judge.

Figure 18–14
Computers at Work in National Defense

"There's no denying the profound impact all this has on the course of human life, but let's never forget one thing. It's still love that makes the world go round."

National Defense: Tomorrow

Of course, there is not much unclassified material on which to base speculation about future uses of computers in the area of national defense. Much of the progress that has been made in the field of computing has resulted from research efforts funded by the Department of Defense. A significant part of the effort to develop fifth-generation computers is being funded by the government.

Virtually all of the warning and weapons systems now in place or planned for the foreseeable future rely upon computer control. Until such time as the world powers feel confident of peace, we can expect large expenditures of public funds on computing for national defense.

A less controversial use of computers has been found in the area of urban affairs. The next section provides a review of some of the activities in that area.

Urban Affairs: Today

The affairs of our cities concern most of us. Beyond the usual organizational uses of computers by cities, two other uses are significant. Neither is a surprise to the city dweller because neither is particularly new. Computers are used in traffic control and urban planning (see Figure 18–15). Computer-controlled traffic signals which receive traffic level inputs from sensors embedded in the streets and adjust traffic lights to ease the flow of cars and trucks throughout the city have been in use since the 1970s.

Urban planners use simulation programs to determine the effects of urban developments upon the flow of traffic, the change in population densities, and the available sunlight. For example, graphics programs can plot three dimensional perspectives of the city skyline to determine the impact of a new high-rise building.

Urban Affairs: Tomorrow

The uses of computers in urban affairs will undoubtedly increase with time. The sheer magnitude of numbers of people living in urban areas make the computer a necessary tool in traffic control, billing for city services, keeping

Figure 18–15
Computers Aid Public Transportation and Traffic Control

track of voters, and so on. We may see citizen access to libraries, to city service departments, and to elected officials via electronic mail or videotex.

The design of parks, urban areas, and neighborhoods has a far-reaching effect on the lives of people who work and live in the city. So do traffic and the scheduling of public transportation. The use of computing systems, it is hoped, will help make our cities more livable.

Urban design is one of the many areas in which the computer has had an impact upon the quality of life. Other impacts have been discussed in the areas of agriculture, art, economics, education, health care, and so on. The changes which occur in the quality of life go far beyond the technological changes themselves, as the next section explores.

Social, Economic, and Political Change

Changes in technology usually trigger changes in other areas. The rapid rate of change in the technology of computing has had, and will continue to have, significant social, economic, and political impact.

Information, for example, is a source of power socially, economically, and politically. People's values change as they absorb more knowledge. Those with better educations are more flexible in adapting to a society in which technological change is occurring. They are better equipped to cope with the changes in skills required by the changing nature of the work force. Superior information is often the determining factor in political struggles for power within organizations of all types.

Societies usually experience significant disruption as a result of great technological advancement. Adjustment in the social, economic, and political spheres usually lags behind technological adaptation. Automobiles, for example, represent a technology which was quickly adapted. They stimulated the development of suburban areas, which eventually led to deterioration of the older central cities. Significant social, economic, and political issues arose which are still unresolved.

How will an affluent society deal with the millions of people who have been displaced from productive work by computing machines? What social, economic, and political changes are necessary in order to hold our society together? Will the computer lead to the best of all possible worlds, the worst of all possible worlds, or some tolerable place in-between? The answers will, in time, become known.

Knowledge of the fantastic capabilities of computers and a desire to put them to intelligent use will help form the future in a positive way. The process has only just begun.

Challenge Update

Thad and the reader should now be able to discuss both the positive and negative impacts that computers have on our lives through their use in agriculture, art, economics, education, health care, national defense, and urban affairs.

Newest Developments

Computers are already becoming more commonplace in our lives, and that trend will continue. Although their contribution to the history of man will continue to be questioned from time to time, as are the contributions of telephones, combustion engines, and nuclear power, they will for the most part be recognized as tools capable of both beneficial and malevolent use.

Personal computers will become as common as televisions and power lawnmowers. They will be as loved as chocolate chip cookies when their services are desperately needed and as hated as telephone answering devices at the end of an important call when not. Their users will be many, but their misuse will continue to be a problem for some time.

Perhaps we should see how Thad is doing in preparing his speech for the Phelonian Assembly.

COMPUTING CHALLENGE: *A Final Note*

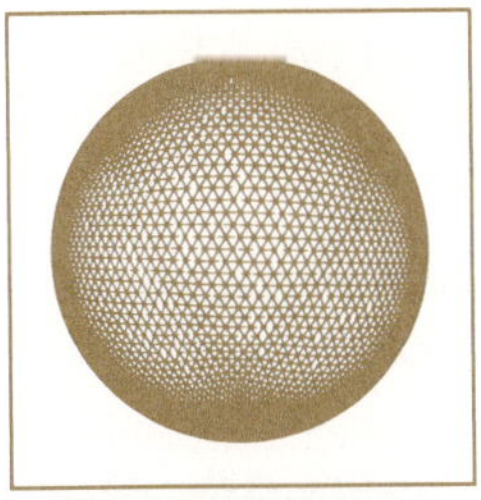

Thad's notes for his presentation were complete, but he worried about his concluding remarks. He became quite disturbed at his assignment and feared for his life. He thought about escape. His thoughts were interrupted by a strange electronic noise . . . bleeem!

Bleeem! Thad bolted upright in his bed. His micropocessor-based wrist-watch alarm had sounded, ending his nap. He had gone to the library to work on a term paper about computers but had fallen asleep. What a dream he had experienced!

What did it all mean?

Why did he have to decide whether or not computers were good or bad?

Who cared anyway?

SUMMARY

- The purpose of this chapter has been to explore some of the many ways in which the quality of life has been enhanced by the use of computers, but a single chapter can only begin to scratch the surface in terms of identifying the many uses to which the computer can be put, for computers can be used to serve many different ends.
- While computers serve our society in beneficial ways, they sometimes contribute in an unfortunate way to a reduction in the quality of life.
- Computers in agriculture, art, economics, education, health care, law enforcement, national defense, and urban planning can improve the society in which we live.

- The acquisition of a computing system represents a typical substitution of capital for labor in the productive process, and such a substitution virtually always increases the productivity of labor.
- The full impact on overall productivity of installing a computer cannot be measured without considering the other factors of production: materials, energy, and capital.
- Productivity improvement needs must be tempered by the other needs of employees and organizations.
- As computers displace workers from their current jobs, unemployment will tend to increase.
- Retraining, relocation, and other effective means must be developed to prevent the impact upon employment from becoming catastrophic to our society.
- Rapid technological change stimulates and leads changes in the social, economic, and political spheres as well, and societies which do not adapt to such changes ultimately fail.
- Vigilance is necessary to minimize the extent to which the quality of life is threatened by a greater incidence of computer crime.
- The existence of large data bases containing personal information, to which remote access is possible, raises the possibility that our informational privacy will be abused.
- Threats to our personal informational privacy can be monitored and minimized through the vigilance of consumer groups, the voluntary compliance with privacy guidelines by organizations, and the development of effective privacy legislation by lawmakers.
- The uses to which computers can be effectively put and the impacts those uses have on the quality of life require that people have a better understanding of the capabilities of computers.
- The purpose of this text has been to contribute in a positive way to that understanding, recognizing that a great deal can be accomplished if we all contribute some of our energies to the development of a better tomorrow.

CASE: The Use of Computing to Conserve Energy

The energy crises precipitated by the Arab Oil Embargo of the early 1970s has had far reaching implications for our society. The threat of insufficient energy resources stimulated research efforts in the field of synthetic fuels, stepped up efforts to develop nuclear power facilities, and caused us all to evaluate our energy consumption patterns. Energy conservation efforts were developed and put into effect across the country, one example of which is illustrated in this case.

The San Diego Gas & Electric Company (SDG&E) provides a valuable energy conservation service to its customers. Energy technicians are available upon invitation to inspect a house for poor insulation, inefficient heating and cooling methods, and excessive gas or electricity usage. Data are fed into a computer in which a specialized program computes a detailed analysis of the home's energy conservation merits (or potential) and recommends possible improvements.

The Home Energy Conservation Analysis is based on specific data about the home that the energy audit technician gathers through both a weatherization inspection and an interview with family members. The data gathered includes quality of insulation, number of members of the household, and average past utility bills. The analysis itself is performed on the central computers of the General Electric Information Services Company in Rockville, Maryland. The data the technician obtains are transmitted from the technician's portable terminal via the homeowner's telephone. The data are processed immediately, and within seconds a synthesized voice from the central computer reports the results of the analysis. The auditor records the results on a report form for the residents.

The audited family benefits from lower utility bills if the recommended actions are taken, and society in general benefits from the resulting conservation of energy. Any utility company could use the same system with the proper equipment and information.

"Audit Program Evaluates Home Energy Conservation," *Infosystems*, September 1981, pp. 144–149. Reprinted from INFOSYSTEMS.

Questions for the Case

1. The energy audit described here is one of many examples in which computers are used to analyze and recommend improvements. Name others.
2. Name some areas in which computers have contributed to a decrease in efficiency or effectiveness.

DISCUSSION QUESTIONS AND EXERCISES

1. Describe the area in which computers have had the greatest positive influence on the quality of life.
2. Describe the area in which computers have had the greatest negative impact on the quality of life.
3. Explain the impact on productivity figures of the substitution of capital for labor which is typical of a computer acquisition.
4. What are the characteristics of data processing systems which cause them to be threats to our informational privacy?
5. Describe the probable impact on unemployment of each of the following:
   (a) Automation.
   (b) Shorter work week.
   (c) Higher retirement age.
   (d) War.
6. Computers have had both positive and negative impacts on the quality of life. Describe particular computer applications which have had both impacts.
7. Discuss examples of the social, economic, and political impacts of other significant technological changes, for example, the airplane, television, electricity, and videos.

8. What can managers of organizations do to improve the impact of computers on the working lives of people in the organization?
9. What should the government do to ensure that computers contribute positively to the quality of life?
10. Think about a day in the life of a manager, other employee, other professional, or a student. In what ways have computers contributed positively to that person's experience. In what ways has the contribution been negative?
11. Survey a group of twenty to thirty students. How many own personal computers? How many expect to buy them within a year?
12. Interview several people in each of the following age groups: over fifty, thirty to fifty, fifteen to thirty. Determine if they feel differently about the impact of computers on the quality of life.
13. Survey current periodicals in agriculture, science, medicine, data processing, and selected areas of the humanities. Are computers viewed differently by each of these areas? Explain.
14. Do something to improve the quality of living for others. Put a nice message in the instructor's electronic mail box. Call home. Pick up litter. Turn down the volume on the stereo. Drive carefully.

ADDITIONAL READINGS

Bequai, August. *How to Prevent Computer Crime: A Guide for Managers.* New York: Wiley, 1983.

Bjorn-Anderson, N., et al., eds. *Information Society: For Richer, For Poorer.* New York: Elsevier Science Publishing, 1982.

Crichton, Michael. *Electronic Life: How to Think about Computers.* New York: Knopf, 1983.

Fossum, Eystein. *Computerization of Working Life.* New York: Wiley, 1983.

Frates, Jeffrey, and Moldrup, William. *Computers and Life: An Integrative Approach.* Englewood Cliffs, NJ: Prentice-Hall, 1983.

Hockey, Susan. *A Guide to Computer Applications in the Humanities.* Baltimore, MD: Johns Hopkins University Press, 1980.

Hoffman, Lance J., ed. *Computers and Privacy in the Next Decade.* New York: Academic Press, 1980.

Laver, Murray. *Computers and Social Change.* New York: Cambridge University Press, 1982.

McCorduck, Pamela. *Machines Who Think.* San Francisco: W. H. Freeman, 1979.

Norback, Craig T. *The Computer Invasion.* New York: Van Nostrand Reinhold, 1981.

Parker, Donn B. *Fighting Computer Crime.* New York: Scribner's, 1983.

Ramo, Simon. *What's Wrong with Our Technological Society—And How to Fix It.* New York: McGraw-Hill, 1983.

Rule, McAdam, Stearns, and Uglow. *The Politics of Privacy.* Westport, CT: Greenwood Press, 1980.

Sparks, Leslie E. *Investment Analysis with Your Microcomputer.* Blue Ridge Summit, PA: Tab Books, 1983.

Appendix A

Problem Solving and Programming

The ability to write computer programs can be quite beneficial. Those who excel in programming have an opportunity to pursue an interesting career. Others, however, will find that a knowledge of programming will help them in other careers. On many occasions we, as users of computers, are asked to work with the program development staff to specify, outline, or judge a particular applications program. Firsthand knowledge of the programming process is a definite advantage in such consultations.

The writing of a computer program to solve a particular data processing task is always challenging, frequently fun, but sometimes very frustrating. The frustrations occur often enough that efforts to reduce them are important. Experienced programmers gradually develop a methodology for program development which is efficient and effective. A beginning programmer must develop good problem-solving techniques and learn early to employ the best in programming practices.

Some programs are short exercises in problem solving written by the user to perform certain tasks for relatively brief periods of time. Others are very large in size, written by teams of programmers for the performance of sizeable data processing tasks. The degree of formality with which a program is developed differs according to its size, its importance, its ultimate role in the data processing systems of the organization, and the size of the programming team.

A small, user-written program intended for limited use would become overburdened by the same set of program development rules that are necessary for the development of standard, production software intended to faithfully serve many users over a long period of time. On the other hand, if production programs were written with the same degree of informality as a small, user-written program, disastrous results would undoubtedly occur.

In this appendix we will explore the program development process at a level of formality which will encourage good programming practice on the part of users and programmers alike. Professional programmers will, of course, need a significant amount of additional material, but nothing here should be wasted effort, even for them.

The program development process will be described as a sequence of five steps:

1. Problem analysis.
2. Algorithm design.
3. Formal representation of program logic.
4. Coding.
5. Testing and debugging.

These steps will lead the programmer through the proper sequence of activities in the development of a program, from an understanding of the problem itself, through a formal representation of the procedure necessary to accomplish the task itself, to the generation and testing of the finished program.

Students new to the art and science of programming are advised not to take any shortcuts. Experienced programmers have developed an understanding of the potential costs incurred by the taking of shortcuts and do not, therefore, need that advice.

Programming is fun. It is also very challenging. The challenge always seems to be: Is the programmer clever enough to outwit the machine? Sometimes it seems to be: Can the programmer overcome the numerous obstacles caused by the machine's obstinance and stupidity in order to produce a working program? In reality, of course, it is only: Can the programmer develop an understanding of the problem adequate enough to specify (and document) the instructions necessary to correctly direct the machine's efforts and provide the user(s) with output that is timely, relevant, accurate, and usable?

The machine, of course, is not really malevolent, but it is sometimes hard for the programmer to keep its neutrality in perspective. It certainly seems, at times, to be the opponent in a win-or-lose struggle. The fact of the matter is that it has been designed to expect a certain well-defined behavior on the part of the programmer. If the programmer departs, however slightly, from the rules of expected behavior, the machine becomes "confused" and unable to perform in the manner the programmer (or user) wishes.

Programming is a cooperative effort between the machine and the programmers. The machine does its part only if the programmer does his or hers; and, in the long run, it will make far fewer errors than its human helper.

Problem Analysis

The purpose of the program development process is to generate a well-designed, well-written computer program designed to accomplish a particular data processing task. The first step in the program development process is problem analysis, assuming that problem identification has been completed elsewhere. Problem identification, of course, is sometimes difficult and is always a most important element. It depends upon the skill and analysis of a talented user.

For some time yet, the beginning programmer will be constrained to the use of the class of languages known as **procedural languages,** in which the programmer must specify the exact procedure the machine is to use to perform the desired task. Although nonprocedural languages are available, most beginners will have to serve an apprenticeship in the procedural languages to provide a quality base upon which to build good programming skills.

It may also be true that the increased use of program development aids will decrease the extent to which a programmer will be asked to develop program logic step by step. There is, however, no substitute for the requirement that programmers be able to develop logical procedures and arrange them in an appropriate way. We continue that emphasis here.

The programmer must be able to identify the outputs which are required and the means by which they are to be generated. The outputs produced by a program and most data values used within a program are identified within the program in association with a variable name. Thus, the variable names to be used in a program for the manipulation of output values must be identified.

The programmer next looks to the inputs that are available and useful in the particular data processing task at hand. These must be identified and appropriate variable names must be assigned.

Attention must then be directed to the *transformations* which are necessary to derive the desired outputs from the available inputs. These transformations may require the temporary storage of intermediate results which will again require that variable names be assigned to them.

The products of the problem analysis phase of program development are an understanding on the part of the programmer of the tasks to be performed by the program and an identification of all variables to be used. These products become an important part of the overall **documentation** of the program itself. The programmer should produce and place in the documentation file a narrative statement of the purpose of the program, the general means by which the purpose will be attained, and a list of the variable names together with their corresponding explanations. As discussed elsewhere in the text, proper documentation also will include flowcharts, decision tables, and pseudocode necessary to clearly identify the logic to be used in solving the problem.

Algorithm Design. The step-by-step procedure which is necessary to solve a particular problem-solving task is known as an **algorithm.** Development of the algorithm is the second step in the program development process.

Only three basic structures are necessary for the statement of any algorithm, hence the statement of any computer program. An algorithm, or a computer program, needs the ability to specify a **sequence** of operations, the ability to **select** from among two or more alternate sequences, and the ability to perform **iterations,** that is, to repeat sequences. With these basic structures virtually any problem-solving procedure (hence any computer program) can be specified.

The algorithm represents the *logic* of the data processing task, the separate sub-tasks which must be completed in order to complete the overall task required of the program. Algorithms for complex data processing tasks could be very complex themselves, so complex that their specification needs to be accomplished in stages.

In the first stage of algorithm development, the overall task is specified only in terms of the major sub-tasks necessary to accomplish it. The second stage, and each successive stage, takes each sub-task and refines it into even smaller tasks. This step-wise refinement of the overall task into a final set of small tasks is the basis for a design method known as **top/down design.** The top/down design method asks the designer/programmer to first devote attention to the overall, logical relationships among the major sub-tasks, and then to consider the logical relationships within the sub-tasks themselves.

Once the logic of the program has been fully specified, the programmer should review this logic by tracing the various paths through the algorithm to develop confidence that the algorithm has been correctly specified. Often the programmer checks the algorithm by assuming the role of a CPU in reading and executing the instructions in the algorithm. This **desk checking** of the algorithm will help detect errors which would later cause the program to fail.

The contribution of this phase to the program's documentation is the final, detailed version of the algorithm itself. The documentation now contains a general narrative of the problem, the general means by which the problem will be solved, the identification of all variables, and a detailed statement of the algorithm which will be developed into the program.

Formal Representation of Program Logic. The next phase of the program development process is that of *representing the logic of the algorithm in some formal way* so that two basic purposes are served. In the first place, the formal representation gives the program designer an opportunity to once again check the logic of the program itself. Most of the methods used to formally represent the logic provide a graphical representation of the program logic, which is easier to check than the narrative of the algorithm itself.

The formal representation of program logic also makes it possible to *share the program development workload* with others. At this point in the process the overall programming task can be divided into subprograms, called **modules,** so that the modules can be developed by several programmers working in parallel. The translation of any of the forms of formal representations of program logic into a computer program is very straightforward and can usually be accomplished by junior programmers or programmer trainees. This frees the senior programmer/designer for other work.

We will explore four methods for formally representing program logic: flowcharts, pseudocode, HIPO, and Warnier/Orr diagrams.

Flowcharts

Flowcharts are network-like drawings, which are drawn to represent the logical paths and relationships within many different types of systems. They are used by chemical engineers, for example, to represent the steps in the processing of chemicals. They are used by data processing professionals to represent the steps in the processing of data.

Flowcharts are used by data processing professionals in two different but related ways. In **systems flowcharting** they are used to graphically represent the flow of information through a data processing system. In **program flowcharting** they are used to represent the various steps in a computer program. An example systems flowchart is shown in Figure A–1, and the symbols used there are explained in Figure A–2.

Systems flowcharts differ from program flowcharts in the level of detail which they are used to illustrate. Systems flowcharts illustrate the overall data flows in a complete system, while program flowcharts illustrate the computing steps within a single program module. An example program flowchart is shown in Figure A–3, and the symbols used there are explained in Figure A–4.

The difference in level of detail and the tie between systems flowcharts and program flowcharts can be seen easily. The program represented in Figure A–3 fits entirely within the process box of Figure A–1. That is, the processing symbol (the rectangle) is used in systems programming to represent computer processing. The particular computer processing which is to be done is represented by the entire program flowchart in Figure A–3.

Systems flowcharting is an extremely useful skill. Systems analysts use it regularly to study current systems and to design new ones. Most texts

FIGURE A–1
Systems Flowchart—Class Scheduling Example

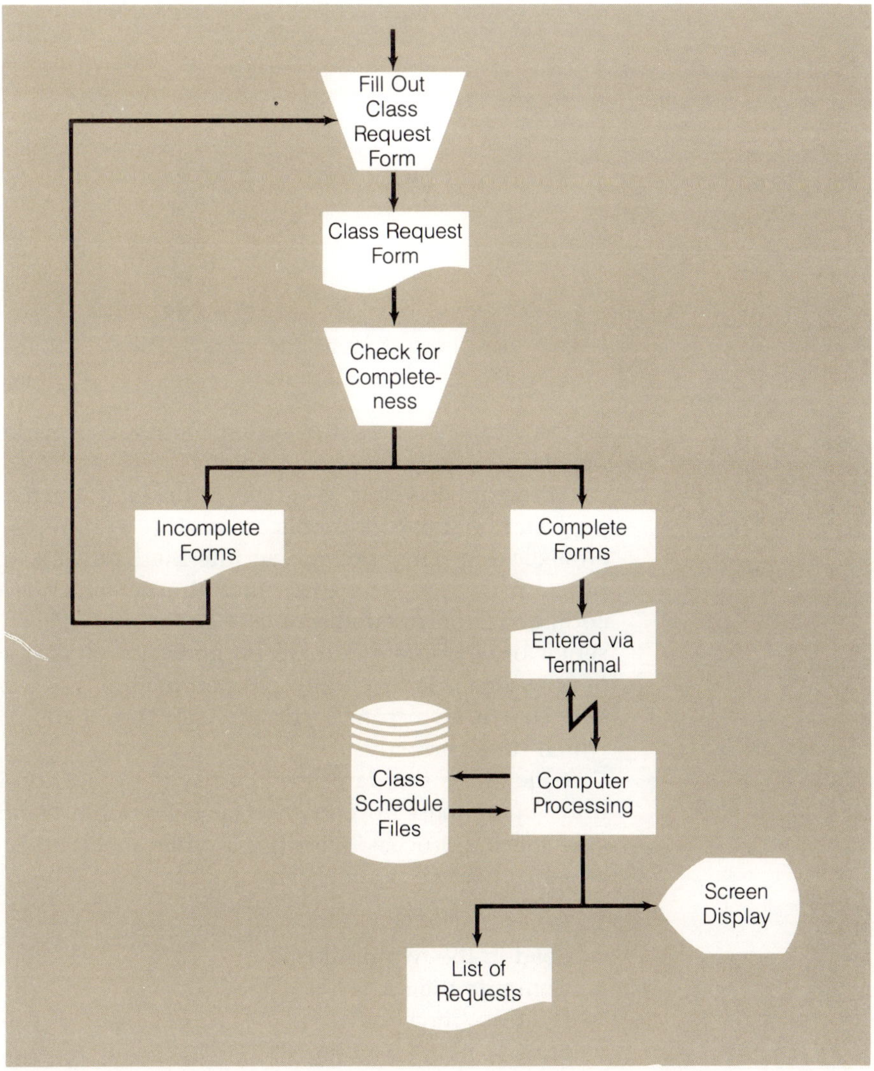

FIGURE A–2
Explanation for Systems Flowchart Symbols Used in Figure A–1

Symbol	Use in Figure A-1
Manual Operation	1. Student preparing request for classes 2. Clerk checking request form
Document	1. Class request form 2. List of requests
Manual Input	1. Keyboard entry of requests
Processing	1. Computer processing of requests
Magnetic Disk	1. Storage of available classes
Display	1. Screen display of student schedule

on the formal processes of systems analysis provide coverage of it in some detail.

A program flowchart is equally as useful in the development of computer programs. Standard symbols are used to graphically represent the logic of an algorithm. They provide an intermediate step in the development of a program in the sense that, once the flowchart is completed, the actual coding of the program becomes significantly easier. In many organizations, senior programmers develop program flowcharts, while the actual coding of programs is left to junior programmers or programmer trainees. A good flowchart drawn from a correct algorithm leads to a computer program which runs correctly.

Some of the standard flowchart symbols are shown in Figure A–5. I will draw upon these to construct a few sample flowcharts to illustrate the flowcharting process. Consider a program which is supposed to read and add together two numbers and print the sum. The algorithm looks like this:

1. Begin.
2. Read in the two numbers.
3. Compute the sum.
4. Print out the sum.
5. Stop.

FIGURE A–3
Program Flowchart—Class Schedule

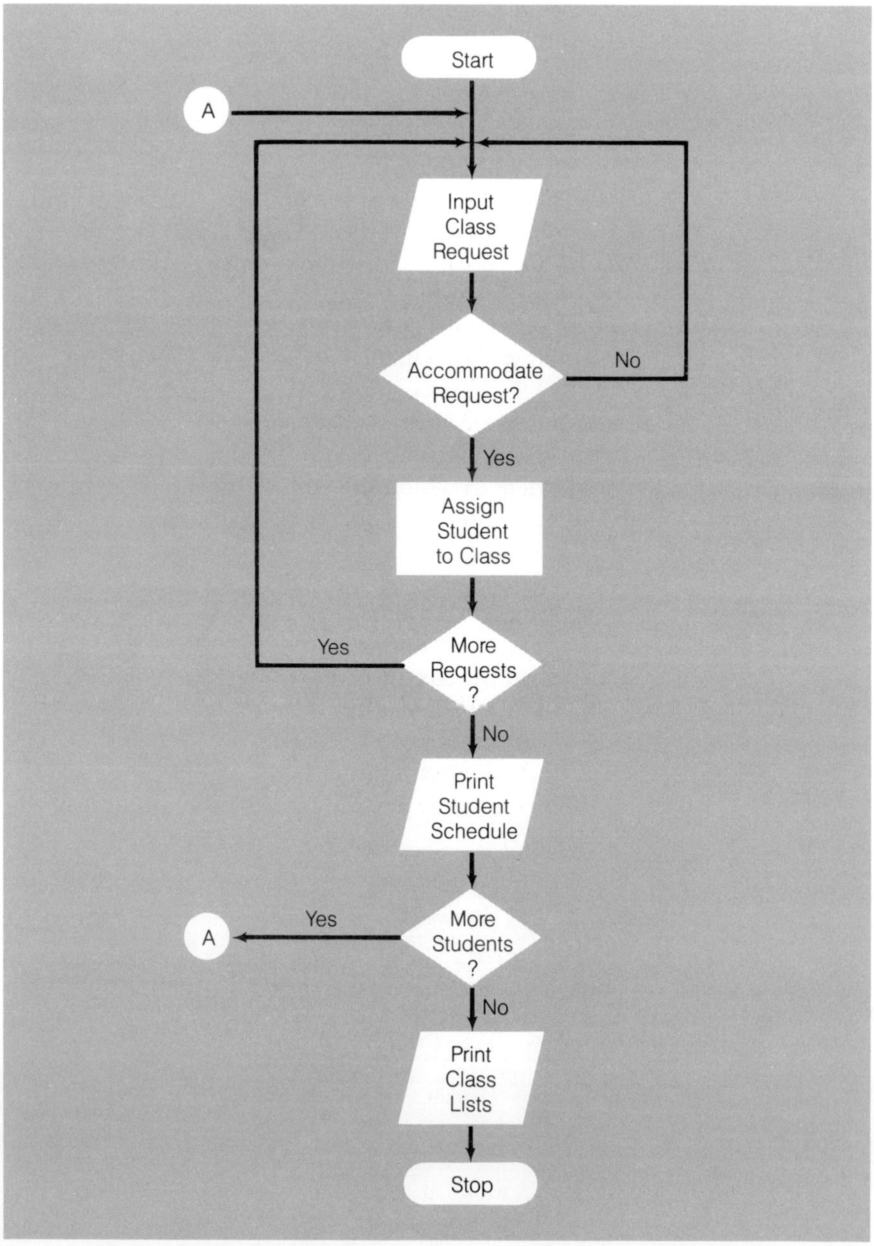

The flowchart which represents this algorithm is shown in Figure A–6.

Suppose we change the assignment to one which requires that the program repeat the processing steps of reading, summing, and printing for a given number of times, say ten times. The algorithm must now include provisions for repeating some of the steps, for counting the number of times the steps have been repeated, and for stopping when ten repeats have been completed. The new algorithm would be:

1. Begin.
2. Initialize counter.
3. Read in two numbers.
4. Compute the sum.
5. Print out the sum.
6. Increase the counter by 1.
7. Check the value of the counter against 10, and
   if less than 10, return to Step 3,
   if not less than 10 go to Step 8.
8. Stop.

The flowchart which represents this algorithm is shown in Figure A–7.

To add more complexity, assume that the program is to print not only the sums associated with each pair of numbers, but to print the overall sum of all the numbers at the end of the program. To do this an *accumulator* is needed, in which the sum of the sums (a running sub-total) can be kept. The new algorithm now looks like this:

1. Begin.
2. Initialize counter.
3. Initialize accumulator.
4. Read in two numbers.
5. Compute the sum.
6. Print the sum.
7. Increase the counter by 1.
8. Increase the accumulator by the amount of the sum.

FIGURE A–4
Explanation for Program Flowchart Symbols Used in Figure A–3

Symbol	Use in Figure A-3
Start/Stop	1. Beginning of program 2. End of program
Input/ Output	1. Entry of student's request 2. Printing of student's schedule 3. Printing of class lists
Process	1. Matching of student's request with available space
Decision	1. Can student's request be accommodated? 2. Are there more requests from this student? 3. Are there more students?
Cont.	1. Discontinue at A 2. Continue at A

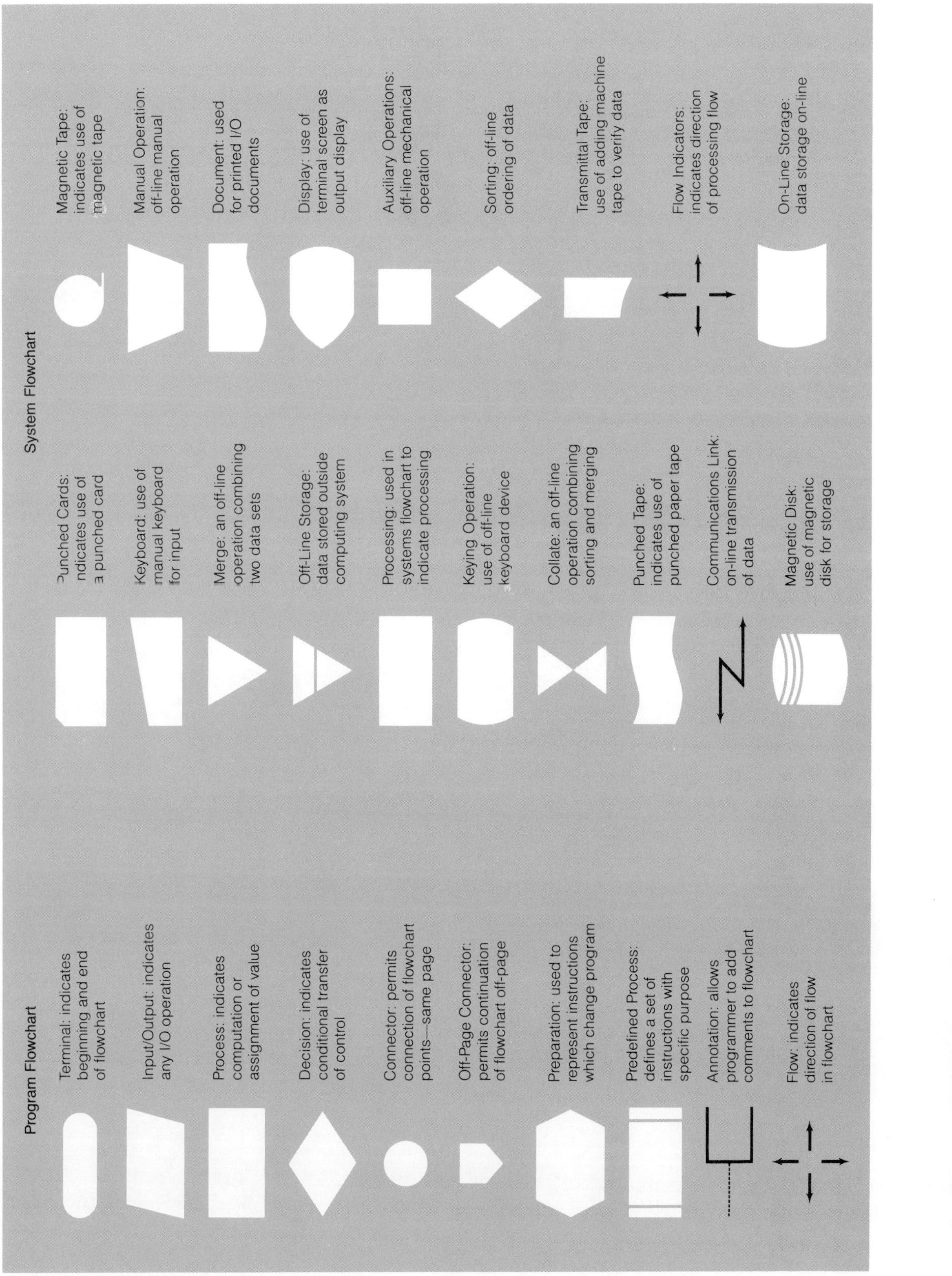

FIGURE A–5 Flowchart Symbols

FIGURE A–6
Program Flowchart to Add Two Numbers

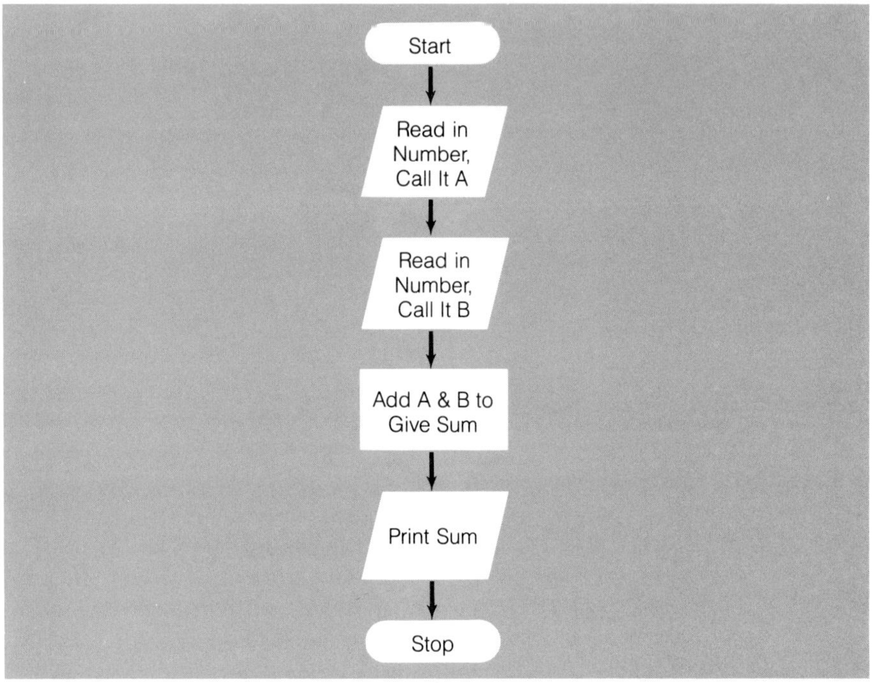

FIGURE A–7
Program Flowchart to Add Ten Pairs of Numbers

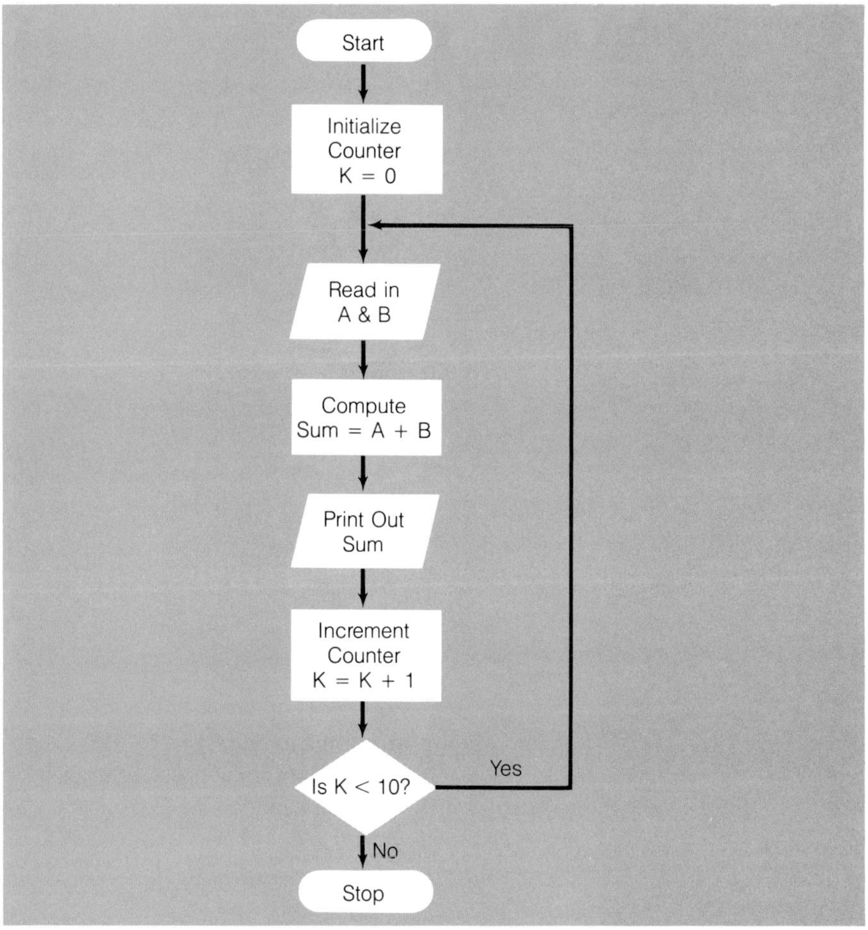

9. Check the value of the counter against 10, and
   if less than 10 return to Step 4,
   if not less than 10 go to Step 10.
10. Print the value of the accumulator.
11. Stop.

The flowchart to represent this algorithm is shown in Figure A–8.

Counters and accumulators such as those used in the last two flowcharts are frequently required in program logic. The reader should review both

FIGURE A–8
Program Flowchart to Add Ten Pairs and Accumulate Total

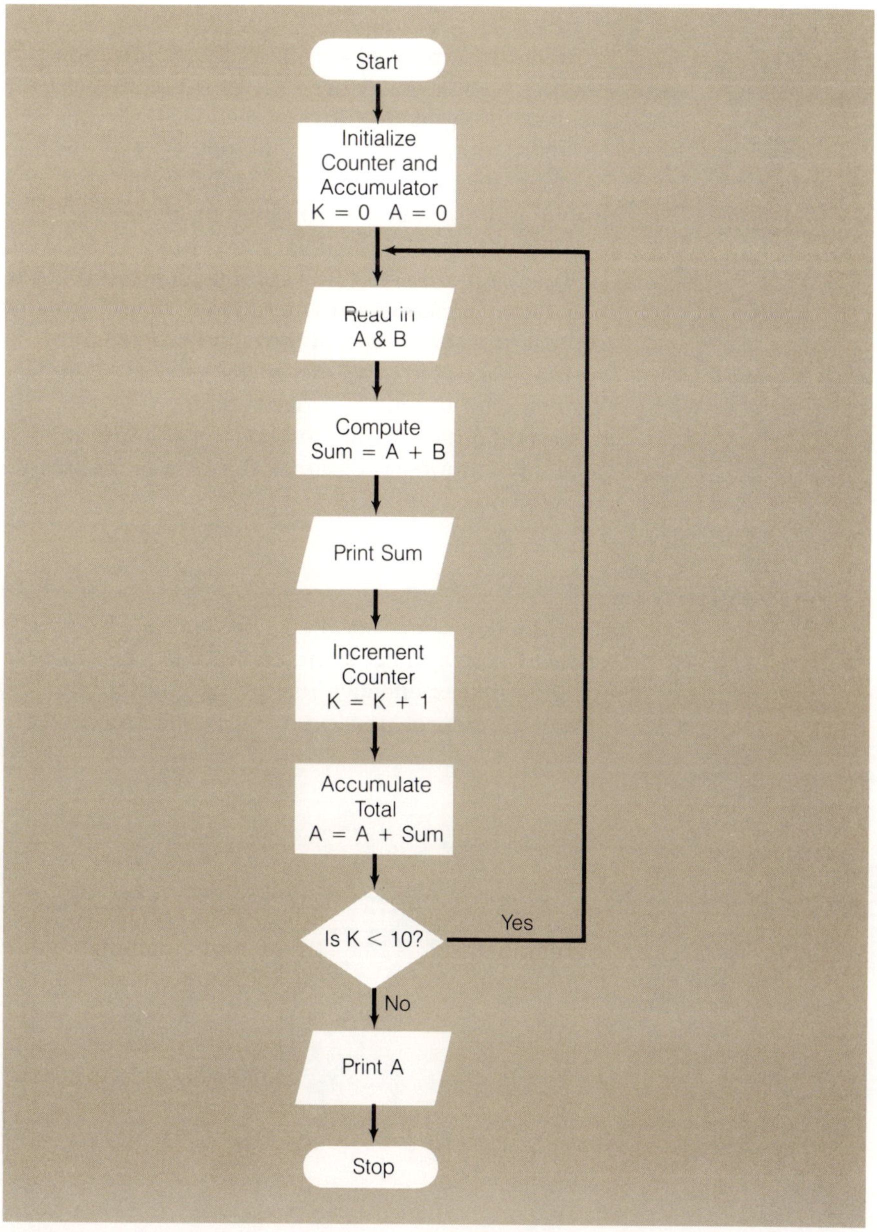

to make sure their use is understood. A look at other fundamental programming structures will help improve the reader's ability to flowchart program logic.

Three fundamental structures are required of a programming language. With them, virtually any program is possible. They are:

1. sequence.
2. selection.
3. iteration.

With flowcharts, the sequence is represented by the flow lines and arrows of the flowchart, and the general upper-left to lower-right flow of program logic. Selection is represented by the IF/THEN/ELSE construct shown in Figure A–9.

Iterations, more often called loops, are represented through the use of the DO/WHILE construct shown in Figure A–10. The DO/WHILE construct is used to implement logic which requires the repetition of certain blocks of instructions as long as a particular test condition is true. For example, it could have been used to repeat, while the count is less than ten, the summation of pairs of numbers in Figure A–7. A flowchart using the DO/WHILE construct to replace the counter is illustrated in Figure A–11.

The standard set of flowchart symbols and the three basic constructs of sequence, selection, and iteration give the programmer the capability of representing the logic of virtually any program through the use of flowcharts. A student who can master the art of flowcharting should have no trouble with the art of programming.

Several other techniques exist for the intermediate representation of the logic of computer programs. The next technique to be presented is that of pseudocode.

Pseudocode

Pseudocode offers an alternative to flowcharting. With it, English phrases instead of graphical symbols are used to represent program logic. Pseudocode makes effective use of indentation and key words, like IF, THEN, and ELSE to provide a brief, logical statement of an algorithm. Pseudocode

FIGURE A–9
IF/THEN/ELSE Construct

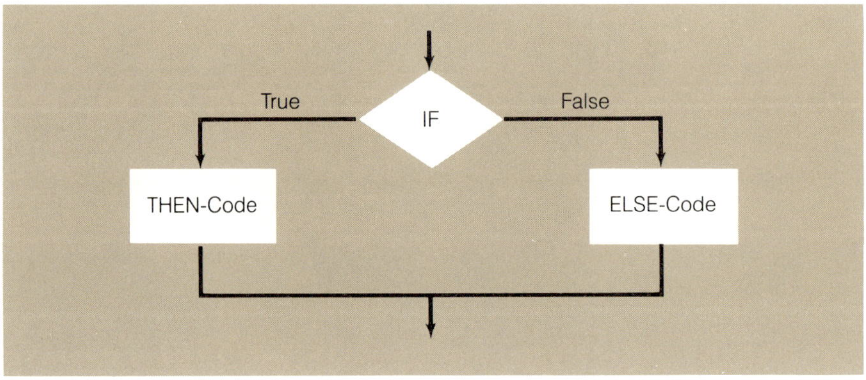

FIGURE A–10
DO/WHILE Construct

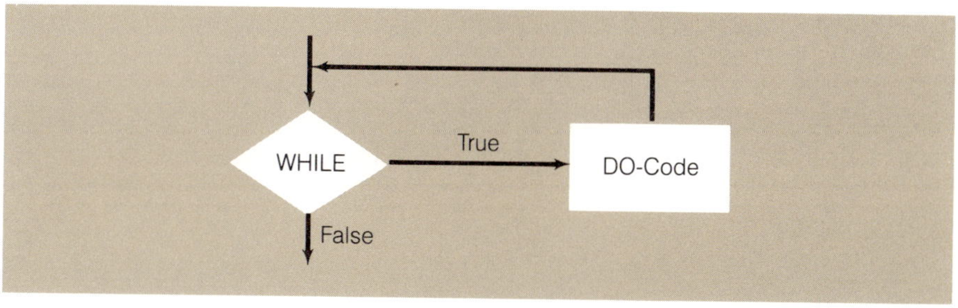

representations are less difficult for some people to generate than flowcharts. On the other hand, the flow of logic of an overall program is not as easy to visualize from pseudocode as it is from a flowchart.

The first of the basic constructs, **sequencing,** is expressed in pseudocode by the top/down arrangement of program logic. The first instruction of the sequence is at the top of the block of pseudocode, with subsequent instructions underneath it.

The second fundamental construct, **selection,** is represented through the use of IF/THEN/ELSE sequences, which in general specify that IF (a particular condition is TRUE) THEN (a set of instructions is to be executed), ELSE (a different set of instructions is to be executed). The instructions for each possibility (TRUE or FALSE conditions of the IF) are indented slightly from the IF itself. Figure A–12 provides an example of an IF/THEN/ELSE represented in pseudocode.

The third fundamental construct, **iteration,** can be represented in pseudocode through the use of DO/WHILE and ENDDO keywords to represent the beginning and ending of loops. The set of instructions between the DO and ENDDO are to be executed WHILE (as long as) the index variable takes

FIGURE A–11
DO/WHILE Construct in Sum Program

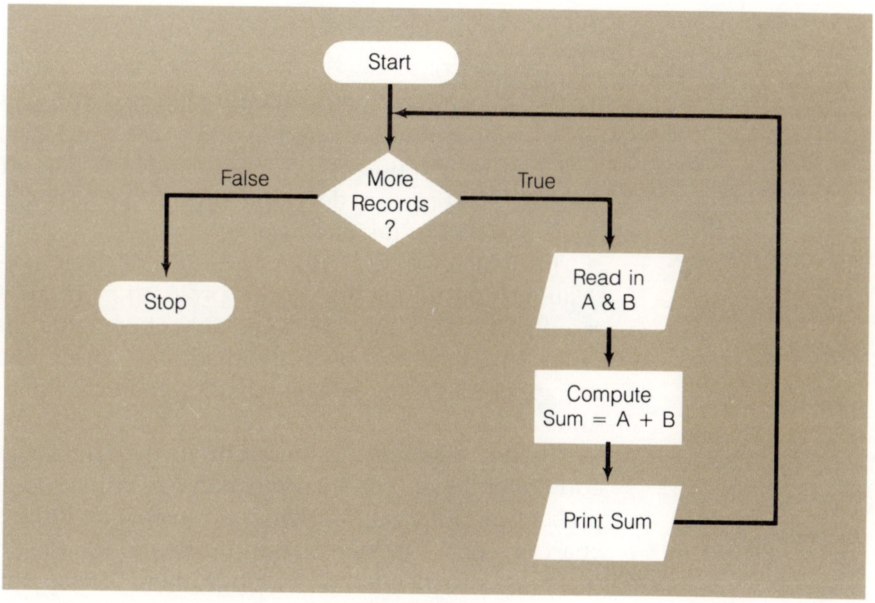

FIGURE A–12
Pseudocode Example

```
Read first number
Read second number
IF first number is greater than second
  THEN write out first number
  ELSE write out second number
```

on a certain range of values. Instructions within the loop are indented slightly from the DO/WHILE and ENDDO statements to visually set the loop apart from the rest of the instructions. An example of the DO/WHILE and ENDDO construct is illustrated in Figure A–13. An IF/THEN/ELSE sequence is included within the range of the loop in Figure A–13 to illustrate the use of indentation to facilitate program clarity.

Pseudocode undoubtedly grew out of necessity. As the pressure on programmers to improve their productivity grew, they must have turned to pseudocode as a quick-and-dirty alternative to the tedious drawing of flowcharts. It provides an efficient alternative to flowcharting, though it probably does not generate a display of program logic which is as effective in the documentation of a program.

FIGURE A–13
Pseudocode with IF/THEN/ELSE and DO/WHILE

```
Read first number
Read second number
  DO WHILE first number is not 99
    IF first number is larger
      THEN print first number
      ELSE print second number
  ENDDO
```

HIPO

HIPO (an acronym for **Hierarchy plus Input-Process-Output**) is the third technique for representing program logic to be discussed. Originally used as a tool for documenting programs, HIPO has evolved into a top/down design aid in program development. HIPO charts are used at three different levels of detail to document program logic.

The first level, the visual table of contents, presents the hierarchical relationships among the various program modules. Program modules, represented by blocks in the visual table of contents, are numbered according to the level they occupy in the hierarchy. These reference numbers tie the general chart to the detailed charts to be developed later for each module. An example visual table of contents chart is presented in Figure A–14.

The next level of the hierarchy in the HIPO system of charts presents additional detail. For each block in the visual table of contents, an input-process-output chart known as an **overview diagram** will be drawn. This chart presents the inputs used in the module, the outputs produced, and the processes needed to generate them. These charts are numbered ap-

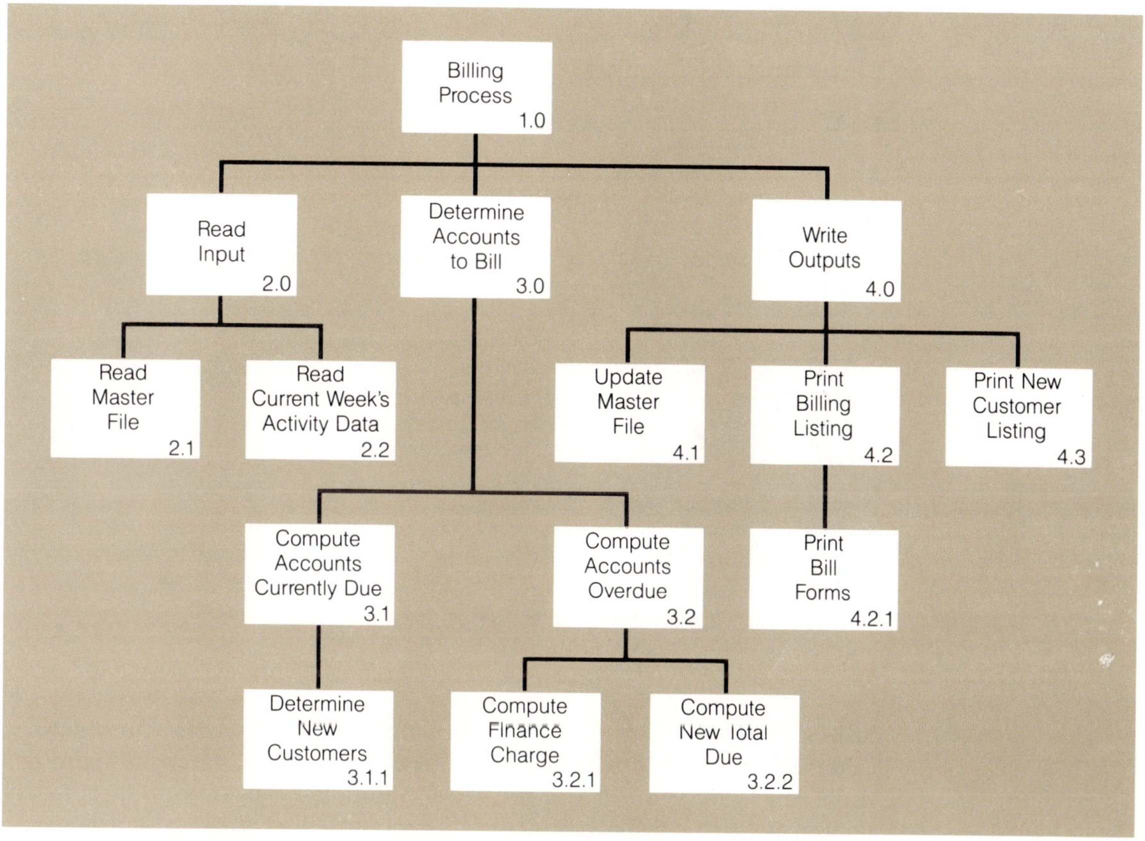

FIGURE A–14
Example of a Visual Table of Contents

propriately to tie them to the general hierarchy discussed above. An example overview diagram is presented in Figure A–15.

At the next level in the hierarchy, even more detail is added. Here the specific data items used are identified, and the processing functions needed are specified. The level of detail here must be sufficient to allow program code to be written from it. Pseudocode might be used at this level to represent the functions to be performed within the module.

HIPO represents a technique useful for several different purposes in the program development process. At the upper levels, the general relationships can be used to explain the role of the program to managers and users. The detailed, lower-level charts provide the necessary intermediate step between algorithm development and program logic. The HIPO system of charts provides a sequence of top/down steps essential to good programming.

Other formal techniques are available which deal with the program development process in a fashion similar to that of HIPO. Of these, Warnier/Orr diagrams are perhaps the most popular. They will be discussed next.

Warnier/Orr Diagrams

Jean-Dominique Warnier, a Belgian mathematician, devised an approach to program development known as **data structure diagrams.** They were

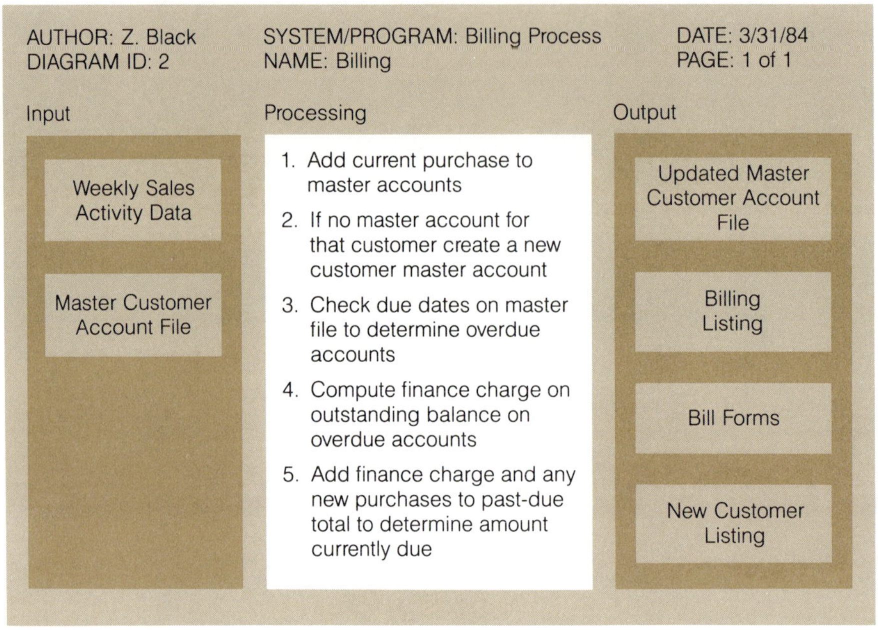

FIGURE A–15
Example of an Overview Diagram

extended by Ken Orr, and the technique is now known as **Warnier/Orr.** Although Warnier/Orr diagrams are hierarchical, the hierarchy is expressed from left to right instead of the more traditional top to bottom representation. Figure A–16 shows a hierarchy chart and the corresponding Warnier/Orr representation.

Warnier/Orr diagrams provide an effective tool with which to develop programs. They provide structure and an emphasis on top/down design techniques in a manner similar to the various levels of the HIPO diagrams. Consider, for example, the processing of transactions to update an account balance. The program must determine whether each transaction represents a debit or credit entry in order to adjust the account balance appropriately. A flowchart of the logic of such a program is presented in Figure A–17. The equivalent Warnier/Orr diagram is shown in Figure A–18.

Each of the three fundamental programming structures can be represented in Warnier/Orr diagrams. Sequences are represented within a par-

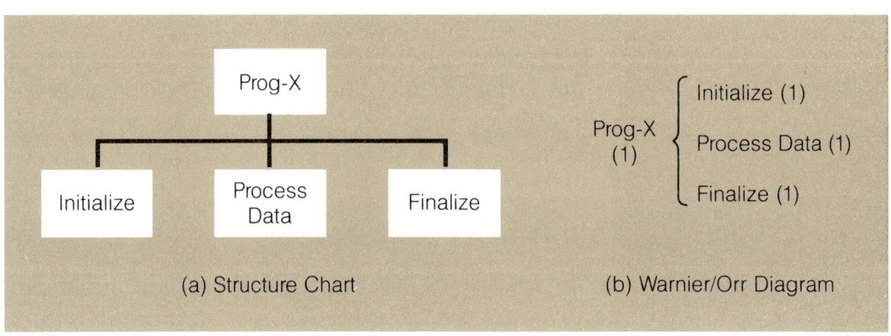

FIGURE A–16
Comparison of Structure Chart and Warnier/Orr Diagram

FIGURE A–17 Flowchart of Warnier/Orr Diagram Shown In Figure A–18

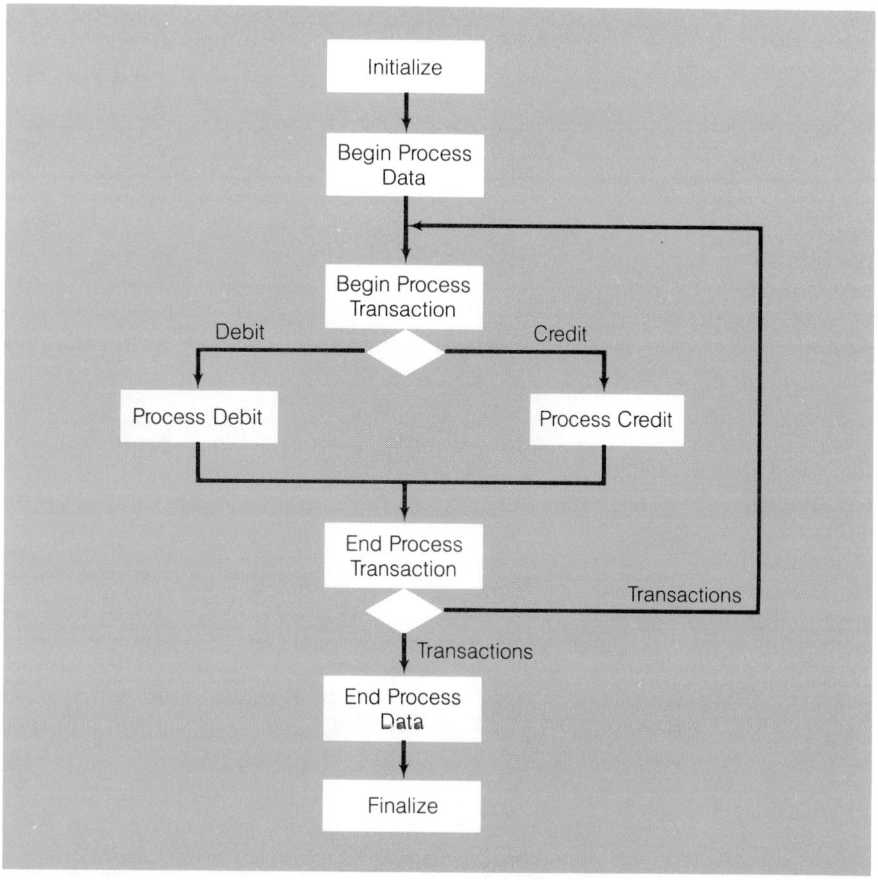

FIGURE A–18 A Complete Warnier/Orr Program Diagram

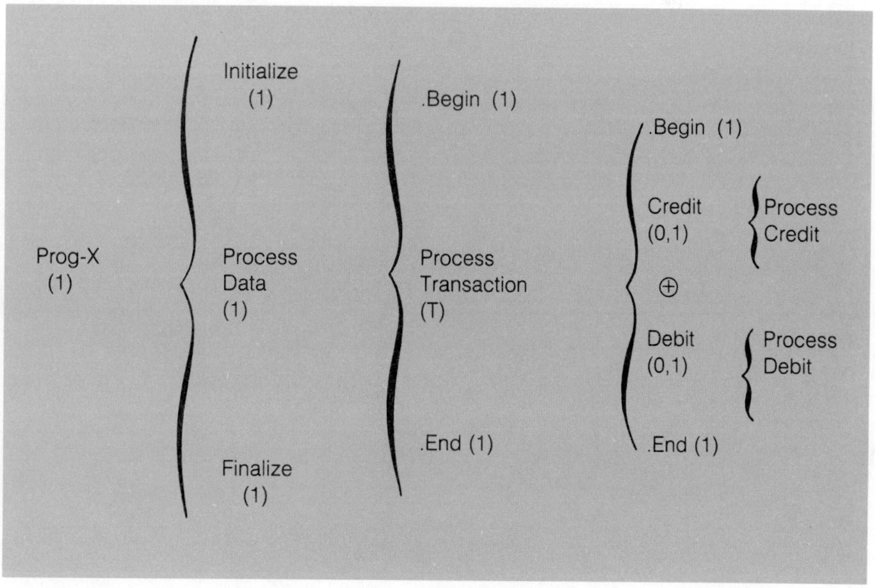

FIGURE A–19
Warnier/Orr Representation of Sequence

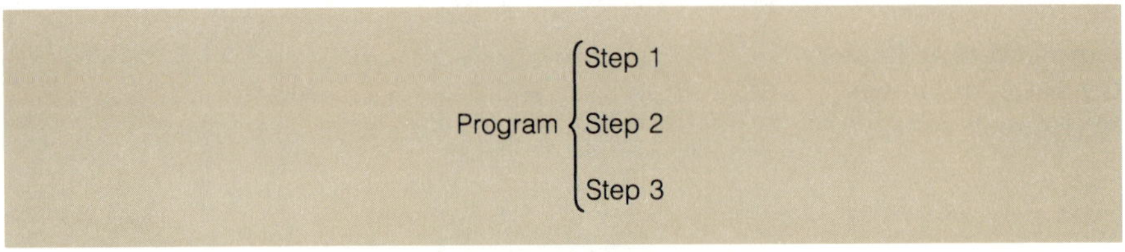

FIGURE A–20
Warnier/Orr Representation of Selection (Alternation)

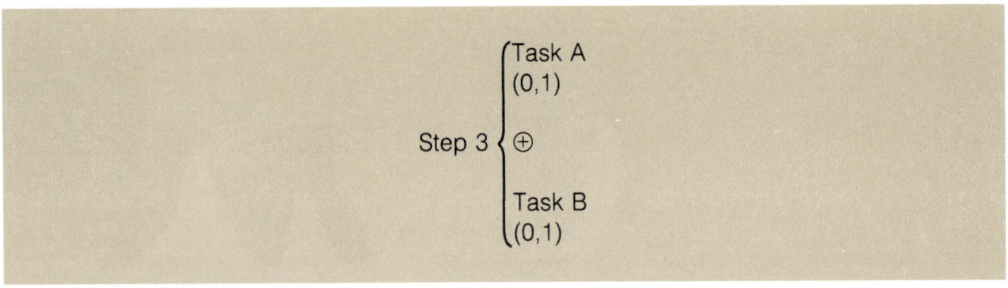

FIGURE A–21
Warnier/Orr Representation of Iteration (Repetition)

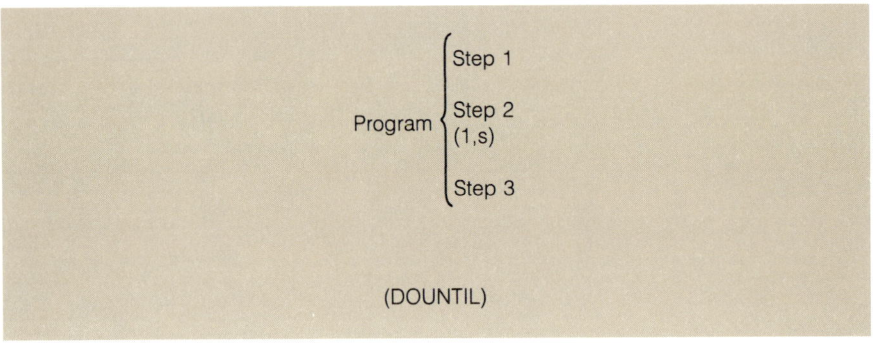

FIGURE A–22
Warnier/Orr Diagram for Overtime Program

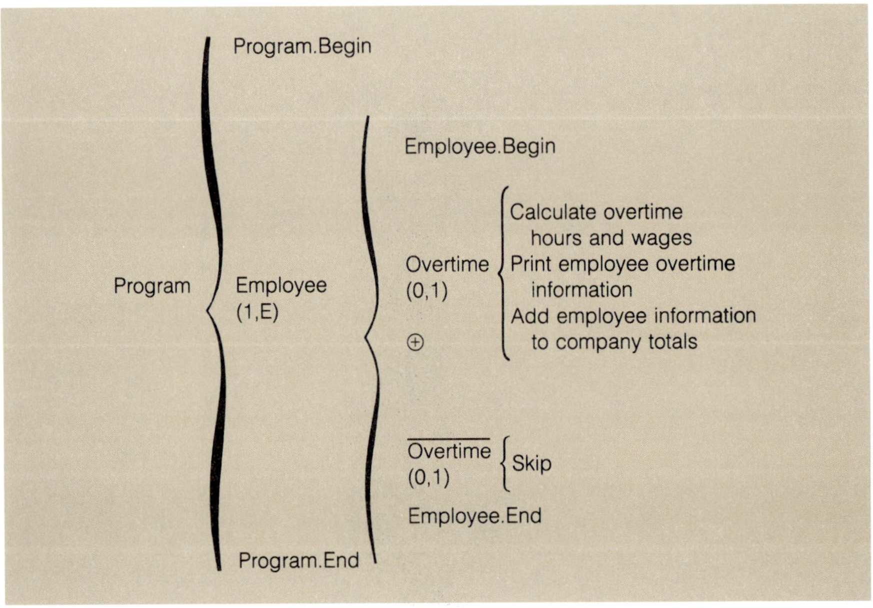

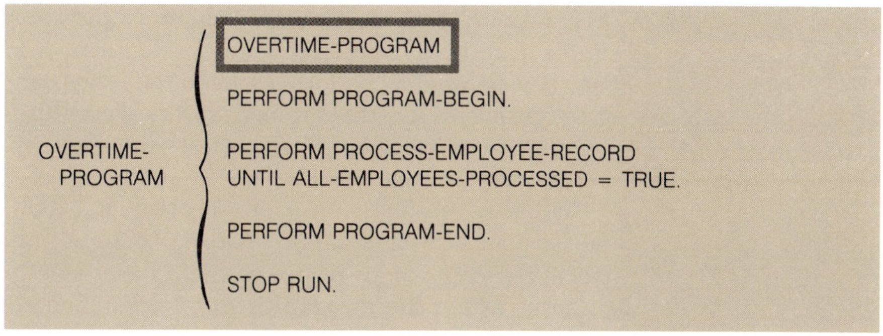

FIGURE A–23
Warnier/Orr Diagram for Overtime Program

FIGURE A–24
Translation of Warnier/Orr Overtime Program to COBOL

```
PROCEDURE DIVISION.
OVERTIME-PROGRAM.
  PERFORM BEGIN-PROGRAM.
  PERFORM PROCESS-EMPLOYEE-RECORDS
    UNTIL ALL-EMPLOYEES-PROCESSED = TRUE.
  PERFORM PROGRAM-END.
  STOP RUN.
```

ticular bracket from top to bottom, as illustrated in Figure A–19. Selection, referred to as *alternation* in Warnier/Orr terminology, is indicated by placing an exclusive OR operator between two steps as illustrated in Figure A–20. The third construct, iteration, is known in Warnier/Orr terminology as *repetition.* It is represented by writing, in parentheses under the name of the step itself, the number of possible repetitions for each step in the sequence. Repetition is illustrated in Figure A–21.

Warnier/Orr diagrams are used to develop the logical design of a program. From them the actual coding of the program is a relatively simple and straightforward process. Figures A–22, A–23, and A–24 show how one program module (for a payroll application) might be developed.

Warnier/Orr diagrams are widely used, but there are other techniques which are also used. These include data flow diagrams, data structure charts, and some proprietary techniques such as Nassi/Schneiderman diagrams, Jackson diagrams, and Yourdon bubble charts. Each is an attempt to provide an efficient and effective mechanism for developing the logic of a program prior to its being coded, the next step in the sequence. The representation used then becomes part of the program's documentation.

Coding

The process of converting the logical steps of a program into statements in a programming language is known as **coding.** Beginners always seem to assume that the writing of program code is the most difficult part of the program development process when, in fact, it is a rather simple task. It is simple if, and only if, the program development work of the previous steps has been adequately performed. If, on the other hand, work on the analysis of the problem, the development of the algorithm, and the formal representation of the program logic has not been properly done, writing program code is next to impossible.

Coding is the first step in the process in which the rules of syntax of the particular programming language become important. Until this step, logical representations of the program have been independent of the language in which the program is to be implemented. Coding, however, requires that each logical element of the program be captured in a set of instructions in a particular programming language.

The conversion from the logical representation of the algorithm into program code is straightforward. If the conversion is from a flowchart to program code, for example, the programming languages have commands which correspond almost directly with flowchart representations. Coding forms, which help the programmer with instruction layout, are available for most of the popular languages.

Care should be taken during the coding process to build documentation into the program. The logical development process which preceded the actual coding should have led to a program whose logic is well-structured. Variable names and program module names should be chosen so that the context of their use will be understood. In addition, remark and comment statements should be incorporated into the program code in order to make the program easy to understand.

Once the program is coded, it is ready for the next phase in the process of program development—testing and debugging. Both are discussed in the next section.

Testing and Debugging

Even though a great deal of effort has gone into the development of a correct program, the programmer has to assume that at this stage of its development it still contains errors. A scheme must be devised which will ensure that the program is adequately tested so that its errors can be detected and corrected.

Errors of Syntax

Three different categories of errors are possible, and different mechanisms are used to detect and correct each. The first type, **errors of syntax,** arise whenever instructions in the program do not satisfy the requirements of the language as it has been defined.

Each language has a well-defined set of rules of syntax which must be followed. Among other things, the rules of syntax specify the reserved words, the correct punctuation, and the structure of each of the instructions in the language. Language compilers and interpreters depend upon these rules in performing the translation of the program. If the programmer violates the rules of syntax, the compiler will not be able to translate the program. If a syntactical error is encountered by the compiler, a diagnostic message is generated to help the programmer discover the nature of the error.

Unfortunately, the diagnostic messages are not always as helpful as one would hope. The number of different syntactical errors that programmers can make is very large. Consider, for example, the many different ways in which the spelling or punctuation of an instruction could be incorrect.

In order to correctly detect all possible errors and provide an accurate diagnostic message, the compiler would have to be impossibly large. Compromises have to be made in order to keep the size of the compiler within reasonable limits. The diagnostic messages are usually terse and general. Interpretation of this rather terse, general set of diagnostic messages is, therefore, left to the programmer. Until the syntactical errors are removed, of course, the program will not run.

Execution Errors

The second category of errors is known as *execution or run-time errors.* Errors of this type are detected by the system during an attempt to run the program. That means that they cannot be discovered by the system until the errors of syntax have been removed so that the program can be moved to execution. Examples of errors of execution include such mistakes as the use of variables in computations before values have been assigned to them, division by zero, trying to read data beyond the end of the data file, or a mismatch between the type of data and the type of variable used for the data.

Execution errors, like errors of syntax, are caused by programmer carelessness or data errors. Most of them will cause the execution of the program to be aborted. The system once again provides a diagnostic message intended to help the programmer find the source of the error.

Errors in Logic

Although errors of syntax and execution errors are troublesome, the third category of errors presents even more grief. While the system is able to find and print diagnostic messages for the previous two categories of errors, the *logical errors* which might remain in the program cannot be given the same treatment. The system has no means by which to detect remaining errors in logic. For example, the programmer might have written an instruction in the program which causes two numbers to be added together when, in fact, they were to be multiplied. If the syntax of the addition is correct, and correct values exist for each of the operands, then no errors will be detectable by the system. The program would be, however, incorrect.

Errors in logic which are not detectable by the system must be found by the programmer. Tests must be devised which will expose any errors which remain in the program. A variety of data should be used to test the program to make sure that the extreme points of all branching instructions, for example, are tested. Consider as an illustration a payroll program which is supposed to calculate overtime pay for those workers who have worked in excess of 40 hours. Test data should include hours worked figures of both 40 and 40.01 hours to ensure that the program treats each correctly.

One very helpful technique in trying to debug programs is the use of output statements temporarily inserted in the program to print the beginning values and intermediate results of computations. A program which prints an incorrect answer may be wrong as a result of an incorrect computation or as a result of a correct computation with incorrect values. Output statements which print the values of all inputs and the values of all intermediate results will help the programmer determine the type of error which exists and narrow down its location. When the errors have been found and corrected, the temporary output statements can be removed from the program.

Program testing and debugging is, for the student in a course in computer programming, a learning opportunity. In a sense, the student who gains the most experience in finding and removing errors will be the student who has learned the most. The unfortunate students who do not make many errors will have to help those who do in order to gain from the experience.

Program testing and debugging is, for the professional programmer, the skill which separates the successful programmers from the unsuccessful ones. Programs implemented in a professional environment must be as error-free as reasonable effort can make them. Users and managers are not tolerant of program errors. They should not be. Programming instructors insist on error-free programs from their students for good reasons.

The process of writing a computer program can be as informal as sitting at a terminal and entering statements without any prior work on the structure of the program. While most such efforts are disastrous for all but the most capable programmers—who know enough not to do it—students seem always to be tempted to operate in that mode. Problem analysis, algorithm development, the formal representation of the program logic, coding, and testing and debugging should be part of every serious attempt to write a program. A well-designed program has a better chance of executing correctly, is easier for others to understand, and is much easier to maintain than one which is not. Good program design is critical.

The testing and debugging phases also contribute to program documentation. Programmers should include with a program's documentation, a description of the testing process, perhaps even a description of the test data. Both would be helpful in determining the reasons for errors encountered later.

Postscript to Program Development

One of the main ingredients of successful program development is the use of proper techniques. Students of programming must develop a tool kit of correct techniques for taking them through the problem analysis, algorithm development, formal representation of the logic, coding, and testing and debugging phases. Good habits, acquired early, will provide an excellent return on the initial investment of the programmer's time.

The reader should now be ready to study a specific programming language. An appendix covering BASIC is provided for that purpose.

Appendix B

The Internal Representation of Data

Analog computers make use of continuous functions to represent data values, but digital computers rely upon the use of discrete internal states. As a matter of fact, most digital computers rely on the use of only two discrete states. The **binary digital** nature of these computers is the characteristic which gives rise to the term **bits,** a shortening of binary digits.

Inside the various elements of computer hardware the representation of these bits takes on several different forms, depending upon the design of the device itself. Bits may be represented by the presence or absence of voltage, by an electronic gate which is open or closed, or by magnetic flux in one direction or the other. This internal, binary representation of data means that computers will use binary arithmetic to perform the basic mathematical operations on data values. It also means that any data value to be stored inside the computer will have to be represented by a pattern of binary digits.

We typically use the symbols 0 and 1 to form the binary representations of data values. If the data to be represented are numeric, then the binary representation could be as straightforward as the use of the equivalent binary number. The binary representations of the decimal numbers 0 to 9 would be represented as:

Decimal	*Binary*
0	0
1	1
2	10
3	11
4	100
5	101
6	110
7	111
8	1000
9	1001

In binary arithmetic, as in decimal arithmetic, the numerical digits have place value. Each digit has its own intrinsic value modified by the number of places it occupies to the left of the right-most, or units, place. Each displacement to the left represents another power of the arithmetic base. In decimal arithmetic the base is ten, and place values increase by powers of ten. Thus we have tens, hundreds, thousands, and so on as place values. The decimal number 4,352 can be evaluated as 4 thousands (10 to the third power), 3 hundreds (10 to the second power), 5 tens (10 to the first power)

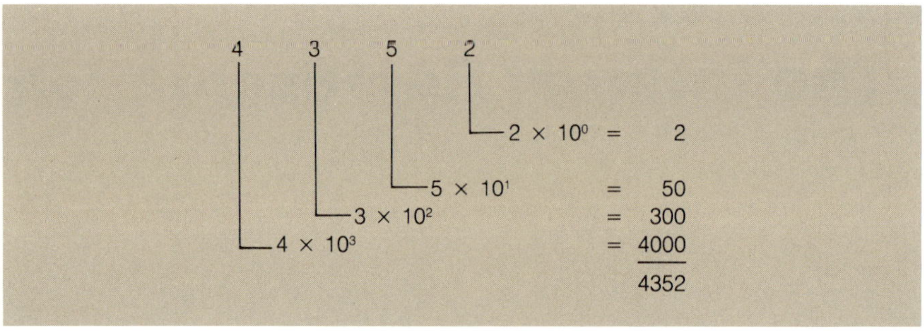

FIGURE B–1
Decimal Representation of Place Values

and 2 units (10 to the zero power). Figure B–1 illustrates this evaluation of 4,352.

The valuation of numbers in the binary representations occurs in the same way, except that the base would be two instead of ten. Figure B–2 illustrates the binary representation of the decimal number 25. A binary representation can be converted to a decimal representation by the process illustrated in Figure B–2. The decimal equivalents to the place values represented in the binary number are computed and then added up to yield the equivalent decimal representation.

To convert a decimal number to its binary equivalent, we use division by 2 and cast out the remainders into a binary representation of the original number. This process is illustrated in Figure B–3. (A conversion table is provided at the end of this appendix.)

Although the representation of whole numbers in binary is very straightforward, some compromises are required when fractions are to be represented. Some decimal fractions would require an extremely long, perhaps even infinite, binary representation. Computer design constraints usually restrict the number of bits which can be used in the representation of any single data value. If the binary representation of a decimal fraction requires more bits than are allowed, some of the bits will be lost. The exact manner in which this "round off" occurs differs from one design to another, but users requiring precise answers need to be aware of any given machine's limitations in this regard.

Arithmetic operations within the computer use binary arithmetic. The rules for **binary addition** are easy to learn. Two 0s add to form a 0. Two 1s add to form a 0 with a carry of 1 to the next higher place. A 0 and a 1

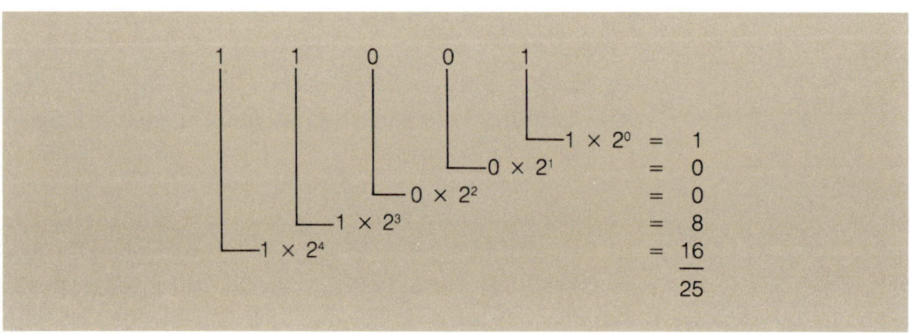

FIGURE B–2
Binary Representation of Place Values

FIGURE B–3
Decimal-to-Binary Conversion

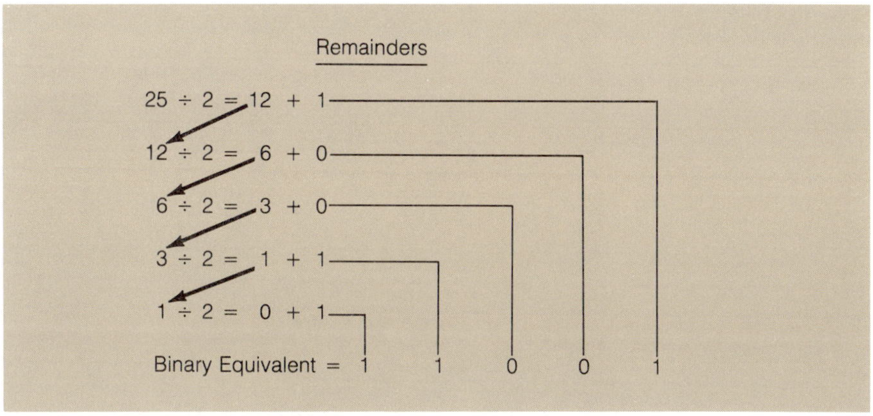

add together to give a 1. Binary addition is illustrated in Figure B–4, which also shows the addition of the decimal equivalents.

Binary subtraction within computers is done in a clever way. The 1's complement of the number to be subtracted is formed and then *added* to the number from which the subtraction was to be done. The final carry, formed by the left-most addition, indicates whether the resulting difference is positive (carry = 1) or negative (no carry). If positive, the carry is added to the units position of the difference to form the answer. If negative, the ones complement of the difference must be formed to give the answer. Binary subtraction, with and without a carry, is illustrated in Figure B–5.

Binary multiplication and **division** are handled as addition and subtraction. The multiplication of 16 by 236 is the same as sixteen additions of 236. Division is the same as figuring the number of times the divisor can be subtracted from the original number. Arithmetic units can, therefore, make use of the principles of binary addition to perform the necessary arithmetic operations on numerical data values.

FIGURE B–4
Binary Addition

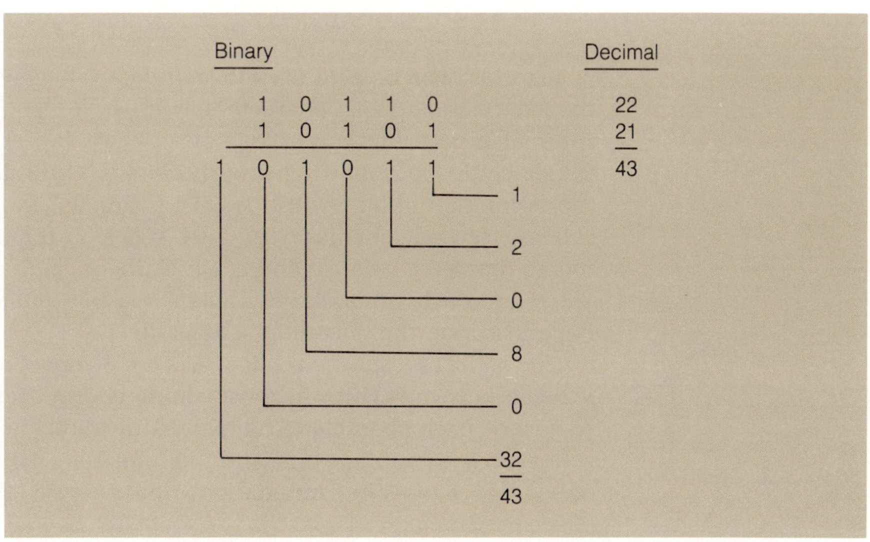

FIGURE B–5
Binary Subtraction

(a) Subtract 13 from 19
Binary equivalent of 19 is 10011
Binary equivalent of 13 is 01101
One's complement* of binary 13 is 10010
Adding binary 19 to one's complement of 13:

```
        10011          19
        10010        - 13
       ------        ----
       100101           6
      ↗
(Carry is 1)→   1
       ------
        00110
        ||||└─0
        |||└──2
        ||└───4
        |└────0
        └─────0
              -
              6
```

(b) Subtract 19 from 13
One's complement of binary19 is 01100
Adding binary 13 to one's complement of 19:

```
        01101
        01100
       ------
       011001
      ↗
(Carry is 0)→ form one's complement,
              negative
        00110 ⇒ -6
```

*One's complement is formed by changing zeros to ones and ones to zeros.

We must also be able to represent data values which are not numerical, for letters and special characters (such as +, −, /, and *) must also have internal representations. While the binary representations of numerical values could be done by using the binary equivalent of the number, the representation of letters and special characters would require some other scheme. Several schemes exist. Each relies on the use of a particular set of bits to represent a single character. Numeric, alphabetic, and special characters are each uniquely identified by a particular pattern of bits which depends upon the encoding scheme in use.

One of the oldest schemes in use is the **Binary Coded Decimal** encoding scheme, known as **BCD.** Its most common form uses 6 bits to form a pattern to encode each character. The two left-most bits in the 6-bit BCD encoding scheme represent zone bits, and the remaining 4 bits are numeric bits. The zone bits are used in combination with numeric bits to encode letters and special characters.

Six bits, each of which has two possible values, allows sixty-four as the maximum number of characters which can be represented by this scheme. We can easily represent twenty-six upper case letters of the alphabet, ten numerical digits, and some special characters as shown in Table B–1. There are not enough patterns left for the lower-case alphabet, however, which is one of the limitations of BCD encoding. Another limitation in BCD is the lack of standardization in the representation of special characters. Different manufacturers used different encoding schemes for the special characters, so a lack of uniformity exists.

An extended version of binary coded decimal, known as **EBCDIC** (for **Extended Binary Coded Decimal Interchange Code**), has become one of the two most popular schemes for data encoding. The EBCDIC code

TABLE B–1 *EBCDIC, ASCII–8, and BCD Encoding Schemes (for Numbers and Upper-Case Letters)*

Character	EBCDIC Binary	ASCII-8 Binary	Binary Coded Decimal
A	1100 0001	1010 0001	11 0001
B	1100 0010	1010 0010	11 0010
C	1100 0011	1010 0011	11 0011
D	1100 0100	1010 0100	11 0100
E	1100 0101	1010 0101	11 0101
F	1100 0110	1010 0110	11 0110
G	1100 0111	1010 0111	11 0111
H	1100 1000	1010 1000	11 1000
I	1100 1001	1010 1001	11 1001
J	1101 0001	1010 1010	10 0001
K	1101 0010	1010 1011	10 0010
L	1101 0011	1010 1100	10 0011
M	1101 0100	1010 1101	10 0100
N	1101 0101	1010 1110	10 0101
O	1101 0110	1010 1111	10 0110
P	1101 0111	1011 0000	10 0111
Q	1101 1000	1011 0001	10 1000
R	1101 1001	1011 0010	10 1001
S	1110 0010	1011 0011	01 0010
T	1110 0011	1011 0100	01 0011
U	1110 0100	1011 0101	01 0100
V	1110 0101	1011 0110	01 0101
W	1110 0110	1011 0111	01 0110
X	1110 0111	1011 1000	01 0111
Y	1110 1000	1011 1001	01 1000
Z	1110 1001	1011 1010	01 1001
0	1111 0000	0101 0000	00 1010
1	1111 0001	0101 0001	00 0001
2	1111 0010	0101 0010	00 0010
3	1111 0011	0101 0011	00 0011
4	1111 0100	0101 0100	00 0100
5	1111 0101	0101 0101	00 0101
6	1111 0110	0101 0110	00 0110
7	1111 0111	0101 0111	00 0111
8	1111 1000	0101 1000	00 1000
9	1111 1001	0101 1001	00 1001

TABLE B–2 *EBCDIC and ASCII-8 Encoding Schemes (for Special Characters and Lower-Case Letters)*

Character	EBCDIC	ASCII-8
Blank	01000000	00100000
¢	01001010	—
.	01001011	00101110
<	01001100	00111100
(	01001101	00101000
+	01001110	00101011
|	01001111	01111100
&	01010000	00100110
!	01011010	00100001
$	01011011	00100100
*	01011100	00101010
)	01011101	00101001
;	01011110	00111011
-	01011111	—
—	01100000	00101101
/	01100001	00101111
,	01101011	00101100
%	01101100	00100101
—	01101101	—
>	01101110	00111110
?	01101111	00111111
:	01111010	00111101
#	01111011	00100011
@	01111100	01000000
'	01111101	00100111
=	01111110	00111101
"	01111111	00100010
a	10000001	01100001
b	10000010	01100010
c	10000011	01100011
d	10000100	01100100
e	10000101	01100101
f	10000110	01100110
g	10000111	01100111
h	10001000	01101000
i	10001001	01101001
j	10010001	01101010
k	10010010	01101011
l	10010011	01101100
m	10010100	01101101
n	10010101	01101110
o	10010110	01101111
p	10010111	01110000
q	10011000	01110001
r	10011001	01110010
s	10100010	01110011
t	10100011	01110100
u	10100100	01110101
v	10100110	01101110
w	10100110	01110111
x	10100111	01111000
y	10101000	01111001
z	10101001	01111010

TABLE B–3 *Number System Conversion Table*

Decimal	Hexa-Decimal	Binary	Octal
0	00	0000 0000	0000
1	01	0000 0001	0001
2	02	0000 0010	0002
3	03	0000 0011	0003
4	04	0000 0100	0004
5	05	0000 0101	0005
6	06	0000 0110	0006
7	07	0000 0111	0007
8	08	0000 1000	0010
9	09	0000 1001	0011
10	0A	0000 1010	0012
11	0B	0000 1011	0013
12	0C	0000 1100	0014
13	0D	0000 1101	0015
14	0E	0000 1110	0016
15	0F	0000 1111	0017
16	10	0001 0000	0020
17	11	0001 0001	0021
18	12	0001 0010	0022
19	13	0001 0011	0023
20	14	0001 0100	0024
21	15	0001 0101	0025
22	16	0001 0110	0026
23	17	0001 0111	0027
24	18	0001 1000	0030
25	19	0001 1001	0031
26	1A	0001 1010	0032
27	1B	0001 1011	0033
28	1C	0001 1100	0034
29	1D	0001 1101	0035
30	1E	0001 1110	0036
31	1F	0001 1111	0037
32	20	0010 0000	0040
33	21	0010 0001	0041
34	22	0010 0010	0042
35	23	0010 0011	0043
36	24	0010 0100	0044
37	25	0010 0101	0045
38	26	0010 0110	0046
39	27	0010 0111	0047
40	28	0010 1000	0050
41	29	0010 1001	0051
42	2A	0010 1010	0052
43	2B	0010 1011	0053
44	2C	0010 1100	0054
45	2D	0010 1101	0055
46	2E	0010 1110	0056
47	2F	0010 1111	0057
48	30	0011 0000	0060
49	31	0011 0001	0061
50	32	0011 0010	0062
51	33	0011 0011	0063
52	34	0011 0100	0064

TABLE B–3 *Continued*

Decimal	Hexa-Decimal	Binary	Octal
53	35	0011 0101	0065
54	36	0011 0110	0066
55	37	0011 0111	0067
56	38	0011 1000	0070
57	39	0011 1001	0071
58	3A	0011 1010	0072
59	3B	0011 1011	0073
60	3C	0011 1100	0074
61	3D	0011 1101	0075
62	3E	0011 1110	0076
63	3F	0011 1111	0077
64	40	0100 0000	0100

uses 8 bits and can therefore form 256 different patterns. EBCDIC can be used to represent both upper- and lower-case letters, numbers, and a large number of special characters. The left-most 4 bits in EBCDIC encoding are known as zone bits and the others are numeric bits. The EBCDIC encoding values are shown in Tables B–1 and B–2.

The other commonly used code is the **ASCII** (for **American Standard Code for Information Interchange**) encoding scheme. Both 7-bit and 8-bit versions of this code exist. A listing of ASCII-8 codes is provided in Tables B–1 and B–2.

The existence of several different encoding schemes for data results in incompatibility problems between two computing devices which use different schemes. In order for them to communicate with each other, an interface must be provided to translate from one scheme to the other.

Schemes for the internal representation of data are best if they use a base which is an even power of two. The decimal numbering system is not a good one for representing computer codes because it cannot be represented as an even power of two. Both octal and hexadecimal numbering systems are more satisfactory. The octal numbering system works well with 6-bit encoding schemes, in which the contents of 3 bits form a unique octal number. For 8-bit encoding, hexadecimal numbers are used to represent each 4-bit segment.

An octal numbering system presents no problems with numerical digits; the digits 0 through 7 are used. Hexadecimal does cause some trouble, however, for no single numerical digit exists to represent the decimal values from 10 to 15. In hexadecimal representations, the letters A through F are used to represent 10 through 15. Binary, octal, decimal, and hexadecimal equivalents are shown in Table B–3.

Although octal and hexadecimal are somewhat more convenient numbering systems for us humans than is binary, the computer still is based upon binary. All data encoding is accomplished by forming binary patterns to represent the various numbers, letters, and special characters. While the bits might be represented by electronic gates, magnetized spots, or voltage differences, the value represented by the binary pattern can only be correctly determined if the underlying encoding scheme is known.

Appendix C

Programming in BASIC

BASIC, which is the acronym for Beginners All-Purpose Symbolic Instruction Code, is an easy-to-learn language best suited for an interactive computing environment. It is a popular language for microcomputers. BASIC programs may be either compiled or interpreted, depending upon the particular implementation choices of the manufacturer.

Although an ANSI standard for **Minimal Basic** exists, many other versions of the language exist. It is extremely unlikely that a BASIC program written in one environment would, without modification, run in a different one. Although the differences among versions are usually small, any difference is usually sufficient to discourage portability of programs.

The discussion of program development in Appendix A indicated that a programming language needs three fundamental constructs in order to support structured programs. These constructs are sequence, selection, and iteration. We will see, in this appendix, the extent to which BASIC provides for each of these constructs.

Building a Foundation: Interactive Programming

BASIC was written for use in a timesharing environment. In order to use it in that environment, some interaction with the system is necessary. A brief discussion of the interaction with the timesharing system will be presented. Discussion of the most common statements in the BASIC programming language will follow the timesharing material.

Logging On

A user of a timeshared system must establish an active session with the host computer by **logging on.** Some systems have direct, hard-wired connections which make it possible to connect simply by turning on the user's terminal. Other terminals gain access to the computer system through use of a modem and a connecting telephone line. Yet other systems will require that the user turn on the terminal, dial the computing system's number on a nearby telephone, and, when the computer's answering tone is heard, place the telephone handset into an acoustic coupler connected to the terminal. An appropriate keyboard entry (sometimes a carriage return is enough) from the terminal will alert the system to the user's presence. The system will ask for an account number so that the user's account can be properly charged. Each entry line from the terminal must be followed by a carriage return. Until the carriage return is struck, the system ignores the terminal and its input.

A shared system will ask for a **password** so that access to the system via that account number can be restricted to authorized users. (Remember the carriage return after the password entry.) Once the log-on procedure has been successfully completed, the system sends a system prompt character to tell the user that work can begin. By typing BASIC and executing a carriage return, the user lets the system know that a BASIC program is going to be written, edited, or executed. Many systems respond to this request with a different prompt to let the user know that the BASIC programming environment has been entered.

Text Entry

Most computing systems have a program whose purpose is to aid the operator in entering a program, a file, or other text. This program is called a **text editor.** Execution of a specific command in the system's job control language (JCL) calls the text editor into operation. The job control commands differ from system to system. The text editor provides an environment within which text can be entered, reviewed, and edited.

The user's entry of BASIC calls a text editor that will enable the user to enter and revise text, and it initiates the BASIC language compiler (or interpreter) that, in effect, will translate commands and instructions which follow. Unlike most other languages, the BASIC language has a built-in text editor. For this reason, the entry of the command BASIC is sufficient to allow the user a wide range of flexibility during the terminal session. The user, upon entering the text editing mode via BASIC, will be allocated some memory space for *working storage,* into which a program can be entered.

A user wanting to enter a new program can indicate that by entering **NEW,** followed by a carriage return. If an old program exists in the system's secondary memory, a copy of it can be brought into the working space by typing **OLD** (or **LOAD**) followed by the program's name and a carriage return. The commands OLD and NEW are known as systems commands.

Two other systems commands are essential to the running of a BASIC program. **LIST,** followed by a carriage return, will cause the program currently in the working space to be listed on the terminal's output device, which is usually either a CRT screen or a printer. **RUN,** followed by a carriage return, will cause the program currently in the working space to execute, or run.

EXERCISE

Obtain an account number and password (if necessary) and practice the log-on procedure. Ask the instructor for any system-specific instructions which might be necessary. Be sure to write them down exactly as they *should be, dotting every "i" and crossing every "t," because the computer will not forgive errors in the log-on procedure.*

We now assume that the reader has:

1. *Logged on properly.*
2. *Entered the password properly.*
3. *Typed BASIC.*
4. *Typed NEW in order to write a new program.*

(Typing BYE will terminate the log-on on most systems. The instructor should provide the appropriate command if it differs from BYE.)

Entering a BASIC Program

A program is entered, from the terminal keyboard into the working space, a line at a time. BASIC requires that each line be a complete statement, and that each statement have a statement number associated with it. Although statements can be entered in any order, and statement numbers can be assigned by the user as he or she sees fit, the system will list and execute the program statements in numerical order by statement number. This number also becomes the reference by which a particular line of text can later be reviewed, altered, or deleted.

Systems vary in the manner in which they treat the contents of the working space when the user's terminal session is ended. Some systems automatically store the contents in long-term storage in case the user wants to continue working on the same material at a later time. Most systems, however, simply cause the contents of the working space to be destroyed when the user terminates the session. On those systems, the user may cause a copy of the contents of the working space to be saved, that is, sent to longer-term secondary storage. The command **SAVE,** followed by a filename, which is followed by the carriage return, causes a copy of the contents of working storage to be saved. The filename is typically some arbitrary combination of letters, numbers, and symbols. The name is subject to specific rules for each particular computer system. A user gains access to the saved file by logging on and executing the OLD command, followed by the filename and the carriage return.

A summary of the terminal session described so far follows:

1. Log-on.
2. Request the text editor system and BASIC language compiler by entering the word BASIC.
3. Enter the text by beginning each line with a line number, followed by the characters of text for the given line, and completed by a carriage return.
4. Save the text by making up a file name and entering the SAVE command, causing the text to be permanently stored.
5. List the program in the working space by entering LIST.
6. Execute the program in the working space by entering RUN.

A copy of the transcript of a terminal session is provided in Figure

FIGURE C–1
Example Terminal Session

```
-TACS @
DPS440 OSU TIMESHARING ON 03/12/83 AT 9.772

USER ID: BA131HAVI @
PASSWORD: XXXXXXXXXXX @

* BASIC @

*  10 REM SAMPLE PROGRAM @
*  20 REM PROGRAMMER   - W. HARRISON @
*  30 REM   VARIABLE LIST @
*  40 REM       H - HEIGHT @
*  50 REM       W - WEIGHT @
*  60 REM       D - POUNDS PER INCH @
*  70 PRINT "ENTER YOUR HEIGHT IN INCHES" @
*  80 INPUT H @
*  90 PRINT "ENTER YOUR WEIGHT IN POUNDS" @
* 100 INPUT W @
* 110 LET D = W / H @
* 120 IF D > 27.5 THEN 160 @
* 130 IF D < 21.5 THEN 180 @
* 140 PRINT "YOU ARE OK" @
* 150 GO TO 999 @
* 160 PRINT "YOU MIGHT BE HEAVY" @
* 170 GO TO 999 @
* 180 PRINT "YOU MIGHT BE LIGHT" @
* 999 END @
* RUN @

ENTER YOUR HEIGHT IN INCHES
? 70 @
ENTER YOUR WEIGHT IN POUNDS
? 190 @

YOU ARE OK

READY
* BYE @

** COST: $  0.38     TO DATE  $   4.23     7%
** ON AT 9.772  - OFF AT 9.875  ON 3/12/83
   -LINE TERMINATED
```

This example is from a Honeywell DPS440 system. Other systems will be different.
The * is the system prompt.
Programmer-entered text is underlined.
The @ has been used to indicate a carriage return.

C–1 so that the reader can see how the terminal session would look. All commands entered by the operator are underlined. A carriage return made by the operator is indicated as a @. The initial "TACS" entry in Figure C–1 is required by the particular system on which the example was run to allow the user to select the computer system on which the example would be run. As it happens, two systems were available, and the user chose TACS.

The computer then sent the date and the name of the specific operating system with which the user would be working. This transmission culminates in a request for a user identification code.

At this point, the user establishes authority to use the system by entering a validation code, which, in this case, is a combination of a user number and password. The computer responds to a valid code by transmitting a message about the amount of money left in the user's account. The * prompt indicates the operating system is ready. Entering the command BASIC results in the system prompt which indicates that the system has entered BASIC. The user then enters a program into the working space and asks that the program be listed and then run. It appears to have run correctly, so the user can save the program under the filename SAMPLE and terminate the session by typing **BYE,** followed by a carriage return.

Data files can be created in exactly the same way, except that statement numbers are not used with lines of data. Data files can also be saved through the use of SAVE.

Table C–1 shows several text editing commands that are typically supplied by the BASIC text editor. These particular commands are used by a Honeywell computer system. Different systems may use slightly different commands.

The operating system in a timesharing environment will take some time to master. It is important to understand that the examples from the Honeywell computer system presented here are not universal. They should provide sufficient foundation for further study of another system, but differences are to be expected. System-specific information is described in the user manuals which accompany each system. The reader should refer to the BASIC user's manual for the system on which the programming will be done.

Some additional text editing capabilities are useful. If it is necessary to insert new lines of text, programming language commands, or additional pieces of raw data into a file, they can be assigned a previously unused line

Table C-1 *Basic Text Editing Commands*

Command	Description/Effect
BASIC	Initiates text editor and calls the BASIC language compiler or interpreter
AUTO	Initiates an automatic line-numbering system that aids the user in entering text by automatically providing integer line numbers that are incremented by tens
OLD filename	Recalls a file from permanent storage that had been earlier saved under the descriptor "filename"
RESEQ	Causes the line numbers of the current text file being used to be resequenced using line numbers by tens (will aid in inserting new instruction lines between existing lines of the file)
LIST	Causes the contents of the file in working storage to be displayed on the operator's screen or other output device
RUN	Causes the program in working storage to execute
SAVE filename	Causes a copy of the contents of working storage to be saved under filename

number and entered. To delete a line is equally simple. Merely enter the line number of the line to be deleted, then execute a carriage return. The BASIC text editor will automatically see to it that this line number is removed from the file currently in working storage. At this point, it is important to recall that if you are working on a file that had been previously created and recalled from storage, the insertions and deletions subsequently made will not be reflected in the permanently stored file until the RESAVE command is executed.

Using a Microcomputer with BASIC

The set of steps necessary to enter and run a BASIC program on a microcomputer is very similar to those just discussed. The differences derive from the microcomputer's more limited abilities and the single-user (as opposed to a timesharing) environment.

To begin, the user must perform the "booting" operation which brings the system from the off condition to one capable of doing BASIC programs. Most microcomputer systems are "booted" by inserting a boot disk into the primary disk drive and turning the system on. The disk drive becomes operative, and the instructions stored on the disk are read into the system. These instructions give the microcomputer the ability to interact with the user, to display characters on the screen, and to send output to a printer. They also provide a text editor with which the user can interact and a BASIC interpreter to execute BASIC programs.

Once the system is booted in BASIC, a prompt appears on the display and the user can begin to enter a program. An old program stored on a disk could be retrieved and brought into the workspace by typing LOAD, followed by the filename associated with the old program and a carriage return. Once the old program has been loaded, it can be listed with LIST and executed with RUN as before. If the listing, or the output from a program's execution, are to be printed, some additional commands are sometimes necessary. These commands are specific to a system and must be determined by reference to the user's manual for the system.

Most memories in microcomputers do not retain their contents once the power switch is turned off. That is why users have to insert a disk to boot the system, to put back into the memory the fundamental operating software which gives the system its capabilities. If the user wants to save a program created in the BASIC working space on a microcomputer, some preliminary work is necessary. Any program to be saved must be copied to some external medium, such as a floppy disk.

Floppy disks come in several sizes with different kinds of sectoring and several different densities of storage. The user must make sure that the correct type of disk is available. Then, it must be **initialized** so that it can receive a stored program. This initialization can be accomplished through the use of a program which is part of the system's utilities programs. The initialization, or formatting, of the disk causes the appropriate storage tracks and a directory to be established. Once the disk has been initialized, it is ready to receive stored files or programs.

A program created in BASIC on the microcomputer can be saved by typing SAVE, followed by the name of the disk on which is it to be saved and the filename under which it is to be saved. If the disk has been initialized with the name of CLASS, and the program has been named PROG1, then the save command would be:

```
SAVE CLASS/PROG1
```

These commands also vary slightly from system to system.

The fundamental procedures for gaining access to a BASIC programming environment have been described, both for a timesharing system and a microcomputer system. Before going further, the reader should try out the access procedure on an available system. It will undoubtedly be different from that described here but should be similar. The logging-on procedure should be within the user's abilities before proceeding to the discussion of the details of programming in BASIC.

In general, the reader would be well advised to try out all procedures described here, or in any other programming text. Programming procedures sound reasonable enough, but only through a firsthand use can the reader be sure that they can be used. The best way to learn a programming language is to write programs, make mistakes, correct them, and move on. It is one area of study which absolutely requires the active participation of the reader.

Elementary Output

BASIC programs consist of a sequence of BASIC statements which direct the computer to perform certain actions. The rules of syntax for each of the various statements will be described in turn. As discussed in Appendix A, the rules of syntax must be observed by the programmer, or the resulting program will not execute.

All instructions in a BASIC program must contain a statement number and a BASIC statement. A BASIC statement consists of one or more **reserved words** in combination with variable names, operators, and operands. Statement numbers are assigned by the programmer and must be between 1 and 99999, inclusive. Each line of a BASIC program can contain a maximum of seventy-two characters, although some implementations of BASIC allow more.

The last statement in a BASIC program (the statement with the highest statement number) must be the END statement. It will consist only of a statement number and the word END, as follows:

```
999 END
```

PRINT Statement

In order to allow the reader to write programs as early as possible in this introduction to BASIC, this section presents the PRINT statement. With it, the reader can write programs immediately. As a matter of fact, a PRINT statement and an END statement can, themselves, make a complete program. Here is an example of such a program:

```
 70 PRINT "THIS IS A SAMPLE PROGRAM"
990 END
```

From the above example we can see that a *PRINT statement* contains a statement number, followed by the BASIC command PRINT, which is followed by a series of words contained within a set of quotation marks. Any characters at all—letters, numbers or special characters—may be contained within the quotation marks. When the program executes, these characters, known as a *character string*, will be sent to the output device. The above program can be executed on the system by typing RUN on the line after the END statement as illustrated below:

```
 70 PRINT "THIS IS A SAMPLE PROGRAM"
990 END
RUN
```

The execution of the program will cause the character string in the PRINT statement to be printed on the screen or printer as below:

```
THIS IS A SAMPLE PROGRAM
```

The PRINT statement can contain several character strings, and if the character strings are separated by commas, each will be sent to a separate print zone on the output device. BASIC in this case sets aside five printing zones within each line of output. Each PRINT statement in a program will cause a new line to be started on the output device. Each item to be printed will be sent to a separate zone. When more than five print items are contained in a single PRINT statement, a new line is begun automatically. A PRINT statement with nothing in the print list which follows it will cause a blank line to be sent to the output device.

PRINT statements with character strings can be used to produce report headings or column headings. They can also be used to allow an executing program to be conversational, as we shall see later. Here is an example of a PRINT statement which contains several character strings:

```
50 PRINT "NAME", "STREET", "CITY", "STATE"
```

EXERCISES

Example: *Write a program to cause the computer to print someone's name and address.*

Solution:
```
70 PRINT "BILL HARRISON"
80 PRINT "2900 NW JOHNSON"
90 PRINT "CORVALLIS, OR 97330"
990 END
```

Output:
```
BILL HARRISON
2900 NW JOHNSON
CORVALLIS, OR 97330
```

1. *Write a program which prints your name and address.*
2. *Write a program which prints this message:*

```
HELLO
I AM A COMPUTER
I HAVE BEEN INVENTED
TO HELP YOU
```

3. *Write a program which prints this message:*

```
DISCRETION IS THE BETTER PART OF VALOR
```

REM Statement. BASIC provides the programmer with a means for inserting remarks into the program in order to make it easier to understand the program logic or flow. The REM (for REMark) statement allows the programmer to insert remarks at any point in the program, without influencing the actual execution of the program. REM statements are ignored by the computer in the execution of the program. A few REM statements added to the previous program will illustrate their use:

```
 10 REM SAMPLE PROGRAM
 20 REM PROGRAMMER: W. HARRISON
 30 REM WRITTEN ON A RAINY DAY IN MARCH
 40 REM CORVALLIS, OREGON
 70 PRINT "THIS IS A SAMPLE PROGRAM"
990 END
```

Execution of the program would be exactly the same as it was before, it is not influenced by the presence of REM statements. REM statements provide a good way for a programmer to provide documentation of a program, within the program itself.

The reader should gain access to a BASIC programming environment and write a few programs using REM, PRINT, and END statements. The clever calendars and posters hanging around computing centers can virtually all be generated by a BASIC program using only PRINT statements and character strings. After some programming practice, the reader can then move to the material which explains the association of data values with variables, which follows in the next section.

EXERCISE

1. *Create a set of REM statements which might be useful at the beginning of all your programs for the course. SAVE it to use later, whenever you start a new programming assignment.*

Variables and Constants

In algebra we use variables to "stand in" for the actual quantities represented in algebraic equations. For example, we use the variables X and Y in the equation

X = Y + 4

to express a relationship between X and Y which is true for an infinite number of values of Y. That is, if Y were 2, then X would be 6; if Y were 5, then X would be 9, and so on. X and Y are variables which can take on many values.

Programming languages use variables for the same purpose, to stand in for the actual values. Programmers write programs using these variables, which then take on specific values as the program executes. As a matter of fact the equation

X = Y + 4

is a valid statement in many programming languages, including many versions of BASIC.

The use of variables in programming makes it possible to write a program in general terms. Consider, for example, a payroll program which computes weekly pay. Such a program would use variable names to "stand in" for the employee's name, the wage rate, the hours worked, and so on. Then, when the program is executed, specific values are assigned to these variable names as each different person's pay is computed. Otherwise, a separate program would be needed for each employee. Consider the following illustrations:

Payroll Program	**Payroll Program**
Repeat for all employees	Read in Jones' hours and wage
Read in employee name, wage, hours	Multiply Jones' hours by his wage
Multiply wage times hours	Print check for Jones
Print check for employee name	Read in Smith's hours and wage
End repeat	Multiply Smith's hours by her wage
	Print check for Smith
	Etc.

Obviously, the program on the left will be much shorter. It will also still be correct long after Smith and Jones have left the employ of the firm in question. Variable names provide the programmer with much-needed flexibility in the writing of programs in general terms.

Many people like to correlate variable names with storage locations within the computer's memory. Each variable name corresponds to a single memory location where a single value can be stored. The programming instruction

X = Y + 4

would be interpreted (correctly) as:

- Make a copy of the number stored at location Y.
- Add 4 to it.
- Store the resulting number at location X.

In the payroll program example, the program would read in and store the specific values (for one employee) for employee name, hours, and wage; then use those values in computing the employee's pay. Then it would read in the specific values for the next employee (discarding the previous ones) and compute that employee's pay, and so on.

All programming languages make use of **variable names** to achieve the writing of programs in general terms. It is a relatively simple concept, but one which beginning programmers do not appreciate fully until much later in their programming careers. Programs use variable names in programming statements to indicate actions which are to be taken with the **contents** of the storage locations (which correspond with those variable names). Programming novices sometimes have difficulty distinguishing between a **variable** (a storage location) and its **value** (the contents of that location) at any particular point in time.

The rules for naming variables in Minimal BASIC are simple ones. A variable name may be used for storage of either numeric values or character strings. Numeric variable names consist of a single letter or a single letter followed by a numerical digit. The following are all legal variable names in BASIC:

A D1 X5 Z

The variable names below are not allowed in Minimal BASIC, although the first two may be allowable in other implementations of BASIC:

```
ALPHA  X495  25X
```

String variables consist of a letter followed by a dollar sign ($). Thus, A$, X$, and D$ are legal, but 1$ and $H are not.

EXERCISE

1. From the BASIC user's manual for your system, or from the instructor, determine which of the following are valid variable names for the BASIC at your school:

```
X        KOUNT
K1       NUMB1
N19      SIXTEEN
Z254     EMPLOYEENAME
```

Printing the Values of Variables

The values associated with variables can be printed by using the PRINT statement. In this use, the command PRINT must be followed by a list of those variables for which values are to be printed. For example, the PRINT statement

```
30 PRINT A, D$
```

specifies that the values associated with the variables A and D$ be sent to the output device at the time the statement is executed.

BASIC assumes there are five print zones for each print line. Use of a comma to separate variables in a print list will cause the value associated with each successive variable to be sent to the next print zone. Sometimes it is desirable to override the print zone assignments. For example, when we would like to print text along with the values of variables, we would like to have normal spacing, not zoned spacing. A semicolon between the text and the variable name in the print list will cause them to be printed next to each other. Consider the following:

```
100 PRINT "THE ANSWER IS "; A
```

This PRINT statement would cause the following to be sent to the output device, assuming the value of A was 24.7:

```
THE ANSWER IS 24.7
```

If we had used a comma to separate the items in the list, the output would have looked like this:

```
THE ANSWER IS    24.7
```

PRINT statements allow other flexibilities which are beyond the scope of this brief treatment of the language, but which can be found in user's manuals or full-fledged language texts. For example, the print list can contain constants, numerical expressions, and tab settings.

Constants. The BASIC programming language can also handle constants, either numerical constants (like 3.14159) or character string constants (like "YES"). Numerical constants can be interspersed with numerical variables in algebraic expressions. Numerical constants may be positive or negative. If no sign is specified, the constant is considered to be positive.

Assignment Statements

Assignment statements derive their name from the fact that value is always assigned with a variable as a result of execution of the statement. In BASIC, the assignment statement is also known as the *LET statement.* An assignment statement which assigns the value 4 to the variable G would be written as:

```
40 LET G = 4
```

Most versions of BASIC require that the command LET be part of the statement, but many implementations allow assignment statements to forego the word LET itself. The proper syntax of the statement requires a statement number, followed by the word LET, followed by a single variable name, an equals sign, and an expression to the right of the equals sign. The general form of the LET statement is shown in Figure C–2.

When assignment statements are used to assign values to numeric variables, the expression to the right of the equals sign must be an arithmetic expression. When they are used to assign values to string variables, the expression must be a string expression—either another string variable or a string of characters included within quotation marks. In both cases, the value of the expression is determined and then assigned to the variable on the left-hand side of the equals sign.

The arithmetic operators which may be used to build numeric expressions allow the programmer to represent complex computations. The allowed operators are:

Symbol	Meaning	Operation
+	(Plus)	Addition
–	(Minus)	Subtraction
*	(Asterisk)	Multiplication
/	(Slant)	Division
^	(Circumflex)	Involution (exponentiation)

Note: Most implementations of BASIC use ** or ↑ for exponentiation rather than ^.

Since we do not have the same degree of flexibility in entering programming statements that we have in algebra, some rules are necessary to prevent ambiguity in algebraic expressions. (In particular, it is difficult to represent numerators and denominators precisely when writing is confined to a single line of text.) Therefore, a set of rules is necessary to ensure that an expression will be executed in the manner intended by the programmer. For example, consider the assignment statement below:

```
65 LET X = 2 * A - B / C + 4.3
```

How should the above expression be evaluated? Some of the possible interpretations are shown in Figure C–3. Ambiguity obviously cannot be tolerated in the evaluation of expressions. Both the programmer and the machine must apply the same rules of operator precedence to determine exactly how the above expression is to be evaluated. The rules for evaluating an expression are:

1. Expressions within parentheses are to be evaluated first.
2. Involution (exponentiation) operations are to be performed next.
3. Then multiplication and division operations are performed.
4. Addition and subtraction operations are of lowest precedence.
5. In case of ties—operators of equal precedence—the operation on the left is performed first.

These rules are sufficient to remove any ambiguity and to assure the programmer that an expression will be evaluated properly.

Three types of problems seem to be encountered by beginning programmers when using the assignment statement. First, they forget that the assignment of value to a string variable requires either another string variable as an expression or a string of characters enclosed within quotation marks. Second, they mix variable types in a single assignment statement. Third, they reverse the correct form of the statement and put the expression on the left and the variable to which value is to be assigned on the right. Assignment of value always takes place from an expression on the right to a variable on the left. Examples of correct assignment statements follow:

```
10 LET K = 0
70 LET K = K + 1
40 LET A = 3 * C
90 LET W = K - 2 * (R + 4.2)
30 LET Q$ = T$
85 LET M$ = "NAME"
```

FIGURE C–2
BASIC LET Command

(Statement Number) LET (Variable) = (Expression)

(a) General Form

230 LET Y = 2 * Z − 5

280 LET B$ = "HELLO"

(b) Examples

FIGURE C–3
Evaluation of BASIC Expression

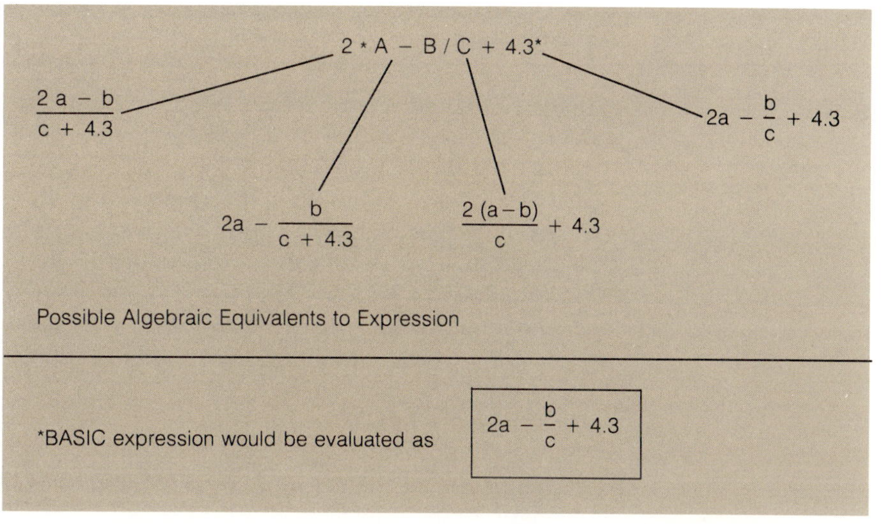

EXERCISES

Example: *Write a program which assigns a numeric value to a numeric variable, assigns a string value to a string variable, and prints out both values.*

Solution:

```
 70 LET X = 23
 80 LET T$  = "SKIDDOO"
 90 PRINT X, T$
990 END
```

Output:

```
23 SKIDDOO
```

1. *Write a program which assigns numeric values to two variables, assigns a string value to one variable, and prints out the values associated with all three.*

2. *Assume the Video Index is computed by dividing the number of hours a student spends watching videos by 24; write a program which calculates your video index. (What does it mean if your video index is 0? What does it mean if your video index is 1?)*

3. *Whenever the temperature in the Willamette Valley of Western Oregon gets above 95 degrees Fahrenheit, students cut their classes and float down the river on inner tubes. One's rate of travel on the river can be calculated from the following equation:*

Rate = Rate of current – Drag coefficient

Write a program which computes the rate of travel if the current is 5.2 miles per hour and the drag coefficient is 1.79.

4. *Assume that you recently bowled three lines with the following scores: 162, 175, 153. Write a program which computes your average score.*

READ and DATA Statements

There are two other statements which cause values to be assigned to variables. They can both be used to allow data to be brought into a program. One is the READ statement, the topic of this section, and the other is the INPUT statement, the topic of the next section. READ can be used to bring data from DATA statements within the program or from files stored outside the program. This discussion deals only with its use in conjunction with DATA statements. A *READ statement* in BASIC requires a statement number, the command READ, and a list of variables to which values are to be assigned as a result of the execution of the statement. Here is an example:

```
40 READ A, F$, V4
```

Variable names in the list must be separated by commas. The above READ statement expects to find a numeric value (to be assigned to A), then a character string (to be assigned to F$), and finally a numeric value (to be assigned to V4).

The values to be assigned to these variables must be part of one or more DATA statements contained within the program. The *DATA statement* contains a statement number, the command DATA, and a list of data values separated by commas. For example, a DATA statement which would satisfy the example READ statement in the previous paragraph would be:

```
600 DATA 24.5, PART.NO, 533
```

Execution of the READ statement above with this DATA statement would cause the variable to take on the values illustrated in Figure C–4. Character string values here may be, but do not have to be, contained in quotes.

The programmer must bear the responsibility for maintaining close coordination between the READ and DATA statements. Execution of a READ statement in a program causes the next-in-line values from DATA statements to be used. If the values in the DATA statements are not in the correct order, improper assignments of value or type mismatches will result. Consider, for example, the following program:

```
10 READ A, B, C$
20 READ D, F$, V
.
.
.
500 DATA 25, 43, STOP
510 DATA 39.4, GO, 12.2
900 END
```

Execution of this program would result in the values illustrated in Figure C–5 being assigned correctly. The same assignments could have been made, however, if the DATA statements had been:

```
500 DATA 25
510 DATA 43, STOP, 39.4
520 DATA GO, 12.2
```

Programmers must make sure that the variables in the list of a READ statement and the values in corresponding DATA statements agree. Anything else will introduce errors. For this reason it is good programming practice to print out, at least initially, the values of variables as they are read into the program, to make sure that the necessary coordination between READ and DATA statements exists.

FIGURE C–4
Variables and Their Associated Values

Variable Name	Value in Storage
A	24.5
F$	PART. NO
V4	533

The READ and DATA statement combination can be used to provide data for a program whenever the data values are known prior to execution of the program. A program can be written with dummy DATA statements, with the real DATA statements to be substituted prior to execution. The location of the READ statement is fixed by the logic of the program; however, DATA statements are not actually executed, so they may be located anywhere in the program as long as they appear before the END statement. If an insufficient amount of data is included in DATA statements in the program, an END OF DATA message is sent to the output device when the supply of data is exhausted.

FIGURE C–5
Data Value/Variable Name Associations

Variable Name	Value in Storage	Variable Name	Value in Storage
A	25	D	39.4
B	43	F$	GO
C$	STOP	V	12.2

Data values assigned by a READ statement must be contained in DATA statements within the program. In the next section we will see that the INPUT statement provides a means for data entry during the actual execution phase of the program.

EXERCISES

Example: *Write a program which reads in three numbers, adds them together, and computes (and prints) the proportion of the total each of the original numbers represents.*

Solution:

```
 70 READ A, B, C
 80 LET T = A + B + C
 90 LET A1 = A/T
100 LET B1 = B/T
110 LET C1 = C/T
120 PRINT A, A1
130 PRINT B, B1
140 PRINT C, C1
150 PRINT T
900 DATA 65, 91, 104
990 END
```

Output:

```
 65     .25
 91     .35
104     .40
260
```

1. *Write a program which reads two numbers from a DATA statement, adds them together, and prints out the sum.*
2. *Write a program which reads (from a DATA statement) a numeric value (into a numeric variable) and a string value (into a string variable) and prints out both.*
3. *Write a program which reads the following DATA statements and produces an address in its correct format.*

```
900 DATA "2694 TEMPLE"
910 DATA "STAFFORD, KANSAS 67578"
920 DATA "ANNABELLE JONES"
```

4. *Assume that your computer account is charged for each of your work sessions at the terminal according to the following scale:*

Terminal connect time:	*\$3 per hour*
Compute (CPU) time:	*\$7.50 per minute*
Output Charge:	*\$0.05 per page*

Given the following statistics from a recent terminal session, compute the charge to your account:

Terminal connect time:	*53 minutes (be careful)*
Compute time:	*.03 minutes*
Output:	*4 pages*

Input Statement

An INPUT statement in BASIC provides an opportunity for programs to be interactive. It will cause execution of the program to be temporarily suspended while the user enters the data necessary for the program's processing. The INPUT statement requires a statement number, followed by the command INPUT, which is followed, in turn, by the list of variables for which values are to be entered. The system displays a prompt (usually a ?) on the output device to indicate that it is waiting for the input to occur. Examples of correct INPUT statements are:

```
10 INPUT A
45 INPUT B$, D, F1
30 INPUT Z3, B4, T$
```

Either character strings or numerical values can be entered via an INPUT statement as long as the appropriate type of variable is used for each case. Character string values may be either quoted or unquoted.

INPUT statements do not utilize DATA statements but wait, instead, for entry of the data values from the keyboard. In order to make sure that the person doing the data entry knows exactly what to do, PRINT statements are almost always used just ahead of INPUT statements to alert the user to the program's need for data entry. The examples which follow illustrate the use of PRINT statements to prompt the user in a conversational manner:

```
10 PRINT "ENTER YOUR AGE"
11 INPUT A


20 PRINT "ENTER YOUR FIRST NAME"
21 INPUT N$


30 PRINT "ENTER VALUES FOR A, B, AND C"
31 PRINT "SEPARATE THEM WITH COMMAS"
32 INPUT A, B, C
```

Execution of the above statements would cause the following displays on the output device:

```
ENTER YOUR AGE
?
ENTER YOUR FIRST NAME
?
```

```
ENTER VALUES FOR A, B, AND C
SEPARATE THEM WITH COMMAS
?
```

After displaying each ?, the program pauses to allow the data to be entered. The user must enter the data and a carriage return before execution of the program will continue. Many computers allow the prompt to be part of the INPUT statement. The above examples could then be done as follows:

```
10 INPUT "ENTER YOUR AGE", A
20 INPUT "ENTER YOUR FIRST NAME", N$
30 INPUT "ENTER A, B, C", A, B, C
```

The reader has now been exposed to three different mechanisms by which values can be associated with variables within a program. The LET statement allows values to be assigned to variables, the READ statement takes values from DATA statements; and the INPUT statement takes values entered by the user during the execution of the program. The reader should write programs using each of these statements to make sure they are fully understood. In the next section you begin to learn how to use control statements in programs to direct the flow of execution.

EXERCISES

Example: *Write a program which carries on a brief conversation with the user.*

Solution:

```
 70 PRINT "WHAT IS YOUR NAME"
 80 INPUT A$
 90 PRINT "HI"; A$, "HOW ARE YOU?"
100 PRINT "SORRY TO HEAR IT"
120 PRINT "HAVE A NICE DAY"; A$
130 PRINT "GOODBYE"
990 END
```

1. *Write a program, different from the example above, which carries on a brief conversation with the user.*
2. *Write a program which asks a user to input four numbers, adds the numbers together, and prints out the sum.*
3. *Write a program which asks the user for an investment amount, an interest rate, and the number of years of the investment and then computes (and prints) the future value of the invested amount according to the formula:*

$$\text{Future value} = \text{Present value X } (1 + \text{Interest rate})^{\text{No. of years}}$$

4. *Write a program which accepts as input a future value, an interest rate, and the number of years of the investment and computes (and prints) the*

present value according to the formula:

$$\textit{Present value} = \frac{\textit{Future value}}{(1 + \textit{Interest rate})^{\text{No. of years}}}$$

The GO TO Statement

One of the easiest (and perhaps one of the most overused) statements is the GO TO statement. A *GO TO statement* requires a statement number, the command GO TO, and another statement number, the object of the GO TO. Execution of the statement causes the executing sequence to be interrupted, and control to be transferred to the statement identified as the object of the GO TO. For example, the following statement:

```
150 GO TO 400
```

would cause statement number 400 to be the next statement to be executed.

A GO TO statement can be used to transfer control in either direction, back in the direction of the beginning of the program to repeat code already executed or in the direction of the end of the program. The GO TO provides an **unconditional branch,** a certain jump to another location in the program. Although the GO TO makes a transfer of control easy to implement, its use in excess can cause problems.

Good programming practice requires that the use of GO TO statements be restricted to only those uses which are absolutely necessary and not detrimental to an understanding of the flow of the program. Most versions of BASIC lack the control structures necessary to eliminate the GO TO entirely, but their use in BASIC and other languages should be kept to a minimum.

EXERCISE

1. *Write a program that accepts as input two numbers, adds the numbers together, prints them out, and goes back to ask for the input of two numbers again.* Important question: *What is wrong with the program?*

The IF/THEN Construct

One of the common uses of the GO TO statement is to form loops in a program, to cause certain segments of the program to be repeated. Consider, for example that we have just written a set of statements which compute the net pay for an employee. Although we could write another set to do the same computation for the next employee, it would be more efficient to reuse the first set of instructions. So, we put a GO TO at the bottom to send us back to the beginning to repeat execution of the net pay calculations as follows:

```
 10 REM SIMPLE NET PAY CALCULATION
 20 REM PROGRAMMED BY W. HARRISON
 30 REM 28 FEBRUARY 1983
 40 REM  VARIABLE LIST
 50 REM      H  = HOURS WORKED
 60 REM      W  = WAGE RATE
 70 REM      G  = GROSS PAY
 80 REM      D  = DEDUCTIONS
 90 REM      N  = NET PAY
100 REM      N$ = EMPLOYEE NAME
110 PRINT "ENTER VALUES FOR N$, H, W, AND D"
120 INPUT N$, H, W, D
130 ---------------------
140 LET G = H * W
150 LET N = G - D
160 PRINT "NET PAY IS"; N
170 GO TO 110
900 END
```

The dashes in statement 130 are meant to indicate that the program is not complete and correct as it is written. The GO TO in 170 has established a loop, but no means has been built into the program to terminate the loop. This program would run as long as someone entered data. If the program had been written to use the READ/DATA combination instead of INPUT, the program would have run until the DATA statements had been exhausted and would then have terminated with END OF DATA.

An IF/THEN statement should be used to terminate the loop in the above program. The IF/THEN statement requires a statement number, the command IF, a relational expression (defined below), the command THEN and a statement number to be the object of the THEN. For example, we could have the user cause the program to be terminated by the entry of a particular, unique value for one of the inputs. Values unlikely to be encountered in normal data should be used. Any of the following IF statements could have been used to terminate the above program, by sending execution to the END statement:

```
130 IF N$ = "END" THEN 900

130 IF H > 0 THEN 900

130 IF W = 0 THEN 900

130 IF D > 0 THEN 900
```

With one of these statements in the program, the user would need only to enter an appropriate value in order to terminate execution of the program. Data used to terminate loops in this manner are known as **trailer data.** A prompt could be added as statement 115 to help the user remember the correct means for stopping the program, that is, the particular value expected for the trailer data. The prompt could say:

```
115 PRINT "ENTER END AS NAME TO STOP"

115 PRINT "NEGATIVE HOURS WILL END PROGRAM"

115 PRINT "ENTER WAGE OF 0 TO STOP"

115 PRINT "NEGATIVE DEDUCTIONS CAUSES STOP"
```

The IF/THEN statement is a very versatile statement. It provides a conditional branch or transfer of control based upon the truth or falsity of the relational expression. The *relational expression* is formed by connecting two expressions by a relational operator. A relational expression has a value which is either TRUE or FALSE. If the relational expression is TRUE, execution is transferred to the statement number which is after THEN. If the relational expression is FALSE, the statement number after THEN is ignored, and execution follows the normal sequence. That means that the statement after the IF is executed next if the relational expression is FALSE. The relational operators allowed are shown in Table C–3.

Symbol	Meaning	Example	Meaning
<	less than	A < B	A less than B
>	greater than	G > F	G greater than F
=	equals	X = Y	X equal to Y
<=	less than or equal to	D <= K	D less than or equal to K
>=	greater than or equal to	S >= T	S greater than or equal to T
<>	not equal to	P <> W	P not equal to W

IF/THEN statements are used to transfer control of the program to other statements, depending upon values encountered at the time the program executes. Some examples are:

`50 IF K = 100 THEN 330`	Transfers control down the program (to statement 330) when the counter (K) reaches a value of 100
`90 IF K = 10 THEN 20`	Keeps the program in a loop by returning control to statement 20 until the counter has become 10 or more

`30 IF A$ = "D" THEN 70`	Checks transaction type for deposit (D) and directs control to the appropriate segment of code (statement 70) for handling deposits.

The ability to incorporate loops and conditional branches in programs greatly increases the programmer's ability to write powerful programs. With the increase in power comes an increase in the difficulty of understanding someone else's program and an increased likelihood of program errors. Programmers will have to develop good programming practices to counter these negative possibilities.

EXERCISES

Example: *Write a program which asks the user for his or her name and grade point average (gpa) then prints an appropriate message, depending upon the value of the gpa. For example, in a 4.0 maximum grading scheme, everyone with a gpa less than 3.0 could be given an encouraging message to study harder.*

Solution:

```
 70 PRINT  "ENTER YOUR NAME"
 80 INPUT N$
 90 PRINT "ENTER YOUR GPA"
100 INPUT G
110 IF G > 2.99 THEN 990
120 PRINT "STUDY HARDER, LEARN MORE"
130 PRINT "GOOD LUCK,"; N$
990 END
```

Output:

```
(a) None if gpa > 2.99
(b) STUDY HARDER, LEARN MORE
    GOOD LUCK, (NAME)
```

1. *Write a program that accepts two numbers as input and declares (by printing) the value of the larger number.*
2. *Modify the program in exercise 1 above to handle a series of number pairs—printing the larger of each pair each time. (Do not worry about stopping this program.)*
3. *Modify the program in exercise 2 above to stop whenever the first number of the pair is zero.*
4. *To counter competition in the long-distance telephone business, one company decided to offer merchandise credits to all customers whose long-distance calls were $15 or more each month. The credits were to be the amount of the long-distance calls for everyone who qualified. For example, a customer who had $14 (or less) of long-distance calls would receive no merchandise credit, while someone with $15 in calls would receive $15 in merchandise credits. Write a program to input a series of*

customer names and long-distance billings and print a message awarding merchandise credits to those customers who qualify. The program should terminate when it encounters a customer whose long-distance billing is less than zero (the trailer data value).

Counters and Accumulators

The use of counters and accumulators has been discussed in Appendix A. Readers who have not read that material should do so before reading the following material on the implementation of counters and accumulators in BASIC.

Counters are used to ensure that execution of a particular segment of code occurs a specified number of times. Any numeric variable can be used as a counter in BASIC. The programmer must initialize the counter before the program enters the loop whose execution is to be controlled by the counter. Code to cause the counter variable to be incremented must be included within the loop, and an IF/THEN statement must be provided to transfer control when the counter has reached the desired value.

Accumulators are used for the storage of totals. Data values encountered by the program are added to the contents of the accumulator variable to provide running subtotals within a loop. When the loop terminates, the accumulator contains the total of the values encountered. Many programs use both counters and accumulators. For example, a program to calculate the average score achieved by students on an examination might look like this:

```
 10 REM TEST SCORE AVERAGES
 20 REM PROGRAMMER - W. HARRISON
 30 REM VARIABLE LIST
 40 REM     S = INDIVIDUAL SCORE
 50 REM     K = COUNTER
 60 REM     T = SCORE ACCUMULATOR
 70 REM     A = AVERAGE SCORE
 80 REM
 90 REM INITIALIZE COUNTER AND ACCUMULATOR
100 LET K = 0
110 LET T = 0
120 REM LOOP TO ENTER AND ACCUMULATE SCORES
130 PRINT "ENTER SCORE OR 0 TO TERMINATE"
140 INPUT S
150 IF S = 0 THEN 220
160 REM INCREMENT COUNTER
170 LET K = K + 1
180 REM ADD SCORE TO ACCUMULATOR
190 LET T = T + S
200 GO TO 130
210 REM COMPUTE AVERAGE AND PRINT IT
220 LET A = T / K
```

```
230 PRINT "THE AVERAGE WAS"; A
240 PRINT "THERE WERE", K; "SCORES"
900 END
```

As was discussed in Appendix A, accumulators and counters are two of the fundamental building blocks used by programmers in putting together programs. They are extremely useful constructs. Readers are encouraged to work with them until their use is fully understood.

EXERCISES

Example: *Write a program to read a series of data statements, each of which contains a salesperson's name and sales volume, and to accumulate the salesperson's commission, figured at 20 percent of sales. The program should terminate when a negative sales value is encountered.*

Solution:

```
 60 LET T = 0
 70 READ A$, S
 80 IF S < 0 THEN 110
 90 LET T = T + S
100 GO TO 70
110 LET C = 0.20 * T
120 PRINT A$; "EARNED", C; "DOLLARS"
800 DATA JONES, 2590
801 DATA JONES, 1450
•
•
980 DATA JONES, -100
990 END
```

Output: JONES EARNED (whatever) DOLLARS

1. *Modify the example program to check the salesperson's name each time and ignore any data statements which do not pertain to JONES.*
2. *Modify the example program to print the answer and stop after reading twenty-five data statements.*
3. *Modify the example program to accommodate two salespeople whose data statements are intermixed.*
4. *Consider a small business which has three products. During the month, data statements are created as products are sold. At the end of the month a program is needed to read all the data statements and compute (and print) the total sales for each product. Design a data statement to use as a trailer.*

The FOR/NEXT Construct

Earlier, this appendix discussed the formation of program loops with the use of the GO TO statement, with an IF/THEN statement embedded within the loop to provide for its termination. In some cases an IF/THEN statement can be used with a counter to terminate a loop after it has been repeated the correct number of times. Use of FOR and NEXT statements in BASIC provides a mechanism for using loops with built-in counters. The FOR statement identifies the variable which will be used as the counter, its initial value, its limit (maximum value), and the counting increment. For example, the following statement creates a loop which uses K as the counter and schedules repetition of the code within the loop for values of K from 1 to 10:

```
100 FOR K   1 TO 10 STEP 1
•
•
•
•
250 NEXT K
```

The *NEXT statement* increments the counter at the end of the loop and checks the new value of the counter against the maximum value specified in the FOR statement. If the newly incremented value of the counter is less than, or equal to, the maximum, the execution of the statements within the loop is begun again. If not, control passes to the next statement in the program (after the NEXT statement).

The statements between the FOR statement and its terminating NEXT statement are referred to as the FOR-body. Execution of these statements must begin with execution of the FOR statement itself; that is, a GO TO (or any other control statement except RETURN) outside the FOR-body may not be used to transfer control to a statement within the FOR-body. (The exception, the RETURN, will be discussed below in the section on subroutines). The following program segment contains an *incorrect* transfer of control:

```
50 GO TO 140
•
•
100 FOR N = 1 TO 5 STEP 1
•
•
140 LET K = 2 * N
•
•
240 NEXT N
```

Notice that the loop's counter, the variable N, can be used in expressions in LET statements within the loop. It *cannot*, however, be used on the left-hand side of a LET statement. Such a use would cause the counting apparatus to be confused by the assignment of a different value to the counter.

If the word STEP and the increment are omitted from the FOR statement, the increment is automatically assumed to be +1. Thus,

```
100 FOR H = 1 TO 35
```

establishes a loop with a counter (H) which will be scheduled to take on the values 1, 2, 3, . . ., 35. These values are only "scheduled" because the execution of loops may be terminated at any time by control statements which transfer control to a statement outside the FOR-body. For example, the following loop would terminate when the appropriate data value (a value for A less than zero) is encountered:

```
100 FOR I = 1 TO 150
110 READ A
120 IF A < 0 THEN 420
•
•
•
270 NEXT I
```

The initial value, limit, and increment parameters in the FOR statement do not need to be integer constants. They can be numeric expressions, so the following are allowed:

```
90 FOR J = 2 TO N STEP L

90 FOR K = 35 TO 1 STEP -.5

90 FOR M = K TO (A - B) / 4

90 FOR E = Z TO 4 STEP B
```

The loop will be executed as expected by the arithmetic used, except in peculiar cases where round-off is a problem, or where the expressions cause the initial value to be greater than the limit. Tests should be run by the user to determine how any particular implementation of BASIC treats the peculiar cases.

Statements within the FOR-body may be of any type. Another FOR/NEXT combination may be embedded within the FOR-body as long as it is completely contained between the original FOR and NEXT statements and does not use the same counter variable.

FOR/NEXT statements provide a convenient mechanism for building loops into programs. They are particularly useful in programs which use arrays, the topic of the next section.

EXERCISES

Example: *At the end of each week, the inventory clerk of a small record store carries a portable computer through the store, entering the stock number and quantity in stock for each record. Write a program which accepts the stock numbers and inventory levels and prints a list of all record stock numbers for which there are fewer than three in stock. Assume that there are exactly 220 stock numbers.*

Solution:

```
 60 FOR K = 1 TO 220
 70    PRINT "ENTER STOCK NUMBER"
 80    INPUT X
 90    PRINT "ENTER QUANTITY IN STOCK"
100    INPUT N
110    IF N > 2 THEN 130
120    PRINT "REORDER"; X; "STOCK IS"; N
130 NEXT K
990 END
```

Output: REORDER (whatever) STOCK IS (however many)
ETC.

1. *Modify the example program above to print out a message to put on sale those records for which there are more then ten in stock.*
2. *Write a program which prints the integers from 1 to 100.*
3. *Write a program which prints the odd numbers from 99 back to 1.*
4. *A few states require deposits on beverage containers to reduce roadside litter. Write a program which reads 50 data statements which contain the state name followed by either YES or NO, computes the number of YES states, and prints out that number.*

Arrays

We have seen how loops provide the power to cause certain portions of a program to be repeated. READ and INPUT statements within the loop can be used to cause variables within the loop to take on the necessary, various values for each execution of the loop. The particular set of data values used in one execution of the loop are destroyed by the subsequent set of values which are in turn destroyed by succeeding sets. This allows us to use, for example, one set of variable names to process a payroll for thousands of employees.

What would happen though, if we needed to keep every employee's name, social security number, wage rate, and hours worked throughout the program's complete execution phase? One set of variable names would certainly not be enough, because each variable name can have, at most, one value at a time. A separate variable name for each data value would seem to be required.

If, however, we used separate variable names such as A1, A2, A3, . . ., B1, . . ., Z9, we would need separate assignment statements for each payroll calculation for each employee. There must be a way in which we can use a standard form of a variable name in program statements but keep storage space for all data values throughout a program. There is such a way, and it is called an **array**.

An array allows the programmer to set aside particular variable names which will be used with subscripts to provide both standard notation and large volume storage. An array is declared through use of a DIM statement, an example of which follows:

```
10 DIM A(100)
```

This *DIM* (short for *DIMension*) *statement* sets up an array variable, A, which, in the above case, would have 100 elements. Figure C–6 provides a representation of such an array. This array contains storage space for 100 data values, each of which can be referred to by the array name A followed by a subscript in parentheses to indicate a unique element in the array. The third element in the array would be referred to as A(3).

If we were only to use constants as array subscripts, we would still not have gained any efficiency over the use of single variable names for each data value. In fact, we may have lost ground if we have to now use A(3) instead of A3. The real efficiency of the array notation comes when we use variable names and expressions as array subscripts. Thus, the array element A(I) could refer to any element in the array, depending upon the value of I. If I is 3 then A(I) refers to A(3). If I is 47, then A(I) is A(47).

We could even use a counter to send I through the values from 1 to 100 and have A(I) refer to each of the elements in the array in turn. Real efficiencies are gained, then, when we use FOR/NEXT loops to provide the counter. The loop control variable, the counter, can then be used as the general subscript in an array, and each element of the array can be processed in turn as the loop executes.

FIGURE C–6
One-Dimensional Array (Numeric Values)

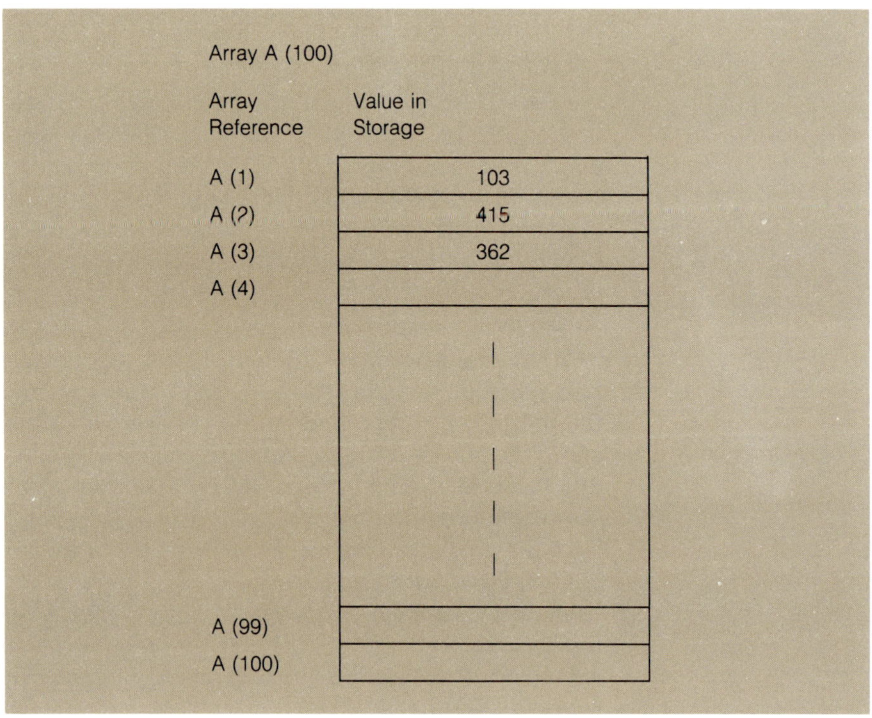

For example, consider a program which is supposed to read names into an array. The following program sets up an array of ten elements and reads names into it:

```
10 REM LIST OF NAMES PROGRAM
20 REM PROGRAMMER W. HARRISON
30 REM LIST OF VARIABLES
40 REM      N$ = ARRAY OF NAMES
50 REM      R  = COUNTER
60 DIM N$(10)
70 FOR R = 1 TO 10
80 READ N$(R)
90 NEXT R
 •
 •
 •
500 DATA JOE, CARRIE, GWEN, JUDY, ROGER
510 DATA RALPH, OLIVER, MARY, PEACHES, OTTO
900 END
```

As the loop executes, R takes on the value 1, N$(1) is read, and JOE is stored into the array. R becomes 2, and CARRIE is stored into N$(2), and so on. The array contents are illustrated in Figure C–7.

Arrays may contain either numeric or character string data values, but the same array may not be used for both. Arrays may be of either one or two dimensions. Two-dimensional arrays have rows and columns (like tables) as illustrated in Figure C–8. The subscripts of a two-dimensional array refer to row number and column number of a particular element in the array. Although the subscript schemes of (row number, column number) and (column number, row number) can be shown to be equivalent, the consistent use of one or the other is essential. The (row number, column number) designation is more commonly used. Thus, C(2,3) refers to the

FIGURE C–7
One-Dimensional Array (String Values)

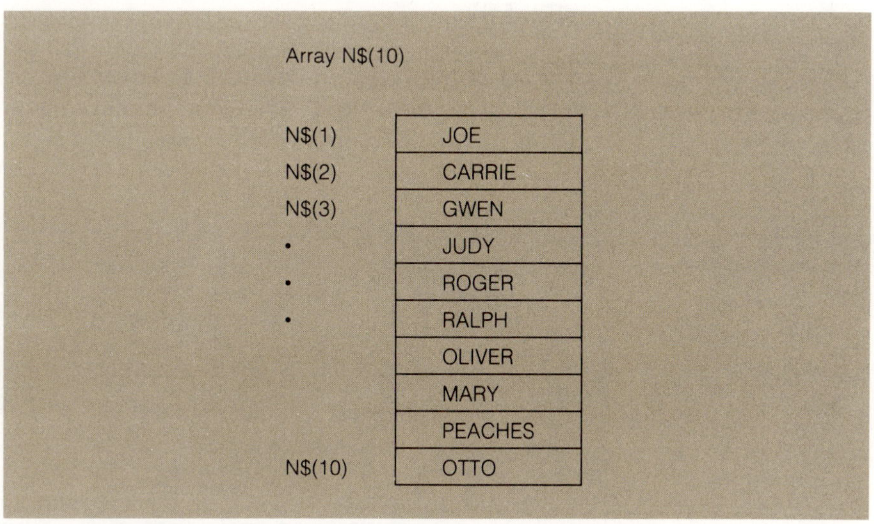

FIGURE C–8
Two-Dimensional Array (Numeric Values)

Array C (3,4)

C (2,3) → row 2, column 3

Rows \ Columns	1	2	3	4
1	27	15	134	76
2	103	88		
3				

array element in the second row of the third column as shown in Figure C–8.

Two-dimensional arrays can make use of FOR/NEXT loops nested one inside the other in order to use the loop control variables as row and column designators. The following program, for example, creates an array, fills it with 0s, and changes the 0s on the diagonal to 1s (as shown in Figure C–9):

```
 10 REM ARRAY WITH 1'S AND 0'S PROGRAM
 20 REM PROGRAMMER W. HARRISON
 30 LIST OF VARIABLES
 40     T = ARRAY
 50     R = ROW DESIGNATOR
 60     C = COLUMN DESIGNATOR
 70 DIM T(4,4)
 80 FOR R = 1 TO 4
 90 FOR C = 1 TO 4
100 LET T(R,C) = 0
110 IF R <> C THEN 130
120 LET T(R,C) = 1
130 NEXT C
140 NEXT R
900 END
```

Execution of the program causes R to be set first to 1, then C to be set to 1, and T(1,1) to be set to 0. The IF statement in 110 is FALSE (R and C are equal), so 120 is executed, which causes the 0 at T(1,1) to be changed to a

FIGURE C–9
Two-Dimensional Array

Array T (4,4)

Rows \ Columns	1	2	3	4
1	1	0	0	0
2	0	1	0	0
3	0	0	1	0
4	0	0	0	1

1. Statement 130 causes C to be incremented to 2 and control to return to the top of the loop on C. Therefore, T(1,2) will be the next element to be stored, followed in turn by T(1,3) and T(1,4). After T(1,4) has received its 0 and control is transferred by 110 to statement 130, the C loop is now fully satisfied, so execution moves to 140. Here R is incremented to 2, and the C loop is entered once again at 90. T(2,1) receives a 0 and filling of the second row follows.

Although the reading of a verbal description of a program's execution gets tedious very quickly, the reader should spend enough time with the above description to ensure that a good understanding of the execution path of the program is reached. The reader should then write other, similar programs and check their actual results against his or her own calculations for further practice.

The combination of FOR/NEXT loops with arrays provides the programmer with an efficient and powerful set of programming tools. In using these tools, the programmer should be careful to:

1. Dimension all arrays before their use.
2. Maintain separation of data types (numeric and string).
3. Keep all array subscripts within the dimensioned boundaries.

Data values stored in arrays can be used in exactly the same ways as data values stored in individual variable names. The appropriate array reference can be used in READ or INPUT statements, in PRINT statements, or on either side of the equals sign in LET statements. As a matter of fact, they may be used wherever expressions are allowed.

EXERCISES

Example 1: *Write a program which sets up a one-dimensional array with room for ten numbers, fills the array with data from data statements, and then prints out the array.*

Solution:

```
 60 DIM A(10)
 70 FOR N = 1 TO 10
 80   READ A (N)
 90 NEXT N
100 FOR K = 1 TO 10
110   PRINT A (K)
120 NEXT K
800 DATA 16, 22, 14, 73, 81
810 DATA 29, 48, 62, 11, 19
990 END
```

Note: *Both the READ and PRINT operations could be accomplished within the same FOR/NEXT loop.*

Output:

```
16
22
14
ETC.
```

1. Modify example program 1 above to compute and print the sum of the numbers in the array.
2. Modify the program in exercise 1 above to compute and print the average of the numbers in the array.
3. Modify example program 1 above to sort the numbers in the array before printing.
4. Write a program which could read 1,000 numbers from data statements, sort them, sum them, compute their average, and print out the sorted array, the sum of the average.

Example 2: *Write a program which sets up a two-dimensional array to maintain inventory information. Each DATA statement will contain:*

	PART NO.	MAXIMUM LEVEL	MINIMUM LEVEL	IN STOCK
e.g.	01394	250	30	196
	01466	120	19	46

Assume there are exactly 500 items in the inventory.

Solution:

```
 60 DIM P(500,4)
 70 FOR I = 1 TO 500
 80    FOR J = 1 TO 4
 90       READ P(I,J)
100    NEXT J
110 NEXT I
•
•
•
990 END
```

5. Modify example program 2 above to print out the array.
6. Modify the program in exercise 5 above to print out only those item numbers for which the actual number in stock is less than the minimum level for that item.
7. Modify the program in exercise 6 above to also print out those item numbers for which the actual number in stock is greater than the maximum level for that item.
8. Write a similar program for an array of inventory information which could accommodate an inventory of 10,000 items and also contains a column for unit costs for each item and a column into which the value of the inventory for each item can be extended.

	PART NUMBER	MAXIMUM LEVEL	MINIMUM LEVEL	IN STOCK	COST	VALUE
Data statement contains:	01233	50	10	21	1.05	

Note: Program must compute and store the extended values.

Use of Functions

Most programming languages provide the programmer with the opportunity to use special segments of code known as functions to perform frequently needed tasks. Some functions are part of the language as it is implemented and are known as **library functions.** The programmer may write and declare other, **user-defined functions.**

The library functions normally provided by minimal BASIC are listed in Table C–2. These functions may be called into use by a programmer wherever the particular task is required within a program. Assume, for example, that the programmer needs to compute the square root of a number. Rather than writing the code for calculating a square root, the programmer may just use the library SQR function as follows:

TABLE C–2 *Minimal BASIC Functions*

Function	Function Value
ABS(X)	The absolute value of X
ATN(X)	The arctangent of X in radians, that is, the angle whose tangent is X. The range of the function is −(pi/2) < ATN(X) < (pi/2) where pi is the ratio of the circumference of a circle to its diameter
COS(X)	The cosine of X, where X is in radians
EXP(X)	The exponential of X, that is, the value of the base of natural logarithms (e = 2.71828 . . .) raised to the power X; if EXP(X) is less than machine infinitesimal, then its value shall be replaced by zero
INT(X)	The largest integer not greater than X; for example, INT(1.3) = 1 and INT(−1.3) = −2
LOG(X)	The natural logarithm of X; X must be greater than zero
RND	The next pseudorandom number in an implementation-supplied sequence of pseudorandom numbers uniformly distributed in the range 0 <= RND < 1
SGN(X)	The algebraic "sign" of X: −1 if X < 0, 0 if X = 0, and +1 if X > 0
SIN(X)	The sine of X, where X is in radians
SQR(X)	The nonnegative square root of X; X must be nonnegative
TAN(X)	The tangent of X, where X is in radians

Taken from: American National Standard for Minimal BASIC ANSI X3.60—1978

```
50 LET X = SQR(Y)
```

The nonnegative square root of Y would be calculated and assigned to X.

User-defined functions require the programmer to define the function in a DEF statement. For example, a user might define a function which converts feet to inches as shown here:

```
30 DEF FNI{X} = 12 * X
```

This function could then be used later in the program whenever the conversion is needed. An example of such a use is:

```
70 LET Z = FNI{9.5}
```

Use of the function in this assignment statement would cause the function's argument, 9.5, to be multiplied by 12 and the resulting product to be assigned to the variable Z.

The syntax of the function-defining statement requires a statement number, followed by DEF, followed by the function name, the parameter(s) used, an equals sign, and an expression by which the function is to be computed. The function name must begin with FN, but the third and final character in the name may be any letter.

EXERCISES

Example: *Write a program which asks for the input of a number, uses the appropriate function to compute the square root of the number, and then prints it out.*

Solution:

```
 70 PRINT "ENTER A POSITIVE NUMBER"
 80 INPUT X
 90 IF X < 0 THEN 130
100 LET Y = SQR(X)
110 PRINT "THE SQUARE ROOT OF"; X; "IS"; Y
120 STOP
130 PRINT "ERROR, X IS NEGATIVE"
990 END
```

1. *Write a program which applies the integer function to an input number and prints both the original number and the result.*

2. *Write a program which generates a series of pseudorandom numbers between 0 and 1 using the appropriate function.*

3. *Modify the program from exercise 2 to print pseudorandom numbers between 0 and 10.*

4. *Write a user-defined function which computes the square of its argument, and use the function to do the squares of a series of inputs.*

Subroutines

A subroutine, or similar subprogram, is provided by most programming languages to allow for modularity in program design. Subroutines are designed to accomplish well-defined processing tasks. They are often program modules which have been previously coded and tested so that they can be used as needed. In BASIC a subroutine is executed as a result of a *GOSUB statement.* For example, the following statement transfers control to a subroutine:

```
80 GOSUB 600
```

In this example, the code to be executed in the subroutine would start at statement number 600. A RETURN statement is placed at the end of the subroutine to return control back to the main part of the program.

Unfortunately, the subroutine implemented in BASIC is little more than another GO TO. It is not well-suited for treatment as a stand-alone module of code. It does allow, however, for the use of a RETURN statement so that control of the program can be transferred back to the statement after the GOSUB, when execution of the subroutine is completed. A RETURN statement needs only a statement number and the word RETURN.

EXERCISES

Example: *Write a program which reads in three numbers and uses a subroutine to compute the average of the three.*

Solution:

```
 70 READ A, B, C
 80 GO SUB 200
 90 PRINT X
100 STOP
200 LET X = (A+B+C)/3
210 RETURN
990 END
```

1. *Write a program which reads ten numbers into an array, sorts them, computes their average, and prints out the sorted array and the average.*
2. *Modify the program in exercise 1 above to use four subroutines, one each for reading, sorting, computing the average, and printing.*

Files

The syntax of file use differs so much from system to system that it is difficult to provide general coverage. The creation and saving of files was treated in the beginning of this appendix. Once the data are stored in a file under a filename, the file must be opened for processing. As an example, a file named RECEIPTS could be opened with the following statement:

```
50 OPEN #1, "RECEIPTS"
```

The #1 in the OPEN statement assigns the number 1 to the file RECEIPTS so that further access can be gained by reference to the number instead of the filename. If, for example, data were to be read from the file, a READ statement would be used which looks like this:

```
60 READ #1, N$, A1, A2
```

The variables N$, A1, and A2 would be assigned the first, second, and third data values, respectively, from this file.

Writing data to the file can be accomplished with either the PRINT statement or the WRITE statement, depending upon the particular implementation of the language. Some implementations require SCRATCH or RESTORE statements to erase old data from a file. Most use the CLOSE command to terminate use of a particular file within a program. An example of a CLOSE command is:

```
690 CLOSE #1
```

A program may work with several different files in the course of the program's execution. Each must be separately opened and closed, using the appropriate commands.

EXERCISES

1. *Discover the file handling commands which work on your system.*
2. *Write a program to create a file.*
3. *Write a program which uses your created file as input.*

This completes a brief treatment of BASIC. The reader should refer to a full-fledged programming text for additional material.

Glossary

Accumulator: A storage location, register, or variable name in which arithmetic results are collected (accumulated).

Accuracy: The extent to which information is a correct representation.

Acoustic coupler: A type of transducer which converts a computing device's electrical signal into an audible one so that data can be transmitted through the telephone network via a standard telephone handset.

Ada: A programming language, named for Ada Augusta, Countess of Lovelace; designed under the direction of the U.S. Department of Defense.

Adder: Electronic logic which performs addition, an essential part of the CPU of any computer.

Algorithm: A statement of the steps necessary to perform a processing task or solve a problem.

Alphabetic data: Data composed (only) of characters contained in the alphabet.

Alphanumeric data: Data composed of characters which are numbers, letters, and/or special characters.

ALU (Arithmetic/logic unit): The electronic logic of the central processing unit which performs arithmetic and logical operations.

Analog signal: A signal which, like a continuous function, can take on an infinite number of values within a particular range.

Analytical engine: A calculating machine, one of the precursors to the computer, designed by Charles Babbage.

APL (A Programming Language): Uses Greek characters as commands to form a very powerful programming language.

Application: A function to which computer expertise has been applied, for example, the payroll application.

Application program: A program written to accomplish a particular function.

Archival storage: A very long-term storage system where records may be kept for years.

ARPANET: A communications network maintained by the Advanced Research Projects Agency of the Department of Defense.

Artificial intelligence: A field of study dealing with the intelligent behavior of machines such as robots.

Ascendancy check: A software check to make sure that the records being processed are in ascending (or descending) order.

Assembler: The program which translates assembly language to machine language.

Assembly language: A programming language, unique for each type of machine, which allows mnemonic codes, variable names and statement labels as improvements over machine language.

Associative memory: A type of memory the contents of which are searched by looking for a known value.

Asynchronous: A mode of telecommunication coordinated through the use of beginning and ending flags; contrast *Synchronous*.

Attributes: From the entity/attribute characterization of records; data elements related to the entity.

Audit trail: A path of examination followed by those trying to verify that activities have been properly completed.

Automatic teller machine (ATM): A microprocessor-enhanced terminal located outside the bank through which customers can transact their banking business.

Backlog: In applications development, the list of recognized projects awaiting development.

Backup file: A copy of a file, stored in a secure place, to be used in case the original is lost or destroyed.

Bar code: A code which uses alternating bars of white and black to encode data.

Baseband: One of the two competing schemes for local area network transmissions of data; uses a narrow transmission bandwidth.

BASIC (Beginners' All-Purpose Symbolic Instruction Code): An easy-to-learn interactive computer programming language.

Batch: A collection of inputs to be processed at one time.

Batch processing: The processing of aggregated collections (batches) of data.

Batch total: A strategic sum used to check processing accuracy.

Baud rate: A measure of data transmission speed, the number of discrete changes in the signal per second; frequently, but not always, synonymous with bits per second.

Benchmark: Use of performance measures to judge a system's performance; also see *Line benchmark* and *Standard benchmark*.

Binary digit (bit): (see *bit*)

Biochip: A biological computer logic chip.

BIPS: Billions of instructions per second, a measure of processing speed.

BISYNC: A data transmission protocol.

Bit (binary digit): The representation of a single value in a two-state device, a single binary element.

Bit-mapping: The transfer of an image, usually from a display screen to a printer, bit by bit.

Blocking: A procedure used to increase the density of data on magnetic tape by grouping records.

Bootstrapping: The initial phase of computer startup in which the computer brings itself up from its inoperative state, that is, by its "bootstraps".

Breadboard: A prototype or unfinished design.

Broadband: One of the competing technologies for local area data transmissions; uses a broad transmission band.

Buffer: A temporary storage area between two devices which process data at different speeds.

Bus network: A single communications line to which a number of computing devices can be connected.

Bypass technology: A telecommunications network which does not use (bypasses) the normal telephone system.

Byte: A collection of bits, usually 8 bits.

CAD/CAM (Computer Assisted Design/Computer Assisted Manufacturing): The use of computers to accomplish design and facilitate movement of the design into manufacturing processes.

CAI: See *Computer-aided instruction.*

Card punch: A device which encodes data into cards by punching holes in them.

Card reader: A computer input device which reads the data punched into cards.

Central processing unit (CPU): The primary component of a computer which houses control and computation functions.

Character printer: A printer which prints a single character at a time.

Characters: The symbols used to represent data.

Chief programmer: The programmer in charge of a programming effort.

Chip: The name given to an electronic device formed by very large-scale integration and used for computer memories and logic.

Client: One whose interests are to be served by a system.

CLOUT: Interface for a relational data base product from Microrim.

COBOL: (COmmon Business-Oriented Language): The programming language most often used for business applications.

Code review: A formal process in which programmers review the programming code written by their fellow programmers.

Coding: Writing statements in a programming language.

COM (Computer Output Microfilm): The use of film to record computer output.

Compatibility: The ability of two or more devices to communicate or connect effectively.

Compiler: A program which translates higher-level language programs into machine language.

Computation: Arithmetic and other data manipulations.

Compute bound: The state in which the speed of data processing is limited by the speed of the central processing unit.

Computer-aided instruction (CAI): The use of computers to assist in educational processes.

Computer crime: A crime made possible by the use of computers.

Computer operator: The person who is responsible for running the computer.

Computer system: A collection of computing devices connected together.

Configuration: A particular assembly of hardware devices.

Content: The meaning associated with data or information.

Contract programmer: A programmer whose services are obtained by formal contract.

Control totals: Significant totals used to ensure that data processing operations have been accurately completed.

Cost/benefit analysis: A comparison of the costs of a system with the benefits expected to be derived from the system.

Counters: Logical constructs which accomplish counting in programs.

CP/M (Control Program for Microprocessors): A microcomputer operating system designed by Digital Research.

CPU: See *Central processing unit.*

Critical path: The longest path in a critical path method network.

Critical path method (CPM): A technique in management science for project management which identifies the longest (most critical) path.

Critical success factors: Those elements of an activity which are essential to a favorable outcome.

Cross-footing check: A software check used to ensure data processing accuracy.

CSMA/CD (Carrier Sense, Multiple Access/Collision Detection): A methodology which allows several computing devices to share a local area network.

Custom software: Software designed and written for a specific purpose.

Cycle time: The time it takes the CPU to complete a full cycle.

Cylinder: In magnetic disk operations, the storage area accessible when all read/write heads are located at the same position above each disk.

Data: A collection of characters which form a representation having meaning within the context of data processing.

Data administrator: The person in charge of an organization's data.

Data base: A large collection of data in support of a set of data processing tasks.

Data base administrator: The person in charge of a data base.

Data base management system (DBMS): A set of programs which manages a data base, controlling access, facilitating report generation and updating of the data, and providing for inquiry access by users.

Data bus: A connecting link between the CPU and primary memory.

Data cell: A device used for large-scale, on-line storage of data; uses an automatic mechanism to access strips of magnetic tape.

Data dictionary: One of the components of a DBMS which identifies and defines each data item stored in a data base.

Data editing: The process of modifying or correcting data.

Data item: A single element of data.

Data processing manager: The manager in charge of a data processing group.

Data processing system: A collection of hardware, software, people, and procedures for the generation of information.

Data redundancy: Duplication of data stored in a system.

Data security: Protection of data from unauthorized access.

Data structure diagram: A diagram used to represent data relationships.

Data validation: The process of ensuring data accuracy.

dBase III: A data base software package marketed by Ashton-Tate.

DBMS: See *Data base management system.*

Decision making: The process of choosing among alternative courses of action.

Decision support system (DSS): A particular kind of management information system requiring interactive use to solve semi-structured problems.

Decision table: A chart which yields a chosen activity according to the values of several input parameters.

Degree of permanence: Used in the text to refer to the extent to which output must be maintained over time, permanently.

Design: To decide upon the features of a scheme or plan.

Desk checking: Judging the correctness of a program by imagining its execution.

Desktop computer: A microcomputer system small enough to fit on a desktop in the office environment.

Difference engine: A calculating machine designed by Charles Babbage; a precursor to the computer.

Digital: Having a finite set of states; most computers are designed on the basis of two-state, digital components.

Digitizer: A computer input device consisting of a drawing board and an electronic mouse, used to input graphical data.

Direct-access file: A file in which records can be located and retrieved directly, that is, without searching through a large portion of the file; also known as random-access file.

Disk drive: A device used to read and write on magnetic disks.

Diskette: see *Floppy disk.*

Disk pack: A set of magnetic disks on a common spindle.

Distributed data processing: A management scheme which distributes computing equipment, data, and programs throughout an organization.

Documentation: Predominantly written material used to explain how a computing device or program works and how to use it.

Domain: A set (from set theory).

Dot matrix: A scheme for printers and video displays which uses a set of points to form characters.

Dot matrix printer: A printer which forms characters through use of a dot matrix.

Econometric model: A complicated set of mathematical relationships which can be used to predict an economy's performance.

Economies of scale: A phrase used to describe the principle that, in certain circumstances, bigger is better. For example, processing speed increases with increases in size of the CPU.

Edit checks: A software check to assist in checking data accuracy during input operations.

Efficiency: The ability to achieve goals with a minimum consumption of resources.

Electronic mail: A procedure by which people use personal computers and a communications network to send each other messages.

Emulation: The process of causing one computer to imitate the operations of another.

Encoding scheme: The set of rules which govern the use of bit patterns to represent characters for data transmissions.

Encryption: The use of secret coding schemes to mask the real meaning of information during communication.

Entity: Name given to the central data element, or "owner," of a record.

Entity-attribute method: A means for describing a record; the entity is the central item of interest and other data values are attributes.

Ethernet: Proprietary name of the local area network developed by the Xerox Co.

Event: An action which takes place.

Exception reporting: A management reporting method which emphasizes only extraordinary information.

Executive workstation: A microprocessor-based terminal for use by executives.

Expert system: A knowledge-based program which is capable of activities normally attributed to an expert.

Extension check: An arithmetical operation to check values on orders and invoices.

Facilities management: The management of a company's computer center by an outside supplier of such services.

Facsimile transmission: The sending of copies (facsimiles) via telecommunications.

Fetch register: A register used to retrieve data from storage.

Fiber optics: The transmission of signals via strands of glass of extremely high quality.

Field: A space, either conceptual or physical, within a record in which a data item can be stored.

File: A collection of records.

File structures: Physical and logical rules which determine the particular form of records in a file.

Firmware: Instructions, such as program instructions, which are permanently implanted in memory.

Fixed-length field: A zone of storage of constant size used for data.

Floppy disk: A secondary storage media in which data are stored on the electromagnetic surface of a thin disk.

FLOPS (floating point operations per second): The number of floating point arithmetic operations performed per second.

Flowchart: A graphical representation of the logic of an algorithm.

Format: The layout or spatial arrangement of output.

FORTRAN: A programming language useful in scientific and engineering applications because of its ease in representing algebraic expressions.

Fourth-generation language: An advanced programming language which allows use of a computer without the specification of a procedural language program.

Framework: An integrated software product from Ashton-Tate.

Frequency: The number of times output is to be generated per period.

Frequency division multiplexing: In telecommunications, the shared use of a single transmission line accomplished by allocating different frequencies to each message; compare *Time division multiplexing.*

Full duplex: A communications scheme in which communications are allowed in two directions, both at the same time; contrast *Half duplex.*

Functional specification: A method of describing a system in terms of the functions it must be capable of performing.

General systems theory: The body of knowledge concerned with the study of characteristics common to all systems.

Goal: An objective to be achieved; the purpose of a system.

Graphics: A computer output mode which allows pictures, drawings, and graphs to be generated.

Graphics printer: A printer capable of printing both text and graphics.

Graphics tablet: A computer input device which makes it possible to enter pictures, drawings, and graphs.

Graphics terminal: A special terminal designed to facilitate the use of graphics in computer output.

Hacker: Originally used to describe avid computer buffs but used more recently to describe those computer buffs who gain unauthorized access to sensitive computer systems.

Half duplex: A communications scheme in which communications are allowed in both directions, though only a single direction at a time; contrast *Full duplex.*

Hardware: The name given to a collection of computer equipment.

Hardware compatability: The ability of two or more pieces of computer equipment to connect and communicate with each other.

Hardware, intelligence in: The inclusion of memory and programmability in computer equipment.

Hard-wired: A direct connection by wire or cable between two computing devices.

Hashing: A method of locating a record within a file which uses algebraic means to compute an address from the key.

Hash total: An arithmetical check on processing accuracy.

Hexadecimal: A numbering system which uses the base 16.

Hierarchical data model: A data structure used in data base management to define logical relationships among data elements.

Hierarchical model: A data structure which defines relationships in terms of parent-child connections.

Higher-level language: Any of those languages superior in development to machine and assembly languages.

HIPO (Hierarchical Input/Process/Output): A means for developing and illustrating the logic within a program or set of programs.

IBG (interblock gap): The blank space which separates data on a magnetic tape to allow the tape drive room to start and stop without missing data.

Icon: A likeness, a graphical image used to help the user select the appropriate software action; usually displayed on a personal computer display.

Implementation: The phase in the system life cycle during which the new system is installed.

Implementation in parallel: An implementation method which continues to run an old system (in parallel) with a new one until confidence can be gained in the new system's ability to run properly.

In-house computing facility: A computing system owned and operated by an organization.

Indexed sequential: A file structure in which records are stored in sequence, but quick access is facilitated through the use of an index.

Indexed sequential file: A sequential file implemented on a direct access device with an index for quick access to strategic locations in the file.

Information: Data which have been processed in order to be useful.

Information requirements analysis: The determination of the information required to support managerial decision making.

Information resource management (IRM): A school of thought which promotes the investment in information as a resource which is to be managed as any other resource.

Initializing: In programming, the setting of variables to their initial values, frequently zero.

Input: The entry of data into an information system.

Instruction decoder: An element of the CPU which translates a command into an appropriate activity on the part of the system.

Instruction set: The fundamental set of commands which the computer can execute.

Integrated circuit: A tiny electronic device which results from the combination of several, perhaps many, transistors, permitting greatly enhanced speed of processing.

Integrated package: In personal computing, a series of software packages coordinated to work together.

Integrated services digital network (ISDN): A network based upon digital techniques which allows a variety of information services to be integrated.

Intelligence: The capability of machines which have memory and can execute a series of instructions.

Inter-record gap (IRG): See *IBG*.

Interactive: A mode of computer access characterized by alternating computer and user actions.

Interactive processing: A means of working with a computer from a terminal in which the user and the system each respond directly to the activities performed by the other.

Interblock gap: See *IBG*.

Interface: The boundary at which two systems come together; used to describe the boundary between human operators and computing devices.

Interface device: A piece of hardware used to connect two otherwise incompatible devices.

Internet: Network containing both long distance and local loops.

Interpreter: A program which translates higher-level language instructions in terms of another language in order to execute the instructions.

Inverted file: A collection of records in which a data element which is an attribute in the original file can be used as a key for the new (inverted) file.

I/O bound (input/output bound): A situation in which computer processing speeds are limited by the speed(s) of the input and/or output device(s).

Iteration: The repetition of a particular set of operations.

Job control language (JCL): The set of commands which allows the user of a computing system to specify the set of resources needed for a particular processing task.

Josephson Junction: A technology based upon the reduced resistance of conductors to the flow of electrons at temperatures near absolute zero; may be used in building the computers of the future.

K (Kilo): A symbol which in computing has a value of 1,024; used loosely to indicate thousands (of storage units in primarty memory), thus 8K is approximately 8,000, but more exactly is 8,192.

Key: A data element in a record which can be used as an access point to the record itself.

Keypunch: A data preparation machine which encodes data by punching holes in cards.

Key-to-disk: A data entry machine in which data are entered on to magnetic disks through keyboard entry.

Key-to-tape: A data entry machine in which data are entered on to magnetic tape through keyboard entry.

LAN: See *Local area network*.

Lap-size (notebook) computer: A microcomputer small enough to set on one's lap.

Large-scale integration (LSI): An extension of integrated electronic circuits on a large scale; an advancement which made transistors obsolete in computers.

Laser card: A card which uses laser-based techniques to store information.

Letter-quality printer: A printer capable of letter-quality printing.

Letter-quality printing: Printing of high enough quality that it would be satisfactory for professional correspondence.

Librarian: A person who is responsible for maintaining a library of tapes, programs, or other documentation; sometimes used to refer to a program which maintains files on a computer system.

Library function: Subprograms provided by a computer system and available to the user (stored in system library).

Library maintenance: A set of programs which are part of the operating system and which enables files to be created, stored, modified, and deleted.

Limit check: An instruction built into a computer program which checks particular values to make sure that certain, reasonable limits have not been exceeded.

Line printer: A printer which prints a line at a time.

Link-edit: A part of the operating system which establishes connections between various program segments whenever necessary.

Lisa: A microcomputer sold by Apple Computer.

Live benchmark: The testing of computer system's performance by running an organization's programs on the system; compare *Standard benchmark*.

Local area network (LAN): Communications connections over short distances made via twisted-pair wires, coaxial cable, or fiber optics cables which allow several computing devices to communicate with each other.

Logging on: Identifying oneself to the system as an authorized user.

Logical description: A description of data relationships independent of the physical description.

Logical design: Used in the development of information systems to distinguish between the conceptual relationships (how they are related) among data elements and their physical relationships (where they are stored).

Logical record: Data elements related to each other in a file, the collection of attributes related to a single entity.

Lotus 1-2-3: An integrated software package sold by Lotus Corp.

Machine dependent: Descirbes a particular program whose execution can be achieved on only a particular type of computer.

Machine independent: Describes a particular program whose execution is not dependent upon the type of computer itself.

Machine language: The most fundamental of computer languages, unique to each type of computer, through which programmers can specify a set of instructions to be executed by the machine.

Machine readable: Capable of being directly input to the computer without modification by manual processes.

Magnetic bubble: A small magnetic domain which can be used to store data.

Magnetic disk: A disk with an electromagnetic surface which can be used to store data.

Magnetic drum: A cylinder with an electromagnetic surface which can be used to store data.

Magnetic ink character recognition (MICR): A system whose use of a special alphabet and ink with magnetic properties to record data allows the banking system to sort, process, and clear checks rapidly.

Magnetic tape: Ferromagnetic tape used to store data.

Mainframe computer: A large-scale computer.

Maintenance programmer: A programmer who works on the correction and modification of programs.

MAN: See *Metropolitan area network.*

Management information system (MIS): A collection of related components designed to generate information to support managerial activities.

Mandatory requirements: Requirements within a request for proposal (RFP) which must be met by any supplier.

Mass storage device: Secondary storage equipment which offers large volume storage of data for relatively low cost per data element.

Master file: The semi-permanent file used to store information for applications; compare *Transaction file.*

Measure of performance: A means by which to determine how well or poorly a system is doing.

Medium: The substance on which output is stored.

Memory management: The use of a set of programs in the operating system to allocate and reconfigure the system's memory.

Menu: A list of possible options in interacting with a computing device which allows the user to select the next activity.

Metropolitan area network: A telecommunications network which operates within the boundaries of an urban area.

MICR: See *Magnetic Ink Character Recognition.*

Microcomputer: A very small but relatively powerful computer.

Microfiche: A small sheet of microfilm images.

Microfilm: Photographic film used to record data.

Microprocessor: A set of electronic devices which form a CPU for a microcomputer.

Minicomputer: A computer system whose size and capability are in between those of a microcomputer and a mainframe.

Minimal BASIC: A version of BASIC defined by ANSI.

MIPS (millions of instructions per second): Used to describe computer processing speeds.

Modem: Shortening of modulator/demodulator, a transducer which converts a computer's digital signals into analog ones (modulation) for transmission over a telephone line and converts analog signals into digital ones (demodulation) at the receiving end.

Modularity: Subdivision of a large program or project into smaller units.

Module: One of the units into which a program can be divided to simplify its preparation.

Mother board: The printed circuit board on which the CPU and memory chips are mounted.

Mouse: A small, hand-held electromechanical device used to control cursor movements for some personal computing systems.

Multiplexing: The combining of many signals in such a way that they can all be sent over a single transmission line without confusion; also see *Frequency division multiplexing* and *Time division multiplexing.*

Multiprocessing: The use of two or more CPUs in a single computer system.

Multiprogramming: The ability of a CPU to have numerous, partially complete programs in its memory at the same time.

Nanosecond: A billionth of a second.

Natural language: A programming language similar to English and therefore usable by novices.

N/C machine: See *Numerically-controlled machine.*

Networking: The connecting together of numerous locations via transmission lines capable of carrying data between the various computing devices.

Network model: A data structure model which captures data relationships in a network of nodes and directed arcs.

Nonprocedural language: A programming language in which results may be achieved without the specification of step-by-step procedures.

Numerical address: The reference to a storage location in a computer's memory.

Numeric data: Data represented solely by numbers.

Numerically-controlled (NC) machine: A manufacturing machine in which the various settings required for proper operation are controlled by numerical sequences.

Object program: The translated version of a source program, usually in binary (machine language).

OCR (optical character recognition): The process of automatic data entry through a machine's reading of handwritten, typed, or printed characters.

Off-line: Not directly connected to a computer system.

OMR (optical mark recognition): The process of data entry through a machine's reading of a special input form on which specific characters are represented by marks within specific delimiters.

On-line: Directly connected to a computer system.

On-line documentation: Explanatory material, stored within the system, that can be accessed while the user is using the system.

Operating environment: Software which provides an interface between the user of a personal computer and the operating system or applications packages on the system.

Operating system: The collection of programs which controls the overall operation of a computing system and makes its resources available to the users.

Operations code: A numerical code, part of a machine language instruction, which corresponds to an elemental activity within the basic instruction set of a computer.

Optical character recognition: See *OCR*.

Optical disk: A disk which uses an optical method, usually a laser, to store and retrieve data.

Optical mark recognition: See *OMR*.

Optional: Used in requests for proposals to indicate specifications which are not absolutely required.

Optional requirements: Those requirements outlined in a request for proposal (RFP) which are not mandatory but might be desirable in a system.

Outcome: The end result of an action.

Output: The information generated by a computer system.

Overlap: A central processor capability which allows two or more activities to take place at the same time.

Overlapped processing: The scheduling of data processing tasks on a computer such that two or more can take place simultaneously.

Overlay: A means of bringing programs into the primary memory in sections as needed so that the entire program does not have to be in the memory at the same time.

Overview diagram: In HIPO, a diagram which illustrates a broad, overall view of the system.

Packet switching: A means of transmitting data in which the original message is divided into a series of packets and packets are sent by the most efficient route to the destination, where they are reassembled into the original message.

Page printers: A printer which prints a page at a time.

Page scanner: An OCR device which has the capability of reading entire pages at once.

Paging: The capability of dividing large programs into sections, called pages, and moving the pages into and out of the memory as necessary.

Parallel operation: Two or more operations which take place at the same time.

Parity bit: A bit which is used in conjunciton with an even or odd bit scheme to detect data errors.

Parity checking: The use of parity bits to ensure data quality.

Parse: To break an instruction into its components.

Partitioning: Dividing the primary memory into sections and allocating different programs to the different sections (partitions) so that they do not interfere with each other.

Pascal: A programming language well suited for teaching structured programming concepts.

Password: A secret code used to deny access to unauthorized users.

Peripherals: Hardware other than the CPU itself.

Perpendicular recording: In magnetic storage, a technology which allows magnetized areas to "stand on end" rather than "lie end to end," and thus allows greater storage densities.

PERT/CPM (Program Evaluation and Review Technique/Critical Path Method): Program management techniques to schedule and control large projects.

Personal computer: A microcomputer used as a personal machine.

Physical description: Details of data storage identifying actual data locations.

Physical record: The actual representation of data on the storage medium.

Picture element: See *Pixel*.

Pixel: Shortening of picture element; a single dot on a television screen.

PL/I (Programming Language/One): A higher-level language which combines some of the strengths of both COBOL and FORTRAN.

Plotter: A computer output device designed to draw (plot) graphical output.

Plug-to-plug compatible: A descriptor used to indicate that two devices can be correctly connected to each other; commonly used to indicate that equipment made by a non-IBM manufacturer is compatible with the corresponding IBM product.

Portable: A computer capable of being carried.

Power: The characteristic of higher-level language which results in one instruction representing many machine language statements.

Precompiler: A program, or set of programs, which processes programmer inputs to produce a program which can them be compiled.

Predefined logic system: A programming aid which allows a programmer to select from a set of prewritten program segments in writing a new program.

Price-to-performance ratio: A ratio used to indicate the value of a potential purchase; in computing, a measure of the cost of a unit of computing power.

Primary memory: That part of a computing system's memory which is housed within the CPU.

Printed circuit board: An electronic component which represents electrical circuits on a board substrata.

Printer: An electromechanical device which produces printed output.

Private branch exchange (PBX): The switching mechanism which connects an organization and its telephone system to the nationwide telephone service.

Procedural language: A language, such as COBOL, FORTRAN, BASIC, or Pascal, in which a programmer must specify a procedure in order to accomplish a task.

Process control: Use of a computer to determine the status of a process and issue commands to bring its performance close to a standard.

Program: A set of instructions in a special language which guides the computer's activities.

Program Evaluation Review Technique/Critical Path Method: See *PERT/CPM*.

Program flowcharting: A graphical representation of the logic of a computer program.

Program generator: A program, or set of programs, which helps programmers generate the code necessary to accomplish a task.

Programmable: Capable of executing instructions.

Programming: The act of creating a set of instructions which accomplish a data processing task.

Protocol: A set of rules which governs the communications between two computing devices.

Protocol converter: A device which allows two devices using different protocols to communicate.

Prototype: A trial or unfinished version of a hardware or software component.

Prototype design (quick-and-dirty design, design-as-you-go design, bread board design): A design technique which emphasizes gradual evolution of the finished product.

Pseudocode: Literally false code; a shorthand method of indicating the logic of a computer program.

Query: An inquiry in nonprocedural language by which a user extracts information from a data base.

Query languages: See *Nonprocedural language*.

Random-access file: A file which allows equally likely access to all records; compare *Direct-access file*.

Range check: A means for checking values within a program to ensure that they are within an appropriate range.

R:Base: A data base software product from Microrim.

Read-only memory (ROM): Primary computer memory whose contents are fixed during manufacture and cannot be changed. Note: PROM (programmable read-only memory) and EPROM (erasable, programmable read-only memory) also exist.

Real time: The time frame necessary to access information to support a particular data processing task. Very frequently used to indicate instantaneous information retrieval or file update.

Real time system: A system which responds instantly.

Record: A set of related data elements.

Register: An electronic location within a computing device in which an individual datum, a storage location, or an instruction can be temporarily stored.

Relation: A subset of a Cartesian Product (from set theory).

Relational data model: A data structure used to represent logical relationships among data elements in a data base.

Remote batch: The ability to process batches of data from remote locations.

Remote batch processing: Batch processing initiated from a site geographically removed from the computer center itself.

Report generator: A program, or set of programs, which facilitates the construction and formatting of a report. Often a capability included in a Data Base Management System.

Request for proposal (RFP): A formal document announcing the requirements for a new computer system issued by a potential purchaser to allow vendors to submit bids (proposals).

Reserved word: One of the words in a programming language set aside for special meaning.

Review: An evaluation of past performance.

Ring network: A network in which all devices are connected in a ring without a central host.

Robotics: The use of robots.

Robot: An electromechanical device which, increasingly, operates under computer control to perform work.

ROM: See *Read-only memory*.

RPG (Report Program Generator): A programming language of limited capability for the generation of reports.

Schema: Logical structure of data within a data base.

Secondary memory: Any one of a number of auxiliary memory devices which supplement the primary memory of a computer system.

Select: To choose from among a set of alternatives.

Selection: A programming structure in which one of two or more possible paths is chosen.

Selection committee: A committee put together to evaluate alternatives and choose the best system.

Sequence: A program structure designating the order of instructions.

Sequencing: Putting in order.

Sequential file: A file structure in which the records are arranged in order (in sequence).

Service bureau: A business which sells computer services, such as programming, data entry, and processing, to other organizations.

Signals: A visible indication that an event has taken place within an organization.

Simplex: A transmission mode in which communication is allowed in one direction only.

Simulation: An analytical procedure in which a computer program is written to capture the important characteristics of a real system, and the program is run to generate statistics which might indicate how the real system would behave.

Software: Computer programs, including systems and applications programs.

Software engineering: The application of good software techniques.

Software package: A set of standardized programs which have been written for resale.

Software portability: The degree to which programs written for one system can be successfully moved to another.

Sort/merge routine: A program, often made available as part of the operating system, which enables the user to sort or merge files.

Source document: An original document which serves as a source of data for data entry operations.

Source program: The original version of a computer program, written in a higher-level language.

Specifications: The detailed description of a desired system.

Spooling: The use of a magnetic disk, or similar secondary memory device, to receive and store (temporarily) output on its way to an output device; spooling allows the CPU to do other things while output operations continue.

Spreadsheet software: The name given to software developed originally for personal computers which made it possible for users to construct tables for a variety of analytical operations.

Standard benchmark: A test of hardware performance using standard programs; compare *Live benchmark.*

Star network: A network arrangement with outlying devices connected to a central host.

Step-wise refinement: A process in which a general outline of a project acquires detail as it moves through a series of steps.

Storage: A data processing function which accommodates a difference in time between the acquisition of data and the use of information.

Stored program: One of the basic concepts of computing; a set of instructions stored within the system itself; computer can execute these again and again at its own speed, without a programmer's input.

Store registers: Electronic components which control the movement of data into memory.

Structured design: A set of formal procedures which guide the design of a data processing project.

Structured programming: A set of formal procedures which guide the writing of a program.

Supercomputer: A very large and very fast computer, capable of executing over 500,000 instructions per second.

Swapping: The mechanism by which programs and segments of programs are swapped into and out of the primary memory of a computer.

Symbol: Something that stands for something else.

Symphony: An integrated software package sold by Lotus Corp.

Synchronous: In telecommunications, a scheme for data transfer which relies on coordination of the sending and receiving units by timing; contrast *Asynchronous.*

Syntax: The formal rules of a computer language, which must be followed in order to code instructions.

System: A collection of related parts which work together to produce a desired result.

System life cycle: A series of steps which describe the various stages of a system's life.

System overhead: The nonproductive activities in which a system engages; in particular, the execution of systems programs contribute to system overhead.

System software: Programs which give the computer certain capability, but which, in and of themselves, are not productive.

Systems analysis: The formal study of a system to establish its ends, means and relationships to other systems.

Systems analyst: A person who engages in the analysis and design of computing systems, who works as liaison between users and the data processing group.

Systems design: To decide upon the features of a system.

Systems flowcharting: The graphical representation of data flows in a systems study.

Systems programmer: A programmer who writes and modifies systems software.

Systems programs: The software which gives a computer the basic capabilities to execute applications programs; coordinates operations and makes computer system operate efficiently.

Tape drive: A device on which magnetic tape is mounted for the purpose of reading from or writing to the tape.

Telecommunications: The movement of data across vast distances using communication facilities such as telephone systems and computer systems.

Teleconferencing: The process of carrying on a conference in which the participants, though perhaps widely separated geographically, communicate via television with each other.

Teletext: Information broadcast electronically to home terminals.

Terminal: A typewriter-like device which can be connected over communications lines to a computer to allow a user to interact with the computer system.

Text editor: A program which allows the user to create, modify, and delete text.

Thin film: A technology which produces a thin ferromagnetic coating on magnetic disk surfaces or read/write heads.

Time division multiplexing: A telecommunications scheme which allows two or more units to share a transmission line by giving a short period of exclusive use to each unit in turn; compare *Frequency division multiplexing.*

Timeliness: Existing within a time frame dictated by an application.

Timesharing: An arrangement in which a number of users share in the use of a computing system, each unaware and unbothered by the others' use.

Token: An electronic signal used in some local area networks to govern use of the network so that conflicting uses are prevented.

Top/down design: A design strategy in which overall (at the top) considerations are resolved and major functions identified before detailed (at the bottom) considerations and subfunctions receive attention.

Trailer data: False data values used to indicate the end of a data file.

Transaction file: The collection of transactions stored temporarily in a file to await processing; eventually used to update master file; compare *Master file.*

Transaction processing: A data processing method which has as its primary task the completion of a fundamental organizational task.

Transaction: A fundamental event in an organization.

Transducer: A device which converts a signal from one form to another.

Transistor: An electronic component whose circuitry replaced that of vacuum tubes for a time in computer development.

Transmission line: A communications connection.

Transparency: A concept in which some functions are performed without an awareness on the part of the user that the system is engaged in the performance of those functions.

Transportable: Used to describe a personal computer small enough to carry (with difficulty).

Tuples: An ordered arrangement of elements.

Turn-key system: A system which has been designed so that the user need only turn on the key to use it.

UCSD p-system: A proprietary operating system for microcomputers designed at the University of California—San Diego.

Unconditional branch: A transfer of control in a program.

Universal product code (UPC): One of the bar codes for the encoding of data, consisting of vertical bars whose ||| pattern identifies manufacturer and product; appears on most grocery products.

Unix: A proprietary operating system for microcomputers designed at Bell Laboratories.

Unstructured: Used to describe problems without identifiable solution techniques.

Usefulness: Can be applied to serve some end.

User-defined functions: Subprograms written by the user.

User program: A computer program written by a user.

Utility programs: A set of programs, part of the operating system, which provides the system with some common data processing capabilities and data conversions.

Vacuum tube: The basic electronic building block of the 1950s.

Validity check: A check applied to data at entry to determine whether or not it is proper.

Value-added network (VAN): A long-distance communications network in which the vendor offers certain added functions such as packet switching.

VAN: See *Value-added network.*

Variable length field: A zone, used to store data, whose length can vary in order to accommodate data of varying lengths.

Variable names: Symbols to which values can be assigned for processing.

Verifying machine: A machine, much like a keypunch, which is used to check the accuracy of punched cards.

Vertical recording: A new means of storing data on magnetic media which takes advantage of new technologies that allow vertical (instead of horizontal) magnetic domains. This results in much greater data densities.

Very-large-scale integration: See *VLSI.*

Videodisc: A disc, shaped like a phonograph record, on which data are recorded and read by lasers.

Videotext (videotex): Information services sent via communications lines to home terminals.

Virtual memory: A memory management technique in which room is made within the primary memory for additional data by moving other data out to secondary storage.

VLSI (very-large-scale integration): The miniaturization of transistor circuits to the point that hundreds of thousands can be placed on extremely small semiconductor chips.

Voice-store-and-forward: A capability offered by sophisticated telephone systems or PBXs to allow messages to be recorded for later delivery.

Wafer technology: An experimental technology that uses a complete silicon wafer to represent a computer's logic.

Walkthroughs: A formal review process in which one programmer explains his or her program design and code to other programmers in an effort to improve the program and provide training to programmers at the same time.

Warnier/Orr diagram: A diagram used to represent program logic.

War room: A phrase used to describe a conference room with extensive information display capabilities.

Well-structured: Describes problems for which solution techniques exist.

Winchester disk: A magnetic disk design which seals the disks and their read/write heads in a dust-proof chamber for greater reliability.

Windows: Video screen partitions which allow information from several applications to be viewed simultaneously.

Word processing: The use of a microprocessor-enhanced keyboard to compose, edit, and format text.

Word processor: A microprocessor-based machine for text editing.

WordStar: A word processing package by MicroPro.

Zero: All that is left of a glossary when one gets to the Zs.

Index

8.6 Courtesy of Hewlett-Packard. **Fig. 8.7** Courtesy of Hewlett-Packard. **Chapter 9** Courtesy of Omnifax Corporation. **Fig. 9.5** Taurus Photos. **Fig. 9.11** NASA. **Fig. 9.13** Taurus Photos. **Fig. 9.16** Courtesy of the San Francisco Examiner. © Copyright 1982 Gordon Stone **Part III** Courtesy of NCR Corporation. **Chapter 10** Courtesy of Hewlett-Packard. **Fig. 10.2** Courtesy of the Burroughs Corporation. **Fig. 10.3** Courtesy of Delta Airlines. **Fig. 10.5** Photo courtesy of Jerry Bushey. **Fig. 10.7** Courtesy of Stock Boston. Photo by Ellis Herwig. **Fig. 10.9** Courtesy of Control Data Corporation. **Fig. 10.10** Courtesy of NCR Corporation. **Fig. 10.11** Courtesy of International Business Machines Corporation. **Fig. 10.12** Courtesy of Hewlett-Packard. **Chapter 11** Courtesy of NCR Corporation. **Fig. 11.2** Courtesy of Los Alamos. **Fig. 11.3** Courtesy of Marathon Corporation. **Chapter 12** Courtesy of Radio Shack—A Division of Tandy Corporation. **Fig. 12.1** Copyright © 1982/83 by C.W. Communications/Inc., Framingham, MA. Reprinted from COMPUTERWORLD. **Fig. 12.4** Courtesy of Stock Boston. **Fig. 12.7** Courtesy of Stock Boston. **Fig. 12.8** Courtesy of Honeywell. **Fig. 12.9** Courtesy of Bechtel Corporation. **Fig. 12.10** Courtesy of Symbolics, Inc. **Chapter 13** Courtesy of Sperry Univac Corporation. **Fig. 13.1** Courtesy of Hewlett-Packard. **Fig. 13.7** Copyright © 1981 by C.W. Communications/Inc. Framingham, MA. Reprinted from COMPUTERWORLD. **Fig. 13.8** Photo by Bob Gaylord. **Fig. 13.10** Reprinted with permission, *High Technology Magazine*. Feb. 1984. Copyright © 1984 by High Technology Corporation, 38 Commercial Wharf, Boston, MA. **Chapter 14** Black Star. Photo by John Marriott. **Fig. 14.1** Courtesy of Nationwide. **Fig. 14.3** Courtesy of Jerry Bushey. **Fig. 14.4** Courtesy of Hewlett-Packard. **Fig. 14.6** Courtesy of Paradyne, Inc. **Fig. 14.7** *(a)* Courtesy of Control Data Corporation; *(b)* Reprinted with permission of International Business Machines Corporation, *(c)* Courtesy of Control Data Corporation. *(d)* Courtesy of Sperry Univac. **Fig. 14.8** Courtesy of Honeywell. **Part IV** Woodfin Camp & Associates. Photo by David Burnett. **Chapter 15** Courtesy of Hewlett-Packard. **Fig. 15.1** Courtesy of Apple Computers, Inc. **Fig. 15.3** Reprinted with the permission of Micro Pro International. **Fig. 15.4** *(a)* Courtesy of Sperry Univac. *(b)* Reprinted with the permission of International Business Machines Corporation. **Fig. 15.5** Courtesy of Activision. **Fig. 15.6** Courtesy of Digital Research. **Fig. 15.7** Reprinted with the permission of International Business Machines Corporation. **Fig. 15.8** Reprinted with the permission of International Business Machines Corporation. **Fig. 15.9** Courtesy of Hewlett-Packard. **Fig. 15.10** Courtesy of Honeywell. **Fig. 15.11** Courtesy of Hewlett-Packard. **Fig. 15.12** Reprinted with the permission of International Business Machines Corporation. **Fig. 15.13** Courtesy of Videotex. **Fig. 15.14** Photo by Bowling Green State University Photo Service. **Chapter 16** Courtesy of Radio Shack—A Division of Tandy Corporation. **Fig. 16.3** Photo by Jerry Bushey. **Fig. 16.5** Courtesy of Panasonic. **Chapter 17** Courtesy of Hewlett-Packard. **Fig. 17.1** Photo by Jerry Bushey. **Fig. 17.2** Fran Heyl Associates. Photo by Dan McCoy. **Fig. 17.3** Ford Motor Company Photo. **Fig. 17.4** Courtesy of Intelledex Corporation. **Fig. 17.5** Courtesy of Computervision. **Fig. 17.6** Courtesy of Chrysler Corporation. **Fig. 17.7** Courtesy of Apple Computers, Inc. **Fig. 17.8** Courtesy of Lanier. **Fig. 17.9** Courtesy of Morrow Company. **Fig. 17.10** Courtesy of Omnifax Corporation. **Fig. 17.11** Courtesy of Paradyne. **Fig. 17.12** Culver Pictures, Inc. **Fig. 17.13** Digital Equipment Corporation. **Chapter 18** Courtesy of Apple Computers, Inc. **Fig. 18.1** Courtesy of NOAA. **Fig. 18.2** Courtesy of NASA. **Fig. 18.3** Courtesy of Artronics, Inc. **Fig. 18.4** Courtesy of Presentation Computer, Inc. **Fig. 18.5** Wide World Photos **Fig. 18.6** Courtesy of Chrysler Corporation. **Fig. 18.7** Courtesy of Commodore Computer Systems Division. **Fig. 18.8** Courtesy of Control Data Corporation. **Fig. 18.9** Medical College of Ohio. **Fig. 18.10** Courtesy of The American Cancer Society. **Fig. 18.11** Courtesy of Honeywell. **Fig. 18.12** Photo by Jerry Bushey. **Fig. 18.13** Reprinted with the permission of International Business Machines Corporation. **Fig. 18.14** Courtesy of the U.S. Air Force. **Fig. 18.16** Courtesy of Stock Boston. Photograph by Peter Menzer.

Color Sections

Computers In Action 1. 1. Courtesy of Pelham and Friends Photography. **2.** Courtesy of Apple Computers, Inc. **3.** Courtesy of Apple Computers, Inc. **4.** Stock Boston. Photo by Julie Houck. **5.** Stock Boston. Photo by John Coletti. **6.** Courtesy of Radio Shack—A division of Tandy Corporation. **7.** Courtesy of Compag. **8.** Courtesy of Hewlett-Packard. **9.** Courtesy of Grid Computers. **10.** Courtesy of Stock Boston. Photo by Gregg Mancuso. **11.** Courtesy of Apple Computers, Inc. **12.** Researchers, Inc. Photo by Richard Hutchings. **Computers In Action 2. 1.** Courtesy of Piper, Jaffery and Hopwood. **2.** Photo by Jerry Bushey. **3.** Courtesy of Piper, Jaffery and Hopwood. **4.** Photo by Jerry Bushey. **5.** Courtesy of Piper, Jaffery and Hopwood. **6.** Courtesy of Piper, Jaffery and Hopwood. **7.** Courtesy of Hewlett-Packard. **8.** Peter Arnold. Photo by Cecile Brunswick. **9.** Taurus Photos. Photo by Philip Jon Bailey. **10.** Courtesy of Apple Computers, Inc. **11.** Courtesy of Xerox Corporation. **Computers In Action 3. 1.** Courtesy of Cray Research. **2.** Photo by Jerry Bushey. **3.** Photo by Jerry Bushey. **5.** Courtesy of Sperry Univac Corporation. **6.** Photo by Jerry Bushey. **7.** Courtesy of Hewlett-Packard. **8.** Photo by Jerry Bushey. **9.** Photo by Jerry Bushey. **10.** Photo by Jerry Bushey. **11.** Photo by Jerry Bushey. **12.** Fran Heyl Associates. Photo by Phillip Harrington. **13.** Courtesy of Hewlett-Packard. **14.** Fran Heyl Associates. Photo by Dan McCoy. **Computers In Action 4. 1.**Taurus Photos. Photo by C.B. Jones. **3.** Photo by Jerry Bushey. **4.** Courtesy of Hewlett-Packard. **5.** Photo by Jerry Bushey. **6.** Photo by Jerry Bushey. **7.** Courtesy of International Business Machines Corporation. **8.** Photo by Jerry Bushey. **9.** Courtesy of Digital Equipment Corporation. **10.** Fran Heyl Associates. Photo by Dan McCoy. **Computers In Acion 5. 1.** Courtesy of AT&T. **2.** Courtesy of AT&T. **3.** Courtesy of Sperry Univac Corporation. **4.** Courtesy of AT&T. **5.** Courtesy of AT&T. **6.** Courtesy of AT&T. **7.** Courtesy of AT&T. **8.** Courtesy of AT&T. **9.** Courtesy of Texas Instruments. **10.** Courtesy AT&T. **11.** Courtesy of AT&T. **12.** Courtesy of AT&T. **13.** Courtesy of NASA. **14.** Courtesy of AT&T. **Computers In Action 6. 1.** Fran Heyl Associates. Photo by Dan McCoy. **2.** Courtesy of Sperry Univac Corporation. **3.** Courtesy of Sperry Univac Corporation. **4.** Courtesy of Hewlett-Packard. **5.** Courtesy of Sperry Univac Corporation. **6.** Courtesy of McAuto, Inc. **7.** Courtesy of McAuto, Inc. **8.** Taurus Photos. Photo by Laima Druskis. **9.** Photo by Jerry Bushey. **10** Courtesy of Gorvus Systems. **11.** Photo by Jerry Bushey. **12** Courtesy of Sperry Univac Corporation. **13.** Courtesy of Control Data Corporation. **Computers In Action 7. 1.** Woodfin Camp and Associates. Photo by David Burnett. **2.** Courtesy of Sperry Univac Corporation. **3.** Courtesy of Hewlett-Packard. **4.** Courtesy of Apple Computers, Inc. **5.** Photo by Jerry

Bushey. **6.** Courtesy of Microm. **7.** Taurus Photos. Photo by Eric Kroll. **8.** Woodfin Camp and Associates. Photo by Chuck Fishman. **9.** Courtesy of Hewlett-Packard. **10.** Courtesy of Texas Instruments. **11.** Courtesy of Radio Shack—A division of Tandy Corporation. **12.** Woodfin Camp and Associates. Photo by David Burnett. **Computers In Action 8. 1.** Woodfin Camp and Associates. Photo by David Burnett. **2.** Courtesy of Apple Computers, Inc. **3.** Photo by Kevin McMahon. **4.** Woodfin Camp and Associates. **5.** Woodfin Camp and Associates. Photo by David Burnett. **6.** Fran Heyl Associates. Dan McCoy. **7.** Courtesy of Eickonix Corporation. **8.** Fran Heyl Associates. Dan McCoy. **9.** Fran Heyl Associates. Dan McCoy. **10.** Photo by Jerry Bushey. **11.** Photo by Jerry Bushey. **12.** Courtesy of TymShare, Inc. **13.** Taurus Photos. Photo by Eric Kroll. **14.** Courtesy of Apple Computers, Inc.